Old Kent:

THE EASTERN SHORE OF MARYLAND;

NOTES ILLUSTRATIVE OF

THE MOST ANCIENT RECORDS OF KENT COUNTY, MARYLAND,

AND OF THE

PARISHES OF ST. PAUL'S, SHREWSBURY AND I. U.

AND

GENEALOGICAL HISTORIES OF OLD AND DISTINGUISHED FAMILIES OF MARYLAND, AND THEIR CONNECTIONS BY MARRIAGE, &c.,

WITH

AN INTRODUCTION,

BY

GEORGE A. HANSON, M. A.

Corresponding Member of the Maryland Historical Society, &c.

CLEARFIELD

Originally published
Baltimore, Maryland 1876

Reprinted
Regional Publishing Company
Baltimore, Maryland 1967

Reprinted for
Clearfield Company, Inc. by
Genealogical Publishing Co., Inc.
Baltimore, Maryland
1990, 1996, 2002

Library of Congress Catalogue Card Number 67-16963
International Standard Book Number: 0-8063-4632-9

Made in the United States of America

TO

THE MEMORY

OF

THE FIRST SETTLERS OF THE EASTERN SHORE OF MARYLAND,

TO

THEIR DESCENDANTS WHERESOEVER DISPERSED,

AND TO

THE PEOPLE OF KENT, MY NATIVE COUNTY,

THESE PAGES

ARE REVERENTLY AND AFFECTIONATELY

INSCRIBED.

PREFACE.

"HONOUR THY FATHER AND THY MOTHER."

THE early records of Kent County, Maryland, which contain the only memorials extant of many of the first settlers of the Eastern Shore, are time-worn, mouldering, falling to pieces, and in a few years will become illegible, decay, and be lost. Upon their faded and perishing pages are chronicled some of the acts and doings of good men who have gone before us—whose graves are unknown—whose tombstones have disappeared—and whose names are forgotten, or are no longer mentioned among men.

To rescue from oblivion, to perpetuate a knowledge of these memorials, and to preserve a memento of our fathers—to whom, under Providence, we are indebted for the blessing of life, for all that we partake of on Earth and may enjoy in Heaven—was the motive which inspired the preparation of these pages, and which, though not contemplated when the foundation was laid, has naturally, at the request of others, led to the publication of this volume.

To clothe with interest the dryasdust and barren details of trivial and ordinary affairs, I have endeavoured—with the light afforded by ancient Tombstones, Wills, Parish Registers of Births, Marriages and

Deaths, and the assistance of friends and their family annals—to connect, genealogically, the first settlers with their children—the present generation—and to weave, as it were, a living garland around the crumbling monuments of the dead.

Many of the genealogies are founded, exclusively, upon public Records, Wills and Parish Registers of unquestionable authority; though they are, in some instances, widely at variance with venerable and long cherished traditions. Others are drawn out from private sources, which are received as authentic by the respective families.

The extent, fullness and accuracy of the histories of families depended, in a great degree, upon the inclination to impart information, ability and concurrence of persons now living, and it is due to myself to say that I have gladly embodied and added to all proper and reliable information furnished to me—and, also, which will explain omissions, that I have been frequently asked to omit names and family connexions, and that with all such requests I have regretfully complied. "*De gustibus non est disputandum.*"

With regard to the mechanical execution of the work, the proof-sheets were entrusted to Peter A. Kelly, Esq., the Superintendent of the Printing Department of Messrs. Kelly, Piet & Co.

The copper-plate engravings were executed by Messrs. Anderson & Son (James M. Anderson and W. Scott Anderson), of Baltimore.

The abbreviations used are b., for born,—d., for died, deceased,—dau., for daughter, child., for children—m., for married, and unm., for unmarried. In the spelling of names, words, etc., and capitalization, I have followed my originals.

It is proper that I should express my appreciation of the considerate courtesy and painstaking politeness of David C. Blackiston, Esq., Clerk, and of Messrs. Henry C. Chase and John W. Palmer, in the Clerk's Office,—and of William Stevens, Esq., Register, and Mr. Harry Rickey, of the Register's Office, at Chestertown.

Remembering, with gratitude all whose sympathy encouraged me in my labor of filial love, I return the warmest expression of my thanks to those who aided me in obtaining information. Their names are many, and are designated in the Index by (*) an asterisk.

Imperfect as this tribute is, I hope that it will be indulgently accepted as an humble effort to repay my debt of gratitude to Maryland and my native County.

GEO. A. HANSON.

83 Edmondson Avenue,
Baltimore, 30th December, 1876.

INTRODUCTION.

KENT COUNTY justly claims the honor of being the most ancient settlement, and of inheriting the oldest organized government, in the State of Maryland, and as such was represented by Captain Nicholas Martin in the Legislative Assembly of Virginia, several years before the first settlement at St. Mary's, and before the grant of Maryland was made by Charles I to Lord Baltimore. The settlement was made on Kent Island by a Protestant Colony, from Virginia, under the leadership of William Clayborne and his Chaplain, Rev. Richard James, of the Church of England, who was the first one who preached the Gospel of Christ in Maryland. They were both (Clayborne and James) driven from Kent Island, and their property confiscated by the Lord Proprietary.

The Kent settlement, *i. e.* Kent county, originally embraced and included the whole of the Eastern Shore, and was under the government of an officer styled the "Commander of the Isle of Kent." The present limits of the county were, from time to time, defined by the boundaries of new counties carved out of her ancient domain; thus, Talbot was taken from it in 1661, Somerset in 1666, Cecil in 1674, Dorchester in 1669, Queen Anne's in 1706, Worcester in 1742, and Caroline in 1773. In 1695 Kent Island was attached to Talbot. In 1706 it was divorced from Talbot and given to a younger sister, Queen Anne's, who values the "Isle of the Olden Time" as the most precious jewel in her dowry—the borrowed pledge of her royal descent.

When James I ascended the throne (24th March, 1603), Virginia was the name applied by the English to the whole Continent of North America. A patent was granted to "The

London Company," in 1606, for lands between the thirty-eighth and forty-fifth degrees of north latitude. This company received a new charter in 1609, with the title of "The Treasurer and Company of Adventurers of the City of London for the First Colony of Virginia," and the grant of all lands north and south of "Cape Comfort," to the extent of two hundred miles in both directions, which embraced the territory of the present State of Maryland. A third charter, in 1611, made no change in the boundaries on the mainland. In 1623 a *quo warranto* was issued, and all these charters were annulled. From that time Virginia ceased to be a "Proprietary," and became a "Royal Government," subject to the pleasure of the King, to be dealt with as he saw fit. This decision was distasteful to the proud Virginians, and they did not snubmit to it cheerfully.

Charles I granted to Cecilius Calvert, Baron of Baltimore, the charter for Maryland, bearing date 20th day of June, 1632, embracing lands which once formed part of the lands granted by the Virginia charter, which had been annulled, as we have seen, by the judgment on the writ of *quo warranto* in 1623. (*Vide "The History of Maryland," by John Leeds Bozman, Vol. II,* pp. 9–21*; "A Relation of Maryland, reprinted from the London Edition of* 1635*;" McMahon,* p. 5, *et sub.*)

At the time of this grant of Maryland no settlement had been made within its prescribed limits, except upon the "Isle of Kent," by one William Clayborne, an influential and prominent colonist of Virginia, who had previously, the 26th day of August, 1624, been nominated by King James "one of the Council," in a commission issued to Sir Francis Wyat and others. When King Charles I renewed the charter for the government of Virginia, Clayborne was continued of the council and assigned to be the Secretary of State in Virginia. In 1627, the 26th day of March, Clayborne was again, for special reasons, reappointed Secretary of the State. It is fair to presume that he was a man of liberal education and of unusual ability. During the years 1627–'28–'29 the Governor of Virginia authorized William Clayborne, "the Secretary of State of this Kingdom, to explore and discover the source of the

Chesapeake Bay, from the thirty-fourth to the forty-first degrees of north latitude." Under this authority, it appears, Clayborne made his settlement on the Isle of Kent. After this, Charles I, in May, 1631, gave Clayborne a license "to trade in all the seas, coasts, harbors or territories, in or near to those parts of America, for the sole trade with which there had been no former grant from the crown."

Under such circumstances, was the charter of Maryland granted to Cecilius Calvert, the 20th day of June, 1632. Lord Baltimore did not accompany the colonists to Maryland; "hee appointed Leonard Calvert to goe Governour in his stead, with whom he joyned in commission Mr. Jerome Hawley and Mr. Thomas Cornwallis (two worthy and able gentlemen)." They arrived at "Point Comfort, in Virginia," the 24th day of February, 1634, and were treated with much "courtesie and humanitie" by the Governor of Virginia. William Clayborne welcomed them, also, with a grim salutation. "At this time one Captaine Cleyborne (one of the Council of Virginia), comming from the parts whether they intended to goe, told them that all the natives were in preparation of defense by reason of a rumor some had raised amongst them that six shippes were to come with many people, who would drive all the inhabitants out of the country." This was a polite declaration of war, for the wish was father to the thought, and Clayborne never took back the gage which he then threw down.

Clayborne was fully acquainted with the scope and objects of the expedition. He had come to Virginia in 1621 as surveyor, and soon became a councillor. When George Calvert, the first Lord Baltimore, visited Virginia, in 1628–'29, and landed at Jamestown, the Governor (West) and Council, composed of William Clayborne and others, called him before them and demanded what his purpose was, being Governor of another plantation (New Foundland), to abandon that, and come thus to Virginia. He replied that he came to plant and to dwell. "Very willingly, my lord," they answered, "if your lordship will do what we have done, and what your duty is to do." Upon his refusal to take the oath of supremacy, they ordered him to depart. Clayborne soon followed him to England, and was prompt, with his partners, William Cloberry, John de la Barre and David Moorhead, to remonstrate against the grant of Maryland to Lord Baltimore, on the ground that it embraced the Isle of Kent, which he had purchased from the "kings of that country." When the charter was granted, his rage was great, and his complaints loud and deep. He exerted, with some success, his utmost efforts to excite the ire of the Virginians. Many of them proclaimed, and made it their familiar talk, that they would rather knock their cattle in the head than sell them to Maryland. His friend, Captain Samuel Matthews, scratching his head and stamping his foot, cried out, "A pox on Maryland!"

It was on the Feast of the "Annunciation of the Blessed Virgin," being the 25th day of March, 1634, the "Pilgrims" first landed in Maryland, on an island called St. Clement by McSherry, but now called Blackistone's Island. The occasion was a solemn one, and was celebrated with such religious ceremonies as were becoming to an event so important to mankind.

A fixed settlement two days afterwards, *i. e.* the 27th day of March, 1634, was made at St. Mary's, and this latter day must be considered as the true date of the actual settlement of this colony. (*Vide "History of Maryland," by McSherry*, pp. 30 and 32.)

From this time until the year 1650, when the erection of new counties curtailed the limits of St. Mary's, the whole of the Western Shore was called "St. Mary's," to distinguish it from the Eastern Shore, or Kent.

The grant to Lord Baltimore created great dissatisfaction among the colonists of Virginia, and they petitioned the King to restore to them their former possessions. The petition was finally acted upon, in the Star Chamber, in July, 1633, when it was adjudged by the Privy Council "that Lord Baltimore should be left in possession of this grant, and the petitioners to heir remedy at law, if they have any such." The Governor and Council of Virginia received the decision sullenly, and not in the spirit of acquiescence. They did not surrender, "rescue or no rescue," but bided their time. It never came.

Clayborne did not remain idle. In March, 1634, he petitioned the Governor and Council of Virginia, asking for advice as to the course he should pursue, informing them that he and his colonists had been required to renounce their dependence upon and subordination to Virginia. The Governor and Council archly expressed surprise that such a question should be propounded. They said they saw no reason why he should surrender the Isle of Kent, and "as the right to my lord's patent is yet undetermined in England, we are bound in duty, and by our oaths, to maintain the rights and privileges of the colony. Nevertheless, in humble submission to his majesty's pleasure, we will keep a good correspondence with them, not doubting that they will not entrench upon the rights of his majesty's plantations." (*Vide McMahon*, p. 12.) They kept *themselves* quiet, and Clayborne chafed like an untamed tiger in leading-strings until the headstrong Harvey was removed, and Sir William Berkeley became Governor, in 1639.

Clayborne refused to submit to the Lord's Proprietary's demand, and in September, 1634, he was forced to withdraw, and fled to Virginia; he was attainted and his property confiscated. Governor Harvey refused to surrender him to the authorities of Maryland or to protect him, but, under the pretense of high respect for the King's license, sent him to England, with the witnesses, to await the royal pleasure. Clayborne never forgot or forgave this conduct of the authorities of Virginia, and brought it bitterly to their remembrance in 1652.

Clayborne went to England a bitter, vindictive and unrelenting enemy to the Lord Proprietary. He petitioned the King for a confirmation of his former license to trade, for a grant of other lands adjoining Kent Island, and the power to govern them. The King, influenced by Sir William Alexander, his Secretary for Scotland, and one of Clayborne's associates in the license, issued a favorable order. The matter was finally adjudicated, in April, 1638, and determined "that the right to all the territory, within which Clayborne's settlements were made, was vested in Lord Baltimore."

The next year, as an humble suppliant, he begged of the Governor and Council of Maryland the restitution of his confiscated property. This was sternly and harshly denied. Failing in this, in 1644, he instigated the Indians to make war upon the colony. As soon as peace was restored to the afflicted people, he associated himself with Richard Ingle, a proclaimed "traitor to the King," excited and led a rebellion against the Proprietary's government, and actually drove the Governor out of the colony. For more than a year he held possession of the government, during which time many valuable records of the province were lost or destroyed.

The Governor, Leonard Calvert, did not long survive his restoration. He died at St. Mary's the 9th day of June, 1647. Among his last acts, and peculiarly interesting to us, was the reconstruction of the government of Kent Island.

After this, when King Charles had been beheaded (30th January, 1649), and the Commonwealth was established, the irrepressible Clayborne, with Fuller and others, was commissioned, in September, 1651, by Cromwell's Council of State, to subjugate the province whence he had lately been driven as a rebel. They were empowered "to reduce and govern the colonies within the Chesapeake Bay." Here was a fine and open field for Clayborne to glut his vengeance, and he was swift to avail himself of the opportunity. Never did a towering hawk more eagerly swoop upon a poor, mousing owl than did Clayborne, straight as an arrow from the bow, seek and find his quarry. He paid his respects first to Virginia—performed his agreeable task of "reduction" neatly, cleanly and expeditiously. Then, like a falcon, he plumed his feathers, and in March, 1652, borne upon the wings of the wind, pounced upon St. Mary's. He treated Governor Stone with insolent indignity, violently seized upon his commission, and deposed him from office.

Clayborne then, the 29th March, 1652, appointed a council, of which Robert Brooke was made president and acting Governor, took possession of the records, and abolished the authority of the Proprietary. In July, 1652, Stone submitted, and was reinstated and permitted to retain and administer the government "in the name of the keepers of the liberty of England." Clayborne again took possession of Kent Island and Palmer's Island, at the mouth of the Susquehanna. Having triumphed, this man of Belial was master of the situation, and the power of Lord Baltimore was overthrown.

A proclamation, in the name of Cromwell, was issued, dated 22d day of July, 1654, and a commission appointed for the government, at the head of which was Captain William Fuller.

As soon as convenient, Lord Baltimore made an effort to regain his rights, and directed Stone to require all persons to take the "oath of fidelity" and re-establish the Proprietary government. This was done in the latter part of 1654, *o. s.* As soon as Clayborne heard of these proceedings, with one fell spring he grappled with his foes. At the battle of Providence (now Annapolis), 25th March, 1655, he took Stone prisoner, and compelled him again to submit. He condemned Stone to be shot, but the soldiers loved the amiable Governor, and refused to execute the cruel order.

In 1658 the government was, happily, restored to the Proprietary by treaty, and the claims of Virginia and of Clayborne at once and forever extinguished.

Isle of Kent.

This beautiful island was settled, as we have seen, between the years 1627 and 1630, by William Clayborne, its government organized as a Colony of Virginia and as such represented in the General Assembly of Virginia, which was "holden at James Citty the 21st of ffebruary 1631–2," *o. s.*

It appears that, towards the latter part of the year 1637, *o. s.*, the Isle of Kent had been in some measure reduced to the obedience of the Lord Baltimore. Clayborne had failed in his attempts to retain possession of it, by force, and had, as before stated, been sent by the Governor of Virginia to England, to seek what remedy he might find there.

It now became necessary to extend and establish the civil authority of the Lord Proprietor over the Island, as a part of the Province of Maryland. Accordingly, on the 30th day of December, 1637, Leonard Calvert, Governor of Maryland, constituted and appointed his "good friend *Captain* GEORGE EVELYN, of the Isle commonly called Kent," "to be Commander of the said Island and the inhabitants thereof," with power to elect and choose a Council, and to call a "court or courts," to hear and determine "all causes and actions whatsoever civil" not exceeding in damages or demands the value of ten pounds sterling, and with the criminal jurisdiction of a "justice of peace in England," not extending to life or member, etc.

Notwithstanding, and although, Clayborne was absent, many of the inhabitants did not hesitate to express their contempt for and resist the constituted authorities; and it was deemed necessary that the Governor, assisted by Captain Thomas Cornwaleys, one of the Council, and a competent armed force, should proceed to the Island and reduce its seditious inhabitants, by *martial law* if necessary.

The Governor thought the emergency a serious one; and he appointed Mr. John Lewger, his secretary, to act in his stead during his absence from St. Mary's.

On the 22nd day of April, 1638, Governor Calvert appointed WILLIAM BRAINTHWAYTE, to be "Commander of the Isle of Kent in all matters of warfare by sea and land necessary to the resistance of the enemy or suppression of mutinies and insolencies," in all matters *civil* and *criminal* to exercise the jurisdiction of a Justice of the Peace, to hold a court or courts, and to hear and determine all causes civil "not exceeding in damages or demands to the value of *one thousand weight of tobacco*."

A General Assembly met at the Fort of St. Mary's (on Monday, the 25th of February, 1638–1639, *n. s*). Mr. Nicholas Browne, planter, and Mr. Christopher Thomas appeared, among the Burgesses, as the delegates from Kent. Their credentials, the returns from the Isle of Kent, were certified by twenty-four (24) signatures. Supposing these signatures to have been the names of all the male heads of families, then on the Isle of Kent, as they most probably were, it would afford a tolerable datum from which might be inferred the aggregate white population of the Island at this period of time. Accounting five to a family, the usual computation, the population would amount to one hundred and twenty souls.

At this Assembly (1638–39) the powers of the Commander were more clearly ascertained, and a "*Court of Record*" was erected, to be called—the HUNDRED COURT OF KENT; of which the Commander of the Island was to be the judge, and from which court an appeal lay to the County Court at St. Mary's. Provision was also made for the Supreme Court at St. Mary's to sit occasionally on the Isle of Kent.

In consequent of dangers arising from the hostility of the "salvages," "*Captain* GILES BRENT, *Esqr.*, one of the Council," was commissioned, February 3rd, 1639, *o. s.*, to be Commander of the Isle of Kent," with *military* powers. This was for special and temporary purposes. He remained on the Isle, in commission, but a few months, for it appears that on the 14th day of August, 1640, WILLIAM BRAINTHWAYTE was acknowledged by the Governor as Commander of the Isle, and "GILES BRENT, *gent.*," as the "treasurer of our province."

The Indians had again become so hostile that the Governor on the 10th day of July, 1641, issued his proclamation, prohibiting all persons whatsoever "to harbour or entertain any Indian," under pain of the penalties of *martial law*, and declaring it "lawful to any inhabitant whatsoever of the Isle of Kent to shoot, wound, or kill any Indian whatsoever coming upon the said island."

On the 16th day of December, 1642, MR. GILES BRENT,

2

was appointed, by commission, "to be Commander of our Isle and COUNTY OF KENT; to be Chief Captain in all matters of warfare; and to be Chief Judge in all matters and things civil and criminal, happening within the said Island, not extending to life or member or freehold." In the same commission, also, "William Ludington, Richard Thompson, and Robert Vaughan, gent., were appointed to be commissioners within our said island to all powers and effects as to commissioners of a *county* by the law of the province do or shall belong." Commissioners of a county appear to have been then considered as having, not only the powers of conservators of the peace at common law, but as thereby authorized to hold a county court. These gentlemen seem, therefore, to have been now first authorized to hold a county court in the Isle of Kent.

If any such court was held by them the record, and all evidence of it, has been lost.

The Isle of Kent, whilom, the proud but beautiful Virgin Queen of the Chesapeake, was now joined in the bonds of holy wedlock with Maryland; changing her state, she also changed her name, and together with all her possessions will hereafter be known as

KENT COUNTY,

until irreverent hands carved away with invisible lines her ancient domains; and herself, sole relic of the olden time, deprived of her marriage crown, was given as a dowry to the daughter of her elder sister.

As seen before, about this time, 1644, William Clayborne was at his old tricks, troubling the Colony, prowling about and instigating the Indians to make war upon the inhabitants. Governor Calvert was much alarmed; accordingly, about the 1st of December, he sent a reconnoitering expedition, under the command of Mark Pheypo and John Genalles to spy out the land, and "to enquire whether Captain Clayborne, or any other, have made any disturbance of the peace, or committed any outrage upon the island, and to learn what force he did it with, and what strength he is of there at sea or shore, and what his intents further be, and how long he means to stay." They were also authorized to publish a proclamation declaring Captain William Clayborne, Esq., and Richard Thompson, enemies of the Province, etc. The result of this expedition is not known. Clayborne did not show his teeth on that occasion; he was not ready to bite.

Another expedition was sent against William Clayborne, who had again resorted to open force to regain his former possessions. We have before seen him, immediately after the dissolution of the old charters of Virginia, placed in the conspicuous stations of Councillor and Secretary of that province. He had also, in the year 1642, experienced the King's favor in appointing him to the office of "King's treasurer within the dominion of Virginia *during his life.*" We may, therefore, consider him as having been for some years past an inhabitant of Virginia, agreeably performing the duties of his office; but now, for interested purposes, he had forsaken his King and benefactor, and arrayed himself under the banner of the Parliament. It is not improbable but that he acted also under the ordinance of Parliament, of November, 1643, whereby the superintendence of the colonies was invested in the Earl of Warwick, with a council of five peers and twelve commoners, who were authorized "to nominate, appoint and constitute all such subordinate governors, councillors, officers and agents, as they shall judge to be *best affected*, and most fit and serviceable for the said plantations, and to remove others." Interest is a powerful persuader of the affections, and they might, with confidence, count upon "one *Captaine* William Clayborne."

WILLIAM BRAINTHWAYTE, Esq., was again, on the 1st day of January, 1644, *o. s.*, commissioned "to be Commander of Kent, with all authority, civil and criminal, which heretofore to any commander hath belonged, and in absence to depute such person as he shall think fit, and John Wyat, Robert Vaughan, gent., John Abbott, William Cox, commissioners."

In the early part of the year 1647, *o. s.*, Governor Calvert proceeded to reclaim and reduce Kent Island to the obedience of the Lord Proprietary. We have no information as to the circumstances, whether peacefully or otherwise, attending the repossession of the island. All that we know is that the inhabitants "submitted themselves again to his Lordship's government," and took the oath of fealty to Lord Baltimore.

The most of Clayborne's adherents fled to parts unknown, an act thought to be "acceptable to God, not displeasing to his Majesty, and an assured happiness unto this colony."

Some few, however, remained, took the oath of fealty, and were pardoned, the 16th of April, 1647. Their names were Thomas Bradnox, Edward Comins, John Metham, Thomas Belt, Robert Short, Francis Lumbard, John Ayres, Zachary Wade, Richard Catesford, Edward Lannin and Walter Joanes.

Governor Calvert, also, the 18th day of April, 1647, *o. s.*, commissioned Robert Vaughan, gent., to be "chief captain and commander," under him (the Governor), "of all the militia of the Isle of Kent, and with it to command and execute whatsoever shall be by him thought requisite for the said island against all intestine mutinies or seditions;" invested him with the power of martial law; "provided that where the offense shall deserve the forfeiture of life or member, that such offender for his trial be referred, and judgment to the *provincial court*, to be held by his Lordship's *Governor and Council* of this province." He further authorized "the said Captain Robert Vaughan to award all process necessary, according to the law and custom of this province," etc.; and he also authorized the said Captain Robert Vaughan, William Cox, Thomas Bradnox, Edward Comins, Philip Conner and Francis Brooke, gent., or the major part of them, whereof the said Robert Vaughan to be always one, to hear, try and judge, according to the laws of this province, all actions and causes civil," except "where the freehold of any one shall come in question," provided that it shall be lawful for any man, at any time before execution served, "to appeal unto the *provincial court;*" and he also invested them with criminal jurisdiction, "excepting when the life or members of any one person shall come in question."

Before the Governor left the island, he issued, on the 20th April, 1647, another commission "to Captain Robert Vaughan and the rest of the commissioners of the Isle of Kent," requiring them to cause all the property "belonging unto any of the late rebels," those who "had fled from thence or were remaining," who had refused "to take the oath of fealty," "to be attached and kept in safe custody," etc.

After his return to St. Mary's, on the 8th of May, he issued a proclamation prohibiting the departure of any person out of the province without leave, or the entertainment of any stranger, "until they had been first at the fort of St. Inigoes."

He further authorized Captain Vaughan, by commission dated the 31st of May, "to collect, demand and receive, for the use of the Lord Proprietary, all customs, confiscations, forfeitures and escheat, by any means and at any time, due to his said Lordship upon the said island," and also by two other commissions, to Mr. Francis Brooke, he was required to take into his custody "all neat cattle belonging to his Lordship in the said island," and particularly "all the estate of John Abbott, late of said island."

These were the last acts of Governor Leonard Calvert. A few days afterwards, on the 9th of June, 1647, he died, after having appointed, by a verbal nomination, Mr. Thomas Greene as his successor.

Having now faithfully traced, by the light of general history, the History of Kent County from its first settlement, I will now confine myself to the channel marked out by

THE OLDEST EXTANT RECORD OF KENT COUNTY.

It commences "on ye 3rd of January, 1647," *o. s.*, to illustrate and impart a knowledge of which is the sole and proper motive of the preparation and publication of these pages.

OLD KENT.

SECTION 1. "By virtue of an Act of Assembly Entituled An Act for Repairing the Damages already sustained in the Records of the Land, Secretary's, Commissary's and County Court Offices and for the security of the same Records for the future, made at a Session of Assembly begun and held at the City of Annapolis the Seventeenth Day of July, Anno Dom. seventeen hundred and sixteen.——

"By Virtue whereof the Commissioners for Kent County mett at the Court house in the Town of Chester in said County this Day of in the twelfth Year of the Dominion of CHARLES, Absolute Lord and Prop'ry of the Province of Maryland, and Avalon Lord Baron of Baltimore—Anno Dom. seventeen hundred twenty and seven, Being present Mr. Lambert Wilmer, Mr. Thomas Ringgold, Mr. Abraham Redgrave, Mr. William Frisby, Mr. Frederick Hanson, Mr. James Wilson Junr., Mr. John Evans, and Mr. George Skirven.

"The above Comm'rs, inspecting into the Record Books of the aforesaid County, do adjudge that reparations are needfull in what relates to Land and that the same be Transcribed by James Smith of the aforesaid County, which are as follows, viz:

May 15, 1727, The Worshp'll.
Mr. Lambert Wilmer,
Mr. Thoms. Ringgold,
Mr. Abram. Redgrave,
Mr. William Frisby,
Mr. Fredk. Hanson,
Mr. Jams. Wilson Junr.
Mr. John Evans,
Mr. Geo. Skirven,
Commrs. Present.

"The aforesaid James Smith proceeds to Transcribe out of an old Record Book what relates to Land as follows, viz—Liber A. No. 1, page 1."

1647–8.

SEC. 2. The first entry in LIBER A., COURT PROCEEDINGS OF KENT COUNTY, is as follows, viz:

"At a Court holden for this Island, at Mr. Philip Conier his house, on ye 3rd of January, 1647,

"Present, Capt. ROBERT VAUGHAN, Commander, Mr. THOMAS BRADNOX, Mr. PHILIP CONIER, Mr. ED. COMMINS, Mr. FRANCIS BROOKE."

The first case is thus recorded:

"JOHN METHAM complaineth against Francis Lumbard, in an action of debt to the value of four hundred pounds of tobacco and cask, and for this he bringeth his suit."

"The Court ordereth, that the plaintiff shall recover one hundred pounds of tobacco and cask, and the defendant to recover of Ed. Commins ninety pounds of tobacco and cask." Fol. 1.

The next case is that of JOHN WINCHESTER, who complaineth against Edward Commins, gent., "in an action of slander," and claims "five thousand pounds of tobacco and cask." "Warrant granted."

"The Court ordereth that the defendant shall ask the Wife of the plaintiff forgiveness in open court, for the slander, and likewise to pay to the woman 500 lbs. of tobacco and cask in satisfaction, with Court charges." Fol. 1.

SEC. 3. "At a Court held for this Island the 29th day of January, 1648,

"*Present*, Capt. ROBERT VAUGHAN, Mr. PHILIP CONNER, Mr. NICHOLAS BROWNE.

"Capt. ROBERT VAUGHAN, Commander of this Island, complaineth against William Laut, planter, for that the said William Laut hath uttered divers reviling, and upbraiding speeches against the person of the said Capt. Vaughan, and his authority, full of insolency, arrogancy, and pride, inciting and animating thereby those people committed to his charge to sedition and rebellion, and the lessening of his power and authority, for which fact of his, the said Capt. Robt. Vaughan requires the said Laut may be censured and punished, as the foulness thereof shall by this Court be found to deserve. Warrant issued.

"The Court ordered, that the Defendant should confess himself sorry for his fact committed in open Court and the action to be dismissed." Fol. 12.

John Winchester, of the Isle of Kent, styles himself "Cordwainer."—*Ibid.*

HENRY MORGAN was Sheriff in Jan., 1648.—*Ibid* Fol. 13.

1648–49.

SEC. 4. "January 13th, 1648.

"I do appoint Jachary Wade to be my lawful Attorney to sue for, recover, and receive all debts belonging unto me, and also to demand the Lord Proprietary his rent corn, and to give discharge for the same, and what my said Attorney shall do therein, I do hereby ratify and confirm.

"Witness my hand, MARGARET BRENT."

Liber A. C. P., Folio 14.

SEC. 4, A. The BRENTS. Mr. GILES BRENT and Mr. Mr. FULK BRENT, brothers, with their two sisters, Mrs. MARGARET BRENT and Mrs. MARY BRENT, came into the province of Maryland, the 22nd day of November, 1638, and were in some way by blood, affinity or friendship connected with the family of Lord Baltimore. They brought with them a considerable number of servants of both sexes.

Mrs. Margaret Brent was the first woman who ever claimed the right of suffrage in America.

There are many descendants of Giles Brent now living in Maryland and Virginia. An article in De Bow's Review, of May, 1859, contains a very interesting sketch of the family in Virginia.

ROBERT BRENT, who d. 4th Feb'y, 1750, aged 46, and Mary Brent, his wife, who d. 15th Jan'y, 1773, aged 68, were the progenitors of the Brents of Maryland. They left a son, Robert Brent.

ROBERT BRENT, son of Robert and Mary Brent, m. 5th Oct., 1756, Anna Maria Parnham, a descendant from the Hon. John Pole, privy councillor, and had child., viz., Francis, b. 23d July, 1757, d. 13th May, 1758,—Robert, b. 17th June, 1759,—Mary, b. 23d Dec., 1762, d. 8th Sept., 1715,—Anna Maria, b. 4th Jan'y, 1765, d. 16th June, 1785,—Teresa, b. 3d May, 1767, who m. Col. James Fenwick, and d. *sine prole*,—Elinor, b. 11th Feb'y, 1770, who m. Francis Digges, d. 21st May, 1822,—James, b. 20th March, 1772,—Elizabeth, b. 13th June, 1774, d. 15th Sept., 1827,—and Francis Wharton Brent, b. 7th Nov., 1776. Robert Brent d. 6th Jan'y, 1790, in the 57th year of his age.

ROBERT BRENT, son of Robert and Anna Maria Parnham Brent, m. 26th Feb'y, 1783, Dorothy Leigh, and had child., viz., William Leigh, b. 20th Feb'y, 1784,—Anna Maria Parnham, b. 15th Feb'y, 1785, and George Brent, b. 28th Oct., 1786.

WILLIAM LEIGH BRENT, son of Robert and Dorothy Leigh

Brent, m. 4th April, 1809, Maria Fenwick, and had child., viz., Hon. Robert James Brent,—James Fenwick Brent, who m. Laura Overton, dau. of Gen. Walter H. Overton, of Louisiana,—Maria Brent, who m. Edward Watkins, of Georgetown, D. C.,—Henrietta, who m. and d. *sine prole*,—William Brent,—Sarah Ann Brent, who m. Allen Luce,—Edward Cole Brent, who m. Fanny Baker, of Louisiana,—Gen. Joseph Lancaster Brent, who m. Frances Rosella Kenner, dau. of Duncan F. Kenner, of Louisiana,—Louisiana Brent, who d. young, and Chas. Vivian Brent, who m. Josephine Merrick, dau. of Hon. William Merrick. Hon. William Leigh Brent d. 1848.

Maria Fenwick was the dau. of James Fenwick and Henrietta Lancaster. James Fenwick was the son of Ignatius Fenwick, Jr., and his wife Sarah Taney, and the only brother of the Right Reverend Edward Fenwick, the first Roman Catholic Bishop of Cincinnati, Ohio. Ignatius Fenwick, Jr., was the son of Ignatius Fenwick, Sr., and his wife Mary Cole. Ignatius Fenwick, Sr., was descended from Mr. Cuthbert Fenwick, an interesting sketch of whom is given by George L. L. Davis, in "The Day-Star," pp. 207–219.

HON. ROBERT JAMES BRENT, son of the Hon. William Leigh and Maria Fenwick Brent, m. Matilda Lawrence, of Hagerstown, and d. 4th Feb'y, 1872, leaving child., viz., Robert Fenwick,—Mary Hoke,—Leila Lawrence,—Emma Fenwick,—Ida Schreve, and Elizabeth (Bettie) Hager Brent.

Hon. Robert James Brent, the Attorney General of Maryland during the administration of Gov. Enoch Louis Lowe, and the life-long intimate bosom friend of Hon. Henry May, was for many years one of the most successful and distinguished leaders of the Baltimore Bar and in the Federal Courts in the city of Washington, D. C.

Mrs. Matilda Lawrence Brent was the dau. of Upton Lawrence and his wife, Elizabeth Hager, who was descended from Jonathan Hager, the founder of Hagerstown, Md. Upton Lawrence was the son of John Lawrence, of Linganore Hills, Md., and his wife, Martha West, who was the dau. of Stephen West, of the Wood Yard, Prince George's county, who came to America about 1711, and first settled in Anne Arundel county. He was the son of John West, Esq., of Horton, Buckinghamshire, England.

The Wood Yard is the old Darnall estate. The tombstone of Col. Henry Darnall, the emigrant, still remains there, and marks his last earthly resting-place.

MARY HOKE BRENT, dau. of Hon. Robert James and

Matilda Lawrence Brent, m. William Keyser, Vice-President of the Baltimore and Ohio Railroad Company, and had child., viz., Robert Brent,—Mathilde and William Keyser.

Leila Lawrence Brent, dau. of Hon. Robert James and Matilda Lawrence Brent, m. Dunbar Hunt, of Mississippi, and had a dau., Anita Dunbar Hunt.

Anna Maria Parnham Brent, dau. of Robert and Dorothy Leigh Brent, m. and was the second wife of Joseph T. Mitchell, of Kent, and had child., viz., Joseph Thomas, b. 18th April, 1817,—Louisa, and Robert Brent Mitchell.

Joseph Thomas Mitchell, son of Joseph T. and Anna Maria Parnham Brent Mitchell, m. twice. His 1st wife was Caroline Horsey, and had child., viz., Eliza and Joseph Mitchell. His 2nd wife was Kate Kent, of Annapolis, and had child., viz., Robert Brent and Adelaide Mitchell.

George Brent, son of Robert and Dorothy Leigh Brent, m. 19th July, 1809, Matilda Thomas, dau. of William and Catharine Thomas, and had several child., only one of whom survives, Judge George Brent, of Charles county, who m. Catharine Merrick, dau. of Hon. William Merrick.

Sec. 5. Some suits for trespass, debt, and other causes, and very many for slander, appear upon this record, about the year 1648. Jno. Salter and his wife are conspicuous in the last-named of cases, but especially Capt. Thomas Bradnox and Mistress Bradnox.

Sec. 5, A. Thomas Bradnox was pardoned by Gov. Calvert the 16th April, 1647. He held many positions of honor in Kent and will soon appear as the Sheriff of Kent by commission sent to him by the hands of Mr. John Coursey, by his "Loving friend Tho. Hatton." He came into the Province of Maryland in 1644 with his wife Mary, and men servants, John Phillips and Edward Williams. (Liber A. No. 1, Fol. 84.) In the same Liber, Folio 157, we find that Mary, his widow, won the affections of an honorable man, who settled all her property upon her for her own exclusive use.

1649–50.

Sec. 6. In the bill of sale from Margaret Brent to Zachary Wade and Edd Claxston, in June, 1649, for a cow she styles herself, "Attorney for my brother Giles Brent." In the gift of "Marie Brent," to John Deane's son George, of a cow and calf, in 1651, she styles herself "Attorney to my brother Giles Brent." Liber A. C. P., Fols. 33 and 35.

1650–51.

SEC. 7. It would appear that there were no colonists of Maryland living upon the mainland of the Eastern Shore as early as the year 1650, and probably none in 1652.

Henry Morgan was one of the Judges at the Court held in the month of January, 1650, *o. s.* Francis Lumbard was sheriff in the year 1650. In the month of January 1650, *o. s.*, Walter Weeks, "of ye County of Northumberland," gave a bill of sale to Geo. Croutch of the Isle of Kent County "for one or more cattle upon the Island."

Liber A, No 1, Fols. 3 & 4.

SEC. 8. The following extract contains the first recorded evidence of the planting of an orchard in Kent county, now so celebrated for its fruit. The extract is from a lease of John Winchester, of the Isle of Kent, of one hundred acres of land to Francis Barnes, dated 12th August, 1650, wherein the said Francis Barnes binds himself as follows: "I the said Francis Barnes do hereby bind myself to seat and plant the said Land this next Ensuing Yeare and to plant an orchard of twenty Apple Trees, ten pear trees, twenty peach trees and twenty Cherry trees and to make a fence about the same and keep it in repair."

Liber A, No. 1, Folio 7.

SEC. 8, A. Col. Edward Wilkens, of this county, had at one time one hundred and forty-five thousand fruit trees growing in his several orchards.

1651-52.

SEC. 8, B. Our ancestors were careful in recording their cattle marks. The following is an illustration of the manner in which it was done, by virtue of "An Order for recording the Mark of Cattle and Hogs." Act of 1650, chap. xiii.

"January, 22, 1651 Thos. Marsh, gent, his mark of hogs and Cattle:—Both ears swallow-tailed, and no other mark." Fol. 26.

SEC. 9. "At a Court held at *St. Mary's* 20th January, Anno Domini 1650, Present GOVERNOR WM. STONE, Esqr., ROBERT BROOKE, Capt. John Price, Mr. Thos. Genrralt, &c. Upon Mr. MORGAN'S petition (this day exhibited by Mr. Francis Brooke, his Attorney) to be relieved for certain fees and charges due to him, who was then Sheriff of Kent, by ye late imprisonment of Thomas Bradnox for felony, who was acquitted therein upon ye trial, as was alleged; and ye question being from whom ye said fees and charges are due; this Court is clearly of opinion, and doth order, that Thomas Bradnox ye prisoner shall pay such fees and charges belonging to ye Sheriff (to be moderated and allowed by ye Commissioners and Commander at Kent), as were duly incurred by reason of ye said imprisonment, and he to be at liberty to seek his relief against ye prosecutors, being quitted upon ye trial."

"Copia vera Tho. Hatton Secre." Folio 35.

SEC. 10. "At a Court holden in Kent County on ye 12th January, 1651:

Present,

Capt. ROBT VAUGHAN, COMMANDER,

Mr. PHILLIP CONNER,	Mr. NICHOLAS BROWNE,
Mr. HENRY MORGAN,	Mr. THOMAS BRADNOX,
Mr. THOMAS RINGGOLD,	Mr. JOSEPH WICKES,
Fol. 38.	Commissioners."

SEC. 11. It appears that "ague" was upon Kent Island as early as 1651. Fol. 61.

Thomas Marsh "was chirurgeosn" in 1651. Fol. 36.

SEC. 12. "The Inventory of Robt. Short,

20th Nov., 1651."	lbs. of tob.
Imprimis, for one gun	250.
For one small bed, with a canvass ticking, and 2 old blankets	140.
For one pair of shoes, 20, for some old lumber, 90	110.
For an old frying pan, 8; and a cow and calf, 600	608.
For a heifer of two years old, and something more in calf	400.
For a 3 years old bull, 500; an old " " " split in the back, and the bottom of an iron pot	515.
For one yearling bull, 200	200.
For one cow, and a two years old heifer, and one yearling heifer	1300.
	3523.

Sworn appraisers } Robt. X. Martin
Rich. X. Blunt.

Folio 75.

1652-53.

SEC. 13. In the year 1652, Mark Benton "petitioned against Robt. Vaughan for order from the Court for his freedom, with corne and clothes." The Court decided in his favor. Folio 52.

SEC. 14. On the 2nd of June, 1652, the Surveyor-General issued the following address to the people of Kent county:

"WHEREAS divers inhabitants of this County of Kent have several warrants to survey land yet unreserved, whereby they fear some danger or prejudice may come to them, in relation to their land, I, ROBERT CLARKE, *Surveyor General* of this Province, do hereby promise to make good all such warrants, wherein it shall appear I am deficient, until such time as I can come, and perform the service.

"ROBERT CLARKE,
"Surveyor General.

"To the inhabitants
of the Isle of Kent.
Recorded this 15th of
June, 1652." Fol. 44.

SEC. 15. JOHN GOULD, aged 40 or thereabouts, sworne and examined in court, saith: That your deponent did carry home a suit of curtains to Francis Brights, by order from his master, Mr. Carlyen; after which time your deponent did see about half a yard of Francis Brights' stuff at his master's house; and further saith not.

JOHN I GOULD.
mark.

Fol. 44.

SEC. 16. In 1652 a hogshead of tobacco contained three hundred pounds. In the same year St. Mary's is called by Kent Islanders "Maryland." To prevent the case between Major Joseph Wickes and Doct. Th. Ward being heard there, an arbitration is made by Thos. Marsh and Jno. Russell. Fol. 57.

Thos. Hynson was Clerk of the County of Kent in 1652. Fol. 49–57.

SEC. 17. At the Court held at Mr. Lumbard's, the 12th of August, 1652, Francis Lumbard was authorized to act as Sheriff for that year, having been elected a second time. From this case it would appear that the Sheriff, at this period, did not wait for the Governor's commission. Fol. 47.

SEC. 18. At the same Court, an inquest was held over the body of James Wilson, a "Scot," and a servant of Capt. Thos. Bradnox. The death occurred on the 19th of August, 1652.

"The Jury having according to their Oaths, and in discharge of their Consciences, made inquiry into the death of James Wilson, and do unanimously conclude that the material cause of the said Wilson his death was an intermitting fever joined with the dropsy or scurvy, as commonly understood, and further that the stripes given him by his Master not long before his death were not material." Wm. Fuller and eleven other Jurors. For the entire case, see Folios 47-49.

SEC. 19. At the August Term of the Court. 1652, Edward Coppedge was found guilty of "living in——" with Elizabeth Risby, before he was able to prove the death of her husband, Wm. Risby; and sentenced to pay 600 lbs. of tobacco, and to remain in the sheriff's hands, until the execution of a bond, "that he company not with her nor come to have any familiarity with the aforesaid Elizabeth Risby." Fol. 50.

At the same session of the Court, Elizabeth Risby was sentenced to receive 15 lashes and to give bond for her good behavior. Fol. 51.

SEC. 20. At the same session of the Court Capt. ROBERT VAUGHAN was fined 300 lbs. of tobacco, for insolent language to the Court. Fol. 52.

A second time, Capt. ROBERT VAUGHAN insulted the Court by using most "opprobious" epithets, bending his "fist" over the "heads" of the Judges and "swearing" at the Clerk as "he sat at table." For this offence the Court imposed a fine of 600 lbs. of Tob. Fol. 56.

Capt. ROBERT VAUGHAN had lately been deposed by the "Keepers of the Liberty of England," and could not stomach and digest the doings of a Court organized by the Puritan Commissioners.

SEC. 21. THOS. WARD, about the same time, was arrested upon "suspicion of felony." The case was referred to the next Court. In one of the depositions, it is stated, that a servant had run away, and upon being taken back, "Mistress Ward did whip her with a peach tree rod & after she had done, she took water and salt, and salted her, and when she was adoing the same the maid cried out, and desired her Mistress to use her like a Christian, and she replied and said: "Oh! ye ——you." "Do you liken yourself like a Christian?" And also after that time, "She ran away several times." (Fol. 54.) The Jury found that the punishment given by Thos. Ward and his wife was not the cause of the "maid's" death, but that it was "unreasonable considering her weak estate of body;" and the Court imposed a fine of 300 lbs. of tob. for the "unreasonable and unchristian-like punishment." Fol. 56.

SEC. 22. Among the Proceedings of the November Court, 1652, is the following: "Whereas the Wife of Francis Hunt hath petitioned unto this Court for a Certificate unto the

Provincial Court, that she was the Wife of said Hunt, which was lately slain by the Indians upon the Isle of Kent, the —— of October, wherefore this Court hath granted her lawful request: These are therefore to certify your Worships, and the rest of the Council of the certainty of the premises." Fol. 56.

SEC. 23. At the November Court, 1652, "THOS. RINGGOLD, aged 43 years," deposed, that about the 1st of the preceeding July, he heard Wm. Jones at Thos. Hinson's house, say, that he would question Thos. Ward, about the death of his "maid" for he would bring him to his twelve God-fathers, which was John Hood, and Elizabeth Risby, and Richard Blunt, and he would prosecute the suit. Fol. 57.

SEC. 24. Upon Folio 58 there is a long and curiously queer deposition of Henry Carlien respecting expressions he heard, in relation to the case of Ed. Coppedge and "Risby's Wife." The deposition of Henry Carlein retails a conversation at his own house with Jane the wife of John Hood. Jane Hood asserts the innocence of Elizabeth Risby, and insists that the latter is the lawful wife of Ed. Coppedge, "but only for the ceremony."

SEC. 25. At the December Court, 1652, Thos. Weest, servant to HENRY MORGAN, gentleman, obtained his freedom, and freedom corn, with whatever besides may "be usual according to the custom of the Country."

The order is conditional, the Master being allowed a certain time to produce the indentures. Fol. 60.

SEC. 26. At the December Court, 1652, the following deposition was made:

"The deposition of THOS. PETT, aged 40 years or thereabouts, sworne, examined, saith, that a little after Will'm Jones came from the *Susquehanahs*, deponent did hear the said Jones say, that he did see Andrew the Sanyeard (Spaniard?), and he asked for the boy Salter, and he said, that if he had him there, he would clothe him, and further saith not." Fol 61.

SEC. 27. "January the 9th being the Lord's Day, one Burton shot a goose, and one Thomas Farington going on the ice towards the goose, was drowned, the said Farington being late servant of Mr. Philip Conier, on the Isle of Kent. Upon this occasion, a Jury was empanelled, and the Coroner sat Jan. 11th, 1652, *o. s.*

"The deposition of CHRSTIAN HILL, the Wife of Thos. Hill, being of age about 45 years, concerning the death of the said

Thos. Farington, the said Christian Hill, sworne & examined, saith, that the boy was at our house upon occasion for his Mistress, and I despatched him away presently, and he said, he was to go with Goodman Burton for a goose, and within a while after, I went to look out after him, and I saw Goodman Burton upon the ice, and he went into the canoe, and the boy went out of the canoe upon the ice upon his knees with a stick afore him, and when he came almost to the goose, he called to Goodman Burton, and said, the ice cracked, and he turned about another way, and presently fell in, and then he called to Goodman Burton to help him, and he went forth out of the canoe, and when he came within a paddle's length to my discerning, he fell in also. I saw him labour with his hands and could endure to see the sight no longer, but went in, and further your deponent saith not." (Fol. 44.) Thos. Hill testified to the same facts as his mother. And the Jury gave the following verdict:

"That the said Thomas Farington came by his death, as far as they can discern, not by his own will, intent, or purpose, nor by the intent of any other, but according to the evidence, fell through the ice, and perished, before any help could come to save his life." Fol. 64.

Mrs. Christian Hill survived her first husband, Thomas Hill. On the 5th day of November, 1657, I find her recorded as being, then, the wife of Thomas Ringgold.

Sec. 28. The license given by the Governor to Thos. Ringgold to kill "any wild, unmarked hogs within any of his Lordship's forests" upon the "Island" was revoked and returned to the Clerk, on this 2nd of Feb. 1652, *o. s.* Fol. 44.

Sec. 29. At the February session of the Court, in 1652, *o. s.*, The Court granted a Certificate to John Conitt, for 300 acres of land, "he coming to this Island, himself, his Wife & Child the first of May last, 1652." Fol. 67.

At this Court, Thos. Marsh, "merchant," obtained judgment against the estate of Wm. Jones. Fol. 67.

Sec. 30. At the same Court Henry Carlien, and Thos. Ringgold testified, that about the last of the previous May, they heard Capt. Jacobs say, "that he had shipped 16 hhds. of Tobacco aboard Mr. Marsh his vessel." Fol. 70.

Francis Lumbard testified, that he heard Capt. Jacobs about the same time say, "that he was to give Mr. Thos. Marsh 4 lbs. a ton for freight in his vessel to New England. Fol. 70. Isaac Iler confirmed the testimony of Mr. Lumbard. Fol. 70.

Sec. 31. At the same Court Thos. Pett testified, "that being at Maryland, at the Court, he heard the Secretary ask Mr. Ward, whether the tobacco and the servant that Mr. Wickes, was to pay for the land, should be for the children's use, and the said Mr. Ward answered, that it was the Mother's, before it was his, and he desired that it might go for their use." (Fol. 71.) Here is an instance in which "Maryland" was used as another name for St. Mary's.

SEC. 32. "Received of Mr. Henry Carlien, six rolls of tobacco, one bear's skin, and five raccoons' skins, which goods abovesaid I shall sell for his use, to the Dutch Plantation, or Boston, after safe arrivement, or to be delivered to Mr. Henry Payne in Boston. Witness my hand, this 25th day of May, 1652. John Jacobs." Fol. 73.

SEC. 33. The County Levy for the year 1652 was estimated at 2,877 lbs. of tobacco, at the rate of "45 lbs. of tob. per poll of all tithable persons throughout this Island." Fol. 68.

SEC. 34. On Folio 45 is recorded the following Proclamation:

BY THE COMMISSIONERS OF THE COUNCIL OF STATE FOR THE COMMONWEALTH OF ENGLAND.

WHEREAS the right honorable the council of State for the commonwealth of England by authority of parliament have committed to us, the commissioners several powers in the reducing, settling and governing of all the plantations within the bay of Chesapeake, as by their commission and instructions, bearing date at Whitehall, the 26th day of September, 1651, may appear, in pursuance whereof the foresaid commissioners, having applied themselves to the governor and council of Maryland, (one of the plantations within the limits aforesaid) requiring them to submit themselves and to act accordingly, and having tendered the same several times unto them, so that they might remain in their places, conforming themselves to the laws of the Commonwealth of England, in point of government only, and not infringing the lord Baltimore's just rights, which they having denied and refused, as being inconsistent with the patent of the lord proprietor and their oaths made to him; In obedience, therefore, to the said council's commands, in their said commission to us directed, for the preservation of the honor and interest of the commonwealth of England for settling the colony of Maryland in their due obedience and peace, and for the true administration of justice and right to the inhabitants thereof, until further order can be taken therein and until the council of State's further pleasure shall be known; We, the said commissioners have hereby thought fit to publish these orders following, requiring all the people of this province to see the same kept and observed;

That all writs, warrants and process whatsoever be issued forth in the name of the keepers of the liberty of England by authority of parliament; that they be signed under the hand of one or more of the council hereafter named, viz: Robert Brooke, esqr., cols. Francis Yardley, Mr. Job Chandler, captain Edward Windham, Mr. Richard Preston, and lieutenant Richard Banks.

That the said council of Maryland, first taking the engagement, do cause the same to be tendered to all the inhabitants in these words,—We, whose names are subscribed, do promise and engage ourselves to be true and faithful to the commonwealth of England, as it is now established, without King or house of lords.

That the said council of Maryland, or any two or more of them, whereof Robert Brooke, esq., to be one, do govern and direct the affairs thereof, and hold courts as often as they think fit for that purpose, as also that they summon an assembly to begin 24th June next coming, the burgesses whereof are only to be chosen by such freemen as have taken the said engagement, and that neither by the said council nor in the said assembly anything be acted contrary to the laws of England there established, or to their obedience due to the commonwealth of England.

That the commissions for the governor and council be hereby declared void and null, and to be delivered into the hands of us, the commissioners, as also that all records and other matters and things relating to the government of Maryland be delivered into the hands of the council herein by us nominated.

RICHARD BENNETT,
EDMUND COURTIES,
WILLM CLAIBORNE.

Dated at St. Mary's the 29th day of March 1652.

Bozman thinks that the Commissioners never proceeded "to any hearing or examination of complaints against Vaughan." He was mistaken, as we will see by the document in the following section, which has never before been published. It is recorded on Folio 66 of LIBER A. *Court Proceedings of Kent county.*

SEC. 35. WHEREAS, the reducing, settling and governing of Virginia, and all the English plantations within the Bay of

Chesapeake, was referred to certain Commissioners, by order from the Council of State for the Commonwealth of England; AND Whereas, the Governor and Council for this Province of Maryland, in obedience and conformity to the said order and power, have authorized and deputed the persons, whose hands are hereunto subscribed, for settling the Isle of Kent, and the rather for that reason of some differences, and complaints by the inhabitants, there, against Capt. ROBERT VAUGHAN, the chief in place and command upon the said Island, the course of justice, and keeping courts for the better administration thereof, hath been of late discontinued:

THESE are, therefore, in the name of the KEEPERS OF THE LIBERTY OF ENGLAND, by authority of Parliament, to signify, and declare, that for the present, till further order out of England, Mr. PHILIP CONNER, Mr. THOS. RINGGOLD, Mr. THOS. BRADNOX, Mr. HENRY MORGAN, Mr. NIC. BROWNE, Mr. THOS. HYNSON, Mr. JOSEPH WICKES, Mr. JOHN PHILLIPS, and Mr. JOHN RUSSELL, be Commissioners for the said Island, and that they, or any four of them, whereof Mr. PHILIP CONNER, or Mr. THOS. RINGGOLD to be always one, shall have power to hear and determine all differences, and to call courts for that purpose as often as they shall see cause, to make choice of a Sheriff, and a Clerk for keeping Records, and Execution of Writs, and all other process, and to act in all things for the peace, safety and welfare of the said Island, and the inhabitants thereof, as they or the former Commissioners did, or might do, by virtue of their commission from the Lord Baltimore, and the Governor & Council of this Province under him.

REQUIRING all the inhabitants of the said Island to take notice of this Order, and to conform themselves accordingly, as they will answer the contrary at their peril.

Given under our hands, at the Isle of Kent the 31st day of July, 1652.

RI: BENNETT,
EAD: LLOYD,
THOS: MARSH,
LEO: STRONG.

SEC. 35, A. EDWARD LLOYD came from Virginia with Leonard Strong, William Durand and others, about the year 1650, and settled on Greenbury Point, near Annapolis. He was a Puritan, and compelled to quit Virginia in consequence of his nonconformity. Leonard Strong says in his "Babylon's Fall" that they were not invited into Maryland, they were only "received and protected."

Edward Lloyd was a gentleman of conspicuous ability, and was commissioned, 30th July, 1650 by Governor Stone, Commander of Anne Arundel County, then, recently erected and named after Lady Anne Arundel, the dau. of Lord Arundel, of Wardour, lately the beautiful wife of Cecilius Lord Baltimore. For many years he was a Privy Councellor of Maryland. He returned to England in 1668, m. a widow, Mrs. Grace Buckerfield, and resided in London until his death. In his will, dated 11th March, 1695, he styles himself "Edward Lloyd, of the Parish of Saint Mary, White Chappel, in the County of Middlesex, merchant, and late a planter of Maryland," and devised "WYE HOUSE" to his grandson Edward Lloyd, who was the son of his son Philemon Lloyd—Philemon Lloyd was the son of Edward Lloyd and his first wife Alice Crouch.

PHILEMON LLOYD, son of Edward and his first wife Alice Crouch Lloyd, was a member of the Legislature of Maryland in the sessions of 1671 and 1674. He m. Mrs. Henrietta Maria Neale Bennett, widow of Richard Bennett, and eldest dau. of Capt. James and Anna Neale, and had children, viz: Edward,—Philemon,—Henrietta,—Anna Maria,—Alice, d. *sine prole*,—Jane, d. *sine prole*,—Mary, d. *sine prole* (the town of Millington, Kent County, Maryland, stands on land once owned by her),—Margaret,—Elizabeth, d. young,—and James Lloyd. Philemon Lloyd d. 2d Jan'y 1698, and his wife 4th May 1697.

SEC. 35, B. Captain James Neale came to Maryland about the year 1650, from Spain, *via* Portugal. The Act of Assembly of 1666, Chapt. VIII, discloses a glimpse of his former history. It is as follows:

"*The Humble Petition* of Capt. James Neale, viz: For naturalization of his four children, HENRIETTA MARIA,—JAMES,—DOROTHY and ANTHONY NEALE, born in Spain, of ANNA, his wife, during his residence there as a merchant, and also employed there by the King and the Duke of YORK in several emergent affairs, as by commissions herewith produced might appear, &c."

James Neale, son of Capt. James and Anna Neale settled and married on the Western Shore of Maryland.

Dorothy Neale m. ——— Taney, and was the ancestress of the late Chief Justice Taney. Mrs. Anna Neale was a great mother, more than a thousand of her descendants are mentioned in this volume.

HENRIETTA MARIA NEALE, eldest dau. of Capt. James and Anna Neale, m. 1st Richard Bennett, who was drowned in early manhood, and left two child., viz: Richard, who m. Elizabeth Rousby, and d. *sine prole*, and a dau. who m. ——— Darnall, or ——— Lowe.

SEC. 35. C, EDWARD LLOYD, of Wye House, Talbot County, Md., eldest son of Philemon and Henrietta Maria Neale Bennett Lloyd, was a member of the Legislature of Maryland in the sessions of 1699, 1701 and 1702. He m. 1st Feb'y 1703, Sarah Covington,—and had six child., viz: Edward, b. 11th Sept. 1705, d. 14th Feb'y 1707,—Philemon, b. 26th March, 1709, d. 5th March, 1729, *sine prole*,—a second Edward, b. 8th May, 1711, d. 27th Jan. 1770,—Rebecca C. b. 11th June, 1713, who. m. William Anderson, merchant, of London,—James, b. 14th Aug. 1715, d. 14th Sept. 1738, *sine prole*,—and Richard Lloyd, b. 19th March, 1717, who m. ——— ——— and had two child., viz: Anna Maria, who m. Jeremiah Nicols, and Major James Lloyd, who m. Elizabeth Tilghman. Edward Lloyd d. 20th March, 1719, and his widow m. 3d May, 1721, James Hollyday, of Readbourne, Queen Anne's Co (see HOLLYDAY). She was a remarkably beautiful woman. She accompanied her dau. Mrs. Rebecca C. Lloyd Anderson to London, and d. there 9th April, 1755. The letter that records her death is stained with tears, and her character through life justified such expression.

EDWARD LLOYD, of Wye House, son of Edward and Sarah Covington Lloyd, was a member of the Maryland Legislature in the session of 1739. He m. 26th March, 1739, Ann Rousby, of Patuxent, and had four child., viz: Elizabeth, b. 10th Jan'y 1742, who. m. Gen'l John Cadwalader of the Revolutionary Army, and had a dau. Maria Cadwalader, who m. Gen'l Samuel Ringgold, of Fountain Rock, Washington Co., Md. (see RINGGOLD),—Edward, b. 15th Dec. 1744, d. 8th July 1796,—Henrietta Maria, b. 28th Jan'y 1746-7, and Richard Bennett Lloyd, b. 13th Aug. 1750, who became a captain in the King's Life Guards, m. in England, Joanna Leigh, of the Isle of Wight, and d. 12th Sept. 1787, and had child., viz: Edward, who settled near Alexandria, Va., and left many descendants,—Richard Bennett,—Henry and Emily Lloyd. The three last d. *sine prole*.

Mrs. Ann Rousby Lloyd d. 1st May 1769, aged 47 years, and her husband, Edward Lloyd, d. 17th Jan'y 1770.

EDWARD LLOYD, of Wye House, son of Edward and Ann Rousby Lloyd, m. 19th Nov. 1767, Elizabeth Tayloe, and had seven child., viz., Ann, b. 30th Jan'y 1769,—d. 20th Feb'y 1840,—Rebecca, b. 16th Oct. 1771,—d. 26th Oct. 1848,—Elizabeth, b. 5th Sept. 1774, d. 6th March 1849,—Eleanor, b, 22d Sept. 1776,—Edward, b. 22d July 1779, d. 2d June 1834,—Maria, b. 11th March 1782, d. 15th Jan'y 1868, and Mary Tayloe Lloyd, b. 26th May 1784 and d. 18th May 1859. Edward Lloyd d. 8th July 1796 and his wife 17th Feb'y 1825. She was b. 17th March 1750.

ANN LLOYD, dau. of Edward and Elizabeth Tayloe Lloyd, m. Richard Tasker Lowndes, of Bostic House, Prince George's Co., Md., and had child., viz., Elizabeth Lloyd, who m. Rt. Rev. William Pinckney, D. D.,—Ann,—Edward Lloyd,—Richard Tasker, a second Edward Lloyd, and Benjamin Ogle Lowndes.

REBECCA LLOYD, dau. of Edward and Elizabeth Tayloe Lloyd, m. 10th Oct. 1793, Hon. Joseph Hopper Nicholson, Chief Justice of the Sixth Judicial District and one of the Judges of the Court of Appeals of Maryland, and had child., viz., Joseph,—Edward,—Edward Lloyd, who m. Margaret Harwood, of Annapolis, and d. 17th July 1846,—Elizabeth,—Joseph Hopper, b. 10th Oct. 1806, d. 2d June 1872, and James Macon Nicholson.

JOSEPH HOPPER NICHOLSON, son of Judge Joseph Hopper and Rebecca Lloyd Nicholson, m. 10th April 1827, Eliza Ann Hagner, of Washington, D. C., and had child., viz., Joseph Hopper, b. Feb'y 1828, d. 10th April 1830,—Fanny Rebecca, b. 23rd Oct. 1829, d. 23rd Feb'y 1847,—Emily, and Mary Hagner Nicholson, b. 29th April 1837, m. 9th Aug. 1859,—James Buchanan Henry, of New York, d. at the Clarendon Hotel, Saratoga Springs, N. Y., 12th Aug. 1867, and had child., viz., Buchanan Henry, b. June 1860, d. 27th April 1862, and Joseph Nicholson Henry.

JAMES MACON NICHOLSON, son of Judge Joseph Hopper and Rebecca Lloyd Nicholson, m. 21st June 1838, Arinthea D. Parker, of Northampton County, Va., and had child., viz., Harriet Burleigh, b. 25th Dec. 1840, d. 23d July 1841,—Rebecca Lloyd, who m. 17th April 1866, John Eager Howard Post, and Lelia Parker Nicholson, recently d.

ELIZABETH LLOYD, dau. of Edward and Elizabeth Tayloe Lloyd, m. 14th Feb'y 1805, Henry Hall Harwood, of Annapolis, and had child., viz., Elizabeth Lloyd,—Mary Anne, and Josephine Nicholson Harwood.

ELIZABETH LLOYD HARWOOD, dau. of Henry Hall and

Elizabeth Lloyd Harwood, m. 12th June 1854, Francis Scott Key, son of Francis Scott and Mary Tayloe Lloyd Key.

MARY ANN HARWOOD, dau. of Henry Hall and Elizabeth Lloyd Harwood, m. William Ghiselin, and had a son, William H. Ghiselin.

JOSEPHINE NICHOLSON HARWOOD, dau. of Henry Hall and Elizabeth Lloyd Harwood, m. 10th Jan'y 1833, Edward Gibson Tilton, U. S. N., a native of Delaware, and had child., viz., Edward, b. 7th Oct. 1833, d. an infant,—McLane, who m. 26th July 1866, Anna M. Wells, of Annapolis,—Clara, who m. 29th Dec. 1864, William Campbell Emory,—Lizzie,—James,—Gibson,—and Edward Gibson Tilton.

ELEANOR LLOYD, dau. of Edward and Elizabeth Tayloe Lloyd, m. Charles Lowndes, a brother of Richard Tasker Lowndes, before mentioned, and had child., viz., Harriet,—Edward Lloyd, b. 5th June 1797, d. 21st Oct. 1797,—Charles,—Lloyd,—Richard Tasker, b. 29th March 1803, d. 24th April 1844,—and Elizabeth Ann Lowndes.

Charles Lowndes survived his 1st wife, Eleanor Lloyd Lowndes, and m. Frances Whiting, of Va., and had child., viz., Frances P., who d. young,—Beverly Bladen,—Frances Whiting and Frances P. Lowndes.

HARRIET LOWNDES, dau. of Charles and Eleanor Lloyd Lowndes, m. Dr. Samuel Scolley, of Jefferson Co., Va., and had child., viz., Charles Lowndes,—Ann Lloyd, who m. —— Beckwith, of Va.,—Samuel,—Eleanor, who m. —— Moore, of Va.,—and Elizabeth Scolley, who m. —— Page.

CHARLES LOWNDES, son of Charles and Eleanor Lloyd Lowndes, m. 4th May 1824, Sally Scott Lloyd, dau. of Gen'l Edward and Sally Scott Murray Lloyd, and had child., viz., Sally Lloyd,—Ellen, b. 15th Sept. 1831, d. 23d July 1845,—Charles, who m. Catharine Tilghman,—Edward Lloyd, b. 11th Oct. 1836, d. 20th June 1837,—Lloyd,—Richard Tasker, b. 14th Feb'y 1843, d. 6th Aug. 1845, and Elizabeth Tayloe Lowndes.

SALLY LLOYD LOWNDES, dau. of Charles and Sally Scott Lloyd Lowndes, m. John W. Bennett, U. S. N., and had child., viz., Ellen Lowndes,—Harriet Gibson, and Charles Lowndes Bennett.

RICHARD TASKER LOWNDES, son of Charles and Eleanor Lloyd Lowndes, m. Elizabeth Black, of Cumberland, Md., and had child., viz., Eloise and Bessie Lowndes.

ELIZABETH ANN LOWNDES, dau. of Charles and Eleanor Lloyd Lowndes, m. Horace Leeds Edmondson, and had child., viz., John,—Horace Leeds,—Maria Lloyd, and Charles Lowndes Edmondson.

Horace Leeds Edmondson survived his 1st. wife, Elizabeth Ann Lowndes Edmondson, and m. Mrs. —— Dawson, of Easton, Md., and had child., viz., William Groome and Alice Leeds Edmondson.

ALICE LEEDS EDMONDSON, dau. of Horace Leeds Edmondson, m. 29th Feb'y 1876, Hon. James Black Groome, ex-Governor of the State of Maryland. (See BLACK.)

HON. EDWARD LLOYD, of Wye House, only son of Edward and Elizabeth Tayloe Lloyd, was Governor of the State of Maryland in 1809–1811, and United States Senator from the 21st of Dec. 1819 to the 24th Jan'y 1826. He m. 30th Nov. 1797, Sally Scott Murray, who was b. 30th Oct. 1775, and had child., viz., Edward, b. 27th Dec. 1798, d. 11th Aug. 1861,—Elizabeth Tayloe,—James Murray, b. 10th Jan'y 1803, d. 22d July 1847,—Sally Scott,—Ann Catharine,—Daniel and Mary Eleanor Lloyd. Gov. Edward Lloyd d. 2d June 1834. Mrs. Sally Scott Murray Lloyd d. 9th May 1854.

EDWARD LLOYD, of Wye House, son of Gov. Edward and Sally Scott Murray Lloyd, m. 30th Nov. 1824, Alicia McBlair, who was b. 5th March 1806, d. 8th July 1838, and had child., viz., Edward,—Elizabeth,—McBlair, b. 6th Jan'y 1831, d. 3d Sept. 1846,—Alicia,—and Sally Lloyd. Edward Lloyd, d. 11th Aug. 1861.

COL. EDWARD LLOYD, of Wye House, son of Edward and Alicia McBlair Lloyd, m. 25th June 1851, Mary Lloyd Howard, dau. of Charles and Phoebe Key Howard (see HOWARD), and had child., viz., Edward, b. 24th Oct. 1853, d. 13th Aug. 1854,—Alicia,—a 2d Edward,—Charles Howard,—McBlair,—John Eager and Elizabeth Phoebe Key Lloyd.

ELIZABETH LLOYD, dau. of Edward and Alicia McBlair Lloyd, m. Nov. 1852, Charles Henry Key, son of Frances Scott and Mary Tayloe Lloyd Key, and had child., viz., Edward Lloyd,—Mary Tayloe,—Philip Barton, b. 26th Nov. 1858, d. 10th Oct. 1862,—Frances Scott,—and Alicia Key.

ALICIA LLOYD, dau. of Edward and Alicia McBlair Lloyd, m. Capt. Chas. S. Winder, U. S. A., and C. S. A., and had child., elsewhere named.

SALLY LLYOD, dau. of Edward and Alicia McBlair Lloyd, m. 9th Nov. 1859, David Churchill Trimble, and had a son, Isaac Ridgeway Trimble.

ELIZABETH TAYLOE LLOYD, dau. of Gov. Edward and Sally Scott Murray Lloyd, m. 1st June 1820, Edward S. Winder, and had child., viz., Edward Lloyd, who m. Helen Thorborn, of Norfolk, Va.,—Levin, b. 13th Nov. 1822, d. 21st March 1843, at Louisville, Kentucky,—James Murray, b. 15th Feb'y 1825, d. 7th Sept. 1847, at Jalapa, Mexico, of a wound received at the battle of Puerto National, 12th Aug. 1847,—Sarah Murray Winder, — Charles Sydney, b. 7th Oct. 1829, d. 9th Aug. 1862, in the battle of Cedar Run,—Elizabeth Tayloe,—Mary and William Sydney Winder.

GEN. CHARLES SYDNEY WINDER, son of Edward S. and Elizabeth Tayloe Lloyd Winder, was a graduate of West Point, and attained the rank of Captain of Infantry in the United States Army. In the Spring of 1861 he resigned his commission and went South, where he served with distinction, and was made a Brigadier General. He was slain in battle at Cedar Run, 9th August, 1862. He m. his cousin, Alicia Lloyd, and had children, viz., Charles Sydney,—Edward Lloyd, and Elizabeth Lloyd Winder, b. 4th August, 1860, and d. 8th November, 1862.

ELIZABETH TAYLOE WINDER, dau. of Edward S. and Elizabeth Tayloe Lloyd Winder, m. Charles J. Pennington, and had children, viz., Josias,—Elizabeth Lloyd and Edward Winder Pennington.

JAMES MURRAY LLOYD (b. 10th January, 1803, d. 22d July, 1847), son of Gov. Edward and Sally Murray Lloyd, m. 1st November, 1836, Elizabeth McBlair, who was b. 3d January, 1818, d. 30th October, 1850, and had child., viz., Edward, b. 11th Aug., 1837, d. 17th May, 1839,—James Murray, b. 30th October, 1840, d. 21st June, 1861,—and Charles Tilghman Lloyd, b. 22d October, 1842, who entered the Confederate Army and was wounded twice in battle, the last time, fatally, at Gettysburg, Pa., 2d July, 1863, and died the next day.

SALLY SCOTT LLOYD, dau. of Gov. Edward and Sally Scott Murray Lloyd, m. 4th May, 1824, Charles Lowndes, son of Charles and Eleanor Lloyd Lowndes.

ANN CATHERINE LLOYD, dau. of Gov. Edward and Sally Scott Murray Lloyd, m. 19th February, 1835, Franklin Buchanan, U. S. N. (Admiral Buchanan, C. S. N.), and had child., viz., Sally Lloyd,—Letitia McKean,—Alice,—Nannie and Ellen, twins,—Elizabeth Tayloe,—Franklin,—Rosa, and Mary Tilghman Buchanan, who m. W. Tilghman Owen.

ADMIRAL FRANKLIN BUCHANAN was a Captain in the United States Navy until the memorable 19th of April, 1861, when he resigned and was commissioned an officer in the Navy of the Confederate States. He was the Admiral in command of the Merrimac during its short and brilliant career of victory, and was wounded in the famous fight with the iron-clad monitor, Ericsson, in Hampton Roads, 9th March, 1862. He was the youngest son of Dr. George Buchanan, a graduate of the Universities at Edinburgh and Paris; who m. 18th June, 1789, Letitia, second dau. of the Hon. Thomas McKean, an eminent lawyer, a member of the Continental Congress from the State of Delaware, and a Signer of the Declaration of Independence.

Dr. George Buchanan was b. in Baltimore County, 19th of September, 1763, the son of Andrew Buchanan. See "Chronicles of Baltimore, by Col. J. Thomas Scharf," pp. 258-9.

SALLY LLOYD BUCHANAN, dau. of Admiral Franklin and Ann Catharine Lloyd Buchanan, m. 30th Oct. 1866, Thomas Forman Screven.

NANNIE BUCHANAN, dau. of Admiral Franklin and Ann Catharine Lloyd Buchanan, m. 4th April 1861, Julius Ernest Meiere, U. S. Marine Corps and C. S. N., and had child., viz., Nannie Lloyd and Ernest Meiere.

ELLEN BUCHANAN, dau. of Admiral Franklin and Ann Catharine Lloyd Buchanan, m. 5th June 1861, George P. Screven, and had child., viz., Franklin Buchanan,—Mary, and Murray Lloyd Screven.

DANIEL LLOYD, son of Gov. Edward and Sally Scott Murray Lloyd, m. 22d Nov. 1832, Virginia Upshur, who was b. 13th Oct. 1812, d. 7th June 1843, and had child., viz., Ann Steele,—Edward,—Arthur Upshur, b. 17th Aug. 1837, *deceased*,—Daniel, and Upshur Lloyd

Daniel Lloyd, m. 2ndly Catharine Henry, and had child., viz., Mary Campbell,—Kate Henry,—Henry, and Tayloe Lloyd.

ANN STEELE LLOYD, dau. of Daniel and Virginia Upshur Lloyd, m. Archibald Stirling, of Baltimore, and had child., viz., Edward Lloyd,—Margaret,—Archibald, and Upshur Stirling.

MARY ELEANOR LLOYD, dau. of Gov. Edward and Sally Scott Murray Lloyd, m. 26th Oct. 1837, William Tilghman Goldsborough, son of Gov. Charles and Sarah Yerbery Goldsborough, and had child., viz., Charles, who m. 7th Nov. 1865, Mary Colquhoun Galt,—William Tilghman,—Edward Lloyd, b. 15th Dec. 1843, d. 29th March 1861,—Ellen Lloyd,—Fitzhugh,—Nannie Lloyd,—Sally Scott, b. 27th Jan'y 1855, d. 6th Dec. 1856,—Richard Tilghman,—Alice Lloyd, and Mary Lee Goldsborough.

Hon. William Tilghman Goldsborough d. in Baltimore city, 23d Jan'y 1876, and was buried at Greenmount Cemetery. (See GOLDSBOROUGH.)

MARIA LLOYD, dau. of Edward and Elizabeth Tayloe Lloyd, m. Richard Williams West, of "The Wood Yard," Prince George's Co., Md., and had child., viz., Richard Williams,—Elizabeth Hannah,—Richard Henry,—Edward Lloyd, and Mary Lloyd West.

ELIZABETH HANNAH WEST, dau. of Richard Williams and Maria Lloyd West, m. 31st July 1832, the Rev. Jonathan Loring Woart, and had a son, Richard West Woart.

Mr. and Mrs. Woart were lost at sea, while coming from Charleston, S. C., to Baltimore, on board the "Pulaski," in 183 .

RICHARD HENRY WEST, son of Richard Williams and Maria Lloyd West, m. Annie Elizabeth Hays, and d., having had one child, Maria Lloyd West. His widow m. Capt. John Williams Tudor Gardiner, U. S. A., and had several children.

EDWARD LLOYD WEST, son of Richard Williams and Maria Lloyd West, m. Lucy Cushing, of Massachusetts, and had child., viz., Edward Lloyd, b. 2d Jan'y 1842, d. 22d Feb'y 1862, at Culpepper C. H., Va.,—Charles Cushing,—Lucy Cushing, and Frank West.

MARY LLOYD WEST, dau. of Richard Williams and Maria Lloyd West, m. Dr. John Burr Hereford, who d. in Alexandria, Va., 26th Oct. 1868. They had a son, Richard West Hereford.

MARY TAYLOE LLOYD, dau. of Edward and Elizabeth Tayloe Lloyd, m. 19th Jan'y 1802, Francis Scott Key, the author of the National Anthem, THE STAR SPANGLED BANNER, and had child., viz., Elizabeth Phoebe, b. 10th Oct. 1803, —Maria Lloyd, b. 13th Feb'y 1805,—Francis Scott, b. 7th Oct. 1806,—John Ross, b. 3d March 1809, d. 21st May 1837, —Ann Arnold, b. 2d March 1811,—Edward Lloyd, b. 26th Sept. 1813, d. 8th July 1822,—Daniel Murray, b. 9th June 1816, d. 22d June 1836,—Philip Barton, b. 5th April 1818, d. 27th Feb'y 1859,—Ellen Lloyd, b. 16th Aug. 1821,—Mary Alicia Lloyd Nevins, b. 20th Nov. 1823, and Charles Henry Key, b. 30th July 1827.

FRANCIS SCOTT KEY was b. 9th Aug. 1780, at the residence of his father, John Ross Key, near Pipe Creek, in Frederick Co., Md., a short distance from Emmittsburg. After his marriage he resided for several years in Frederick city, Md., afterwards he removed to Georgetown, D. C., and finally settled in Washington. He died in the city of Baltimore while on a visit to his daughter, Mrs. Charles Howard, on the 13th Jan'y 1843, aged 63 years.

ELIZABETH PHOEBE KEY, dau. of Francis Scott and Mary Tayloe Lloyd Key, m. 9th Nov. 1825, Charles Howard, of Baltimore, and had child., viz., Francis Key Howard, who m. 27th Jan'y 1853, Lydia E. Hollingsworth Morris,—John Eager Howard,—Charles Howard, who m. 11th July 1855, Mary C. Winder, of Northampton Co., Va.,—Mary Lloyd Howard, who m. 5th June 1851, Edward Lloyd, of Talbot Co., Md.,—James Howard,—Alice Howard,—Edward Lloyd Howard,—McHenry Howard, who m. 18th June 1867, Julia Douglass Coleman,—Ellen Key Howard, who m. 7th Dec. 1865, Charlton Hunt Morgan, of Lexington, Ky.,—Elizabeth Gray Howard, b. 16th Oct. 1841, d. 14th Nov. 1862, and Anna Arnold Key Howard, b. 3d Aug. 1845, and d. 24th May 1846.

For lineage and descendants of Charles Howard, see HOWARD.

MARIA LLOYD KEY, dau. of Francis Scott and Mary Tayloe Lloyd Key, m. 3d June 1823, Henry Maynadier Steele, of Dorchester Co., Md., and had child., viz., Mary Nevett,—Elizabeth Frances,—Sarah Isabella,—Maria Lloyd, b. 2nd Feb'y 1831, d. 20th May 1834,—Henry M.,—Frank Key,—Anna Key,—Ellen Key, and Billings Steele.

Henry Maynadier Steele was b. 5th Oct. 1798, the son of James and Mary Nevett Steele, and d. 29th March 1863.

MARY NEVETT STEELE, dau. of Henry Maynadier and Maria Lloyd Key Steele, m. Dennis Claude, of Annapolis, Md, and had child., viz., Jessie,—Ellwood Wilson, and Herbert Claude.

ELIZABETH FRANCES STEELE, dau. of Henry Maynadier and Maria Lloyd Key Steele, m. Charles Calvert Steuart, and had a dau. Alice Steuart.

For Lineage of Charles Calvert Steuart, see STEUART.

SARAH ISABELLA STEELE, dau. of Henry Maynadier and Maria Lloyd Key Steele, m. Alexander Wylie Habersham (U. S. N.), of Georgia, and had child., viz., Wylie, Henry Steele, Edward Heddon and Ellen Habersham.

HENRY M. STEELE, son of Henry Maynadier and Maria Lloyd Key Steele, m. Emma Brush, and had child., viz., Edward and Constance Steele.

FRANK KEY STEELE, son of Henry Maynadier and Maria Lloyd Key Steele, m. 23d December, 1867, Sallie K. Spalding.

ANNA KEY STEELE, dau. of Henry Maynadier and Maria Lloyd Key Steele, m. 6th January, 1864, Jacob Field Bartow, and had child., viz., Henry Steele and Nevitt Steele Bartow.

FRANCIS SCOTT KEY, son of Francis Scott and Mary Tayloe Lloyd Key, m. 4th April, 1826, Elizabeth Lloyd Harwood, and had child., viz., Henry Harwood,—Elizabeth Lloyd,—John Ross,—Fanny Scott,—Mary Ellen,—Alice Turner,—Daniel Murray,—Anna Arnold, and Wilfred Key, b. 4th March, 1845, d. 24th February, 1865, a prisoner of war, at Washington, D. C.

Francis Scott Key d. 4th April, 1866, in the 60th year ot his age.

JOHN ROSS KEY, son of Francis Scott and Mary Tayloe Lloyd Key, m. 25th September, 1834, Virginia Ringgold, daughter of Gen. Samuel Ringgold, of Fountain Rock, and his 2d wife, Marie Antoinette Hay (see RINGGOLD), and had two child., viz., Clarence Key, who m. at Galveston, Texas, 21st March 1867, Mrs. Priscilla Hadley Skiff, and John Ross Key, who m. Mabel Thayer.

ANNA ARNOLD KEY, dau. of Francis Scott and Mary Tayloe Lloyd Key, m. 25th Feb'y 1829, Daniel Turner, of Warrenton, N. C., who was b. 26th Sept. 1796, the son ot James and Mary Turner, of N. C., and had 11 children, viz., Alice Key Turner, who m. 27th Nov. 1856, Dr. John M. Browne, U. S. N.,—Ellen Key Turner, who m. 28th Feb'y 1860, John S. Messersmith, U. S. N., and had 2 child., viz., Edward Turner and Anna Key Messersmith,—Rebecca Turner, who m. Philip Thomas Norwood, of N. C., and had a dau., Ellen Key Norwood,—Anna Key Turner, b. 14th June 1834, d. 13th Jan'y1859,—Francis Scott Turner,—Mary Anderson Lloyd Turner, b. 6th March 1839, d. 16th July 1855,—Daniel Turner,—Elizabeth Phoebe Howard Turner,—Edward Turner, b. 10th May 1845, died 8th Nov. 1851,—Janet Turner, who m. 27th July, 1865, Otis Wardwell, and Emily Virginia Turner.

PHILIP BARTON KEY, son of Francis Scott and Mary Tayloe Lloyd Key, m. in Nov. 1845, Ellen Swann, of Baltimore, and had child., viz., Elizabeth Swann, who m. Robert A. Dobbin,—Mary Lloyd, who m. 24th April 1874, William Gilmor,—Ellen Donnell, b. 2d Sept. 1850, d. 18th Jan'y 1857,—James Swann, and Alice Key.

Mrs. Ellen Swann Key, d. 20th March 1855. Philip Barton Key d. 27th Feb'y, 1859.

ELLEN LLOYD KEY, dau. of Francis Scott and Mary Tayloe Lloyd Key, m. 27th Jan'y 1846, Simon Fraser Blunt (U. S. N.), of Virginia, and had child., viz., Alice Key,—John Y. Mason, and Mary Lloyd Blunt.

Simon Fraser Blunt died at his residence in Baltimore, 27th April 1854.

MARY ALICIA LLOYD NEVINS KEY, dau. of Francis Scott and Mary Tayloe Lloyd Key, m. 2d June 1846, Hon. George Hunt Pendleton, of Cincinnati, Ohio, and had child., viz., Francis Key,—Mary Lloyd, and Jane Frances Pendleton.

CHARLES HENRY KEY, son of Francis Scott and Mary Tayloe Lloyd Key, m. in November 1852, Elizabeth Lloyd, dau. of Edward and Alicia McBlair Lloyd, and had child., viz., Edward Lloyd,—Mary Tayloe,—Philip Barton, b. 26th Nov. 1858, d. 10th Oct. 1862,—Francis Scott, and Alicia Scott Key.

SEC. 35, D. COL. PHILEMON LLOYD, son of Philemon and Henrietta Maria Neale Bennett Lloyd, was a member of the Legislature of Maryland in the sessions of 1701 and 1702. He m. Mrs. Freeman, of Annapolis, and had a dau. Henrietta Maria Lloyd.

HENRIETTA MARIA LLOYD, dau. of Philemon Lloyd, married Samuel Chew, and had child., viz., Samuel (of Herring Bay),—Henrietta Maria, who m. Edward Dorsey, Attorney-at-Law,—Philemon Lloyd,—his twin brother, Bennett, who m. Anna Maria Tilghman, dau. of Edward and Ann Turbutt Tilghman, d. *sine prole*,—Margaret, and Mary Chew.

MARGARET CHEW, dau. of Samuel and Henrietta Maria Lloyd Chew, m. John Beale Bordley, son of Thomas and Ariana Vanderleyden Frisby Bordley, and had child., viz., Thomas,—Matthias, who m. Susan Heath,—Henrietta Maria, who m. Major David Ross, and John Bordley.

MARY CHEW, dau. of Samuel and Henrietta Maria Lloyd Chew, m. twice. Her 1st husband was William Paca, who signed the Declaration of Independence, and had a son, John Paca. Her 2nd husband was Daniel Dulany and had two sons, viz: Lloyd, who was run through with a sword in a duel with Rev. Bennett Allen, and Walter Dulany.

HENRIETTA LLOYD, dau. of Philemon and Henrietta Maria Neale Bennet Lloyd, m. Henry Blake, and had child., viz., John Sawyer (of Wye),—Henrietta Maria, who m. —— Stringfellow,—Dorothy, who m. Dr. Charles Carroll and had a son, Charles Carroll, Barrister (see CARROLL), and Philemon Blake, of Chester.

ANNA MARIA LLOYD, dau. of Philemon and Henrietta

Maria Neale Bennet Lloyd, m. Richard Tilghman, son of Dr. Richard and Marie Foxley Tilghman. She was the ancestress of all the Tilghmans of Maryland. (See TILGHMAN.)

SEC. 35, E. JAMES LLOYD, son of Philemon and Henrietta Maria Neale Bennett Lloyd, m. 12th Jan'y 1709, Ann Grundy, a lady celebrated for her beauty, who was b. 25th April, 1680, d. 18th Nov. 1731, the dau. of Robert Grundy and Deborah, his wife, formerly Deborah Impey, widow of Thomas Impey, whose maiden name was Deborah Boynton, and had child., viz., Henrietta Maria, b. 26th Jan'y 1710,—Robert, b. 19th Feb'y 1712,—Margaret, b. 16th Feb'y 1715,—James, b. 16th March 1717,—Deborah, b. 19th May 1719,—Philemon, b. 4th Nov. 1721,—and Anne Lloyd, b. 13th Feb'y 1724.

James Lloyd d. 29th Sept. 1723.

HENRIETTA MARIA LLOYD, dau. of James and Ann Grundy Lloyd, m. Samuel Chamberlaine, and had child., viz., Thomas,—James,—Lloyd,—Anne, who m. Richard Tilghman Earle,—Henrietta Maria Chamberlaine, and Samuel Chamberlaine.

Samuel Chamberlaine, b. 17th May 1697, d. 30th April 1773. Mrs. Henrietta Maria Lloyd Chamberlaine, b. 26th Jan'y 1710, d. 29th March 1748.

SAMUEL CHAMBERLAINE, son of Samuel and Henrietta Maria Lloyd Chamberlaine, m. Henrietta Maria Hollyday, of Radcliffe, and had child., viz., Anna Maria, who m. John Goldsborough,—Sarah Hollyday, who m. Hon. John Leeds Kerr,—Harriet Rebecca, who m. Levin Gale,—James Lloyd,—Henry,—Samuel and Richard Lloyd Chamberlaine, who d. *sine prole.*

ROBERT LLOYD, son of James and Ann Grundy Lloyd, m. Anna Maria Tilghman Hemsley, widow of William Hemsley and dau. of Richard Tilghman, of the Hermitage, and had child., viz., Richard,—Deborah, who m. Col. Peregrine Tilghman (see TILGHMAN), and Anna Maria Lloyd, who m. William Tilghman. (See TILGHMAN.)

MARGARET LLOYD, dau. of James and Ann Grundy Lloyd, m. William Tilghman, of Groces. (See TILGHMAN.)

JAMES LLOYD, son of James and Ann Grundy Lloyd, m. Elizabeth Ward, of Cecil Co., Md., and had a numerous family.

DEBORAH LLOYD, dau. of James and Ann Grundy Lloyd, m. Jeremiah Nicols, and had child., viz., Robert Lloyd Nicols and Jeremiah Nicols.

SEC. 35, F. CHARLES HOWARD, who m. Elizabeth Phoebe Key, dau. of Francis Scott Key and Mary Tayloe Lloyd, was descended from JOSHUA HOWARD. The following interesting memorandum, in the hand-writing of Col. John Eager Howard, records the early history of the family in Maryland:

"JOHN EAGER HOWARD was born the 4th day of June 1752, in Baltimore County, in Maryland, at the place settled by his grandfather, Joshua Howard, who came from England to this country about the year 1667. He was from Manchester, where the people generally turned out, and he with them, at the time of Monmouth's invasion, though very young, to support James. They marched to London, where, Monmouth being defeated, they were discharged; and he preferred coming to this country rather than return to his father, who was displeased at his leaving home in the manner he did. He obtained a grant for the land where he settled, which is still in the family, soon after he came to this country. He married Joanna O'Carroll, from Ireland, and had a number of children, one of whom, Cornelius, father of J. E. Howard, married Ruth Eager, whose grandfather, George Eager, as appears by the records, purchased, in 1668, the estate now held, near, and including part of the City of Baltimore.

"It is supposed the family of Eagers came from England to Maryland soon after the charter to Lord Baltimore, but the records afford but little information prior to 1668.

"It appears by the records that the above-named George Eager left three sons,—Thomas,—John and George. Thomas married and died without leaving children—his widow married Samuel Merryman. George died young, without being married. JOHN married Jemima Murray and had two children. George and RUTH, who were infants when he died. The widow married Philip Jones, and by him had one daughter, who married Joseph Murray, from whom are descended a part of the Cromwells and Chenoweths. On the death of Jemima, Philip Jones married again, and from this second marriage are descended Thomas Jones, Philip and Nicholas Rogers and others.

"Philip Jones was guardian and had the estate of the younger George Eager, —— and whether owing to too much restraint, or a natural propensity, George was bound an apprentice to the sea,—and afterwards was captain of a ship. He sailed from West River, in the year 1752, aged about thirty-three, in a vessel belonging to Galloway, of that place, loaded with wheat, and was never afterwards heard of.

"RUTH married Cornelius Howard, as above stated.

"The above is mostly from record testimony,—and where that failed, the defect is supplied by tradition."

(Signed) " JOHN E. HOWARD.
Feb'y 17th 1810."

JOSHUA HOWARD m. Joanna O'Carroll and had child., viz., Francis Howard,—Cornelius Howard,—Violetta Howard,—Sarah Howard,—Mary Howard, who m. Nathaniel Gist,—Elizabeth Howard, and Edmund Howard, who d. about 1750. Joshua Howard d. in 1745, and his wife died in 1763.

SEC. 35, G. CORNELIUS HOWARD, son of Joshua and Joanna O'Carroll Howard, m. Ruth Eager, dau. of John and Jemima Murray Eager, and had child., viz., George, who m. Mrs. Hannah Jones Edward, dau. of Thomas Jones, and left no descendants,—Joshua,—Ruth,—John Eager, b. 4th June 1752, d. 12th Oct. 1827,—Rachel,—Philip,—Cornelius, d. 12th Feb'y 1844, aged 89 years,—Violetta, who m. Joseph West, had one son, Joseph West (who d. young), and d. 21st Feb'y 1844, aged 84 years,—Ann, and James Howard.

RUTH HOWARD, dau. of Cornelius and Ruth Eager Howard, m. Charles Elder, and had two child., viz., George Elder, and Charles Elder, b. 1774, d. 1829.

CHARLES ELDER, son of Charles and Ruth Howard Elder, m. Sally Howard (of another Howard family), and had child., viz., Violetta,—Ruth, b. 1801, d. 1854,—George, b. 1802, d. 18th July 1866,—Juliana,—Rebecca, b. 1814, d. 1846,—Cornelius Howard,—Cornelius Henry, and Achsah Howard.

Mrs. Sally Howard Elder, b. 1773, m. 1798 and d. in 1839.

VIOLETTA ELDER, dau. of James and Sally Howard Elder, m. twice. Her 1st husband (1831) was Thomas Barnes, and had 2 child, viz., Archibald, and Sally Barnes, who d. 30th Oct. 1851, aged 15 years. Her 2d husband (1846) was Wilson Lee Soper.

RUTH ELDER, dau. of Charles and Sally Howard Elder, m. William Shipley, and had child., viz., Sally, b. 1818, d. in 1834,—Robert (who m. Sophia Haines, and had child, viz., Alverda,—Clara, and William Hopkins Shipley),—Ruth E., b. in 1821, d. 1851,—Juliana (who m. 1st George W. Gray, who d. in 1852, *sine prole,* and 2d in 1854, John W. Marlow, and had 2 child., viz., William H., d., and William H. Marlow),—Cornelius H. (who m. 29th May 1866, Lizzie M., dau. of Samuel M. Barry),—William Henry,—Charles Elder, b. 1829, d. 20th Oct. 1858 (who m. June 1858, Mary E. Bottomly),—and Frank L. Shipley.

William Shipley, b. in 1782, m. 1816, and d. 1835. Mrs. Ruth Elder Shipley, b. 1801, d. 1854.

GEORGE HOWARD ELDER, son of Charles and Sally Howard Elder, m. in 1832, Ellen North Moale, and had child, viz., Frances Moale (who m. her cousin, William H. Shipley),—Robert North (who m. in 1862, Susan Voss, and had child., viz., Elizabeth H., and Ellen North Moale Elder),—Cornelia Howard, b. in 1838, d. 18th March 1864 (who m. 12th April 1859, Douglass Stirling, and had a son, George H. Stirling),—George H.,—Ellen North, and Elizabeth Elder, who m. in 1875, Jervis Spencer, son of Jervis Spencer.

SEC. 35, H. COL. JOHN EAGER HOWARD, son of Cornelius and Ruth Eager Howard, is one of those immortal few whose name and history will always be cherished with affectionate veneration by the sons of Maryland. He was gallant, brave, true to his native State, and faithful to his country. When the Revolutionary War broke out, he immediately volunteered for any service, and was elected a Captain in the Second Battalion of the Flying Camp of 1776, under the command of Col. Josias Carvil Hall. When the Battalions were re-arranged, as Regulars, in March 1777, he was appointed Major of the Fourth Battalion, Col. Hall commanding. He was commissioned Lieutenant-Colonel of the Second Regiment, 11th March 1779. He served through the whole war with brilliancy.

After the conclusion of the War for Independence, Col. Howard returned to civil life. He was three times elected Governor of the State of Maryland, viz., in 1788, 1789 and 1790. Always willing to serve his State when called upon, he disliked office-holding, and though warmly pressed by Gen. Washington, who knew his ability and worth, he declined a seat in the Cabinet, as Secretary of War. He was elected 30th Nov. 1796, United States Senator, and occupied that position until the 4th of March 1803.

Col. John Eager Howard, m. 18th May 1787, Margaret Chew, a lady celebrated for loveliness, elegance, and refinement, the eldest dau. of Hon. Benjamin Chew, of Philadelphia, and had child., viz., John Eager, b. 25th June 1788, d. 18th Oct. 1822,—George, b. 21st Nov. 1789, d. 2d Aug. 1846,—Benjamin Chew, b. 5th Nov. 1791,—William, b. 16th Dec. 1793, d. 25th Aug. 1834,—Juliana Elizabeth, b. 3d May 1796, d. 22d May, 1821,—James, b. 17th Dec. 1797,—Sophia Catherine, b. 6th March 1800,—Charles, b. 26th April 1802, d. 18th June 1869, and Mary Anne Howard, b. 16th Feb'y 1806, d. 20th May 1806.

JOHN EAGER HOWARD, eldest son of Col. John Eager and Margaret Chew Howard, m. 20th Dec. 1820, Cornelia Annabella Read, who d. 28th Dec. 1862, and had one son, John Eager Howard, b. 3d Sept. 1821, and d. near Boston, Mass., 1862. John Eager Howard d. at Mercersburg, Pa., 18th Oct. 1822.

GOV. GEORGE HOWARD, son of Col. John Eager and Margaret Chew Howard, was Governor of Maryland in 1831–32, m. 26th Dec. 1811, Prudence Gough Ridgely, and had child., viz., John Eager, b. 27th Nov. 1812, d. 3d July 1838,—Priscilla Ridgely, b. 31st July 1814, d. 5th May 1837,—Margaret Elizabeth,—Charles Ridgely, b. 1st Sept. 1818, d. 30th Jan'y 1859,—Sophia C,—George, b. 9th May 1822, d. 7th July, 1876, Jacob Hollingsworth, b. 24th Jan'y 1824, d. in Jan'y 1825,—William,—Cornelius,—Rebecca Hanson, b. 7th Jan'y 1829, d.,—James, b. in January 1830, d.,—David Ridgely, b. 27th Jan'y 1831, d. 2d Feb'y 1831,—Eliza Carroll. b. in 1832, d., and James Carroll b. in Aug. 1833., d. an infant.

PRISCILLA RIDGELY HOWARD, dau. of George and Prudence Gough Howard, m. 9th July 1835, Eugene Post, and had one son, Eugene Howard Post, who m. 19th Sept. 1865, Mary Adams, and had child., viz., Eugene and Margaret Elizabeth Post, b. 4th Sept. 1868, d. 17th April 1869. Mrs. Priscilla Ridgely Howard Post d. 5th May 1837, and her husband, Eugene Post, m. her sister, Margaret Elizabeth Howard.

MARGARET ELIZABETH HOWARD, dau. of George and Prudence Gough Howard, m. 2d Oct. 1838, her brother in law, Eugene Post, and had child., viz., Mary Magdalene,—John Eager Howard, who m. 17th April 1866, Rebecca Lloyd Nicholson, and d. 12th Feb'y 1876,—Sophia Howard (who m. 4th June 1858, Ridgely Duvall, and had child., viz., Ridgely, and Eugene Post Duvall, b. 18th June 1867, d. 17th Aug. 1867),—Richard (who m. 1st Nov. 1866, Ella Stump),—George Howard, and William Voss Post, who m. Miss Boice.

CHARLES RIDGELY HOWARD, son of George and Prudence Gough Howard, m. 24th Dec. 1844, Elizabeth Ann Waters, and had child., viz., Prudence Rebecca,—Sophia Read, who m. Thomas W. Ward, of New York,—Elizabeth Waters, b. 4th Oct. 1849, d. 10th Nov. 1849,—James Round Morris,—a second Elizabeth Waters, and Cornelia Howard.

Charles Ridgely Howard d. 30th Jan'y 1859, in the harbor of Panama, and Mrs. Elizabeth Ann Waters Howard m. 21st Feb'y 1860, William George Read, son of William George and Sophia Catharine Howard Read, and had a dau. Florence Mary Read.

Sophia C. Howard, dau. of George and Prudence Gough Howard, m. 12th May 1840, Richard Norris.

William Howard, son of George and Prudence Gough Howard, m. Octavia Duvall, and had child., viz., Eliza Ridgely,—William, b. in 1857, d. 12th July 1858,—James Herbert, b. 3d May 1860, d. 5th May 1860,—Gustave Beauregard, and John Duvall Howard.

Hon. Benjamin Chew Howard, son of Col. John Eager and Margaret Chew Howard, m. 24th Feb'y 1818, Jane Grant Gilmor, who was b. 30th March 1801, and had child., viz., Louisa Sherlock (who m. 1st June 1841, George Brice Hoffman, and had child., viz., Howard, and George Hoffman, b. 10th Aug. 1844, d. 6th May 1846),—Robert Gilmor, b. 3d Sept. 1821, d. 20th Dec. 1821,—Sophia, b. 3d Sept. 1822, d. at Rome, 23d May 1852,—Marian,—Ann Williams,—Jane Gilmor (who m. 1st June 1869, Joseph King),—William Gilmor, b. 20th Feb'y 1829, d. 16th March 1829,—Juliana McHenry (who m. 28th June 1853, Richard W. Tyson, and had child., viz., Sophia Howard,—George Hoffman, b. 8th March 1856, d. 23d Dec. 1858,—Benjamin Howard,—Jessie, b. in 1862, at Nice, d. at Rome, 24th Feb'y 1863, and Jesse Tyson),—Ellen Gilmor (who m. 20th Dec. 1860, Richard Basset Bayard, and had child., viz., Ellen Howard,—Richard Howard, and Jean Gilmor Bayard, b. 4th Aug. 1866, d. 2d April 1867),—William Gilmor, who m. 18th June 1864, Annie Doyle, and afterwards Lucy Brent of Va.,—Benjamin Chew, b. 21st March 1837, *deceased*,—and Charles Gilmor Howard, b. 15th May 1839, d. 18th May 1839. Hon. Benjamin Chew Howard d. 6th March 1872.

William Howard, son of Col. John Eager and Margaret Chew Howard, m. 14th May 1828, Rebecca Ann Key, and had child., viz., William Key (who m. 9th Feb'y 1854, Agnes Schley, dau. of William and Ann Cadwalader Ringgold Schley (see Ringgold), and had child., viz., Agnes, b. 17th Nov. 1854, d. July 6th 1856, and William Key Howard, b. 20th Sept. 1857, d. 20th Oct. 1857. Mrs. Agnes Schley Howard d. 23d Sept. 1857, and he married 2dly Clara Haxall Randolph, and had child., viz., William Key and Allan Randolph Howard),—Louisa Emily, b. 5th Dec. 1830, d.,—and Philip Barton Key Howard, b. 5th Jan'y 1834, d.

William Howard d. 25th Aug. 1834, and Mrs. Rebecca Ann Key Howard m. 2dly Alexander H. Tyson, and had child., viz., Alexander Hamilton, b. 19th April 1840, d. 26th Dec. 1855,—Mary Lloyd,—Henry Johnson, b. 13th April 1845, d.

16th Feb'y 1858, and Anna Key Tyson, who m. Robert Mitchell.

JULIANA ELIZABETH HOWARD, dau. of Col. John Eager and Margaret Chew Howard, m. 7th Dec. 1819, John McHenry, who d. at Mercersburg, Pa., 9th Oct. 1822. Mrs. Juliana Elizabeth Howard McHenry d. at Belvidere, the residence of her father, 22d May 1821, leaving one son, James Howard McHenry.

JAMES HOWARD MCHENRY, son of John and Juliana Elizabeth Howard McHenry, m. 25th June 1855, Sally Nicholas Cary, and had child., viz., Julia Howard,—James, b. 30th Sept. 1857, d. 10th July 1858,—Wilson Cary,—Ellen Carr, and John McHenry.

JAMES HOWARD, son of Col. John Eager and Margaret Chew Howard, m. twice, his 1st wife was Sophia Gough Ridgely, and had child., viz., Juliana Elizabeth, d,—Charles, Ridgely (who m. 23d April 1861, Mary Holly Austin, and d. in 1862),—Margaret Sophia (who m. Charles Ridgely, of Hampton, and had child., viz., John, who m. Helen Stewart, —Charles, b. 19th July 1853, d. 1873,—Howard,—Otho Eichelberger,—Eliza,—Juliana Elizabeth Howard, and Edgar Howard Ridgely, b. 11th Oct. 1863, d. 13th Aug. 1864, and Margaret Ridgely),—and John Eager Howard who d. in 1876. His 2d wife was Catharine M. Ross, of Frederick city, Md., dau. of William Ross and his wife Catharine W. Johnson, dau. of Col. Baker Johnson, and had child., viz., Anna Harrison,—William Ross, who m. Elizabeth Mary Ridgely, and had a son, Charles Ridgely,—James McHenry,—Harry Carroll, and David Ridgely Howard. James Howard d. 19th March 1870.

SOPHIA CATHARINE HOWARD, dau. of Col. John Eager and Margaret Chew Howard, m. 7th May 1825, William George Read, and had child., viz., William George, who m. 21st Feb'y 1860, Elizabeth Waters Howard, widow of Charles Ridgely Howard, and had a dau. Florence Mary Read),—Mary Sophia,—Howard, b. July 1838, d. 22d Feb'y 1839, and Mary Cornelia Read.

MARY SOPHIA READ, dau. of William George and Sophia Catharine Howard, m. Arthur Thomas Weld, of Leagram, England, and had child., viz., Mary Edith,—William George,—Arthur John, b. at Lytham, Lancashire, England, 24th Nov. 1857, d. at Gravesend, 15th Feb'y 1866,—Edward Joseph,—Mary Sophia,—Albert Henry, and Louisa Maria Weld.

MARY CORNELIA READ, dau. of William George and

Sophia Catharine Howard Read, m. 4th May 1858, Albert Henry Carroll, of Howard Co., and had child., viz, Mary Sophia,—Mary Ellinor, and Agnes Carroll.

Albert Henry Carroll joined the army of the Confederate States, and was killed in a skirmish near Martinsburg, 7th Sept. 1862.

Mrs. Mary Cornelia Read Carroll m. 25th June 1866, Col. James Fenner Lee, and had a dau. Mary Cornelia Lee.

CHARLES HOWARD, son of Col. John Eager and Margaret Chew Howard, m. 9th Nov. 1825, Elizabeth Phoebe Key, who was b. 10th Oct. 1803, the dau. of Francis Scott Key, the author of "The Star Spangled Banner," and his wife Mary Tayloe Lloyd Key (see LLOYD), and had child., viz., Francis Key, who d. in London 29th May 1872,—John Eager.—Charles,—Mary Lloyd,—James,—Alice,—Edward Lloyd,—McHenry,—Ellen Key,—Elizabeth Gray, b. 16th Oct. 1841, d. 14th Nov. 1862, and Anna Arnold Key Howard, b. 3d Aug. 1845 and d. 24th May 1846.

FRANCIS KEY HOWARD, son of Charles and Elizabeth Phoebe Key Howard, m. 27th Jan'y 1853, Lydia E. H. Morris, and had child., viz., John Morris, b. 1st Dec. 1853, d. 14th Jan'y 1856,—Lydia Hollingsworth,—Elizabeth Phoebe, b. 30th Aug. 1857, d. 29th July 1858,—Nancy Hollingsworth,—Frank Key, and Charles Howard.

CHARLES HOWARD, son of Charles and Elizabeth Phoebe Key Howard, m. 11th July 1855, Mary C. Winder, and had child., viz., Charles Eager,—Elizabeth Key,—Ruth, and Nannie Bruce, and Rosa Howard.

MARY LLOYD HOWARD, dau. of Charles and Elizabeth Phoebe Key Howard, m. 5th June 1851, Edward Lloyd, and had child., viz., Edward Lloyd, b. 24th Oct. 1853, d. 13th Aug. 1854,—a 2d Edward,—Charles Howard,—McBlair,—John Eager, and Elizabeth Phoebe Key Lloyd.

MCHENRY HOWARD, son of Charles and Elizabeth Phoebe Key Howard, m. 18th June 1867, Julia Douglass Coleman, dau. of Gen. C. G. Coleman, of Jerdone Castle, Louisa Co., Va., and had child., viz., Elizabeth Gray Howard,—Charles Howard, and Mary Howard.

ELLEN KEY HOWARD, dau. of Charles and Elizabeth Key Howard, m. 7th Dec. 1865, Charlton Hunt Morgan, and had child., viz., Thomas Morgan,—Charlton Morgan, and Ellen T. Morgan.

ELIZABETH HOWARD, youngest dau. of Joshua and Joanna O'Carroll Howard, m. William Welles, and had child., viz.,

Frank, who m. ——— Tevis, and had a son, Joshua Wells, who m. Mrs. Reinecker, whose maiden name was Fite,—Joseph, —James, and Nancy Wells, who m. ——— Crawford.

SARAH HOWARD, second dau. of Joshua and Joanna O'Carroll Howard, m. Christopher Gist, and had child, viz., Nancy, who d. unmarried,—Thomas, who was taken prisoner at Braddock's Defeat, and lived 15 or 16 years with the Indians,—Nathaniel Gist, and a son who m. and has descendants living ing in South Carolina.

GEN. NATHANIEL GIST, son of Christopher and Sarah Howard Gist, m. Judith Bell, and had a dau., Eliza Violetta Howard Gist, who married Francis P. Blair, and had child., viz., Montgomery Blair, Frank P. Blair,—James, and Elizabeth Blair.

VIOLETTA HOWARD, eldest dau. of Joshua and Joanna O'Carroll Howard, m. William Gist, and had child., viz., Joseph,—a dau. (who m. ——— McGee, and had a dau., Polly McGee, b. 5th May 1782, m. 16th Sept. 1802, John Kirby, and had 3 child., viz., Samuel Owings, b. 1st Oct. 1803,—Ann, b. 17th June, 1806, and Mary Kirby, b. 9th Sept. 1809),—and Joseph Gist.

John Kirby, d. 5th July 1861. Polly McGee Kirby d. 3d June 1812.

ANN KIRBY, dau. of John and Polly McGee Kirby, m. John P. Miller, who was b. 2d Dec. 1804, d. 3d Sept. 1851, and had a son, John F. Miller.

ANN GIST, dau. of William and Violetta Howard Gist, m. James Calhoun, and had child., viz., William, b. 30th Nov. 1767, d. in June 1808,—James, b. 4th Nov. 1770, d. 30th Aug. 1819, and Elizabeth Calhoun, b. 26th April 1774, d. 21st Aug. 1815.

WILLIAM CALHOUN, son of James and Ann Gist Calhoun, m. Lydia Cattel, and had child., viz., Mary,—Eliza,—Ann,—Lydia, and Sidney Calhoun, who m. Horace Bliss,—William Calhoun b. 30th Nov. 1767, d. June 1808.

MARY CALHOUN, dau. of William and Lydia Cattel Calhoun, m. 9th June 1812, Benedict Wm. Hall, and had child., viz., Janet Smith, b. 10th July 1813, d. Dec. 1857,—Lydia, b. 20th Feb'y 1815, d. 8th May 1817,—Elizabeth Buchanan, —and Mary Calhoun, b. 4th June 1818, d. Dec. 1847.

JANET SMITH HALL, dau. of Benedict Wm. and Mary Calhoun Hall, m. Wm. Fitzhugh Turner, and had child., viz., Marian Calhoun, b. 6th Oct. 1834, d. 19th March 1858,—Eliza Randolph, b. 22d Dec. 1835, d. 1854,—Thomas Shirley, b. 4th

Aug. 1837, d. 29th Oct. 1865,—Lydia Calhoun, b. 22d July 1839, d. 12th April 1867,—William Hall, d.,—Sophia Cooke, —Virginia Caroline, b. 2d Jan'y 1843, d. 1849,—William Fitzhugh, d.,—Henry Julian, and Horatio Whitridge Turner.

Wm. Fitzhugh Turner and Janet Smith Hall were m. 17th Sept. 1833. He d. 4th Dec. 1852, and she in Dec. 1857.

Marian Calhoun Turner, dau. of Wm. Fitzhugh and Janet Smith Hall Turner, m. William Carrere, and had a son, John Fitzhugh Carrere.

Elizabeth Buchanan Hall, dau. of Benedict Wm. and Mary Calhoun Hall, m. 20th April 1843, Horatio L. Whitridge, and had child., viz., Olivia Cushing, who m. 23d Jan'y 1868, Alexander Nisbet Turnbull,—Mary Calhoun, b. 4th Dec. 1845, d. 9th June 1856,—Elizabeth Hall, b. 15th Dec. 1847, d. 20th April 1850,—Benedict Wm. Hall,—Alice Dickenson,—Thomas, 10th July 1853, d. 5th Feb'y 1855, —Lydia Calhoun, b. 14th July 1857, d. 30th June 1864, and James Hindman Barney Whitridge. Horatio L. Whitridge d. in 1875.

Ann Calhoun, dau. of William and Lydia Cattel Calhoun, after the death of his sister, Mary Calhoun Hall, m. and was the 2d wife of Benedict Wm. Hall, and had child., viz., Sidney Calhoun Hall, who m. 2d Oct. 1851, James Morrison Harris, and had a son William Hall Harris,—Margaret Louisa Hall, who m. 20th Jan'y 1857, Dr. Alexander C. Robinson, and had three child., viz., Ann Calhoun,—Carvil Hall, and Louisa Hall Robinson,—Lydia Abbot Hall, b. 4th June 1829, d. 15th Aug. 1856,—Anna Maria Hall, who m. 22d Feb'y 1855, Edward Wyatt Blanchard, and had child., viz., John Gowan and Sidney Blanchard,—and William Carvil Hall, who m. 21st Feb'y 1867, Agnes Robinson.

Elizabeth Calhoun, dau. of James and Ann Gist Calhoun, m. 1st Jan'y 1793, James A. Buchanan, and had child., viz., Eliza,—James,—William Boyd,—James Calhoun,—Eliza,—Esther,—John,—Robert Smith,—Samuel Smith, and Harrison Buchanan.

William Boyd Buchanan, son of James A. and Eliza Calhoun Buchanan, m. Ellen Boucher Carr, d. 30th April 1857, aged 63 years, and had child., viz., James Calhoun,—Peter Carr,—Maria Jefferson,—William,—a second Peter Carr,—Elizabeth Calhoun,—Wilson Cary,—Esther S., and Dabney Carr Buchanan. Mrs. Ellen B. C. Buchanan d. 12th Jan'y 1876, in the 70th year of her age.

Robert Smith Buchanan, son of James A. and Elizabeth

Calhoun Buchanan, m. Ellen B. McMechen, and had child., viz., James A. Buchanan (who m. 17th Sept. 1857, Rosa Parran of Shepherdstown, Va., and had child., viz., Richard Parran,—Esther Smith, and Laura Isabella Wallace Buchanan), —Eliza S. Buchanan (who m. Walter C. Smith, and d. 10th Feb'y 1860, in the 29th year of her age, and had one child, Clement Carroll Smith),—Ellen A. Buchanan,—Wm. McMechen Buchanan,—Robert S. Buchanan, d. 6th May 1861, and a second William McMechen Buchanan.

SEC. 35, J. The JOHNSON FAMILY, of Maryland, are descended from Thomas Johnson, a grandson of Sir Thomas Johnson of Great Yarmouth, Norfolk County, England, who was of an old family of distinction. The Johnsons had been members of Parliament, and Bailiffs, or Mayors of Yarmouth, since 1585.

THOMAS JOHNSON, the emigrant, was a lawyer in London, eloped with Mary Baker, a Ward in Chancery, and came to America prior to the year 1700. He died in 1714, leaving an only son, Thomas Johnson, who was b. 19th Feb'y 1702.

THOMAS JOHNSON, son of Thomas Johnson and Mary Baker, m. Dorcas Sedgwick, who was b. 2d Nov. 1705, the dau. of Joshua and Elizabeth Sedgwick, and had child., viz., Thomas, b. 13th Dec. 1725, d. an infant,—Benjamin, b. 6th July 1727, who m. twice, had six sons and two daus., and d. in May, 1786,—Mary, b. 5th Aug. 1729, who m. in 1801, Walter Hellen, had two sons and two daus., and d. in 1801,—Rebecca Johnson, b. 8th Nov. 1730, who m. Thomas McKensie, and d. 11th March, 1767, *sine prole*,—Thomas, b. 4th Nov. 1732, who m. Ann Jennings, and d. 26th Oct. 1819, aged 87,—James, b. 30th Sept. 1736,—Elizabeth, b. 17th Sept. 1739 (who m. Capt. George Cook, a Scotchman, the commander of the Maryland Ship Defence, in the Revolution, and had one dau. and six sons),—Joshua, b. 25th June 1742 (who went early in life to London, where he m. Catharine ———, retired to Nantes, in France, during the Revolution, returning to London, 1783, was appointed the first American Counsul at that Port, and had a dau., Louisa Catharine Johnson, who m. 26th July, 1797, John Quincy Adams),—Dr. John, b. 9th Aug. 1745 (who had a dau. Dorcas Johnson, who m. Samuel Clapham, of Loudon Co., Va.),—Col. Baker, b. 30th Sept. 1747, who m. Catharine Worthington, and d. 18th June 1811,—and Roger Johnson, b. 18th March 1749, who m. Betzy Thomas, a Quakeress, dau. of Shepherd Thomas, and had seven sons and 4 daus., and d. 3d March 1831.

GOVERNOR THOMAS JOHNSON, son of Thomas Johnson and Dorcas Sedgwick, was the leading man in Maryland during the Revolution, if there could be a leader among so many able men who stood beside him in those trying times.

At the Convention of the Province of Maryland, held in Annapolis, 22d to 25th June 1774, he was elected to the Continental Congress, which assembled in Philadelphia the following September, and was re-elected at each successive election, by the Conventions of Maryland to Congress, until 13th Feb'y 1777, when he was chosen the first Chief Magistrate of the free and independent sovereign STATE OF MARYLAND.

At the meeting of the Deputies of the counties of the province of Maryland, held in Annapolis, on the 8th to the 12th of Dec. 1774, he was appointed one of the "committee of correspondence for this province."

At the meeting of the Delegates appointed by the several counties of the province of Maryland, which met in Annapolis, Wednesday, 28th July, and continued till 14th Aug. 1775, he was chosen one of the "council of safety for this province."

He was a prominent member of the Convention of the Delegates which met at Annapolis, on the 7th of Dec. 1775, and on the 13th Dec., with Charles Carroll, of Carrollton, Smith Bishop, Nathaniel Ramsey, and Joseph Gilpin, was elected by ballot on a committe to "devise the best ways and means to promote the manufacture of salt-petre." On the 6th Jan'y 1776, he was elected by the Convention a Brigadier General, and afterwards displayed much military talent while in command of the Flying Camp. The people of Maryland had such implicit confidence in his judgment as a statesman, and relied so much upon his wisdom and discretion in council, that the Convention of Maryland, on the 4th July 1776, felt compelled to withdraw his military commission, for the following modest and complimentary reasons:

"Thereupon the convention considering that the said "Thomas Johnson, Esq., cannot discharge the duty of briga-"dier of the forces to be raised in this province, in consequence "of the resolves of congress, of the third day of June last; "to which command the convention, from a confidence in his "capacity and abilities to fill the same with advantage to the "public cause, and honor to himself, had appointed him, and "also execute the trust reposed in him as a deputy in congress "for this province; and being of opinion, that it is of very "great importance to the welfare of this province, that it "should not be deprived of the advice and assistance of the "said Thomas Johnson in the public councils of the united "colonies, and that his place can be supplied with less incon- "venience in the military than in the civil department, therefore, "*Resolved*, That a brigadier general be elected by ballot in the "room of the said Thomas Johnson, esquire."

So important was his presence esteemed, that having refused to serve in the Convention, under the instructions of the people of Anne Arundel, that Col. Richardson, of Caroline, resigned his own seat, conveyed to him a farm in Caroline County, went home and had Thomas Johnson returned in his place.

He was, with William Paca, George Plater and James Hollyday, of that celebrated committee, elected 24th May 1776, which politely invited "his Excellency, ROBERT EDEN, Esq., Governor of Maryland," to vacate.

Upon his motion, George Washington was elected, 15th June, 1775, Commander in Chief of all the Continental forces, raised, or to be raised for the defence of American liberty.

Thomas Johnson was an ardent patriot, never doubting or hesitating, and when on the 28th of June, 1776, he, with others, secured the passage by the Convention of the resolution authorizing the deputies from Maryland, in Congress, "to concur with the other united colonies, or a majority of them, in declaring the united colonies free and independent states," he felt, to quote the words of one of his family, that "his work was done." The rest was with GOD—who, always, "helpeth them to right who suffer wrong."

On the 4th of July the Declaration of Independence was passed by Congress, the deputies from Maryland, of which he was one, concurring. The instrument itself was not ready to be signed until the 2d of August 1776, on which day Thomas Johnson was necessarily absent on account of illness in his family, and this is the sole and proper reason that his signature was not affixed to that, the noblest roll of honor possessed by mankind.

On the 13th of February 1777, by the two houses of the Legislature of Maryland, he was, almost unanimously, elected the Chief Magistrate of the State, receiving forty out of fifty-two votes. He was inaugurated 21st of March 1777, the FIRST GOVERNOR OF THE STATE OF MARYLAND.

When his gubernatorial term expired he retired to private life, and so remained until General Washington prevailed upon him, 5th of August 1791, to accept a seat upon the bench, as an Associate Justice of the Supreme Court of the United

States, in place in of John Rutledge, resigned. This position he held, and discharged its duties with great ability, until his resignation in 1793. Afterwards General Washington pressed upon him the portfolio of Secretary of State, which he declined. He, with Dr. Stuart and Mr. Daniel Carroll, commissioners, laid off the City of Washington, and selected the sites of the Capitol, President's House, and other public buildings.

Governor Johnson died at Rose Hill, 26th Oct. 1819, aged 87. Take him all in all he was one of the most beautiful characters found upon the pages of American history. Gentle and lovable as a woman,—there was no one who drew a more eager sword, or whose clarion voice rang more musically in the headlong charge than his. Knowing no fear upon the battle field, he possessed also that honest moral courage which feels no misgivings in the performance of sacred duties however hazardous and uncertain the consequences might be. His intuitive perception of right was quick and keen as a damascene blade; in decision he was calm and deliberate, and his will was so firm that no vicissitude could shake his purpose when once resolved.

He was a lawyer of great ability aud learning, of conspicuous integrity and very successful in his practice. It is said that when John Adams was asked why so many Southern men occupied leading positions and possessed great influence during the struggle for independence he replied that "if it had not been for such men as Richard Henry Lee, Thomas Jefferson, Samuel Chase, and Thomas Johnson, there never would have been any revolution."

He m. 16th Feb'y 1766, Ann Jennings, of Annapolis, only dau. of Thomas Jennings, Justice, who d. 26th Aug. 1759; and had child., viz., Thomas Johnson,—Ann Johnson, who m. Major John Graham, of Calvert, and removed to Frederick County,—Rebecca Johnson, who m. her cousin, Thomas Johnson, of Loudon Co., Va.,—Dorcas Johnson, who remained unmarried,—and Joshua Johnson, who m. Miss Beall.

THOMAS JOHNSON, eldest son of Gov. Thomas Johnson and Ann Jennings, m. twice. His 1st wife was Miss Hessilius, of Annapolis, who d. *sine prole.* His 2d wife was Elizabeth Russell, dau. of William Russell, of Baltimore, and had child., viz., Mary Ann, who m. Hugh W. Evans, of Baltimore,—Eliza Johnson, who d. in 1860, unmarried,—and Fanny Russell Johnson.

FANNY RUSSELL JOHNSON, dau. of Thomas Johnson and Elizabeth Russell, m., in December 1823, Col. John McPherson, of Frederick County, and, in 1873, had the blessed privilege of celebrating her golden-wedding. Her husband d. the March following, aged 78 years, after a long, useful and honorable life. They had child., who survived to maturity, viz., Ann Graham McPherson (who m., 22d Jan'y 1850, Worthington Ross, Attorney at Law, a leading member of the Frederick bar, son of William and Catharine Worthington Johnson Ross, who d., leaving a dau., Fanny McPherson Ross),—Alice McPherson (who m. Col. George R. Dennis, and d. young, leaving several children),—Fanny McPherson, who m. and is the 2d wife of Col. George R. Dennis, and has several children.

COL. JAMES JOHNSON, son of Thomas Johnson and Dorcas Sedgwick, was a large manufacturer of iron and a distinguished patriot. He m. Margaret Skinner, of Talbot County, and had child., viz., James, Thomas and Rebecca Johnson.

THOMAS JOHNSON, son of Col. James and Margaret Skinner Johnson, m. Rebecca, dau. of Gov. Thomas Johnson, and had child., viz., Ann Jennings,—Margaret, who m. James Graham, and Thomas James Johnson.

JAMES JOHNSON, son of Col. James and Margaret Skinner, m. Ann Richards, and had child., viz., Margaretta, who m. Samuel Hough and had 3 child.,—Anne,—Mary, who m. Lambert Hopkins,—John, who m. Mary Overstreet and had 6 child.,—Thomas, who m. Miss Spedon and had 6 child.,—and James A. Johnson, who m. in Mexico.

ANNE JOHNSON, dau. of James and Ann Richards Johnson, m. Maj. M. M. Clark, and had child., viz., James L.,—Duncan, —Thomas Johnson,—Juliet, and Anne J. Clarke.

SEC. 35, K. COL. BAKER JOHNSON, of Frederick County, son of Thomas Johnson and Dorcas Sedgwick, was a member of the Convention of Maryland which met in Annapolis, 21st June 1776, commanded a battalion in his brother's brigade, and distinguished himself at Paoli, near Philadelphia. He m. 9th Dec. 1784, Catharine Worthington, dau. of Col. Nicholas Worthington, of Summer Hill and Belvoir, Anne Arundel Co., and had child., who lived to maturity, viz., Baker Johnson,—Catharine Worthington Johnson,—William Johnson,—Juliana Johnson, who m., and was the 1st wife of the Rt. Rev. Bishop Johns, D. D., of Virginia, and d. leaving several children,—Matilda Chase Johnson,—Caroline Worthington Goldsborough Johnson,—Worthington Johnson, and Charles Worthington Johnson.

CATHARINE WORTHINGTON JOHNSON, dau. of Col. Baker Johnson and Catharine Worthington, m. 4th March 1806,

William Ross, an eminent lawyer of Frederick, son of Major William Ross and Mary Hannah, and had child., viz., William J. Ross, a distinguished member of the Maryland bar (who m. twice, 1st in 1831, Maria Davis, who d. young, leaving two child., viz., John, d., and Charles W. Ross, who m. 12th Dec. 1861, Cornelia Ringgold Potts, dau. of George M. Potts and Cornelia Ringgold (see RINGGOLD). His 2nd wife, m. in 1841, was Eliza Hughes Stokes, whose mother was the dau. of Capt. John Hughes, who bandaged with his own uniform scarf, the eyes of Major Andrè, who also d. young, leaving a dau., Eliza Ross),—Baker Ross (who d. in 1830, at the residence of his uncle, Rev. John Johns, in Baltimore),—Catharine Mary Ross (who m. in 1832, James Howard, son of Col. John Eager Howard and Margaret Chew, (see HOWARD),—Ann Elizabeth Ross (who m. in 1832, William G. Harrison, of Baltimore, and d. in 1833, aged 20 years, *sine prole*),—John W. Ross, now of Baltimore,—Juliana J. Ross (who m. in 1839, Rev. John F. Hoff, D. D., of the Protestant Episcopal Church, and has several children),—Matilda J. Ross, "a perfect woman, nobly planned," who d. 29th July 1866,—Worthington Ross (who m. 22d Jan'y 1850, Ann Graham McPherson, and left a dau., Fanny McPherson Ross)—Caroline Ross,—and Charles Johnson Ross, d.

SEC. 35, L. MAJOR WILLIAM ROSS came from Scotland, with his cousin John Ross, to America, with the 42d Highlanders, commanded by Sir Hugh Montgomery, "The Sodger Hugh of Burns," and was taken prisoner by the Indians at Grant's defeat, but succeeded in escaping and regained the British camp. After the term of their service expired, the cousins separated, never to meet again. At parting, with vows of lasting remembrance and affection, they exchanged "bonnets." John Ross went to Canada, married, settled and died there, leaving children, whose descendants are now living in Montreal and Quebec.

William Ross settled at Lancaster, Pennsylvania, and m. Mary Hannah. When the Revolutionary war broke out he espoused the cause of the colonies, and entered the American army, and served with distinction as a major.

Major William Ross was b. 16th Dec. 1727, in Ross-shire, Scotland, and d. 4th Dec. 1797, leaving three child., viz., John,—Ann, and William Ross, who m. Catharine Worthington Johnson.

More than seventy years after the cousins parted, Mr. Charles W. Ross, of Frederick, a descendant of Major William Ross, while in Canada, made himself known to the descendants of John Ross, and since then mutual visits have been made and returned, and the two branches of the family in America are closely united in freindship.

WORTHINGTON JOHNSON, son of Col. Baker Johnson and Catharine Worthington, m. 14th May 1822, Mary Jane Fitzhugh Potts, dau. of Judge Richard Potts, of Frederick, and had child., viz., Worthington Ross Johnson,—Dr. Richard Potts Johnson,—Ross Johnson, and Dr. George Johnson.

JUDGE RICHARD POTTS, of Frederick, was m. twice. His first wife was Elizabeth Hughes, a sister of Capt. John Hughes, who bandaged the eyes of Major André, and had one son, Richard Potts, who m. Annie S. Murdock, and d. *sine prole.* He m. 2dly, 19th Dec. 1799, Eleanor Murdock, and had child., viz., Mary Jane Fitzhugh Potts, who m. Worthington Johnson,—Harriet Murdock Potts, who m. Judge Richard H. Marshall, and had a dau., Nannie Marshall,—George Murdock Potts, who m. Cornelia Ringgold, dau. of Gen. Samuel Ringgold and Maria Cadwalader (see RINGGOLD),—and Eleanor M. Potts.

WORTHINGTON ROSS JOHNSON, son of Worthington Johnson and Mary Jane Fitzhugh Potts, m. 18th June 1844, Ann Rebecca Graham, and had child., now living, viz., Thomas Worthington, — Caroline Graham, — Richard Potts, — John Graham, and Catharine Worthington Ross Johnson.

DR. RICHARD POTTS JOHNSON, son of Worthington Johnson and Mary Jane Fitzhugh Potts, m. twice. He m. 1st, 17th April 1850, Elizabeth Lee Taylor, who d. in 1860, *sine prole.* He m. again 22d Aug. 1865, Mary G. Saunders, and had child., now living, viz., Edward Stanfield,—Mary Eleanor, and Blair Johnson.

ROSS JOHNSON, son of Worthington Johnson and Mary Jane Fitzhugh Potts, m. 12th Aug. 1850, Maria L. Hammond, and had child., now living, viz., Mary Potts,—Worthington,—John Ross, —Richard Potts,—Eleanor Murdock,—Nathan Hammond,—Maria Hammond,—Harriet Marshall,—Ross,—and Jane Beall Johnson.

DR. GEORGE JOHNSON, son of Worthington Johnson and Mary Jane Fitzhugh Potts, m. 19th April 1855, Emily Crawford, dau. of William H. and Lydia L. Crawford, of Philadelphia, and had child., now living, viz., William Crawford,—Baker,—George Potts, and Nannie Marshall Johnson.

CHARLES WORTHINGTON JOHNSON, son of Col. Baker Johnson and Catharine Worthington, b. 28th Sept. 1805, m. Eleanor

Murdock Tyler, of Frederick, who was b. 10th Aug. 1810, dau. of Doctor Bradley Tyler and Harriet Murdock, and had child., viz., Harriet Johnson, and General Bradley T. Johnson.

HARRIET JOHNSON, dau. of Charles Worthington Johnson and Eleanor Murdock Tyler, m. in 1849, Charles Schley, son of Maj. Henry Schley and Sarah Maria Worrell (see WORRELL), and had child., viz., Bradley,—Lucy,—Eleanor,—Jessie, and Sybil Schley.

SEC. 35, M. GENERAL BRADLEY T. JOHNSON, son of Charles Worthington Johnson and Eleanor Murdock Tyler, m. 25th June 1851, Jane Claudia Saunders, of North Carolina, and has a son, Bradley Saunders Johnson.

Mrs. Jane Claudia Saunders Johnson is the dau. of the Hon. Romulus M. Saunders, of North Carolina, and Anna Hayes Johnson, dau. of Hon. William Johnson, of Charleston, South Carolina, Associate Justice of the United States Supreme Court.

Hon. R. M. Saunders was formerly member of Congress, Attorney General, and a Judge of the Supreme Court of North Carolina, and United States Minister to Spain. He was the mover and author of the famous two-third rule adopted by the Democratic party, at the first national Democratic convention, at Baltimore, 21st May 1832.

General Johnson was graduated at Princeton College, in the class of 1849, read Law with Mr. William J. Ross, of Frederick, Maryland, and finished his legal course in 1850-51, at Dane Hall, University of Cambridge, Mass., and was admitted to the Bar in North Carolina in 1851. In the same year he was elected States Attorney for Frederick County, Maryland. In 1859 he was the Democratic candidate for Comptroller of the State, was a member of the National Democratic Conventions which assembled in 1860, at Charleston and Baltimore, and supported with energy and zeal the regular nominee of the party, John C. Breckenbridge. In 1860–61 he was Chairman of the Democratic State Central Committee of Maryland.

On the 8th day of May 1861, he left Frederick, Maryland, in command of the first organized company that went South, composed of Frederick men, all volunteers, sixty in number, who marched armed to Point of Rocks, Va. He was mustered into the army of the Confederate States, 21st May 1861, as captain of Company A, First Maryland Regiment, his friend, George K. Shellman, being the first lieutenant. On the 17th June 1861, he was commissioned major of the same regiment. This regiment was officially thanked 22nd June 1861, by Gen. Jos. E. Johnson, for their faithful and exact obedience to orders. On the 21st July 1861, he was promoted to lieutenant colonel of the First Maryland Regiment, and on the 16th Dec. 1862, commissioned colonel of cavalry.

In the first Maryland campaign he was the colonel commanding the 2d brigade. On the 22d of June 1863 he was appointed colonel of the 1st regiment of the Maryland Line, and on the 4th of February 1864, though absent on duty, he was unanimously elected by the officers, at Fisher's Hill, colonel and commander of the Maryland Line. On the 28th of June 1864, he was commissioned brigadier-general of cavalry, in recognition of his extraordinary service, defeating, with a battalion of sixty men, the main object and purpose of the famous raid of Kilpatrick and Dahlgren, to destroy Richmond.

General Johnson was in active and arduous service all through the whole war. In 1861 he was in the battles of Manassas, Munson's Hill and Mason's Hill. In 1862 he participated in the engagements at Rappahannock Station,—Front Royal,—Winchester,—Harper's Ferry,—Harrisonburg,—Cross Keys,—Port Republic, in Jackson's Valley campaigns,—at Coal Harbour,—Malvern Hill,—Westover,—2d Manassas,—Chantilly,—Warrenton Springs, and Grovetown. In 1863, he was engaged at Gettysburg,—Martinsburg,—Hainesville,—Chester Gap,—Culpepper,—Brandy Station and Centreville,—and in 1864, at Pollard's Farm,—Trevillian's Section,—Frederick,—Beltsville,—Winchester,—was with General McCausland in the Chambersburg raid,—at Winchester 19th Sept.,—at Fisher's Hill 21st Sept.,—at Cedar Creek 8th Oct.,—and at Woodstock 19th Oct. 1864.

In Early's raid into Maryland, and around Washington, General Bradley T. Johnson commanded the advance guard, in the invasion, and the rear guard, on the retreat.

From the 3d of July to the 1st of November 1864, he fought every day, with a few exceptions of occasional rest, and continued in active service until the surrender at Appomattox Court House, on the 10th day of April 1865.

Major General Ewell, in his official report of the Valley Campaign, said:

"The history of the Maryland regiment, gallantly com-" manded by Colonel Bradley T. Johnson during the campaign" of the Valley, would be the history of every action from" Front Royal to Cross Keys. On the 6th, near Harrisonburg," the Fifty-eighth Virginia Regiment was engaged with the

"Pennsylvania 'Bucktails,' the fighting being close and bloody. "Colonel Johnson came up with his regiment in the hottest "period, and by a dashing charge in flank drove the enemy "off with heavy loss, capturing Lieutenant-Colonel Kane, "commanding. In commemoration of this gallant conduct I "ordered one of the captured 'Bucktails' to be appended as a "trophy to their flag. The action is worthy of acknowledg- "ment from a higher source, more particularly as they avenged "the death of the gallant Ashby, who fell at the same time. "Four color-bearers were shot down in succession, but each "time the colors were caught before reaching the ground, and "were finally borne by Corporal Daniel Shanks to the close of "the action."

"On the 8th inst., at Cross Keys, they were opposed to "three of the enemy's regiments in succession."

General Bradley T. Johnson at the close of hostilities remained in Virginia, and is now (1876) successfully engaged in the practice of the law. Though his junior in years, the writer has known, intimately, Gen. Bradley T. Johnson from early boyhood, and never knew, heard, believed or suspected, that he was capable of doing any act unbecoming to a Christian soldier, or unworthy of a Maryland gentleman.

SEC. 36. Upon folio 42 is recorded the following important document, and interesting list of names:

ISLE OF KENT,
5th *April*,
1652.

WE, whose names are hereafter subscribed, do promise and engage ourselves to be true and faithful to the Commonwealth of England, without King or House of Lords.

Tho. Ward,
Tho. South,
* Tho. Wetherell,
Tho. Pett,
* Tho. Taylor,
* Hen. Carlyen,
Fran. Lumbard,
* John Hud,
* Robert Martin,
* John Smith,
* Henry Ashley,
* John Philips,
John gould,
* Edw. ebes,
* John Smyth,
* John Richeson,
* Hen. Taylor,
Will Leedes,
John Sepsen,
* Anthony Calliway,
* John Gibson.
Robert Vaughan,
Philip Commins,
Thos. Ringgould,
* Thos. Bradnox,
* Hen. Morgan,
Joseph Wickes,
William Elliot,
* Robert halters,
Richard Blunt,

* Matthew Read,
* Will Jones,
* John Ringgold,
* Francis Bright,
Edw. Copedge,
Edmt. Weebe.
John Russell,
Rich. Salter,
Marke Benton,
* John Maconick,
* Will Band,
* Francis Barnes,
* Hen. Clay,
* Roger Baxter,
* James Horner,
* Hen. Weest,
Isa. Ilive,
* Tho. Weest,

George Croutch,
Edward Burton,
Abraham hollman,
John Winchester,
Nicholas Picurd,
Nic. Browne,
* David geldersen,
* Will Price,
Tho. Hill,
John Dean,
* Edw. Coxe,
Robert Dunn,
To ye truth of this
I here subscribe
John Coursey,
John Errickson,
Andrew Hanson,
Andrew Anderson,

NOTE.—* Made his mark.

SEC. 36, A. This list of sixty-six names undoubtedly includes all the adult white male colonists living in Kent county in 1652–53, or nearly all; and we may therefore infer that the white population, upon the Island, then numbered about 330 souls. Many of these signatures may be autographs; some of them are certainly not. THOMAS RINGGOLD never pronounced or spelled his name *Rin-gould*. JOHN COURSEY could not have signed it before the month of February 1653, as we will presently see.

ANDREW HANSON, who died in 1655, did not arrive until the year 1653: which date is ascertained by the deposition of Andrew Hellena, who married his widow, Annika Hanson, as follows:

SEC. 36, B. "Andrew Hellena makes 350 acres of Land appear upon Oath as Rights due him viz: first himself, next ANDREW HANSON, Annikeck Hanson, Hanse Hanson, Frederick Hanson, Katharine Hanson, Margarett Hanson which rights came in, in the year 1653."

folio 42 Lib: B. Sworn in Court.

John Coursey Clk.

LIBER A NO. 1. *For transcribing old Records.* Folio 61.

SEC. 36, C. THOMAS RINGGOLD, being in the fortieth year of his age, came to Kent, with his two sons John and James, in the year 1650.

About or before the year 1657 he m. a second time Mrs. Christian Hill, widow of Thomas Hill, Sr., and on the 5th of of Nov. 1657, by deed, secured to Thomas Hill, Jr., all his father's landed estate. On the 2d of Dec. 1661, he gave to his sons, James and John Ringgold, "*the one-half of my land called Huntingfield, which is in estimation twelve hundred acres, lying on the east side of Chesapeake Bay.*"

It does not appear that he had any children by his second marriage.

MAJOR JAMES RINGGOLD, of Huntingfield, "lord of the manor on Eastern Neck," son of Thomas Ringgold, was twice m. By his 1st wife he had one son, Thomas Ringgold. His 2d wife was Mary Vaughan, dau. of Capt. Robert Vaughan, the Commander of Kent from 1647 to 1652, and had child., viz., William,—John,—James, and Charles Ringgold. Maj. James Ringgold d. 1686.

CHARLES RINGGOLD, son of Maj. James Ringgold and Mary Vaughan, m. 17th Jan'y 1705, Elizabeth Burke, and had child., viz., James, b. 30th June 1709,—Charles, b. 27th April 1713, and Vincent Ringgold, b. 12th Aug. 1716.

WILLIAM RINGGOLD, son of Maj. James Ringgold and Mary Vaughan, had child., viz., Susanna, who m. Benjamin Wickes (see WICKES),—John,—James,—Thomas, and Rebecca Ringgold.

William Ringgold survived his wife Martha, and d. in 1754.

THOMAS RINGGOLD, eldest son of Maj. James Ringgold, by his 1st wife, was m. three times. His 1st wife, Sarah Ringgold, d. and was buried 20th April 1699, leaving an only son, Thomas Ringgold. He m. again, 17th Sept. 1699, Mary Tylden, dau. of Marmaduke and Rebecca Tylden, who d. and was buried 9th Sept. 1708, leaving child., viz., Sarah, who was baptized 29th Sept. 1700,—Elias, b. 6th Sept. 1702,—James, and Joseph Ringgold.

Thomas Ringgold was buried 10th Oct. 1711, leaving his 3d wife, Frances Ringgold, with two small child., viz., Josias, and Mary Ann Ringgold,—the latter of whom was baptized 16th April 1712, after her father's death.

SEC. 36, D. JOSIAS RINGGOLD, youngest son of Thomas and Frances Ringgold, m. 11th Aug. 1730, Sarah Smith, and had child., viz., Thomas, b. 14th Dec. 1732,—a 2d Thomas, b. 25th March 1734,—Josias, b. 28th Sept. 1735,—Sarah,—Mary,—Ann,—Hannah, and Rebecca Ringgold.

Josias Ringgold d. in 1770.

JOSIAS RINGGOLD, son of Josias Ringgold and Sarah Smith,

left three child., viz., Josias, b. in 1762,—Sarah,—and Henrietta Ringgold, who m. William Perkins, son of Col. Isaac Perkins. (See PERKINS.)

JOSIAS RINGGOLD, b. in 1762, m. in 1802, Mary Groome, dau. of Charles and Sarah Kennard Groome, and had child., viz., Josias,—Sarah Ann,—Charles,—Mary Ann,—Henrietta Groome, and William Groome Ringgold.

JOSIAS RINGGOLD, son of Josias and Mary Groome Ringgold, m. in Dec. 1826, Ann Eliza Cruikshanks, and had child., viz., William Groome,—Ann Elizabeth,—Sarah Henrietta, — Mary Groome,—Josias, — Isabella Sluby, — Laura Eugenia, and Catharine Browne Ringgold.

LAURA EUGENIA RINGGOLD, dau. of Josiah and Ann Elizabeth Cruikshanks Ringgold, m. Nov. 1862, John Kennard Aldridge, and d. leaving child., viz., William Ringgold, and John Henry Aldridge.

ISABELLA SLUBY RINGGOLD, dau. of Josias and Ann Elizabeth Cruikshanks Ringgold, m. 31st Oct. 1866, Dr. James A. Cruikshank, of Louisiana, and had child., viz., James, and Robert Cruikshank.

JOSIAS RINGGOLD, son of Josiah and Ann Eliza Cruikshanks Ringgold, m. 14th of Dec. 1865, Kate Gamble, and had child., viz., Emily W.,—Wm. Groome,—Robert Gamble, and Edna Ringgold.

MARY GROOME RINGGOLD, dau. of Josias and Ann Eliza Cruikshanks Ringgold, m. 7th of Oct. 1857, Dr. Jas. Henry Price, and had child., viz., Anna,—Josias,—Mary Belle, and Annie Price.

SARAH HENRIETTA RINGGOLD, dau. of Josias and Ann Eliza Cruikshanks Ringgold, m. Medford Blackiston, and had child., viz., Emma Ringgold,—Laura, and James Thomas Blackiston. Mrs. S. H. R. Blackiston m. a second time Maj. Richard Smyth.

ANN ELIZABETH RINGGOLD, dau. of Josias and Ann Eliza Cruikshanks Ringgold, m. 31st of Oct. 1867, John Kennard Aldridge, and has one child, Lizzie Bella Aldridge.

SEC. 36, E. MARY ANN RINGGOLD, dau. of Josias and Mary Groome Ringgold, m. 6th of Feb'y 1827, Dr. Jacob Fisher, who was b. 2d of Dec. 1796, son of Rev. Isaac and Bathsheba Fisher, and had child., viz., Mary Matilda,—Alfred Henry,—Samuel Groome,—Jacob Frederick,—Josias Ringgold,—Isaac Montgomery,—Clorinda Cornelia,—Ringgold Williams,—Chas. Joseph Groome,—Henry Theodore, and Ella Theodora Fisher. Doctor Jacob Fisher, was the

Register of Wills of Kent county. He d. 18th Feb'y 1859.

MARY MATILDA FISHER, dau. of Dr. Jacob and Mary Ann Ringgold Fisher, m. 8th of Feb. 1849, William Groome Frisby, and had child., viz., Mary,—William Groome,—Charles Jacob,—Matilda, and William Groome Frisby.

ALFRED HENRY FISHER, son of Dr. Jacob and Mary Ann Ringgold Fisher, m. Mary Hodges, who d. leaving one child, Mary Fisher. He m. again, 14th Oct. 1857, Sep. Abell, of Illinois.

DR. SAMUEL GROOME FISHER, son of Dr. Jacob and Mary Ann Ringgold Fisher, m. 4th of Nov. 1858, Martha Isabella Constable, a descendant of Philip Conner, the last Commander of Kent, and had child., viz., Henry,—Stevenson,—Ellen Constable,—Edgar, and Samuel Groome Fisher.

Jacob Frederick Fisher, son of Dr. Jacob and Mary Ann Ringgold Fisher, m. 8th Jan'y 1869, Maria Elizabeth Asprill, and had child., viz., Joseph Alfred, and William Fisher.

CLORINDA CORNELIA FISHER, dau. of Dr. Jacob and Mary Ann Ringgold Fisher, m. 23d Jan'y 1867, George Hamilton Thompson, and had child., viz., Ella Clorinda, — Jacob Fisher,—Mary Julia,—Clorinda Fisher,—and Ella Matilda Thompson.

ELLA THEODORA FISHER, youngest dau. of D. Jacob and Mary Ann Ringgold Fisher, d. unmarried, 13th Nov. 1875, The following notice of her death appeared in "*The Chestertown Transcript:*"

"ELLA THEODORA FISHER.

"The deceased, the youngest daughter of Dr. Jacob and "Mrs. Mary Ann Ringgold Fisher, of Kent county, Md., was "born the 10th day of September, 1847, and departed this life "at the residence of her widowed mother, in Chestertown, in "the early morning of the 13th of November, 1875, aged 28 "years, 2 months and 3 days.

"Tenderly and judiciously reared by affectionate and pious "parents, her whole life was but a preparation for that quiet "resting place on earth, which she loved so well, and the home "prepared in heaven. She was unaffectedly pious, a sincere "Christian, and her faith was so much a part of her being, "that between her pure soul and the vanities of this world "there was a great gulf fixed. Her character and disposition "were unknown and unappreciated outside of the circle of "her most intimate friends, for she was so modest and retiring "that she never unveiled the beauties of her mind or the "graces of her disposition except to those who loved her. She "made no enemies, cherished no enmities, and was a sincere "and unselfish friend. Her character was transparently true "and pure. The perfect frankness with which she expressed "her sentiments attested the candor of her disposition and the "sincerity of her convictions, and was only equaled by the "modest firmness with which she gave utterance to her views. "It is a blessed comfort to us, to know that she had quietly and "silently, in her own closet, prepared herself to meet her "God. Months ago, while in the enjoyment of her usual "health, she expressed, fully, her wishes in regard to her "interment, and less than two weeks before her fatal sick-"ness she reiterated the same wishes, and intimated that "she believed she would die before the spring of the year. "Though this presentiment was fresh and full in her mind "it did not deter her from nursing and watching at the "bedside of a sick and dying relative. There she con-"tracted the typhoid fever, and fell, as many noble women "have done before, a martyr to her affections. She died as we "would all like to die—in the path of duty, at peace with God "and man. A star hath fallen heavenward."

HENRIETTA GROOME RINGGOLD, dau. of Josias and Mary Groome Ringgold, m. Joseph Rasin, and had two child., viz., Allee Rasin and Joseph Rasin, who m. Miss Sarah Paca.

MRS. MARY GROOME RINGGOLD and her second husband, Benjamin Blackiston Wroth, had child, viz., Charles,—Kiuvin,—Elizabeth,—Benjamin Blackiston, and William Groome Wroth.

SEC. 36, F. ELIAS RINGGOLD, son of Thomas and Mary Tylden Ringgold, m. 15th April 1725, Mary Bordley, and had a son, Thomas Ringgold, who was b. 30th Oct. 1726, and d. in Aug. 1728.

Elias Ringgold d. in Nov. 1737. In his Will, dated 19th Oct. 1737, he speaks of his "loving wife Mary," and provides for "the child then unborn."

SEC. 36, H. THOMAS RINGGOLD, son of Thomas and his 1st wife Sarah Ringgold, m. 1st May 1712, Rebecca Wilmer, dau. of Simon and Rebecca Wilmer (see WILMER), and had child., viz., Thomas, b. 5th Dec. 1715,—Rebecca, baptized 4th June 1727,—William, and Sarah Ringgold, who m. Alexander Williamson.

MAJOR WILLIAM RINGGOLD, of Eastern Neck (estate now called "Hermitage"), son of Thomas Ringgold and Rebecca Wilmer, was one of the Committee of Safety, Observation and

Correspondence, during the Revolutionary War, a member of the Convention which met in Annapolis, 14th Aug. 1776, and formed the first Constitution for the STATE OF MARYLAND. He received his military commission from Matthew Tilghman, President of "The Delegates of the Freemen of Maryland in Convention." He m. twice, 1st on the 9th of Jan'y 1750, Sarah Jones, and had child., viz., Dr. Jacob Ringgold,—Mrs. Blunt, and Rebecca Ringgold, who m. John Williamson, and had a dau., Sarah Williamson, who m. James Ringgold, and had child., viz., James,—Alexander,—William,—Richard Willaimson (who was President of Washington College),—Thomas,—Sarah W.,—Anne Rebecca,—Mary,—Jacob, and Washington Ringgold.

Major William Ringgold survived his 1st wife, and m. his cousin Mary Wilmer, dau. of William and Rosa Blackiston Wilmer (see WILMER), and had child., viz., William,—Peregrine,—Hester, who m. Mr. Holland,—Henrietta, who m. Capt. Thomas Harris (see HARRIS),—Mrs. Miller,—Sarah,—Rebecca,—Eliza, and Fannie Ringgold.

James Ringgold, above-mentioned, was the son of James Ringgold, who had child., viz., James,—Mary (who m. Thomas Carvill, and had child., viz., James,—Edward,—Marianne,—John,—Harriet, and Orlando Carvill),—Richard (who m. Elizabeth Smith, dau. of Dr. Walter Smith, of Georgetown, D. C., and had child, viz., Walter S.,—Mary Melvina,—Richard C.,—Eliza,—Clement S.,—James S.,—Matilda C., who m. Hon. James Alfred Pearce,—Sophia S.,—and Harriet Ringgold, who m. Rev. William Henry Wilmer (see WILMER), and d. *sine prole.*

DR. WILLIAM RINGGOLD, son of Major William and his 2d wife, Mary Wilmer, m. Martha Hanson, dau. of Hans and Mary Hynson Hanson (see HANSON), and had child., viz., William, b. in 1794,—Peregrine, b. in 1796,—Harriet Rebecca, b. in 1798,—James Alexander, b. in 1800,—Frederick Gustavus, b. in 1801, and Mary Hanson Ringgold, b. 10th September, 1803.

WILLIAM RINGGOLD, son of Dr. William Ringgold and Martha Hanson, m. Maria Nicholson.

PEREGRINE RINGGOLD, son of Dr. William Ringgold and Martha Hanson, m. 29th Dec. 1822, Mary C. Coe, dau. of William Coe and Mary Sears, and had child., viz., Mary H. Ringgold, who m. 5th Aug. 1848, Edward P. Roberts,—William H. Ringgold, who m. 29th Dec. 1864, Ann Frances McKew,—John P. Ringgold, who m. 14th July 1853, Louisa

A. Wickes, dau. of John Wickes and Mary Jewell,—Maria L. Ringgold, who m. 17th Nov. 1853, James W. Weatherby, and C. Frederick Ringgold, who m. 22d Jan. 1868, Sarah V. Wickes.

HARRIET REBECCA RINGGOLD, dau. of Dr. William Ringgold and Martha Hanson, m. 7th Sept. 1820, John Stevenson Constable, and had child., viz., William Ringgold,—Martha Isabella,—Mary,—Stevenson and Ellen Constable (see CONSTABLE).

MARY HANSON RINGGOLD, dau. of Dr. William Ringgold and Martha Hanson, m. 9th Oct. 1821, Hon. James Hodges, of Liberty Hall, Kent County, and had child., viz., James Hodges,—William Ringgold Hodges,—Mary Hodges,—Frances Harriet Hodges, and Robert Hodges. (See HODGES.)

PEREGRINE RINGGOLD, son of Major William Ringgold and Mary Wilmer, m. Barbara Smith, a sister of Gen. Walter Smith, of Georgetown, D. C., and had child., viz., Alexander Hamilton Ringgold,—Lieutenant William Ringgold, U. S. N., *deceased*, and a dau., who died young.

SEC. 36, J. THOMAS RINGGOLD, merchant, son of Thomas Ringgold and Rebecca Wilmer, was a member of the Congress of 1765, and was a member of the Legislature of Maryland in the sessions of 1762, 1763, 1765, 1766, and 1768. He m. Anna Maria Earle, dau. of James and Mary Tilghman Earle, and had one son, Thomas Ringgold.

He d. 1st April 1772, in the 57th year of his age. She d. in July 1794, in the 70th year of her age.

THOMAS RINGGOLD, of Chestertown, only son of Thomas Ringgold and Anna Maria Earle, was a member of the Convention of Maryland which met at Annapolis, 8th May 1776. He m. Mary Galloway, and d. 26th of Oct. 1776, aged 32 years, leaving child., viz., Thomas,—Samuel, b. 15th Jan'y 1770,—Anna Maria, b. 9th March 1772, who m. 24th March 1795, Colonel Frisby Tilghman, son of James and Susanna Steuart Tilghman (see TILGHMAN)—and Benjamin Ringgold.

Mrs. Mary Galloway Ringgold was the dau. of Samuel Galloway, of Tulip Hill, Anne Arundel County.

Samuel Galloway had four child., viz., John Galloway, whose only dau. m. Virgil Maxey, and had two daus.—one m. Francis Markoe, of Washington, and the other m. Col. G. W. Hughes, of the Topographical Engineer Corps,—Benjamin Galloway, who was educated at Eton, read Law at Lincoln's Inn, m. Miss Chew, settled and d. at Hagerstown,—Mary Galloway, who m. Thomas Ringgold,—and Anne Galloway, who m. James Cheston, son of Daniel Cheston and Francina Augustina Frisby.

General Samuel Ringgold, son of Thomas Ringgold and Mary Galloway, m. 3d May 1792, Maria Cadwalader, dau. of Gen. John Cadwalader. Soon after or about the time of his marriage, he removed from Kent county and settled upon his estate, *Fountain Rock*, in Washington county, Maryland. This was an immense tract, containing several thousand acres of the most productive land in the State of Maryland, or in America. Here he built a magnificent mansion, which resembled in many particulars the President's house in Washington; it was adorned with beautiful stucco work, and elaborate wood carving. Many of the doors, perhaps the greater number, were of solid mahogany. All the appointments, stables and other offices were in style, befitting the most elegant private residence in Maryland. After many years the estate passed into other hands. New buildings were subsequently added to the mansion and it became the seat of the College of St. James; during which period the writer spent six very happy years there, as a student.

Gen'l Cadwalader d. 11th of Feb'y 1786, at his country seat in Kent county, Md., aged 44 years, 1 month and 1 day, and was buried in the Church yard of Shrewsbury Parish, Kent county, Md. Upon his tomb is inscribed a noble tribute, a beautiful epitaph, written by Thos. Paine, "who during his lifetime was his violent political enemy."

Gen. Samuel and Maria Cadwalader Ringgold, of Fountain Rock, had child., viz., Anna Maria, b. 10th of July 1793, d. 4th March 1828,—John Cadwalader, b. 15th Nov. 1794, d. young,—Samuel, b. 16th Oct. 1796,—Mary Elizabeth, b. 18th Dec. 1788, d. 9th of March 1836,—Ann Cadwalader, b. 10th Jan. 1801,—Cadwalader, b. 20th August 1802,—Cornelia, b. 2d Sept. 1805,—Edward Lloyd, b. 19th April 1807,—Chester, b. 17th Jan'y 1809,—and Charles and Frederick, twins, b. 22d and 23d of July 1810.

Maria Cadwalader Ringgold, wife of Gen. Samuel Ringgold, d. 28th August 1810.

Gen. Saml. Ringgold m. in Washington, at the President's House, a second time, Marie Antoinette Hay, and had child., viz., George Ringgold, U. S. A., d.,—Fayette Ringgold, U. S. Consul in Peru, South America,—Virginia Ringgold, who m. John Ross Key, and Rebecca Ringgold, who m. Dr. Hay, of Chicago.

Gen. Samuel Ringgold d. at the residence of his son-in-law, William Schley, in Frederick City, Md., Sunday, 18th Oct. 1836.

MAJOR SAMUEL RINGGOLD, U. S. A., son of Gen. Samuel and Maria Cadwalader Ringgold, greatly distinguished himself and fell at the battle of Palo Alto, in Mexico, 8th May 1846.

REAR-ADMIRAL CADWALADER RINGGOLD, U. S. N., son of Gen. Samuel Ringgold and Maria Cadwalader Ringgold, d. in the city of New York, 29th April, 1867.

ANN CADWALADER RINGGOLD, dau. of Gen. Samuel and Maria Cadwalader Ringgold, m. William Schley, a distinguished lawyer of Frederick City, Md., 28th Sept. 1824, and d. June 1870. William Schley d. March 1872, in Baltimore, where he had resided for many years previous to his death. They had child., viz., William, b. 9th of Sept. 1825, d. 16th Sept. 1833,—Cadwalader Ringgold, b. 20th March 1828, d. 30th of July 1828,—Ann Cadwalader,—Agnes,—Allen, b. 20th Feb'y 1835, d. 10th July 1835,—Samuel Ringgold,—William Cadwalader, and Alice Schley, b. 26th Dec. 1844, d. 10th July 1847.

ANN CADWALADER SCHLEY, dau. of William and Ann Cadwalader Ringgold Schley, m. 9th Jan'y 1855, William Woodville, Jr.

AGNES SCHLEY, dau. of William and Ann Cadwalader Ringgold Schley, m. 9th Feb'y 1854, William Key Howard, and d. 23d Sept. 1857. She had one child, William Key Howard.

WILLIAM CADWALADER SCHLEY, son of William and Ann Cadwalader Ringgold Schley, m. 17th of Dec. 1868, Ellen Teackle, second dau. of St. George W. Teackle, of Baltimore city, Md., and had child., viz., Ann Teackle Schley, William Cadwalader Schley and St. George T. Schley.

CORNELIA RINGGOLD, dau. of Gen. Samuel and Maria Cadwalader Ringgold, of Fountain Rock, Washington county, Md., m. 16th Nov. 1826, George M. Potts, of Fountain Rock, Frederick county, Md., and had child., viz., Richard,—Arthur,—George M.,—Cornelia Ringgold, and Eleanor Potts.

DR. RICHARD POTTS, U. S. A. and C. S. A., son of George M. and Cornelia Ringgold Potts, m. twice. His 1st wife (2d June 1852) was Rebecca B. McPherson. His 2d wife (9th Sept. 1862) was Eugenia Dunlap, dau. of Hon. G. W. Dunlap of Kentucky. He left one child, George Dunlap Potts.

ARTHUR POTTS, son of George M. and Cornelia Ringgold Potts, m. 21st Jan'y 1869, Hellen Mobberly, dau. of Dr.

Mobberly, of New Market, Frederick county, Md., and had child., viz., Eleanor,—Louisa,—Richard, and Cornelia Potts.

CORNELIA RINGGOLD POTTS, dau. of George M. and Cornelia Ringgold Potts, m. 12th Dec. 1861, Charles W. Ross, son of William J. Ross, an eminent lawyer of Frederick, Md., and had child., viz., William J. Ross, Jr.,—Cornelia Ringgold Ross,—Charles W. Ross, and George Murdock Potts Ross.

ELEANOR POTTS, dau. of George M. and Cornelia Ringgold Potts, m. Arthur S. Johns, son of Right Rev. John Johns, Bishop of Virginia, and d. leaving one child, Eleanor Johns, since deceased.

SEC. 37. February 2d, 1652, I ROBERT CLARKE, Gentleman and Surveyor Generall, of this Province, do hereby attest that in the year 1640 I did survey and lay out unto William Brantwell Gent and Thomas Bradnox, planter ten thousand Acres of Land upon the Northernmost part of the Isle of Kent commonly called Love Point, in the year 1650. The said Thomas Bradnox to Invite Inhabitants to seatt the said Island did lay down his rights of 1400 Acres of Land, now posses't of other Tennants, that he might have his Right, in some other place, the truth hereof is known to divers of the Inhabitants as well as to my self.

ROBT. CLARKE Survyr. Genll.
PHILLIP CONNER,
JOHN RUSSELL. Fol. 64.

SEC. 38. The Clerk of the Court in 1652 signs his name THOM'S HYNSON, SEN. Folio 66.

1653–54.

SEC. 39. The following is a curious epistle:

For the Worl. Mr. Philip Conner, and Mr. Thos Ringgold, and the rest of the Commissioners,

Gentlemen:

My dear respects to you being remember'd, I would entreàt you to take into your serious consideration, the griefs and sorrows, w'ch I have sustained, and do sustain, through my great oversight, caused by My infirmity, I committed in Court, in using very unfitting language, which I can confess, I am very sorry for. But I hope, the measure of grief is no further good, than it makes way for joy; for a bad action salved up with a free forgiveness, is as not done; and as a bone once broke, is stronger after well setting, so is love after reconcilement. I know, how easy it is to detest some faults in others, w'ch we flatter in ourselves; for, in the best Men, nature is Partial in itself.

Therefore it is good to sentence others' frialties, with the remembrance of our own. But, God Willing, it shall be my duty hereafter to keep myself from all violent passion, w'ch causeth discontent, knowing, that all things happen from Him (from ?) Whom Himself came.

I pray, look upon the crosses and wants that God hath laid upon me at present, withal, having lost almost all my hogs, and the greater part of my cattle, being wanting and dead. Yet methinks, I see some men, ready to add to my afflictions, rather than to yield me any comfort in my sorrow.

The end, for which I write these lines unto you, is that you would be pleased to remit the fines that were laid upon me for my offence committed; and it shall be understood, a thankfulness, from him, that is,

Yr. poor friend to love you
ROBERT VAUGHAN.

Kent, the 1st of
April, 1653.

The Commissioners in consideration that Capt. Vaughan "submitteth himself" and acknowledged "his offences to be from frailty," and also considering the sorrow he hath expressed and the "losses" he has "suffered," "freely remit" the fines for his "misdemeanors" to the Court, "in 1652," so far as it lies in their power, with an "earnest admonition unto him, to be careful to keep his promises, in his petition, not to run himself into the like prœmunires." Fols. 72 & 73.

SEC. 40. Among the proceedings of the Court, which was holden 3d August 1653, Francis Lumbard, for neglect of duty, was removed from the Office of High Sheriff, and Thomas Bradnox appointed, in his place.

SEC. 41. On the 18th day of March, 1653 *o. s.*, Gov. Stone granted a license to Thomas Adams, "with his vessel to trade or traffic with those of the Swedish nation in Delaware Bay, or in any part of this province, not being enemies to the Commonwealth of England." It may be asked why should such a license be deemed necessary or proper! Perhaps the only explanation may be found in the excited state of feeling at this period. It must be borne in mind that the Swedes had planted their Colony within the ancient Dominion of Virginia, and located themselves in that part of Virginia which Charles I, by Charter, on the 20th June, 1632, had granted to Lord Baltimore. The Proprietary of Maryland claimed, by Charter, the very ground the Swedes held in possession; and asserted this right in 1642–43 by sending George Lamberton to establish an English Colony on the western bank of the Delaware. This claim was forcibly resisted by the Swedes, and Governor Printz expelled the English settlers, took Lamberton, by *ruse de guerre*, prisoner and did not release him until he had exacted a "weight of beaver." This, of course, produced much ill feeling in Maryland, which was aggravated and intensified by the current report and belief that the Swedes had taught the "Susquehannock Indians" the use of firearms. The people of Maryland, therefore, and especially the inhabitants of Kent Island, who had suffered much from the guns of the savages, regarded the Swedes as private and public enemies. In consequence of this personal hostility, evidence of which sufficiently appears upon the Record, but few of the Swedes who came to Kent in 1653 remained upon the Island: some returned to the Delaware, and one at least, Randal (Randolph) Hanson, went to St. Mary's to carve out his fortune at the point of his sword.

SEC. 42. MR. DAVIS says: "The settlement and subsequent fate of the Swedes suggest a subject for one of the saddest, yet sweetest, chapters in the history of American colonization. Planted upon the Delaware, under the auspices of a crown distinguished for its noble qualities, but overlaid, if not crushed, in the infancy of the colony by the superior numbers, first of the Dutch and then of the English, they still retained in the midst of all their reverses the fond remembrance of their native land; and cherished, with a gentle but glowing love, the faith and traditions of their original ancestry. Eight generations also have lingered around the gravestone and the hearth of their early American forefathers; nor have they yet lost those elements so characteristic of their race, and which, in spite of so much that is mean in every age, have imparted such real dignity to human nature.—THE DAY STAR, p. 78, *note* 1.

SEC. 43. Until the publication of the "Annals of the Swedes on the Delaware," by Rev. JEHU CURTIS CLAY, very little was known with accuracy in regard to the arrival and first settlement of the Swedes. Every writer felt at liberty to assume as correct the dates of his favorite author, and even our own Bozman fell into error.

SEC. 44. It was in the reign of that glorious King, the lion-hearted GUSTAVUS ADOLPHUS, the benefactor of humanity as well as of his own people, that an attempt was first projected to plant a colony of Swedes in America. That great man resolved to invite to his colony "colonists from all the nations of Europe," of all conditions of honest and industrious men, and to make it "a blessing to the common man," and to the "whole Protestant world," a home for "all oppressed Christendom." In this wise and generous resolve he was encouraged by the advice and zeal of William Usselinx, an eminent merchant of Antwerp, who suggested to the King the idea of a Commercial Company, and urged it upon the ground that it would be the means of planting the Christian religion among the Indians, that his Majesty's dominions would be enlarged, the treasury enriched from abroad, the taxes lessened at home, and that the piety, sobriety and frugality of the Swedes, peculiarly fitted them to carry such an enterprise to a successful accomplishment.

Sec. 45. A company was chartered with power to trade to America, Asia and Africa. The King issued his Proclamation or Edict, dated at Stockholm, the 2d July 1626, in which he offered the most liberal terms of subscription to his subjects of all ranks. The proposal was received by all classes with great enthusiasm. The King's mother, his brother-in-law, Prince John Cassimir, the members of his Majesty's council, many civil and military officers of high rank, bishops and clergy, merchants and citizens, country gentlemen and farmers, gladly and eagerly became liberal subscribers to the undertaking. Officers of rank and qualification were selected, and proper ships and all necessaries were provided. Every preparation was made and the work was ripe for execution and accomplishment, when the German wars broke forth, which taxed all the resources of the nation; and Gustavus Adolphus found it necessary to draw his sword to vindicate upon the plains of Europe the sacred rights of conscience before he could plant religious freedom upon the banks of the Delaware. It is not necessary to recount the story of the wonderful campaigns of Gustavus Adolphus, to tell how, like a conquering hero, with his brave army he won possession of large tracts of country from the borders of Hungary and Silesia to the banks of the Rhine, and from the Lakes of Constance to the Black Sea, taking three hundred cities and fortified places in the German Empire, and how he frustrated the cruel schemes of the bigoted Ferdinand against the Protestants, and by a tactics, all his own, defeated the two most renowned warriors of his age, Tilly and Wallenstein; for every student of Religious Freedom is familiar with that heroic episode in history.

Sec. 46. The bustling scenes of camp and battle life

deepened the desires of Gustavus Adolphus to establish a colony in America; and amid the most stirring events, a few days before his death, while at Nuremberg, he drew up a matured plan for the colony.

On the 16th November 1632, in the full tide of success and in the moment of glorious achievement, Gustavus Adolphus was slain in battle at Lützen: Religious Freedom gained one of its most memorable triumphs and Humanity shed a tear over one of her ablest and most glorious defenders.

SEC. 47. Gustavus Adolphus, sixth of the line of Vasa, son of Charles IX and Christina of Schleswig-Holstein, born in Stockholm, Dec. 2, 1594, married in 1620 Maria Elleonore, of Brandenburg, whose court he visited in disguise to choose a wife. Their daughter, Christina, was his successor.

The Chancellor Oxenstiern published the Proclamation, which had been left unsigned by Gustavus Adolphus, and added:

"Though the above declaration and amplification of the before mentioned privileges, of his majesty of glorious memory, could not have been signed on account of the multifarious and incredible affairs of war, I cannot, in consequence of my duty, and good personal knowledge but certify, that the same has been the highest desire and wish of his royal majesty; therefore, I, by the crown of Sweden, and plenipotentiary minister general, have signed it, with my own hand, and affixed my seal to it, at Hilebrum, April 10th 1633."

SEC. 48. In the year 1637, the indefatigable Usselinx broached the subject again to Count Oxenstiern. Oxenstiern, then prime minister, laid the subject before Queen Christina; who approved the plan proposed. Peter Menewe, who had been the Dutch Governor of New Netherlands, 1624–1632, was appointed commander of the expedition. The colonists sailed from the port of Gottenburg, on the West Coast of Sweden, some time, it is supposed, in the autumn of the year 1637, in two vessels; one an armed ship, called the "Key of Kalmar," the other a transport, named the "Bird Grip" or "Griffin." The expedition numbered about one hundred and fifty souls. The colonists brought with them a plentiful supply of necessaries for trade, subsistence and defence, and with them also came Reorus Torkillus, a clergyman; who was the first that ever preached the Gospel on the banks of the Delaware. The colonists sailed up Minquas creek (which they named CHRISTINA in honor of their young Queen), and landed at the Rocks, which form a natural wharf of stone, and are situated at the foot of Sixth street, in the city of Wilmington, Delaware. The Swedes by purchase from the Indians obtained a grant of all the land from Cape Henlopen to the Falls of Trenton and there fixed up land-marks. This purchase, however, was not made until they had built Fort Christina, and felt secure from the attacks of the Dutch; who by William Kieft, Director General of New Netherlands, protested, energetically, against the occupation of the Swedes; saying, among other things, that the land in question "has been in our possession many years, and has been secured by us with forts above and below, and sealed with our blood." All which, it is charged, is *well known to Menewe, having been done while he was Director General of New Netherlands.* Notwithstanding the prosperity of their trade, the Swedes at Fort Christina became discouraged, and in the Spring of 1640 determined to abandon the settlement; but the very day of their intended departure, a Dutch ship, the Fredenburg, arrived with tidings and succor from Sweden, laden with men, cattle, and everything necessary for the cultivation of the country. In this vessel, it is said, arrived Peter Hollendare who, afterwards, succeeded Menewe as Governor of Delaware. Menewe appears to have been an energetic and just man. Acrelius, says, "he did great service to the first Swedish colony." Vanderdonk, in his description of New Netherlands, quotes a letter of Menewe's, which shows that he took great interest in the development of the agricultural interests of the colonies. He died in 1641 and was buried in the old Swedish church-yard at Wilmington, where also rest the remains of Reorus Torkillus. Upon the death of Menewe, PETER HOLLENDARE, an officer of the Swedish army, became Governor. Of his administration little is known. He held the office for about eighteen months and then returned to Sweden, and was made commander of the Naval Arsenal at Stockholm.

SEC. 49. On the 16th day of August, Lieutenant-Colonel JOHN PRINTZ was commissioned Governor of New Sweden. Queen CHRISTINA was very precise in her instructions to him in regard to his conduct to the English, the Dutch and the Indians. In all which, much liberality of sentiment and practical wisdom is displayed, as well as womanly, queenly solicitude for the welfare of her subjects; "but before all to labor and watch that he renders all things to ALMIGHTY GOD, the true worship which is His due."

SEC. 50. Governor PRINTZ sailed, the day he received his commission, from Stockholm for New Sweden, in the ship

RENOWN (called by Campanius the FAME), accompanied by the STORK. Some writers say that, in addition to the FAME, two ships of war, called the SVAN (SWAN) and CHARITAS accompanied him. After a passage of five months they arrived at Fort Christina, 15th Feb. 1642, *o. s.* With them came, as Chaplain, CAMPANIUS (JOHN CAMPANIUS HOLM), justly celebrated for being the first to translate Luther's Catechism into the Indian language; but more widely known as the author of the journal of his visit to New Sweden, which is the foundation of the interesting "Description of the Province of New Sweden," compiled by his grandson, Thomas Campanius Holm.

SEC. 51. GOVERNOR PRINTZ selected as the site of his residence Tinacong (TINICUM ISLAND). It is now the Lazaretto of Philadelphia. Here the Governor built Fort Gottenburg and a very handsome mansion for himself and family, Printz Hall, with a fine orchard, pleasure-house, and many conveniences attached. On this island, also, the principal colonists had their dwellings and plantations. A church was also erected here which, on the 4th of September 1646, Dr. John Campanius consecrated for divine service, and also its burying place. Campanius records that the first corpse ever buried there was Catharine, daughter of Andrew Hanson, the 28th October 1646, being the Feast of St. Simon and St. Jude. *Vide* Campanius, p. 73.

SEC. 52. The traffic of the Swedes being interfered with by the Dutch, Gov. Printz erected another fort at Elsingburg (Salem Creek), but it was taken possession of by an enemy more blood-thirsty and more enterprising than the Dutch then were. It was stormed and carried by mosquitoes; the garrison ignominiously fled, and was afterwards known in song and story as *Myggenborg*, or Mosquito Fort. About the time of the erection of this fort it was that Gov. Printz expelled the English at Varkenkill (Salem Creek) and captured George Lamberton, who afterward, 1647, was lost at sea.

SEC. 53. On the 6th Nov. 1643, Queen Christina granted New Gottenburg or Tinicum Island to Governor Printz. For further protection, Gov. Printz erected a fort on the Schulkill (so named by the Dutch), and means "hidden creek or sculk creek," from the retired position of its mouth. In December 1645, Fort Gottenburg was blown up and destroyed, an accident occasioned by the carelessness of a sleepy servant.

SEC. 54. In the year 1646, ANDREAS HUDDE, an active, pertinacious man, appeared on the stage as the Governor of the Dutch on the Delaware, and a series of disputes commenced which culminated, finally, in the overthrow of the Swedish power in America. The answer of Printz to Hudde is characteristic of the man and the times. Andreas Hudde urged upon Printz the older claims of the Dutch to the Delaware. To which Governor Printz replied, "that the Devil was the oldest possessor of Hell, but that he sometimes admitted a younger one." "This," said the indignant Dutchman, "he declared at his own table, on the 3d of June, in the presence of me and my wife." In the same year the colonists were more encouraged than strengthened by the arrival of the *Svan* (Swan), the *Black Cat*, the *Key of Calmar*, and the *Lamb*, which brought ammunition, people, and goods for the Indians.

SEC. 55. Many attempts were made to settle the disputes in regard to bounds and the rights of possession by diplomacy, but the Dutch and Swedes were equally unyielding, and many outrages were committed on both sides. Finally, on the 19th of July 1651, Stuyvessant, Governor of New Netherlands, convened all the Indian Sachems who lived near the Delaware, and obtained from them a deed of all the land from Fort Christina to Bombay Hook, and immediately proceeded to erect a fort to secure possession. He chose the spot where New Castle now stands and built *Fort Cassimir.* This was fatal to the peace and prosperity of New Sweden. The Swedes became discouraged, and the Governor having long waited in vain for reinforcements, finding all his protests unheeded by the Dutch, and the Mother Country unwilling or unable to assist him in enforcing his demands, resolved to return home. Governor John Printz performed his last official act on the 1st October 1653, and some time afterwards returned to Sweden. Some Swedes returned with him, and a few of his personal friends wandered to other colonies.

SEC. 56. On the 12th of December 1653, the College of Commerce appointed John Claudius Rising as commissioner and assistant to Gov. Printz. But upon his arrival he found that Printz had departed, and he immediately assumed the office of Governor. Rising was a gallant, chivalric man, and one of his first acts was to capture Fort Cassimir. This aggression was the death-blow to the peace and existence of New Sweden. War ensued, and the Swedes after a gallant but unavailing resistance were overpowered, and in September 1655 the jurisdiction of the *Dutch* over *New Sweden* was established, which in a few years was destined to be pushed aside by the domination of a prouder, haughtier, more aggressive and more powerful race—the *Anglo-Saxon.*

SEC. 57. "Such," says the historian, Bancroft, "was the end of *New Sweden*, the colony that connects our country with Gustavus Adolphus and the nations that dwell on the Gulf of Bothnia. It maintained its existence for a little more than seventeen years, and succeeded in establishing permanent plantations on the Delaware. The descendants of the colonists, in the course of generations, widely scattered and blended with emigrants of other lineage, *constitute probably more than one part in two hundred of the present population of our country.* * * * Free from ambition, ignorant of the ideas which were convulsing the English mind, it was only as Protestants that they shared the impulse of the age. They cherished the calm earnestness of religious feeling; they reverenced the bonds of family and the purity of morals; their children, under every disadvantage of want of teachers and of Swedish books, were well instructed. With the natives they preserved peace. A love for Sweden, their dear mother country, the abiding sentiment of loyalty toward its sovereign, continued to distinguish the little band; at Stockholm they remained for a century the objects of a disinterested and generous regard; affection united them in the New World; and a part of their descendants still preserve their altar and their dwelling round the graves of their fathers."

SEC. 58. The following sections are taken from the second part of Liber A., Court Proceedings of Kent County:

WHEREAS by exercise of the Chiefe MAGISTRACY, and Administration of the Government, over England, Scotland, Ireland, and Dominions thereunto beelonginge, doth now reside in his Highness the LORD PROTECTOR; assisted with a COUNCIL; IN whose name all *writs*, process, Commitions, Graunts or orders are to runne; AND from whom all MAGISTRACY, and powers, in the three Kingdoms, or Nation aforesaid, and the DOMINIONS thereof, is to be derived;

AND this PROVINCE OF MARYLAND, by lawfull power from the supreme AUTHORITIE of the Commonwealth of England, formerly and since from the LORD PROTECTOR, and COUNSELL, now beeinge COMMITTED, to the *Honorable Richard Bennett, Esq.*, and Colonell *Wm. Claiborne*, is subscribed to the present GOVERNMENT OF ENGLAND, and established therein, by a COMMITION GRAUNTED in the name of his HIGHNESS the LORD PROTECTOR, unto *Capt. Wm. Fuller*, Mr. *Ritch. Preston*, Mr. *Wm. Durand*, Mr. *Edwd. Loyd*, *Capt. Jno. Smith*, Mr. *Leo. Strong*, Mr. ——— *Lawson*, Mr. *Jno. Hatch*, Mr. *Wm. Parker*, Mr. *Ritch. Wells*, and Mr. *Ritch.*

Ewen, for the orderinge, directinge and Governinge, all the AFFAYRS OF MARYLAND:

THEREFORE the sayd *Capt. Wm. Fuller*, and the rest of the Commitioners, present at a Court houlden at PROVIDENCE, the 28th Day of februari 1654, ACCORDINGE to order of this Court in Pursuance, of the Discharge of that trust, which is Committed to them, for the more eassie aud speedy ADMINISTRATION of JUSTICE, Conservation of the peace, prevention of insurrections and disturbances which may arise, and for the suppressinge of the same HAVE in the name of the LORD PROTECTOR, and doe by these presents nominate, and appoint Mr. *Phillip Connier Chiefe Commander*, of the *County of Kent*, within the PROVINCE OF MARYLAND, GIVINGE and *Grauntinge*, in the name of his *Highness*, the LORD PROTECTOR of *England, etc.*, unto the sayd *Phillip Conier*, *Power* and *Authoritie*, in the sayd COUNTIE, to COMMAUND all persons therein, in all things relatinge necessarily to the defence thereof, from the INSURRECTIONS of INDIANS, and attempts of any persons whatsoever, unlawfully made, against the peace and libertie of the people, as also to Commaund them, in that which concerns the due ADMINISTRATION of JUSTICE and RIGHT, the Execution of Lawes, upon delinquents and the lawfull and necessary use of the MILITIA.

REQUIRINGE the people of the sayd Countie to bee subject to all his lawfull Commaunds, AND also wee doe by these presents Nominate and appoint Mr. *Joseph Wickes*, Mr. *Tho. Ringgold*, Mr. *Thomas Hynson*, Mr. *Jno. Russell*, Mr. *Henry Morgan*, Mr. *Wm. Eliot*, and Mr. *Henry Carline*, to bee Commitioners for the sayd County of Kent ASSISTANT to the sayd Mr. *Philip Conier* (who is hereby appointed PRESIDENT of the Commition) for the Conservation of the peace, Administration of Justice, and right EXECUTINGE of JUDGMENT to all persons indiferently, in all Causes, of which they shall bee allowed Capable to have Cognizance, and for the present as they have formerly done, untill further order bee published, AND that any foure of the sayd Commitioners whereof Mr. *Philip Conier*, or Mr. *Joseph Wickes*, or Mr. *Tho. Ringgold*, or Mr. *Tho. Hinson*, to bee all ways one, shall have power to Keepe Courts, at such times and in such places as to them shall seem Convenient and necessary, AND that all writs, proces, warrants, supenas, etc., which concerne the County Court, shall bee signed by the sayd Mr. *Philip Conier*, but in his absence by Mr. Joseph Wickes, and upon extraordinarie or sudden occation, which endangers the Saftie of the County, preventinge or supressinge of any dangerous action, the nearest Commissioners shall have power to give out a warrant directed to the Sheriffe or Constable and in case of Extremitie depute one to serve the same, AND lastly the sayd Mr. *Philip Conier*, and the sayd Commissioners are Required to Cause the Clerk of theire Court to transcribe the Court *prosedings* and to deliver them to the Secretarie of the Province, every six Months, at the GENERALL PROVINCIALL COURT.

GIVEN at Providence under my hand this first day of March 1654.

WILL FULLER,
WILLIAM DURAND.

Copia vera testis
Me Clar. Coms. Kent.
Tho. Hill. Liber A. Fol. 97.

SEC. 59, A. Mr. *Philip Conier, Commander of Kent,* is a very interesting personage in the history of our County. We first met with him on the 18th day of April 1647, when he was appointed, one of the Commissioners of Kent County, by a Roman Catholic Governor; and he was not a Roman Catholic.

When the commission for the Government of Kent County was re-organized, 11th Dec. 1648, by Gov. Greene, "for special reasons him thereunto moving," Mr. Conner, alone, with Capt. Vaughan, was retained upon the bench. Again, on the 31st July, 1652, when all the other Commissioners were ousted by Bennet, Lloyd, Marsh and Strong, the Puritan Commissioners, he was retained, and placed at the head of the new Commission, with such gentlemen as Mr. Thomas Ringgold and Major Joseph Wickes, who were of the *élite* of the Province. And now we find him, though he was not a Puritan, sought out and chosen, by the minions of Oliver Cromwell, to be the COMMANDER OF KENT, in order to give the prestige and dignity of respectability to the administration of their rule, among the gentlemen of Kent County.

PHILIP CONNER (or Conier, as his name was sometimes spelled), THE LAST COMMANDER OF OLD KENT, left one son, Philip, who "ye 28th day of January 1667, made choice of Mr. John Wright to be his guardian," and d. left a son, by his first wife, James Conner, who m. 1st Jan'y 1705 Elinor Flannagan, and had a son, James Conner.

JAMES CONNER, the last named, and his wife, Catharine Conner, left a dau., Isabella Conner. He d. 5th April 1740.

ISABELLA CONNER, dau. of James and Catharine Conner, was b. in 1735, d. 29th Nov. 1782. She m. twice. Her 1st husband was John Bordley. She m. 2dly, 1st Sept. 1761, William Stevenson, and had child., viz., William, b. in Chestertown, Md., 8th June 1762, d. 15th Nov. 1766,—Mary, b. in Chestertown, 12th Sept. 1763, d. 12th Jan. 1765,—John, b. 13th Aug. 1765, and d. the following November,—James, b. 17th Aug. 1766, at Bath, England,—Francina Augustina, b. 5th Feb'y, at Bristol, England,—Isabella, b. 6th July, 1769, at Bristol England,—Ariana, b. 19th Sept. 1770, in England,—Mary, b. 17th Feb'y 1772, in England,—William, b. 17th June 1774,—John Conner, b. 11th Nov. 1775,—and Charles Willliam Washington Stevenson, b. 1st April 1778, and d. 17th Nov. 1779. Mrs. Isabella Stevenson d. 29th Nov. 1782, and her husband, William Stevenson, d. 23d Oct. 1786, aged 47 years. They were both buried at Chestertown.

William Stevenson, the husband of Isabella Conner Bordley Stevenson was the son of William Stevenson, of Lancashire, England, who m. in 1738, Francina Augustina Frisby, who was b. 16th Aug. 1719, the 3d dau. of James Frisby and his wife Ariana Vanderleyden, who m. 9th Feb'y 1713, James Frisby, b. 18th June 1676, the son of James and Sarah Frisby.

Ariana Vanderleyden, b. in 1690, the dau. of Matthias Vanderleyden and his wife, Anna Margaretta Herman, who was the dau. of Col. Augustine Herman and his 2d wife, Miss Ward.

Sec. 59, B. Col. Augustine Herman was a native of Prague, in Bohemia, who, after being educated in Holland, came to America at an early age, remained a few years in New York, where he m. his 1st wife, and finally settled a colony at Bohemia Manor, in Maryland. He m. a Miss Ward, of Cecil county, and became a distinguished and useful citizen of Maryland. He was twice m. and had child., viz., Ephraim,—George,—Casparus,—Anna Margaretta,—Judith, and Francina.

Matthias and Anna Margaretta Herman Vanderleyden had child., viz., a dau., *name unknown*,—Anna Francina,—Augustina, b. in 1685, and Ariana Vanderleyden, b. in 1690.

Anna Francina Vanderleyden, 2d dau. of Matthias and Anna Margaretta Herman Vanderleyden, m. Edward Shippen and had one dau. Margaret, who m. Mr. Jekyl and had child., viz., Frances, who m. Mr. Hicks, and Margaret, who m. Mr. Chalmers, and went to Scotland, and had a son, George Chalmers, who was the father of the Historian.

Augustina Vanderleyden, 3d dau. of Matthias and

Anna Margaretta Herman Vanderleyden, m. James Harris, had one son, Matthias Harris, and d. in 1775, aged 90 years.

James and Sarah Frisby, of Cecil county, had child., viz., James, b. 18th June 1676,—Mary, b. 4th Feb'y 1678,—Sarah, b. 28th March 1680,—Thomas, b. 8th Feb'y 1681,—William, b. 3d July 1684,—Benjamin, b. 28th Feb'y 1688,—Mary, b. 2d July 1690,—Jacob, b. 19th Oct. 1693,—Frances, b. 15th May 1696, and William Frisby, b. 22d Aug. 1699.

The first mentioned James Frisby was a brother of William Frisby, who was a vestryman of St. Paul's in 1693.

JAMES FRISBY, son of James and Sarah Frisby, m., 9th Feb'y 1713, Ariana Vanderleyden, 4th dau. of Matthias and Anna Margaretta Herman Vanderleyden, and had child., viz., Sarah, b. 7th Dec. 1714,—Ariana Margaret, b. 18th Sept. 1717, who m. James Harris, and had one son, James Harris, who dying unm. left his estate to his friends, James Brice, of Annapolis, and James Cheston, of West River,—and Francina Augustina Frisby, b. 16th Aug. 1719, who m. 1st, in 1738, William Stevenson, and 2dly Daniel Cheston.

James Frisby d. 18th Dec. 1719, aged 35 years, and his widow m., in Sept. 1723, Thomas Bordley, of Bordley Hall, Yorkshire, England, and had child., viz., Thomas,—Matthias and John Beale Bordley.

JOHN BEALE BORDLEY, son of Thomas and Ariana Vanderleyden Frisby Bordley, was m. twice. His 1st wife was Margaret Chew, dau. of Samuel and Henrietta Maria Lloyd Chew (see LLOYD), and had child., viz., Thomas,—Matthias, who m. Susan Heath, and had 13 child.,—Henrietta Maria, who m. Major David Ross, of Kent, and had 9 child.,—and John Bordley, who d. 27th March 1761, and had 3 child. His 2d wife was Mrs. Mifflin (the mother of Gov. Thomas Mifflin, of Pennsylvania), and had a dau., Elizabeth Bordley, who m. James Gibson, of Philadelphia.

John Beale Bordley d., and his widow m. a 3d time, in 1728, Hon. Edmund Jennings, and had child., viz., Peter,—Ariana, b. in 1729,—Edmund, b. in 1731, who resided in London, and d., in 1819, unm., and Charles Jennings.

ARIANA JENNINGS, dau. of the Hon. Edmund and Ariana Vanderleyden Frisby Bordley Jennings, m. John Randolph, Attorney-General of Virginia, under the Royal Government. They resided at Williamsburgh, Va., until the Revolution, and then accompanied the Royal Governor, the Earl of Dunmore, to England. They had child., viz., Edmund,—Susan Beverly, and Ariana Jennings Randolph.

HON. EDMUND RANDOLPH, son of John and Ariana Jennings Randolph, was, at the time of the departure of his parents, about 19 years of age, and, being sincerely devoted to the cause of independence, remained in America.

He m. Eliza Nicholas, dau. of Robert Carter Nicholas, formerly Treasurer of Virginia, and had child., viz., Lucy Randolph, who m. Peter V. Daniel, of Richmond, Va.,—Peyton Randolph, who m. Maria Ward, of Amelia Co., Va.,—Edmonia Randolph, who m. Thomas Lewis Preston, 5th son of Col. William Preston, of Smithfield, Va., and had child., viz., John Thomas Lewis Preston (a Professor in the Virginia Military Institute, who m. Miss Caruthers), and Elizabeth Preston, who m. William A. Cocke, of Cumberland Co., Va.,—and Susan Beverly Randolph, who m. Mr. Tayloe, and had two child., viz., John, and Charlotte Tayloe who m. Moncure Robinson, of Richmond, Va.

SUSAN BEVERLY RANDOLPH, dau. of John and Ariana Vanderleyden F. B. Jennings Randolph, m. Major John Gaines, of Virginia, a British officer, and d. in England, leaving three children.

ARIANA JENNINGS RANDOLPH, dau. of John and Ariana Vanderleyden F. B. Jennings Randolph, m. Capt. James Wormsley, a British officer, and d. in England, leaving four child.

SEC. 59, C. SARAH FRISBY, eldest dau. of James and Ariana Vanderleyden Frisby, m., 9th Sept. 1730, John Brice, son of John Brice, of Haversham, England, and had child., viz., Ariana, b. 19th June 1732,—Sarah, b. 3d June 1735,—John, b. 22d Sept. 1738,—Denton, b. 1740,—Ann, b. 1744,—James, b. 1746,—Benedict, b. 1749,—Charles, b. 1750,—Edmund, b. 1751,—a 2d Denton, b. 1753,—Margaretta Augustina, b. 1755, and Elizabeth Brice, b. in 1757.

ARIANA BRICE, dau. of John and Sarah Frisby Brice, m., 4th Sept. 1750, Dr. David Ross, and had child., viz., Sarah, who m. Dr. John Steuart, of Bladensburg,—Marian, who m. Mr. Corbutt, of Scotland,—David, who m. Miss Bordley,—Horatio, who d. unm.,—Ariana, who was the 2d wife of Dr. John Steuart,—Archibald,—Elizabeth, who m. Mr. Smith, of New Hampshire,—Ann, and Augustina Margaretta Ross.

SARAH BRICE, dau. of John and Sarah Frisby Brice, m., Nov. 1761, Richard Henderson, of Bladensburg, and had child., viz., Richard,—a daughter, who m. Gen. James Maccubbin Lingan, who was killed by a mob in Baltimore, 28th July, 1812,—Ariana, and Archibald Brice Henderson.

John Brice, son of John and Sarah Frisby Brice, m. Mary Maccubbin, dau. of Nicholas and Mary Clare Carroll Maccubbin, and had child., viz., John, b. 24th Jan'y 1770,—Nicholas, b. 23d April 1771,—Henry, b. 25th Oct. 1777,—Edmund, b. 22d Nov. 1780,—and Margaret Clare Brice, b. 9th July 1783.

John Brice, son of John and Mary Maccubbin Brice, m. Sarah Lane, of Baltimore, and had child., viz., John, who m. and removed to Kentucky,—Mary, who m. Christian Keener, of Baltimore,—Providence, who m. Mr. Claggett, of Washington,—Nicholas, who m. Miss Russell, and Eliza Brice, who m. J. P. Kraft, Prussian Consul.

Hon. Nicholas Brice, son of John and Mary Maccubbin Brice, m. Anna Maria Tilghman, eldest dau. of Richard and Margaret Tilghman, of Chestertown, and had child., viz., Margaret Elizabeth,—Richard Tilghman,—John Henry, who m. Sophia Howard, of Baltimore Co.,—George Hoffman,—Anna Maria, and Charles Carroll Brice, who m. Susan Selby.

Hon. Nicholas Brice was Chief Judge of the Baltimore City Court for many years.

Henry Brice, son of John and Mary Maccubbin Brice, m. Harriet Tilghman, of Chestertown, dau. of Richard and his 2d wife, Mary Tilghman, and had child, viz., James,—Ann,—Juliana Paca,—Edmund Henry,—Richard Tilghman,—William Nicholas,—John Charles,—George Alfred,—Thomas, and Harriet Maria Brice.

Edmund Brice, son of John and Mary Maccubbin Brice, m. Charlotte Moss.

Margaret Clare Brice, dau. of John and Mary Maccubbin Brice, m., in 1809, Clement Smith, of Georgetown, and had child., viz., Joseph Brice,—Mary Clare, who m. Wm. B. Thompson,—Richard Henry,—Matilda Sophia,—Susan Eliza,—Clement,—Walter,—Margaret C,—and Sarah Frisby Smith, who m. Richard Tilghman.

James Brice, son of John and Sarah Frisby Brice, m. Juliana Jennings, dau. of Thomas Jennings, of Annapolis.

Benedict Brice, son of John and Sarah Frisby Brice, m., in January 1775, Mary Goldsborough, dau. of John and his 1st wife, Ann Turbutt Goldsborough, and had a dau., Sarah Goldsborough Brice, b. 10th Aug. 1776.

Sarah Goldsborough Brice, dau. of Benedict and Mary Goldsborough Brice, m. Andrew Price, of Baltimore, and had child., viz., Greenbury Goldsborough,—Ariana Frisby, b. 9th March 1799, who m., 4th July 1822, Capt. John G. Johnson,—

Elizabeth Greenbury, who d. 25th Dec. 1816,—Nicholas, who d. 4th Aug. 1810,—Sarah Caroline, who d. in September 1812,—and Benedict Price.

EDMUND BRICE, son of John and Sarah Frisby Brice, m. Harriet Woodland, and had a son, James Brice, who d. unm. Mrs. Harriet Woodland Brice m. 2dly Dr. William Murray, of West River, and had child., viz , William, Mary Anne, and Alexander Murray.

MARGARETTA AUGUSTINA BRICE, dau. of John and Sarah Frisby Brice, m. Major Andrew Leitch, and had child., viz., James, and Sarah Leitch, who m. John Addison, of Prince George's Co.

Maj. Andrew Leitch was killed in a skirmish, at King's Bridge, New York, in 1776, and his widow m. again and had a dau., Mary, who m. Dr. John Shoaff, of Annapolis, and had child., viz., Arthur, who m. Miss Forsyth, and left 5 child.,—Jane, who m. the Right Rev. John Johns, of Va.—Mary, who m. Rev. Andrew Stevenson,—Ann,—and Charles Shoaff.

ELIZABETH BRICE, dau. of John and Sarah Frisby Brice, m., in 1773, Lloyd Dulany, a Royalist. They went to England, where he was killed in a duel by the Rev. Bennett Allen. The duel was fought on the 18th of June 1782, and Mr. Dulany died on the 26th day of the same month.

After the death of Mr. Dulany, she m. Maj. Walter Dulany, of the British Army, and subsequently returned to Annapolis, and left three child., viz., Mary, who m. Henry Rogers, of Baltimore,—Grafton, and Sarah Dulany.

FRANCINA AUGUSTINA FRISBY, dau. of James and Ariana Vanderleyden Frisby, m. twice. Her 1st husband, m. in 1738, was William Stevenson, of Lancashire, England, and had one son, William Stevenson. Her 2d husband, m. in 1746, was Daniel Cheston, and had three child., viz., James, b. in 1747,—Francina Augustina, b. in 1752, who accompanied her half-brother, William Stevenson, to England, and m. William Bordley,—and Daniel Cheston.

JAMES CHESTON, son of Daniel and Francina Augustina Frisby Stevenson Cheston, m., in 1775, Ann Galloway, of Tulip Hill, West River, Md., and had child., viz., Ann, b. in 1776,—Francina Augustina, b. in 1777, and James Cheston, b. in 1779.

SEC. 59, D. WILLIAM STEVENSON, only son of William and Francina Augustina Stevenson, m., 1st Sept. 1761, at Chestertown, Isabella Conner Bordley, widow of John Bordley, and dau. of James and Catharine Conner, and had child., which were named in SECTION 59, A.

James Stevenson, son of William and Isabella Conner Bordley Stevenson, m. Miss Miller, and d. 1805, leaving two child., viz., Charles,—and Isabella Stevenson, who m. Mr. Burgess, and left child.

Isabella Stevenson, dau. of William and Isabella Conner Stevenson, m. John Constable, of Kent, and had child., viz., James, who d. unm.,—John Stevenson, d. young,—Harriet, d. unm.,—Maria, who m. Rev. James Hanson, and d. *sine prole*,—Selina, who m. —— Bangs, and d. *sine prole*,—a 2d John Stevenson,—Henry, d. young,—Albert, b. 3d June 1805, d. 22d Aug. 1855,—William Stevenson, d. 31st Dec. 1851,—Elizabeth, d. 20th Sept. 1875, in the 66th year of her age,—and Mary Constable, b. 1812, who m. Dr. Joseph Browne, of Chestertown, and d. *sine prole*.

John Stevenson Constable, son of John and Isabella Stevenson Constable, m. twice. He m. 1st, 7th Sept. 1820, Harriet Rebecca Ringgold, dau. of Dr. William and Martha Hanson Ringgold (see Ringgold), and had child., viz., William Ringgold,—Martha Isabella,—Mary,—Stevenson, and Ellen Constable.

His 2d wife, m. 3d Oct. 1865, was Harriet Wilmer, of Baltimore, dau. of John Williamson and Elizabeth Gittings Croxall Wilmer.

He died in 1866, aged 66 years.

William Ringgold Constable, son of John Stevenson and Harriet Rebecca Ringgold Constable, m., 1st July 1852, Frances Harriet Hodges, dau. of James and Mary Hanson Ringgold Hodges (see Hodges), and had child., viz., Harrie Clarence,—William Stevenson,—Charles Hodges,—Mary Rebecca,—Roberta Hodges, and Martha Hanson Constable.

Martha Isabella Constable, dau. of John Stevenson and Harriet Rebecca Ringgold Constable, m., 4th Nov. 1858, Dr. Samuel Groome Fisher, son of Dr. Jacob and Mary Ann Ringgold Fisher, and had child., viz., Henry Groome, b. 19th Aug. 1859, d. 27th July 1860,—Jacob Stevenson, b. 25th Sept. 1860, d. 30th June 1861,—Ellen Constable,—Samuel Edgar, b. 8th Feb'y 1863, d. 7th April 1865, and Samuel Groome Fisher.

Mary Constable, dau. of John Stevenson and Harriet Rebecca Ringgold Constable, m., 29th Jan'y 1852, Richard W. Jones, and had child., viz., George Stevenson, b. 13th April 1853, d. 22d Oct. 1865,—Henry Miller, b. 24th July 1854, d. 30th Jan'y 1855,—Albert Constable, b. 18th Dec. 1855,—Mary Rebecca,—Elma Virginia, b. 17th Nov. 1858,

d. 12th Nov. 1872,—Richard Sterling,—and Laura Jones, b. 21st Jan'y 1865, and d. 14th Nov. 1865.

STEVENSON CONSTABLE, son of John Stevenson and Harriet Rebecca Ringgold Constable, m., in Nov. 1860, Alice Anna Riley, and had child., viz., Mary Blanche,—Harriet Lillian,—John Stevenson,—Horatio Beck, and Albert Constable.

ELLEN CONSTABLE, dau. of John Stevenson and Harriet Rebecca Ringgold Constable, m., 15th Jan'y 1863, Dr. Samuel Beck, of Kent, and had child., viz., Harriet Ringgold,—Horatio Wright,—Mary Isabel,—William Walker,—Walter Constable, b. 12th Oct. 1872, d. 13th Jan'y 1876,—Samuel,—and Ellen Constable Beck.

ALBERT CONSTABLE, son of John and Isabella Stevenson Constable, m. Hannah Archer, dau. of Dr. John and Ann Stump Archer, of Rock Run, Harford Co., Md., and had child., viz., John Ann,—Isabel Stevenson,—Alice Maria, and Albert Constable.

ISABEL STEVENSON CONSTABLE, dau. of Albert and Hannah Archer Constable, m., 7th Nov. 1861, Thomas Erskine Gittings, of Baltimore Co., Md., and had child., viz., Albert Constable, b. 25th Sept. 1862, d.,—Thomas Erskine,—Alice Constable, and John Ann Gittings.

ALICE MARIA CONSTABLE, dau. of Albert and Hannah Archer Constable, m. 4th Sept. 1862, John Charles Gittings, and had one child, Rebecca Nicols Gittings, b. 1st Sept. 1863, and d. 28th Sept. 1864.

John Charles Gittings and his wife are deceased and are buried in Greenmount Cemetery.

HON. ALBERT CONSTABLE (at present, 1876, member of the Maryland Legislature for Cecil county) son of Albert and Hannah Archer Constable, m. 12th June 1866, Elizabeth Black Groome, dau. of Gen. John Charles and Elizabeth R. Black Groome, of Elkton, and had child., viz., Alice,—Arline,—John, and Albert Constable.

WILLIAM STEVENSON CONSTABLE, son of John and Isabella Stevenson Constable, m. twice. His 1st wife was Susanna Mummey, of Baltimore, who d. *sine prole*. In May 1840, he m. Catharine Mummey, a sister of his d. wife, and had child., viz., Isabel Stevenson (who m. 12th Nov. 1863, Freeman Skinner, of Va., and had two child., viz., William Constable and Freeman Skinner, *twins*),—Susannah Mummey,—Catharine Mummey (who m. 21st May 1871, Dr. Josiah R. Bromwell),—Maria Matilda (who m. 22d April 1873, Thomas Courtney

Jenkins, and d. 14th Feb'y 1874. Her husband d. in Sept. 1875),—Grimilda Spencer, and William Anna Constable.

SEC. 59, E. ELIZABETH CONSTABLE, dau. of John and Isabella Stevenson Constable, m. John W. Walker, of Chestertown, and had child., viz., Mary Elizabeth,—John Constable, d.,—William Stevenson,—Anna Isabel, and Thomas Walker, d. John W. Walker d. 10th Aug. 1844, and his wife 20th Sept. 1875.

MARY ELIZABETH WALKER, dau. of John W. and Elizabeth Constable Walker, m. 7th June 1849, Henry W. Archer, of Harford Co., and had child., viz., Elizabeth,—John, b. 22d Jan'y 1853, d. 1855,—Henry Wilson,—William Stevenson,—Mary Angela,—Robert,—Ann,—James,—Isabel Stevenson,—Rosalie, b. 12th July 1864, d. Aug. 1864, and Christian Grahame Archer.

WILLIAM STEVENSON WALKER, son of John W. and Elizabeth Constable Walker, m. 27th Dec. 1855, Mary Rebecca Ricaud, dau. of Judge James B. and Anna E. F. Gordon Ricaud, of Kent, and had child., viz., Anna Elizabeth,—John William, b. 8th Jan'y 1861, d. 9th July 1861,—Cornelia Ricaud, and William Stevenson Walker.

The Ricaud family, of which Judge James B. Ricaud was a member, has been identified with St. Paul's Parish since the year 1699. The present (1876) Register of the Parish, Charles Gordon Ricaud, is the son of the late Dr. Laurence Ricaud and Mrs. Caroline Rebecca Frisby Gordon Ricaud.

John W. Walker was the son of John Walker, of Scotland, and his wife Christiana Grahame, also a native of Scotland.

ANNA ISABEL WALKER, dau. of John W. and Elizabeth Constable Walker, m. 28th Sept. 1858, Dr. William H. Gale, of Somerset County.

SEC. 59, F. MARY STEVENSON, dau. of William and Isabella Conner Bordley Stevenson, m. Henry Hall, of Anne Arundel County, and had one son, Henry Hall.

HENRY HALL, of Tudor, Anne Arundel Co., son of Henry and Mary Stevenson Hall, m. Mary Estep, and had child, viz., Edward, b. in 1816, who m. Louisa Fenwick, dau. of Dr. Martin Fenwick,—Eleanor, who m. twice: 1st, James McCaleb, 2dly, Dr. Elliot Burwell,—Ann, who m. Dr. William Frederick Steuart (see STEUART),—Estep, who m. Sarah Webster,—Mary,—Maria, who m. William Meade Addison,—Hamilton, who m. Mary Thomas,—Francina Cheston, who m. 14th of Nov. 1854, Robert Lemmon, son of Richard and Sarah Stevenson Lemmon,—Augustus, who m. Mary Cheston, dau. of Dr.

James Cheston,—and Fenwick Hall, who m. Nannie Cheston, sister of Mary Cheston, and d. 4th April 1876.

WILLIAM STEVENSON, son of William and Isabella Conner Bordley Stevenson, m. in 1800, Ann Foster, and had child., viz., Sarah,—Mary, and William Stevenson.

WILLIAM STEVENSON, son of William and Ann Foster Stevenson, m. Elizabeth Taney, dau. of the Hon. Roger B. Taney, late Chief Justice of the United States.

SARAH STEVENSON, dau. of William and Ann Foster Stevenson, m. Richard Lemmon, and had child., viz., Sarah,—Robert, who m., 14th Nov. 1854, Francina Cheston Hall, dau. of Henry and Mary Estep Hall, and had a son, Richard Lemmon,—Ann Stevenson,—George,—William Stevenson,—John Southgate, and Isabel Lemmon.

SARAH LEMMON, dau. of Richard and Sarah Stevenson Lemmon, m. Henry Randall, of Philadelphia, and had child., viz., Richard,—Annie,—Grace,—Betty, and Matthew Randall.

MARY STEVENSON, dau. of William and Ann Foster Stevenson, m. Dr. William Brogden, of Roe Down, Anne Arundel Co., Md.

SEC. 59, G. DR. WILLIAM BROGDEN, of Roe Down, was descended from William Brogden, who came from Leeds, England, to Calvert county in 1712, and had one son, William Brogden, who was educated in England and ordained a clergyman of the Church of England in 1735.

REV. WILLIAM BROGDEN was commissioned to preach on the 8th Aug. 1785, by "Edmund, by Divine permission Bishop of London," and returned to America, and took charge of the Parish of All Hallows, Anne Arundel Co. In 1751 he was inducted by Lt. Governor Samuel Ogle, Rector of Queen Anne's Parish, Prince George's Co., and officiated in both until 1763, when he resigned the latter and continued in the former to the day of his death, in Nov. 1774. Soon after his return from England he purchased from the original patentee the estate called Roe Down, where he resided. It remains to this day in the family. He m. 24th Dec. 1740, Elizabeth Chapman, and had child., viz., William, b. in 1741,—John L. S.,—Rebecca,—Samuel,—Richard,—Elizabeth, and Robert Brogden.

MAJOR WILLIAM BROGDEN, son of Rev. William and Elizabeth Chapman Brogden, served with credit in the Revolutionary army. His commission is dated 1st March 1778. He. m. 18th Dec. 1795, Margaret McCulloch, d. 13th Sept. 1824, and had child., viz., William, b. in 1797, d. 3d July

1863,—David McCulloch, b. in 1802, d. 4th May 1875, and Mary Brogden, d. unm.

DR. WILLIAM BROGDEN, son of Major William and Margaret McCulloch Brogden, m. 28th April 1828, Mary Stevenson, dau. of William and Ann Foster Stevenson, and had child., viz., Anna,—William,—James McCulloch,—Richard, —Henry H.,—Arthur,—Mary, and Meta Brogden.

JAMES McCULLOCH BROGDEN, son of Dr. William and Mary Stevenson Brogden, m. Eleanor Addison Gittings, and had child., viz., Mary Stevenson,—James Charles,—William, —Rebecca Nicols,—Margaret Smith Gittings,—Arthur,— John, and Harry Brogden.

ARTHUR BROGDEN, son of Dr. William and Mary Stevenson Brogden, m. Mary Mercer, dau. of Col. John Mercer, of Cedar Rock, West River, d. 5th Jan'y 1875, and had child., viz., Sophia, and Mary Brogden.

MARY BROGDEN, dau. of Dr. William and Mary Stevenson Brogden, m. Daniel Murray, son of Dr. James H. Murray, of West River, and had child., viz., Meta and Mary Murray.

META BROGDEN, dau. of Dr. William and Mary Stevenson Brogden, m. Thomas W. Brundige, of Baltimore Co., and had a dau. Mary Brundige.

DAVID McCULLOCH BROGDEN, son of Maj. William and Margaret McCulloch Brogden, m. Margaret Sellman, dau. of Gen. Jonathan Sellman, and had child., viz., Priscilla,—Sellman,—Mary,—Elizabeth,—Hellen, who m. John W. Iglehart, Jr., of Anne Arundel Co., and James Dick Brogden.

PRISCILLA BROGDEN, dau. of Daniel McCulloch and Margaret Sellman Brogden, m. Thomas J. Wilson, and had child., viz., Margaret,—Clarence,—Henry, and Priscilla Wilson.

SEC. 59, H. MAJOR JOSEPH WICKES was a gentleman of birth, breeding, refinement, and culture. He made his first appearance to us "on ye 12th January 1651," *o. s.*, in an elevated position, upon the Bench of Kent County Court. In this honorable position he remained by successive appointments, and on the 1st of July 1656, he appeared as the presiding Judge of the Court. A few years after, when the affairs of the Province had been brought to the verge of ruin by the Puritans, he was chosen a Burgess to represent Kent County, in the Assembly which was begun and held at St. Leonard's, on the 27th April 1658. It would be interesting to know how he bore himself in that famous Assembly. Of one thing we are sure, that his conduct was consistent with his usual deportment, for again, on the 25th day of July 1678, he appears as the presiding Justice of Kent County Court.

I find no mention of his holding an office of emolument, but he worthily filled positions of great trust and responsibility. Independent of the marked ability which distinguished him, his chief and noticeable characteristics were constitutional purity and dignity of character, amiability of disposition and discerning generosity.

One of the Justices of Kent county, by the weight of his personal worth, he added lustre to the office,—to that office, concerning which, my lord Coke says that, "the whole world hath not the like, if it be duly executed." He was one of the WORTHIES of Kent county.

The year of the arrival of Major Joseph Wickes, on Kent Island, is ascertained by the following entry, dated July 13th 1658, in "Liber A. For Transcribing Old Records," Fol. 40:

"*Joseph Wickes* doth enter a Caveat of Land for 15 Servants or Rights, due to him vizt: Joseph Wickes, John Meconnichin, William Davies in the year 1650,—John Morgan, Edward Tarant, in the year 1654,—Anne Gold & a Negro, in the year 55,—Mrs. Wickes and her two Children, in the year 56,—John Longthorne, Richard Huson and Elizabeth Ellis, in the year 57, & Francis & Thoms Brookes, in the year 56. These Rights are Entered to be taken up, on the Eastern Neck against the Upper part of Kent."

The above is a very interesting entry. It discloses the fact, that Mistress Marie Hartwell was a widow with two children, when she married Maj. Wickes, and that Major Joseph Wickes was the first slave owner in Kent county, Maryland. We can have no doubt that he was an exceptionally kind master to his slaves; for his servant Edward Tarant, in his Will, left to Major Joseph Wickes one hogshead of tobacco, "for his tender care of me in my sickness."

In connection with a deposition, made by Major Joseph Wickes, on the 11th of Oct. 1656, it is stated that he was then "aged 36 years or thereabouts."

It appears that *Major Joseph Wickes*, with his family and servants, came to Kent county, Maryland, in the year 1650, and was then in the 30th year of his age. On the 19th day of July 1656, he married Mrs. Marie Hartwell, and, on the 18th day of August 1656, his son Joseph, by a previous marriage, died.

The earliest descendant of Major Joseph Wickes, of whom I have found any record or detailed information, was a grandson:

Samuel Wickes, son of Joseph Wickes, signer of the Address of Protestants of Kent county, November 1689, who was the son of Major Joseph Wickes.

SAMUEL WICKES married Frances Wilmer, 13th Jan'y 1705. He d. in 1732, and in his Will mentions "his loving wife Frances," and the following child., viz., Samuel,—Benjamin,—Simon (died 1737),—Joseph,—Lambert,—Martha,—Rebecca, and Ann Wickes. Frances Wilmer Wickes died in 1756. She was the dau. of Simon and Rebecca Wilmer.

SAMUEL WICKES, son of Samuel and Frances Wilmer Wickes, died in 1767. In his Will, dated 25th Feb'y 1761, he mentions his "dear loving wife Mary," and the following child., viz., Samuel,—Lambert,—Richard,—Joseph (who died 1784),—Martha,—Mary and Sarah Wickes, and Francis Dunn.

SAMUEL WICKES, son of Samuel and Mary Wicks, m. Ann Kennard, and left the following child., viz., William,—Maria,—Sally, and Lambert Wickes.

COL. WILLIAM WICKES, son of Samuel Wickes and Ann Kennard, greatly distinguished himself as a Major in the Battle of Caulk's Field, and was afterwards promoted to be Colonel.

SEC. 59, I. BATTLE OF CAULK'S FIELD.—Copy of a letter from Col. Philip Reed, of the First Regiment of Maryland Militia, to Brigadier General Benjamin Chambers:

CAMP AT BELLE AIR,
3d Sept., 1814.

SIR—I avail myself of the first moment I have been able to seize from incessant labor, to inform you that about half-past 11 o'clock on the night of the 30th ult. I received information that the barges of the enemy, then lying off Waltham's farm, were moving in shore. I concluded their object was to land and burn the houses, &c., at Waltham's, and made the necessary arrangements to prevent them, and to be prepared for an opportunity, which I had sought for several days, to strike the enemy. During our march to the point threatened, it was discovered that the blow was aimed at our camp. Orders were immediately given to the Quarter Master to remove the camp and baggage, and to the troops to countermarch, pass the road by the right of our camp, and form on the rising ground about three hundred paces to the rear—the right towards Caulk's house, and the left retiring on the road, the artillery in the centre, supported by the infantry on the right and left. I directed Captain Wickes and his second lieutenant, Beck, with a part of the rifle company to be formed, so as to cover the road by which the enemy marched, and with this section I determined to post myself, leaving the line to be formed under the direction of Major Wickes and Capt. Chambers.

The head of the enemy's column soon presented itself, and received the fire of our advance party at seventy paces distance, and, being pressed by numbers vastly superior, I repaired to my post in the line, having ordered the riflemen to return and form on the right of the line. The fire now became general along the whole line, and was sustained by our troops with the most determined valor. The enemy pressed our front; foiled in this, he threw himself upon our left flank, which was occupied by Capt. Chambers's company. Here, too, his efforts were equally unavailing. His fire had nearly ceased, when I was informed that in some parts of our line the cartridges were entirely expended, nor did any of the boxes contain more than a very few rounds, although each man brought about twenty into the field. The artillery cartridges were entirely expended. Under these circumstances, I ordered the line to fall back to a convenient spot, where a part of the line was fortified, when the few remaining cartridges were distributed amongst a part of the line, which was again brought into the field, where it remained for a considerable time, the night preventing a pursuit. The artillery and infantry, for whom there were no cartridges, were ordered to this place. The enemy having made every effort in his power, although apprized of our falling back, manifested no disposition to follow us up, but retreated about the time our ammunition was exhausted.

When it is recollected that very few of our officers or men had ever heard the whistling of a ball; that the force of the enemy, as the most accurate information enables us to estimate, was double ours; that it was commanded by SIR PETER PARKER, of the MENELAUS, one of the most distinguished officers of the British navy, and composed (as their officers admitted in a subsequent conversation) of as fine men as could be selected from the British service, I feel justified in the assertion that the gallantry of the officers and men engaged on this occasion could not be excelled by any troops. The officers and men performed their duty. It is, however, but an act of justice to notice those officers who seemed to display more than a common degree of gallantry. Major Wickes and Capt. Chambers were conspicuous; Captain Wickes and his Lieutenant Beck, of the rifle corps, Lieutenant Eunick and Ensign Shriven, of Captain Chambers's company, exerted themselves, as did Captain Hynson and his Lieutenant Grant, Captain Ussleton, of the brigade artillery, and his Lieutenants Reed and Brown. Lieutenant Tilghman, who commanded the guns of the volunteer artillery, in the absence of Captain Hands, who is in ill health and from home, was conspicuous for his gallantry; his Ensign Thomas also manifested much firmness.

I am indebted to Captain Wilson, of the cavalry, who was with me, for his exertions, and also to Adjutant Hynson, who displayed much zeal and firmness throughout; to Dr. Blake, Dr. Gordon, and to Isaac Spencer, Esq., who were accidentally in camp, I am indebted for their assistance in reconnoitering the enemy on his advance.

You will be surprised, sir, when I inform you that in an engagement of so long continuance, in an open field, when the moon shone brilliantly on the rising ground occupied by our troops, while the shade of the neighboring woods, under the protection of which the enemy fought, gave us but an indistinct view of anything but the flash of his guns; that under the disparity of numbers against us, and the advantage of regular discipline on the side of the enemy, we had not one man killed, and only one sergeant, one corporal and one private wounded, and those slightly. The enemy left one midshipman and eight men dead on the field, and nine wounded, six of whom died in the course of a few hours. Sir Peter Parker was amongst the slain; he was mortally wounded by a buck-shot, and died before he reached the barges, to which he was conveyed by his men. The enemy's force consisted of marines and musqueteers, was in part armed with boarding pikes, swords and pistols, no doubt intended for our tents, as orders had been given by Sir Peter not to fire. Many of these arms, with rockets, muskets, &c., have fallen into our hands, found by the picket guard under Ensign Shriven (Skirven?), which was posted on the battle-ground for the remainder of the night. Nothing but the want of ammunition saved the enemy from destruction.

Attached are the names of the wounded; and as an act of justice to those concerned, I inclose you a list of every officer and soldier engaged in this affair. Certain information from the enemy assures us that his total loss in killed and wounded was forty-two or forty-three, including two wounded lieutenants.

I am, sir, your most obedient humble servant,

PHIL. REED,
Lieut. Col. Commandant.

Benjamin Chambers, Brigadier General, 6th Brigade Maryland Militia.

Names of the Wounded of Capt. Chambers' Company.—John Magnor, sergeant, slightly in the thigh; Philip Crane, corporal, a ball between the tendons and the bone of the thigh, near the knee.

Of Capt. Page's Company.—John Glanville, a private, in the arm.

SECTION 59, J. COL. WILLIAM WICKES m. Milcah Page, and had child., viz., William Henry,—James Page,—Augusta, and Antoinette Wickes. Col. William Wickes m., a 2d time, Anne Spencer, dau. of Richard Spencer and Martha Wickes.

LAMBERT WICKES, son of Samuel and Ann Kennard Wickes, m. Alethea Ireland, and had child., viz., Emeline L. Wickes, who m. David Davis,—and Louisa Maria Wickes, who m. Peregrine Wethered, and left child., viz., Lewin and Ann Elizabeth Wethered.

CAPT. LAMBERT WICKES, son of Samuel and Mary Wickes, was one of the most gallant officers of the Continental navy. On the 10th June 1776 he was ordered to repair with the Continental ship, the "Reprisal," to the West Indies for arms and ammunition, carrying with him Mr. William Bingham, commercial agent for the government, at Martinique. Soon after leaving the Capes of the Delaware, on the 11th July 1776, he captured the English merchant ship "Friendship," of between 400 and 500 tons burden. Two days after, he captured the English schooner "Peter," and before he arrived at his destination he captured, also, the "Neptune" and the "Duchess of Leinster." On the 21st Sept. 1776, he was directed to convey Dr. Benjamin Franklin to France, and to perform other services, which instruction he faithfully complied with. On his way he made prizes of two English brigantines, and was the first American naval officer, and commanded the first American man-of-war that ever appeared in European waters. On the 5th Feb'y 1777, he captured the "Lisbon Packet," Capt. Newman, two days out from Falmouth. He also captured the "Polly & Nancy," the "Hibernia," the "Generous Friends," the "Swallow," and the "Betty." Subsequently Capt. Wickes commanded a squadron, consisting of "Lexington," Capt. Henry Johnson; the "Dolphin," Capt. Samuel Nicholson, and his flag-ship, the "Reprisal," captured many prizes of considerable value, and performed many gallant exploits.

His vessel foundered, 1st Oct. 1777, on the Banks of Newfoundland, and all on board perished, except the cook. Capt. Lambert Wickes d. unm.

SEC. 59, L. MARTHA WICKES, dau. of Samuel and Mary Wickes, m. 23d Dec. 1771, Richard Spencer, who was b. 4th Oct. 1734, the son of James Spencer (of the ancient and noble House of Spencer, now represented by Earl Spencer, of England) and Ann Benson (aunt of Gen. Perry Benson, of the Revolutionary Army), and had child., viz., Anne Spencer, b. in Aug. 1774,—Lambert Wickes Spencer, b. 11th July 1776,—Richard Spencer, b. in July 1779,—Emma Spencer, b. in Sept. 1781,—Samuel Spencer, b. 16th Aug. 1784,—Samuel and Gower Spencer, twins, b. 9th Aug. 1792.

ANNE SPENCER, dau. of Richard Spencer and Martha Wickes, m. Col. William Wickes.

RICHARD SPENCER, of Spencer Hall, Kent, son of Richard Spencer and Martha Wickes, m. Sophia Gresham, descended from the noble family of Sir Thomas Gresham, of London, founder of the Royal Exchange and of Gresham College, who was knighted by Queen Elizabeth, and had child., viz., Martha Sophia, d. young,—Charlotte Anna (who m. James Page Wickes, son of Col. William Wickes and Milcah Page, and had child., viz., Mary Anna, Charlotte Augusta, who m. T. Romie Strong, William Henry, who m. Matilda Ruth, Mary Antoinette, Martha Spencer, James Page, Richard Spencer, Robert, Samuel De Coursey, and Maria Spencer Wickes),—and Maria Louisa Spencer.

MARIA LOUISA SPENCER, dau. of Richard Spencer and Sophia Gresham, of Spencer Hall, m. 28th Nov. 1843, Alexander Harris, son of Capt. Thomas Harris, of Rock Hall, and Henrietta Ringgold, dau. of Maj. William Ringgold, of Eastern Neck (see RINGGOLD), and had child., viz., Alexander, d. young,—Anna Maria, m. 23d Nov. 1869, Daniel Chase Chapman, of Baltimore,—Emma,—Spencer, and Allan Alexander Harris.

LAMBERT WICKES SPENCER, son of Richard Spencer and Martha Wickes, settled in Talbot County, and m. Anna Spencer, dau. of Col. Perry Spencer, of Perry Hall, Talbot, and had child., viz., Dr. Samuel Wickes,—Perry,—Lambert,—George,—Martha, and Anne Spencer.

Richard Spencer, who m. Martha Wickes, was the grandson of James Spencer, who, when about the age of twenty years, came from England, and settled in Talbot county, in 1670, and d., leaving a son, James Spencer.

JAMES SPENCER, of Spencer Hall, Talbot county, son of James Spencer, m. Ann Benson, and had child., viz., Robert,—Richard,—James, and Nicholas Spencer.

Robert Spencer, son of James Spencer and Ann Benson, m. Mrs. Lydia Sherwood Ennalls, and had child., viz., Perry,—Samuel,—John,—Henry, killed in the Revolutionary Army,—Jonathan,—Rebecca,—Mary,—Dorothy, and Richard Spencer.

Col. Perry Spencer, of Perry Hall, Talbot county, son of Robert and Lydia Sherwood Spencer, m. twice. His 1st wife was Mary Hopkins, and had child., viz., Jonathan,—Richard,— Mary,— Dorothy,— Eleanor, and Anne Spencer, who m. Lambert Wickes Spencer, son of Richard and Martha Wickes Spencer. His 2d wife was Eliza Hayes.

Col. Spencer d. in 1822. He was a Presidential Elector in 1801 and 1805, and voted for Thomas Jefferson.

Jonathan Spencer, son of Col. Perry and Mary Hopkins Spencer, m. Miss Robinson, of Talbot, and left child., viz., Mary, who m. W. B. Willis,—Elizabeth, who m. John Willis,—and Ellen Spencer, who m. Mr. Jewell, of Washington, D. C.

Hon. Richard Spencer, Member of Congerss, 1829-1831, son of Col. Perry and Mary Hopkins Spencer, m. Anna S., dau. of William Baker, of Baltimore, and had child., viz., William Baker, d.,—Mary Anne, who m. Rev. John Keener, Bishop of the M. E. Church, South,—and Emma Spencer.

Mary Spencer, dau. of Col. Perry and Mary Hopkins Spencer, m. John Kennard, and had child., viz., John H.,—Perry,—Robert, and Elizabeth Spencer.

Eleanor Spencer, dau. of Col. Perry and Mary Hopkins Spencer, b. 4th Sept. 1793, d. 4th March 1838, m. 21st May 1816, Alexander B. Harrison, and had child., viz., Mary Harrison, b. 4th Oct. 1818, d. 5th Aug. 1820,—Dr. Samuel Alexander Harrison (who m. 2d Sept. 1847, Martha Isabella Denny, and had child., viz., Patty Belle, and Mary Spencer Harrison, who m. Mr. Noble and has a dau., Katy Bell Noble),—Mary Eleanor Harrison (who m. Rev. John Ruth, and had two child., viz., Dr. Melancthon Ruth, U. S. N., and Mary Anna Ruth),—Emily Harrison (who m. William H. Harrison, son of Stephen Harrison and Susanna Spencer, and had a dau., who m. William Willis),—and Jonathan Perry Harrison, who m., 1st, Caroline Denny, and had child., viz., Bradford and Blaney Spencer. His 2d wife was Elizabeth P. D. Bird, of Galveston, Texas.

Richard Spencer, of Beverley, son of Robert Spencer, m. 25th Dec. 1787, Eleanor Hopkins, sister of his brother Perry's wife, and had child., viz., Robert Spencer,— Rev. Joseph Spencer, D. D., of the P. E. Church, who m. Francis Mitchell,—Henry Spencer (who m. Anna Matilda Martin, and had child., viz., Richard Henry, and Anne, wife of Dr. Matthews, of Talbot),—Susanna Spencer (who m. Stephen Harrison, and had child., viz., Will H., Eduard, Theodore, Samuel, Stephen, Susan, Emily and Eleanor Harrison),—Perry Spencer, who m. Mary J. Wiseman,—Jeremiah Spencer,—Edward Spencer (who m. Grisselda Mummy),—Matthew Spencer, who m. Elizabeth Ann Skinner, and left child., viz., Rev. Charles S. Spencer,—Matilda,—Selina, and Eliza Spencer.

SECTION 59, M. MARY WICKES, dau. of Samuel and Mary Wickes, m. Capt. Thomas De Coursey, and had a son, Gerald De Coursey.

GERALD DE COURSEY, son of Capt. Thomas De Coursey and Mary Wickes, m., 9th Jan'y 1816, Sarah Wickes, dau. of Samuel Wickes and Ann Kennard, and had child., who lived to maturity, viz., Mary, who m. W. J. Gibson,—Thomas Wickes, who m. Sarah F. Nichols, and left three child., only one of whom, Samuel Gerald De Coursey, is now living,—and Samuel Wickes De Coursey.

SAMUEL WICKES DE COURSEY, son of Gerald De Coursey and Sarah Wickes, m., 20th Feb'y 1834, Sarah Jane Lafourcade, dau. of P. M. Lafourcade, of Bordeaux, France, and had child., viz., Gerald De Coursey, d.,—Edward De Coursey, d.,—Mary Augusta De Coursey, who m., 5th Jan'y 1863, Hugh Hamilton,—Juliette De Coursey, who m., 17th Jan'y 1861, J. B. Sartori,—Marcelus De Coursey, who m., 12th Nov. 1861, Mary Stovell,—Sarah Jane De Coursey, who m., 26th Dec. 1872, Dillwyn Parrish,—Emma De Coursey, and Samuel Wickes De Coursey, Jr.

SEC. 59, N. BENJAMIN WICKES, son of Samuel and Frances Wilmer Wickes, m. Susanna Ringgold (dau. of William Ringgold, who was the son of James Ringgold and his wife, Mary Vaughan, who was the dau. of Capt. Robert Vaughan, the Commander of Kent from 1647 to 1652), and had child., viz., Joseph,—Samuel,—Benjamin and Martha Wickes.

JOSEPH WICKES, son of Benjamin and Susannah Ringgold Wickes, m. Miss Dunn, of Poplar Neck, d. 1786. His Will is dated 21st Nov. 1783, and its codicil 24th Dec. 1785. In them he mentions the following child., viz., Joseph,—Simon,—Frances (who m. Peregrine Cooper, and had two child., Peregrine, and Willamina, who m. William Maxwell, and left two child., Frances and James Henry Maxwell),—and Ann Wickes, who m. Mr. Brown, and left the following child., viz., Joseph,—William,—James,—John,—Thomas,—Rebecca and Ann Brown.

JOSEPH WICKES, son of Joseph Wickes and Miss Dunn, m.

Mary Piner. He d. 1822, aged 63 years. Mrs. Mary Piner Wickes d. 1823, aged 59 years. They had the following child., viz., Joseph Wickes,—Thomas Wickes,—Simon Alexander Wickes, and Sarah Piner Wickes, who d. 1844.

COL. JOSEPH WICKES, son of Joseph and Mary Piner Wickes, m. Elizabeth Caroline Chambers, dau. of Gen. Benjamin Chambers. He d. 1864, in the 76th year of his age. She d. 1872, aged 72 years. Their child. were as follows, viz., Mary Elizabeth Wickes,—Benjamin Chambers Wickes,—Joseph A. Wickes,—Hester H. Van Bibber Wickes,—Ezekiel Chambers Wickes,—Peregrine Lethbury Wickes, and Sarah Augusta Wickes.

HON. JOSEPH A. WICKES, son of Col. Joseph and Elizabeth Caroline Chambers Wickes, is now (28th June 1875), one of the Judges of the second Judicial Circuit of Maryland, which is composed of the counties of Caroline, Talbot, Queen Anne's, Kent and Cecil.

He m. twice. His 1st wife 13th June 1848, was Anna Maria Tilghman, dau. of William Cook Tilghman (see TILGHMAN), and had child., viz., Chambers Wickes, who m. 7th May 1875, Elizabeth Houston, dau. of Dr. Benjamin F. and Anne Louise Hynson Houston, of Chestertown,—Anna Maria Tilghman Wickes, who m. 10th June 1874, Dr. William Houston, U. S. N., son of the above-named Dr. Benjamin F. Houston,—Hester Van Bibber Wickes,—Steadman Tilghman Wickes, and Carrie Barney Wickes.

He m. 2dly, 29th Nov. 1865, Ann Rebecca Wickes, dau. of Capt. Simon Wickes and Mary Freeman, and had child., viz., Joseph A. Wickes, d., and Josephine Rebecca Wickes.

SIMON WICKES, son of Joseph and Mrs. Dunn Wickes, m. Mary Freeman, d. 1815, and left child., viz., Mary Wickes,—Hannah Wickes (who m. Benjamin Houston, who was the father of Dr. Benjamin F. Houston, now residing in Chestertown, Md.), and Simon Wickes.

CAPTAIN SIMON WICKES, son of Simon and Mary Freeman Wickes, m. Elizabeth Blake. He d. 1848, and left the following child., viz., Mary Henrietta Wickes,—Simon Wickes,—Charles Henry Wickes,—William Nicols Earle Wickes,—Isaac Freeman Wickes,—Ann Rebecca Wickes,—Elizabeth Wickes, and Thomas Stockton Wickes.

WILLIAM NICOLS EARLE WICKES, son of Capt. Simon and Elizabeth Blake Wickes, m. 2d June 1857, Anne Elizabeth Wethered, dau. of Peregrine and Louisa Maria Wickes

Wethered, and had child., viz., Louisa Maria, d.,—William Nicols Earle d., and Lewin Wethered Wickes.

SAMUEL WICKES, son of Benjamin and Susanna Ringgold Wickes, had two daus., viz., Martha, and Mary Wickes.

BENJAMIN WICKES, son of Benjamin and Susanna Ringgold Wickes, had child., viz., Joseph,—Benjamin,—John,—Samuel, and Susannah Wickes. Susannah Wickes m. 23d Aug. 1765, William Houston, and left child., viz., Hon. James Houston, Judge of the United States District Court for Maryland (who m. Augusta Chambers, dau. of Gen. Benjamin Chambers), and Benjamin Houston, who m. Hannah Wickes, dau. of Simon Wickes.

SEC. 59, O. THOMAS HYNSON was the Clerk in 1652. He came to Kent in 1650, and was then about twenty-nine years of age. He had four sons, viz., John,—Charles,—Thomas, and Henry Hynson, who left many descendants.

JOHN HYNSON, d., was buried at St. Paul's, 10th of May 1705. His wife's name was Ann Hynson. They had the following child., viz., John,—Nathaniel,—Sarah,—Elizabeth (who m. Mr. Rodgers),—Jane (who m. Philip Holeager, and had one son, Nathaniel Holeager), and Mary Hynson, who m. Mr. Glanville.

Nathaniel Hynson, son of John and Ann Hynson, d. 1721, *o. s.* By his 1st wife Hannah Hynson, he had three child., viz., Nathaniel, b. 12th Jan'y 1709, d. 1712,—Mary and Hannah. His 1st wife was buried at St. Paul's, 26th Nov. 1713. He m. again, 6th of Aug. 1714, Mary Kelley. In his Will, dated 4th May 1721, he mentions his wife Mary, and the following child., viz., Nathaniel,—Hannah,—Martha, and Rebecca Hynson.

NATHANIEL HYNSON, son of Nathaniel and Mary Kelley, m., 29th Oct. 1735, Mary Smith, and had a son, Nathaniel Hynson, b. 24th Oct. 1736.

NATHANIEL HYNSON, son (?) of Nathaniel and Mary Smith, m. Mary Richardson, of Wye, Talbot county, and left one son, Nathaniel Hynson, who was b. 15th Jan'y 1781.

NATHANIEL HYNSON, son of Nathaniel and Mary Richardson Hynson, m. Sophia Ringgold, eldest dau. of Jas. and Ann Roberts Ringgold, of Annapolis, Md., and had the following child., viz., James Ringgold,—Sophia Ann,—Henry Ringgold,—Nathaniel Thornton,—James Ringgold,—Joseph Nicholson,—William Scott,—Charles Edward, and John Ringgold Hynson.

NATHANIEL THORNTON HYNSON, son of Nathaniel and

Sophia Ringgold Hynson, m. twice. His 1st wife (m. 6th Dec. 1832) was Anna Maria Smyth Willson, eldest dau. of Dr. Thomas Willson, of Trumpington, Eastern Neck, Kent Co., Md., by whom he had two child., viz., Helen Anna Maria, and Henry Thornton Hynson. In Dec. 1836 he m. Anna Maria Medford, dau. of Macall and Anna Maria Parr Medford, of Hanover Square, London, Eng., by whom he had the following child., viz., Medford,—Anna Sophia,—Adele Freeman,—Nathaniel Thornton,—Frances Louisa,—Theodore Freeman,—Henry Parr,—Ida, and Percy Ringgold Hynson. Nathaniel Thornton Hynson d. 12th May 1876, aged 66 years and 6 months.

MEDFORD HYNSON, son of Nathaniel and Anna Maria Medford Hynson, m. Fanny Rigby, of Queen Anne's Co., Md.

JOHN RINGGOLD HYNSON, youngest son of Nathaniel and Sophia Ringgold Hynson, was a gallant officer in the U. S. Navy, and died during the Mexican war.

SEC. 59, P. CHARLES HYNSON m., 25th day of March 1687, Margarett Harris, d., was buried at St. Paul's, 24th May 1711. In his Will, dated 10th Jan'y 1703, he mentions his "loving wife Margaret," and the following child., viz., Thomas,—Charles,—Dorcas,—Jane,—and Margaret Hynson.

THOMAS HYNSON, son of Charles and Margaret Harris Hynson, m., 19th Oct. 1710, Wealthy Ann Tilden, dau. of Marmaduke and Rebecca Wilmer Tylden. He d. in 1738. In his Will, dated 26th of May 1738, he mentions the following child., viz., Charles,—Martha,—Waltham, and Mary Hynson. Mary Hynson m. Mr. Jones, and had a son, Thomas Jones.

CHARLES HYNSON, son of Thomas and Wealthy Ann Tilden Hynson, m., 30th Nov. 1739, Phoebe Carvill. He d. in 1782. In his Will, dated 21st of Sept. 1782, he mentions his sons, Charles Hynson,—John Carvill Hynson, and Richard Hynson; grand-daus., Waltham and Martha Rolph, dau. of Phoebe Rolph, wife of John Rolph; grand-dau. Martha Hanson, dau. of his dau. Mary Hanson, wife of Hans Hanson, grand-dau. of Sarah Hynson; Waltham Hynson, dau. of John Carvill Hynson and Rebecca his wife, his sisters Mary Jones and Elizabeth Dunn, wife of James Dunn, his grand-child. Charles Hynson, son of his son Charles, and Phoebe Hynson, dau. of his son John Carvill Hynson and Rebecca his wife.

CHARLES HYNSON, son of Charles and Phoebe Carvill Hynson, m. Sarah Waltham, and had the following child., viz., Charles,—John,—Thomas, — Sarah, — Hannah,—Richard,—Edward, and Martha Hynson.

JOHN CARVILL HYNSON, son of Charles and Phoebe Carvill Hynson, d. 1816. In his Will, dated 29th Dec. 1814, he mentions his child., viz , John Carvill Hynson, and Phoebe Wright,—Mary Worrell,—Wealthy Ann Hardesty, and Rebecca Redding, and his five grand-child., viz., Edward Wright,—William Carvill Wright,—Ann Rebecca Livesay,—Eliza Jane Redding, and Sarah Ann Hynson. He also speaks of James Hynson Wright.

RICHARD HYNSON, son of Charles and Phoebe Carvill Hynson, m. Araminta Bowers, a sister of Major James Bowers. He d. 1801, and had the following child., viz., Thomas Bowers Hynson,—Amelia Sophia Charlotta Hynson,—Harriet Hynson,—Araminta Hynson, and Mary Ann Hynson.

THOMAS BOWERS HYNSON, son of Richard Hynson and Araminta Bowers Hynson, m. Ann Dunn, dau. of Robert Dunn, and had the following child., viz., Richard Hynson,—Thomas Bowers Hynson,—Mary Elizabeth Hynson,—Anna, and Anna Louise Hynson.

RICHARD HYNSON, son of Thomas Bowers and Ann Dunn Hynson, m. Caroline Louisa Marsh, dau. of Elias and Louisa Eccleston, of Philadelphia, and had the following child., viz., Augusta Eccleston,—Caroline Louisa,—Marion, and Richard Dunn Hynson.

MARY ELIZABETH HYNSON, dau. of Thomas Bowers and Ann Dunn Hynson, m. Thomas R. Brown, and had the following child., viz., Dr. Thomas R. Brown,—Dr. James Brown,—Wm. Brown, and Mary Louisa Brown, who m. Richard Merryman, of Baltimore County, Md.

ANNA HYNSON, dau. of Thomas Bowers and Ann Dunn Hynson, m. Samuel W. Spencer, and left two sons, Joseph Gordon Spencer, and Samuel Wright Spencer.

ANNE LOUISE HYNSON, dau. of Thomas Bowers and Ann Dunn Hynson, m. Dr. Benjamin F. Houston. They have the following child., viz., Dr. William Houston, U. S. N., who m. Anna Tilghman Wickes,—Lucy Houston, who m. George Thomas Beal, of Baltimore, Md., and Elizabeth Houston, who m. Benjamin Chambers Wickes.

AMELIA SOPHIA CHARLOTTA HYNSON, dau. of Richard and Araminta Bowers Hynson, m. her cousin, Thomas Hynson ("Adjutant Hynson"). They had the following child., viz., T. W. Hynson, d.,—Chas. H. Hynson,—Thomas William Hynson,—George Washington Hynson,—Lavinia Elizabeth Hynson (who m. Samuel Griffith),—William Hynson,—Harriet Amelia Hynson, and Caroline Willamina Hynson.

THOMAS WILLIAM HYNSON, son of Thomas and Amelia Sophia Charlotta Hynson, m. Mary Sophia Walker, dau. of Rev. Thomas Walker and Elizabeth Miller (Rev. Thomas Walker was the son of John Walker, of Edinburgh, Scotland, and Ann Grieves, a sister of Lord John Grieves), dau. of Nathaniel Miller, of Swan Creek, Kent Co., Md., and have the following child., viz., William Thomas Hynson,—Christopher Columbus Hynson,—Andrew Jackson Hynson,—Virginia Walker Hynson (who m. Mr. James Thomas Moody),—Franklin Pierce Hynson, and George Washington Hynson.

HARRIET HYNSON, dau. of Richard and Araminta Bowers Hynson, m. Matthew Tilghman, and left the following child., viz., Richard Tilghman, who was lost at sea in the Frigate Hornet,—James Bowers Tilghman, now living in Virginia,—William M. Tilghman, removed to Arkansas,—Tench Tilghman, done to death, while defending his castle, by a California posse comitatus,—Henrietta Louisa Tilghman, who m. William B. Everett,—Anna Maria Tilghman, who m. Dr. Benjamin F. Houston,—Harriet Tilghman, who m. William B. Tilghman, of Queen Anne's county, Md., and Catharine Tilghman, who m. James L. Davis.

ARAMINTA HYNSON, dau. of Richard and Araminta Bowers, m. William Wakeman, son of William B. Wakeman. She m. 2dly William Crane, and had child., viz., William B. Crane, and Thomas R. Crane.

MARY ANN HYNSON, dau. of Richard and Araminta Bowers Hynson, m. George B. Westcott, and left one child., Harriet Louisa, who m. Thomas Hill, of Baltimore, Md.

SEC. 60. *To all the free subjects of the Commonwealth of England dwelling in the Province of Maryland our lovinge friendes and neighbors.*

WHEREAS by the supreme AUTHORITY of the Commonwealth of England this PROVINCE is reduced to the obedience of the sayd Commonwealth, by a special power Committed to the Honowrable RICHARD BENNETT Esquire Governor of Virginia and Colonell WM. CLAIBORNE and CAPT. Edmund Curtis Commaunder of the Ginney frigate a man of Warre sett forth by the Commonwealth, for that purpose as is aparantly knowne, to all the people of this Province and an engagement taken by the sayd people to bee obedient thereunto, WHICH power of the sayd Commissioners and Reducement of this PROVINCE thereunto hath been Confirmed by the aforesayd supreme AUTHORITIE under theire hand and sealles to the sayd Commissioners of State, and nothinge hath appeared nor doth yet appear for the *Countermaundinge* or *Alteringe* the acte of *Reducement* in this PROVINCE either by his Highness the LORD PROTECTOR or Parliament of England, yet sume persons formerly by instruction from the Lord Baltimore undertook to work an alteration in the Government, settled in Maryland by the Authority aforesaid; which occasioned the Commissioners of the Commonwealth of England the second time to appear for the setlinge thereof in the obedience of the sayd Commonwealth and in special expression to his Highness the LORD PROTECTOR, by a Commission graunted to Capt. WM. FULLER, Mr. RITCHARD PRESTON and others in the Commissions nominated, for the orderinge, directinge and Governinge the people and Affayrs of MARYLAND, which hath CONTINUED in Peace untill this time.

NOW againe uppon what ground or pretence wee know not the sayd power is Contradicted, the Acts of a lawfull and full Assembly violated the records taken away by force, the peace of the Province disturbed, the Administration of Justice obstructed and hindered, the hearts and minds of the people distracted and amazed; yet no power, Commission or graunt from his Highness the Lord Protector is showen or published.

THEREFORE in Obedience to his Highness the LORD PROTECTOR, who by his *Proclamation* hath Confirmed the magistracy Established by the Parliament and Councel of State: untill his Highness shall signifie his pleasure to the contrary: WEE doe by these presents publish, declare and proclaime to all the free subjects of England, Inhabitants of the Province of Maryland, THAT they continue in that Ingagement which they have taken in that Reducement which they gave, owned and Acknowledged by their Representatives in a lawfull orderly and full Assembly of the Province, untill an express power and Commission from his Highness is published to the Contrary.

WHICH we doe by this our ACTE and declaration publish to all for the discharge of our CONTIENCE to the SUPREME GLORIOUS MAJESTY OF HEAVEN the LORD OF HOSTS HIMSELF,—the Trust Committed to us, the Honor of his Highness the LORD PROTECTOR, the peace and wellfare of the Province, and the satisfaction of all the free subjects of England that are in this Province: SOE GOD help us as wee speake and intend Really what wee declare.

WILL. FULLER
WILLIAM DURAND
LEO. STRONG
RI: EWEN.

Liber A. Fol. 98.

1655–1656.

Sec. 61. At a Court holden for Kent the 25th day of April 1655, at the house of Lieutenant Hinson, high sheriff for ye Countie. Folio 99.

Present Capt. Jos. Wickes Mr. Tho. Ringgold
Mr. Philip Conier Mr. William Eliot
Mr. Hen. Carline.

Whereas Mr. Nicolas Browne desired of ye Provincial Court a Reference to ye Court at Kent, Concerninge an Action of slander wherein ye sayd Mr. Browne is defendant, & *John Deane* plaintife: And it hath appeared by three sufficient witnesses that ye sayd Mr. Nicolas Browne hath slandered ye sayd John Deane, in sayinge that he was a Thieffe, & that he had stolen Mr. Littleton's plate:

The Court doth therefore order that ye sayd Mr. Nicolas Browne shall in open Court, ask ye sayd Deane forgiveness, & shall pay towards ye reparation of ye plaintiff's credit, five hundred pounds of tob. and cask, & for a fine five hundred pounds of tobacco & cask for publick uses, as ye Court shall think fit, and sayd tobacco to bee payd upon all demands with Court Charges, and he remain in ye sheriff's hands till he performs ye Order.

John Deane by his Attorney Lieutenant Hinson complains against Mr. *Nicolas Browne*, in an action of slander against his Wiffe, having proved by three witnesses that the slander is evident and apparent.

The Court in Consideration of ye sayd slander hath Ordered that ye sayd Mr. Nicolas Browne shall in open Court ask forgiveness of ye sd Deane's wife and acknowledge his Offence & shall pay a fine of three hundred pounds of tobacco in Cask towards ye reparation of ye plaintiff's credit with Court Charges els Execution.

Whereas Mr. Nicolas Browne hath been cast in Court in two actions of defamation, ye one against John Deane & the other agst his Wife, both beinge proved by sufficient wittnesses, yet notwithstandinge, ye sayd Mr. Browne refuses to obey ye sd Order of Court, and desires, an Appeall to ye Provincial Court, pretendinge his further testimony, to make his slander appear there: Therefore ye Court is pleased to Ansr. his desire, and graunt him an Appeall to ye next Provinciall Court, provided hee put in sufficient Securitie to ye Sheriffe for treble damages, if hee bee Cast in ye suit, & till hee give securitie to remain in ye sheriff's hands. Ibid Folio 99.

SEC. 62. Bee it known unto all men by these presents, That whereas my husband HENRY CARLINE is indebted to Mr. *Henry Morgan* a certaine summe of tobacco, I RACHEL CARLINE doe by virtue hereof for securinge of the sd tobacco to Mr. Henry Morgan bynd over foure head of cattell, vid. one cow, one two yeare ould all marked with a * * * * in the left eare and cropt on the Right eare, I do also bind over all oure stocke of hoggs marked as aforesayd & all the sayd goods for to rest and remaine for securitie to the sd Mr. Henry Morgan his Heirs, Executors, Administrators and Assigns, till such time as the sayd tobacco bee satisfied and payd & for confirmation hereof I have hereunto put my hand this of June 1655. Liber A. C. P. folio 100.

SEC. 63. Know all persons by these presents, That I WILLIAM CLAPHAM, doe hereby give full power and authoritie, unto my well-beloved Friendes, Mr. HENRY CARLINE and Mr. WILLIAM ELIOTT, to apprehend and take into their custodie the bodies of *James Boothward,* and *Marie* his wife, *John a Dutchman,* and *Elizabeth Ganeere,* beinge runaway servants, and havinge feloniously taken away the particulars within specified, firmly ingaginge myselfe, by these presents, to save harmlesse & indamnifie the sayd Carline and Eliott or either of them in what one or both shall doe, in or concerninge the servants.

In witness hereof I have set my hand this 28th of June 1655.

Signed WM. CLAPHAM.

Test. Thomas Madeslard
John Carroll.

Copia vera testis
Me Clar Com.
Kent. Tho. Hill.

Liber A. C. P. Fol. 100. (21)

SEC. 64. *To Mr. Philip Conier, Commander, and the rest of the Commissioners of the countie of Kent in Mariland:*

WHEREAS THE COMMONS of the Countie of Kent in Marieland by their representatives or Burgesses chosen by them to attend the General Assembly, October the 20th 1654, did desire that they might retaine their ancient privilidge to have a Court of Judicature continued in the sayd Countie, AND THE ASSEMBLY by a particular acte in that case provided, did determine that they should enjoy that privilidge as formerly and that the next Provincial Court should Consider of the persons nominated & propounded to bee commissioners for the said Countie of Kent and receive their engagement to the present Government settled in Mariland under his Highness the LORD PROTECTOR and for graunt them power in his name to act as Commissioners for the Countie of the Isle of Kent, AND accordinge to the sayd act of Assembly Mr. PHILIP CONIER *Commander* of the sayd County and the rest of the Commissioners nominated did appeare beefore the *Provinciall Court* and there ACCEPTED of a power of JUDICATURE AND ENGAGED THEMSELVES BY OATH to serve the LORD PROTECTOR and Commonwealth as Commissioners for the Countie of Kent;

These are therefore to declare to all whom it may concerne, That the sd power of Judicature soe graunted as aforesayd to the sd Philip Conier Commaunder and the rest of the Commissioners of Kent ought and shall continue in force, accordinge to the Act of Assembly notwithstanding any thinge that hath happened since by occasion of the late, arisinge, or any other cause whatsoever. And the sayd Commaunder & Commissioners of the sayd County of Kent are HEAREBY REQUIRED in the NAME of his Highness the LORD PROTECTOR of England to attend to their duty and trust committed to them, to the best of their knowledge & abilitie: Whereof they may not to faill uppon Their perill, given the 24th of September 1655.

WILL FULLER.

To be published by the Sheriffe.

8th mo 29th This day all whatever hath been written Entered on Record in the Court Boocke since the last Court houlden Aprill 25th, '55, was published by ye Courts apointment.

Liber A. C. P. Folio 102.

SEC. 65. 8th Moneth 1655 At a Court houlden for Kent the 29th of October 1655 at the house of Mr. Thomas Hinson high sheriffe for the County.

JAMES HORNER (by his Attorney Mr. Tho. Hinson) havinge petetioned the Court for 14 dayes work, upon his own diet, wrought for *Andrew Hanson, Valerus Leo & Swan Swanson,* in their crope the sd 14 dayes beinge confest by sume of the Swedes present in Court & further hath made appear that there is due to him out of the Swedes cropp two barrels of Corne.

The Court doth therefore Order that the sd *James Horner*

shall bee payd out of the cropp of the forementioned three Swedes two barrels of Corne and for his 14 days worke 25 lbs. of tob. a day, to bee payd upon demaund with Court Charges els execution.

(2) HENRY MORGAN havinge petitioned the Court for 10 dayes work & diet wrought for *Andrew Hanson, Valerus Leo & Swan Swanson* in their cropp, the sayd 10 dayes beeinge made apeare to the Court to be unsatisfied.

The Court doth therefore order that the three Swedes before mentioned shall pay out of their crops to Mr. Morgan upon all demaunds for the 10 dayes work & diet 25 lbs. of tob. a day & Court charges els execution.

This bill byndeth me, ROBERT GAMMER of ye Isle of Kent Planter, my Heirs, Executors, Administrators & Assigns to pay or Cause to bee payd unto ANTHONY CALLOWAY his heirs, Executors, Administrators or Assigns ye full & Just sume of twelve hundred and fiftie pounds of good & sound merchantable tobacco in leaf with Casks at or upon the tenth of November next ensuing the date hereof; And for the better performance of ye same I the sd Robert Gammer doe bynd over my Crope of tobacco & corne untill ye sd Bill bee satisfied as wittnes my hand 16th of July 1655.

ROBERT GAMER.

Witness John Russell
John Winchester.

SEC. 66. Moneth 29th 1655 At a Court houlden for Kent November 29th 1655 at Mr. Thos. Hinson's High Sheriffe for ye Countie.

THOS. HINSON Complains against JNO. SALTER for tobacco, which upon Accompt & part by bill & tobacco also due for Court Charges. And the sd Jno. Salter doth acknowledge in Court that hee is Indebted to the plaintiff 622 lbs. of tob.

Sd Court doth therefore order that the sd Salter shall make present payment of the sd debt of 622 lbs. of tob. with Court Charges els Execution.

MR. HENRY MORGAN hath made his Complaint that for the tyme of eight weekes hee harbored in his house, Cherished and kept with meat, drink & Attendance in the tyme of his sickness Valerus Leo, & was at Charges in funeral Expenses and desires satisfaction.

THE COMPLAINT CLEARED.—The Court doth therefore Order that in full satisfaction for all the aforementioned Charges present payment shall be made out of the estate of Valerus Leo to the sd Mr. Morgan 600 lbs. of tobacco, els execution.

ANICAH HANSON Complains Against the Estate of VALERUS LEO that the sd Leo was Indebted to her husband ANDREW HANSON 680 lbs. of tob.

A DEPOSITION.—Mr. Thos. Hinson Sheriffe of the Countie, aged 35 years or thereabouts, sworne, examined and saith, That he heard *Valerus Leo* a little before his death Owne & acknowledge that hee Owed to Andrew Hanson 680 lbs. of tob. & further saith not.

Signed THO. HYNSON Sh.

A DEPOSITION.—Anicah Hanson widow, aged 36 years or thereabouts, sworne, Examined & saith that there is due to her from the Estate of Valerus Leo 680 lbs. of tob. & that shee hath recd no part nor parcell thereof & further saith not.

ANICAH HANSON havinge made her Complaint * * The Court doth therefore Order that out of the Estate of the sd Leo present payment bee made of the sd 680 lbs. of tob. els Execution.

Whereas ANICAH HANSON, Relict of Andrew Hanson, deceased, hath petitioned this Court and renownst her husband's estate desiring the Court to take order Concerninge the same as in discretion it shall think fitte, ffor the ye satisfying of Creditors & her Relief:

The Court doth therefore Order that Mr. THOMAS HYNSON, high sheriffe of the Countie shall take the sd estate into his Custodie, and Edeavour to find out everi part & parcell thereof & bringe it into an Inventorie or order, to bee brought into the Court, that the sayd Estate may be disburst accordinge to lawe & contience.

Hanson.

SEC. 67. AN ACT OF ASSEMBLY, NUMBER 16.

*The names of all that shall bee borne, marriea, or buried within the * * * shall be exhibited to the Clarke of everie Court, who shall keep a Just Register thereof, who shall bee allowed five pounds of tobacco as a fee aue to him for every such Register made and kept as aforesaid.*

A List of the names according to Acte followeth:

BIRTHES.

Moneth.	Day.	
		1654.
12	3	Richard Blunt.
		1655.
2	25	Marie Baxster.
8		AnicahHa nson's daughter Barberi.
5	22	Henery Clay.
8	30	Capt. Vaughan's child Charles.
6		Dean's child Christian.
8	19	Picket's daughter Elizabeth.
		1656.
2	23	John Winchester's daughter.
8	1	Mr. Henry Morgan, a daughter borne.

MARRIAGES.

Moneth.	Day.	
		1655.
8		John Dabbs, with Nan Eates.
11	6	Roger Baxster. with Mary Croutch.
1	4	Thomas Hill, Jr., with Margret Balie.
		1656.
3	5	Andrew Elenor with Anica Hanson.
5	7	Capt. Jos. Wickes, with Marie Hartwell.

BURRIALLS.

Moneth.	Day.	
		1865.
5	4	Mr. Bradnox's servant.
5	6	Mr. Nicholas Browne.
8	4	Valerus Leo.
9	14	Joane Baxster.
9	22	Thomas Boulton.
9	23	Edward Tarant.
10	2	George Croutch.
10		Baxter's daughter Elizabeth.
4		Andrew Anderson Hanson
6		Mr. Bradnox servant, John Pritchet.
7	15	John Smith's child John.
		1656.
5	16	John Elise's child, named John Ellse.
5	19	Robert Dunne's child, his name, William Dunne.
6	6	Mr. Wickes' child Joseph.
6	14	Anne Gould, Mr. Wickes' servant.
8	12	Thomas Hawkins, of Poples.
8	19	Edward Purlin : Scott.

NOTE.—All the dates contained in the above List are set down according to the OLD STYLE, the Julian Calendar. In the month of February 1751, *o. s.*, Lord Chesterfield introduced into the House of Lords a Bill for reforming the Calendar and adopting the Gregorian style of reckoning, which was used by all Christendom, except Russia, Sweden and England.

By the statute of GEORGE II, CHAP. XXIII, A. D. 1751, it was enacted that the "Supputation, according to which the year of our Lord beginneth on the twenty-fifth day of *March*, shall not be made use of from and after the last day of *December* one thousand seven hundred and fifty one; and that the first day of *January* next following the said last day of *December* shall be reckoned, taken, deemed and accounted to be the first day of the year of our Lord one thousand seven hundred and fifty-two:—and from and after the said first day of *January*, one thousand seven hundred and fifty-two, the several days of each month, shall go on and be reckoned and numbered in the same order,—as they now are, until the second day of *September* in the said year, one thousand seven hundred and fifty-two inclusive; and that the natural day next immediately following the said second day of *September*, shall be called, reckoned and accounted to be the fourteenth day of September," 1752.

The reader will now be able to reduce with ease the dates of the Old Style to the new. In the above list, according to a *puritan* enactment, the months are deprived of their time-honored names and numbered like convicts; MARCH being the first month.

SEC. 67, A. ANDREW HANSON, whose death is recorded in the List, was b. in Sweden, in 1618, the son of Col. Hanson, of the Swedish Army, and grandson of John Hanson, of London, was descended from Roger de Rastrick, who was seated at Rastrick, in the Parish of Halifax, York county, England, in the year 1251.

ROGER DE RASTRICK, of Rastrick, left three sons, viz., Hugh de Rastrick, of Linlands,—Rev. John de Rastrick, and Simon de Rastrick.

HUGH DE RASTRICK, of Linlands, and his wife Agnes were living in 1257, and had sons, viz., John de Rastrick, and William de Rastrick.

JOHN DE RASTRICK, son of Hugh de Rastrick and Agnes, his wife, left a son,

JOHN DE RASTRICK, whose eldest son,

HENRY DE RASTRICK, left a son,

JOHN DE RASTRICK, who in the year 1330, assumed the

surname of HANSON (a diminutive of Henry's son) and signed his name, JOHN HANSON, to a deed in 1337. He m. Alice (dau. of Henry de Woodhouse, and granddau. and heiress of Alexander de Woodhouse by his wife Beatrice, dau. and heiress of Thomas de Toothill), and had a son, John Hanson.

JOHN HANSON, of Woodhouse, son of John Hanson and Alice de Woodhouse, m. Cicely de Windebanke, and left a son, John Hanson.

JOHN HANSON, of Woodhouse, son of John Hanson and Cicely de Windebanke, m. Cicely, dau. of John Ravenshaw, and left a son, John Hanson.

JOHN HANSON, of Woodhouse, son of John Hanson and Cicely Ravenshaw, m. Catharine, dau. of John Brooke (whose wife was a great-grandchild of Thomas Beaumont, of Whitely), and left a son, John Hanson.

JOHN HANSON, of Woodhouse, son of John Hanson and Catharine Brooke, m. Agnes Savile (eldest dau. of John Savile, Esq., of New Hall, by Margery, dau. of John Gledhill), and had sons, viz., John Hanson, of Woodhouse, b. 1517, d. 1599,—Edward Hanson, of Nether Hall, b. 1520, d. Dec. 1601,—Thomas Hanson, of Rastrick, and Arthur Hanson.

THOMAS HANSON, of Rastrick, son of John Hanson and Agnes Savile, m. Janet, dau. of John Gledhill, of Little-even, in Barkisland, and had sons, viz., Roger Hanson,—Thomas Hanson, of Rastrick,—John Hanson, of London, and Robert Hanson, of Rastrick.

JOHN HANSON, of London, son of Thomas Hanson and Janet Gledhill, m. Frances, dau. of John Prichard, and had sons, viz., John Hanson,—Thomas Hanson, and Edward Hanson.

HANSON ARMS—*English.*

ARMS: Or, a chevron, countercomponed, argent and azure, between three martlets, sable.

CREST: On a helm, a chapeau, argent, lined argent, a martlet, volant, sable, mantled gules, double argent.

MOTTO: SOLA VIRTUS INVICTA.

N. B. Certified by William Ryley, Norroy King at Arms, 17th Jan'y 1652.

JOHN HANSON, of London, son of John Hanson and Frances Prichard, while taking a summer tour in Sweden, fell in love with and m. a Swedish lady, who was closely connected, in friendship, at least, with the Royal Family. He and his wife d. young, leaving a son, who was reared in familiar intimacy with Gustavus Adolphus, then a youth about the same age. At a suitable time he entered the army, served with credit, rose to the rank of Colonel, became a trusted officer, and was always retained near the royal person in action. While defending and attempting to shield his King, he fell, slain in battle, with Gustavus Adolphus, at Lützen, 16th Nov. 1632. He left four sons, viz., Andrew Hanson,—Randal or Randolph Hanson,—William Hanson, and John Hanson, all of whom were taken under the immediate protection of the Royal Family of Sweden. In August 1642 QUEEN CHRISTINA placed them in the special care of Lieutenant Colonel John Printz, Governor of New Sweden, with whom they came to the Delaware, and remained there, on Tinicum Island, until the year 1653, when they came to Kent Island.

COL. HANSON, of the Swedish Army, was authorized to bear a coat of arms, which was preserved by his eldest son and has been retained by his descendants to the present day. It was appropriate to a Christian soldier, and the cause for which he died—Religious Liberty.

The following is a correct definition :

HANSON ARMS—*Swedish.*

ARMS : Azure, a cross, betonée cantoned by four fleur-de-lis, argent.

CREST : A martlett, proper.

MOTTO : SOLA VIRTUS INVICTA.

[*See Title Page.*]

ANDREW HANSON, eldest son of Colonel Hanson, settled on Kent Island in 1653, and died there in 1655.

RANDOLPH HANSON (second son of Col. Hanson), or Randal Hanson, as he called himself, and Randle, for short, among his comrades, when the military fit was upon him did not tarry long on Kent Island. He was a bold, enterprising, ambitious and restless man. He went to the seat of Government, at St. Mary's, to carve out his fortune at the point of his sword, and was engaged in all the military operations of his day.

That he was a man of marked distinction, and regarded as a "gentleman of condition," is sufficiently attested by the fact that his dau., Barbara Hanson, was the first love and wife of Thomas Hatton, gent., of one of the proudest families of England, a grand-nephew of Sir Christopher Hatton, Lord High Chancellor of England, the famous courtier, who bewitched the Court of Queen Elizabeth with the exquisite grace of his manners.

I am inclined to think that Randolph Hanson was of so restless and aspiring a disposition that he "cared for none of these things," though he did not forget that his mother was a Swede, and that his father was a gallant soldier, and a loyal subject of Gustavus Adolphus; but Col. Hans Hanson, of Kimbolton, did keep up the intercourse with his grandfather's family, and it was maintained until the Revolutionary war. A magnificent silk dress, inwrought with bullion thread, was sent over as a wedding present to the bride of his grandson Gustavus Hanson, by the family in England, and a portion of it is in the possession of her great-grandson.

William Hanson, next in age, accompanied his brother Randolph to St. Mary's. He returned to Kent, and died in in 1684, leaving only his "loving wife Alice."

Col. John Hanson, the youngest son of Col. Hanson, of the Swedish Army, was b. in Sweden, about the year 1630, came to New Sweden, on the Delaware, in 1642, removed to Maryland in 1653, and, after a short sojourn on Kent Island, went to St. Mary's: finally, about, or after, the year 1656, he settled in Charles County, and lived there until his death. In his Will, dated 12th Dec. 1713, he styles himself "planter of Charles County," and mentions seven child., viz., Robert,—Benjamin,—Mary (wife of Rev. William Maconchie),—Anne,—Sarah,—John,—Samuel, and his grandson Samuel Hanson.

Robert Hanson, eldest son of Col. John Hanson, represented Charles County in the Legislature of Maryland in the sessions of 1719, 20, 28, 32, 34, 39 and 1740. In his Will, dated in 1746, and admitted to probate in 1748, he mentions his child., viz., Samuel,—William,—Dorothy,—Mary,—Sarah,—Violetta, and Benjamin Hanson. He bequeathed to his grandson Robert Hanson (the son of his son, Samuel Hanson, and his wife, Mary Hanson) a tract of land called "Betty's Delight," which, the testator says, was "left me by the Will of my father, John Hanson."

Dorothy Hanson, dau. of Robert Hanson, m. Richard Harrison, and had a son, Robert Hanson Harrison, who was a very distinguished man. "He was a lawyer of fine talents "and legal acquirements, was Military Secretary, with the "rank of Colonel, to General Washington during the Revolu-

" tionary War, and, upon the unanimous election of the latter " as President, and the organization of the Government under " the Constitution of 1787, Colonel Harrison was selected and " appointed by him one of the Supreme Court of the United " States."—*Extracted from a letter of Col. W. H. S. Taylor to Hon. Frederick Stone.*

MARY HANSON, dau. of Robert Hanson, m. John Briscoe (see BRISCOE).

SAMUEL HANSON, son of Col. John Hanson, represented Charles Co. in the Legislature of Maryland in the sessions of 1716 and 1728, was the Commissary of Charles Co. in 1734, and Clerk of the same in 1739. His eldest dau. m. Dr. Daniel Jenifer (see JENIFER). Another dau. m. David Stone (see STONE). In his Will, dated 22d Oct. 1740, he mentions, then living, his wife Elizabeth, and child., Judge Walter Hanson (of Harwood),—William Hanson,—Samuel Hanson (of Greenhill),—John Hanson (of Mulberry Grove),—Elizabeth Hanson (who m. Benjamin Douglas and had a dau., Elizabeth),—Charity Hanson,—Jane Hanson, and Chloe Hanson, then a minor.

SAMUEL HANSON was buried at Equality, an estate then owned by his son-in-law, David Stone, " the inheritor of Paynton Manor, with Court Leet and Court Baron," a lineal descendant and representative of Governor William Stone, and the great-grandfather of the Hon. Frederick Stone, of Port Tobacco, Md.

SEC. 67, B. DAVID STONE (son of Thomas, the son of John, who was the son of Hon. William Stone, Governor of Maryland from 1649 to 1654) m. twice. His 1st wife was Miss Hanson, the dau. of Samuel and Elizabeth Hanson. His 2d wife was Elizabeth Jenifer, dau. of Dr. Daniel Jenifer and his wife, a dau. of Samuel and Elizabeth Hanson (see JENIFER).

He left child., viz., Samuel Stone,—Thomas Stone, who signed the Declaration of Independence,—Hon. John Hoskins Stone, who was Governor of Maryland, from 1794 to 1797,—Judge Michael Jenifer Stone,—Walter Stone,—Frederick Stone, and Daniel Stone.

SAMUEL STONE, son of David Stone and his 1st wife, m. his cousin, Mrs. Ann Hanson Mitchell, widow of Hugh Mitchell and his wife, a dau. of Judge Walter Hanson.

The following letter, dated 30th May 1874 (a portion of which is quoted), contains an interesting history of this branch of the family:

" SAMUEL STONE (son of David), by his wife and cousin,

" the widow of Hugh Mitchell, and dau. of Walter Hanson, " left four child. who grew up, to wit: Walter Hanson Stone, " the eldest (named after his grandfather Walter Hanson), " —David Stone,—Alexander Stone, and Sarah Stone. David " and Alexander d. unm., the former in 1840, over 70 years of " age (the oldest of the name that I ever heard of, and the *only* " *Jeffersonian Democrat of the family*), and the latter when he " was 19 or 20 years of age. Walter Hanson Stone, oldest " son of Samuel, m. Rachel Muncaster, the oldest child and " dau. of his father's neighbor, James Muncaster, before he " was twenty-one years old (a runaway match), and whose pre- " sent representative and descendant is James Muncaster " Brown, a millionaire, and partner in the great banking " firm of 'Brown Brothers & Co.,' New York.—He d. " on his hereditary place, Paynton Manor, at the early age " of 27, leaving two daus., Ann, b. 1788, and Sarah S., b. " in 1790. Ann Stone, the oldest, m. in 1805, Captain John " Taylor, of St. Mary's county, and d. in 1815, aged only 27, " leaving three child., to wit: Walter Hanson Stone, the " oldest (named after his grandfather, Walter Hanson Stone), " Sarah Ann and John Arthur Taylor, who before the late " civil war was a wealthy planter and Physician in Louisiana. " All now living and m., but once each, having had families, " numbering altogether thirty child., 17 sons and 13 daus. " Sarah S. Stone (second dau. of Walter Hanson) m. Doctor " W. Dunnington, in June 1812, and d. May 1830, childless. " Sarah Stone, the only dau. of Samuel Stone, the second " husband of the dau. of Walter Hanson, m. John Briscoe, " somewhere about the year 1793, and after surviving her " husband about 20 years, d., leaving five child., to wit: Sam- " uel,—John,—William (m. to his pretty cousin, Elizabeth " Mitchell),—Walter Hanson Stone (named after his uncle, " and Janet, the two first having d. many years ago, " but the two last, Walter Hanson Stone (m.), and Janet " (a maiden), are both still living, now old people over 70 years " of age, being grandchild., and the only surviving of them, " of the daughter of Walter Hanson, the son of Samuel, the " son of John Hanson the ancester before mentioned. * * * " The fact is, that for more than one hundred years there was " no family so wealthy, prominent and powerful in Charles " county, and their relatives and descendants in the State, as " the Hansons, hardly excepting the *Stones*, including the first " proprietary Governor, after Leonard Calvert, and descendants " with whom the Hansons were nearly allied by marriage and "consanguinity. The ancient records in the Clerk's and "Register's offices still show that the principal offices of the "county, within that period, Judges of Courts, Clerks of "ditto, Registers of Wills, High Sheriffs, Inspectors, &c., were "held and filled by members of that remarkable family, "besides the State Chancellor, members of Congress, and "Judge of Baltimore City Court before mentioned.

"From having been the most, they are now the least nume- "rous of the old families still residing in the county. There "was a Samuel Hanson, a near neighbor of my father, who "was a brave officer of the old Maryland Line of the Revolu- "tionary War. He m. Margery McConchie, his relative, and "d. leaving an only son, Robert Winder Hanson, who d. in "1853, and left two sons, Earnest, and Alban, now m. and "living upon their old farm, a part of Paynton Manor of the "Stones. There was another Samuel Hanson (Samuel appear- "ing to have been a favorite name in the family) likewise a "brave Revolutionary officer of the same old Maryland Line, "who left an only son, named Josias H. Hanson, whom "as my cousin 'Si,' I knew very well. He lived the "last thirty years of his life in Washington and Baltimore, "and died in or near the latter city, leaving an only son, "whose name I do not now remember, but when I last saw "him he was a wounded Confederate soldier, in a hospital in "Richmond, Va. I knew two other Hansons of the same "family, Thomas H., who m. a dau. of Colonel William Dent "Beall, a distinguished Revolutionary officer (Maryland Line), "who d. in Fredericksburg, Va., leaving many child., and "Isaac Hanson, who was Clerk in one of the Departments all "his manhood life, and d. there, an old man, leaving a family. "I also knew another family of Hansons, but do not know "from what branch they descended or the name of their father. "They were William, the oldest,—Francis B.,—Chloe Ann, "and Jane. Neither of the males m., both are now d., the "younger was an Episcopal clergyman of good talents and "very high character, who d. in Baltimore in the early part of "the present year. Of the females, Jane, the youngest, m. "Joseph Young, and d. many years ago, and Chloe Ann, the "oldest, m. Henry A. Stone, and is still living, a fine old "lady, 72 or 73 years of age.

"I wish I knew more than I have here related of this fine "and by no means undistinguished race, in which I feel a "*personal* as well as a public interest, as I am connected with "them by blood, and with the Stone family also, as is indica-"ted by my *name*, which I herewith subscribe in full as,

"Very truly your friend and relative,

"WALTER HANSON STONE TAYLOR,

"Late second Military Auditor of the Confederates States."

JUDGE MICHAEL JENIFER STONE, son of David Stone, and his 2d wife, Elizabeth Jenifer, m. his cousin, Mary Hanson Briscoe (granddau. of John Briscoe and Mary Hanson, dau. of Robert Hanson), and had child, viz., Frederick D.,—William B.,—Michael J.,—Elizabeth J., and Eleanor Stone. Of whom Michael J. and Eleanor (29th May 1876) survive.

FREDERICK D. STONE, eldest son of Judge Michael Jenifer Stone and Mary Hanson Briscoe, m. in 1819, Eliza Patton, of an ancient Virginia family, who d. in 1820, leaving an only son, Frederick Stone.

HON. FREDERICK STONE, only son of Frederick D. Stone and Eliza Patton, has been a prominent and leading citizen of Charles County for many years. In 1852 he and Samuel Tyler, with William Price, were appointed by the Legislature of Maryland, Commissioners to "simplify and abridge the rules of Pleading, Practice, and Conveyancing" in this State. In 1864 he was elected a member of the Maryland Constitutional Convention, and in the fall of the same year was elected to the Legislature. He was elected in 1866 a member of the 40th Congress, and re-elected in 1868. Again, in 1871 he was called upon to represent his native county in the Legislature of Maryland. He has been m. twice. He m. 10th of June 1852, Maria Louisa Stonestreet, dau. of Nicholas and Ann E. Stonestreet, who d. in Nov. 1867, leaving four child., viz., Annie,—Elizabeth,—Ellen (generally called Bessie),—Jennie, and Maria Louisa Stone. He m. 2ndly, 15th of June 1870, Jennie Fergusson, a sister of his 1st wife.

ANNIE STONE, eldest dau. of Hon. Frederick Stone and Maria Louisa Stonestreet, m. 19th Nov. 1875, her relative Henry Gerard Robertson, son of Walter Hanson Robertson and Catharine Barnes.

SEC. 67, C. JUDGE WALTER HANSON, of Harwood, son of Samuel and Elizabeth Hanson, was Commissary of Charles County in 1740, m. Miss Hoskins, and had child., who survived to maturity, viz., Hoskins,—Anne, who married Hugh Mitchell, and Elizabeth Hanson, who m. Daniel Jenifer, commonly called "Squire Jenifer," and d. Nov. 1757, aged 25 years.

HOSKINS HANSON, son of Judge Walter Hanson, m. Sarah Thompson, and had three child, viz., Richard Thompson Hanson (who emigrated about the year 1812 to Georgia, settled in Oglethorpe County, m. Eliza Ray, and had child., viz., Darthula, — Philip, — Anne, who m. Major Moss, of the Confederate Army, — George, — Richard, — Catharine, and Mary Hanson, who m. Doctor Stiles Hopping),—Sarah Hanson (who m. Major William Penn, of Charles County, and had three sons, viz., Dr. Hanson Penn,—William Hanson Penn, and Richard Thompson Penn),—and Catharine Hanson.

CATHARINE HANSON, youngest dau. of Hoskins Hanson and Sarah Thompson, m. in 1804, Gerard Robertson, d. 15th Oct. 1861, and had five child., who lived to maturity, viz., Walter Hanson, — Catharine, —John Richard, — Alexander Hanson, b. in 1813, and Hoskins Hanson Robertson, b. in 1816.

WALTER HANSON ROBERTSON, son of Gerard Robertson and Catharine Hanson, m. in 1835, Catharine Barnes, d. in 1852, leaving six child., viz., Ellen Robertson (who m. in 1859, H. Clay Nally, who d. in 1862, leaving her with one dau., Ellen Clay Nally),—George Robertson, who d. in the military hospital, at Richmond, in 1863,—Jane Robertson (who m. in 1863, Samuel Hawkins, and had child., viz., Walter,—Harry, —Arthur,—Charles,—Catharine, and George Robertson Hawkins),—Mary Robertson, unm., — Henry Gerard Robertson (who m. 19th Nov. 1875, Annie Stone, eldest dau. of Hon. Frederick Stone), and Ann Key Robertson, unm.

CATHARINE ROBERTSON, dau. of Gerard and Catharine Hanson Robertson, m. 1834, Henry Middleton Brawner, Attorney at Law, of Charles County, who d. in 1837, leaving two child, viz., John A. Brawner, and Henrietta M. Brawner, who m. 10th July, 1861, Lemuel Wilmer, son of Rev. Lemuel Wilmer, and Jane Henrietta Frisby (see WILMER).

JOHN A. BRAWNER, son of Henry Middleton Brawner and Catharine Robertson, m., 10th June 1856, Catharine C. Briscoe, and had child., viz., Henry Middleton,—Gerard Briscoe,—John A.,—Verlinda Fowke,—Mary Catharine,—Washington and Hugh Brawner.

JOHN RICHARD ROBERTSON, son of Gerard Robertson and Catharine Hanson, m., in 1835, Margaret Cox, dau. of Col. Hugh Cox, who d. in 1839, leaving an only son, Hugh Robertson, who d. unm. He m. again, in 1841, Rebecca Cox, sister of his 1st wife, who d. in 1847, leaving two sons, viz., Samuel, who took the name of Cox, and Henry G. Robertson, killed while in the Confederate Army, in 1864. His 3d wife,

m. in 1849, was Roberta Wallace, of Montgomery County, and has child., viz., Harriet,—Edward, and Jeff Davis Robertson.

DOCTOR ALEXANDER HANSON ROBERTSON, son of Gerard Robertson and Catharine Hanson, m., 28th Dec. 1842, Verlinda Stone Fowke, dau. of Gerard Fowke, of Charles Co., and had child., viz., Catharine Fowke,—William Augustus, who took the name of Fowke, by act of Assembly, 1862, and Alexander Hanson Robertson. Mrs. Verlinda Stone Fowke Robertson d. in 1870.

ALEXANDER HANSON ROBERTSON, son of Doctor Alexander Hanson Robertson and Verlinda Stone Fowke, Attorney at Law, in the city of Baltimore, m., 11th Jan. 1876, Estelle Fisher, only dau. of the late William Fisher, of Baltimore.

HOSKINS HANSON ROBERTSON, son of Gerard Robertson and Catharine Hanson, m., 1839, Catharine Robertson, who d. in 1850, leaving two child., viz., George Hanson, and Elizabeth Catharine Robertson. He m. again, in 1853, Elizabeth Mitchell, dau. of Rev. Richard Henry Barnes Mitchell (see MITCHELL), who d. in 1859, leaving a dau., Lucy Compton Robertson.

SEC 67, D. ANNE HANSON, dau. of Judge Walter Hanson, m. Hugh Mitchell, a Scotchman, who d. in 1761, leaving one son, John Mitchell, and two daus., viz., Jeannette Hanson Mitchell, and Catharine Mitchell, a great belle and a very beautiful woman, who d. unm.

Mrs. Anne Hanson Mitchell m., a 2d time, her cousin, Samuel Stone, the son and only child of David Stone by his wife, the dau. of Samuel Hanson. (See STONE, *Col. Taylor's letter*.)

GENERAL JOHN MITCHELL, only son of Hugh Mitchell and Anne Hanson, entered the Revolutionary Army, when a mere youth, as Ensign, served through the whole war with credit and rose to the rank of Captain. He retained through life a fondness for military affairs, and at the time of his death was an officer of the militia of his native State, with the rank of General. He m. twice. His 1st wife was Lucy Stoddert, and had one son, John T. Heberd S. Mitchell, who had a son William, who left a son, William Heberd Mitchell, who m. Emily E. Mitchell, dau. of Gen. Walter Hanson Jenifer Mitchell.

His 2d wife was Catharine Barnes (sister of John Barnes, formerly Clerk of Charles County), and had child., viz., Richard Henry Barnes Mitchell,—Walter Hanson Jenifer Mitchell,—

Mary Mitchell, who m. James Brawner, and d. young, *sine prole*,—and Elizabeth Mitchell, who m. William D. Briscoe, of Charles County, and left three child., only one of whom survives, Mary Briscoe Page, wife of H. Clagett Page.

General John Mitchell d. in 1812, aged 56 years.

REVEREND RICHARD HENRY BARNES MITCHELL, of the Protestant Episcopal Church, was m. twice. His 1st wife was Lucinda Compton, and had 8 child., viz., John W. Mitchell,—Richard H. Mitchell, of Baltimore,—Rev. Walter A. Mitchell, of St. John's Parish, Hagerstown,—Lucinda Mitchell, who m. Richard H. Hebb, of St. Mary's County,—Elizabeth, who m. Hoskins Hanson Robertson, and d. in 1859, leaving an only dau., Lucy Compton Robertson,—Catharine, d., who m. Josiah Dent, of Georgetown, D. C.,—Mary, who m. John B. Bateman, and Violetta Mitchell, now (2d May 1876) residing in St. Mary's Co.

His 2d wife was Susan Binney, and had three child., viz., Rev. James A. Mitchell, of Centreville,—Dr. Andrew Mitchell, of Wilmington, Delaware, and the Rev. Whittingham Doane Mitchell, who d. in Florida.

Rev. Richard Henry Barnes Mitchell was the Rector at Elkton, at the time of his death, in 1869.

GENERAL WALTER HANSON JENIFER MITCHELL, son of Gen. John Mitchell and his 2d wife Catharine Barnes, m. Mary Fergusson, dau. of Judge John Fergusson, and had child., viz., Bettie Fergusson Mitchell,—Mary Matilda Mitchell, who m. 18th July 1861, Philip Henry Muschett (see MUSCHETT),—Hugh Mitchell,—Robert Fergusson Mitchell,—Emily E. Mitchell, who m. William Heberd Mitchell, a grandson of Gen. John Mitchell and his 1st wife Lucy Stoddert,—John Hanson Mitchell, Attorney-at-Law, Port Tobacco, and Cassie Mitchell.

SEC. 67, E. JEANNETTE HANSON MITCHELL, dau. of Hugh Mitchell and Anne Hanson, m. Doctor Mungo Muschett, a Scotchman, and had child., viz., Mary Hanson Muschett, b. 7th June 1788,—Wm. Muschett, b. 22d Feb'y 1790,—Henry Alexander Muschett, b. 5th Nov. 1792,—Anne Hanson Muschett, b. 16th May 1794,—Philip Hanson Muschett, b. 25th Dec. 1796,—Robert Muschett, b. 27th June 1798, John Mitchell Muschett, b. 20th Aug. 1799, and Mungo Muschett, b. 1st April 1803.

JOHN MITCHELL MUSCHETT, son of Dr. Mungo Muschett and Jeannette Hanson Mitchell, m. Jane Alice Barnes, dau. of Humphrey Barnes, and had child., viz., Anne Key Muschett,

Briscoe.

who m. Robert Speake,—Philip Henry Muschett,—George Humphrey Muschett,—Jeannette Mitchell Muschett, and Catharine Robertson Muschett.

PHILIP HENRY MUSCHETT, son of John Mitchell Muschett and Jane Alice Barnes, m. 18th July 1861, Mary Matilda Mitchell (dau. of Gen. Walter Hanson Jenifer Mitchell and Mary Fergusson), who d. leaving two child., viz., Walter Mitchell Muschett, and Mary Matilda Mitchell Muschett.

GEORGE HUMPHREY MUSCHETT, son of John Mitchell Muschett and Jane Alice Barnes, m. Nellie Barnes, dau. of Judge Richard Barnes, and had child., viz., Nellie Lee Barnes Muschett,—Richard Lee Muschett, and Mary Muschett

SEC. 67, F. CHLOE HANSON, dau. of Samuel and Elizabeth Hanson, m. Philip Briscoe, of St. Mary's County, and had child., viz., Dr. John Hanson Briscoe,—Samuel Hanson Briscoe, who d. unm.,—Hanson Briscoe, and Eliza Storer Briscoe.

DR. JOHN HANSON BRISCOE, son of Philip Briscoe and Chloe Hanson, was b. near the village of Chaptico, St. Mary's County, in 1752. At the age of eight years he was sent to Edinburgh, Scotland, to receive a classical and professional education. He was graduated at the University of Edinburgh, in 1773, and, returning to Chaptico, entered upon the practice of his profession. On the 6th day of Jan'y 1776 he was elected, by the Convention of Maryland, Major in the Upper Battalion of St. Mary's County, Col. Jeremiah Jordan commanding. Soon after, he was commissioned Surgeon in the Continental Army, and served as such in the 2d Maryland Regiment, Major General William Smallwood's Division, from which he and others withdrew, 11th Jan'y 1778, in consequence of some unwise *Resolves* of the Field Officers of that Division. Dr. Briscoe was then assigned to Hospital duty. At the close of the Revolutionary War he was in charge of the Government Hospitals in the city of Philadelphia. Upon the conclusion of the war, he returned to Chaptico, and d. 26th Sept. 1796, without having received from the United States Government any compensation for his services, and which remain unpaid for to this day. He m. Elizabeth Attaway Bond, and had child., viz., Thomas Briscoe, who m. his cousin, Eleanor Buchanan,—Philip Briscoe,—Dr. John Hanson Briscoe,—Cecilia Briscoe, who m. 1st Mr. Clagget, 2dly Mr. Lyles,—Ellen Briscoe, who m. Bernard Hooe, of Virginia, and Elizabeth Attaway Briscoe, who m. 1st John Sothoren, and 2dly Rev. A. M. Jones.

PHILIP BRISCOE, son of Dr. John Hanson Briscoe and Elizabeth Attaway Bond, b. 9th Nov. 1786, was for many years an eminent and celebrated teacher, and was twice elected the Principal of his Alma Mater, Charlotte Hall, St. Mary's County. He d. 26th of Sept. 1842, leaving a name and memory venerated and cherished by the wise and good of Lower Maryland.

He m., 19th July 1817, Maria Thompson, who was b. 8th Dec. 1796, and had child., viz., Lucretia Leeds,—William Thomas,—Rachel Ann,—Jas. Thompson,—Gustavus Brown,—John Hanson,—Edward Tayloe, and Elizabeth Ellen Cecilia Briscoe.

LUCRETIA LEEDS BRISCOE, dau. of Philip and Maria Thompson Briscoe, m., in 1840, Henry J. Carroll, and had a son, Philip Michael Carroll.

WILLIAM THOMAS BRISCOE, son of Philip and Maria Thompson Briscoe, the eminent teacher, and for 20 years Vice Principal of Charlotte Hall, m., in Dec. 1847, his cousin, Sarah Ann Thompson.

RACHEL ANN BRISCOE, dau. of Philip and Maria Thompson Briscoe, m. Albert Young, and had child., viz., Robert Alexander,—Lucy Briscoe,—Evelina,—Susan Maria,—Albert, and Rachel Young.

HON. JAMES THOMPSON BRISCOE, son of Philip and Maria Thompson Briscoe, several times in the Legislature and a Senator of Maryland, m. Anna Maria Parran, and had child., viz., John Parran,—Philip,—James Thompson, and William Christian Briscoe.

GUSTAVUS BROWN BRISCOE, son of Philip and Maria Thompson Briscoe, m. Elizabeth Sasscer, and had child., viz., Henry St. James Linden, and Fannie Briscoe.

EDWARD TAYLOE BRISCOE, son of Philip and Maria Thompson Briscoe, a Professor at Charlotte Hall, m., 21st Oct. 1873, Sallie Ferguson Vaughan, and had a dau., Maria Briscoe. Mrs. Sallie Ferguson Vaughan Briscoe is the dau. of John Merriwether Vaughan and his wife, Rebecca Pocahontas Ferguson, the dau. of James Boswell Ferguson and his wife, Sallie Gay. Sallie Gay was the dau. of William Gay, who was a son of Dr. William Gay and his wife, Elizabeth Bolling. Elizabeth Bolling was the dau. of Col. John Bolling and Mary Kennon. Col. John Bolling was the only son of Jane Rolfe and Col. Robert Bolling, m. in 1675. Jane Rolfe was the only child of Thomas Rolfe and his wife, Jane Poyers, of England, and Thomas Rolfe was the only child of

John Rolfe and his wife, POCAHONTAS, called also MATOA, who were m. "about the 1st of April," A. D. 1613.

ELIZABETH ELLEN CECILIA BRISCOE, dau. of Philip and Maria Thompson Briscoe, m., 19th Feb'y 1869, Dr. John Allen Billingsley, and had child., viz., Philip Briscoe,—Marie Alice,—Jennie Reeder, and Wm. Thomas Billingsley.

DR. JOHN HANSON BRISCOE, son of Dr. John Hanson Briscoe and Elizabeth Attaway Bond, served as Captain in Gen. Steuart's Regiment during the war of 1812–14, was Judge of the Orphans' Court in St. Mary's County, and also in Baltimore City. He was appointed Naval Officer by President Pierce, and held that position at the time of his death, in 1853. He m., 23rd May 1823, Mary Key, and left a dau., Sophia Key Briscoe.

HANSON BRISCOE, son of Philip and Chloe Hanson Briscoe, m. Miss Jordan, sister of Justinian Jordan, and had child., viz., Charles Briscoe, who emigrated to Kentucky,—Elizabeth Briscoe, who m. Mr. Shanks,—Mary Briscoe, who m. Mr. Cressap, of Cumberland,—Harriet Briscoe, who m. Mr. Pigman, of Cumberland,—Maria Briscoe, who m. Mr. Cressap, of Cumberland,—and Nancy Briscoe.

ELIZA STORER BRISCOE, dau. of Philip and Chloe Hanson Briscoe, m. Barnet Barber, and had child., viz., Dr. Philip Barber, who m. Miss Yates, of Charles County,—Jennet Barber, who m. Thomas Marshall, of Prince George's County,—Chloe Barber,—Betsey Barber, and Rebecca Barber, who m. 1st Richard Bond, and 2dly, her cousin William Briscoe, son of John and Mary Hanson Briscoe.

MARY HANSON, dau. of Robert Hanson, m. John Briscoe, of Charles County, a brother of Philip Briscoe, of St. Mary's County, and had child., viz., John,—Samuel, and Eleanor Briscoe.

JOHN BRISCOE, son of John and Mary Hanson Briscoe, m. Jane Llewelyn (Mrs. Dent), and had child., viz., Llewelyn Briscoe,—Eleanor Buchanan Briscoe, who m. her cousin Thomas Briscoe,—Mary Eden Briscoe, who m. Peter Carnes,—Caroline Briscoe, who m. James Shemwell,—William Briscoe, who m. 1st Miss Barber, of St. Mary's County, 2dly Miss Harris, of Frederick,—and Charles L. Briscoe, who m. Miss Lee.

SAMUEL BRISCOE, son of John and Mary Hanson Briscoe. m. Miss Dent, of Charles County, and had child., viz., William Briscoe, who m. his cousin, Sarah Stone, a niece of Judge Michael Jenifer Stone,—Grace Briscoe,—Nancy Briscoe, who

m. John Robertson, of Scotland,—Judah Briscoe, who m. William Bayne, of Prince George's County,—Mary Hanson Briscoe, who m. Judge Michael Jenifer Stone (see STONE),—and Eleanor Briscoe.

ELEANOR BRISCOE, dau. of John and Mary Hanson Briscoe, m. James Buchanan, of Scotland, and d. *sine prole*.

SEC. 67, G. DR. DANIEL JENIFER, m. the eldest dau. of Samuel and Elizabeth Hanson, and had child., viz., Daniel Jenifer,—Daniel of St. Thomas Jenifer, who signed the Constitution of the United States, 28th April 1788, and Elizabeth Jenifer, who m. David Stone (see STONE).

DANIEL JENIFER, son of Dr. Daniel Jenifer, m. Elizabeth Hanson, dau. of Judge Walter Hanson, and had child., viz., Dr. Walter Hanson, b. 1751, d. 1785, *sine prole*,—Daniel of St. Thomas, d. unm., and Doctor Daniel Jenifer, b. 1756, d. 1809. Daniel Jenifer was b. 1727, d. 1795. His wife, Elizabeth Hanson Jenifer, d. Nov. 1757, aged 25 years.

DOCTOR DANIEL JENIFER, son of Daniel Jenifer and Elizabeth Hanson, m. 25th Jan'y 1785, Sarah Craik, dau. of Dr. James and Mariamne Craik, and had child., viz., Betty, b. 1785, d. 1809, unm.,—Elizabeth, b. 1787, d. an infant,—Ann, b. 1788 (who m. John B. Norris, and had a dau., and d. 1814),—Daniel of St. Thomas, b. 1789, d. 1822, *sine prole*,—Daniel, b. 15th April 1791, d. 18th Dec. 1855,—Walter Hanson, b. 1792, d. 1832 (who m. Helen Patton, dau. of James Patton, and had three daus., m., and settled in Louisiana, and Mariamne Jenifer, b. 1797, who m. George Forbes, and d. 1818, *sine prole*.

COL. DANIEL JENIFER, son of Doctor Daniel Jenifer and Sarah Craik, was a member of Congress in 1831–1833, and 1835–1841, and Minister to Austria, during the administration of Harrison and Tyler. He m. Eliza Trippe Campbell, dau. of John Campbell, of Charles county, and had child., viz., John Campbell, b. 1813, d. 1846, *sine prole*,—Daniel of St. Thomas, b. 1814, d. 1843, *sine prole*,—Ann Ophelia (who m. William S. Triplett, of Richmond, Va., and had four child.),—Marion Eliza (who m. William S. Barton, of Virginia, and had four child.),—Col. Walter Hanson, now of Baltimore, lately an officer in the service of the Khedive of Egypt, formerly an officer in the U. S. army, and during the late war distinguished in the Confederate States Army,—James Craik, b. 1825, m. a dau. of William Tayloe, and d. 1868, *sine prole*,—Mariamne (who m. Seth Barton, of Virginia, and had two sons), and Daniel Jenifer.

DANIEL JENIFER, son of Col. Daniel Jenifer and Eliza Trippe Campbell, m. Mary E., dau. of Dr. Thos. C. Risteau, of Baltimore county, and had child., viz., Ann Courtnay, b. 1849, d. 1867,—Eliza Trippe, who m. John Hanson Mitchell, of Charles county, and has four child.,—Mary Risteau, who m. Hugh Mitchell, of Charles county,—Thomas Risteau,—Marion,—Bettie,—Daniel,—Walter Hanson, b. in 1861, d. 1862,—John B. Morris,—Emily Barton, b. in 1864, d. 1867, —Courtnay, b. in 1867, d., and Florence Campbell Jenifer.

It is observed that none but those named Daniel left male descendants.

SEC. 67, H. SAMUEL HANSON, of Green Hill, son of Samuel and Elizabeth Hanson, was noted for his patriotism, and "it is related of him that he presented General Washington 800 pounds sterling silver to cover the bare feet of his soldiers with shoes."

WILLIAM HANSON, son of Samuel and Elizabeth Hanson, was "Examiner General of Maryland," *see Genealogical Record of the Family of Thomas, compiled from papers in possession of Dr. J. Hanson Thomas, by Douglas H. Thomas, Baltimore*, 1875.

JOHN HANSON, of Mulberry Grove, son of Samuel and Elizabeth Hanson, was a very remarkable and distinguished man. Of his early life but little is known beyond a few incidents, which displayed great decision of character and moral intrepidity at a time when men's hearts were quaking with apprehension. "In the early part of the Revolutionary war, some high-toned and decided resolutions were proposed in the House of Delegates of which he was a member; and when the question was put there was an awful pause, members hesitating to stake their heads and fortunes by any hasty or overt act: then, at the critical moment, John Hanson rose and said, 'Mr. President, these resolutions ought to pass, and it is high time.' With these words he sat down, and the resolutions were passed amidst much patriotic enthusiasm."

I am permitted to quote the following interesting and carefully written memoir:

"John Hanson was born in Charles Co., Maryland in 1715. "He represented his native county in the House of Delegates "every session, with few exceptions, from 1757 to 1773, when "he removed to Frederick Co., which he likewise represented "till 1781. He bore an active and prominent part in opposi- "tion to the arbitrary Acts of Parliament, and as early as "22d June 1769, he, with others, signed the Non-Importation

"Agreement of Maryland. On the 20th June 1774, he was "elected Chairman of a meeting held in Frederick Co., when "resolutions were adopted 'to stop' all exports from and im-"ports to Great Britain and the West Indies, until the Acts "of Parliament blockading the Port of Boston were repealed.

"John Hanson was elected Chairman of the Committee of "Observation for Frederick County upon its formation, Sept. "14th, 1775, and continued to hold that position until the "formation of the State Government. He filled positions on "various Committees, including the Committee for Licensing "Suits, a Committee authorized by the Convention of the "Province, and was also on the Committee of Correspond-"ence, as well as on one for building a Jail (the 'Barracks') "for prisoners of war, large numbers of whom were constantly "delivered at Frederick for safe-keeping. It was during his "Chairmanship that Cameron, Smith and Conolly, partici-"pators in the Dunmore-White Eyes conspiracy, were appre-"hended in Frederick County. He was appointed by the "Convention of Maryland to establish a gun-lock factory at "Frederick, and was commissioned Treasurer of the County, "21st June 1775.

"He, with Jas. Lloyd Chamberlaine, Benjamin Rumsey and "Thomas Contee, were appointed Commissioners by the Con-"vention of Maryland, Oct. 9th 1776, 'to appoint officers "and to encourage the re-enlistment of Maryland Militia and "regular troops, whose terms of service in the Continental "army were about expiring.'

"John Hanson was elected to the Continental Congress and "presented his credentials 22d Feb'y 1781, was elected Presi-"dent, Nov. 5th following, which position he filled for one "year with distinguished credit to himself and to the marked "satisfactiou of that body, receiving the thanks of Congress "Nov. 4th 1782. General Washington, upon his return to "Philadelphia, after the surrender of Lord Cornwallis, was "received by Congress, and welcomed in a congratulatory "address by President Hanson. John Hanson and Daniel "Carroll, under instructions from the Legislature, signed the "Articles of Confederation, on the part of the State of Mary-"land, March 1st 1781. He was a man of great moral intre-"pidity and decision of character, and but few men, even in "the exciting times of the Revolution, and prior thereto, "enjoyed in a greater degree the confidence of the community, "as is fully evinced by the fact that he was elevated by his "countrymen to the very highest and most responsible offices,

" and was in the service of the State almost without intermis-
" sion from 1757 to 1782.

"He was a member of the Protestant Episcopal Church, " and was very zealous in its interests. He m. Miss Jane " Contee, dau. of Alexander Contee, and was the father of " Alexander Contee Hanson, Chancellor of Maryland.

"He d. Nov. 22d 1783, aged 68, at Oxen Hill, Prince " George's county, while on a visit to his nephew, Thomas " Hanson."

The above memoir was delivered at Independence Hall, Philadelphia, the 1st of July 1876, by Douglas H. Thomas, at the request of the "Committee on the Restoration of Independence Hall, Col. Frank M. Etting, chairman."

Mr. Thomas was a member of the "Centennial State Board of Maryland," appointed by the "United States Centennial Commission."

The Centennial State Board of Maryland consisted of the following:

REV. JOHN G. MORRIS, COL. J. THOMAS SCHARFF, COL. GEORGE A. HANSON, DOUGLAS H. THOMAS, and WILLIAM H. CORNER.

JOHN HANSON, of Mulberry Grove, son of Samuel and Elizabeth Hanson, m. Jane Contee, and had child., viz., Catharine Contee Hanson, b. 16th Nov. 1744 (who m. Philip Alexander, Attorney at Law, the owner of Alexander's Island, near Alexandria, Va., and d. *sine prole*),—Jane Contee Hanson, b. 23d Feb'y 1747, d. 17th June 1781,—Alexander Contee Hanson, b. 22d Oct. 1749, d. in 1806,—Elizabeth Hanson, b. 9th Dec. 1751, d. 12th Oct. 1753,—John Hanson, b. 18th March 1753, d. 6th March 1760,—Samuel Hanson, b. 25th Aug. 1756, who studied medicine with Dr. Philip Thomas, and served as surgeon of Gen. Washington's Life Guards, and d. 29th June 1781,—Peter Contee Hanson, b. 9th Dec. 1758, who, at the age of 19 was lieutenant in the 1st Battalion of Maryland Infantry, Major Otho H. Williams commanding, was mortally wounded while bravely fighting at Fort Washington, and d. a few days after, in November 1776,—and Grace Hanson, b. 19th Sept. 1762, and d. 10th Aug. 1763.

"MRS. JANE CONTEE HANSON d. 21st Feb'y 1812, in the 85th year of her age, being 84 in the September preceding."

She was the dau. of Alexander Contee, who, with his uncle, John Contee, emigrated to Maryland, and settled in Prince George's county. Alexander Contee, baptized "ye 22d day of April 1693," was the son of Peter and Catharine Contee, who lived at Barnstable, Devonshire, England. The family came originally from Rochelle, France, and, being Protestants, emigrated to England during the reign of Louis XIV. "Adolphe de Comtee was High Sheriffe of London and Middlesex in 1643."

The motto under his "Arms" in Guild Hall, London, is "Pour Dieu et mon Roi." The following is a definition of the Contee arms:

ARMS:—*Gules and azure, a chevron, ermine between three wolves passant, or,*

A relic of the exquisite taste, wealth, refinement and culture of the family, viz., a tea service of silver, bearing the family arms and the Tower of London Stamp, for the year 1620, is now possessed in beautiful preservation by a descendant, Dr. John Hanson Thomas, of Baltimore.

ALEXANDER CONTEE HANSON, son of John Hanson and Jane Contee, was in early life Assistant Private Secretary to General Washington. He was one of the first Judges of the General Court of Maryland, under the Constitution of 1776. In 1789 he was appointed Chancellor of Maryland, and held that position until his death, in 1806. At the request of the Legislature, he compiled the Laws of the State. The volume is known as "Hanson's Laws." In 1789 he was appointed to digest a Testamentary System for Maryland. He was offered the appointment of United States District Judge, by General Washington, but declined it. Chancellor Hanson was a writer of great force and clearness. A few of his productions are carefully preserved by the Maryland Historical Society, under the name of "Hanson Pamphlets." He m. Rebecca Howard, of Annapolis, and had child., viz., Charles Wallace Hanson,—Alexander Contee Hanson, and a dau. who m. Thomas Peabody Grosvenor, a distinguished Member of Congress from New York, who d. in 1815. She d. in 1817.

JUDGE CHARLES WALLACE HANSON, son of Chancellor Alexander Contee Hanson and Rebecca Howard, m. Rebecca Ridgely, of Hampton, the eldest dau. of Hon. Charles Ridgely, who was Governor of Maryland from 1815 to 1818. He d. 8th Dec. 1853, *sine prole.*

HON. ALEXANDER CONTEE HANSON, son of Chancellor Alexander Contee Hanson and Rebecca Howard, was United States Senator 1816–1819. I extract the following from the letter before quoted from Col. Taylor to Hon. Frederick Stone:

"*Alexander Contee Hanson* was a man of great notoriety "and fame in his time. He like all his family and name,

" with the exception before mentioned, was a staunch and " unflinching Federalist of the George Washington and Alex- " ander Hamilton school, and was editor and proprietor of the " 'Federal Republican,' the leading Federal paper in the State " if not in the United States. He was also a member of Con- " gress, when no nobody and *upstart* could be such, was of the " indomitable and unconquerable energy, full of talent, and " I suppose, as brave a man as any that ever belonged to the " race of man, at any time or anywhere. He was mobbed by " the Democrats, in Baltimore, just before the war of 1812, " and his press and types destroyed, as is in the personal recol- " lection of persons still living. He defended himself and " premises with the most reckless and undaunted bravery, and " shot dead the first man (a Dr. Gales) of the mob that entered " his door, and to this same courage and firmness, alone, he owed " his life, when afterwards with a few friends, including the two " Revolutionary Generals, Lingan and 'Light-Horse' Harry " Lee, he surrendered to the Democratic authorities of the " city, upon an assurance and promise of protection, was " locked up in a jail, and then basely and treacherously aban- " doned in the night to the wild fury of the cowardly and " vindictive mob that first assailed him. He soon however " got safe to the old home of his family, and with his head " still bound up and the bloody stains of his recent wounds " visible, addressed a large crowd in Port Tobacco, commenc- " ing with, 'In Charles county now rest the bones of my " ancestors,' &c. The excitement in the almost unanimous old " Federal county, where his name and family had for so many " years played such prominent parts, was almost inconceiv- " able, and fifty of the leading men, it was said, armed them- " selves as well as they could, and offered, or did actually go " on horseback to defend him from a threatened and appre- " hended attack of the same Baltimore mob at Annapolis. I " am not old enough to remember these things, though I think " I have a dreamy indistinct recollection of some of them, but " I have learned what is here written, mainly, from my father, " who was what was called '*a very bitter Federalist*,' indeed. " This same *Hanson*, whilst in Congress, fought a duel with an " officer of the United States Navy (Capt. Charles Gordon), " when, with marvellous coolness and nonchalance, he badly " wounded his antagonist, hitting him exactly where he said " he would."

HON. ALEXANDER CONTEE HANSON m. Priscilla Dorsey and had several child., only one of whom survives, Charles

Grosvenor Hanson, who m. 16th Jan'y 1840, Annie Maria Worthington (who was b. 17th Sept. 1821, and d. 11th March 1873, the dau. of T. H. Worthington, of Baltimore county), and had child., viz., Charles Contee, b. 2d Nov. 1840, d. 28th May 1857,—Mary Worthington, b. 12th Jan'y 1842, d. 23d Sept. 1863,—John Worthington,—Priscilla,—Charles Edward,—Murray,—Samuel Contee,—Grosvenor,—Nannie, —Florence Contee, and Alice and Bessie Hanson, twins, who d. in infancy.

JOHN WORTHINGTON HANSON, son of Charles Grosvenor Hanson and Annie Maria Worthington, m. 1st June 1876, Alice A. Armistead, dau. of the late Anderson H. Armistead, of Baltimore.

SEC. 67, I. JANE CONTEE HANSON, dau. of President John Hanson and Jane Contee, m. 18th Feb'y 1773, Dr. Philip Thomas, and had child., viz., James Thomas, b. in August 1774, d. an infant,—Catharine Hanson, b. 15th Oct. 1775,—Rebecca Bellicum Thomas, b. 8th Feb'y 1777, and John Hanson Thomas, b. 16th May 1779. Mrs. Jane Contee Hanson Thomas, b. in Feb. 1747, in Charles county, d. 17th of June 1781.

DOCTOR PHILIP THOMAS was b. near Chestertown, 11th June 1747, and "commenced the practice of Physic and Surgery in Fredericktown, 1st Aug. 1769, after studying four years under Dr. Thomas Vandyke." He also attended the professional lectures, and the hospital and a bettering house in Philadelphia, under Professors Bond, Shippen and Morgan, "and, at the same time, Dr. Smith's Lectures on Natural and Experimental Philosophy, and matriculated in the college." See a memoir of his family, by Dr. Philip Thomas, in the "*Genealogical Record*," *&c.*, by Douglas H. Thomas.

He was a very prominent and active citizen. He was Chairman of the Committee of Safety for Frederick County during the Revolution, and was one of the Presidential Electors who voted for General Washington when first made President. He was the first President of the Medical Society of Maryland. He died 25th of April 1815. He was the son of James Thomas and Elizabeth Bellicum, of Kent. James Thomas was b. in Kent, the son of James Thomas and Elizabeth Hacket, who were m. about the year 1710. The last named James Thomas was a native of Wales or West England. Elizabeth Bellicum was a sister of Christopher Bellicum, a prominent Vestryman of Shrewsbury Parish.

CATHARINE HANSON THOMAS, dau. of Dr. Philip Thomas

and Jane Contee Hanson, m. Dr. Ashton Alexander, and had child., viz., Ashton,—George, who m. Miss Levering, and Elizabeth Ashton Alexander.

REBECCA BELLICUM THOMAS, dau. of Dr. Philip and Jane Contee Hanson, m. Judge Alexander Contee Magruder, and had child., viz., Rebecca Thomas Magruder, who m. Major Scott, U. S. A.,—Jane Magruder, who m. Mr. Byias,—John Hanson Thomas Magruder, State Librarian at Annapolis, and Philip Magruder.

HON. JOHN HANSON THOMAS, son of Dr. Philip Thomas and Jane Contee Hanson, m. 5th of Oct. 1809, Mary Isham Colston, and had child., viz., Philip Hanson, b, 10th Sept. 1810, d. 11th Nov. 1821,—Rawleigh Colston, b. 12th Aug. 1812, d. 16th June 1826, and Charles Edward Thomas, b. 23d of Sept. 1813, whose name was changed by Act of Assembly to that of his father, John Hanson Thomas. Hon. John Hanson Thomas possessed brilliant talent, and was gifted with eloquence of high order. He was Chairman of the Committee of Defence in 1812–14. In 1814 he was a leading member of the Maryland Legislature. "He was the person selected by the Federalists of Maryland, who were in the ascendency, to be elected to the United States Senate, but dying before the time, Alexander Contee Hanson, his cousin, was elected. He d. May 2d 1815, being exactly one week after the death of his father, from whom he contracted the same disease whilst faithfully attending him during his sickness. They are both buried in Frederick." See "*Genealogical Record*," *&c.*, by D. H. Thomas.

MRS. MARY ISHAM COLSTON THOMAS was descended through a long line of knightly ancestors, from Robert de Colston, of Colston Hall, in the County of Lincoln, who was living at the time of the Conquest. William Colston, of Bristol, England, amassed an immense fortune in the Spanish and Levantine trade, and d., leaving child., viz., Edward Colston, his heir, the great Philanthrophist, and William Colston, who emigrated to America and became the Clerk of Rappahannock county, Va., and left a son, William Colston, who had two sons, viz., William and Charles Colston. Charles Colston m. Susan Traverse, and had child., Traverse, and Susanna Colston, who m. Mr. Eustice, and d. *sine prole*.

TRAVERSE COLSTON, son of Charles and Susan Traverse Colston m. twice. His 1st wife was Alice Corbin Griffin, dau. of Col. Thomas Griffin, of Richmond county, Va., and had child., viz., Charles, who m. Ann Fauntleroy, and Elizabeth

Griffin Colston, who m. Col. William Peachy. His 2d wife was Mrs. Susanna Opie Kenner, and had child., viz., Traverse, who d. young,—William (who m. Lucy Carter, dau. of Col. Landon Carter, of Sabine Hall, and had child., viz., William, —Traverse,—Elizabeth and Susanna),—Rawleigh, and Samuel Colston, who was a Captain in the Revolutionary Army, and d. unm.

RAWLEIGH COLSTON, of Honeywood, son of Traverse Colston and his 2d wife Susanna Opie Kenner, m. Elizabeth Marshall, a sister of Chief Justice John Marshall, the dau. of Col. Thomas Marshall and Mary Keith, and had child., viz., Edward (who m. 1st, Jane Marshall, and 2dly Jane Brockenborough, and had child., viz., Elizabeth,—Jane,—Mary,—Rawleigh,—William, —Lucy,—Judith and Edward),—Susan (who m. B. Watkins Leigh, and had child., viz., William, who m. Mary White Colston, and Mary Susan, who m. Conway Robinson), Mary Isham (who m. John Hanson Thomas), Thomas Marshall (who m. Elizabeth Fisher, and had child., viz., Rawleigh, —Nancy and Elizabeth),—Rawleigh Traverse (who m. Mrs. Kellerman, the widow of the Duke Valmey, one of Napoleon's Marshals),—Lucy Ann, and John James Marshall Colston.

SEC. 67. J. MRS. ELIZABETH MARSHALL COLSTON was the granddau. of John Marshall, who came from Wales, and settled in Westmoreland county, Va., who m. Miss Markham, and had 9 child., of whom Col. Thomas Marshall was the eldest.

COL. THOMAS MARSHALL, eldest son of John Marshall, m. Mary Keith, dau. of a clergyman, from Scotland, and his wife, formerly a Miss Randolph, of James River. Col. Thomas Marshall and Mary Keith had 15 child., viz., John (the Chief Justice),—Thomas,—James,—William,—Charles, —Alexander,—Lewis,—Elizabeth (who m. Rawleigh Colston, of Honeywood),—Anna Maria,—Judith,—Lucy,—Susan,— Charlotte,—Jane, and Nancy, all of whom m.

CHIEF JUSTICE JOHN MARSHALL, eldest son of Col. Thomas Marshall and Mary Keith, m. 3d January 1783, Mary Willis Ambler, the 2d dau. of Jacquilin Ambler, (Treasurer of Virginia, who was the 3d son of Richard Ambler, who came from England to Yorktown, and had child., viz., Thomas,—Jacquilin Ambler,—Mary,—John),— James Keith, and Edward Carrington Marshall, the youngest, and now (6th June, 1876) the only surviving child of the great Chief Justice.

THOMAS MARSHALL, eldest son of Chief Justice John

Marshall and Mary Willis Ambler, m. in 1810, Margaret Wadrop Lewis, and had child., viz., John,—Agnes Harwood, —Mary,—Fielding Lewis,—Ann Lewis,—Margaret Lewis, and Thomas Marshall.

FIELDING LEWIS MARSHALL, son of Thomas Marshall and Margaret Wadrop Lewis, m. 10th April 1843, Rebecca Francis Coke, and had child., viz., Richard Coke,—Margaret Lewis,—Mary Willing Byrd,—Susan Lewis,—Thomas,—Evelyn Byrd,—Fielding Lewis,—Rebecca Francis,—Agnes Harwood, and Eleanor Warner Marshall.

RICHARD COKE MARSHALL, eldest son of Fielding Lewis and Rebecca Francis Coke, m. 21st Nov. 1865, Mary Catharine Wilson, a sister of Lieutenant St. Julien Wilson, of the Confederate Army, who was slain in battle 31st July 1864, and the dau. of Samuel M. Wilson and Mira Rosanna Barraud, dau. of Dr. Daniel Cary and Mary Lawson Barraud, of Norfolk, Va. (see BARRAUD), and had child., viz., Mira St. Julien,—Rebecca Coke,—Susan Lewis,—Samuel Wilson, and Kate Marshall, d.

DR. JOHN HANSON THOMAS, son of John Hanson Thomas and Mary Colston, was b. in Frederick, Maryland, and raised in Virginia. He came to Baltimore 23d of September 1834, and commenced the study of medicine in Dr. Alexander's office. He was appointed one of the resident students of the Baltimore Infirmary, was graduated in March 1836, and practiced medicine a short time. "He has been identified with the interests of the city of Baltimore since his removal thereto. He was a member of the City Council, State Legislature, and President of the Farmers' and Merchants' Bank for 35 years, besides filling other positions of trust and honor, including directorship in Insurance Companies, and President of the Academy of Music.

"During the war 1861-64, when a member of the Legislature, he with ten others were arrested on 12th September 1861, and confined in various United States forts for six months."

DR. JOHN HANSON THOMAS, m. 15th of November 1837, Annie Campbell Gordon, dau. of Basil and Anna Campbell Gordon, of Falmouth, Virginia, and had child., viz., Basil Gordon Thomas,—John Hanson Thomas,—Raleigh Colston Thomas,—Douglas Hamilton Thomas,—Nannie Gordon Thomas,—Mary Randolph Thomas, and John Marshall Thomas.

"Mrs. John Hanson Thomas' family on the paternal side, Gordon, were from Scotland.

"The first of whom we have ancestral record is *Samuel Gordon*, who was b. in 1656. He m. Margaret McKinnell; they lived at "Stockerton" in the Parish of Kirkcudbright, Scotland. He was the first of the name on Stockerton farm, where he d. 15th April 1732, aged 76. It is known that he was a respectable farmer, and was in some way related to the families of Lord Kenmuir and the Gordons of Greenlaw, and was visited by both families, especially by Sir Alexander and Lady Gordon, of Greenlaw.

"John Gordon, son of Samuel, m. Miss Grace Newall; he d. August 23d 1738, aged 56 years.

"Samuel Gordon, the first of Lochdongan, son of John, m. Nicholas Brown, dau. of John Brown, of Craigen Callie, and Margaret McClamrock, of Craigen Bay. Mrs. Nicholas Brown Gordon was from the Carsluth family; her grandfather and uncle were ministers in the Parish of Kirkinabrook.

"Samuel Gordon and his wife, Nicholas Brown Gordon, of Lochdongan, had a large family, many of whom were born at 'Stockerton' before their removal to 'Lochdongan.' One dau. m. Mr. Herron, of Kegton, and d. leaving one son, John; the other dau. m. John Bell, of Gribdae, and d. June 3d, 1826, at the age of 77. Samuel Gordon d. Feb'y 22d 1799 and his wife Nov. 18, 1795, aged 71. Their oldest son, John, m. Miss Brown, and at his father's death inherited the two "Lochdongans.

"Three younger sons, Samuel Bazil and Alexander migrated to Virginia, where they engaged in mercantile business. Alexander afterwards returned to Scotland, and d. in the year 1819. Samuel Gordon m. Susannah Knox,—Bazil Gordon m. her sister, Annie Campbell Knox, and had child., viz., Douglas Hamilton,—Bazil Brown,—Annie Campbell,—Susan, and others who d. young.

"The family of Mrs. John Hanson Thomas, on the maternal side Knox, were from Scotland, the first of whom that came to this country were William Knox, Robert and John; their mother's name was Janet Somerville, father's name not remembered. Annie Knox, sister of the immigrants, m. Mr. Campbell, and lived and d. in Scotland.

"John Knox lived a bachelor at 'Orchard Fields,' Stafford county, Va., where he was murdered by his slaves, whom he had promised to set free by his Will, some 150 in number, and which not being made at the time of his death they were inherited by his brother William.

"Robert Knox settled in Maryland, where he m. and had child., but all traces of them are lost.

"The Knoxes owned large landed property in Virginia, consisting of 'Windsor Lodge,' Culpepper county; 'Berry Hill,' Stafford county; 'Orchard Fields,' Stafford county; 'Bellmont,' same county, where most of the old members of the family are buried; 'Smith's Mount,' and 'Vancluse' in Westmoreland county.

"William Knox, of 'Windsor Lodge,' in 1766 m. Susannah, only dau. of Thomas Fitzhugh, Sr., of 'Boscobel,' Stafford county; her mother's name was Sarah Stuart, of King George county, and a descendant of the Royal Stuarts.

"William and Susannah Knox had child., viz., Dr. Thos. Fitzhugh,—Susannah Fitzhugh,—Agnes,—Annie Campbell,—Jessie,—Sarah Stuart,—Caroline,—William A., and John Somerville Knox.

"Dr. Thomas Fitzhugh Knox m. Mary Reiley, dau. of James Reiley, of Winchester, and Miss McBryde, of Delaware; they had child., viz., Henry Knox,—Ann Somerville,—Thomas Fitzhugh,—William Henry, and James McBryde.

"Susannah Knox m. Samuel Gordon of 'Kenmuir,' and d. 10th July 1869, aged 94; they had child.,—William Knox,—Samuel,—Alexander,—John,—Bazil,—Wellington,—Mary, wife of Dr. John H. Wallace, of Fredericksburg,—Agnes, wife of C. Hughes Armistead, of Baltimore, and Susan, widow of Mr. Ryan, of Baltimore. Agnes Knox m. Samuel Gordon, nephew of Samuel and Bazil Gordon, they lived at the old place, 'Lochdongan' for some time, but afterwards settled near Falmouth, Virginia. They had child., John,—Samuel,—William,—Bazil, and Marian, who m. Mr. Edmund Taylor, of Caroline county. Bazil was a very celebrated engineer, and built the High Bridge near Farmville, Virginia. He was afterwards killed in St. Louis, Mo., by two deserters from the United States fort, under the supposition that he had money, large sums of which he had been collecting for several weeks, and which he had sent away the night before his death; the murderers were afterwards hanged."

"Annie Campbell Knox m. Bazil Gordon, of Falmouth, and had child., as already stated.

"Jessie Knox m. William Edward Voss, and lived in Rappahannock county, Virginia. They had child.,—William,—Robert,—Benjamin Franklin, and Susan, who m. Mr. Richard Norris, of Baltimore.

"Sarah Stuart Knox and Caroline d. unm. William

A. Knox m. Sarah Alexander, and had child.,—Agnes Gordon,—William,—Henry,—Mary Eliza,—Jessie,—Bolivar, and Annie Bell Knox. Agnes Gordon m. Mr. James T. Soutter, who by right of birth was heir of the Marquisate and Earldom of Annandale of Scotland, and, although frequently pressed by lawyers from Temple Bar to apply for his rights, steadfastly refused.

"John Somerville Knox m. Elizabeth Selden and had child.,—Churchill,—Annie,—John,—Janet, and Robert.

"Douglas Hamilton Gordon, son of Bazil and Annie Campbell Gordon, m. Mary Ellen Clarke, dau. of Colin Clarke, of Glouchester, Virginia, and had a dau. Ellen D. Gordon.

"His 2d wife was Ann Eliza, dau. of J. Hampden Pleasants, of Richmond, and have child., now living, Bazil,—Douglas Hamilton,—Annie Campbell,—Mary, and Rose Stanly Gordon.

"Bazil Brown Gordon, son of Bazil and Annie Campbell Gordon, m. Elizabeth Bolling Skipwith, dau. of Henry Skipwith, April 24th, 1840, had child., Bazil F., b. 10th Feb'y 1841, and Henry Skipwith, b. October 25, 1844. Bazil B. Gordon, d. Oct. 9th 1846, and his son Bazil F., March 9th, 1866. Henry Skipwith Gordon, m. Mary T. Wheeler, of Washington, January 9th 1866, and have child., now living,—Bazil and Henry Skipwith."—See "*Genealogical Record*," by Douglas H. Thomas.

John Hanson Thomas, Jr., son of Dr. John Hanson Thomas and Annie Campbell Gordon, m. Mary Howard Beirne, dau. of Hon. George P. Beirne, of Huntsville, Alabama.

Mrs. Mary Howard Beirne Thomas d. 7th October 1867, leaving a son, Howard Beirne Thomas.

Raleigh Colston Thomas, son of Dr. John Hanson Thomas and Annie Campbell Gordon, m. 25th of Nov. 1868, Mary McDonald, dau. of William McDonald, of "Guilford," Baltimore County, and had child., viz., Mary McDonald Thomas, and Raleigh Colston Thomas.

Douglas Hamilton Thomas, son of Dr. John Hanson Thomas and Annie Campbell Gordon, m. 25th of Jan'y 1870, Alice Lee Whitridge, dau. of Dr. John and Catharine C. Whitridge, and had child., viz., Douglas Hamilton Thomas, and John Hanson Thomas.

Mary Randolph Thomas, dau. of Dr. John Hanson Thomas, and Annie Campbell Gordon, m. 21st of April 1870, Gen. John Carroll (sometimes called Gen. John N. Carroll), of "The Caves," a son of John Henry Carroll and Matilda Hol-

Thomas.

lingsworth, and had child., viz., John Nicholas Carroll and Charles Carroll. (See CARROLL.)

SEC. 67. K. Among the leading and most prominent citizens of Maryland during the Revolution, were the three distinguished representatives of the antient Carroll Family, viz., CHARLES CARROLL, barrister,—CHARLES CARROLL, OF CARROLLTON, and REVEREND JOHN CARROLL, D. D., who were descended from Daniel Carroll and his wife, Dorothy, dau. of Kenedy and Margaret O'Bryon,—dau. of More Carroll of Ely and O'Neil, whose mother was the dau. of the Earl of Argyle in the Highlands of Scotland.

The origin of this family is veiled in the mists of remote antiquity, but enough is known to establish its identity through many generations and centuries.

The first authentic source and recognized authority of the present day we have of the Carroll family is that of Sir Bernard Burke, the compiler of the great "English Peerages," and by virtue of his office the "Ulster King of Arms," who says:

"Kean, third son of Olioll Olum, King of Munster in the third century, was ancestor of the great house of Carroll. His descendant, Cearbhal, gave the name of Carroll to his posterity. The territory of Ely comprised the present Barony of Lower Ormond, County Tipperary, with the Barony of Clonlisk and part of Ballybrit in the King's County, extending to the Sleive Bloom mountains on the borders of the Queen's County. The Carrolls, as Princes and Lords of Ely, were very powerful from the 12th to the 16th century.

"A pedigree contained in Keating's History commences with Noah, thence through many generations to Feniusa Farsa, King of Scythia, and first founder of the Universal Schools at the plain of Magh Senair, thence to the Lords of Gothia (Dragotha, Lord of Gothia), thence to Milesius, King of Spain, thence to Duach Donn Delta Droghadh, monarch of Ireland, A. M. 3912, thence to Carroll, from whom this ancient family took the name, thence through many generations to Daniel Carroll, King of Ely, who founded the famous Abbey of Mellifont in the county of Lowth A. D. 1142, the Abbey of Newry 1148, and Cnocksingan Abbey 1182—'he was a pious prince, and left a glorious character behind him'—thence through many generations to Carroll the fourth, who founded the fine Convent of Roscrea for the Franciscans or Gray Friars A. D. 1490. He m. the dau. of O'Dimpsy, Lord of Clanmallia, thence to Carroll the fifth, 'whose daus.

were all married to the prime nobility of the nation—one to the Lord Muskery, another to the great Earl of Desmond,' &c.

"The next Carroll m. Sara O'Bryen, dau. of the Earl of Thurmond and niece of the Lord Clare. The next Carroll m. the Earl of Meath's dau.; and now lastly comes Daniel Carroll, 'who m. Dorothy, dau. of Kenedy by Margaret O'Bryen, dau. of More Carroll of Ely and O'Neill, who had for mother the dau. of the Earl of Argile in the Highlands of Scotland.' 'This Daniel Carroll had twenty sons whom he presented in one troop of horse, all accoutred in habiliments of war, to the Earl of Ormond, together with all his interest for the service of King Charles the First. Most of these died in foreign service, having followed the hard fate of King Charles the Second.' From this Daniel's many sons is presumed to have sprung all the different branches of the house of Carroll.

"The next in descent, and eldest son, was Daniel Carroll, who had two sons, 1st Charles, and 2d John.

"Charles the 1st m. Clare Dunn, had two sons, Charles and John, and one dau. It was the *last* Charles who emigrated to America about the beginning of the eighteenth century, and settled at Annapolis, in Maryland—his brother John having been lost at sea.

"Charles Carroll m. Dorothy Blake, and was the father of Charles Carroll, afterward barrister-at-law, and of Mary Clare Carroll. Dorothy Blake was 'descended from an ancient family of that name in Hampshire, in England, and of the same family as Admiral Robert Blake,' whose silver is now in the Carroll family."

The Reverend John Carroll was born in Upper Marlborough, Maryland, in 1735, and was educated for the priesthood at the College of St. Omers, in France, and at Liege, in Belgium, where he was ordained in 1769. On the suppression of the Jesuits in France, he took refuge in England, and was employed by Lord Houston as the tutor of his son. In 1773, he was a professor at Bruges, but returned to England and resided with the family of the Earl of Arundel until the eve of the Revolution, when he returned to America to share the fortunes of his native State. He settled in Baltimore city, where he spent the remainder of his life. His reputation for piety, learning, eloquence, and patriotism was so widely extended that it was thought he might exercise great influence over the Roman Catholic population of Canada, and, therefore, in February 1776, at the request of the Continental Congress, he accompanied his cousin Charles Carroll, of Carrollton, Judge Samuel Chase, and Dr. Benjamin Franklin to Canada, on a mission from the united colonies, to solicit the co-operation of that province. In 1786, he was created Vicar-General of the Roman Catholic Church for the United States. On the 15th of August 1790, at Ludworth Castle, England, he was consecrated Bishop of the See of Baltimore. He remained for several years the only Roman Catholic Bishop in this country. His diocese embraced the whole of the thirteen States and all the territories. On the 7th of July 1806, he laid the corner-stone of the Cathedral in Baltimore. In the year 1803, he was elevated to the dignity of Archbishop, and discharged with fidelity his arduous and constantly increasing duties until the 3d of December 1815, when he died in the eighty-first year of his age.

Charles Carroll, of Carrollton, the grandson of Charles Carroll, the son of Daniel Carroll, of King's County, Ireland, was b. 20th Sept. 1737, the son of Charles Carroll and Elizabeth Brook. At the age of eight years he was sent to France to be educated. He remained six years at the College of English Jesuits, at St. Omers; one year at a College of French Jesuits, at Rheims; two years at the College of Louis Grand; one year at Bourges, to study civil law, and then returned to college at Paris. In 1757 he visited London, and commenced the study of law in the Temple. He returned to Maryland in 1764, and in June 1768, m. Mary Darnall, dau. of Henry Darnall, Jr. She was spoken of "as an agreeable young lady, endowed with every accomplishment necessary to render the connubial state happy." He achieved distinction among the ablest political writers of that day, and in a controversy with Daniel Dulany, he won a reputation for wisdom and solidity of reasoning which placed him in the front rank of patriots, and decided his career for life.

In December 1774, he was appointed one of the "Committee of Correspondence for this Province," and in the following year was elected one of the "Council of Safety." He was elected a delegate from Anne Arundel County to the Convention which met 7th Dec. 1775, at Annapolis, and adjourned 18th Jan'y 1776. In Feb'y 1776, with Dr. Benjamin Franklin, Judge Samuel Chase, and Dr. John Carroll, he was appointed a Commissioner to Canada to endeavor to induce the people of that province to coöperate in the struggle for independence. When the Commissioners returned from their unsuccessful mission, Congress was debating the propriety of a Declaration of Independence, and the situation was critical. The deputies from Maryland were bound by their instructions given by the Convention 12th Jan'y 1776, as follows: "We further instruct you that you do not, without the previous knowledge and approbation of the Convention of this Province, assent to any proposition to declare these colonies independent of Great Britain," and which instructions had been unanimously reiterated and confirmed 21st May 1776.

Judge Chase and Mr. Carroll were much disquieted by the emergency; apprehensive and anxious for the honor of their State, they hastened to their posts of duty.

The Convention of Maryland was in session. With burning eloquence, ably seconded by Thomas Johnson, they told their story, and pressed upon eager and willing ears the necessity of withdrawing the instructions. On the 28th of June 1776, it was unanimously resolved that the deputies from Maryland in Congress "be authorized and impowered to concur with the other united colonies, or a majority of them, in declaring the united colonies free and independent states."

On the 4th of July 1776, the following were elected deputies to represent Maryland in the Continental Congress: Matthew Tilghman, Thomas Johnson, William Paca, Samuel Chase, Thomas Stone, Charles Carroll, of Carrollton, and Robert Alexander. Two days afterwards, 6th July, Maryland solemnly declared her independence.

Mr. Carroll took his seat in Congress 18th July 1776, and on the 2d of Aug. 1776, signed to the Declaration of Independence his name, CHARLES CARROLL, of CARROLLTON—that being his usual signature, and the name he had been known by since his entrance into public life to distinguish him from his elder kinsman, CHARLES CARROLL, BARRISTER. He was made a member of the Board of War, and served in Congress until 10th Nov. 1776, with marked ability.

In December 1776 he was chosen a member of the first Senate of the State of Maryland; in 1777 was returned to Congress; in 1781 was re-elected to the Senate of Maryland, and in 1788 was elected United States Senator, in Congress. In 1791 he was returned to the Senate of Maryland, and again re-elected in 1796. In 1797 he was one of the commissioners appointed to settle the boundary line between Maryland and Virginia. He continued in the Senate of Maryland until 1801, when he retired from political life.

On the 23d of April 1827, he was elected a member of the first Board of Directors of the Baltimore and Ohio Railroad, and on the 4th of July 1828, laid the foundation-stone of that railroad. He continued to take a deep and lively interest in the progress and welfare of his native State until his death. He died on the 10th of Nov. 1832, in the 96th year of his age, the last surviving signer of the Declaration of Independence.

Mr. John H. B. Latrobe, in his very interesting and exhaustive memoir of Charles Carroll, of Carrollton, says, "In "1825, one of Mr. Carroll's granddaughters was married to "the Marquis of Wellesley, then Viceroy of Ireland; and it is "a singular circumstance, that one hundred and forty years "after the first emigration of her ancestors to America, this "lady should become vice-queen of the country from which "they fled, at the summit of a system which a more imme-"diate ancestor had risked everything to destroy; or, in the "energetic and poetical language of Bishop England, 'that "in the land from which his father's father fled in fear, his "daughter's daughter now reigns as Queen.' See *Biography of the Signers to the Declaration of Independence*, Vol VII, p. 259.

Charles Carroll, the grandfather of Charles Carroll, of Carrollton, was at one time a clerk in the office of Lord Powis, in the reign of James II, and came to America before the accession (1689) of William and Mary. In 1691 he was appointed in the place of Col. Henry Darnall, Judge and Register of the Land Office, and also agent and receiver of rents for Lord Baltimore. He was a Roman Catholic, but in 1718 was expressly exempted from any disqualification on account of his religion. He d. previous to the year 1747. His son, Charles Carroll, the father of Charles Carroll, of Carrollton, was b. in 1702, and d. in 1782.

Charles Carroll, of Carrollton, left three child., viz., Charles Carroll,—Elizabeth Carroll, who m. Richard Caton, and was the mother of Lady Wellesley, Duchess of Leeds, and Lady Stafford,—and Catharine Carroll, who m. General Robert Goodloe Harper. Richard Caton d. 19th May 1845, aged 82–83. Gen. Goodloe Harper, b. 1765, d. 14th Jan'y 1825.

Charles Carroll, eldest son of Charles Carroll, of Carrollton, m. in 1799, Harriet Chew, dau. of Hon. Benjamin Chew, Chief Justice of Pennsylvania, and had child., viz., Charles Carroll,—Mary Carroll, who m. Richard H. Bayard, —Louisa Carroll, who m. Mr. Jackson,—Harriet Carroll, who m. Hon. John Lee, and Elizabeth Carroll who m. Dr. Richard Tucker.

Charles Carroll, eldest son of Charles Carroll and Harriet Chew, b. in Baltimore, in July 1801, m. in October 1825, Mary Diggs Lee (a granddau. of Hon. Thomas Sim Lee, Governor of Maryland, in 1792-94), and had child., viz., Mary Carroll,—Charles Carroll,—Thomas Lee Carroll, who d. young,—Hon. John Lee Carroll,—Louisa Carroll,—Oswald Carroll, who d. young,—Albert Henry Carroll,—a 2d Thomas Lee Carroll,—Robert Goodloe Harper Carroll, and Helen Sophia Carroll.

Mary Carroll, eldest dau. of Charles Carroll and Mary Diggs Lee, m. in 1866, Dr. Acosta, and resides in Paris.

Charles Carroll, son of Charles Carroll and Mary Diggs Lee, m. in 1858, Caroline Thompson, of Staunton, Virginia.

Hon. John Lee Carroll, for many years a distinguished member of the Senate of Maryland, and, at present (1876), the Governor of the State, son of Charles Carroll and Mary Diggs Lee, m. 24th April 1856, Anita Phelps, dau. of Royal Phelps, a leading merchant of New York, and had child., viz., Charles Lee Carroll,—Mary Louisa Carroll,—Anita Carroll,—Royal Phelps Carroll,—Charles Carroll,—Albert Henry Carroll,—Irene Carroll,—John Lee Carroll, and Helen Carroll. Mrs. Anita Phelps Carroll d. 24th March 1873.

Louisa Carroll, dau. of Charles Carroll and Mary Diggs Lee, m. in 1858, George Cavendish Tayloe, of England, a grandson of Lord Waterpark, and had two sons and three daus.

Albert Henry Carroll, son of Charles Carroll and Mary Diggs Lee, m. 4th May 1858, Mary Cornelia Read, dau. of William George Read and Sophia Catharine Howard, a dau. of Col. John Eager Howard (see Howard), and had child., viz., Mary Sophia,—Mary Ellinor, and Agnes Carroll. Albert Henry Carroll joined the army of the Confederate States and was killed in a skirmish, 7th Sept. 1862, near Martinsburg, Va. Mrs. Mary Cornelia Carroll m. again, 25th June 1866, Col. James Fenner Lee, and had a dau., Mary Cornelia Lee.

Robert Goodloe Harper Carroll, son of Charles Carroll and Mary Diggs Lee, m. in 1863, Miss Thompson, of Virginia, who d. in 1864, and in 1872 he m. Mary D. Lee, of Frederick County, and had two sons.

Helen Carroll, dau. of Charles Carroll and Mary Diggs Lee, m. in 1868, J. Oliver O'Donnell, of Baltimore, and had one son and two daus.

Charles Carroll, barrister, was the grandson of Daniel Carroll, the son of Daniel and Dorothy Carroll, before mentioned.

DANIEL CARROLL, eldest son of Daniel and Dorothy Carroll, m. and left two sons, viz., Charles and John Carroll.

JOHN CARROLL, second son of the last named Daniel Carroll, "was the father of Sir Daniel O'Carroll, who at the instance of the Duke of Ormond was made a lieutenant colonel 1st March 1709, and 2d Sept. 1710 was made a colonel of a regiment of horse, being also by Queen Anne created a baronet, was knight of the order of Aragon in Spain, and died Lieutenant General of his Majesty's forces 1750 (vide *Lodge Peerage*, vol. iv)."

Sir John O'Carroll, son of John Carroll ("John O'Carroll of Beaugh, Esqr."), died 12th Aug. 1723.

CHARLES CARROLL, eldest son of the last named Daniel Carroll, m. Clare Dunn, who was the dau. of the great O'Connor Dun (or Don), her mother being Jane Bermingham, dau. of Edward FitzRichard, the 17th Lord Athenry (vide *Lodge Peerage*, John Carroll of Baugh). The above Charles' brother m. Margaret, dau. of Ocrean of Sligo, her mother being Margaret Bermingham, dau. of Edward FitzRichard, the 17th Lord Athenry (vide *Lodge Peerage*).

Charles Carroll and Clare Dunn had child., viz., Dr. Charles Carroll, and John Carroll, who was lost at sea, and a dau., Dorothy Carroll.

DR. CHARLES CARROLL, eldest son of Charles Carroll and Clare Dunn, was the first one of his branch of the family that settled in America. He was the eldest of the elder branch of the great house of Carroll, known as of Ely O'Carroll, as is shown by his armorial bearings of gold. He accumulated an immense landed estate, among the largest, perhaps the very largest, in the Province of Maryland, consisting of large tracts of land on the Eastern Shore,—in Frederick County,—in Anne Arundel County,—and in and near the City of Baltimore, including "Carroll's Island,"—"Mount Clare" (the property of James Carroll),—"The Plains," near Annapolis,—"Clare Mont" (the residence of Hon. Carroll Spence, late Minister to Turkey),—and "The Caves," the present residence of General John Carroll. Dr. Charles Carroll was active and prominent in the public affairs of the State, and in the session of 1738 was the representative of the City of Annapolis in the Legislature of Maryland. In religion he was a Protestant, which is fully disclosed in some of his letters still extant.

Dr. Charles Carroll m. Dorothy Blake, dau. of Henry Blake (of an ancient family in Hampshire, England), and his wife Henrietta Lloyd, dau. of Philemon Lloyd and Henrietta

Maria Neale (see LLOYD), and had child., viz., Charles Carroll, barrister, b. Sunday, 22d March 1723, d. 23d March 1783,—Mary Clare Carroll, b. Saturday, 13th May 1727, and John Henry Carroll, who d. *sine prole.*

In the year 1748 the following interesting and suggestive correspondence took place between Dr. Charles Carroll and his first cousin, Sir Daniel O'Carroll, previously mentioned:

"LONDON, May 1st, 1748.

"SIR: Since cousin Jno. Carroll, your brother, went to "see you, I have not heard a word of him or of any of the family. "It would be a great pleasure to me to know of the happiness "not only of the sons of so near a relation as cousin Charles, "your father, but of a still nearer, if possible, of cousin Clare "Dun, your mother, and could I be of any service, either here "or elsewhere, to any of your family, I should embrace with "pleasure every opportunity.

"I received some time ago a letter from Ireland, from my "brother, Major Carroll; in it he acquaints me that his two sons, "Romy and James, both young and well-bred to accounts and "book-keeping, have lately gone to St. Christophers to settle "either there or in Maryland, recommended to you and friends "by your near relation, that worthy nobleman, Lord Athenry. "I am yet ignorant where they settle, that I may when known "take proper measures to obtain all needful recommendations "to the military for protection, and from such merchants here "as you may judge necessary for such business as they are "capable of. My most kind love to all your good family and "to my nephews if there, and please to believe me to be, dear "cousin, your most loving kinsman and humble servant,

"DANIEL O'CARROLL.

"P. S.—All letters directed to me at St. James Coffee "House will come safe. We have surely a peace, and a suspen-"sion of hostilities was expected in a few days."

To the above the following reply was sent:

"ANNAPOLIS, IN MARYLAND,
"September 9th, 1748.

"SIR:—This day I received the favor of yours dated Lon-"don, the 1st of May last, and embrace the first opportunity "of acknowledging the same with an assurance of pleasure I "have in hearing the health of a gentleman of my name, and "so nearly related in family, tho' by the destinies and revolu-

" tions of time and States, separated from our native soil, " where our predecessors time immemorial inherited both " ample estates and honors. Nothing more contributes (next " to christian patience) to alleviate my concern for such mis- " fortunes than the consideration that the Macedonian and " Roman Empires are no more, that the Grecian States, with " many more within the compass of Europe, have been over- " turned. I therefore comfort myself and endeavor to be " satisfied in this wild part of the globe. I have not had the " pleasure of seeing either of your nephews, or hearing of or " from them, and I cannot say but I am glad they have chosen " to fix at St. Christophers rather than here, by reason I think " that, or other West India islands, are the most probable " places for young gentlemen to get into business and make " something of a fortune. I assure you if I were young and " had not the charge of a family and an interest which I can- " not get rid of, I would not stay here. My brother John " some years ago had resolved to go to the West Indies, Span- " ish Islands and Main, and in his passage with other gentle- " men from Barbadoes to Antigua, the vessel and all were lost, " which leaves me the only son of the family you mention. " But by this I do not expect to inherit Clonlisk, Ballibritt " Leap, Castle Town, or any other part, or a foot in Ely " O'Carroll. Transplantations, sequestrations, acts of settle- " ments, infamous informations for loyalty and other evils " forbid. It will be a singular pleasure to me at all times to " hear from you and of your health and happiness and that " of all your family, to which I sincerely wish the same. " Any letters directed for me here and left under cover for " Messrs. John Philpot & Co., merchants, in London, at the " Virginia and Maryland Coffee House, near the Exchange, " will come safe. If I hear anything of your nephews shall " not fail to acquaint you. I am with great esteem and respect " your affectionate kinsman and most humble servant,"

"CHARLES CARROLL."

CHARLES CARROLL, barrister, son of Dr. Charles Carroll and Dorothy Blake, was b. 22d March 1723. At a tender age his father sailed with him, intending to place him at school in England, but by stress of weather they were driven to Portugal. Dr. Carroll was so much pleased with Lisbon that he placed him at college there, under the immediate tuition of the Rev. Edward Jones, at the English House, on Bairo Alto, West Lisbon. When about 16 years of age he was removed to the celebrated school of Eton, in England. The correspondence between him and his father is still extant, and is creditable to the heads and hearts of both. It displays on the parent's part an unceasing watchfulness and tender solicitude for the comfort and welfare of the child, only equalled by his confidence in the manliness and integrity of his son. In one letter the dutiful behavior of Charles to his deceased mother is thankfully and touchingly dwelt upon.

While at Eton, he received a letter from his father, dated 21st July 1739, which contains the following:

"In point of religion be not too much attached to any opin-
" ions, grown up with you. Examine well that of those, you
" converse with, whose you find good, and lives moral and
" virtuous. Bigotry and superstition in religion is a grand
" error. The Church of England as by Law established is
" worthy of your consideration. Therein consult with the
" virtuous, sober and learned."

In 1740 Charles Carroll made known to his father that his desire was to devote himself to the legal profession. In this choice his father concurred and directed that he enter the University of Cambridge, at the same College Daniel Dulany was entered. While at Cambridge, he received a letter from his father, dated 4th Oct. 1742, which contains the following: "This money I hope you will lay out in necessaries for your person or endowment of your mind, and not spend in wine or riot. Remark that women and wine are the bane of youth! Pray take opportunities to improve in your dancing. Some of this money may be applied that way. A genteel carriage in person and behaviour is becoming. Make good choice of your company, avoid such as are profane or extravagant." With a mind thoroughly educated and trained, he commenced the study of law, in the Middle Temple, Garden Court, Library Staircase, No. 2. At this period his father remitted to him an allowance of three hundred pounds sterling, per annum, a large sum at that time.

He returned to Maryland in 1746 and took charge, in a great measure, of his father's large landed estate, and commenced the practice of his profession. One of his favorite resorts for relaxation, amid the cares of professional life and public employments, was "The Caves," a beautiful valley containing three thousand acres of land. This estate he improved and made it a charming place of residence. It remains, to-day, in the family, and with its broad acres undiminished and intact, it is not only one of the oldest ancestral homes, but is also one of the largest and most valuable estates in the State of Maryland. It is now the elegant residence of General John Carroll, its present hereditary owner. Being thoroughly conversant with affairs at home and abroad, he was early called into public life, and became one of the most trusted guides and leaders of the people before and during the stormy period of the Revolution. He was an elegant, fluent, exact and terse writer, and was selected to serve on every committee which required wisdom in council, and the ability to embody its expression in forcible language. To his facile pen our revolutionary ancestors were indebted for many of their ablest public papers. "The Declaration of Rights," which was adopted by the Convention of Maryland, 3d Nov. 1776, emanated from his pen. This is true, also, in a large measure, of the first constitution and form of government of the State of Maryland. His assured and leading position among the acknowledged great men of the State is shown by naming the various committees, with their members, upon which he served.

At a meeting of the deputies of the counties of the province of Maryland, held at Annapolis, from the 8th to 12th of December 1774, it was,

"*Resolved unanimously*, That the Honorable Matthew " Tilghman and John Hall, Samuel Chase, Thomas Johnson, jun., Charles Carroll, of Carrollton, Charles Carroll, " barrister, and William Paca, Esquire, or any three or more " of them, be a committee of correspondence for this province."

At a meeting of the Delegates of the province of Maryland, which was convened at Annapolis, 25th July 1775, and continued till the 14th Aug. 1775, it was,

"*Resolved*, That the Honorable Matthew Tilghman and " John Beale Bordley, Esqs., and Robert Goldsborough, " James Hollyday, Richard Lloyd, Edward Lloyd, Thomas " Smyth, and Henry Hooper, Esqrs., residents of the Eastern " Shore, and the Honorable Daniel of St. Thomas Jenifer, Esq., " and Thomas Johnson, Jun., William Paca, Charles Carroll, " barrister, Thomas Stone, Samuel Chase, Robert Alexander, " and Charles Carroll, of Carrollton, Esqr., residents of the " Western Shore, or any nine, or more of them, be a council " of safety for this province."

He was a member of the Convention of Delegates which met at Annapolis, 7th Dec. 1775, and on the 16th of Dec., when the convention resolved itself into a committee of the whole house, he presided over the committee and reported its action. Again on the 19th of the same month he presided over the committee of the whole house. On the 29th of the same month, it was, on motion,

"*Resolved*, That a committee be appointed to prepare a "draught of instruction for the deputies representing this "province in congress; and Mr. Hollyday, Mr. Carroll, bar-"rister, Mr. J. Tilghman, Mr. Scott, and Mr. Rumsey were "elected by ballot a committee for that purpose."

The committee reported the instructions on the 11th, "which were read, considered and agreed to" on the 12th of January, 1776.

He again, 1st January 1776, presided over the committee of the whole house, and the same day it was, on motion,

"*Resolved*, That a committee be appointed to report resolu-"tions for raising clothing and victualing the forces to be "raised in this province; and Mr. Johnson, Mr. Stone, "Mr. Carroll, barrister, Mr. Rumsey, and Mr. Ware were "elected by ballot a committee for that purpose."

Charles Carroll, barrister, was chosen president of the Convention of Delegates of the province of Maryland which met at Annapolis, 8th May, and remained in session until 25th May 1776. On which last day the following gentlemen were elected a council of safety "until the end of the next session of convention: Daniel of St. Thomas Jenifer, Charles Carroll, barrister, John Hall, Benjamin Rumsey, George Plater, James Tilghman, Thomas Smyth, Thomas Bedingfield Hands, and William Hayward." It was this convention that relieved Gov. Robert Eden of power, and "signified to the governor that the public quiet and safety in the judgment of this convention require that he leave this province, and that he is at full liberty to depart peaceably with his effects."

He was a member of the convention which met at Annapolis 21st June 1776, and, on the 5th of July 1776, was a third time elected one of the council of safety; the council consisting of John Hall, George Plater, Charles Carroll, barrister, Daniel of St. Thomas Jenifer, Thomas B. Hands, Benjamin Rumsey, Thomas Smyth, James Tilghman and Joseph Nicholson, Jr. He was also a member of the convention which convened at Annapolis, 14th Aug. 1776. On the 17th of the same month the convention "proceeded to ballot for a committee to prepare a declaration and charter of rights, and a form of government for this state; and Mr. President, Mr. Carroll, barrister, Mr. Paca, Mr. Carroll, of Carrollton, Mr. Plater, Mr. Samuel Chase and Mr. Goldsborough were elected a committee for that purpose." In the proceedings of 27th Aug. 1776, is recorded the following:

"Brice T. B. Worthington, Charles Carroll, barrister, and "Samuel Chase, Esqrs., having informed the convention that, "they having received instructions from their constituents "enjoining them in framing of a government for this state, "implicitly to adhere to points in their opinion incompatible "with good government and the public peace and happiness, "were obliged, extremely against their inclination to resign "their seats, and that they resigned accordingly."

On the 10th of Nov. 1776, the convention

"*Resolved*, That the Honorable Matthew Tilghman, Esq., "and Thomas Johnson, junr., William Paca, Thomas Stone, "Samuel Chase, Benjamin Rumsey, and Charles Carroll, "barrister, Esquires, or any three or more of them, be del-"egated to represent this state in Congress until the first day "of March next, or until the general assembly shall make "further order therein; and that the said delegates, or any "three or more of them be authorized and empowered to con-"cur with the other United States, or a majority of them, "in forming a confederation, and in making foreign alliances, "provided that such confederation, when formed, be not "binding upon this state without the assent of the general "assembly; and the said delegates, or any three or more of "them are also authorized and empowered to concur in any "measures which may be resolved on by Congress for carrying "on the war with Great Britain, and securing the liberties of "the United States, reserving always to this state the sole "and exclusive right of regulating the internal police thereof.

"And the said delegates, or any three or more of them are "hereby authorized and empowered, notwithstanding any "measures heretofore taken, to concur with the congress, or a "majority of them in accommodating our unhappy differences "with Great Britain, on such terms as the congress, or a "majority of them shall think proper."

In 1777, Charles Carroll, barrister, was elected to the first Senate of the State of Maryland, and was also appointed Chief Justice of the General Court,—the first Chief Justice of Maryland, which he declined.

He married 3d June 1763, Margaret Tilghman, dau. of Hon. Matthew Tilghman, and had two child., twins, who d. in infancy.

Charles Carroll, barrister, d. at his residence, Mount Clare, near Baltimore on the 23d day of March 1783, aged 60 years and 1 day, leaving his estate to his nephews, Nicholas and James Maccubbin, the sons of his sister, Mary Clare Carroll and her husband, Nicholas Maccubbin, upon condition that they took their mother's maiden name, Carroll, "and that only, and use the coat of arms forever after." The will was dated 7th Aug. 1781 and the codicil 23d March 1783.

MARY CLARE CARROLL, dau. of Dr. Charles Carroll and Dorothy Blake, m. 21st July 1747, a Scotchman, Nicholas Maccubbin, as he was called in the Lowlands (in his native Highlands his name was Mac Alpine), who claimed descent from Kenneth II, surnamed Mac Alpine, who d. in 858, and who, having united the Scots and Picts under one sceptre, was the first King of all Scotland. (See STEUART.)

MARY CLARE CARROLL and Nicholas Maccubbin had child., viz., Nicholas Maccubbin,—James Maccubbin,—John Henry Maccubbin,—Samuel Maccubbin,—Susan Maccubbin, who m. Mr. Ligon, and Mary Maccubbin, who m. John Brice, son of John and Sarah Frisby Brice (see BRICE).

Nicholas and James Maccubbin, sons of Mary Clare Carroll and Nicholas Maccubbin, assumed the name and arms of CARROLL in compliance with the testamentary injunction of their uncle, Charles Carroll, barrister.

NICHOLAS CARROLL, eldest son of Mary Clare Carroll and Nicholas Maccubbin, m. Anne Jennings, dau. of Hon. Thomas Jennings, an eminent lawyer, by appointment the first Attorney General of Maryland, and had child., viz., Nicholas Carroll, who d. 11th Nov. 1869, aged 83, *sine prole*,—John Henry Carroll,— Thomas Carroll, who d. *sine prole*,—Anne Elizabeth Carroll, who m. Temple Mason, of Temple Hall, Virginia, and Mary Clare Carroll.

Mrs. Anne Jennings Carroll d. 20th Sept. 1830, in the 69th year of her age.

Hon. Thomas Jennings was the son of Hon. Edward Jennings, formerly Attorney General of the Province of Maryland, who was brought up at Blenheim, being a cousin of the Duchess of Marlborough, and also a cousin of William Jennings, of Acton Place, county of Suffolk, England, the wealthy banker of London, whose estate was so long in Chancery.

JOHN HENRY CARROLL, of "The Caves," son of Nicholas Carroll and Anne Jennings, m. 21st Dec. 1842, Matilda Hollingsworth, the dau. of Horatio Hollingsworth and Emily Ridgely, and a great-granddau. of Judge Samuel Chase, who signed the Declaration of Independence. He d. 1856, aged 56 years, and left a son, John Carroll.

GENERAL JOHN CARROLL, of "The Caves" (sometimes called General John N. Carroll), was elected to the Maryland Legislature in 1869, in the 22d year of his age, and was commissioned 5th of April 1870, Chief of Cavalry, in Maryland, with the rank of Brigadier General. He m. 21st of April 1870, Mary Randolph Thomas, dau. of Dr. John Hanson Thomas and Annie Campbell Gordon, and has two child., viz., John Nicholas Carroll and Charles Carroll.

MARY CLARE CARROLL, dau. of Nicholas Carroll and Anne Jennings, m. Captain Robert Trail Spence, U. S. N., and had child., viz., Anne Josepha Spence (who m. Franklin Smith, of Mississippi, and had child., viz., Carroll Smith,—Mary Clare Smith, who m. Mr. Stephenson, and Anne Smith),—Carroll Spence,—Dr. Robert Trail Spence (who was a surgeon in the Mexican War),—Mary Clare Spence (who m. Oliver P. MacGill, formerly a member of the Legislature, and Register of Wills in Baltimore County, and had child., viz., Mary Clare, d.,—Roberta, who m. Mr. Howard, Rebecca Carroll,—Carroll, and Lillie MacGill), — Charles Stewart Spence (who represented the City of Baltimore, in 1845, in the Legislature of Maryland, and was appointed by President Buchanan to exchange the ratification of the treaty made between the United States and Persia, and resides in Paris, France),—Stephen Decatur Spence (who was appointed midshipman in the U. S. Navy by President Tyler, resigned, and was afterwards appointed by President Buchanan Lieutenant in the Marine Corps, and resigned in 1861),—and Roberta I. Spence, who m. Charles Brooke.

CAPTAIN ROBERT TRAIL SPENCE was b. in Portsmouth, New Hampshire, in 1788, and entered the United States Navy in 1800. He rose rapidly to distinction, and in 1815, at the age of 27 years, he held the rank of Post Captain, the highest grade then in our Navy. He was one of those daring young officers whose gallant exploits, in our war with Tripoli, presaged the future glory of the Navy of the United States. A letter which has never been published, written by Captain Stephen Decatur to Keith Spence, Esq., the father of Captain Spence, giving an interesting account of Decatur's successful conflict with the Turkish gunboats, speaks in flattering terms of the gallant conduct of Midshipman Spence on that occasion.

"U. S. Ship Congress,
"Tunis Bay, Jan'y 9th, 1804.

"Dear Friend: I had the pleasure of receiving yours " of the 20th of Nov., with a letter for Captain Stewart and " Robert, which I shall keep until their return, which is ex- " pected shortly. Your son has displayed a manliness of " conduct that will make every American proud of him as a " countryman. After the accident which befel his boat he " served in the boat with me; his conduct with me was such " as you would have wished. As to his being confirmed, " there can be no doubt of it. Commodore Preble has given " me his word it shall be done. He has earned it,—it needs " but a statement, and it will be done.

" You will see in my report to Commodore Preble, on the " 7th of August, your son is mentioned in a way that will not " be displeasing to you. I shall be happy to have him with " me, but Captain J. Barron wishes him to sail with him in " the *Essex*. You see he is in great demand.

" You will observe I am in the return of the wounded, on " the 3rd of August. My wounds were slight, as follows: " On the arm by a sword, and in the breast by a pike. I " found that hand to hand is not child's play,—'tis kill or be " killed. You no doubt recollect the conversation we had " when in the City of Washington. I then informed you " that it was my intention to board if ever I had an opportu- " nity, and that it was my opinion there could be no doubt as " to the issue. You will not doubt me, I hope, when I say " that I am glad the event has proved my ideas were correct. " I always thought we could lick them their own way and " give them two to one. The first boat they were 36 to 20; " we carried it without much fuss,—the second was 24 to 10, " they also went to the leeward.

"I had 18 Italians in the boat with me who claim the " honor of the day. While we were fighting, they prayed. " They are convinced we could not have been so fortunate " unless their prayers had been heard. This might have been " the case, therefore, we could not contradict it. Some of the " Turks died like men, but much the greater number died " like women.

"I leave to-morrow for Tripoli. If you are suffered to " walk out, you will know my ship by her having stump top " gt. mast.

"Believe me to be yours sincerely,

"Stephen Decatur."

Keith Spence, Esq., to whom the above letter was written, was purser on board of the U. S. Frigate *Philadelphia* when she grounded, and was captured by the Turks in the bay of Tripoli, and at this time was a prisoner in the Castle of Tripoli, and a witness of the gallant conduct of his son and countrymen. He also witnessed the recapture and destruction of the *Philadelphia*, by his friend Decatur, "an achievement, viewing the manner in which it was accomplished, and the circumstances attending it, equals any thing of the kind on record."

In 1822, the manly protest of Captain Spence, as senior naval officer of the United States, in reply to the proclamation of Francisco Morales, General-in-Chief of the Spanish forces on the Main, threatening with imprisonment and death all foreigners found in the Spanish colonies, whose countries were at war with Spain, was much applauded. "The conduct of Captain Spence," said a leading writer, "has been honorable to humanity and the country which gave him birth. His noble, manly and dignified Protest does him great honor, and will be read by Americans with pleasure."

In 1826, Captain Spence was assigned to the command of the West India Squadron. He d. 26th Sept. of the same year.

The Cutt family, maternal ancestors of Captain Spence, according to Brewster and Adams, as stated in their Annals of Portsmouth, settled in New Hampshire previous to the year 1646. Brewster says that "they were the largest landholders in Portsmouth in 1660." His maternal grandfather, John Cutt, was appointed by the King the first President of New Hampshire, and in 1760, President Cutt convened the first Assembly ever held in that Colony. His maternal uncle, Gen. William Whipple, commanded the 1st New Hampshire Brigade at the surrender of Burgoyne, was a member of the Continental Congress from New Hampshire, in 1776, and signed the Declaration of Independence.

Hon. Carroll Spence, son of Captain Robert Trail Spence and Mary Clare Carroll, was educated at St. Mary's College, where he was graduated and received the degree of A.M. At Dickinson College he received the degree of L. L. B. In 1842, he was elected to the Legislature of Maryland, and in 1854 was chosen Presidential Elector. He received the degree of LL. D. from St. Mary's College. In 1854 he was appointed Minister to the Sublime Porte, by President Pierce, and under very difficult and extraordinary circumstances, made the first treaty ever concluded between the United States and Persia. A New York paper, speaking of Hon. Carroll Spence, said, "Mr. Spence has represented this country near the Sublime Porte during an exciting period of European politics, and has proved himself a diplomatist of no little ability. His powerful protest in behalf of the unfortunate Greeks, at the commencement of the war, induced the Turkish Ministry to rescind their harsh measures against them, and obtained for him the thanks of every lover of humanity. (For his interference in behalf of the Greeks, he received the thanks of the King of Greece, and a tender of a decoration, which he declined.)

"His earnest appeal to the Sultan for religious toleration in the Ottoman Empire, was instrumental in procuring the late firman in behalf of the Christians there, while it was, chiefly, owing to his strenuous efforts that the exiled patriots from the Principalities were permitted to return to their country. As a striking proof of his influence with the Turkish Government, he has lately prevailed upon it to send two of its principal officers to procure a Steam-Line-Battle-Ship in the United States."

HON. CARROLL SPENCE m. his cousin, Rebecca Carroll, dau. of Charles Ridgely Carroll and Rebecca Anne Pue, and had child., viz., Kate Stiles Spence, and Rebecca Carroll Spence.

JAMES CARROLL, son of Mary Clare Carroll and Nicholas Maccubbin, m. in December 1787, Sophia Gough, dau. of Harry Dorsey Gough, of Perry Hall, Baltimore County, and had child., viz., James Carroll,—Harry Dorsey Gough Carroll, who m. Eliza Ridgely, dau. of Gov. Charles Ridgely, of Hampton,—Prudence Gough Carroll, who m. John Ridgely, son of Gov. Charles Ridgely, of Hampton,—and Charles Ridgely Carroll.

JAMES CARROLL, eldest son of James Carroll and Sophia Gough, m. 7th Nov. 1811, Achsah Ridgely, dau. of Gov. Charles Ridgely, of Hampton, and had child., viz., Charles Ridgely Carroll, d.,—Sophia Carroll, d.,—Prudence Gough Carroll,—James Carroll,—Priscilla Ridgely Carroll, d.,—and Achsah Ridgely Carroll.

HON. JAMES CARROLL, son of James Carroll, and Achsah Ridgely, m. 5th Oct. 1837, Mary Wethered Ludlow, dau. of Robert C. Ludlow, U. S. N., and Ann Catharine Wethered (see WETHERED) and had child., viz., Achsah Ridgely Carroll,—Sally Wethered Carroll,—James Carroll, b. 27th Nov.

1841, d. 16th Feb'y 1842,—James Carroll, b. 20th April 1843, d. 24th Jan'y 1846,—Mary Ludlow Carroll,—Sophia Gough Carroll,—Harry Dorsey Gough Carroll,—and Catharine Ludlow Carroll.

CHARLES RIDGELY CARROLL, son of James Carroll and Sophia Gough, m. 21st Nov. 1823, Rebecca Anne Pue, dau. of Dr. Arthur Pue, and had two sons and six daus., viz., James Carroll,—Charles Arthur Carroll, who m. 13th July 1871, Sallie H. White,—Rebecca Carroll, who m. Hon. Carroll Spence,—Sophia Gough Carroll, who m. 5th Feb'y 1852, George B. Milligan,—Susan Carroll, who m. 26th Dec. 1850, Thomas Poultney,—Achsah Ridgely, who m. 1st Nov. 1855, William Shippen, of Philadelphia,—Mary Carroll (now d.), who m. Robert M. Denison,—and Gough Carroll, who m. in 1871, Edwin Schenck.

The following notes are carefully extracted from papers and documents in possession of the Carroll family:

"The Sept of O'Carroll was early established in Lowth, being then popularly styled Princes of Orgeil. Previous to the English invasion, immediately after the great Synod of Mellifont in 1152, is recorded the expulsion of their chief from that country, of which he had been the acknowledged lord, from Drogheda to Asigh in the County of Meath. These annalists, however, notice O'Carrolls as Chiefs of Orgeil and Ely O'Carroll down to the year 1193; and it is especially recorded that when in 1166, on the eve of Strongbow's invasion of Ireland, Roderic O'Connor, then king of this country, seeking to ascertain the feeling of allegiance towards himself, encamped with an army hereabout, Daniel Carroll, with the other chiefs of Lowth, came into his tent, delivered hostages for their fealty, and received in return, as related in the *Annals of Innisfallen*, 'a present of two hundred and forty beeves.'

"The O'Carrolls were, at that time and previously, settled in a territory of Tipperary, from them called Ely-O'Carroll. The death of Amergin Carroll, Lord of Ely, is recorded in 1033. This inheritance comprised the present Barony of Lower Ormond, with that of Clonlisk and part of Ballibritt in the King's County, and to the Sleive Bloom Mountains in the Queen's. The name was one of power and possession in the Counties of Cavan and Leitrim (vide *Annals of Innisfallen*, and *King James' Army List; Funeral Entries Dublin Castle*).

"In 1168 died John Carroll, Bishop of Ross.

"In 1171 Charles Carroll, Lord of Orgeil, joined Roderick O'Connor, the last native King of Ireland, in the ineffective siege of Dublin, then occupied by the English. In 1178 he made a gallant and successful attack upon De Courcy, and, dying in 1189, was interred in the Abbey which he had founded for Cistercians at Mellifont.

"In 1327 John Carroll became Archbishop of Cashel.

"Thomas Carroll became Bishop of Tuam, 1349.

"Fergan Carroll surrendered his possessions (1615) to Edward the Sixth, who restored them to him on English tenure, with the addition of the dignity of Baron. (See Sir Bernard Burke, and vide *Records of Parliament.*)

"Perrot's Parliament of 1585 was attended by Lord Carroll of Ely (vide *Records of Parliament.*)

"In the Office of Arms of Dublin is recorded the death of Sir Wm. Carroll, August 15th, 1630 (vide *Office of Arms*).

"Amongst the active measures concerted by James I for reducing Ireland, a commission was appointed 'for ascertaining the bounds and limits of O'Carroll's County, commonly called Ely O'Carroll.' (See Surveyor General's Office, 1641.)

"On 11th of April, 1691, 1,500 men, commanded by General Carroll, came to Inniskean, with a design to have that place as a step further upon our frontiers. (Vide *Story's History.*)

"The attainders of 1691 included those of John Carroll of King's County, John Carroll (who is buried in the churchyard of Dunkerron, near Roscrea), and John Carroll of the County Sligo—also Eugene Carroll of the Queen's County. (Vide Attainders 1691.)

"1549. Carroll submitted to Lord Justice Brabazon, agreed to find foot and horse, surrendered Ely O'Carroll, and had it regranted and was created Baron of Ely. (Vide *Betham MSS.* vol. iv. p. 287. Also Burke.)

"1460. The counties of Kilkenny and Tipperary paid Carroll for peace. (*Betham MSS.* and Sir Bernard Burke, vol. iv. p. 166.)

"1540. One of the accusations against Lord Deputy Grey was that he took O'Carroll's castle from a loyal Carroll. (*Betham MSS.* p. 264.)

"O'Carroll, Prince of Ely, was taken prisoner by James, 3d Earl of Ormond, 1399, but made his escape 1400.

"Ellen, only dau. of Pierce Butler, eldest son of Sir Edmund Butler of Roscrea, whose younger brother, John of Kilcash, was father to Walter, 11th Earl of Ormond, was wife

Carroll.

of John Carroll, chief of his name: she d. in 1620. (Vide *Betham MSS*. vol. ii, p. 20.)

"In 1532 Carroll, Prince of Ely, m. a dau. of Gerald, ninth Earl of Kildare, and was loyal to Henry ye 8th. (*Betham MSS*. vol. i., p. 33.)

"1548. O'Carroll took the Castle of Nenagh, demolished it and drove the English out. (See Sir Bernard Burke.)

"Leim-Ui-Bhanain, now the Leap Castle, the seat of H. Darby, Esq., in the King's County, about five miles to the north of Roscrea (vide O'Donovan, LL. D., M. R. I. A). This castle bears its name to the present day—Ely O'Carroll (Hist. of O'Donovan). Leim-Ui-Bhanain, now the Castle of the 'Leap' in Ely O'Carroll near Roscrea. This fine old castle now forms a part of the residence of H. Darby, Esq. It occupies a high bank immediately under the Hill of Throch, and commands a splendid view of the lofty acclivities of the mountains of Sliath Bladhma, the ancient bulwark of the Carrolls (vide *Ware's Annals*), 'Clonlisk,' giving name to a barony in the south of the King's County.

"In a manuscript missal, preserved in the library of Trinity College, Dublin, Class B., Tab. 3, No. 1, there is recorded the death of Carroll, as follows: 'Hic obiit vir sine nomine [Ferganoninini (that is without a name) O'Carroll] qui fuit dominus et princeps Elie occissus in Castro suo proprio in Clurintis morte incognita, et nisi predicitur improvisa, et qui fuit magne sapientia et mirabilis fortitudinis; cujus anime propitietur Deus. Amen. In anno Domini millessimo ccccexli.

"The present chief of this family is unknown, but the grandfather of the Marchioness of Wellesley was a representative (vide *Annals Four Masters*, note, vol. v., p. 1835). Charles Carroll (barrister) was the chief of the Carroll family.

"It is stated a barony was granted to Carroll as Baron of Ely O'Carroll in 1552 (vide Sir Bernard Burke's *Extinct Peerages*, p. 407).

"Carroll was originally chief of all the tract of country now divided into the baronies of Clonlisk and Ballibritt, in the King's County, and of the adjoining barony of Ikerrin in the county of Tipperary, but for many centuries his county was considered as co-extensive with the two baronies in the King's County above mentioned. O'Carroll's strongest castle was Leim-Ui-Bhanain, now the Castle of the Leap.

"Sir Charles O'Carroll, in a letter to the Lord Deputy, written in 1595, preserved in the Library at Lambeth Palace, complains that the Right Honorable the Earl of Ormund had subtracted several territories from Thomond, which he added to his 'Countie Pallentine of Tipperarie, though there be no coullir for it, particularly Muskryhyry, which he improperlye and usurpedly called the Heither Ormund, though it was ever heretofore reputed, knowen and taken as of Thomond, until of late subtracted by the greatnesse, countenance, and export power of the said Earle.'

"On the 8th March, 1576, Carroll, lord of Ely O'Carroll, made his submission to Queen Elizabeth, as appears from the following indenture, enrolled in the record branch of the office of Paymaster of Civil Services :

"This Indenture, made the 8th day of Marche, Anno Domini 1576, betwyxte Sir Henry Sidney, Knt. lorde Deputy of Ireland, for and in behalfe of the Queenes most excellent M atie, of thone parte: and Sir William O'Karroll of Lemyvanan, in the countrie called Elye O'Kerroll and now to be made parcell of the King's Countie; McOney O'Kerroll, Daniel O'Kerroll, McCallogh O'Kerroll, in the said countrie, freeholders of the other part: Witnesseth, that the said Sir William and the rest above named, do covenant, agree and condscend to and with the said Lorde Deputy, to surrender and give up in the Queenes most Honorable Courte of Chauncerie of Ireland, all such manors, castells, lands, tenements, rents, revisems, and all other hereditaments that they and every of them have within the said countrie called Elye O'Karroll. And the said Lorde Deputy doe promise and graunte that the same shall be by letters patents, given back to the said Sir William, and theires males of his bodi, lawfullie begotten and to be begotten, and for want of such issue to John O'Kerroll, brother to the said Sir William, and the heires males of his bodie, lawfullie begotten and to be begotten. To have and to hold the said countrie called Elyie O'Karrell, by two Knights' fees in chiefe. And the said Sir William, and the rest above named, to be wholie discharged from the Bonaght accustomed to be payd out of the said country, and all other cesses and ymposcions, other than the rents hereafter specified.

"Signed, SR WILLIAM O'KARRELL.

"Lord Rosse is the present owner of Birr Castle, one of the ancient seats of the Carrolls. (Vide Burke's *Peerage*, p. 94.)

"The estate of the Carrolls, consisting of upwards of three hundred and seventy-nine thousand acres of land, comprising the King's and Queen's counties and part of

Tipperary, was confiscated about 1691, and the titles and persons attainted." (See records of Attainders and Confiscations.)

SEC. 67, L. ANDREW HANSON, eldest son of Col. Hanson, of the Swedish Army, was b. in Sweden in 1618, and came to this country with his wife, Annika Hanson. Their dau., Catharine Hanson, d. on Tinicum Island and was buried 28th of Oct. 1646. Campanius records that hers was the first corpse ever interred upon that Island. Andrew Hanson d. on Kent Island, in June 1655, leaving his wife, Annika Hanson, with four small child., viz., Hans Hanson,—Frederick Hanson,—Katharine Hanson, and Margarett Hanson. A posthumous child, Barbara Hanson, was b. in November 1655. Annika Hanson administered upon the estate of her deceased husband. She was a woman of singular independence and decision of character. Finding that his estate was complicated with that of Valerus Leo, d., and involved with the affairs of Swan Swanson, she, 29th Nov. 1655, in open Court, renounced the administration, and Thomas Hynson, High Sheriff of Kent, was appointed in her stead.

COL. HANS HANSON, eldest son of Andrew and Annika Hanson, was b. on Tinicum Island, New Sweden, in 1646. He was one of the Judges of Kent from 1685 to 1697, inclusive, and a Delegate from Kent in the Legislature of Maryland, in the sessions of 1694–95, 1696–97, from Cecil County in 1699, and a member of the first Vestry of St. Paul's Parish, Kent, elected the 24th of Jan'y 1693. On the 29th day of March 1679, he m. Martha Kelto Ward, and on the 22d day of Sept. 1679, purchased from Charles Vaughan the estate, Kimbolton, "lying on the North side of Chester river, and on the West side of Langford's bay—near the mouth of the North west branch called Broad Neck's Branch," where he afterwards resided.

COL. HANS. HANSON, of Kimbolton, was buried at St. Paul's, Kent, 2nd Sept. 1703. He had child., viz., Mary Hanson, b. the 16th of Dec. 1680,—William Hanson, b. 2nd of Jan'y 1682, was buried at St. Paul's 4th July 1708,—Hans Hanson, b. 16th April 1685 (who m. 29th May 1707, Anne Hamer, and had a dau., Martha Hanson, baptized 4th Jan'y 1712),—Martha Hanson, b. 16th April 1685, buried at St. Paul's 2nd March 1698,—Sarah Hanson, b. 16th March 1687, buried at St. Paul's 6th Sept. 1693 (hers was the first recorded interment in the church yard of St. Paul's),—Ann Hanson, b. 17th April 1689,—George Hanson, b. 26th April 1691, d. 1727,—Frederick Hanson, b. 22nd May 1693, d. 1738, and Samuel Hanson, b. 23rd Oct. 1696.

MARY HANSON, eldest child and dau. of Col. Hans and Martha Kelto Ward Hanson, m. Col. St. Ledger Codd, and left two child., viz., Mary and Beatrice Codd.

BEATRICE CODD, dau. of Colonel St. Ledger and Mary Hanson Codd, m. 6th June 1734, Gideon Pearce, a grandson of William Pearce, who was High Sheriff of Cecil in 1787.

The PEARCES came to Maryland about the year 1660 and settled in that portion of Kent County which was given to Cecil in 1674 and returned to Kent in 1706. They were active, prominent and influential members of Shrewsbury Parish.

WILLIAM PEARCE, son of the High Sheriff of Cecil, represented Cecil in the Legislature of Maryland in the sessions of 1694, 1706 and 1707, was instrumental in having restored to Kent that portion of her territory which had been taken from her in 1674, and was distinguished in the early annals of Kent. In the years 1714 and 1715 he was the presiding Judge of Kent County Court. He d. March 1720. His wife, Isabella Pearce, d. 1729, leaving child., viz., Gideon Pearce,—Benjamin Pearce,—Daniel Pearce,—Elizabeth Ward,—Isabella Johnson and Sarah Hopkins, afterwards Sarah Rogers, and grandchild., viz., Rachel Blay,—Catharine Blay,—Benjamin Hopkins,—Joseph Hopkins and Philemon Church.

GIDEON PEARCE, son of William and Isabella Pearce, m. Beatrice Codd, dau. of Col. St. Ledger and Mary Hanson Codd, and d. in August 1751, leaving child., viz., James Pearce,—George Pearce,—David Pearce,—Andrew Pearce,—Nathaniel Pearce,—Mary Pearce,—Sarah Kennard,—Elizabeth Scott,—and Isabella Pearce, also a grandson, William Pearce.

JAMES PEARCE, for many years a Vestryman of Shrewsbury Parish, son of Gideon and Beatrice Codd Pearce, m. 17th August 1771, Catharine Susanna Shannon. He d. in 1802, leaving child., viz., Isabella Pearce Freeman, b. 27th July 1772, James Pearce,—Gideon Pearce,—William Pearce,—Elizabeth Pearce,—Ann Pearce and Catharine Pearce.

GIDEON PEARCE, son of James and Catharine Susanna Shannon Pearce, m. Julia Dick, dau. of Dr. Elisha Cullen Dick, of Alexandria, Va., and left two child., viz., James Alfred Pearce and Ann Ophelia Pearce.

ANN OPHELIA PEARCE, dau. of Gideon and Julia Dick Pearce, m. D. M. Wharton, of Botetourt County, Va., and had child., viz., J. A. P. Wharton,—Edmund L. Wharton,—John A. Wharton,—Catharine Julia Wharton,—and D. M. Wharton.

Hon. James Alfred Pearce, son of Gideon and Julia Dick Pearce, m. Martha J. Laird, who d. leaving child., viz., Catharine Julia Pearce,—Charlotte A. Lennox Pearce (Mrs. Crisfield, the gifted poetess),—and James Alfred Pearce.

After the death of Mrs. Martha J. L. Pearce, Mr. Pearce m. Matilda C. Ringgold, dau. of James Ringgold (see Ringgold, p. 65). He d. 30th Dec. 1862, leaving his widow, Mrs. Matilda C. R. Pearce, with one dau., Mary C. Pearce, his other child. surviving. He was a gentleman of great and varied culture, and a Statesman of enlarged conservative views. He was not a politician in the usual acceptation of the word, and yet was one of the most successful public men in Maryland during the period of his life. Honors and offices waited upon him. His success was due entirely to his own individual merit,—to his unsullied integrity and capacity for public affairs,—and the appreciation of his eminent qualities, by his fellow citizens. His death was regarded by men of all parties as a loss to the country, and deplored as a national calamity. He was reputed to be one of the wisest and safest statesmen in that august body, the Senate of the United States; and the minds of the people were turning towards him as a proper candidate for the Presidency, when death removed him from the Councils of the Nation. He d., leaving behind him a reputation which adds to the treasury of national honor, and a name which adorns the History of Maryland, and will be cherished in Kent by generations unborn.

Mr. Pearce was born the 14th of Dec. 1805, at the residence of his grandfather, Dr. Elisha Cullen Dick, in Alexandria, Va. His mother d. when he was very young, and his early education was received in Alexandria, under the direction of his grandfather. He entered Princeton College at the early age of fourteen, and was graduated in 1822, before he had completed his sixteenth year, dividing the honors of his class with Hugo Mearns, of Pennsylvania, and Edward D. Mansfield, of Ohio, both of whom were men of mature years and minds, and were distinguished in after life: the first for general scholarship, and the latter in the Law, being the Professor of Constitutional Law, for many years, in the Cincinnati College. Among his classmates, also, were George R. Richardson, Attorney General of Maryland, one of the brightest ornaments of the Maryland bar in his day, and Albert B. Dod, of New Jersey, afterwards a Professor in Princeton College, and one of the most brilliant rhetoricians and lecturers in this country.

It was the custom of the College at that period for one

member of each class, at graduation, to write verses descriptive of the character of each one of the class, in the order of the roll-call, which was called the "Honoriad;" and was written by him best qualified by the voice of the class for the task. The HONORIAD for the class of 1822 was written by William Augustine Washington, of Virginia. The verses descriptive of Mr. Pearce will show the estimate placed on him by his associates and class-mates. They are as follows:

"PEARCE!

" With undissembled joy and homage free
Attractive Genius, next we turn to thee!
'Tis good to pause, and ponder on the mind,
Where all thy charms, thy countless charms, we find;
Where all thy vast and varied powers are shown,
And where thy pleasure 'tis to place thy throne.
In thee, admired Pearce! a mind is found,
Where all these charms and all these powers abound.
Yes! Fancy,—Wit,—and Judgment all appear
To meet and shed their mingled radiance here.

Hence JIM, we like to linger on thy name,
To tell thy value,—hear thy merit's claim,
Display thine honest excellence, and pause
To pay our trifling tribute of applause.
Fain would the Muse have all thy worth expressed,
But dreads to put her talent to the test.
Oh! could she borrow but one tithe of thine,
Around that brow, that honored brow, she'd twine
As fair a wreath as ever learning's lore
Or princely pride in proudest moment bore."

After leaving College, Mr. Pearce studied law in Baltimore, with the late Judge Glenn, and was admitted to the Bar in 1824. Shortly after his admission, he commenced the practice of his profession in Cambridge, where he remained about a year; after which, he went to Louisiana and engaged in sugar planting, on the Red River, with his father. He remained there about three years, and then returned to Kent, where he spent the rest of his honored life. On his return to Maryland he resumed the practice of the law, at the same time carrying on the farm, upon which he resided. He was not, however, permitted to devote himsef to his profession, as he desired, for he was early called into public life. In 1831 he was sent to the Legislature of Maryland, and in 1835 he was elected a member of the House of Representatives, and with the exception of a single Term in 1839, when he was defeated by a small majority by the Hon. Philip F. Thomas, he was re-elected, from time to time, till 1843. In 1843 he was transferred to the United States Senate, where he was continued, by four successive elections, until his death, the 20th day of December 1862. During this long period of public service, the Library of Congress, the Botanical Gardens, the Smithsonian Institute, and the Coast Survey Department were favorite objects of his fostering care, and received great and valuable attention from him, while at the same time he faithfully, conscientiously, and with distinguished ability discharged all the Senatorial duties of a Legislator.

He was offered a seat on the Bench of the United States District Court, for the State of Maryland, by President Fillmore, and during the same Presidential Term was nominated and confirmed Secretary of the Interior; both of which positions he declined, preferring to remain in the Senate, where he believed he could be more useful to his country. He left a son, now residing in Chestertown, who worthily bears his honored name, James Alfred Pearce, and illustrates, at the bar, the "honest excellence" of his distinguished father. He is now (9th Aug. 1875) the capable State's Attorney in and for Kent County, Maryland.

SEC. 67, M. GEORGE HANSON, son of Col. Hans and Martha Kelto Ward Hanson, m. 3 times. His 1st wife was Mary Hurtt. His 2nd wife was Sarah Pearce, dau. of Capt. Daniel Pearce, who represented Kent in the Legislature of Maryland in the sessions of 1709, 1711, 1712 and 1713, and was a Vestryman of Shrewsbury Parish in 1718. His 3rd wife was Jane Hynson. He d. 1727, and left child., viz., Martha,—Frederick (who was a Church Warden of Shrewsbury Parish, 16th April 1750),—William,—Christina,—Mary, who m. John Crew,—and George Hanson.

FREDERICK HANSON, son of George and Sarah Pearce Hanson (in his Will dated 31st Dec. 1771, he says his mother's maiden name was Sarah Pearce), had child., viz., Rebecca (Mrs. Williams), b. 20th Nov. 1744,—William, b. 19th Feb. 1747, d. 1789,—Mary, b. 17th March 1750,—James, b. 20th March 1752,—Elizabeth, and Sarah Hanson, who m. Jacob Freeman. His wife's name was Martha Hanson. He d. 1772.

MARY HANSON, dau. of Frederick and Martha Hanson, m. William Granger, who was a member of the Maryland Convention which ratified the Constitution of the United States 28th April 1788, and had two daus.; one, Maria Granger, m. Bennett Mitchell, and the other m. Joseph T. Mitchell.

Elizabeth Hanson, dau. of Frederick and Martha Hanson, m. twice. Her 1st husband was Dr. William Frisby. She m. again 7th Feb'y 1792, Dr. Edward Worrell, son of William Worrell, of Fairy Meadow, who was b. 3d April 1753, and had child., viz., Edward H. Worrell, who m. Elizabeth Ringgold, dau. of Samuel Rinngold,—William Henry Page Worrell,—Sarah Maria Worrell, b. 13th Feb'y 1797,—Frederick Worrell, b. 13th Feb'y 1800, d. 19th June 1822,—James Worrell, b. 27th July 1802, d. 5th Nov. 1824, and Elizabeth Pearce Worrell, b. 17th March 1804. Dr. Edward Worrell, d. 18th Oct. 1804.

Dr. William Worrell, of Fairy Meadow, was the son of Edward Worrell and Mary Tilden, dau. of Marmaduke and Sarah Tilden. Edward Worrell was b. 1719, the son of Edward and Mary Worrell. The last named Edward Worrell was elected a vestryman of St. Paul's Parish, 27th Feb'y 1716.

William Henry Page Worrell, son of Dr. Edward and Elizabeth Hanson Frisby Worrell, b. 27th Aug. 1795, m. 27th Jan'y 1829, Catharine Tilden, dau. of Dr. Charles Tilden, of Kent, d. 11th March 1858, and had child., viz., Ann Elizabeth Worrell, b. 5th Dec. 1829, d. 4th June 1830,—Elizabeth Ann Worrell, b. 31st Jan'y 1831, d. June 26th, 1845,—Frederick Worrell,—Mary E. Worrell, who m. Joseph W. Howard, of Kent,—Charles Edward Worrell, b. 30th Sept. 1839, d. 14th Dec. 1843,—Maria Louisa Worrell,—William Edward Worrell and Catharine Worrell.

Dr. Frederick Worrell, son of William Henry Page and Catharine Tilden Worrell, m. 14th Oct. 1863, Mary Willis Houston, of Lancaster, Pa., and had child., viz., Alice Mary Worrell, b. 29th Nov. 1864, d. 14th Oct. 1865,—Franklin Houston Worrell,—Frederick Worrell, b. 31st March 1867, d. 27th July 1867,—Catharine Worrell, and Charles Worrell.

Sarah Maria Worrell, dau. of Dr. Edward and Elizabeth Hanson Frisby Worrell, m. Maj. Henry Schley, son of John and Mary Schley, of Frederick, and had child., viz., John Edward Schley,—Charles Schley,—Fairfax Schley, and Clara Schley. Mrs. Sarah Maria W. Schley d. 1868, and Maj. Schley, 1st April 1871.

JOHN EDWARD SCHLEY, son of Major Henry and Sarah Maria Worrell Schley, m. 1844, Mary V. Towner, of Shepherdstown, Va., and has a son, Towner Schley, and daus. viz., Anna,—Mary Virginia,—Ida,—Clara,—Helen, and Florence Schley.

CHARLES SCHLEY, son of Maj. Henry and Sarah Maria Worrell Schley, m. 1849, Harriet Johnson, a sister of General Bradley T. Johnson (see JOHNSON), who greatly distinguished himself in the Confederate army, and with other sons of Maryland emulated the glorious deeds of the old Maryland Line. They have a son, Bradley Schley, and daus. viz., Lucy,—Eleanor,—Jesse, and Sybil Schley.

DR. FAIRFAX SCHLEY, son of Maj. Henry and Sarah Maria Worrell Schley, m. 1847, Ann Rebecca L. Steiner, and has 4 child., viz., Steiner Schley,—Jennie Schley,—Louis Henry Schley, and Agnes Schley.

CLARA SCHLEY, dau. of Maj. Henry and Sarah Maria Worrell Schley, m. 1863, Dr. Howard Pinckney, of New York, and has a son, William Henry Pinckney.

HON. FREDERICK HANSON, son of Col. Hans and Martha Kelto Ward Hanson, b. at Kimbolton, Kent, 22d May 1693, m. 14th Feb'y 1711, Mary Lowder, was Chief Justice of Kent County Court in 1732, d. in 1738. His wife, Mary Lowder Hanson, d. 1747. They had child., viz., Hans Hanson, b. 28th Nov. 1712,—Benjamin Hanson, b. 28th Nov. 1714,—Frederick Hanson,—Gustavus Hanson,—Mary Hanson,—Sarah Hanson, and Ann Hanson, who m. Thomas Perkins, son of Daniel and Susanna Starton Perkins (see PERKINS).

HANS HANSON, son of Judge Frederick and Mary Lowder Hanson, d. in 1753, leaving his wife, Margaret Hanson, and child., viz., Hans,—George,—Mary,—Martha, and Anne Hanson. George Hanson was appointed, 19th June 1777, by Governor Thomas Johnson, Captain in the 20th Battalion of Militia, and was High Sheriff of Kent, 1785–1787.

HANS HANSON, son of Hans and Margaret Hanson, m. Mary Hynson, dau. of Charles and Phœbe Carvill Hynson, who d. 1st Feb'y 1774. Hans Hanson, d. in 1777, leaving two child., viz., Martha and William Hanson.

MARTHA HANSON, dau. of Hans Hanson and Mary Hynson, m. Dr. William Ringgold, son of Major William Ringgold, of Eastern Neck (see RINGGOLD), and had child., viz., William Ringgold, who m. Maria Nicholson,—Peregrine Ringgold, who m. 29th Dec. 1822, Mary C. Coe,—Harriet Rebecca Ringgold, who m. 7th Sept. 1820, John Stevenson Constable (see CONSTABLE),—James Alexander Ringgold,—Frederick Gustavus Ringgold, and Mary Hanson Ringgold, who m. 9th Oct. 1821, Hon. James Hodges, of Liberty Hall (see HODGES).

GUSTAVUS HANSON, son of Judge Frederick Hanson and Mary Lowder, m. Catharine Tilden, dau. of John Tilden and Catharine Blay (see TILDEN), and had child., viz., George Adolphus Hanson,—Edward Hanson,—Gustavus Hanson,—Margaret Hanson,—Sarah Hanson,—Elizabeth Hanson, and Catharine Hanson.

GUSTAVUS HANSON was one of the Committee of Safety, Observation and Correspondence, for Kent County, during the Revolutionary War. He d. in 1788, and his wife, Mrs. Catharine Tilden Hanson, d. in 1794.

Catharine Blay was the dau. of Col. William Blay, of Blay's Range, and Isabella Pearce, dau. of Judge William Pearce, of Kent, a son of William Pearce, High Sheriff of Cecil in 1687 (see PEARCE).

MARGARET HANSON, dau. of Gustavus and Catharine Tilden Hanson, m. Thomas Granger, a younger brother of the William Granger before mentioned, and had child., viz., William,—Thomas,—Mary (who m. John Wroth, see WROTH),—Elizabeth, — Peregrine, — Theodore, — Frederick, and Anna Granger.

GEORGE ADOLPHUS HANSON, of Radcliffe Hall, son of Gustavus and Catharine Tilden Hanson, was b. 15th Sept. 1762, and m. 17th March 1789, Rebecca Baird, dau. of Alexander Baird and Elizabeth Ellis. George Adolphus Hanson, d. at Radcliffe Hall, Kent, 16th Oct. 1823, and his wife, Rebecca Baird Hanson, at the same place, 1st June 1810. They had child., viz., Alexander Baird Hanson, b. 8th Feb'y 1790, Catharine (who m. 3d Oct. 1839, Dr. Peregrine Wroth (see WROTH) and d. 28th Dec. 1854,) and Elizabeth Hanson, twins, b. 26th Oct. 1791,—George Hanson, b. 1st Nov. 1793,—Lavinia Hanson, b. 5th Dec. 1794, d. 6th Nov. 1851,—Harriet Hanson, b. 12th Feb'y 1799,—George Washington Hanson, b. 12th May 1799, and Sarah Rebecca Hanson, b. 31st July 1806, d. 4th Nov. 1835.

ALEXANDER BAIRD, the father of Rebecca Baird Hanson, m. 30th Oct. 1746, Elizabeth Ellis, b. 3d April 1724, d. 3d Feb'y 1778, and had child., viz., Francis, b. 25th Sept. 1747, —Mary, b. 22d Aug. 1749,—Catharine, b. 18th March 1751, —Alexander, b. 8th April 1753,—Ann, b. 1st Dec. 1754,—a 2d Ann, b. 6th Jan'y 1756,—a 2d Alexander, and Arthur, *twins*, b. 7th March 1758,—Elizabeth, b. 9th Feb'y 1760,

—a 2d Catharine, b. 2d Feb'y 1762,—Sarah and Rebecca, *twins*, b. 20th April 1764, and a 3d Ann Baird, b. 30th March 1766.

GEORGE WASHINGTON HANSON, youngest son of George Adolphus and Rebecca Baird Hanson, m. 1st June 1830, Margaret Ann Wilmer, d. 16th July 1839, and had child., viz., Gustavus Adolphus Hanson, b. 16th March 1831, d. 11th Aug. 1831,—Catharine Rebecca Hanson, and Pere Wilmer Hanson, who m. Sarah Maria Hopper, dau. of Judge Philemon Blake and Ann Hopper, of Queen Anne's, and had child., viz., Margaret McLean,—Ann Hopper,—Pere Wilmer, — Ella Anderson, — Lucy Wright, — Charles Edgar, and Eugene Douglas Hanson.

SEC..67, N. COL. ALEXANDER BAIRD HANSON, eldest son of George Adolphus and Rebecca Baird Hanson, b. the 8th Feb'y 1790, at Radcliffe Hall, was educated at Washington College. In early manhood he was a bright and zealous Mason, of the Royal Arch Degree, and by his exertions the Masonic Hall in Chestertown was erected. At this period of his life he commanded the Republican Blues, nick-named the "Silk Stocking Company," the crack military company of Kent county. On the 22d day of December 1829, he m. Susan Wilson Black, dau. of Dr. James and Margaret Wilson Black, of Fairfields, Kent, and resided at his country seat, Woodbury, near the head of Sassafras river, in Kent. Subsequently he removed to Frederick City, where he spent the remainder of his active and useful life. Through his unaided efforts the Act of the Assembly of Maryland, of 1839, chapter 217, was passed, and the Frederick Female Seminary, at Frederick City, owes its existence to him. He remained at the head of its direction till the building was completed, and until the Board of Directors, by a majority vote, elected an individual to be the principal teacher who was considered by him unworthy of the position. Then, with a proper sense of personal dignity and honor, he withdrew from the Board of Directors. He was elected, 4th of June 1850, President of the Frederick County Bank (now, and since the 7th of June 1865, The Frederick County National Bank), and filled that position until the 19th of Nov. 1867, when he resigned. He was appointed on the 14th of July 1852, by the Governor (E. Louis Lowe) of Maryland, Commissioner of the Hospital for the Insane, which was established by the Act of 1852, chapter 302; and was also appointed by the Governor, then being, 19th Dec. 1854, a delegate to represent the State of Maryland in the Commercial Convention, which was held in the City of New Orleans, the 12th Jan'y 1855. On the 30th of March 1855, he was appointed by the Hon. Jefferson Davis, Secretary of War, one of the Board of Visitors to attend the Annual Examination of the Military Academy at West Point. For many years and at different times he was a Director of the Baltimore and Ohio Railroad Company, and of the Chesapeake and Ohio Canal Company.

MRS. SUSAN WILSON BLACK HANSON, d. 24th Oct. 1864, in the 65th year of her age, and Col. Alexander Baird Hanson, d. 21st Sept. 1868, in the 79th year of his age; and were both interred in the family vault at Frederick, Md. They had four child., viz., George Adolphus Hanson,—Margaret Wilson Hanson—Edward Alexander Hanson, and Margaret Black Hanson; of whom only two survive, George A. Hanson, the author of OLD KENT, and Edward Alexander Hanson, of the City of New York.

MRS. SUSAN WILSON BLACK HANSON was descended from James Black, of Londonderry. (See BLACK.)

GEORGE ADOLPHUS HANSON, Attorney-at-Law, son of Col. Alexander Baird and Susan Wilson Black Hanson, m. 23d Sept. 1857, Courtney Cordelia Barraud, dau. of Dr. Daniel Cary Barraud and Mary Lawson Chandler, of Norfolk, Va., and had child., viz., Alexander Barraud Hanson,—Barraud Hanson,—St. George Courtney Hanson,—Mary Susan Hanson,—Edward Anderson Hanson, d., and Catharine Annika Hanson, d.

MRS. COURTNEY C. HANSON was a lady of refined culture, and rare womanly intellectual endowment. In character and disposition, she was as gracefully feminine as any lady that ever graced a fireside, adorned a household or gladdened a home. On her father's side a Huguenot, she was the granddau. of Dr. Philip Barraud, one of the distinguished personages of Norfolk, fifty years or more ago, who was the son of Daniel Barraud, the intimate friend of the Earl of Dunmore, in ante-Revolutionary times. Her father, on his mother's side, was a descendant of Thomas Hansford, who, 13th Nov. 1676, triumphingly surrendered his mortal life, "*a martyr to the right of the people to govern themselves.*" (See Bancroft's *United States*, vol. ii, p. 230.)

Her mother, MRS. MARY LAWSON BARRAUD, still living, is the granddau. of Col. Anthony Lawson, of Revolutionary fame, who was the great-grandson of Col. Anthony Lawson, conspicuous in the suppression of the Bacon Rebellion, 1676, in Virginia, who was the son of Thomas Lawson, who came to Virginia with Capt. John Smith (see *History of Virginia*, by Captaine Iohn Smith, London, 1629).

MRS. COURTNEY C. HANSON departed this life 4th of Aug. 1871, at Radcliffe Hall, Kent County, Md., and lies buried, with her two little children, in Chester Cemetery, near Chestertown.

SEC. 67, O. DANIEL BARRAUD, m. Catharine Curle, and had child., viz., Sally Curle Barraud,—Philip Barraud,—Eleanor Barraud, who d. unm.,—Fanny Barraud (who m. Dr. Applewhite), and Catharine Curle Barraud, who m. John Cornwell.

SALLY CURLE BARRAUD, dau. of Daniel and Catharine Curle Barraud, m. Robert Taylor, and had child., viz., Gen'l. Robert Taylor,—Anne Taylor, who m. Governor James Patton Preston, of Va.,—Sarah Taylor, who m. William Eyre, of Va., and Catharine Taylor.

GOVERNOR JAMES PATTON PRESTON was descended from John Preston, whose father and three uncles (Englishmen) served under King William and aided in defending Londonderry, when it was besieged by the Roman Catholics in 1698. "He was a Protestant of the Presbyterian denomination, a man of strong and correct principles."

JOHN PRESTON, b. in Londonderry, Ireland, m. Elizabeth Patton (a sister of Col. James Patton, of Donegal, the ancestor of Gov. John Floyd, of Va., James D. Breckenridge, of Kentucky, and Col. W. P. Anderson, U. S. A.), removed to Virginia in 1740, and had child., viz., Laetitia Preston, b. 1728, in Ireland,—who m. Col. Robert Breckenridge, of Kentucky,—Margaret Preston, b. 1730, in Ireland, who m. Rev. John Brown, and d. 1802,—William Preston, b. 1732, in Ireland, d. at Smithfield, Va., in June 1783,—Ann Preston, who m. Francis Smith, of Va., and d. 1813, in Kentucky,—and Mary Preston, b. 1740, in Virginia, who m. John Howard, of Va.

COL. WILLIAM PRESTON, only son of John Preston and Elizabeth Patton, m. Susanna Smith, dau. of Francis Smith and Elizabeth Waddy, and d. in June 1783, aged 53 years, leaving 11 child., viz., Elizabeth, who m. William S. Madison,—John, who m. 1st Miss Radford and 2dly Mrs. Mayo,—Francis, who m. Miss Campbell,—Sarah, who m. Col. James McDowell,—William, who m. Miss Hancock,—Susanna, who m. Nathaniel Hart,—Governor James Patton,—Mary, who m. John Lewis,—Laetitia, who m. John Floyd,—Thomas Lewis, who m. Edmonia Randolph,—and Margaret Preston, who m. her relative, Col. John Preston.

GOVERNOR JAMES PATTON PRESTON (b. 27th March 1778, d. 4th May 1843, at Smithfield, Va.), son of Col. William Preston and Susanna Smith, was in 1813 a Colonel in the U. S. Army, and Governor of Virginia, 1816–1819, m. 23d June 1801, Anne Taylor, dau. of Robert Taylor and Sally Curle Barraud, who d. 8th June 1861, aged 84 years, and had child., viz., Sarah Barraud Preston, b. 26th May 1804, d. 30th Aug. 1804,—Hon. William Ballard Preston, b. 29th Nov. 1805,—Gen. Robert Taylor Preston, b. 26th May 1809,—James Francis Preston, b. 8th Nov. 1813, d. 20th Jan'y 1861 (who m. 18th Jan'y 1855, Sarah A. Caperton, dau. of Hugh Caperton, and had child., viz., Hugh Caperton,—William Ballard, and James Fancis Preston, Jr., b. 9th April 1860, d. Feb'y 1862),—Virginia Ann Preston, b. 10th Dec. 1815, d.,—Susanna Edmonia Preston, b. 19th Oct. 1818, d.,—and Catharine Jane Grace Preston, b. 1st Feb'y 1821, who m. 27th Nov. 1845, George A. Gilmer, and d. *sine prole*.

HON. WILLIAM BALLARD PRESTON, son of Gov. James Patton Preston and Ann Taylor, was a member of Congress 1847–1849, Secretary of the Navy under President Taylor, 1849–1850, a Senator in the Congress of the Confederate States, and d. 16th Nov. 1862. He m. 28th Nov. 1839, Lucinda Staples Redd, and had child., viz., Waller Redd (who m. 20th Feb'y 1867, Harriet Means, dau. of Edward Means, who d. 22d March 1869),—Ann Taylor (who m. 1st Dec. 1864, Walter Coles, and d. 12th July 1868, leaving child., viz., Lucy,—Walter, and Nannie Preston Coles, d.),—James Patton,—Lucinda Redd (who m. 27th Feb'y 1866, William R. Beal, and had child., viz., Ballard Preston, d.,—and Annie Preston Radford Beal), Jane Grace, and Mary Rezin Preston, b. 29th March 1854, d. 12th Jan'y 1861.

GEN. ROBERT TAYLOR PRESTON, son of Governor James Patton Preston and Ann Taylor, m. 21st Jan'y 1833, Mary Hart, dau. of Benjamin Hart, of Hartwood, South Carolina, and had child., viz., Virginia Ann Emily Preston,—Benjamin Hart Preston, b. 1st Feb'y 1836, at Smithfield, Montgomery Co., Va., d. 22d June 1851, and James Patton Preston.

VIRGINIA ANN EMILY PRESTON, dau. of Gen. Robert Taylor Preston and Mary Hart, m. 26th Aug. 1856, Robert Stark Means, M. D., son of Governor John Hugh Means, of South Carolina, and had child., viz., Robert Preston Means,—Sally Stark Means, b. 6th Jan'y 1860, at Oakland, Fairfield District, South Carolina, d. 30th Dec. 1861,—Mary Hart Means, b. 20th Feb'y 1861, at same place, d. 17th Aug. 1861,—John Hugh Means, and Courtney Hanson Means.

MAJOR ROBERT STARK MEANS, M. D., C. S. A., was desperately wounded at South Mountain, Md., shot through both legs while leading his command. He was promoted, for his gallantry and faithful discharge of duty, to be a Colonel. He was brave, handsome, gentle, patient in suffering, and very amiable. He d. in 1874.

GOV. JOHN HUGH MEANS, son of Thomas and Sarah Means, b. at Hampton, Fairfield District, South Carolina, 18th Aug. 1812, m. 23d Jan'y 1833, Sally Stark, dau. of Robert Stark, of Columbia, S. C., and was slain in battle at the 2d Manassas. They had child., viz., Col. Robert Stark Means, M. D., b. in Columbia, S. C., 10th Dec. 1833, and Emma Sally Means.

DR. PHILIP BARRAUD, son of Daniel and Catharine Curle Barraud, m. 22d of July 1783, Ann Blows Hansford (who was a half-sister of the Robert Taylor who m. Sarah Curle Barraud, and was descended from Col. Thomas Hansford who was executed by Gov. Berkeley, 13th Nov. 1676, "*a martyr to the right of the people to govern themselves*"), and had child., viz., Ann Blows, b. 26th Nov. 1785, d. 27th Dec. 1816,—John Taylor, b. 4th Jan'y 1788, d. 5th June 1821,—Daniel Cary, b. 14th Feb'y 1790, d. 22d of Oct. 1867,—Catharine Curle, b. 27th Oct. 1791, d. 8th Feb'y 1794,—Robert Francis, b. 12th April 1794, d. 3d June 1800,—a second Catharine Curle, b. 11th Aug. 1796, d. 26th June 1797,—Lewis Hansford, b. 9th June, and d. 18th June 1800,—Otway Byrd, b. 11th Nov. 1801, d.,—and Leliana Barraud, b. 11th Feb'y 1805. Dr. Philip Barraud d. 26th of Nov. 1830, in the 73d year of his age. Mrs. Ann Blows Hansford Barraud d. 6th Nov. 1836, in the 76th year of her age.

ANN BLOWS BARRAUD, dau. of Dr. Philip and Ann Blows Hansford Barraud, of Norfolk, Va., m. 25th Dec. 1802, Gen. John Hartwell Cocke, of Fluvanna Co., Va. He was the son of John Hartwell Cocke, the son of Hartwell, who was the son of Richard Cocke. Mrs. Ann Blows Barraud Cocke d. at Bremo Recess, Fluvanna Co., Va., 27th Dec. 1816, in the 31st year of her age, and had child., viz., John Hartwell Cocke, b. 25th Jan'y 1804, d. Sept. 1846, *sine prole*,—Louisiana Barraud Cocke, b. 29th June 1806, who m. Dr. John N. Faulcon, of Surrey, and d. 9th Dec. 1829, *sine prole*,—Gen. Philip St. George Cocke, b. 17th April 1809, who m. Sally

Elizabeth Courtney Bowdoin, and d. 26th Dec. 1861,—Ann Blows Cocke, who m. Nicholas Francis Cabell, and d. Feb'y 1862,—Dr. Charles Cary Cocke, b. 1st Jan'y 1814, who m. Lucy W. Oliver,—and Sally Faulcon Cocke, b. 8th Sept. 1816, who m. Dr. Arthur Lee Brent.

GEN'L PHILIP ST. GEORGE COCKE, of Belmead, Powhatan Co., Va., son of Gen'l. John Hartwell and Ann Blows Barraud Cocke, m. Sally Elizabeth Courtney Bowdoin, and had child., viz., John Bowdoin,—Louisiana Barraud,—Sally Browne,—Lucy Cary,—Philip St. George,—William Ruffin,—Courtney Bowdoin,—Charles Hartwell,—Mary Augusta,—Helen Hansford,—and Ann Blows, b. 19th, and d. 24th March 1857.

ANN BLOWS COCKE, dau. of Gen'l. John Hartwell and Ann Blows Barraud Cocke, m. Nicholas Francis Cabell, of Nelson Co., Va., and had child., viz., Elizabeth Nicholas Cabell (who m. William D. Cabell, and had child., viz., Ann Blows and Mary Cornelia),—Philip Barraud Cabell (who m. Julia Bolling, and had child., viz., Joseph Hartwell,—Francis Barraud, and Philip Mason),—Sally Faulcon Cabell, and Francis G. Cabell.

DR. CHARLES CARY COCKE, of Bremo, Fluvanna Co.,Va., son of Gen'l. John Hartwell, and Ann Blows Barraud Cocke, m. Lucy W. Oliver, and had child., viz., Mary Braxton,—John Hartwell, and Lelia Barraud Cocke.

DR. DANIEL CARY BARRAUD, son of Dr. Philip Barraud and Ann Blows Hansford, of Norfolk, m. 16th Sept. 1819, Mrs. Mary Lawson Chandler Boush, who was b. 4th Nov. 1797, the dau. of George Chandler and Mary Lawson, dau. of Col. Anthony Lawson (of the Revolutionary Army), and Mary Calvert.

DR. DANIEL CARY BARRAUD and Mary Lawson Barraud had child., viz., Ann Blows Barraud, b. 13th Oct. 1820, d. 22d July 1822,—Mira Rosanna Barraud, b. 22nd Sept. 1822, m. Samuel Mazyck Wilson, and d. 17th Aug. 1850,—Philip St. George Barraud, b. 23rd May 1825, d. 15th June 1825,—Lieutenant John Taylor Barraud, U. S. Navy, b. 23d April 1826, m. 25th May 1857, Honoria Allmand, and d. from the effects of a fever contracted on the coast of Africa, 29th Oct. 1860, leaving his wife and one child, Mira Wilson Barraud,—Captain Thomas Lawson Barraud, 16th Regiment of Virginia Infantry, Mahone's Brigade, C. S. Army, b. 26th May, 1828, m. his cousin, Mary Baker, was slain in battle at Bristow Station, Va., on the 14th of Oct. 1863,—Mary Jane Barraud, b.

29th Aug. 1830, d. 8th Dec. 1852, unm.,—Ann Roy Barraud, b. 17th Jan'y 1833, d. 12th Sept. 1834,—Lelia Baker Barraud, b. 27th Jan'y 1835, d. 10th June 1835, and Courtney Cordelia Barraud, b. in Norfolk, 1st of July 1836, m. 23d Sept. 1857, George Adolphus Hanson, son of Col. Alexander Baird and Susan Wilson Black Hanson, and departed this life, at Radcliffe Hall, 4th Aug. 1871, leaving 4 child. Her remains repose in Chester Cemetery, near Chestertown (see HANSON).

LELIANA BARRAUD, dau. of Dr. Philip and Ann Blows Hansford Barraud, m. 25th April 1825, Judge Richard H. Baker, of Norfolk, and had child., viz., Richard H. Baker, who m. 12th Nov. 1850, Nannie M. May, dau. of David and Maria Ward Pegram May,—Dr. Philip Barraud Baker,—Mary Baker, who m. her cousin, Captain Thomas Lawson Barraud, son of Dr. Daniel Cary Barraud,—Lelia Ann Baker, b. 5th Aug. 1832, d.,—Ann Barraud Baker, b. 14th Aug. 1834, d.,—Catharine Beverley Baker, who m. 7th Feb'y 1870, Capt. Samuel Wilson, C. S. Army,—Lelia Baker, who m. 7th Oct. 1863, Dr. Robert B. Taylor,—and Emily Baker, b. 21st Jan'y 1846, who m. 23d Oct. 1873, Theodore S. Garnett, and d. 23d Feb'y 1876.

SEC. 67, P. MRS. MARY LAWSON BARRAUD is descended from Thomas Lawson, who settled at a very early period in Virginia. His name is reported in a printed book, "*set out by the Treasurer and Councill in this present year* 1620." He m. Miss Bray, and had two child., viz., Anthony Lawson, and George Lawson.

COL. ANTHONY LAWSON, son of Thomas Lawson, above named, was appointed Sheriff of Princess Anne Co., Va., by John Blair, "Commander-in-Chief of the Colony and Dominion of Virginia," served in the army of Virginia during the administrations of Governors Sir William Berkeley, Herbert Jeffreys, and Henry Chicheley, and was conspicuous in the suppression of the Bacon Rebellion of 1676; he m. Elizabeth Westgate, and had child., viz., Thomas, and Margaret Lawson, who m. John Thorowgood.

THOMAS LAWSON, son of Col. Anthony Lawson and Elizabeth Westgate, m. Miss Rose, and had child., viz., Anthony,—Ann,—Frances,—George, and Thomas Lawson.

THOMAS LAWSON, son of Thomas Lawson and ——— Rose, m. Frances Sayer, dau. of Charles Sayer, and had child., viz., Anthony,—Thomas, and Charles Lawson.

COL. ANTHONY LAWSON, son of Thomas Lawson and

Frances Sayer, studied law in early life and was admitted, after an examination by Peyton Randolph and George Wythe, 15th May 1750, to practice in the Courts of Virginia. When the Revolutionary War commenced he abandoned the profession and joined the Army of Virginia. Early in the war he was captured and sent to East Florida, where he was detained until released by the following:

EAST FLORIDA:

SEAL. By his Excellency Patrick Tonyon Esq. Captain General Governor and Commander-in-Chief in and over the said Province.

Permission is hereby given to Anthony Lawson, Esq., to pass from hence to Virginia, he being upon his Parole to release or cause to be Released, at the desire of the Earl of Dunmore, any person or Prisoner there, otherwise to deliver himself up again.

Given under my Hand and Seal, at St. Augustine, this twenty-third day of November 1776.

PAT. TONYON.

TO ALL WHOM IT MAY CONCERN.

COL. ANTHONY LAWSON, was b. in 1729, m. Mary Calvert and d. 16th Feb'y 1785. She was b. in 1742, and d. 18th Jan'y 1787, and had child., viz., Thomas,—Richard,—Henry Lee, — Anthony, — Mary, — Elizabeth (Mrs. Cartwright),— Helen,—and Frances Sayer Lawson, who m. Dr. Evans.

THOMAS LAWSON, son of Col. Anthony Lawson and Mary Calvert, m. Sarah Robinson (dau. of Tully Robinson, son of William Robinson), and had child., viz., Anthony Lawson, b. 14th Aug. 1787, d. unm.,—Dr. Thomas Lawson, late Surgeon General of the United States Army, b. 29th Aug. 1789, who was commissioned, 14th Feb'y 1811, Surgeon mate, by James Madison, President of the United States; commissioned 7th Sept. 1816, Surgeon in sixth regiment of Infantry, "to rank as such from the 21st of May 1813"; commissioned 1st Feb'y 1837, Surgeon General by Andrew Jackson, "to rank as such from 30th Nov. 1836," and "for distinguished and meritorious services in the field before and during the Mexican War" was promoted to the rank of Brigadier General by Brevet, by commission dated 3d March 1849, "to rank as such from 30th May 1848," and d. at the residence of Dr.

Daniel Cary Barraud, in Norfolk, Va., 14th of May 1861, unm.,—and Tully Robinson Lawson, b. 8th June 1793, who d. unm.

RICHARD LAWSON, son of Col. Anthony and Mary Calvert Lawson, m. Miss Godwin, dau. of Joseph Godwin, of Nansemond, Va., and left one child, Mary Frances Lawson, who m. James Edward Wilson, and left child., viz., Indiana E., who m. John W. Young,—Catharine, who m. Dr. John O. Payne, —Lucy, A., who m. Charles D. Willard,—Mary F., who m. Thomas C. Hanford,—and Roscoe T. Wilson, who d. *sine prole.*

ANTHONY LAWSON, son of Col. Anthony Lawson and Mary Calvert, m. Miss Marvolt and left one dau., Elizabeth W. Lawson, b. 23d Dec. 1805, who m. 29th Nov. 1844, James Hill Ransone, who was b. 19th April 1795, and d. 17th April 1860, leaving one son, Dr. Alexander Lawson Ransone.

MARY LAWSON, dau. of Col. Anthony Lawson and Mary Calvert, m. George Chandler, son of George Chandler and Elizabeth Matlock, and had child., viz., George Washington Chandler, who d. young,—John Adams Chandler,—and Mary Lawson Chandler.

JOHN ADAMS CHANDLER, of the Norfolk Bar, son of George Chandler and Mary Lawson, m. Sarah Woodward, and had child., viz., Sarah M. Chandler, who m. William A. Niemeyer,—Mary E. Chandler, who m. John Hill,—Martha W. Chandler, who m. Rev. Leo Rosser,—Georgiana M. Chandler, who m. Henry F. Woodhouse,—and Henrietta C. and Virginia F. Chandler, who were the 1st and 2d wives of Henry Harwood.

MARY LAWSON CHANDLER, dau. of George Chandler and Mary Lawson, m. 1st Mr. Boush, a member of the Legislature of Virginia, who d. *sine prole*; 2dly 16th of Sept. 1819, Dr. Daniel Cary Barraud, and had child (see BARRAUD).

SEC. 67, Q. JAMES BLACK came to this country from Londonderry, about the year 1740, with his wife and child., viz., James Black, who m. Jennette Wallace,—William Black, whose descendants are now living in the Carolinas,—Martha Black, who m. Andrew Kerr,—George Black, who m. Margaret Wallace, and two daus., one of whom m. John Kilgour, of Pennsylvania. The Blacks were Scotch-Irish and members of the Presbyterian Church.

JAMES BLACK, son of the first named James Black, m. 11th May 1762, Jennette Wallace, dau. of Andrew and Elianor Wallace. She d. 22d April 1774, in the 33d year of her age, leaving child., viz., Elizabeth Black, b. 24th Jan'y 1763,—John Black, b. 3d Nov. 1767,—Mary Black, b. 17th April 1773.

ELIZABETH BLACK, dau. of James Black and his 1st wife Jennette Wallace Black, m. 23d Jan'y 1787, Dr. Joseph Wallace, son of Joseph Wallace, who d. 28th May 1777, who was the son of Andrew Wallace, before mentioned. Dr. Joseph Wallace was a surgeon in the Revolutionary army and d. in Elkton, in 1796, aged 44 years, and left child., viz., James Black Wallace, b. 10th June 1788, and d. at Natchez 3d Sept. 1825,—Mary Wallace, b. 17th Sept. 1789, and Dr. Joseph Wallace, b. 5th Feb'y 1791.

MARY WALLACE, dau. of Dr. Joseph and Elizabeth Black Wallace, m. Governor Thomas W. Veazey, who d. 1st July 1842, in the 69th year of his age,—Mrs. Mary Wallace Veazey, d. 9th July 1867.

GOVERNOR THOMAS WARD VEAZEY was descended from John Veazey, of Cherry Grove, who was of an old Norman family, De Veazie, which removed to England in the 11th century. John Veazey settled in Kent prior to the year 1670, and received by grant a portion of the tract of land bounding on Elk and Bohemia rivers, known as Veazey's Neck, now in Cecil County. His Will is dated Feb'y 28th 1697, and mentions child., viz., William Veazey,—George Veazey (who m. Alice, dau. of William and Elizabeth Ward, and had a son, William),—Robert Veazey, who m. Lucy Dermot,—James Veazey (who m. Mary Mercer, and had a son, Edward, who was captain of the 7th Independent Company, Maryland Line, and was killed at the battle of Long Island, Aug. 27th 1776,—and Edward Veazey.

WILLIAM VEAZEY, eldest son of John Veazey, m. Rosamond ——, and had one dau. Susannah Veazey, b. 20th Jan'y 1696.

SUSANNAH VEAZEY, dau. of William and Rosamond Veazey, m. 23d March 1717, John Ward, son of William and Elizabeth Ward, and had 8 child., one of whom was John Ward, b. Mch. 13th, 1730.

JOHN WARD, son of John and Susannah Veazey Ward, m. Elizabeth Wilson, of Kent Island, and had a son Joshua Ward, b. 31st July 1769.

JOSHUA WARD, son of John and Elizabeth Wilson Ward, m. in 1793, Sarah, dau. of Edward and Elizabeth De Coursey Veazey, and had child., viz., John W. Ward, who m. Elizabeth Roberts, of Cecil Co.,—Elizabeth Ward; who m. Dr. Joseph Wallace, of Cecil,—Edward Veazey Ward, who m.

Harriet, dau. of John Fergusson, of Cecil,—Dr. James Robert Ward, of Baltimore County, who m. Ellen, dau. of John McClenahan, of Penna.,—Henry Veazey Ward, who m. Caroline, dau. of William B. Reynolds, of Boston, and afterwards Ann E., dau. of Judge Merrill, of Haverhill, Massachusetts, and d. at Dresden, where he was Consul-General for the Republic of Chili, and has descendants living in Boston,—and George Washington Ward, of Baltimore, who m. Mary J., dau. of Henry and Sophia Wilson, of Fauquier County, Va.

EDWARD VEAZEY, fifth son of John Veazey, m. Susannah ———, and had one son, Col. John Veazey, Jr., b. 12th Feb'y 1701.

COL. JOHN VEAZEY, JR., of Cherry Grove, son of Edward and Susannah Veazey, received an additional grant of land, 11th Aug. 1753. In 1754, he was Deputy Surveyor for Cecil County. He represented Cecil County in the Convention of Maryland, of 1774, 1775, and 1776. On the 6th Jan'y 1776 he was elected Colonel of the Bohemia Battalion. He m. Mary ———, d. 4th May 1777, had child., viz., Edward,—William,—John Ward, and Thomas Brocus Veazey.

EDWARD VEAZEY, of Cherry Grove, son of Col. John and Mary Veazey, b. 1730, m. 19th Jan'y 1755, Elizabeth De Coursey, of Queen Anne's, and had child., viz., Edward,—Edward Henry, who m. Rebecca Ward,—Ann,—Sarah, who m. Joshua, son of John and Elizabeth W. Ward,—Rebecca,—and Thomas Ward Veazey.

ANN VEAZEY, dau. of Edward and Elizabeth De Coursey Veazey, b. 9th April 1766, m. 25th Nov. 1784, William Ward, son of William and Rebecca Davis Ward, and had child., viz., William Henry,—James,—Sarah, who m. Dr. John T. Veazey, —Juliana,—Eliza,—Ann, who m. Thomas B. Veazey,—Susan, and Thomas Veazey Ward.

JUDGE WILLIAM HENRY WARD, of Baltimore, son of William and Ann Veazey Ward, m. Miss Redding, of Delaware, and had a dau. Ellen Ward, who m. Robert Gilmor, of Baltimore, and had eleven child., viz., Judge Robert Gilmor, who m. Ella M., dau. of B. M. Hodges, Jr., of Baltimore,—Wm. Gilmor, who m. Mary, dau. of Philip Barton Key,—Ellen Gilmor, who m. Alexander MacTavish, had a child, Francis Osborne MacTavish, and afterwards m. Dr. G. Halsted Bojland,—Charles Gilmor,—Col. Harry Gilmor, the celebrated Confederate officer, who m. a dau. of Col. Strong, of Pensacola, and had 3 child.,—Howard Gilmor, C. S. A., d. 1862, Richard Tilghman Gilmor, d., Campbell Graham Gilmor,—Arthur Gilmor, C. S. A., d. 1864,—Lt. Meredith Gilmor, C. S. A.,—and Mary Gilmor.

JULIANA WARD, dau. of William and Ann Veazey Ward, m. Dr. George Read Pearce, of Pearce's Neck, Cecil Co., a grandson of George Read who signed the Declaration of Independence. Her 2d husband was Ambrose C. Richardson.

SUSAN WARD, dau. of William and Ann Veazey Ward, m. Andrew Fisher Henderson, son of Frisby and Amelia Fisher Henderson, and had child., viz., Amelia Henderson, who m. James W. Barroll, of Baltimore, son of James Barroll, of Kent,—Lavinia Henderson, who m. James Henry Ferguson, of Baltimore, son of Thomas and Caroline Heide Ferguson, of Middlesex Co., Va.,—Julia W. Henderson,—Susan Henderson, who m. Wilson C. N. Carr, son of Hon. Dabney S. Carr,—Ellen Henderson, who m. John A. Whitridge, son of Dr. John Whitridge,—Thomas Frisby Henderson, who m. Charlotte Kelsey, of Long Island,—and William Ward Henderson, who m. Flora, dau. of Samuel Hollingsworth.

THOMAS VEAZEY WARD, of Woodlawn, son of William and Ann Veazey Ward, m. Mary Thompson, dau. of Robert McLane, of Cecil, and had child., viz., Julia M., who m. Dr. Henry W. Cruikshank,—William Ward, of Rosehill, who m. Charlotte, dau. of William and Arabella Veazey Knight, of Essex Lodge, and represented Cecil county in the Legislature of 1875,—Thomas Ward, of Woodlawn and Eliza M. Ward. Thomas Veazey Ward d. Nov. 1873.

REBECCA VEAZEY, dau. of Edward and Elizabeth De Coursey Veazey, m. Joseph Lusby of Cecil, and has one descendant living, Eliza De Coursey Lusby, of Baltimore.

HON. THOMAS WARD VEAZEY, son of Edward and Elizabeth De Coursey Veazey, b. 31st Jan'y 1774; was Colonel of Militia in the war of 1812–14; was several times a member of the Maryland Legislature; was Presidential elector in 1809 and 1813, and voted for James Madison, and was Governor of Maryland 1835–1838; was 1st m. 18th Nov. 1794 to Sarah Worrell, of Kent county, and had a dau. Sarah, who d. in childhood. His 2d wife was Mary Veazey, m. March 29th 1798, and had five child., Dr. Edward Veazey,—Mary L.,—Thomas Ward,—George Clinton,—Maria Elizabeth, and May L. Veazey. His 3d wife was Mary, dau. of Dr. Joseph and Elizabeth Black Wallace, m. 24th Sept. 1812, and had five child., James Wallace Veazey, of Cherry Grove,—Joseph Wallace Veazey, d.,—Ellen Matilda, who d. in childhood,—Elizabeth Black Veazey, who m. Benjamin B. Craycroft, of Philadelphia,—and Mary Emma Veazey, who m. Dr. Samuel E. Mills.

DR. THOMAS BROCUS VEAZEY, of Essex Lodge, son of Colonel John Veazey, b. March 29th 1750, m. 29th March 1781, Mary Thompson, dau. of Rev. William Thompson, of St. Stephen's Church, Cecil county, and Miss Ross, dau. of Rev. Geo. Ross, of New Castle, Del., a sister of George Ross, who signed the Declaration of Independence. He d. 6th Feb'y 1826, and had four child., viz., John Thompson,—Juliana Ross, who m. Thomas Savin, of Port Deposit, Cecil county,—Maria, who m. Isaac B. Parker, of Burlington, New Jersey, and Thomas Brocus Veazey.

DR. JOHN THOMPSON VEAZEY, of Mount Harmon, son of Dr. Thomas Brocus and Mary Thompson Veazey, b. 22d July 1783, m. 23d Jan'y 1815, Sarah, dau. of William and Ann Veazey Ward, of Woodlawn. He d. March 30th 1839, and had four sons, viz., William T.,—John T.,—George Ross,—and Thomas Brocus, who was captured in the Lopez Expedition and shot by the Cubans 16th Aug. 1851.

GEORGE ROSS VEAZEY, son of Dr. John Thompson and Sarah Ward Veazey, b. 17th Jan'y 1820, was a member of the Baltimore bar, m. 16th May 1850, Eliza Duncan, dau. of Rev. John Mason and Eliza McKim Duncan, and grand-dau. of John McKim, Jr., of Baltimore, d. 12th Sept. 1856, and had four sons, viz., Duncan,—Geo. Ross, d.,—Isaac Parker—and McKim Veazey, d.

ISAAC PARKER VEAZEY, Attorney-at-Law, son of George Ross and Eliza Duncan Veazey, m. April 13th, 1875, Grace Gaddess, dau. of Thomas Stockton and Elizabeth Revely Gaddess, of Baltimore.

THOMAS BROCUS VEAZEY, of Essex Lodge, son of Dr. Thomas Brocus and Mary Thompson Veazey, b. Jan'y 30th, 1792, m. Ann Ward, dau. of William and Ann V. Ward, and had one child, Arabella Veazey.

ARABELLA VEAZEY, dau. of Thomas Brocus and Ann Ward Veazey, m. William Knight, of Cecil. She d. in Dec. 1873, and had six child., viz., Catharine, who m. Robert Barton, of Winchester, Va.,—Charlotte, who m. William Ward, of Rosehill, son of Thos. Veazey and Mary McLane Ward,—Annie,—Julia,—Arabella, d., and Nellie Knight, of Essex Lodge.

DR. JOSEPH WALLACE, son of Dr. Joseph and Elizabeth Black Wallace, m. Elizabeth Ward, and left four child., viz.,

George F. Wallace,—Dr. Joseph Veazey Wallace,—Caroline Wallace, and Laura Virginia Wallace.

Mrs. Elizabeth Black Wallace survived her 1st husband, Dr. Joseph Wallace, and m. 31st Aug. 1799, Dr. John Groome, who was the son of Charles Groome, of Kent County.

SEC. 67, R. CHARLES GROOME, son of Samuel Groome, a Church Warden of St. Paul's Parish in the year 1726, m. twice. By his 1st wife he had eight child., of whom the following survived him, viz., James Groome (who m. Sarah Perkins, dau. of Col. Isaac Perkins, and had child., viz., Isaac,—Charles and James Groome),—John Groome,—Daniel Groome,—Charles Groome, and Sarah Groome, who d. in 1798. By his 2d wife, Sarah Kennard, he, also, had eight child., viz., Milcah, b. 2d Sept. 1773, d. 2d Sept. 1792,—Ann, b. 23d July 1775,—Samuel, b. 7th May 1777,—Henrietta, b. 23d March 1779 (who m. William Pearce),—Elizabeth, b. 20th April 1781,—Mary, b. 2d March 1785,—William Hynson Groome, b. 13th June 1788, and Joseph Groome, b. 3d Oct. 1791. Charles Groome, d. of small-pox, 20th March 1791: that year being memorable in Kent for the general inoculation of the inhabitants, to prevent the ravages of that loathsome disease. He was the Register of Chester Parish, Kent, from the 4th of Feb'y 1766, until his death.

WILLIAM HYNSON GROOME, son of Charles and Sarah Kennard Groome, m. 13th Nov. 1833, Elizabeth Matilda Kennard, his first cousin (a dau. of Owen and Ann Kennard), who was b. 2d May 1807, and d. 4th Jan'y 1863. He d. 9th Jan'y 1869. They had child., viz., Charles Owen (who m. 24th Nov. 1858, Helen Virginia Daingerfield, who d. 15th March 1875),—Ann Kennard,—William Hynson and Samuel Thomas,—Sarah Elizabeth,—Susan Amelia,—Maria Elizabeth and Robert William Groome, who m. 28th Sept. 1871, Elizabeth Ann Trippe, of Newtown, L. I., and has a dau. Elinor Condit Groome.

ANN KENNARD GROOME, dau. of William Hynson and Elizabeth Matilda Kennard Groome, m. 6th Feb'y 1862, Elias O. Dawson, of Easton, and had child., viz., Elizabeth Groome,—William Groome,—Edith,—Ann Kennard,—Edith Offley and Claude Brownrigg Dawson.

MARY GROOME, dau. of Charles and Sarah Kennard Groome, m. in 1802, Josias Ringgold, and had child., viz., Josias,—Sarah Ann,—Charles,—Mary Ann,—Henrietta Groome, and William Groome Ringgold. Mrs. Mary Groome Ringgold survived her husband and m. Benjamin Blackiston Wroth. (See RINGGOLD and WROTH.)

SAMUEL GROOME, son of Charles and Sarah Kennard Groome, m. 1st of Oct. 1812, Deborah Morris, dau. of James Morris a descendant of Anthony Morris, who was b. at St. Dunstan's Stepney of London, 23d Aug. 1654. He d. 14th March 1828, and she d. 2d Jan'y 1821, in the 39th year of her age. Two of their child. survived, viz., Anna Matilda (who m. 25th Nov. 1840, Philip Henry Feddeman, and had a son, Morris Groome Feddeman), and Mary Elizabeth Groome.

MARY ELIZABETH GROOME, dau. of Samuel and Deborah Morris Groome, m. 9th June 1840, William Smyth Thompson, and had child., viz., Elizabeth Morris,—Samuel Groome,—Sarah Matilda,—Mary Rebecca,—William Augustine (who m. 9th June 1875, Florence Hungerford), and Charles Doudle Thompson.

DR. SAMUEL GROOME THOMPSON, son of William Smyth and Mary Elizabeth Groome Thompson, m. 8th July 1864, Miss Caroline Nixon Winchester, and had child., viz., Mary Groome,—Jacob Winchester, and Elizabeth Morris Thompson.

SARAH MATILDA THOMPSON, dau. of William Smyth and Mary Elizabeth Groome Thompson, m. 28th Feb'y 1867 Frederick G. Eareckson, and had child., viz., Frederica Rose, —Mary,—William Augustine Thompson,—Ellen Sophie,— and Matilda Groome Eareckson.

ANN GROOME, dau. of Charles and Sarah Kennard Groome, m. James Buchanan, and had a dau., Mary Ann Buchanan.

MARY ANN BUCHANAN, dau. of James and Ann Groome Buchanan, m. Richard Frisby, and had child., viz., William Groome,—Richard (who m. Catharine Humphreys),—Elizabeth, and Mary Ann Frisby.

WILLIAM GROOME FRISBY, son of Richard and Mary Ann Buchanan Frisby, m. 8th Feb'y 1849, Mary Matilda Fisher, dau. of Dr. Jacob and Mary Ann Ringgold Fisher, and had child., viz., Mary,— William Groome,— Charles Jacob,— Matilda, and William Groome Frisby.

ELIZABETH FRISBY, dau. of Richard and Mary Ann Buchanan Frisby, m. Sylvester Sanner, and had child., viz., Mary Virginia,—Albert, — James, — Annie Elizabeth,—George,— Martha,—William, and Matilda Sanner.

DR. JOHN GROOME, son of Charles Groome and his 1st wife, m. 31st Aug. 1799, Mrs. Elizabeth Black Wallace, dau. of James and Jennette Wallace Black, and the widow of Doctor Joseph Wallace, of Elkton. She d. 7th May 1817, in the

55th year of her age, and Dr. John Groome d. 18th May 1830, in the 62d year of his age. They had child., viz., John Charles Groome, b. 8th of June 1800, d. 30th Nov. 1866; Samuel William Groome, b. 26th July 1802, d. May 1843; and Elizabeth Jennette Groome, b. 12th Feb. 1805, and d. 20th Aug. 1866.

GEN. JOHN CHARLES GROOME, son of Dr. John and Elizabeth Black Wallace Groome, m. 6th December 1836, Elizabeth Riddle Black, dau. of Judge James Rice and Maria E. Stokes Black. He d. in Elkton, 30th Nov. 1846, and had child., viz., James Black Groome,—John Charles Groome, who d. at the verge of a promising manhood,—Maria Stokes Groome,—Elizabeth Black Groome, and Jane Sarah Groome, who m. Dr. John Janvier Black, of New Castle.

HON. JAMES BLACK GROOME, son of Gen. John Charles and Elizabeth R. Black Groome, was Governor of Maryland in 1874 and 1875. He m. 29th Feb'y 1876, Alice L. Edmondson, dau. of Col. Horace Leeds Edmondson.

MARIA STOKES GROOME, dau. of Gen. John Charles and Elizabeth R. Black Groome, m. 27th April 1864, Hon. William M. Knight (at present member of the Senate of Maryland, and a son of William Knight and Rebecca D. Ringgold, dau. of Samuel Ringgold), and had child., viz., William,—John Charles Groome,—Elizabeth Groome,—Ethel, and James Groome Knight.

ELIZABETH BLACK GROOME, dau. of Gen'l. John Charles and Elizabeth R. Black Groome, m. 12th June 1866, Hon. Albert Constable, son of Albert and Hannah Archer Constable, and had child., viz., Alice,—Arline,—John,—and Albert Constable (see CONSTABLE).

DR. SAMUEL WILLIAM GROOME, son of Dr. John and Elizabeth Black Wallace Groome, m. 26th Jan'y 1830, Elizabeth Allen, of Phila., and d. May 1843, leaving two child., viz., Anna Groome, who m. Charles C. Whittlesey, and Samuel W. Groome, who m. Frances Connelly, of Phila., and had child., viz., Henry Connelly Groome,—John Chas. Groome, and Eliza Andrews Groome.

ELIZABETH JENNETTE GROOME, dau. of Dr. John and Elizabeth Black Wallace Groome, m. Capt. Matthew C. Pearce. She d. at Elkton, 20th Aug. 1866, and left three child., viz., Mary Wallace Pearce, who m. Andrew Mitchell,—Jennette Pearce and Ella Pearce.

MARY BLACK, dau. of James Black and his 1st wife Jennette Wallace Black, m. James Scott, of Kent, and left child., viz., Eliza,—John,—Mary Ann, and Maria Jane Scott.

SEC. 67, S. JAMES BLACK, son of James Black, the first named, m. a 2d time 14th Feb'y 1775, Margaret Evans, who d. 13th Sept. 1779, aged 35 years, leaving one dau. Ann Black, b. 16th Nov. 1776, who m. Capt. William Hollingsworth, and d. 20th July 1830. He m. a 3d time, 22d Nov. 1780, Mary Rice, dau. of Evans Rice, and had child., viz., Jane Black, b. 2d Nov. 1781, d. 18th May 1786,—Martha, b. 9th Aug. 1783, d. 27th Sept. 1783,—James Rice Black, b. 14th May 1785,—Sarah Black, b. 26th Sept. 1787, d. 3d Dec. 1861,—Catharine Maria Black, b. 5th Oct. 1789, m. John Donaldson, of Phila., d. Jan'y 9th, 1865, and Jane Black, b. 12th Oct. 1791, d. 18th Dec. 1845,—James Black, d. 30th Oct. 1794, in the 63d year of his age. Mrs. Mary Rice Black, d. 10th Sept. 1833, aged 77 years.

JUDGE JAMES RICE BLACK, of New Castle, Delaware, son of James and Mary Rice Black, m. Maria E. Stokes, of Phila., and left child., viz., Mary Black, who m. Dr. James Couper, of New Castle, Delaware,—Elizabeth Riddle Black, who m. Gen'l. John Charles Groome, of Elkton, and Sarah Black, who m. Commander William L. Young, U. S. N., and had child., viz., James Black Young,—Betty Conrad Young (who m. Samuel Welsh, Jr., of Phila., and had a son Samuel Welsh Young),—Robert Young,—Wm. L. Young,—Catharine Maria Donaldson Young, and Philip R. Fendall Young.

JAMES BLACK YOUNG, son of William L. and Sarah Black Young, m. Miss Welsh, a sister of the said Samuel Welsh.

MARTHA BLACK, dau. of the first named James Black, m. Andrew Kerr, and had child., viz., Mary, who m. Mr. Sharpe, of Kentucky,—Samuel, who m. Miss Corre, dau. of Jas. Corre, of Kent,—Elizabeth (who m. Henry Pearce, and had a child, Sarah Ann Pearce),—Patty (who m. Benjamin Merritt, and had child., viz., William K., George A., and Adelina K. Merritt),—James,—Andrew, and Charlotte Kerr, who m. Joseph Hossinger.

ANDREW KERR, son of Andrew and Martha Black Kerr, m. Hannah Gillespie, and had child., viz., Mary, who m. Francis G. Parke, of Cecil, and had a son, Andrew Kerr Parke,—George G., and James Black Kerr.

GEORGE BLACK, son of the first named James Black, resided at Fairfields, Kent; about the year 1770, he m. Margaret Wallace, dau. of Andrew and Elianor Wallace, before mentioned. He d. Jan'y 1797, and left child., viz., James Black,—Ann Black, who m. James Salsbury,—George Black, —John Black,—Elizabeth Black, who m. Mr. Giles,—Andrew Black, and Thomas Black.

JOHN BLACK, son of George and Margaret Wallace Black, m. Mary Perkins, dau. Col. Isaac Perkins, and left two child., viz., Eliza Jane Black, and Caroline Ann Black.

ELIZA JANE BLACK, dau. of John and Mary Perkins Black, m. in 1822, Benjamin Merritt, before mentioned, and had child., viz., Thomas Albert Merritt (who d. 1857),—Benjamin Gustavus Merritt,—James Black Merritt,—Samuel Augustus Merritt,—Mary Ann Merritt, and Caroline Rebecca Merritt.

REV. JAMES BLACK MERRITT, son of Benjamin and Eliza Jane Black Merritt, m. Hannah P. Webb, dau. of Dr. Samuel Webb, of Kent Co., Delaware.

CAROLINE ANN BLACK, dau. of John and Mary Perkins Black, m. John Carvill Sutton, d. 6th July 1875, leaving child., viz., Mary Ann,—John Carvill,—Sarah,—Caroline,—James, and Ann Matilda Sutton.

DR. JAMES BLACK, eldest son of George and Margaret Wallace Black, was b. at Fairfields, Kent, 4th Jan'y 1772, and m. 12th Dec. 1798, Margaret Wilson, dau. of John and Mary Perkins Wilson. Dr. James Black d. 27th Oct. 1804. Mrs. Margaret Wilson Black was b. at the White House, Kent, 29th Dec. 1779, and d. 7th Sept. 1815. They were both buried at Shrewsbury. They left two child., viz., Susan Wilson Black, who m. Col. Alexander Baird Hanson, of Woodbury, Kent (see HANSON), and Maj. John Gustavus Black.

MAJ. JOHN GUSTAVUS BLACK, son of Dr. James and Margaret Wilson Black, was b. at Fairfields, and m. 4th June 1833, Alphonsa Cummins, of Smyrna, Delaware, dau. of John and Susan Wilson Cummins, and has child., viz., James Edgar Black,—Susan Cummins Black,—Margaret Wilson Black (who m. 3d Nov. 1870, Dr. George S. Culbreth, U. S. N., and has a dau., Susan Black Culbreth), and Eugenia Black.

SEC. 67, T. The WILSONS came from England to the Province of Maryland about the year 1700, and settled in Shrewsbury Parish, Kent.

JAMES WILSON, of Old Field Point, d. at a very advanced age in 1732, leaving his wife, Catharine Wilson, and child., viz., James Wilson,—John Wilson,—George Wilson, and Mary Wilson, who m. Thomas Woodland.

GEORGE WILSON, of Broad Oak, son of James and Catharied Wilson, m. Mary Kennard. He was a delegate from Kent County in the Legislature of Maryland in the sessions of 1728, 1731, 1732, 1734, 1735, 1736, 1740, 1745, 1746, and 1747. He d. in 1748, and left child., viz., George Wilson,—Mary Wilson (who m. Andrew Hynson, and had child., viz., Sarah, b. 9th Aug. 1750,—Thomas, b. 10th April 1752, and Andrew Hynson, b. 9th Dec. 1753),—Sarah Wilson,—Frances Wilson (who m. William Woodland and had a son, William Woodland, b. 15th Oct. 1754),—Rachel Wilson (who m. William Downs and had a child, Araminta Wilson Downs, b. 9th April 1760),—Araminta Wilson, who d. 1760, and Millison Wilson, who m. Dr. William Rogers, a brother of Hon. John Rogers, Chancellor of Maryland from 20th March 1778 until his death in 1780.

GEORGE WILSON, of Castle Cairy, son of George and Mary Kennard Wilson, m. Margaret Hall, and left child., viz., George Wilson,—John Wilson,—William Wilson,—Mary Wilson, who m. Col. William Henry, of the Revolutionary Army, and Sarah Wilson, who m. George Wilson and was the mother of Richard Wilson. Mrs. Margaret Hall Wilson survived George Wilson, and m. Gen. St. Clair, of the Revolutionary Army, by whom she had a son, Dr. Campbell St. Clair, of Sussex Co., Delaware. The old Dowager, as she was called, Mrs. Mary Kennard Wilson, survived her and was living at Broad Oak, and was so enraged with her for marrying a second time that she would not allow Mrs. St. Clair to be interred with her child. and 1st husband in the Wilson family vault.

GEORGE WILSON, eldest son of George and Margaret Hall Wilson, m. Susan Holliday (who was the dau. of Robert and Phoebe Morris Holliday. Phoebe Morris Holliday was the dau. of James and Margaret Cook Morris. James Morris was the son of Anthony Morris, who was b. at St. Dunstans Stepney of London, 23d Aug. 1654, m. Mary Jones, 30th Jan'y 1676, and d. 24th Oct. 1721), and had the following child., viz., George,—Phoebe,—Robert,—George William,—Milicent,—Susan,—Rachel, who m. Edward Price Wilmer (see WILMER), —John,—and Margaret Wilson.

PHOEBE WILSON, dau. of George and Susan Holliday Wilson, was b. 4th Feb'y 1779, m. 8th Dec. 1801, Philip Freeman Rasin, who was b. 4th Oct. 1771, and had child., viz., Jacob Freeman Rasin, b. 24th Feb'y 1803 (who m. 17th Feb'y 1825, Mary Reyner, dau. of John and Araminta Crew Reyner),—George Wilson Rasin, b. 6th Jan'y 1805,—Robert Wilson Rasin, b. 16th Sept. 1806,—Edward Freeman Rasin, b. 16th April 1809,—James Morris Rasin, b. 6th Feb'y 1811,—Henry Holliday Rasin, b. 29th Dec. 1812,—Ann Editha Rasin, b. 12th Sept. 1814,—Caroline Rasin, b. 26th Jan'y 1816,—Sophia Lavinia Rasin, b. 28th Feb'y 1817,—and Philip Alexander Rasin, b. 3d Nov. 1820.

Robert Wilson Rasin, son of Philip Freeman and Phoebe Wilson Rasin, m. 8th May 1832, Mary Rebecca Ringgold, dau. of Edward and Martha Ringgold, and had child., viz., Isaac Freeman,—Phoebe Wilson,—Robert Wilson Lowber,—and Alfred Ringgold Rasin.

Isaac Freeman Rasin, son of Robert Wilson and Mary Rebecca Ringgold Rasin, m. 4th March 1862, Julia Ann Claypool, and had child., viz., Martha Anne Rasin,—Genevieve Ringgold Rasin,—Howard Claypool Rasin,—John Thomas Rasin, and Morris Claypool Rasin.

Robert Wilson Lowber Rasin, son of Robert Wilson and Mary Rebecca Ringgold Rasin, m. 19th June 1860, Margaret Ann Johnson, and had child., viz., Mary Ringgold Rasin,—Lelian Maria Rasin, d.,—Robert Cooper Rasin,—Grace Rasin,—Bessie Rasin, and Viola Rasin.

Alfred Ringgold Rasin, son of Robert Wilson and Mary Rebecca Ringgold Rasin, m. 8th May 1866, Mary E. Hook, who d. 20th Sept. 1867, and left one child, Mary Clara Rasin. He m. 2ndly 17th Oct. 1869, Frances Dorsey, and has one child, Matilda Dorsey Ringgold Rasin.

Dr. Edward Freeman Rasin, son of Philip Freeman and Phoebe Wilson Rasin, m. 14th April 1838, Jannette Turner. His 2nd wife was Ann Cacy, and had child., viz., Erastus,—John,—Ethland, and Hellen Rasin.

Henry Holliday Rasin, son of Philip Freeman and Phoebe Wilson Rasin, m. 11th April 1849, Anna E. Woodland, and had child., viz., Augusta Lavinia,—Henry Turner,—Walter W., and Albert Norris Rasin.

George W. Wilson, son of George and Susan Holliday Wilson, m. Williamann Ringgold, dau. of James and Ann Roberts Ringgold, and had child., viz., Susan Elizabeth,—Mary Henry,—Georgianna Sophia,—John William,—James Ringgold,—George Holliday,—Julianna Virginia,—William George,—Ann Williamina, and Maria Deborah Wilson.

Susan Elizabeth Wilson, dau. of George William and Williamann Ringgold Wilson, m. 2d June 1829, Dr. James Heighe, and had child., viz., Ann Virginia,—Laura Jane,—Georgina Louisa,—William Handy,—Mary Ellen,—Evelina

Rosamond,—Margaret E. (who m. 13th Nov. 1859, George Wilson Spencer), and Susan Elizabeth Heighe. Mrs. Susan Elizabeth Wilson Heighe d. 28th Dec. 1875, aged about 70 years.

JULIANNA VIRGINIA WILSON, dau. of George William and Williamann Ringgold Wilson, m. Thomas Stephens, and had child., viz., Olivia Virginia,—Henry Rasin,—Ann Louisa,—Maria Caroline,—George W. Wilson, and Genevieve Geraldeen Stephens.

WILLIAM GEORGE WILSON, son of George William and Williamann Ringgold Wilson, m. Margaret Travilla, and had one child, William George Wilson.

MARIA DEBORAH WILSON, dau. of George William and Williamann Ringgold Wilson, m. John Dunlap, and had child., viz., Ann Wilson,—James Heighe,—Edwin Wilmer,—Alexander Hart, and Maria Wilson Dunlap.

MILICENT WILSON, dau. of George and Susan Holliday Wilson, m. Jervis Spencer, and had child., viz., Louisa Virginia,—Ann Caroline,—Alexander Hambleton,—George Wilson and William Spencer.

MILICENT WILSON SPENCER survived her first husband, Jervis Spencer, and m. William Reading, and had child., viz., Delia and Louisa Reading.

GEORGE WILSON SPENCER, son of Jervis and Milicent Wilson Spencer, m. 19th May 1836, Margaretta Ringgold, and had child., viz., Helen Spencer—Jervis Spencer (who m. 21st Jan'y 1862, Catharine Staples),—Charlotte Spencer, and Laura Spencer. He survived his wife, Margaretta R. Spencer, and m. 13th Nov. 1869, Margaret E. Heighe, dau. of Dr. James and Susan E. Wilson Heighe, and had child., viz., George W. Spencer and Lizzie Spencer.

HELEN SPENCER, dau. of George Wilson and Margaretta Ringgold Spencer, m. 15th Jan'y 1859, Nathaniel W. Comegys, son of John M. Comegys, and had child., viz., George Spencer Comegys, and John M. Comegys.

CHARLOTTE SPENCER, dau. of George Wilson and Margaretta Ringgold Spencer, m. 16th Jan'y 1862, John Lathem Wethered, son of Peregrine Wethered, and had child., viz., Margaretta Spencer,—Mary Elizabeth, and John Lathem Wethered. (See WETHERED.)

Mrs. Charlotte Spencer Wethered survived her husband, John Lathem Wethered, and m. 25th May 1875, Thomas W. Wickes, of Chestertown, a son of Simon, son of Capt. Simon Wickes.

LAURA SPENCER, dau. of George Wilson and Margaretta Ringgold Spencer, m. Oct. 1867, Addison Emory, son of William Emory, of Queen Anne's, and had a dau., Laura Spencer Emory.

SUSAN WILSON, dau. of George and Susan Holliday Wilson, m. John Cummins, of Smyrna, Delaware, and had child., viz., Susan Holliday (who m. Dr. Daniel M. Fisler, and had a dau. Mary Caroline Fisler),—George Wilson,—John Holliday,—Alphonsa (who m. Maj. John G. Black, see BLACK),—William,—Daniel,—Mary (who m. Daniel B. Cummins, and had a dau., Mary Ellen Cummins),—Martha (who m. Alfred Barratt, and had child., viz., Alfred,—Clara and Adele Barratt),—David James,—Robert Holliday, and Alexander G. Cummins, who m. Louisa Hayes.

GEORGE WILSON CUMMINS, son of John and Susan Wilson Cummins, m. Evelina M. Denny, and had child., viz., George Wilson Cummins, Jr.,—Sarah A.,—Louisa A., and Walter Cummins.

JOHN HOLLIDAY CUMMINS, son of John and Susan Wilson Cummins, m. Martha Ringgold, and had child., viz., Martha R. and Mary J. Cummins. His 2d wife was Rebecca B. Ringgold, and had child., viz., John Ringgold, and Thomas Henry Cummins.

DR. WILLIAM CUMMINS, son of John and Susan Wilson Cummins, m. Ellen Theresa Lowber, dau. of John and Margaret Wilson Lowber, and had child., viz., Margaret,—William A. and Robert L. Cummins.

DANIEL CUMMINS, son of John and Susan Wilson Cummins, m. Martha Ann Raymond, and had child., viz., Eliza B. and Alfred L. Cummins.

DAVID JAMES CUMMINS, son of John and Susan Wilson Cummins, m. Juliet V. Polk, and had child., viz., William P.,—Margaret P.,—Susan F., and Juliet A. Cummins.

MARGARET WILSON, dau. of George and Susan Holliday Wilson, m. John Lowber, and had child., viz., Charles A.,—Ellen Theresa (who m. Dr. William Cummins),—Robert Wilson,—Edward S.,—Rachel Maria (who m. David Smith, and had child., viz., Otis,—Evans, and David L. Smith),—Jane,—John H.,—Catharine (who m. Gov. William Temple, and had child., viz., John C., and Robert L. Temple),—Margaret and James H. Lowber.

CHARLES A. LOWBER, son of John and Margaret Wilson Lowber, m. Catharine Dougherty, who d. leaving child., viz.,

Margaret,—Catharine, and Martha Lowber. His 2nd wife was Emily Safford, who had a child, Emily Lowber.

ROBERT WILSON LOWBER, son of John and Margaret Wilson Lowber, m. Maria Bergen. His 2nd wife was Elizabeth Redfield, who had a dau., Elizabeth Lowber.

EDWARD S. LOWBER, son of John and Margaret Wilson Lowber, m. Elizabeth Ellsworth, and had child., viz., Isabella,—Mary, and Ida Lowber.

JOHN H. LOWBER, son of John and Margaret Wilson Lowber, m. Priscilla Strover, and had a child, Elizabeth Lowber.

JOHN WILSON, son of George and Margaret Hall Wilson, m. 27th Feb'y 1779, Mary Perkins, of the White House, dau. of Thomas and Ann Hanson Perkins, and d., leaving his wife and child., viz., Frederick Wilson,—William Rogers Wilson, Thomás Wilson (who m. Margaret Kane, and d. 1829), and Margaret Wilson, who m. Dr. James Black. (See BLACK.)

CAPT. FREDERICK WILSON, son of John and Mary Perkins Wilson, m. Sarah L. Stuart, dau. of Dr. Alexander Stuart, by his 1st wife, Sally Rasin. He commanded the troop of horse at the battle of Caulk's Field.

WILLIAM ROGERS WILSON, son of John and Mary Perkins Wilson, fell in a duel with Edward Pearce. The fatal bullet is still in existence, in the possession of the writer.

SEC. 67, U. Three or more members of the Perkins family came to America about the year 1700. One of them settled in New England, and two, David Perkins and Daniel Perkins, settled in Kent. They were Quakers, and came from Wales. The name was sometimes spelled Pearkins. They were extensive land owners, and for several generations possessed great wealth.

DAVID PERKINS m. 18th Feb'y 1723, Sarah Reding, and had child., viz., Elizabeth Perkins (who m. 18th Aug. 1745, William Wilson), and Sarah Perkins.

SARAH PERKINS, dau. of David and Sarah Reding Perkins, m. 31st July 1746, and was the 1st wife of Ebenezer Reyner, and had child., viz., Amelia, b. 8th May 1747,—Margaret, b. 14th Oct. 1749,—Rebecca, b. 7th Sept. 1751,—Sarah, b. 14th July 1753,—Hannah, b. 15th April 1756,—Ebenezer, b. 11th Feb'y 1758, and Margaret Reyner, b. 10th Aug. 1760.

DANIEL PERKINS m. in May 1715, Susannah Starton, and d. in 1744. They had child., viz., Ebenezer Perkins, b. 7th April 1717,—Elinor Perkins, b. 16th March 1718,—Thomas

Perkins, b. 12th March 1720,—Susannah Perkins, b. 3d Dec. 1723,—Daniel Perkins, b. 27th Oct. 1725,—Elizabeth Perkins, b. 11th April 1728, and Sarah Perkins, b. 16th Oct. 1739.

ELIZABETH PERKINS, dau. of Daniel and Susannah Starton Perkins, m. 28th June 1764, and was the 2nd wife of Ebenezer Reyner, and had child., viz., Susana, b. 15th May 1765,—Martha, b. 5th Nov. 1766, and Elizabeth Reyner, b. 10th Feb'y 1771.

EBENEZER REYNER survived his 2nd wife and m., 5th Dec. 1771, Rachel Boyer. He was Clerk or Register to the Vestry of Shrewsbury Parish, and thus, minutely, records the birth of his child., viz., Amelia Reyner, "b. the 28th day of June, at four o'clock in the morning, 1773,"—John Reyner, "b. 25th of Oct. 1775,"—Stephen Reyner, "b. Dec. 12th, at 55 minutes past three o'clock in ye morning, 1777,"—Rachel Reyner, "b. the 2d day of Feb'y 1780, 20 minutes of ten of the clock in the evening," and Elizabeth Reyner, "b. 31st day of July, at eleven o'clock in the morning, 1783." He was elected a second time, 16th April 1770, Register of Shrewsbury Parish, and filled that office more than twenty-three years. He recorded the proceedings of the meeting of the vestry of the 5th Aug. 1793. At the meeting of the 2d of Sept. 1793, Mr. James Pearce officiated as the Register pro tem., and Mr. John Hurtt was elected Register, "in consequence of the death of Mr. Ebenezer Reyner." In the Family Record contained in the Prayer Book which Ebenezer Reyner used when he acted as Lay Reader, the birth of John is thus recorded: "John Reyner, son of Ebenezer Reyner by Rachel, his wife, was b. the 20th day of Oct., 25 minutes after eleven o'clock at night, in the year 1775."

RACHEL REYNER, dau. of Ebenezer and Rachel Boyer Reyner, m. 1799, Joseph Stavely, a son of John Stavely, who was a son of James Stavely, son of John Stavely, who settled in Kent (a part which was then in Cecil) about 1680.

JOHN STAVELY, m. 15th April 1755, Margaret Redgrave, and had child., viz., James Stavely, who m. into the Moore family of Still Pond and has a descendant, now living, Mrs. Joseph Webb,—Wilson Stavely, who m. a Miss Vansant,—John Stavely, who m. Elizabeth Reyner, a dau. of Ebenezer Reyner, and m. a 2nd time, Miss Turner, and left a dau. Mrs. Araminta Skirvin,—Isaac Stavely,—Joseph Stavely, and Mary Stavely, who m. John Hepbron, of Still Pond, and left a son, Sewell Hepbron.

JOSEPH STAVELY and Rachel Reyner Stavely had child., viz., William,—Elizabeth, who m. Henry Kelley, and Joseph Stavely, who m. a sister of Francis Cann, and had child., viz., James Reyner, who m. Margaret Elizabeth Hepbron,—Laura Edes,—William Frank, and J. Thomas Stavely, of Philadelphia.

WILLIAM STAVELY, of Lahaska, Pa., son of Joseph and Rachel Reyner Stavely, m. 27th Aug. 1822, Margaret Sheed, dau. of George Sheed, of Southwark, Pa., and on the 27th Aug. 1875, had the blessed privilege of celebrating his Golden Wedding. They had child., viz., Lavinia Sheed,—Olivia,—Isabella Leary,—Ermina Reyner (who m. 8th March 1860, William Jones Biles),—William Reyner,—Margaret,—Virginia, and Rosabella Stavely.

DR. WILLIAM REYNER STAVELY, son of William and Margaret Sheed Stavely, m. Nov. 1856, Julia E. Kelley, and had child., viz., Caroline Shreve,—Albert Livingston,—Margaret Cornell, and Sarah M. Stavely.

MARGARET STAVELY, dau. of William and Margaret Sheed Stavely, m. 3d June 1857, Elijah Mitchell Cornell, and has a son, William Stavely Cornell.

ROSABELLA STAVELY, dau. of William and Margaret Sheed Stavely, m. 6th June 1872, James Woods Jones, and had child., viz., Ermina Biles, and Nelly Stavely Jones.

JOHN REYNER, son of Ebenezer and Rachel Boyer Reyner, m. Araminta Crew, and d., leaving a dau., Mary Reyner, who m. Jacob Freeman Rasin, son of Philip Freeman and Phoebe Wilson Rasin.

DANIEL PERKINS, son of Daniel and Susannah Starton Perkins, d. leaving his wife, Susannah Perkins (who d. 1753) and had child., viz., Daniel Perkins,—Thomas Perkins,—Sarah Perkins,—Susannah Day,—Elizabeth Perkins, and Martha Perkins

DANIEL PERKINS, son of the last named Daniel and his wife, Susannah Perkins, m. 1787, Susanna Wickes, and had child., viz., Sarah—Ann,—Eliza,—Daniel, and Caroline Perkins.

THOMAS PERKINS, son of the 2nd Daniel Perkins, m. Mary Malden, and had child., viz., John,—Susan,—Mary, and Ebenezer Perkins.

EBENEZER PERKINS, son of Thomas and Mary Malden Perkins, m. 1817, Sarah Perkins, dau. of Daniel and Susanna Wickes Perkins, and left child., viz., Caroline Louisa Perkins, —Ann Augusta Perkins,—George Washington Thomas Perkins,—Benjamin Bond Perkins,—Eben Francis Perkins, and James Alfred Perkins.

ANN AUGUSTA PERKINS, dau. of Ebenezer and Sarah Perkins, m. Daniel C. Hopper, son of Daniel Hopper, of Queen Anne's, and had child., viz., Susanna Perkins,—Sarah Maria,—Daniel C.,—Ann Augusta, and Ella Hopper.

GEORGE WASHINGTON THOMAS PERKINS, son of Ebenezer and Sarah Perkins, m. Caroline Chambers, dau. of Hon. Ezekiel Forman Chambers, who, b. 28th Feb'y 1788, was United States Senator from 1826 to 1834, and Judge of the Court of Appeals of Maryland from 1834 to 1851. They had child., viz., George Thomas Perkins,—Ezekiel Forman Chambers Perkins,—Eben Francis Perkins,—Mary Clare Perkins,—Carole Chambers Perkins, and Genevieve Lee Perkins.

DR. GEORGE THOMAS PERKINS, son of George W. Thomas and Caroline Chambers Perkins, m. 17th June 1874, Mary Rebecca Ringgold, dau. of John Fletcher and Sarah Catharine Haldene Baird Ringgold, and a granddau. of Edward Ringgold and Rebecca Smith Ringgold. They have one dau., Marie Clare Perkins.

BENJAMIN BOND PERKINS, son of Ebenezer and Sarah Perkins, m. Margaret K. Emory, dau. of William Emory, of Queen Anne's, and had child., viz., William Emory,—Caroline,—James Alfred,—Benjamin Franklin, and Emory Perkins.

WILLIAM EMORY PERKINS, son of Benjamin Bond and Margaret K. Emory Perkins, m. 10th June 1875, Harriett Althea Davis, dau. of James Lambert and Catharine Araminta Eloise Tilghman Davis, of Chestertown.

EBEN FRANCIS PERKINS, Attorney-at-Law, son of Ebenezer and Sarah Perkins, m. 9th June 1864, Mary E. Warwick, dau. of Edward Warwick, of Philadelphia, and had child., viz., Charles Edward,—Daniel,—George,—Eben Francis,—Clarence Warwick, and Thomas Wickes Perkins.

DR. JAMES ALFRED PERKINS, son of Ebenezer and Sarah Perkins, m. Mary Malvina Blackiston, dau. of Thomas and Mary Malvina Blackiston, and had child., viz., James Alfred,—Thomas Blackiston,—Walter Wickes,—David Blackiston,—Benjamin,—Francis, and Henry Norman Perkins.

SEC. 67, V. THOMAS PERKINS, of the White House, son of David and Susannah Starton Perkins, m. 1751, Ann Hanson, dau. of Judge Frederick and Mary Lowder Hanson, and had child., viz., Frederick Perkins,—Thomas Perkins, b. 1st Feb'y 1754,—Ann Perkins, and Mary Perkins, b. Oct. 1763.

Thomas Perkins d. the 21st Feb'y 1768, at the White House, Kent, leaving a very large estate. His dau., Mary Perkins, while yet a minor, by the death of her brothers and sister, inherited the whole. Four of the wealthiest and most respectable gentlemen of Kent were appointed her guardians, viz., Ebenezer Reyner, Jonathan Turner, Jonathan Worth and John Maxwell. Thomas Perkins was a vestryman, at one time, of Shrewsbury Parish, and one of the first vestry of Chester Parish when it was organized, 4th of Feb'y 1766.

MARY PERKINS, of the White House, dau. of Thomas and Ann Hanson Perkins, m. 2d Feb'y 1779, John Wilson, son of George Wilson and Margaret Hall, who d. leaving child., viz., Capt. Frederick Wilson, who m. Sarah L. Stuart, dau. of Dr. Alexander Stuart by his 1st wife, Sally Rasin,—William Rogers Wilson, who fell in a duel with Edward Pearce,—Thomas Wilson, who m. Margaret Kane, and Margaret Wilson, who m. Dr. James Black, of Fairfields, Kent Co., Md. (See BLACK.)

MRS. MARY PERKINS WILSON survived her 1st husband, John Wilson, and m. 5th Aug. 1794, Dr. Alexander Stuart, a Delawarean. She d. 8th Jan'y 1803, aged 39 years and 3 months, leaving child. by her 2nd husband, viz., Mary Perkins Stuart, b. 29th Oct. 1776, who m., in March 1817, Unit Corse, of Kent, and had three child., viz., Susan,—Alexander, and Sarah Corse,—Rebecca Rasin Stuart, b. 25th March 1798, —Anne Maria Stuart, b. 9th March 1800, and Benjamin Stuart, b. 3d Jan'y 1803.

REBECCA RASIN STUART, dau. of Dr. Alexander and Mary Perkins Wilson Stuart, m. Isaac Williams, of Dorchester, and had child., viz., Mary Perkins,—John,—Rebecca Stuart,—Dr. Thomas Henry Stuart Williams, U. S. A. and C. S. A.—James Polk, and Anne Maria Williams.

ANNA MARIA STUART, dau. of Dr. Alexander and Mary Perkins Wilson Stuart, m. 27th March 1817, Colonel James Polk, son of Judge William and Nancy Purnel Polk, and had child., viz., Euphemia Arbuckle,—Littleton Purnel Dennis,—Mary Stuart,—William Littleton,—Alexander Stuart,—Esther Winder,—Mary Anne,—Elizabeth Stuart,—Ariana Frazier Stuart,—Thomas Hampden,—Lucius Carey, and Josiah Bayley Polk, who m. Oct. 1868, Julia Parker.

WILLIAM LITTLETON POLK, son of Colonel James and Anne Maria Stuart Polk, m. 1855, Virginia Estis, and had child., viz., James,—William Estis, and Alexander Stuart Polk.

ESTHER WINDER POLK, dau. of Col. James and Anne Maria Stuart Polk, m. 1st June 1845, Gov. Enoch Louis Lowe, of Frederick City (whose ancestors settled in Maryland about the year 1675), and had child., viz., Adelaide Vincindier,—Anne Maria,—Enoch Louis,—Paul Emil,—Vivian,—Victoire Vincindier,—Enoch Louis,—Alexander Stuart,—Esther Winder,—Mary Gorter, and James Polk Lowe. Hon. Enoch Louis Lowe was Governor of Maryland, 1850–1854. Subsequently was appointed U. S. Minister to China, but declined.

ADELAIDE VINCINDIER LOWE, dau. of Gov. Enoch Louis Lowe and Esther Winder Polk Lowe, m. 16th Oct. 1867, Edmund Austin Jenkins, and has four child., viz., Austin,—Louis Lowe,—Edward Joseph, and Martin Spaulding Jenkins.

MARY ANNE POLK, dau. of Colonel James and Anne Maria Stuart Polk, m. 12th Aug. 1847, Gosse Onno Gorter, and had child., viz., Onno Gosse,—Thomas Hampden,—Albert Lucius,—Margarita Elizabeth,—Littleton Purnell,—James Polk,—Nathan Rino,—Leopold Maximilian, and Marie Alida Gorter.

Gosse Onno Gorter, the present (1876) Consul of Belgium, at Baltimore, is the son of Onno Gosse Gorter, who was b. 15th May 1776, in Holland, d. 8th Oct. 1826, at Amsterdam, and Margaret Elizabeth Hilkes, b. 12th April 1788, m. in 1813, and d. 9th Jan'y 1868 at Utrecht.

ONNO GOSSE GORTER, son of Gosse Onno and Mary Anne P. Gorter, m. 13th June 1867, Alice Howell Edmondson, and had child., viz., Alice Edmondson,—Gosse Onno, and Arthur Edgar Gorter.

ARIANA FRAZIER POLK, dau. of Col. James and Anne Maria Stuart Polk, m. 13th Feb'y 1857, Lucilius Henry Briscoe, of Georgia, and had child., viz., Mary Stuart,—Martha Wellborn, and Edward Hanson Briscoe.

JAMES POLK, son of Col. James and Mrs. Anne Maria Stuart Polk, m. 1844, Annie Maddox, and had child., viz., Anne Maria,—Catharine Maddox,—James,—William, and Lucius John Polk.

LUCIUS CARY POLK, son of Col. James and Anne Maria Stuart Polk, m. 7th Nov. 1867, Mary E. Clark, dau. of Gabriel D. Clark, of Baltimore, and had child., viz., Gabriel Clark, and Lucius Cary Polk.

SEC. 67, W. EBENEZER PERKINS, son of David and Susannah Starton Perkins, m. 14th May 1740, Mrs. Sarah Barney, and had child., viz., Araminta Perkins, b. 22d April

1741,—Isaac Perkins, b. 5th Aug. 1743, and Mary Perkins. He d. at Perkins' Hill the 27th Aug. 1750, in the 34th year of his age, and was buried in the family burial ground at the White House, the estate of his brother, Thomas Perkins, now owned by Maj. John G. Black, a great-grandson of Thomas Perkins. Ebenezer Perkins possessed great wealth. In his Will, dated the "14th day of the 5th month 1750," he gave to his son, Isaac Perkins, "my two grist mills and saw mill with all to them belonging, with my new dwelling-house."

COL. ISAAC PERKINS, son of Ebenezer and Sarah Barney Perkins, was a distinguished officer in the Revolutionary army, and commenced his military service as Captain in the Fourth Battalion of the "Flying Camp" of 1776. He was known as, and called, a "flaming patriot" in those days. He was a member of the Maryland Convention which ratified the Constitution of the United States 28th April 1788. He survived his wife, Ann Perkins, and d. in 1794. He left a very large and valuable estate. In his Will, dated 27th of April 1781, he mentions his child. then living, viz., William Perkins,—Araminta Perkins, who was b. 16th Nov. 1765,—Ebenezer Perkins, who was b. 25th Nov. 1767,—Sarah Perkins (who m. James Groome, son of Charles Groome), and Mary Perkins, who m. John Black, son of George and Margaret Wallace Black.

WILLIAM PERKINS, son of Col. Isaac and Ann Perkins, m. Henrietta Ringgold, dau. of Josias Ringgold (see RINGGOLD), and had child., viz., Sally Maria,—William,—Isaac,—Anne Wallis,—Henry,—Margaret, and John Perkins.

ISAAC PERKINS, son of William and Henrietta Ringgold Perkins, m. Elizabeth Wroth, dau. of Levi and Martha Wroth, and had child., viz., Levi Wroth Perkins, a gallant Confederate soldier, slain in battle,—William Perkins,—Margaret Elizabeth Perkins,—Dr. Peregrine Wroth Perkins (who m. Annie S. Nolly, of Kentucky),—Martha Wroth Perkins,—Henrietta Maria Perkins,—Albert Perkins,—Isabella Perkins, and Thomas Perkins, who d. 29th July 1876, aged 19 years.

HENRY PERKINS, son of William and Henrietta Ringgold Perkins, m. twice: his 1st wife was a Miss Ringgold. His 2nd wife was Anna Brown. They have child., viz., Elizabeth,—Catharine,—Julius, and Leonard Perkins; all living in Illinois.

JOHN PERKINS, son of William and Henrietta Rinngold Perkins, m. Jan'y 1844, Mary Nicholson, and had child., viz., Sarah Henrietta (who m. 6th Jan'y 1865, Thomas N. Naudain, and d. 5th Sept. 1866, and left a dau., Alice Naudain),—Annie Maria,—John Wesley (who m. 9th Jan'y 1874, Sarah Elizabeth, dau. of Robert Cohen, of Washington, D. C., and has a dau. Marie Maria Perkins),—William Edward,—George Walter, and James Alfred Perkins.

SEC. 67, X. The following letter will explain itself:

"CHESTERTOWN, 23d June 1875."

"*Col. George A. Hanson, of Radcliffe Hall, Kent County, Md.:*

"DEAR SIR—In compliance with your requests I write "you the following short sketch of the Hepbron family of "Kent Co., Md.; but before doing so, I would like to tell "you, in connection with your History of Kent County and "its early settlers, a tradition, I received from my father, re-"specting some of your immediate ancestors on the maternal "side of your family.

"After the battle of Brandywine, Washington's army was "compelled to retreat, which left the way open for the British "to Philadelphia. The British, in order to cripple the re-"sources of the Continental Government, and impede the "supplies of the American army, did not burn and utterly "destroy the mills at Brandywine, as our Northern friends "did all through the South, during our late civil war, but "simply broke the mill-stones, and cast them into the river: "even that was considered a barbarous and vandal outrage, "in the days of our virtuous ancestors. During the hard "winter that Washington's army was encamped at Valley "Forge the men were often in a starving condition, and sup-"plies had to be obtained from a great distance and with "much labor. Robert Morris, with the aid of Col. Isaac "Perkins, bought up all the wheat that could be obtained in "Kent County. It was ground into flour at Perkins' mill, "and waggoned at the expense of much toil and danger to "Valley Forge, via Elkton and other round about routes, to "avoid the British pickets, whose army was then in possession "of Philadelphia. Your great-grandfather, George Black, "of Fairfields, commanded the military escort of the supply "train to its destination, and repeatedly and successfully ac-"complished the responsible and hazardous duty.

"Col. Isaac Perkins was a man of much wealth and of great "credit and influence in Kent County. Had it been otherwise "Robert Morris could not have obtained the wheat in such "hard times. Col. Isaac Perkins owned two grist mills, a saw

" mill, other mills and much other valuable property, then in " improved condition, which has since gone down. It is said " that he raised a company and fully equipped it, with all its " necessary appointments, for the service of his country, at his " own charge and expense.

" Somewhere between the years 1646 and 1668, four broth- " ers, who were grandsons of the Earl of Bothwell, emigrated " to this country. One of them settled in Virginia, another " one on the Susquehanna in Pennsylvania, and two on the " head waters of Fishing Creek (at one time in Cecil County), " but now Lloyd's Creek, in Kent County, Md. These two " were named James and Joseph Hepbron. Joseph Hepbron " died without leaving a family. James Hepbron, from whom " all of the name of Hepbron, now living in Kent County, " claim their descent, leased or patented much land from the " Lord Proprietor of the Province of Maryland; all of which " has been sold or alienated from the family, except a small " farm of about two hundred acres, now belonging to William " Thomas Hepbron, of Still Pond. On this farm, which was " never sold, is situated the family burying ground, in which " lie buried all the Hepbrons that d. in this county previous " to the year 1829, and some who have d. since.

" James Hepbron, the first of the name here, m., late in life, " and left only one son, Thomas Hepbron. Thomas Hepbron, " when he was getting old, m. Miss Wilkerson and left an " only son, whose name was, also, Thomas Hepbron. This " Thomas Hepbron m. Mary Sewell, by whom he had child., " viz., Thomas,—Nancy,—Sally,—John, and Joseph Hep- " bron. Thomas Hepbron m. Miss Duyer, by whom he had " one son, Thomas, and two daus. This son was also known " as and called 'Branch Tom,' because he lived by a big " branch, and to distinguish him from his father and cousin of " the same name. This Thomas Hepbron, or 'Branch Tom,' " m. Elizabeth Wilson, by whom he had four sons, viz., Wil- " liam Thomas Hepbron, the present owner of the old home- " stead,—George Hepbron,—John Hepbron, and James Hep- " bron, all living.

" John Hepbron m., in 1785, Mary Stavely, a dau. of John " and Mary Redgrave Stavely, by whom he had 12 child., " viz., Thomas, lately known as Col. Tom,—Nancy,—Eliza- " beth,—Joseph,—James and John, *twins*,—Samuel,—Mary,— " Cassandra,—Sewell,—William, and one that d. unnamed. " The writer of this is the only one now living.

"The name as I find from old papers and parchments has "been variously spelled, Hepporn, Hepbourn, Hepron, and "Hepburn, which latter mode I have no doubt is the correct "way of spelling it.

"Much of what I have written I have received from my "old Uncle Thomas Hepbron, who if he were now living "would be 135 years old, and has been d. over 45 years. He "used to delight me much when a boy exhibiting to us boys "the old family jewels that had regularly descended to him "as the oldest heir male. Among them were many quaint "old rings, knee and shoe buckles, bracelets, &c., of massive "gold with brilliants, that were heir looms, which he said had "regularly descended from his Scottish ancestors. I have "been with him to the family graveyard, where he has pointed "out to me the spot where old James Hepbron lies buried, "over whose grave is now growing, as was then, a large wal-"nut tree. In searching over the old records of this county "you will find the name but rarely mentioned. The Hep-"brons were a quiet, honest and unobtrusive race; not one of "them up to this time, that I have ever heard, has ever held "or asked for an office. It may be that we are descended from "James Hepburn, Earl of Bothwell, out of whose bones am-"bition was probably squeezed when he fled his native land "to Denmark, because of his complicity in the murder of Lord "Darnly, the husband of Mary, Queen of Scotland, divorcing "his own wife and marrying the Queen himself.

"The first generation or two in this country, as I suppose "they were in Scotland, were Roman Catholics.

"I have seen the old parchment, the first grant of land to "James Hepbron or Hepbrun, as it was then spelled, from "Lord Baltimore. It was burned up with many other old "and quaint relics with the old mansion about the year "1844.

"I was m. in 1828 to Jane Cavender, who d. in 1829, "leaving one child, Louis Spearman Hepbron, who m. Mary "Elizabeth Roseberry, dau. of James Roseberry, and has four "child., viz., James,—Archer,—Lewis, and Lelia Hepbron.

"I m. 2ndly, 12th March 1832, Martha Priscilla Maslin, "dau. of Thomas and Elizabeth Wroth Maslin, and had "child., viz., Margaret Elizabeth Hepbron, wife of Reyner "Stavely,—Rev. Sewell Hepbron, the present Rector of St. "Paul's and I. U. Parishes, in Kent County, who m. Selina "Lloyd Powell, dau. of Charles Powell, of Alexandria, Va.,

" who has two child., Charles Powell, and Sewell Hepbron,—
" and Edward Wroth Hepbron, who m. Mary Alice Jackson,
" of Loudon Co., Va.

" Very respectfully yours,

" SEWELL HEPBRON."

MARY ELIZABETH ROSEBERRY, spoken of in the above letter, was descended from Samuel Roseberry, whose son, James A. Roseberry, m. twice. His 1st wife was Elizabeth Godwin, and had child., viz., Mary Elizabeth, above named,—Samuel James (who m. Emma Godwin, and had child., viz., Alice,—Mary Elizabeth, and Samuel), and Alphonsa Roseberry (who m. William Hepbron, Jr., and had child., viz., Elizabeth Godwin Lee,—Frank Roseberry,—Ida,—Maxwell, and an infant unnamed at present). His 2nd wife was Margaret Snyder, and had child., viz., James C. (who m. Edvina Kelley, and had child., viz., Edna, and James Roy),—and Dr. Benjamin Snyder Roseberry, who m. 27th Oct. 1874, Maria Emily Price (dau. of Henry Price and Rachel Ringgold, dau. of Thos. Jefferson Ringgold, a descendant of the 1st named Thomas Ringgold (see RINGGOLD), and had a dau., Margaret Ringgold Roseberry.

SEC. 67, Y. JAMES WROTH, of Durance, England, m. Ann Kinvin, d. and was buried 21st Nov. 1706, at St. Paul's, Kent. In his Will, dated 31st Oct. 1706, he styles himself "Gentleman," and mentions child., viz., John, who m. 3d Feb'y 1705, Katharine Conaway, — Kinvin, — Mary,—James,—Anne,—Deborah, and Susanna Wroth; and Elizabeth Lumbley and her son George Lumbley. He also mentions his 2nd wife, Mary Wroth.

KINVIN WROTH, son of James and Ann Kinvin Wroth, in his Will, dated 9th June 1750, mentions his sons, viz., Kinvin,—John,—Benjamin, and James Wroth, and also speaks of his wife, Sarah Wroth.

KINVIN WROTH, son of Kinvin and Sarah Wroth, had an only son, Kinvin, whose only son, Levi Wroth, m. 18th Oct. 1808, Martha Wroth, dau. of Kinvin and Priscilla Blackiston Worrell Wroth, and had a dau. Elizabeth Wroth, who m. Isaac Perkins, son of William and Henrietta Ringgold Perkins.

JOHN WROTH, son of Kinvin and Sarah Wroth, d. 8th Jan. 1770, and left four sons, viz., Kinvin,—John,—Benjamin, and Thomas Wroth. His wife, Priscilla Wroth, d. 14th April 1783.

KINVIN WROTH, son of John and Priscilla Wroth, was b. 3d April 1754, m. 23d Sept. 1773, Mrs. Priscilla Blackiston Worrell, who was b. 24th Oct. 1741, a dau. of Benjamin and Sarah Blackiston, of Delaware, and the widow of Simon Worrell. Kinvin Wroth, d. 9th Nov. 1804, and Priscilla B. W. Wroth, his wife, 10th April 1812. They had child., viz., Priscilla Wroth, b. 10th Sept. 1774, whose first husband was William Smith ; she m. again 26th April 1810, Jesse Comegys, —Elizabeth Wroth, b. 1st March 1777, who m. 2d Sept. 1802, Thomas Maslin, and had a dau., Martha Priscilla Maslin, who m. Sewell Hepbron,—Martha Wroth, b. 17th Oct. 1778, who m. 18th Oct. 1808, Levi Wroth, before mentioned, and left descendants which will hereafter be given in proper place,—John Wroth, b. 26th Aug. 1781,—Benjamin Blackiston Wroth, b. 30th Sept. 1783, and Peregrine Wroth, b. 7th April 1786.

JOHN WROTH, eldest son of Kinvin and Priscilla Blackiston Worrell Wroth, m. 11th June 1805, Sarah Worrell, dau. of William Worrell, of Fairy Meadow. His 2nd wife was Mary Granger, dau. of Thomas and Margaret Hanson Granger, and left child., viz., Thomas Granger,—Edward Theodore,—Benjamin,—Margaret, and Louisa Wroth, who m. William Kennard, and had a son William Kennard.

DR. THOMAS GRANGER WROTH, son of John and Mary Granger Wroth, m. Mary Elizabeth Wroth, dau. of Dr. Peregrine and Martha Page Wroth, and had child., viz., Rev. Peregrine Wroth,—Rev. Edward Worrell Wroth (both of the Protestant Episcopal Church),—Martha Page Wroth, and Mary Eugenia Lane Wroth.

EDWARD THEODORE WROTH, son of John and Mary Granger Wroth, m. Eugenia Maria Wroth, dau. of Dr. Peregrine and Martha Page Wroth, who was b. 26th Feb'y 1817, and d. 30th of Sept. 1861.

BENJAMIN BLACKISTON WROTH, son of Kinvin and Priscilla Blackiston Worrell Wroth, m. 2d Feb'y 1808, Mrs. Martha Ann Gleaves Granger, widow of William Granger, the eldest son of the last-mentioned Thomas Granger, who left one child, Editha Gleaves Wroth, who m. Francis A. Ruth. His 2nd wife was Mrs. Mary Groome Ringgold, b. 2d March 1785, a dau. of Charles and Sarah Kennard Groome, and the widow of Josias Ringgold, son of Josias Ringgold, who was the father of Henrietta Ringgold Perkins, before mentioned. Benjamin Blackiston and Mary Groome Ringgold Wroth left two child., viz., Benjamin Blackiston Wroth and William Groome Wroth.

BENJAMIN BLACKISTON WROTH, son of Benjamin Blackiston and Mary Groome Ringgold Wroth, m. 16th Nov. 1848, Anne Caroline Clayton, dau. of Walter Jackson Clayton, of Queen Anne's, and had child., viz., William Frisby,—Thomas Granger,—Clinton Wright,—Emory Sudler, and Margaret Perkins Wroth.

Mrs. Anne Caroline Clayton Wroth d. 5th Oct. 1875, in the 49th year of her age.

WILLIAM GROOME WROTH, son of Benjamin Blackiston and Mary Groome Ringgold Wroth, m. Mary Poits, dau. of Dr. Poits, of Baltimore, and has a son, Henry Atkinson Wroth.

SEC. 67, Z. DR. PEREGRINE WROTH, son of Kinvin and Priscilla Blackiston Worrell, was b. 7th April 1786, and was educated at Washington College, Kent; commenced the study of medicine, 18th July 1803, with Dr. Edward Worrell, who d. Oct. 1804; finished the preparatory study with Dr. Morgan Browne, in April 1807, and became his partner, and practiced the profession until the 1st Feb'y 1857, a period of fifty years, less six months and nineteen days. He now (20th Dec. 1876) resides in the city of Baltimore, in the 91st year of his age, and is hale and hearty, in the full enjoyment of all his faculties. Until the period above mentioned he was an active and distinguished practitioner of medicine in Kent County, and was considered one of the ablest and most learned physicians on the Eastern Shore of Maryland. He is the author of a "History and Treatment of the Endemic Bilious Fever of the Eastern Shore of Maryland;" which work is commonly called and known as "Wroth on Bilious Fever." In 1846 he was elected Lecturer and Professor of Chemistry in Washington College, and ably filled that position until 1854. In early life he was appointed one of the Visitors and Governors of Washington College, and at the death of Judge Ezekiel F. Chambers he was elected President of the Board. He was m. four times. He m. 27th of Aug. 1807, Martha Page, dau. of John and Milcah Page, who was b. 5th of Aug. 1779, and d. in 1826, and had nine child., only three of whom survived, viz., Eugenia Maria, b. 26th Feb'y 1817, who m. Edward Theodore Wroth, before mentioned,—Edward Worrell Wroth, who m. Louisa Clark, of Baltimore, and has one child, Eva Page Wroth,—and Mary Elizabeth Wroth, b. 6th of July 1820, who m. Dr. Thomas Granger Wroth. He m. 2ndly 19th of June 1827, Margaret Smythe Nicols, dau. of Samuel and Eliza Nicols, who was b. 31st March 1802, and had four child., only two of whom survived, viz., Dr. William

Jackson Wroth, who m. Miss Bowie, who d., leaving a dau. Margaret Elizabeth Wroth,—and Margaret Priscilla Wroth, who m. Thomas C. Nicols, of Easton, and has three child., viz., Henrietta Maria,— Edward Theodore, and Margaret Eugenia Nicols. He m. 3dly 3d of Oct. 1839, Catharine Hanson, dau. of George Adolphus Hanson, of Radcliffe Hall. She d. 28th Dec. 1854. He m. 4thly 30th Sept. 1856, Mrs. Louisa Tilden Ringgold, a dau. of Dr. William Blay Tilden, and the widow of George W. Ringgold, son of Edward Ringgold.

JAMES WROTH, son of the first named James Wroth and his 2nd wife, Mary Wroth, m. Ann Walmsley, and had a son who m. Mary Pennington, and had child., viz., George,—William Frederick,—Tamor,—Mary Anne, and Julianna Wroth. He m. again, and had two child., viz., James and John Wroth.

JAMES WROTH, son of James Wroth, last mentioned, and his 2nd wife, m. A. Wroth, dau. of Kinvin, son of the first mentioned Kinvin Wroth, and had child., viz., Kinvin Wroth, and Samuel Wroth, who had sons, viz., William Henry, and James Kinvin Wroth.

JOHN WROTH, also son of James Wroth and his 2nd wife, m. Miss Rothwell, and had child., viz., William M.,—James M. (who m. Caroline E. Wright, and had child., viz., John W.,—Alice, and James Henry Wroth),—Anne E., who m. J. Walmsley, and had one child, Margaret Walmsley, and John W. Wroth.

JOHN W. WROTH, son of John Wroth and Miss Rothwell, m. A. M. Morgan, and had child., viz., Benjamin P.,—Lydia, —Eliza,—Sarah Ward,—John,—James,—Thomas and Araminta Wroth.

SEC. 68.— 11th Men 1: 1655.

At a Court holden for Kent January the first 1655 at ye house of Mr. Thos. Hynson high Sheriffe for the Countie.

Present—MR. PHILIP CONIER

MR. JOSEPH WICKES	CAPT. JNO. RUSSELL
MR. HENRY MORGAN	MR. WM. ELIOT.

ANTHONY CALLOWAY havinge made his Complaint or declaration by way of petition; That two men belonginge to Accomacke, named Tho. Price & Wm Johnson not long since came upon this Island & Carried away Contrarie to an Act of Assembly one Robert Gamer, which standeth indebted to your petitioner by bill three hundred & fifty pounds of tob, and one barrell and a half of Indian Corne, And your petitioner begs an Attachment upon their boat & saill with twoe Oares: Hee humbly Craves an Order for present payment accordinge to ye sd Act.

The Deposition of John Winchester, aged 29 yeares or thereabouts, sworne Examined & saith.

Interrogatarie first. Whether Price & Johnson Carried away Gamer & where he was landed?

Ans. Gamer went in their boat, with them, and landed to the best of their knowledge at ye head of Elke River.

2. Intr. Whether ye boat was not designed to ye head of Elk River before they went off ye Island?

Ans. No: but to goe to Swane Island.

3. Intr. By whom & whether you were hired to bring or Carie the boat or men?

Ans. Noe: we were not hired.

The deposition of Henrie Telion, aged 26 years or thereabouts, sworne, Examined and saith the same which ye sd Winchester doth affirm or ans., being likewise Examined upon ye same Interrogatories.

The Complaint, Charge & debt beinge made appeare by two sufficient witnesses

The Court doth therefore Order that seissure by way of Execution be made upon ye sd boat, saills, & Oares for ye satisfaction of ye sd debt of three hundred & fiftie pounds of tob. & one barrell & a halfe of Indian Corne with Court Charges.

SEC. 69. Whereas the Court hath received Information that Edward Kyers hath trangrest the law in the breach of an Act of Assembly; Evidence followeth:

The deposition of Mr. Isake Ilive, aged 40 yeares or thereabouts, sworne, Examined & saith,—That Ned Kyers Cominge to his house in October last went into the tobacco house to loock for a sticke, that he left there, & in going kild a Turkey & brought it into ye deponent's house & sayd hee had shot a Turkey, & holding his hand on his face, sayd his gun had hurt his face, and sayd to your deponent, if you will give mee two shots of pouder & shot, you shall have ye turkey; & sayd further; I'll goe out againe & you shall have more shooting againe, all this was upon a Sabbath day; and further saith not. ISA. ILIVE.

James Horner, aged 43 yeares or thereabouts, sworne, examined and saith, In all particulars ye same which is declared in ye former Deposition and further saith not.

Signed JAMES I H HORNER.

CAPT. ROBT. VAUGHAN Complaines against the Estate of Andrew Hanson, deceased, for seven hundred and fiftie pounds of tob. due to the said Vaughan by bill and accompt; and having made appear to ye Court, that his demand is Justly due & ye bill and accoumpt still Owinge: The Court doth therefore Order that out of ye Estate, of ye sd Hanson, present payment bee made of ye seven hundred & fiftie pounds of tob to ye plaintiff, els Execution.

SEC. 70. MR. WM. ELIOT & JOHN RINGGOLD Complaine against John Salter & William Price & Jane the wife of John Salter in an action of suspicion of theft; many hoges being lost amongst the neighbours & sume of theire owne hoges gone that disappeared about whom very strangely of a sudon; & pork, often seene in theire house & had no hogs of theire owne to kill, other particulars suspicions about killinge of hoggs & havinge porke in theire houses, sumetymes denieinge, sumetymes affirminge, off & on, in their Answers; with many other circumstances givinge just occasion of suspicion and and moreover A piece of pork Singed & fatt taken in the search by the Constable, & shoed in Court at the board, could no way be convinced to bee as the defendant Ansd to the Charge; that the thick fatt, singed piece of meat was part of a wild small hog that was kild; the eares were demanded in Court, the plaintiff's answer was, that hee layd them by him, & the dogge eat them.

Mr. Elliott plaintiffe desires ye parties or defendants may be examined apart, that two of the three may bee taken away, which is graunted.

Ques.—William Price Examined. Q. Where had you all this meat that hath beene found in your house, havinge no hogs of your own to kill?

Ans.—I kild none, but hee kild a couple, and then one; the eares are at home but the doggs eat the eares of one (it was replied) but piggs & small shoates are not fatt pork, his answer proving the Charges. I'll answer your law or suffer ye law.

Ques.—Where were they kild and when were they killd?

Ans.—One was kild about October & December thereabouts; (where?) about the house.

Mr. Loid said It appears you kild a wild hogg or hoggs; make it appear by the eares or satisfy the law (Price). I kild not this hoggs, he saith it was a wild hogg.

Ques.—John Salter, Examined. When kild you those hoggs & what one?

Ans.—I kild one, two months agoe; one I kild was white, another grisled, & I kild one sow shote, of a year and a half ould that this piece is of; (was this piece unmarkt) Ay and it was this that the dogge eate ye eares.

Deposition.

MRS. FRANCIS MORGAN, aged 30 yeares or thereabouts, sworne, examined and saith, That ye morn after Leo was buried Jane Salter Coming to your deponents house, shee asked her if shee had kild any hogg lately that your deponent might borrow some; shee sayd no; your deponent asked her, then whence had you that singed pork that was taken in your house; and shee answered, It was the shoulder that widdow Bright gave her, And that Mathew Reed kild two hoggs at the head of the new Ordinarie & her husband helpt him whome with them and granny Bright gave him for his paynes a shoulder, & that shee stewed with potatoes & goodie Winchester eat of it, & your deponent answered, I warrant it was ye hogg that was kiled and the gutts cast into ye creek, and shee Answered Ay bee God was it; your deponent answered; tis strange Mathew Reed would singe his hoggs & cast the gutts into ye creeke & lose the fatt; And she answered; Ay bee God did he, & further saith not.

Signed FRANCES MORGAN.

The determination of this Action
Reserved to the next Court.

MR. MORGAN Complaines against the Estate of Andrew Hanson, late deceased, for one hundred and two pounds of tob. & produst an accompt.

Mr. Henry Morgan sworne, Examined and saith that the accoumpt hee hath brought into ye Court amounting to ye sume of one hundred & two pounds of tob. is a Just & true debt & that he hath received no part nor parcell thereof.

The Court doth therefore Order out of ye Estate of ye sd Hanson present payment to bee made of the aforesaid debt, els Execution.

MRS. MARSH by her Attorney Mr. Hynson Complaines against the estate of Andrew Hanson, deceased, for ten thousand seven hundred and fifteen pounds of tobacco and Cask. The debt being proved;

The Court doth therefore Order that present payment be made out of ye Estate of the sayd Hanson of the two thousand seaven hundred and fifteen pounds of tob. and cask to ye plaintiff els Execution.

MRS. MARSH, Widdow, by her Attorney Mr. Thos. Hynson, Complaines against the estate of Valerus Leo, deceased, for One thousand two hundred twenty-eight pounds of tob. and Cask, The debt being proved.

The Court doth therefore Order that present payment be made out of the Estate of ye sayd Valerus Leo of the one thousand two hundred twentie eight pounds of tob. and caske to ye plaintiffe els execution.

Wm. Leedes Complaines against ye estate of Edward Tarrent, deceased, for five hundred pounds of tob. which the sd Tarrent stood indebted to ye plaintiff to bee payd the next ensuinge Cropp: Capt. Wickes being overseer. The plaintiff havinge proved his Complaint, The Court doth therefore Order that the affore-mentioned debt be payd out of the estate of ye sd Tarrent by Capt. Joseph Wickes overseer to ye estate, the last of November next ensuinge this present date.

The Court doth order that John Winchester & John Elis shall make a legal appraisement of the estate of Edward Tarrent, deceased.

SEC. 71. Bee it known unto all men by these presents That I, Roger Baxter of ye County of Kent planter, beinge truly effected in love to Marye Croutch, Widdow, ye late relict of George Croutch deceased and am fully determined God willing to take her to my wedded wife, & soe to make her one with my selfe; The sayd Mary, having Children of her own, desires to reserve sume part of ye estate which was her husband Croutch's, to her own proper use, namely these particulars hearein hereafter exprest.

Imprim. One Redde Cow, called Cherrie, fformerly bought of Capt. Vaughan, her mark, ye right eare Cropt ye left eare under keeled.

Item. One Cowe of a redish coloure, called Clixke, havinge but one Eye, fformerly bought of John Dean.

Item. The whole plantation that was in ye possession, & did lately belonge to her husband Croutch with all ye Appurtenances thereunto belonginge or any wise appurtaininge.

Item. One single bedd, with all belonginge to it, which bedd her husband Croutch gave to theire daughter.

Item. One Boxe, containinge in bigness about halfe a bushell.

Item. One Iron Kettle, containinge about foure gallons.

Now I, the said Roger Baxter, Joininge my selfe in matrimony with ye sd Marie Croutch, doe, notwithstandinge, by virtue heareof disclaim all right, title, claime or interest for mee my heirs, Executors, Administrators or Assignes to all & every particulare of ye sd Cattell & goods formerly mentioned and exprest.

And doe allso further covenant, bind & engage my selfe that ye sd Mary shall have free liberty all ye tyme of her life to dispose all or any part of ye forementioned Cattell and goods, And at ye expiration of her time heare upon Earth If God give her will & opertunitie, then by will, gift or bequest to dispose of ye same to her Childrene or whom she please as beinge her owne proper Estate without ye left or hindrance of me ye sd Roger Baxster my heires, Executors, Administrators or Assignes or any person or persons claimings right or interest from or under me or mine; And if it so happen that ye sayd Marie depart this life without will or diposal of ye sayd Cattell and goodes, that then ye same bee left to bee disposed of at ye discretion of ye Court to her children, then beinge or otherwise accordinge to equitie and conscience:

I doe further covenant & bind my selfe as before that ye sd Marie shall have free libertie to dispose of either or both her children to any person or persons for their better Education & bringing up Allways provided that this disposall bee not done rashly, but to take ye advice of some two honest neigboures or have ye approbation of ye Court, and for Confirmation I have heareunto put my hand in ye presence of ye Court, this first day of January 1655.

Signed
ROGER
BAXSTER. R B

Test. Tho. Hill Clar.

Liber A. Fol. 112.

SEC. 72. The deposition of Mr. Isack Ilive, aged — years or thereabouts, taken in Court the first of January 1655, sworne, examined & saith, That beeinge at ye house of Georg Croutch in ye tyme of his sickness: The sd Croutch desired to make his will, or to speak something concerning ye disposition of his estate, which was as followeth; Sayd hee, Mr. Ilive I entreat you to take notes what I intend to give to my Wife and Children, To my sonne George two gunnes, a great one & a little one, and allso I give him a heiffer called genttle, and yearling coloured black called nanie: to my daughter Marie the heiffer called melenore, two years ould, & one sowe and piggs that Capt. Vaughan had given her formerly; And for ye rest of my Cattell, the plantation, movables & immovables I give to my Wife, and further saith not.

ISA. ILIVE.

SEC. 73. NICOLUS PICHARD aged — yeares or thereabouts, his deposition taken in Court the first of Januarie 1655, sworne, examined and saith

That at ye same tyme when Mr. Isak Ilive was with George Croutch in his sickness your deponent was allso present & heard the same words, formerly exprest in Mr. Ilive's deposition, spoken or uttered by the sd Croutch & further saith not.

NICOLUS PICHARD.

Jurat coram
Phill Conier.

SEC. 74. At a Court houlden for Kent Februarie ye first 1655 at Mr. Tho. Hynson's.

Present—MR. PHILIP CONIER, CAPT. JNO. RUSSELL, CAPT. JOS. WICKES, MR. WM. ELIOT, MR. THO. RINGGOLD, MR. HEN. CARLINE.

Mr. Tho. Bradnox Complaines agst Capt. Jos. Wickes for taking a Cannoe off his land. The Complaint not proved. no Order past.

THOMAS HYNSON, high Sheriffe of ye Countie, Complaines agst John Salter & John Deane for seven hundred pounds of tob. due to his highness the Lord Protector, six hundred by Order of Court & one hundred by breach of an Act of Assembly as is exprest in a bill under their hand dated the 28th of Feb. 1654, a note also under Mr. Durand's hand Sec. for ye Province, to remit, of the seven hundred, three hundred, provided the foure hundred bee payd.

The bill beeinge proved & ye debt made appeare altogether unsatisfied;

The Court doth therefore Order that ye sd John Salter & Jno. Dean shall pay to his highness ye Lord Protector or his substitute foure hundred pounds of tob. beefore the expiration of tenne dayes, and in default thereof, then present payment to bee made by ye sd Jno. Salter and Jno. Dean to his highness ye Lord Protector of England, or his substitute, of seven hundred pounds of tob. with Court Charges, els Execution.

SEC. 75. MR. WM. ELIOT & JNO. RINGGOLD ye last Court havinge made a proceeding by Course of Law, putting into ye Court their complaint or declaration agst John Salter, Wm. Price & Jane, the wife of Jno. Salter, in an Action of suspicion of Theft. The suit remaininge still in dependence, ye plaintiff desires a hearinge, and entreat for Justice agst ye defendants, and that ye suit may be issued without further delay.

The deposition of Margret Balioay, aged 21 or thereabouts, sworne, examined and saith, That Jane Salter beeinge at ye deponent's master's house, talking with her mistress she heard Jane say, that, her husband had a shoulder of pork of ye widdow Bright because hee helpt to carie whom ye hoggs, and her mistress sayd what of ye hoggs that Moll Croutch saw ye garbish of, & Jane swore that it was ye same, & further saith not.

The Deposition of Margret Winchester, aged 25 yeares or thereabouts, sworne, examined & saith;

That about ye last of October your deponent was at ye house of John Salter & his Wife gave her to eate some singed pork which was a good growth, and further saith not.

MARGRET WINCHESTER,
her I mark.

By mee John Russell
19th December Ano. 1655.

The Plaintiffs Mr. Eliot & John Ringgold havinge proved their charge or complaint to ye Court, which ye sd plaintiffs put in ye last Court & have made this Cause, agst John Salter, that there is just cause of suspicion of Theft, evident by many undeniable circumstances & depositions, and making ye suspition now appear. The Court doth therefore Order that ye sd Salter shall not kill any hogg or hoggs without sume two of his honest neighbours, with him, at the killinge of them, or beefore they bee cut up; that they may be able to give evidence of ye marks, beinge thereunto called, & this Order to remaine in force till ye Court signifie their pleasure to ye contrary, this to bee performed with Court Charges, els Execution.

Mr. Wm. Eliot & John Ringgold upon ye forementioned declaration; entreat for Justice agst Wm. Price also, bēinge one of ye defendants in this Action of Suspission of Theft.

The deposition of Henry Morgan, aged 42 years, or thereabouts, sworne, examined & saith; That about ——— your deponent went into ye woods & had in his company his owne boy & Nicolus Pickard & Wm. Price & beeinge in ye woods ye boy and Price parted from them, and afterwards we heard a gun goe off & conceived it to bee Price that shott, & in ye eveninge when wee mett together at Browne's house, your deponent asked him if he kild anythinge, & he answered No! & swore it with bitter Othes, and wee wisht him if hee kild anythinge to confess it, but he still denied that hee kild any thinge; afterwards your deponent's boy that was with Price, when hee shott, tould ye wenches, what he kild, but at present was loth to tell his master, but after ye boy tould your deponent, that Price shott at hoggs once & mist, & shot again & kild a markt shote of Mr. Southes; hearing this your deponent went to Salter's to speake with Price, but Salter & Price beeinge neither of them at home, your deponent left word with Salter's wife that it was Price's best course to goe to South & make his peace with him, & shee lettinge her husband & Price know what your deponent had sayd, they went to South & Price acknowledged he had done him an injury & made an end & further saith not.

Signed HENRY MORGAN.

Nickolas Pickard, sworne, affirmes ye same in ye former deposition till it come to the boy telling ye wenches & further saith not.

The plaintiffes havinge made appeare to ye Court that there is just cause of suspicion agst ye sd Wm. Price of his unlawfull killinge of hoggs: And that he is alsoe culpable of ye breach of an Act of Assembly in killing of a markt hogg contrarie to ye sd Act.

The Court doth therefore Order that ye sd Price (beeinge conceived unable to pay a fine exprest in that Act afforementioned) for his punishment shall attend the next Court & shall in open Court stand with a papper upon his brest declaringe his offence; soe longe tyme as ye Court shall appoint, And shall make a public acknowledgment of his fault; And also shall repair Cranie bridge soe as to be halfe a foot above a common high water, with a Raill to it, & ye bridge to be well staked & made fast in his place, & this to bee performed before the next Court.

And whereas ye said Salter & Price have lived together, in one house & familie, in this time of suspition. It is therefore Ordered that there shall bee a separation, & that sd Price shall forthwith remove & noe longer abide or remaine in house or familie with ye said John Salter; and shall pay Court Charges els execution.

Whereas ye Court hath received information that Wm. Price & Jane Salter have been much accustomed to take ye name of GOD in vain, thereby transgressing both ye Lawes of God & man, but in particular that Wm. Price swore three Othes, hearby transgressinge An Act of Assembly against that sinne, provided; dated Octob. 20. 54 No. 11.

The Court doth therefore Order that ye sd Wm. Price shall pay tenne pounds of tob. for Everie Oath, particularized in ye information; And that John Salter shall pay tenne pounds of tob. for each of those Oathes sworne by his wife forementioned; the one halfe to ye publick use & ye other halfe to ye Informer to bee collected by ye Sheriffe with Court Charges els Execution.

SEC. 76. The Deposition of Mr. Tho. Hynson, aged 35 years or thereabouts, taken in Court February ye first 1655, sworne, examined, saith

That Winter last was twelve months, beeinge with Mr. Marsh when Roger Baxster & hee made up their accoumpts, & Roger Baxster had a bill of Mr. Marshes, which did near discoumpt a bill which Mr. Marsh had of his, when ye sd Mr. Marsh promised to deliver to ye sd Roger Baxster and at that tyme there was a verre small matter beetwixt them, & ye deponent beeing present was desired by both parties to make up their accoumpts and further saith not.

THO. HYNSON.

The deposition of Capt. Jno. Russell, aged 34 years or thereabouts, taken in Court ye first of Feb. 1655, sworne, examined and saith,

That Mr. Marsh beeinge at your deponents house hee desired your deponent to receive two hoggsheads of tob. at Francis Barneses, either one or both as received from Wm. Price & when your deponent delivered ye weight of ye tob. to Mr. Marsh Wm. Price desired to accoumpt with him to see whether hee had payd him all hee Owed him or no, and it appeared that it was payd & Price desired a discharge & Mr. Marsh Answered, it neede not for I'll send over my bill & further saith not.

JOHN RUSSELL.

The deposition of Anthonie Calloway, aged 26 years or thereabouts, taken in Court 11th Mo. first 1655, sworne, examined & saith,

That when Mrs. Bradnox came home from Virginia, ye first night ye deponent heard her tell Mr. Ringgold that Carline coming to Capt. Fleet's & this woman with him, which he carried from Kent, Capt. Fleet provided lodginge for them & for another man, which was there, & provided a bed for ye two women, ye woman with Carline & another woman & Mr. Carline said to yt woman yt hee carried from Kent, "Hunnie thou art a could, wilt thou go to bed." She said "No, Sweetheart;" and he took her in his armes, and threw her upon ye bed yt was provided for Capt. Fleet & ye other stranger, & in ye night Capt. Fleet heard them make a noise, and was very angrie, & call'd to his folkes & bade turn them out at doores, and that ye said Mr. Carline did disown his Wife, beeinge verie angrie, saying that shee had under ye Commissioners hand & ye Court's; & more than that, in ye Chest that her husband brought down there was a Certificate, & ye Chest was broke open, & ye Certificate was found; & there was a Court at Rappahannock's, & this woman that went with Mr. Carline was ordered 30 lashes by ye Court, & Mr. Carline was fined for keeping ye servant away so longe, & disowning of his Wife & was banisht out of ye place, & hee went away intending to come to Kent, but Mrs. Bradnox said that hee could not have ye face to come to show his face, & further saith not.

Sec. 77. At a Court houlden ffor Kent, March the first 1655 at ye house of Mr. Hynson, high sherife of ye Countie.

Whereas a Warrant was lately issued forth agst Edward Rogers for his personal appearance at this Court; to answer his breach of an Act of Assemblie, and hath not made his appearance:

The Court doth therefore Order that if ye sd Edward Rogers shall not make his personal appearance ye next Court; Mr. Tho. Hynson, high sheriff ffor the countie, shall pay the fine exprest in the afforesd Act with costs of suite.

Sec. 78. Aprill ye 24th, 1656. George Hall his mark off Cattell & hoggs: Both eares Cropt and ye right eare overkeeled or a small notch on ye upper side.

Liber A. Fol. 119.

At a Court houlden ffor Kent, May the ffirst 1656, at ye house of Mr. Tho. Hynson, high sheriffe for ye Countie.

The Court havinge received information upon Oath that Edward Rogers is guiltie of a breach of an Act of Assembly; the sd Rogers allso Confessinge in Court that hee shott & kild a turkey upon Sunday Contrarie to the sd Act; pleading for himselfe that this was his first offence, of that nature, & that hee was Ignorant of ye Act of Assembly prohibiting shootinge on Sundayes; & is sorie for his Offence, promissing never to do the like

The Court is pleased for this tyme to accept his plea, & to inflict noe further penaltie upon him, save only, ye sd Rogers shall pay the Charges of ye suitt, els Execution.

Wm. Price hath made his appearance, to satisfie ye Law, for his demerits, standinge in ye Open Court, with a paper upon his brest, declaringe his offence, accordinge to an Order of Court dated Februarie ye first 1655.

MR. THOS. BRADNOX hath arrested to ye Court Jno. Smith in an Action of ye case, sume of his witness beeinge absent, desires a Reference to ye next Court, which the Court is pleased to graunt.

JOHN SMITH, defendant, havinge subponed twoe witneses, for his defense agst ye aforesd action of ye Case, for ye avoidinge of further trouble & charges, desires their Oathes may bee taken, to be of use, for his defence, when occasion shall bee ofered.

The deposition of Tho. Wetherell, aged 47 yeares or thereabouts, sworne, examined & saith,

That Mr. Bradnox came to ye deponent & sd hee had lost a kocke Turkey, and your deponent tould him that Jno. Smith that morninge kild a turkey & Mr. Bradnox sayd that his turkey was alive after George Hall was come from his house about noon, & Mr. Bradnox sayd I heard a gune after George was gone, about ye head of ye spring, & I thought that gunne kild my Turkey; Then sd your deponent to him againe, then it cannot bee your Turkey for ye Turkey that John Smith kild, was kild in ye morning & further saith not.

Signed THO. WITHERELL.

The deposition of George Hall, aged 34 yeares or thereabouts, sworne, examined & saith,

That what ye aforesd Tho. Witherell hath exprest in his Oath, your deponent George Hall affirmes ye same verbatim and further saith not.

GEORGE HALL.
his **H** mark

SEC. 79. The deposition of Wm. Price, aged 30 yeares or thereabouts, taken in ye presence of Mr. Henry Morgan ye 11th of June 1656, sworne, examined & saith:

That about ye middle of May last, on a Saturday, at night, cominge home verie late, your deponent was to goe to Goodman Martin's to work, and Thos. Reade, also, & Goodie Martin was to go home with us, & coming downe to ye water side, readie to put off ye Cannoe, the wind rose, & your deponent was not willinge to goe, but to return back, & stay all night, & cominge backe againe into ye house where Henry Ashley dwells we went to supper, and after supper Goodie Martin made ye bedd, and said "I have turned ye bedd and made it large enough for us all three," and shee and Henry Ashley, & young Robin Martin went all to bedd together, and Robin lay betweene them in ye middle; and in ye morning, when your deponent rose hee found them all three in bedd together and young Robin between; and Goodie Martin and Henry were ye last that rose out of bed, and further saith not.

Signed WM. PRICE.

SEC. 80. At a Court houlden for Kent, July the first 1656.

Present—CAPT. JOSEPH WICKES MR. HEN. MORGAN,
CAPT. JOHN RUSSELL MR. WM. ELIOT.

CAPT. ROBT. VAUGHAN, Attorney to Mr. Abbot, complaines agst Jno. Deane that he stands indebted to ye sd Abbot one thousand two hundred and five pounds of tob. & hath produst a bill of sixteen hundred pounds of tob & cask due to bee payd ye tenth of November next of ye which bill 1205 lbs. of tob. remain still unsatisfied. The sd Deane havinge confest a Judgment & that there remaines unsatisfied of ye sd bill one thousand two hundred and five.

The Court doth therefore Order that ye sd Deane shall make payment of one thousand two hundred & five pounds of tob. & cask to Capt. Robt. Vaughan, Attorney to ye sd Abbot, ye tenth of November next accordinge to ye tenor of ye sd bill with Court Charges els Execution.

SEC. 81. At a Court houlden for particular Occasions, at ye house of Mr. Philip Connier, Commander for the Countie, July the 5th 1656, present Mr. Philip Connier, Capt. Jo. Wickes, Mr. Tho. Hynson, Mr. Henry Morgan, Capt. Jno. Russell.

Whereas Mr. Henry Carline ye first of May last past was in open Court sworne to perform ye Office of a Sheriffe, truly & faithfully for sum present Occasion & not fully Established for want of Securitie; hee promisinge to bringe securitie for his place the next Court followinge, which was the first of July last past; Security by him then tendered, but in such manner, as could not with saftie be accepted. Securitie by ye sd Carline this day tendered, such as ye Court was pleased to accept.

The Court doth therefore Order that ye sd Henery Carline shall act & officiate in ye place & office of a Sheriffe for this Countie of Kent, according to his Oath, and Charge, given him, ye first of May last past, beeing ye said first of May alsoe chosen & elected, & now upon his securitie, by ye Court accepted.

SEC. 82. The Copie of the bond for securitie followeth.

Bee it Knowen unto all men by these presents that we and either of us Thomas Hawkins of Popler Island, & Thomas Coll of ye Countie of Providence doe bind & engage ourselves, our Heirs, Executors, Administrators or Assignes, Joyntly & severally in ye sume of fourtie thousand pounds of tobacco in cask, to save & keep harmless ye Court & Countie of Kent from all damadge, detriment or loss which shall any way be occasioned by Mr. Henery Carline, in ye office of a Sheriffe, without damadge to any person; And for confirmation hereof have hereunto put our hands & seales this 2d of July 1656.

THOMAS HAWKINS.
The mark **TC** of
THOMAS COLE.

Signed, sealed and delivered in ye presence of us.

PHILL SPRYE.
The mark **I** of
JOHN SALTER.

This is signed and seal'd & delivered in ye presence of Mr. Wm. Fuller.

Vera Copia Testis. THO. HILL, Clar.

Fol. 122

SEC. 83. The following deposition alludes to a very early meeting-house (more probably of the Quakers than of the Puritans) if not the earliest within the Province of Maryland:

August, ye 12th 1656. The deposition of Mr. Thos. South, aged about 35 yrs. or thereabouts, taken in ye presence of Mr. Thomas Hynson (upon Kent) sworne, examined & saith,

That about March last your deponent & Ritchard Blunt bought a plantation of Mr. Thomas, at Severne (that hee was then seated upon) as both plainly appear, by a bill of sale, under Mr. Thomas his hand, The bounds of which land, Mr. Thomas made known to us by word of mouth, as followeth: Bounded one way with ye meetinge-house path, but he never understood that it exceeded that; And bounded like-wise to a valley, in ye way to Mr. Owines, where ye fence runs, & ye your deponent further saith, that to ye best of his knowledge, the point of land that ye Meeting-house stands upon was included in ye bargain; and further saith not.

THO. SOUTH.

SEC. 84. At a Court houlden for Kent, September ye first 1656
Present—MR. THO. RINGGOLD MR. HENERY MORGAN
MR. THO. HYNSON MR. WM. ELIOT.

WILLIAM PRICE complaines agst Elizabeth Martin ye wife of Rob. Martin, that shee hath defamed him by callinge him Perjured Rogue: and brings his evidence.

The Deposition of Mr. Tho. Hill, aged 52 years or thereabouts, sworne, examined and saith,

That beeinge at the house of Rob. Martin a little before July Court last, Goodie Martin was enquiringe of an Oath that had lately been taken agst her by William Price & Tho. Reade & askt your deponent what it was that Price had taken his oath of agst her, & your deponent gave her this answer, His Oath was that you were in bedd with Henery Ashley; & hath this in it, you were in bedd together: she replied, Iff hee had taken such an Oath, hee was Perjured Rogue, and further saith not.

THO. HILL.

SEC. 85. The deposition of Thos. South, aged 38 years or thereabouts, sworne, examined and saith,

That your deponent being present at ye same tyme, affirmes ye same verbatime as is exprest & deposed in ye former deposition, to the best of his knowledge, with this addition, that shee sayd Tom Reed sayes no such thinge, and further saith not.

THOS. SOUTH.

The defendant doth acknowledge ye charge made by ye sd Price in his Complaint & that the twoe depositions prove that ye charge was true.

The Court doth therefore Order that the defendant shall pay to ye sd Wm. Price for ye reparation of his credit three hundred pounds of tob. in caske, or acknowledge her offence and aske ye plaintiffe forgives in open Court, & for a fine shall pay three hundred pounds of tobacco in caske for publick uses as ye Court shall think fitt, with Court charges, els execution.

7th Mo. 9th 1656. The deposition of Wm. Price, taken in ye presense of Mr. Thos. Hynson, aged 30 years or thereabouts, sworne, examined & saith:

That your deponent in June last or thereabouts, went to Mr. Hatton's at Siverne (& had in his companye John Salter, Jno. Ringold & Thos. Hinson) to lay out a hogshead or twoe of tob. to buye necessaries, for his use; & he asked for soape & women's shoes & there beeinge none to be had, your deponent, & ye rest that were in his company, went to Mr. Utie's store, & Mr. Utie went into ye store house door, & your deponent saw Jno. Salter handlinge & cheapeninge of a hat, & ye hats lay upon a box that was halfe open, & about halfe full of soap, & as one hand was upon ye hats hee slide ye other downe, into ye box, which made your deponent suspect hee might take sume soap out of ye box, & comminge out of ye store your deponent lookt upon his pocket, & saw it moist, & your deponent askt him what hee had got in his pocket, & hee answered "I tould Mr. Utie my wife was at great want of soap & hee verie kindly gave me a piece," & pulled it out of his pocket & showed it him & it was a small cake of soap & further saith not.

Signed WM. PRICE.

7th Mo. 9th 1656. The deposition of Jno. Ringold, taken in ye presence of Mr. Thos. Hynson, aged 20 years or thereabouts, sworne, examined & saith:

That your deponent beeinge in ye company of Jno. Salter, Wm. Price & Thos. Hinson; Price had occasion to goe to Mr. Hatton's store to lay out a hogshead or twoe of tob. but Mr. Hatton not having such necessaries as Price wanted, wee went to Mr. Utie's store to gett some soap & your deponent spoke to Mr. Utie for soape, & his answer was that his brother had denied divers gentlewomen in that place of soape, & there was little possibilitie of having any. Salter also made a great complaint for soap to Mr. Utye & tould him his "wife had none to wash his linnen," & Mr. Utie goinge into ye store brought forth a pair of shoes, that were spoke for, & Salter seeinge ye store door open went in & went to a parcell of hattes, that lay upon a soap-chest, & was cheapeninge one, Mr. Utie & mee beeinge come to him into the store; & your deponent seeinge ye out side of his pocket & saw a cake of soape, at that present, in his pocket, beefore they went out of ye store-house, & further saith not.

Folio 124 JOHN RINGGOLD.

SEC. 86. MR. THO. BROADNOX agst Anthony Calloway, in an Action of ye Case: The sd Calloway conditioned to serve him ye last yeare; but failinge of ye performance of his conditions; the sd Broadnox enters his Action for a yeare's service to be made good ye next year.

The deffendant brings two Oathes for his defence as followeth:

The deposition of Mr. Tho. Hynson, aged 36 years or thereabouts, taken in the presence of ye Court, sworne, examined & saith,

That being at ye house of Mr. Broadnox about January last, Mr. Broadnox desired y'r deponent to write a Condition between Anthony Calloway and him at that tyme, but had spoke to ye deponent divers tymes before to ye same purpose; And of writing thereof your deponent did Arrest ye sd Calloway at ye suit of Jno. Deane for ye performance of a bargain of service which hee had made with him before, and ye said Anthony being cald to put his hand to ye condition made betwixt Mr. Broadnox and himself formerly mentioned; after hee was arrested, the sd Anthony desired he might speak with Jno. Deane first; Mr. Broadnox replied again, hee might put his hand to it without any questions, for if Deane have you by order of Court then I cannot have you.

Liber A. Folio 125.

SEC. 86, A.— STATE OF MARYLAND,
KENT COUNTY, SCT.

I hereby certify that the aforegoing extracts, contained in Old Kent, written by COL. GEORGE A. HANSON, of Radcliffe Hall, Kent Co., Md., and embraced within the following sections, viz.: Sec. 1, Sec. 8, Sec. 36 B, Sec. 36 C, and within all the *unlettered* sections, from Sec. 59 to Sec. 86, both included, are true and correct extracts from the Court Proceedings and the Land Record Books of Kent County, aforesaid.

Seal of Circuit Court for Kent Co., Maryland.

In Testimony Whereof, I hereunto set my hand and affix the seal of the Circuit Court for Kent County, on this sixteenth day of August, in the year of our Lord eighteen hundred and seventy-five.

D. C. BLACKISTON,
Clerk.

SEC. 87. The following are extracts from Liber C. Liber B. is lost.

At a Court houlden for the County of Kent ye 28th day of January 1667.

Present—CAPT. ROBT. VAUGHAN, MR. JOHN VICKERIS,
MR. RICHARD BLUNT, MR. JOHN DABB,
MR. WILLIAM HEAD, MR. THO. OSBORNE,
Commissioners.

This day Philip the son of Philip Conner late of this county, deceased, comes into Court and made choice of Mr. John Wright to be his guardian and requesteth this Court soe to order it; this Court taking it into consideration doth order that the said Mr. Wright may be his guardian & to perform the part of a guardian by the said Philip according as the law doth require.

[When I examined this Liber in 1865, there was recorded on folio 5 a Commission dated 10th Feb. 1667, from Governor Charles Calvert to John Wright, appointing him Clerk of Kent county in the place of Tobey Wells. Some vandal hand has cut the Commission out, and it is missing.]

1668.

SEC. 88. At a Court houlden ye 31st March 1668, for ye Lord Proprietor in 36th year of his Dominion and for Kent county.

Henry Downs was appointed Constable for the Upper Hundred and John Magruder for the Lower Hundred.

SEC. 89. At a Court houlden ye 25th August 1668, for the Lord Proprietor, in the 37th yeare of his Dominion, and for Kent county, present

CAPT. ROBERT VAUGHAN, MR. WILLIAM HEAD,
CAPT. JOHN VICARIS, MR. RICHARD BLUNT,
MR. MORGAN WILLIAMS, MR. THOMAS OSBORNE,
MR. JOHN DABB,
Commissioners.

SEC. 90. At a Court held the 13th of October 1668, for the Lord Proprietor, in the 37th yeare of his Dominion, at Mr. Richard Blunt's, for Kent county.

Whereas information hath been given to some of the Commissioners of this county that Hannah Jenkins, Daughter in Law to Mr. George Harris of this county hath been delivered of a man child

The Court finding a suspition of Murther ordered a Jury of women to be called to Search the body of the said Hannah whether she was delivered of a child or noe, which accordingly was done.

The names of the Jury-women:

Mary Vicaris	Elizabeth Winchester
Rebecca Denny	Hannah Dabb
Christian Ringgold	Katharine Osborne
Elizabeth Coppage	Ann Blunt
Dorothy Williams	Mary Southern
Margrett Jones	Katharine State.

The Jury's verdict is that the said Hannah Jenkins is clear from the bearing and never had a child to the best of their knowledge.

Mary Vicaris, Fore-woman.

Hannah Jenkins desires her Father-in-Law, Mr. George Harris, to be her Attorney, which the Court doth allow of.

According to the Jury's verdict the Court doth order that the said Hannah Jenkins shall be cleared by proclamation and ordered the Sheriff to doe it.

In the year 1668 the County Levy was 40,300 pounds of tobacco; 115 persons, 260 lbs. per poll.

1669.

Sec. 91. At a Court houlden the 26th of January 1668 *o. s.* (1669 *n. s.*) for the Lord Proprietor, in the 37th year of his Dominion & in Kent Court. Present,

Henry Coursey, Esq.,	Mr. William Head,
Capt. John Vicaris,	Mr. Richard Blunt,
Mr. Matthew Read,	Mr. Thomas Osborne,
Mr. Morgan Williams,	Mr. John Dabb,

Commissioners.

At this Term Mrs. Mary Vaughan, the Relict of Capt. Robert Vaughan, brought a suit against John Muggison.

Desborough Bennett was appointed Clerk in the place of Robert Dunn, and Robert Dunn, John Vicaris, Matthew Read, Morgan Williams, Richard Blunt, Thos. Osborne, Wm. Head, John Wright, and Wm. Bishop were appointed, by Gov. Chas. Calvert, Commissioners of Kent County.

JOHN RINGGOLD, WILLIAM PRICE and "ye three Swedes, RANDOLPH HANSON, WILLIAM HANSON and JOHN HANSON, were together at ye store of Mr. Utye at Severne in ye month of June 1656 . . JOHN HANSON was 26 years of age or thereabouts.

SEC. 92. I do hereby license you to join Francis Pine and Mary Vicaris in marriage, without further publication.

Given under my hand and seal, this 22d day of February 1669.

PHILIP CALVERT.

To all Priests, Ministers or Magistrates whom these presents doe or may concern.

FRANCIS PINE afterwards spoke of Capt. John Vicaris, the former husband of his wife Mary, as his predecessor.

1670.

SEC. 93. At the October Term for the year 1670, John Dabb was made overseer of the high ways for the Upper Hundred, and Ed. Burton for the lower one of the county. The old roads made the previous year, are to be cleared and made good, a sufficient bridge to be made at the head of "Pig Quarter," and another at the "head of the Tarkeels," also a road to be made from the said "Pig Quarter Creek," to the road at the head of Broad Creek, a bridge be made "over the spring by Little Creek, passable both for horse and foot." The inhabitants, who are taxable, are to be called upon to furnish their respective quotas.

In the Records of this year appear the names of Charles de la Roch, Atty., Michael DeCoursey, Physician, Richard Tilghman, Physician, and William Granger, Planter.

At this time Maj. John Ingram was Sheriff and Peter Sayer Clerk of the County.

In the year 1670 there were 163 "Titheables," persons who were liable to taxation, in Kent County.

1671.

SEC. 94. On folio 54, Liber C., is recorded the following:

To all persons to whom these may come, these are to certify, that I have ordered & appoynted & doe hereby order and appoynt that for the future the North East side of Chester, as far as the bounds of Talbott county were formerly on that side, shall now bee added to Kent county and I doe declare that part to belong to Kent as alsoe Poplars Island, and doe hereby require that the Sheriffe of Talbott county presume not to recover any quitt rents or dues from the inhabitants living & residing uppon the places above specified, they being within the county of Kent. Given under my hand this 4 June 1671.

CHARLES CALVERT.

SEC. 95. At a session of the Commissioners, held at the house of Mr. Robert Dunn, November 13th, 1671.

By his Excellency the Generall:

MARYLAND, SS.—I have thought fitt to add to your Commission Tho. South, Joseph Wickes, Henry Horsier and Francis Pyne of your County Gents, to be Justices of Peace of your County, and I doe hereby appoint Tho. South and Joseph Wickes of the Quorum & the sd Thomas South to be Chairman, the which Commissioners I doe hereby order and empower you to swear according to the usual forms & to admitte of them in your County & County Courts as his Lord's Commissioners & Justices of peace in the sd county in as full and ample manner as any of you that are constituted by Commission under the great seal of this province, and of this all persons are to take notice.

Given under my hand and seale att armes this eighteenth day of October, Fortieth year of the Dominion of Cecilius Proprietor. Annoq. Dom. 1671.

CHARLES CALVERT.

To the Commissioners of Kent county.

At the November Court, 1671, John Ringgold was appointed Overseer of the High-ways for Chester Hundred and Philip Thomas for the Lower Hundred.

From the short Register of Burials upon Folio 57, it appears that Robert Dunn "dyed on ye 12th of May 1676," and that Alice, daughter of Joan Dunn, dyed the 9th day of August 1678.

1674.

SEC. 96. Liber C. skips over the period between the Court's session of November 1671 and that of August 1675. The following extract from Liber E. will show who were the Commissioners in 1674:

1674.

At a Court houlden for ye County of Kent, September ye 28th, 1674,

Present—Mr. Thomas South

Mr. Joseph Wickes Mr. John Hinson

Mr. James Ringgold Mr. William Lawrence

Commissioners.

The Complaint of William Drake, servant to Mr. John Wells.

To the worshipfull Justices of ye peace, Commissioners for said County, or to any or either of them. The humble petition of William Drake, servant to Mr. John Wells, showeth yt the sd John Wells your petitioner's master, have severall times abused by giving of me unlawfull correction, by tying my two handwrists together, hanging me up to ye gunne racks, and whipped me without mercy giving me at least one hundred blowes upon my bare skin. And let me hang so long, by the handwrists upon ye sd Gunn Racks, yt ye blood started through and out of my fingers and all my hands pealed, and his chiefest ayme was to strike me upon my members, when he was whipping of me. After he commanded me to goe with him into ye wood along with him; which I did, accordingly, to his desire, and when he had me there he was so unmercifull in beating of me, that, he broke a hycory stick all in pieces—severall other matters I could alege, but loath to be tedious, wherefore your humble petitioner desires yt your worshs. will take it into youer wise consideration and think upon my misery, I doe endure, and your poor servant will pray for you, &c.

A true copy. Charles Bankes, Clk.

Hans Hanson, aged 28 yeares, sworne in open Court, saith yt John Wells stript his servant, William Drake, about ye spring of ye yeare & bound him cross-handed & so hung him on ye Gunn Racks, & he was hung up so high yt his toes touched ye ground, & there the said Wells gave his sd servant fifty lashes upon his naked body, and furthermore your deponent spoke to James Curlow to speak to Mr. Robert Wells to take away ye whipp out of his hands for he thought he had enough, & yt sd. Mr. Wells tould me your deponent, with his own mouth, that he had basted him, afterwards, in the wood, & further saith not.

Hans. Hanson.

1675.

SEC. 97. At a Court holden for ye County of Kent, December ye 7th 1675, and adjourned untill ye 9th day of December.

Present—MR. JOSEPH WICKES MR. JNO. HYNSON
MR. JAMES RINGGOLD MR. HENRY HOSIER,
Commissioners.

MR. CORNELIUS COMEGYS was appointed "Overseer for ye highways of Langford's Bay Hundred and yt he make cleare a road from Richard Joanes his house to Swan Creeke road, according to Act of Assembly, which road is to bee tenn (10) foot wide, & yt sufficient bridges be made in ye sd Roade, passable for horse & foot, if need require."

JNO. DABB was appointed Overseer of the High-ways for the Upper Hundred, Isaac Winchester for the Lower Hundred, and ordered "yt ye old roads, yt were repaired ye last yeare be all cleared & made good from Mr. Joseph Wickes house to Swan Creek roade."

JAMES STOUP recordeth his mark of Cattle and Hoggs w'ch is a Cropp & a slitt on ye right eare, & a Cropp & an under keile on ye Left.

CHARLES BANCKES recordeth his marke of Cattle & Hoggs, w'ch is a swallow forke on ye left eare & an under-kield & an over-kield on ye right eare.

Dec. ye 8th 1675.

HANS HANSON recordeth his mark, a swallow forke on ye left eare & a Croppe & two slitts on ye Right.

SEC. 97, A. CORNELIUS COMEGYS came to Kent about the year 1670. By the Act of Assembly of 1672, chapter xxix, he and his whole family were naturalized. The title of the Act is, "The humble petition of Hans Hanson, Cornelius Comegys, the elder, Millimenty Comegys, his Wife, Cornelius Comegys the younger, Elizabeth Comegys, William Comegys, and Hannah Comegys their children." (See Bacon's *Laws of Maryland.*)

They settled on the Chester River and the old homestead remained in the family until within a few years past. Cornelius Comegys, the elder son of the emigrant, inherited the home farm, and from him is descended the Quaker Neck family.

WILLIAM COMEGYS, younger son of Cornelius and Millementy Comegys, went to Crumpton, then known as McAllister's Ferry. He had one son William Comegys, who m. 28th of Nov. 1734, Ann Cosden, and d. 29th of March 1764. He had child., viz., John, b. 4th of Feb'y 1736,—Alethea, b. 9th of June 1737 (who m. Joseph Ireland),—Alpharis and Alphonso, *twins*, b. 15th of Dec. 1738,—Edward, b. 13th of Jan'y 1741,—Nathaniel, b. 23d of Feb'y 1745,—Ann, b. 28th of June 1747,—Jesse, b. 30th of Oct. 1749,—Edward William, b. 2d of April 1752,—Jonathan,—Elizabeth, b. 7th of Feb'y 1757, and Cornelius Comegys, b. 4th of July 1758.

John Comegys, son of William and Ann Cosden Comegys, m. 15th of Oct. 1757, Sarah Spencer, and had child., viz., Samuel, b. 29th of Aug. 1758,—John,—Ann, b. 4th of Sept. 1763,—Isaac, b. 9th of June 1765,—Jervis, b. 8th Aug. 1768, —William,—Sarah, and Nathaniel Comegys, b. 16th of Dec. 1771.

Samuel Comegys, son of John and Sarah Spencer Comegys, m. 15th of Jan'y 1780,—Mary Gleaves, and had child., viz., John Gleaves,—Sarah,—George,—Margaret, and Samuel Comegys. He m. again 14th of Feb'y 1791,—Mary Freeman, and had child., viz., Freeman,—Mary,—Nathaniel,—Samuel,—Edward F., b. 13th of April 1797 (still living at this date, 16th Sept. 1875, in Alabama),—William,—Milliminta, and Washington Comegys.

Edward F. Comegys, son of Samuel and Mary Freeman Comegys, m. Miss Erly, of Alabama, and had child., viz., George,—John,—Kate, and Ella Comegys. He m. again, and had sons, viz., William and Edward Comegys.

Milliminta Comegys, dau. of Samuel and Mary Freeman Comegys, m. Thomas J. Mann, and had child., viz., Mary Ann,—Joseph Comegys, and Samuel Mann.

Washington Comegys, son of Samuel and Mary Freeman Comegys, m. Miss Palmer, and had child., viz., Samuel William,—George W., and John E. Comegys. He m. a 2nd time, Leonora Newnam, and had child., viz., Washington,—Mary, and Henry Comegys.

Samuel William Comegys, son of Washington Comegys, m. 26th of June 1848, G. A. C. Massey, and had child., viz., Annie M. and Charles E. Comegys.

Nathaniel Comegys, son of John and Sarah Spencer Comegys, m. Hannah Myers, and had child., viz., John Myers, and Samuel Comegys.

John Myers Comegys, son of Nathaniel and Hannah Myers Comegys, m. 26th Nov. 1824, Mrs. Anna W. Comegys Ringgold, dau. of Nathaniel and Francina Worrell Comegys, and widow of James Ringgold, and had child., viz., Nathaniel W.,—Hannah, and Anna Comegys.

JOHN M. COMEGYS, d. 18th Feb'y 1876, in the 77th year of his age.

NATHANIEL W. COMEGYS, son of John Myers and Anna W. C. Ringgold Comegys, m. 15th of Jan'y 1859, Helen Spencer, dau. of George Wilson and Margaretta Ringgold Spencer (see SPENCER),—and had child., viz., George Spencer, and John M. Comegys.

HANNAH COMEGYS, dau. of John Myers and Anna W. C. Ringgold Comegys, m. 27th of Nov. 1849, John F. Newnam, and had child., viz., John F.,—Emma,—Ella,—Bessie, and Robert Lee Newnam.

ANNA COMEGYS, dau. of John Myers and Anna W. C. Ringgold Comegys, m. 15th of Dec. 1853, Stuart R. Emory, and had child., viz., Kate,—Anna Comegys,—Stuart R.,—John M. C., and William N. Emory.

SAMUEL COMEGYS, son of Nathaniel and Hannah Myers Comegys, m. 26th of Nov. 1832, Ann Rebecca Ringgold, dau. of James Ringgold and Sarah Williamson, and had child.,viz., Sarah Williamson,—Mary Rebecca,—Anna Elizabeth,—John Myers, — Samuel, — William, — Alexander, — Milliminta,—Hannah Myers,—Richard Williamson, and Edward Thomas Comegys.

SARAH WILLIAMSON COMEGYS, dau. of Samuel and Ann Rebecca Ringgold Comegys, m. William Emory, and had child., viz., William Comegys—Mary,—Anna,—Alice, and Samuel Comegys Emory.

MARY REBECCA COMEGYS, dau. of Samuel and Ann Rebecca Ringgold Comegys, m. John W. Ireland, and had child., viz., Emma,— Eugenia,—William, — Herman, — Louisa,— Mary, and Hannah Ireland.

NATHANIEL COMEGYS, son of Samuel and Ann Rebecca Ringgold Comegys, m. Kate Rose, of Talbot, and had child., viz., Sophia Rose,—Walter,—Charles,—Edward, and Clarence Comegys.

ALEXANDER COMEGYS, son of Samuel and Ann Rebecca Ringgold Comegys, m. Fannie Cochran, of Delaware, and had one son, Robert Comegys.

HANNAH MYERS COMEGYS, dau. of Samuel and Anne Rebecca Ringgold Comegys, m. William R. Rose, of Talbot, and had child., viz., Willie, and Anna Rose.

ALPHONSO COMEGYS, son of William and Ann Cosden Comegys, had two sons, John and Francis Comegys.

John Comegys, son of Alphonso Comegys, m. Ann Comegys, dau. of Jonathan and Mary Grifith Comegys, and had child., viz., Alphonso (who m. Sarah E. Morgan, and had a son, John E. Comegys),—and Anne Maria Comegys.

NATHANIEL COMEGYS, son of William and Ann Cosden Comegys, m. Hannah Wallace, and had child., viz., William, —Hannah, and John Comegys. He m. a 2nd time Francina Worrell, and had one dau., Ann Worrell Comegys.

WILLIAM COMEGYS, son of Nathaniel and Hannah Wallace Comegys, m. Elizabeth Ward, dau. of Col. John Ward, of Cecil County, Md. (Col. Ward was a Revolutionary soldier, and his great-grandchild. living in Kent now possess the epaulets which he wore at the battle of Long Island), and had one son, John Ward Comegys.

JOHN WARD COMEGYS, son of William and Elizabeth Ward Comegys, m. 6th of Aug., 1826, his cousin, Ann Maria Comegys, dau. of John and Ann Comegys, and had child., viz., Georgia,—Virginia E.,—William,—Indiana M., and John Ward Comegys.

GEORGIA COMEGYS, dau. of John Ward and Ann Maria Comegys, m., 25th Feb'y 1845, Edward W. Comegys, and had child., viz., Mary Virginia,—Columbia,—Sommerfield,—Edward Glanville, and John Ward Comegys.

HANNAH COMEGYS, dau. of Nathaniel and Hannah Wallace Comegys, b. 1771, m. Benjamin Comegys, and had one son, Bartus Comegys.

BARTUS COMEGYS, son of Benjamin and Hannah Comegys, m., 13th of Oct. 1818, Evelina M. Dorsey, dau. of Vachel Dorsey, of Baltimore County, and had child., viz., Elizabeth D. (who m. Robert W. Cliffe),—Benjamin (who m. Mary, dau. of William E. Bartlett),—John P.,—Essex D.,—Philip T.,—Catharine C.,—Sallie M., and Mary C. Comegys.

JOHN P. COMEGYS, son of Bartus and Evelina M. Dorsey Comegys, m. Georgianna Mitchell, and had child., viz., Bartus,—Evelina M.,—Harry D.,—Persehouse, and Caroline Comegys.

ANN WORRELL COMEGYS, dau. of Nathaniel and Francina Worrell Comegys, m. James Ringgold, and had child., viz., Mary and Francina Ringgold. She survived and m. John Myers Comegys, and had child., viz., Nathaniel W.,—Hannah, and Anna Comegys.

JESSE COMEGYS, son of William and Ann Cosden Comegys, m. Mary Everett, and had child., viz., Cornelius Maria and Sarah Comegys.

SARAH COMEGYS, dau. of Jesse and Mary Everett Comegys, m. John Wallace, and had child, viz., Frank,—Sophia,—Cornelius,—Araminta, — Comegys, — Benjamin,—John, and Arthur Wallace.

JONATHAN COMEGYS, son of William and Ann Cosden Comegys, was b. 7th Feb'y 1757, m. Mary Grifith, and had child., viz., Ann, — Edward, — Elizabeth, — Mary,—Ariana, and Jonathan Comegys.

ANN COMEGYS, dau. of Jonathan and Mary Grifith Comegys, was b. 21st June 1775, m. 29th Aug. 1797, John Comegys, and had child., viz., Alphonso, — Francis, and Ann Maria Comegys.

ELIZABETH COMEGYS, dau. of Jonathan and Mary Grifith Comegys, m. Jacob Abbott, and had a son, Jacob Abbott. She m. 2dly, Samuel Brown, of New Jersey, and had a son, Thomas Comegys Brown.

JONATHAN COMEGYS, son of Jonathan and Mary Grifith Comegys, m. Harriet Stradley, 12th of Jan. 1815, and had child., viz., Mary,—Edward William,—Sarah A.,—Eliza, and Ariana Comegys, who m. Mr. Stewart, of Pennsylvania, and had child., viz., Frank,—Harriet,—Ianthus,—Edward,—Mansfield, and Ida Stewart.

EDWARD WILLIAM COMEGYS, son of Jonathan and Harriet Stradley Comegys, m. Georgia Comegys, dau. of John Ward Comegys, and had child., viz., Mary Virginia,—Columbia,—Sommerfield,—Edward Glanville, and John Ward Comegys.

SARAH A. COMEGYS, dau. of Jonathan and Harriet Stradley Comegys, m. B. F. Harris, of Pittsburg, and had child., viz., Cornelia and Franklin Harris. She m. again, Mr. McLain, and had one dau., Emma McLain.

CORNELIUS COMEGYS, the youngest son of William and Ann Cosden Comegys, b. the 4th of July 1758, was a gallant soldier and in many respects a remarkable man. On the 1st of July 1776, he left Chestertown as sergeant in the Flying Camp. On its way to Fort Washington the regiment stopped in Philadelphia, and he was in the city on that memorable day, the 4th of July 1776, and participated in the dread and sublime emotions and rejoicings of that awful moment. After the fall of Fort Washington he was placed in charge of the invalid soldiers and conducted them to Hackenseek in New Jersey. At the expiration of his term of service he again entered the army and served as ensign in Gen. Washington's army, at White Marsh, after the battle of Germantown. In Sept. 1778, immediately after the British had evacuated the city, he removed to Philadelphia, and upon the organization of the Government, under the Articles of Confederation, he received the appointment of a clerkship in the Treasury Department of the infant Republic. He was also assigned to the duty of preparing and signing the Continental currency. In the year 1782 he retired from public life and entered the counting-room of Willing & Morris & Robert Morris. He soon became a great favorite with the firm, and in 1784, with the assistance of the credit of the acting partners, was enabled to commence business as an importing merchant of dry goods. Into his business he carried the same habits and qualities which made him a brave and faithful soldier and won the esteem of all who knew him, whether in the tented field, in Governmental employ, in the counting-room, or behind his own desk. On the 4th of July 1840, being then 82 years of age, he wrote this history of his eventful and honorable life for the use of his children. A shorter sketch, written in July, 1842, is now in the possession of his nephew, Mr. Samuel Comegys. He m. Miss Paul, of Philadelphia. His 2nd wife was Catharine Baker, and had child., viz., Hannah Comegys, who m. Mr. Mason, and had one child, Kate Mason, who m. Mr. Smith,—Julia A. Comegys, who m. Mr. Sargent,—Josephine Comegys and Ella Comegys, who were the first and second wives of Mr. Gilmore,—Jacob Comegys, who m. Miss Lee, of Boston, and Mortimer Comegys, who d. young.

Sec. 98. At the December Term of Court, 1675, the following proceeding was had:

To the Worsh'll Commissioners of Kent County.

The humble petition of Richard Tilghman sheweth,

That whereas yr petitioner about two months since did take Mr. George Hayes to Cure ye bones of his Cubit, being lacerated and torne, by an Accident, in your County, wheareby he is like to lose ye use of his Right Cubit forever, as by the patient may plainly appear; And whereas William Smith of your county, in ye presence of Mr. James Ringgold & others, did promise assume to pay for one halfe of ye Cure, the said George Hayes not being in any capacity to make satisfaction for ye other halfe, & indeed incapable to subsist of himself: your petitioner humbly craves your Care and Assistance to see him satisfied for his full Cure & like wise Order yt ye poore man may be maintained; And yr petitioner as in duty bound shall ever pray, &c.

Vera copia test Chas. Banckes, Clk.

Upon ye delivery of this petition ye Court ordered yt William Smith should be summoned to make his personal appearance ye next Court, which was accordingly done, and then ye abovesd petition was read over in open Court, wheareupon ye sd William Smith declared yt Doctor Tilghman had not made a Cure of George Hayes his arme, yet Nevertheless ye sd William Smith Ingaged in Open Court yt he would satisfie Doctor Tilghman himselfe for ye full Cure of George Hayes his arme according as ye provinciall Court should Order him *satisfaccon:* And yt ye County should not be damnified for ye sd George Hayes Cure, nor for his Maintainance, for he ye sd Smith Ingaged in open Court to provide a sufficient Maintenance for ye sd Hayes, so yt he should not be burdensome to any within ye County; wheareupon ye Court ordered yt should be recorded.

At a Court holden for ye County of Kent, March 25th 1676,

Present—Mr. Joseph Wickes Mr. John Hinson
Mr. James Ringgold Mr. Henry Hosier.

Whereas Mr. Henry Hosier was summoned . . . . to show cause whearefore Mrs. Mary Tilghman, Executrix of Richard Tighman, might not have Execution upon an order of Court, detained against him in March Court 1674-5 for two thousand one hundred pounds of Tob. with Costs of Suit ye sd Mr. Hosier having satisfied neither debt nor costs of suit, as is made apparent;

This Court doth order Execution to ye sd Tilghman for ye sd Debt with Costs of Suite.

SEC. 98, A. Dr. RICHARD TILGHMAN, and Mary Tilghman, his widow and executrix, mentioned in the previous section, came to America in the year 1660 and settled at the Hermitage, on Chester River, in Talbot, now in Queen Anne's county. It is said that Dr. Richard Tilghman was one of the petitioners to have justice done upon Charles the first. It is undeniable that one Richard Tilghman signed the Petition, and as Dr. Richard Tilghman had been a surgeon in the British Navy, and was at this period a Parliamentarian, the signature in question was probably his. He was descended from Richard Tighman, of Holloway Court, in the Parish of Snodland, Kent county, England, who lived about the year 1400; from his son Thomas Tilghman; from his son William Tilghman, who d. 27th Aug. 1541; from his son Richard Tilghman, who d. in 1518; from his son William Tilghman, who d. in 1594, and from his son, Oswald Tilghman, of London, who was b.

4th Oct. 1579, d. in 1628, and was the father of Dr. Richard Tilghman the emigrant, who emigrated to America, in the ship *Elizabeth and Mary*, 1661, to settle upon the tract of land, on Chester river, granted to him by Lord Baltimore in a Patent dated 17th Jan'y 1659. This *lineage* was obtained from Mr. William M. Tilghman, of Philadelphia.

DR. RICHARD TILGHMAN, the emigrant, son of Oswald Tilghman, of London, b. 3d Sept. 1626, m. Marie Foxley, and had child., viz., Samuel, b. in England, 11th Dec. 1650, —Maria, b. in England, in Feb'y 1655,—William,—b. in England, 16th Feb'y 1658,—Deborah, b. at the Hermitage, 12th March 1666, and Richard Tilghman, b. at the Hermitage, 23d Feb'r 1672. Dr. Richard Tilghman d. 7th Jan'y 1675, leaving two child., Maria and Richard Tilghman, and his wife, Mary Tilghman, who was his executrix, and survived him more than twenty years.

MARIA TILGHMAN, dau. of Dr. Richard and Marie Foxley Tilghman, m. Matthew Ward, of the Bay-Side, Talbot, and had a son, Matthew Tilghman Ward, who was the Clerk of St. Paul's Parish 18th Feb'y 1695, *o. s.*, and d. 25th May 1741, in the 64th year of his age, and was at that time President of the Council of the State of Maryland. His 1st wife was Mabel Murphey, widow of Capt. James Murphey. His 2nd wife was Margaret Lloyd, dau. of Col. Philemon Lloyd. He had no sons and adopted his cousin Matthew, son of Richard, and Anna Maria Lloyd Tilghman.

RICHARD TILGHMAN (b. 23d Feb'y 1672, d. 23d Jan'y 1738), of the Hermitage, son of Dr. Richard and Marie Foxley Tilghman, was one of the Lord Proprietor's Council, a zealous member of the English Church, and when the 2nd Chester Church was built, 1697, he advanced the means for its erection, "the vestry engaging to reimburse him the necessary expenses." He m. 1700, Anna Maria Lloyd (see LLOYD), third dau. of Col. Philemon Lloyd, and had child., viz., Mary, b. 23d Aug. 1702,—Philemon, b. 1704, d. young,—Richard b. 28th April 1705, d. 29th Sept. 1768,—Henrietta Marie, b. 18th Aug. 1707,—Anna Maria, b. 15th Nov. 1709,—William, b. 22d Sept. 1711, d. in 1782,—Edward, b. 3d July 1713, d. 9th Oct. 1785,—James, b. 6th Dec. 1716, d. 24th Aug. 1793, and Matthew Tilghman, b. 17th Feb'y 1718, d. 4th May 1790,—Anna Maria Lloyd Tilghman, d. in 1748.

SEC. 98, B. MARY TILGHMAN, dau. of Richard and Anna Maria Lloyd Tilghman, m. 12th Oct. 1721, James Earle, and had child., viz., Michael, b. 19th Oct. 1722,—Anna Maria, b.

8th May 1725,—Richard Tilghman, b. 18th July 1727, d. 17th Jan'y 1728,—a 2nd Richard Tilghman, b. 10th Feb'y 1728,—Henrietta Maria, b. 26th March 1730,—Joseph, b. 11th Nov. 1732, d. 12th Dec. following, and James Earle, b. 21st April 1734. His wife, Mary Tilghman Earle, d. 10th of Jan'y 1736. He m. again, 6th Nov. 1738, Sarah Chatham, widow of Edward Chatham, of Queen Anne's, and had one son, Joseph Earle, b. in 1739, who m. Ann Stevenson, dau. of Rev. Mr. Stevenson, Rector of the Church at Church Hill, Queen Anne's, had child., viz., George W. and William Earle, and d. 1778-9. James Earle d. in May 1739, aged 45 years. He was the grandson of James Earle the immigrant, who was b. 25th July 1631, of the family of Earles of Craglethorpe, Lincolnshire, England, and emigrated to Maryland 15th Nov. 1683, with his wife, Rhoda Earle, and a large family of sons and daus. He d. 24th Sept. 1684, in the 54th year of his age. Michael Earle, his 2nd son, m. 14th Oct. 1686, Sarah Stevens, who d. childless, 7th March 1688. He m. again, 27th Dec. 1690, Ann Carpenter, at Trumpington, Kent, on Chester River, and had child., viz., Elizabeth and James, *twins*, b. 17th of Feb. 1694, and Carpenter, b. 26th of Dec. 1697. Michael Earle and Ann Carpenter Earle, his wife, d. 5th April 1709, and rest in the same grave. Michael Earle was an eminent lawyer at the bar of Kent County Court, and in this profession he was followed with like distinction by his eldest surviving son, James Earle, who m. Mary Tilghman.

CAPT. MICHAEL EARLE, eldest son of James and Mary Tilghman Earle, followed the sea for several years, sailing from Frederick Town, Cecil County. When he retired from a sea-faring life he settled upon his farm, Swan Harbor, in Cecil, and m. Mary Carroll, a sister of his uncle Edward Tilghman's wife, and a relative of Lord Baltimore. They d. without child., in 1787, the same day, and were buried in the same grave at St. Stephen's Church.

ANNA MARIA EARLE, dau. of James and Mary Tilghman Earle, m. Thomas Ringgold, merchant, of Chestertown. He d. 1st April 1772, in the 57th year of his age. She d. in July 1794, in the 70th year of her age. They had one son, Thomas Ringgold (see RINGGOLD).

HON. RICHARD TILGHMAN EARLE, son of James and Mary Tilghman Earle, was a member of the Convention which met in Annapolis 22d June 1774, to oppose the tyrannical proceedings of the Mother-Country and continued through the war an ardent patriot. He m. Ann Chamberlaine, dau. of Samuel

Chamberlaine, of Plaindealing, Talbot, and had child., viz., Samuel,—James,—a 2nd James, b. 26th Feb'y 1764, d. May 1790,—Richard Tilghman,—Henrietta Maria,—Deborah, b. 20th March 1769 (who m. May 1790, Charles Whright, and d. May 1790),—Thomas Chamberlaine (who was b. 29th April 1771, m. Henrietta Maria Hemsley, dau. of William Hemsley, of Cloverfields, Queen Anne's),—Mary,—Margaret, —Susanna, and Ann Earle.

SAMUEL EARLE, son of Richard Tilghman and Ann Chamberlaine Earle, b. 3d of Feb'y 1756, d. 1790, was a Captain in the Revolutionary Army and afterwards practiced law. He m. Henrietta Maria Nicols, and had child., viz., William Nicols,—Ann, and Maria Earle.

HON. RICHARD TILGHMAN EARLE, son of Richard Tilghman and Ann Chamberlaine Earle, b. 23d June 1767, was educated at Washington College and was graduated in May 1787. He studied law with Thomas B. Hands, of Chestertown, and in May 1809, upon the death of his Father-in-law, he was appointed Chief Judge of the second Judicial District of Maryland, and one of the Judges of the Court of Appeals. He was an eminent lawyer, an able Judge, and a good man in all the relations of life. He m. 3d Dec. 1801, Mary Tilghman, dau. of Judge James Tilghman. He d. 8th Nov. 1843, and had child., viz., Elizabeth Ann,—Mary Maria,—Susanna Frisby, — Henrietta Maria, — James Tilghman, — Richard Tilghman,—Samuel Tilghman,—George,—John Charles, and Sarah Catharine Earle, who m. Dr. Joseph E. M. Chamberlaine, of Easton.

ELIZABETH ANN EARLE, dau. of Hon. Richard Tilghman and Mary Tilghman Earle, m. Philip Henry Feddeman, and had child., viz., Philip Henry (who m. Mrs. Lydia Seafield, *née* Cott, and had a dau., Annette Feddeman),—Richard E.,—Mary T.,—Margaret E., and Elizabeth Ann Feddeman.

RICHARD EARLE FEDDEMAN, son of Philip Henry and Elizabeth Ann Earle Feddeman, m. twice. His 1st wife was Ellen Douglas Baker Clayton, and had child., viz., Philip H., and Charles Feddeman. His 2nd wife was Deborah Wright, and had child., viz., Mary Nicholson,—Deborah Wright,—Elizabeth Ann,—Richard E.,—Robert Wright,—Margaret E., and Mabel Lee Feddeman.

PHILIP H. FEDDEMAN, son of Richard Earle and Ellen Douglas Baker Clayton Feddeman, m. Mary Elizabeth Earle, dau. of Samuel T. Earle, and had child., viz., Ellen Douglas, —Samuel Earle Feddeman, and an infant dau.

Mary Maria Earle, dau. of Hon. Richard Tilghman and Mary Tilghman Earle, m. Philip T. Davidson. She survived her husband, and resides at Queenstown. Their child. were, Philip T., who d. in early manhood in Cuba,—Richard E. (who m. Anna Maria, dau. of Capt. Samuel Ogle Tilghman),—George (who m. Marcella Blunt),—Mary Tilghman,—Catharine Thomas, and Susan E. Davidson.

Henrietta Maria Earle, dau. of Hon. Richard Tilghman and Mary Tilghman Earle, m. Dr. David Steuart, now of Fort Penn, Delaware, and had child., viz., Henrietta Maria (who m. Thomas Dilsworth, and had a dau., Henrietta Maria Dilsworth), and David Steuart.

Hon. James Tilghman Earle, eldest son of Hon. Richard Tilghman and Mary Tilghman Earle, was educated at Harvard University, Cambridge, Mass., and was graduated in the class of 1834, and after devoting three years to the study of the law, under the direction of his father, turned his energies and attention to agricultural pursuits, in which he won marked distinction and prominence. In 1849, with Charles B. Calvert and others, he reëstablished the Maryland Agricultural Society, was one of its active Vice Presidents for several years, and in 1856 was elected President. In the stormy and hazardous campaign of 1864 he was nominated by the Democrats of Queen Anne's County to the Senate of Maryland, and was rëelected in 1866, and also under the New Constitution in 1867 and 1871. He was therefore a member of the Senate of Maryland during the trying sessions of 1865, 1866, 1867, 1868, 1870, 1872 and 1874, and was reputed to be among the most upright, soundest, safest, ablest, and most useful members of that honorable body. By his last public services to his State he has connected his name honorably and inseparably with the Centennial Exhibition of 1876. He m., 15th of Dec. 1841, Ann Johns, dau. of Kensey Johns, Jr., Chancellor of the State of Delaware. She d. 8th Oct. 1842. He m. again, 20th of Dec. 1849, Ann Catharine Tilghman, dau. of Col. John Tilghman, of Queen Anne's, and had child., viz., Elizabeth and Ann Johns Earle. Mrs. Ann Catharine Tilghman Earle d. 22d Nov. 1876.

Ann Johns Earle, dau. of Hon. James Tilghman and Ann Catharine Earle, m., 18th June 1874, William H. Babcock, attorney-at-law, of Washington, D. C., and had a dau., Rosa Earle Babcock.

Richard Tilghman Earle, son of Hon. Richard Tilghman and Mary Tilghman Earle, m. twice. His 1st wife was

Catharine Spencer, dau. of Captain Isaac Spencer, of Kent, and had one son, Richard Tilghman Earle. His 2nd wife was Elizabeth A. Spencer, sister of his 1st wife.

SAMUEL T. EARLE, son of Hon. Richard Tilghman and Mary Tilghman Earle, m. Mary W. Brundige, dau. of William Brundige, and had child., viz., James T., who d. a gallant Confederate soldier, after suffering many hardships,—William B.,—Richard T.,—Mary Elizabeth (who m. Philip H. Feddeman),—Samuel T.,—Rosetta W., and Sarah Catharine Earle.

WILLIAM B. EARLE, son of Samuel Tilghman and Mary W. Brundige Earle, m. Louisa Stubbs, of Norfolk, Va., and had child., viz., James T., and Fanny Shepherd Earle.

DR. SAMUEL T. EARLE, of Centreville, son of Samuel T. and Mary W. Brundige Earle, m. Mary Isabel Ringgold, dau. of Thomas Ringgold, of Kent, and had a dau., Mary Isabel Earle.

HENRIETTA MARIA EARLE, dau. of Richard Tilghman and Ann Chamberlaine Earle, was b. 15th March 1761, and d. in June 1828, the widow of Samuel W. Thomas. Her 1st husband was Solomon Clayton, Register of Wills for Queen Anne's, and had child., viz., Richard Earle (who m. Juliana Roberts, and afterwards her sister, Sophia Roberts),—Solomon, drowned in Corsica creek,—Walter Jackson, and Juliana Clayton.

WALTER JACKSON CLAYTON, son of Solomon and Henrietta Maria Earle Clayton, m. Sarah Hacket, and had child., viz., Thomas Earle,—John Hacket,—Juliana Maria (who m. John Eastwick, of Phila.),—Anna Maria Hacket,—Henrietta Maria,—Ann Caroline, and Sarah Elizabeth Clayton.

THOMAS EARLE CLAYTON, son of Walter Jackson and Sarah Hacket Clayton, m. Ellen Douglas Baker, and had one son, Walter Thomas Clayton, who resided in Mobile, Alabama, and m. Carrie Threwer.

ANNA MARIA HACKET CLAYTON, dau. of Walter Jackson and Sarah Hacket Clayton, m. Clinton Wright, of Queen Anne's, and had child., viz., Robert Theodore DeCoursey, b. 5th Sept. 1840, d. 6th Jan'y 1862,—Mary Feddeman, and Clinton Wright, who m. in Tennessee, Feb'y 1871, Frances Kirby, and has child., viz., Clinton, and Nannie Wright.

HENRIETTA MARIA CLAYTON, dau. of Walter Jackson and Sarah Hacket Clayton, m. her brother-in-law, Clinton Wright, and had a dau., Henrietta Clayton Wright, who m. William Samuel Carroll, and had a son, James Lambert Carroll.

ANN CAROLINE CLAYTON, dau. of Walter Jackson and Sarah Hacket Clayton, m. 16th Nov. 1848, Benjamin Blackiston Wroth, of Chestertown, and had child., viz., William Frisby,—Thomas Granger,—Clinton Wright,—Emory Sudler, and Margaret Perkins Wroth. She d. Oct. 5th 1875, in her 49th year.

SARAH ELIZABETH CLAYTON, dau. of Walter Jackson and Sarah Hacket Clayton, m. and was the 3rd wife of her brother-in-law, Clinton Wright, and had child., viz., William Henry DeCoursey and Thomas Clayton Wright. She survived him.

GEORGE EARLE, son of Hon. Richard Tilghman and Mary Tilghman Earle, m. Mary Chamberlaine, dau. of Dr. Joseph Chamberlaine, of Newark, Delaware, and had child., viz., Richard Tilghman,—Elizabeth,—George,—Mary T.,—Charles Thompson,—Susan F., and Catharine Chamberlaine Earle.

DR. JOHN CHARLES EARLE, of Easton, son of Hon. Richard Tilghman and Mary Tilghman Earle, m. Clara E. Goldsborough, dau. of Col. Nicholas Goldsborough, of Talbot, and had child., viz., Elizabeth G.,—Mary Tilghman,—Clara G.,—Matthew Tilghman Goldsborough,—James Tilghman, and Henry Hollyday Earle.

ELIZABETH G. EARLE, dau. of Dr. John Charles and Clara E. Goldsborough Earle, m. Richard Hollyday, of Readbourne, Queen Anne's, and had child., viz., John Charles,—Anna Maria,—Clara E., and Margaret Carroll Hollyday.

MARGARET EARLE, dau. of Richard Tilghman and Ann Chamberlaine, b. 8th March 1765—d. in 1795—m. Philip Feddeman, and had child., viz., Philip H. Feddeman (who m. Elizabeth Ann Earle), and Mary Earle Feddeman.

MARY E. FEDDEMAN, dau. of Philip and Margaret Earle Feddeman, m. Robert Theodore DeCoursey Wright, and had child., viz., Clinton Wright and William Henry Wright.

JAMES EARLE, the fifth son of James and Mary Tilghman Earle, b. 1st April 1734, was appointed after the Revolution Clerk of the General Court for the Eastern Shore of Maryland, and resided in Easton until his death, in October 1810. He m. Elenor Carroll, sister of his brother Michael's wife, and had child., viz., Michael,—James,—Richard Tilghman,—Edward, and Henrietta Maria Earle.

JAMES EARLE, son of James and Elenor Carroll Earle, m. Anna Maria Tilghman, dau. of Peregrine Tilghman, of Hope, Talbot, and had child., viz., Henrietta Maria (who m. Ezekiel Forman, and had child., viz., William and Ezekiel T. M. Forman),—Anna Maria Lloyd, and Ariana Earle. James Earle succeeded his father in the Clerkship of the General Court, and at the time of his death, 1813, was Clerk of the Court of Appeals on the Eastern Shore and cashier of the Bank at Easton.

HENRIETTA MARIA EARLE, dau. of James and Mary Tilghman Earle, b. 26th March 1730, m. William Hemsley, of Cloverfields, Queen Anne's, and had child., viz., William (who m. Maria Lloyd, dau. of Maj. James Lloyd),—Mary, and Charlotte Hemsley.

MARY HEMSLEY, dau. of William and Henrietta Maria Earle Hemsley, m. Joseph Forman, and had child., viz., William,—Ezekiel (who m. Henrietta Maria Earle),—Henrietta Maria, and Augustine Forman.

HENRIETTA MARIA FORMAN, dau. of Joseph and Mary Hemsley Forman, m. Robert Lloyd Tilghman, of Hope, and had child., viz., Robert Lloyd,—Anna Maria (who m. Gen. Tench Tilghman),—Augustine, and Henrietta Tilghman.

SEC. 98, C. RICHARD TILGHMAN (b. 28th April 1705, d. 29th Sept. 1768), 3d of the Hermitage, son of Richard and Anna Maria Lloyd Tilghman, was appointed Judge of the Provincial Court in March 1754. He m. Susanna Frisby, dau. of Peregrine Frisby, of Cecil, and had child., viz., Richard, b. 11th May 1739,—Peregrine, b. 24th Jan'y 1741,—James,—William,—Edward,—Elizabeth,—Susanna, b. 1751, and Anna Maria Tilghman, who m. Henry Ward Pearce, of Cecil, and d. 1834, aged 75.

RICHARD TILGHMAN (b. 11th May 1739), 4th of the Hermitage, son of Richard and Susanna Frisby Tilghman, m. his first cousin, Elizabeth Tilghman, dau. of his uncle Edward Tilghman and Elizabeth Chew, and had one child, Richard Edward Tilghman.

COL. PEREGRINE TILGHMAN (b. 24th Jan'y 1741, d. 1807), son of Richard and Susanna Frisby Tilghman, m. in 1769, Deborah Lloyd, dau. of Col. Robert Lloyd, of Hope, and Anna Maria Hemsley *née* Tilghman. The said Col. Robert Lloyd was the son of James Lloyd and Ann Grundy, of Caroline. James Lloyd was the 3rd son of Capt. Philemon Lloyd, of Wye House, and brother-in-law of the 2d Richard Tilghman of the Hermitage. Col. Peregrine Tilghman resided at Hope, Talbot, and had child., viz., Robert Lloyd,—Anna Maria,—Tench,—William Hemsley, and Elizabeth Tilghman.

ROBERT LLOYD TILGHMAN (b. 13th May 1778, d. 12th June 1823), son of Col. Peregrine and Deborah Lloyd Tilghman, m. 16th April 1807, Henrietta Maria Forman, dau. of Col. Joseph and Mary Hemsley Forman. He resided at Hope, and had child., viz., Mary Forman, who d. in infancy,—

Anna Maria, b. 4th Feb'y 1811 (who m. 1st May 1851, Gen. Tench Tilghman),—Augusta, b. 29th Sept. 1814,—Henrietta Maria, b. 17th June 1817, and Robert Lloyd Tilghman, b. 4th May 1821.

TENCH TILGHMAN (b. 18th April 1782, d. 16th April 1827), son of Col. Peregrine and Deborah Lloyd Tilghman, m. Ann Margaretta Tilghman, dau. of Col. Tench Tilghman, of the Revolutionary Army, and afterwards lived at Plimhimmon, the residence of his mother, near Oxford, Talbot. He had two sons, viz., William, who d. in infancy, and Tench Tilghman.

Gen. Tench Tilghman (b. 25th of March 1810, d. 22d Dec. 1874), of Plimhimmon, son of Tench and Ann Margaretta Tilghman, was a graduate of West Point, and while an officer in the U. S. Army served with credit in the Black Hawk war. He m. twice. His 1st wife was Henrietta Maria Kerr, dau. of Hon. John Leeds Kerr, of Easton, to whom he was m. Nov. 1832, and had child., viz., Tench Francis, b. 25th Sept. 1833, d. 1867,—William Arthur, b. 15th Sept. 1835, d. in 1853,—John Leeds, b. 30th Sept. 1837, d. at the age of 27, an efficient and brave officer in the Confederate Army,—Oswald,—Anna Maria,—Ella Sophia,—Henrietta Kerr (who m. John Richard Burroughs),—Rosalie (who m. Thomas Shreve),—Ann Margaretta, and Sarah Chamberlaine Tilghmam. He m. a 2nd time, 1st May 1851, Anna Maria Tilghman, dau. of Robert Lloyd and Henrietta Maria Forman Tilghman.

TENCH FRANCIS TILGHMAN (b. 25th of Sept. 1833, d. in 1867), son of Gen. Tench and Henrietta Maria Kerr Tilghman, m., 1st, Anna Cox, dau. of Dr. C. C. Cox, and had 3 child. His 2nd wife was Elizabeth Bannon Camp, of Norfolk, Va., and had 2 child.

OSWALD TILGHMAN, son of Gen. Tench and Henrietta Maria Kerr Tilghman, m., in 1869, Martina Martin, who had one son. Mother and child are d.

WILLIAM HEMSLEY TILGHMAN (b. 16th Dec. 1784, d. in Dec. 1863), son of Col. Peregrine and Deborah Lloyd, m. Maria Lloyd Hemsley, dau. of Philemon Hemsley and Elizabeth Lloyd Hemsley, and d. *sine prole*. Elizabeth Lloyd Hemsley was the dau. of Gen. James Lloyd, of Farley, Kent, and Elizabeth Tilghman, the 2nd dau. of James Tilghman, the 4th son of the 2nd Richard Tilghman of the Hermitage.

ANNA MARIA TILGHMAN, dau. of Col. Peregrine and Deborah Lloyd Tilghman, m. James Earle, of Easton, and had three daus., viz., Ariana,—Henrietta Maria (who m.

Ezekiel Forman, son of Col. Joseph Forman and Mary Hemsley, and had child., viz., William H. and Ezekiel T. M. Forman) and Anna Maria Lloyd Earle.

ELIZABETH TILGHMAN, dau. of Colonel Peregrine and Deborah Lloyd Tilghman, m. John Custis Wilson, of Somerset, and had child., viz., Henrietta Maria Wilson, who m. Dr. Handy, of Princess Ann,—Peggy Custis Wilson,—Elizabeth Wilson, who m. the Rev. Dr. Campbell, of Albany, N. Y., a Presbyterian clergyman,—Anna Maria Wilson, who m. Levin Handy, of Somerset, and Mary Ellen Wilson, who m. Gen. George Handy, of Somerset.

JUDGE JAMES TILGHMAN (b. 2nd Aug. 1743, d. 19th of April 1809), 3rd son of Richard and Susanna Frisby Tilghman, was a member of the Conventions of Maryland, 1774–76, a member of the Council of Safety from 17th Jan'y 1776, Chief Judge of the Judicial District composed of Cecil, Kent, Queen Anne's and Talbot Counties, in 1791, and a member of the Court of Appeals, 1804–1809. He was the 1st Attorney General of Maryland. He m. 29th June 1769, Susanna Steuart, dau. of Dr. George Steuart of Annapolis (see STEUART), and had child., viz., George, b. 11th Oct. 1771, d. 30th July 1792,—Frisby, b. 4th Aug. 1773,—Susanna, and Anna Maria Tilghman. Mrs. Susanna Steuart Tilghman d. 24th of Oct. 1774. Judge James Tilghman survived and m. 19th Feb'y 1778, Elizabeth Johns, sister of the first Chancellor Johns, of Delaware, and a dau. of Kensey Johns, of West River, Anne Arundel Co., Md., and had child., viz., Anna Maria, b. 10th March 1779 (who m. Peregrine Blake, and had child., viz., Peregrine Frisby, — Mary Ann Catharine, and Elizabeth Eleanor Blake),—Samuel, b. 30th Aug. 1781, d. 19th Aug. 1782,—Mary, b. 6th Feb'y 1783 (who m. Judge Richard Tilghman Earle),—John, b. 8th of March 1785,—Charles Carroll, b. 26th Jan'y 1788,—Peregrine, b. 31st March 1790, —Mrs. Elizabeth Johns Tilghman, d. 22d Jan. 1809, aged 59 years.

COL. FRISBY TILGHMAN (b. 4th Aug. 1773, d. 14th April 1847), of Rockland, Washington County, son of Judge James and Susanna Steuart Tilghman, m. 24th March 1795, Anna Maria Ringgold, and had child., viz., Mary, b. 8th Feb'y 1796,—George, b. 11th of May 1797,—Thomas Edward, b. 15th April 1800,—Susan Ann, b. 31st March 1801,—Frisby, b. 23rd Oct. 1807, and Ann Cheston, b. 20th Feb'y 1810 (who m. William Hollyday). Mrs. Anna Maria Ringgold Tilghman d. 21st Feb'y 1817. He survived and m. 23d of Sept.

1819, Louisa Lamar, who was b. 30th Aug. 1789, the dau. of Colonel William Lamar, of Alleghany, and had child., viz., Louisa Lamar (who m. and was the 2nd wife of William Hollyday),—Margaret Ann (who m. Gen. Thomas J. McKaig, and had child., viz., Frisby Tilghman, and Nina Lamar McKaig), and Sarah Lamar Tilghman.

MRS. ANNA MARIA RINGGOLD TILGHMAN was the dau. of Thomas Ringgold and Mary Galloway, who had child., viz., Thomas, b. 4th Sept. 1768, d. March 1818 (who m. 10th Feb'y 1795, Mary Gittings, and had child., viz., Thomas and James, *twins*, b. 11th Nov. 1795,—Benjamin, b. 31st. Dec. 1797, and John Galloway Ringgold, b. 20th Dec. 1799),—Samuel, b. 15th Jan'y 1770,—Anna Maria, b. 9th March 1772, d. 21st Feb'y 1817,—Benjamin, b. 15th Feb'y 1774, d. 24th Aug. 1798, and Tench Ringgold, b. 6th March 1776, who m. 10th April 1799, Mary Christian Lee. When page 66 was printed the author did not have access to a transcript from the Ringgold Bible, containing this full list of the child. of Thomas Ringgold, and therefore inserts it here.

MARY TILGHMAN, dau. of Col. Frisby and Anna Maria Ringgold Tilghman, m. Dr. William Hammond, and had child., viz., Ann,—Richard Pindle,—Mary,—William,—Caroline,—George, and Rebecca Hammond.

ANN HAMMOND, dau. of Dr. William and Mary Tilghman Hammond, m. Buchanan Hall, formerly of Washington county, now of Stockton, California, and had child., viz., William and Mary Hammond Hall.

MARY HAMMOND, dau. of Dr. William and Mary Tilghman Hammond, m. Col. Sprague, Paymaster, U. S. A.

DR. WILLIAM HAMMOND, son of Doctor William and Mary Tilghman Hammond, m. Eliza Mitchell, of Washington County, Md., and is now residing in California, and has child., viz., Georgie and Charles Tilghman Hammond.

GEORGE TILGHMAN (b. 11th of May 1797, d. 25th Aug. 1831), son of Col. Frisby and Anna Maria Ringgold Tilghman, m. twice. His 1st wife was Ann E. Lamar, dau. of Col. William Lamar, of Alleghany County, Md., and child., viz., Anna Maria and Mary Tilghman, who m. Phineas Janney. His 2d wife was Anna B. Lynn, dau. of Capt. David Lynn, of Alleghany County, and had child., viz., Fanny Lynn,—Susan (who m. Mr. W. Bowene, and had a dau. Mary Bowene),—George, b. 3d March 1830, and Frisby L. Tilghman, b. 4th July 1831, who m. Anna Bolling, dau. of Col. Bolling, of Petersburg, Va., and had child., viz., Martha and Anna Tilghman.

THOMAS EDWARD TILGHMAN (b. 15th April 1800), son of Col. Frisby and Anna Maria Ringgold Tilghman, m. Rebecca Hammond, and had child., viz., Edward Sommerfield, b. 21st Jan'y 1827,—William Frisby, b. 23d Feb'y 1828,—Thomas Hammond, b. 7th Jan'y 1830. He m. 2dly Sarah Bugbee, and had child., viz., William Ridgely,—Anna Maria,—Sarah, —Charles Ringgold,—Antoinette,—Ida, and Harry Tilghman.

DR. FRISBY TILGHMAN, son of Col. Frisby and Anna Maria Ringgold Tilghman, m. Henrietta Maria Hemsley, dau. of Alexander and Henrietta Maria Tilghman Hemsley. Henrietta Maria Tilghman Hemsley was the dau. of Lloyd Tilghman, son of Matthew the youngest son of the 2nd Richard Tilghman of the Hermitage.

COL. JOHN TILGHMAN (b. 8th March 1785), of Centreville, son of Judge James and Elizabeth Johns Tilghman, m. twice. His 1st wife was Ann Catharine Tilghman, dau. of Richard Tilghman, son of Matthew the son of the 2nd Richard Tilghman of the Hermitage, and had child., viz., John Henry, who m. Octavia Hollinger, of Mobile,—Mary Elizabeth and Ann Catharine Tilghman, who m. Hon. James T. Earle. His 2d wife was Ann Tilghman, dau. of Lloyd Tilghman, son of the above mentioned Matthew Tilghman, and had child., viz., Matthew Ward,—James, b. 16th June 1820, and Lloyd Tilghman, b. 15th Dec. 1821, d. 29th Nov. 1876.

JAMES TILGHMAN, son of Col. John, and his 2nd wife, Ann Tilghman, m. his cousin Harriet, dau. of his uncle Peregrine Tilghman, and had child., viz., John,—George, and Anna Tilghman.

LLOYD TILGHMAN, son of Col. John, and his 2nd wife, Ann Tilghman, m. Mary M. Johns, dau. of the second Chancellor Johns, of Delaware, and had child., viz., Henrietta and Mary Tilghman.

CHARLES CARROLL TILGHMAN (b. 26th of Jan'y 1788), son of Judge James and Elizabeth Johns Tilghman, m. Mary Lloyd Tilghman, dau. of Richard Tilghman, son of Matthew the son of the 2nd Richard Tilghman of the Hermitage. He d. in Dec. 1861, and had child., viz., Charles Henry, b. 9th of Sept. 1821 (who m. Ann Carmichael, dau. of Judge Richard B. Carmichael),—William Brice, b. 3d of June 1823,—Anna Maria, and Mary Elizabeth Tilghman.

WILLIAM BRICE TILGHMAN, son of Charles Carroll and Mary Lloyd Tilghman, m., 6th Feb'y 1849, Harriet Eliza Tilghman, dau. of Matthew and Harriet Hynson Tilghman, and had child., viz., Mary Anna,—Anna Maria, who d. Feb'y

1853,—Charles Carroll, who d. Jan'y 1854,—William Brice, who d. 1st Sept. 1861,—Isabella Wyatt,—Anna Maria, who d. 9th Sept. 1861,—Charles Carroll, and Alice Lee Tilghman, who d. 26th June 1864.

Peregrine Tilghman (b. 31st March 1790, d. 1874), son of Judge James and Elizabeth Johns Tilghman, m. Harriet Hadaway, and had child., viz., James, b. 8th of Sept. 1815,—Peregrine, b. 21st of Sept. 1822 (who m. Anna McKenney, dau. of John McKenney),—Araminta,—Sarah,—Harriet,—Francis,—Jane,—Maria, and Mary Ann Tilghman.

James Tilghman (b. 8th Sept. 1815), son of Peregrine and Harriet Haddaway, m. Augusta Steele, of Cambridge, and had child., viz., Chester,—Daniel, b. 30th Oct. 1851, and J. Cooke Tilghman.

William Tilghman (b. 11th of March 1742, d. Dec. 1800), of the White House, Queen Anne's County, 4th son of the 3d Richard of the Hermitage and Susanna Frisby Tilghman, m. 3 times. His 1st wife was Ann Kent. His 2nd wife was Anna Maria Lloyd, dau. of Col. Robert Lloyd, of Hope. His 3rd wife was Mrs. Eleanor Hall Rosier, widow of Thomas Whetenhall Rosier and dau. of Francis Hall, and had a dau., Anna Maria Tilghman, who m. Edward Tilghman, grandson of Edward Tilghman, of Wye, the 3rd son of the 2d Richard Tilghman of the Hermitage.

Elizabeth Tilghman (b. 24th April 1749, d. in 1836), dau. of the 3rd Richard of the Hermitage, and Susanna Frisby Tilghman, m. William Cooke, of Annapolis, and had child., viz., Richard Cooke (who added Tilghman to his name in compliance with the testamentary injunction of his uncle, the 4th Richard Tilghman of the Hermitage),—William,—Francis,—George,—Catharine,—Anna Maria,—Elizabeth,—Sophia, and Susanna Frisby Cooke, who m. William Williams, and had child., viz., William S.,—Otho Holland,—Henry,—Elizabeth E., and Mary Smith Williams.

Richard Cooke Tilghman of the Hermitage, son of William and Elizabeth Tilghman Cooke, m. Elizabeth Van Wick, of Baltimore, and had child., viz., William Cooke,—Richard Cooke,—Henry Cooke,—John Charles Cooke,—Steadman Cooke,—Elizabeth Cooke (who m. Mr. Purnell, of Caroline, and had child., viz., Isaac and Martha Purnell),—Sophia Cooke,—James Cooke Tilghman, and Fanny Van Wick Tilghman, who m. Mr. Fernandis. His 2nd wife was Frances Van Wick, a sister of his 1st wife.

WILLIAM COOKE TILGHMAN, son of Richard Cooke and Elizabeth Van Wick Tilghman, m. S. Worrell, dau. of Judge Thomas Worrell, of Kent, and had one child, Anna Maria Tilghman (who m. Judge Joseph A. Wickes). His 2nd wife was Sally Emory, dau. of General Thomas Emory, of Poplar Grove, Queen Anne's, and had child., viz., Elizabeth,—William,—Richard,—Sally, and Fanny Tilghman, who m. Dr. Johnson, of Baltimore.

COL. RICHARD COOKE TILGHMAN of the Hermitage, son of Richard Cooke and Elizabeth Van Wick Tilghman, was graduated at West Point, the 2nd in a class of 33, in July 1828, was an intimate friend Gen'l. Robert E. Lee, and one of his groomsmen. He was promoted to Brevet 2nd Lieutenant of Artillery, U. S. A., served 8 years and aided in the construction of the National Road through Ohio. He resigned 31st March 1836. As a Civil Engineer, he served the State of Maryland, 1836–37, and the United States, 1837–46. "He surveyed sites for fortifications on Lake Champlain; located and built roads in the Indian Reservation in Iowa Territory; and made reconnoissances of the approaches to the City of New Orleans, and superintended the harbor improvements at the Lakes Erie and Michigan" (see *Matthew Tilghman*, &c., by George Tilghman Hollyday in *Potter's Monthly*, June 1876).

In 1846, he was elected a Judge of the Orphans' Court for Queen Anne's Co., and appointed by the Governor Chief Judge—the position he now occupies. He m. his cousin, Elizabeth Williams.

HENRY COOKE TILGHMAN, son of Richard Cooke and Elizabeth Van Wick Tilghman, m. Milcah Skinner, dau. of Andrew Skinner, of Fair View, Talbot, and had child., viz., Richard Cooke,—Elizabeth,—Louisa (who m. William Carroll),—Fanny (who m. Richard Hough),—Susan,—Sally and Milcah Tilghman.

RICHARD COOKE TILGHMAN, son of Henry Cooke and Milcah Skinner Tilghman, m. Agnes Owen, dau. of Col. Kennedy R. Owen and his wife Anna Maria, dau. of William Gibson Tilghman, of Groces, Talbot. He d. in 1873, and had a son, Richard Tilghman.

JOHN CHARLES TILGHMAN, son of Richard Cooke and Elizabeth Van Wick Tilghman, m. E. B. Williams, and had child., viz., Steadman,—C. Herman,—Mary,—Susan, and Elizabeth Ellen Tilghman.

James Cooke Tilghman, son of Richard Cooke and Elizabeth Van Wick Tilghman, m. Anna M. Brown, of Queen Anne's, a great-granddau. of James Tilghman, the 4th son of the 2nd Richard Tilghman of the Hermitage.

William Cooke, son of William and Elizabeth Tilghman Cooke, m. Elizabeth Tilghman, dau. of Edward and Elizabeth Chew Tilghman, of Phila., and had child., viz., George,—Francis,—James,—Mary,—Sophia (who m. Robert Gilmor),—Anna Maria,—Elizabeth,—William, and Edward Cooke.

George Cooke, son of William and Elizabeth Tilghman Cooke, m. Ellen A. Dall, of Baltimore, and had child., viz., Ellen Dall,—James Dall,—Elizabeth Catharine,—Georgiana,—Anna Maria,—William,—Meliora,—Mary Clapham,—Julia,—Emily Louisa, and George Addison Cooke.

Catharine Cooke, dau. of William and Elizabeth Tilghman Cooke, m. James Clapham, of Baltimore, and had child., viz., Elizabeth Ann,—Sophia,—Mary,—Henrietta,—Rebecca,—William, and John Clapham.

Anna Maria Cooke, dau. of William and Elizabeth Tilghman Cooke, m. Benjamin Ogle, son of Hon. Benjamin Ogle, Governor of Maryland, 1798–1801; who was the son of Hon. Samuel Ogle, who was three times, in 1732, from 1735 to 1742, and from 1747 to 1752, Proprietary Governor of the Province of Maryland. Hon. Samuel Ogle was eldest son of Samuel Ogle, Esquire, of Northumberland County, England, who d. in the year 1718. Gov. Samuel Ogle d. the 3d of May, 1752, aged 58 years.

Benjamin Ogle and Anna Maria Cooke Ogle, had child., viz., Benjamin,—William Cooke,—George Cooke,—Richard Lowndes,—Elizabeth,—Henrietta,—Anna,— Sophia,— Mary,—Susan,—Louisa,—Catharine (who m. Rev. Chas. Goodrich),— Ellen, and Rosalie Ogle.

Dr. George Cooke Ogle, son of Benjamin and Anna Maria Cooke Ogle, m., 12th Oct. 1853, Anna Maria Cooke, dau. of George and Ellen Dall Cooke, and had child., viz., Benjamin and George Cooke Ogle.

Richard Lowndes Cooke, son of Benjamin and Anna Maria Cooke Ogle, m. Priscilla, dau. of Robert W. Bowie, and had child., viz., Catharine,—Fanny,—Caroline,—Louisa,—Susan, and Richard Lowndes Ogle. His 2nd wife was Fanny Knight, of Vermont, and had child., viz., Mary,—Rosalie,—Randolph, and Henry Ogle.

Elizabeth Ogle, dau. of Benjamin and Anna Maria Cooke Ogle, m. William Woodville, of Baltimore, and had child., viz., Richard Caton,—William,—Middleton,—Ann, and Elizabeth Woodville.

HENRIETTA OGLE, dau. of Benjamin and Anna Maria Cooke Ogle, m. William H. Tayloe, of Virginia, and had child., viz., Henry A.,—Sophia, and Emma Tayloe.

ANNA OGLE, dau. of Benjamin and Anna Maria Cooke Ogle, m. Robert Neilson, of Baltimore, and had one dau., Emily Neilson, who m. Dr. Blackburn, of Virginia.

SOPHIA OGLE, dau. of Benjamin and Anna Maria Cooke Ogle, m. Julius Forrest, and had child., viz., Anna Maria and David Crawford Forrest. Her 2nd husband was Rev. Alexander Marbury, and had child., viz., William,—Benjamin Ogle,—Melville,—Sophia,—Annie, and Ada Marbury.

MARY OGLE, dau. of Benjamin and Anna Maria Cooke Ogle, m. Edward T. Tayloe, of King George's County, Va., and had child., viz., Edward,—Poinsett,—Bladen,—William Ogle,—George Ogle,—Julia,—Mary,—Imogen, and Catharine Tayloe.

SUSAN OGLE, dau. of Benjamin and Anna Maria Cooke Ogle, m. John Hodges, of Prince George's, and had child., viz., John,—Richard,—Lewis,—Upton,—Maria,—Caroline,—Mary,—Susan,—Anna, and Ellen Hodges.

LOUISA OGLE, dau. of Benjamin and Anna Maria Cooke Ogle, m. Rev. Upton Beall, P. E. Church, and had child., viz., Edward Sinclair,—Brooke,—Ellen Louisa, and Amelia Beall.

ELLEN COOKE OGLE, dau. of Benjamin and Anna Maria Cooke Ogle, m. Richard B. Mullikin, and had child., viz., Richard,—William,—Walter,—Arthur,—Edward,—Louisa,—Ellen,—Elizabeth,—Mary,—Emily,—Susan, and Annie Ogle Mullikin.

SEC. 98, D. HENRIETTA MARIA TILGHMAN (b. 18th Aug. 1707, d. 7th of Nov. 1771), dau. of Richard, 2nd of the Hermitage, and Anna Maria Lloyd Tilghman, m. 22d April 1731, George Robins, of Peach Blossom, Talbot, who was b. in the year 1698, d. 6th Dec. 1742, the son of Thomas Robins and Susanna Vaughan. Thomas Robins was b. in 1672, d. 29th Dec. 1721, the son of George Robins, of Peach Blossom, and Margaretta Howes Goldsborough. George Robins, d. 12th of May 1677, buried at Peach Blossom 14th May 1677, was the son of Thomas Robins, who was b. at Bloxham, 10th Oct. 1601, m. 16th of July 1632, Mary, the eldest dau. of Thomas Halhead, of Banbury. Mary Halhead Robins was b. 15th Nov. 1612, d. 27th Feb'y 1648. Thomas Robins m. a 2nd time, 5th Aug. 1650, Mary Eyre, and d. 17th Feb'y 1667. He was the son of George Robins, of Banbury, Oxford county, England, who was b. in 1574, d. 24th Aug. 1641. His wife d. 1st of March 1618, and with him "lieth buried in Banbury, England."

GEORGE ROBINS and Henrietta Maria Tilghman Robins, had child., viz., Anna Maria, b. 13th March 1732,—Margaret, b. 20th April 1734,—Henrietta Maria, b. 16th March 1736 (who m. April 1757, James Lloyd Chamberlaine),—Susanna, b. 10th June 1738,—Thomas, b. 9th Aug. 1740, and Elizabeth Robins, b. 17th Oct. 1742. Mrs. Henrietta Maria Tilghman Robins survived her husband and m. William Goldsborough, and were both buried at Peach Blossom. (See GOLDSBOROUGH.)

ANNA MARIA ROBINS (b. 13th March 1732, d. 16th Aug. 1804), dau. of George and Henrietta Maria Tilghman Robins, of Peach Blossom, m. 9th Dec. 1749, Henry Hollyday, of Ratcliffe, Talbot. They lived, died and were buried at Ratcliffe, and had child., viz., Henrietta Maria, b. 5th Dec. 1750, —Sarah, b. 29th Jan'y 1753 (who m. Henry Nicols, of Darley, and d. 14th Oct. 1829),—Anna Maria, b. 9th Dec. 1756 (who m. George Gale, of Cecil, and had child., viz., Levin,—George, —Ann,—Leah,—Sarah,—Henrietta,—Georgeanna, and Harriet Gale, and d. in 1817),—James, b. 1st Nov. 1758,—Thomas, b. 2d Oct. 1760, d. 1823,—Rebecca, b. 5th Dec. 1762, d. July 1801 (who m. Nicholas Hammond, of Easton, and had child., viz., Dr. Nicholas,—Anna Maria, and Rebecca Hammond),—Elizabeth, b. 7th Aug. 1768, d. 18th Oct. 1810, —Henry, b. 11th Sept. 1771, and Margaret Hollyday, b. 12th May 1774, d. May 1848, who m. Lyttleton Gale, brother of George Gale, and had child., viz., Henry,—Robert,—Levin,—Anna Maria,—Leah,—Susanna, and Elizabeth Gale.

HENRY HOLLYDAY, of Ratcliffe, was the grandson of Col. Thomas Hollyday (of consanguinity with Sir Leonard Hollyday, Lord Mayor of London, 1605) who m. Mary Truman, of England, settled in Prince George's Co., d. 1703, and left sons, viz., James Hollyday, of Readbourne, Queen Anne's, and Col. Leonard Hollyday, of Brookfield, Prince George's.

HON. JAMES HOLLYDAY, of Readbourne (b. 18th June 1696, d. 8th Oct. 1747), son of Col. Thomas Hollyday and Mary Truman, m. 3d May 1721, Mrs. Sarah Covington Lloyd, widow of Edward Lloyd (see LLOYD) and had child., viz., James Hollyday, b. 30th Nov. 1722, d. 5th Nov. 1786, the eminent lawyer and colonial Statesman,—Henry Hollyday, of

Ratcliffe, b. 9th March 1725, d. 11th Nov. 1789, and Sarah Hollyday, b. 5th Oct. 1727, d. 30th March 1729.

COL. LEONARD HOLLYDAY, of Brookfield, son of Col. Thomas Hollyday and Mary Truman, b. 4th May 1698, m. Sarah Smith, and 2ndly Mrs. Eleanor Waring (widow of Marsham Waring and dau. of Clement Hill and Eleanor Darnall, a dau. of Henry Darnall, "a kinsman of Lord Baltimore"), and left child., viz., Thomas (who m. Ann Waring),—Dr. Leonard (who m. 1st Miss Holland, 2ndly Miss Weems),—Elizabeth (who m. Mr. Semmes),—Mary (who m. Maj. Frank Waring), and Clement Hollyday, who m. Miss Priggs, and had a son, Urban Hollyday, who d. 1862, leaving a dau. Amelia Hollyday. Col. Leonard Hollyday d. 6th May 1747. His numerous descendants intermarried with the families of Contee, Bowie, Greenfield, Semmes and Waring.

HENRIETTA MARIA HOLLYDAY (b. 5th Dec. 1750), dau. of Henry and Anna Maria Robins Hollyday, m. 15th Jan'y 1772, Samuel Chamberlaine, of Oxford Neck, and had child., viz., James Lloyd,—Lloyd,—Samuel,—Henry,—Anna Maria (who m. 24th Jan'y 1797, John Goldsborough, see GOLDSBOROUGH),—May,—Sally Hollyday (who m. 8th April 1801, Hon. John Leeds Kerr, see KERR), and Harriet Rebecca Chamberlaine.

JAMES LLOYD CHAMBERLAINE, son of Samuel and Henrietta Maria Hollyday Chamberlaine, m. Anna Maria Hammond, dau. of Nicholas Hammond (a native of the Island of Jersey) and his wife Rebecca Hollyday Hammond, and had child., viz., Samuel (who m. Hannah A. Bullock, of Phila., and had 2 daus., Mary A. and Annie Hammond Chamberlaine),—Rebecca Hollyday,—James Lloyd (who m. Margaret A. M. Chamberlaine, dau. of Samuel and Ariana Worthington Chamberlaine, and had child., viz., Margaret Robins,—Henry,—Samuel,—Anna Maria and Marion Chamberlaine),—Henrietta Maria, and Mary Hammond Chamberlaine.

SAMUEL CHAMBERLAINE, son of Samuel and Henrietta Maria Hollyday Chamberlaine, m. Ariana Worthington, of Cambridge, and had child., viz., Marion (who m. William R. Trippe, and had child., viz., Henrietta Maria,—John H. and Samuel C. Trippe),—Henrietta Maria (who m. Mr. Thomas, of Cecil, and had a dau., Ariana Thomas),—Samuel (who m. Elizabeth Dickenson, of Talbot, and had child., viz., Joseph E. M.,—William and Bertha Chamberlaine),—Margaret A. M. (who m. James Lloyd Chamberlaine, of Oxford), and Dr. Joseph E. M. Chamberlaine, who m. 1st Elizabeth

B. Hayward, and had child., viz., Elizabeth B. (who m. Nov. 1876, R. E. Hayward, of Cambridge, son of Dr. Hayward, "Commissioner of the Land Office of Maryland," and Joseph E. M. Chamberlaine. He m. 2ndly Sarah Catharine Earle, dau. of Hon. Richard Tilghman Earle (see EARLE).

HENRY CHAMBERLAINE, son of Samuel and Henrietta Maria Hollyday Chamberlaine, m. Henrietta Maria Gale, dau. of George and Anna Maria Hollyday Gale, and had child., viz., Anna Maria,—Samuel Lloyd,—Henry (who m. Mary Chambers, of Balto., and had child., viz., Esther,—Nicholson, —Henry Richmond, and Henrietta E. Chamberlaine, who m. Dr. James Bordley, of Centreville),—George Gale (who m. Margaret Gunther, of Phila., and had child., viz., Henry,—George,—Alfred, and Lloyd Chamberlaine),—Sally Rebecca (who m. Rev. Richard Whittingham (brother of Rt. Rev. W. R. Whittingham) and had child., viz., Helen Winnefred,—William Henry,—Richard,—George Herbert, and Louisa Whittingham), and Georgeanna E. Chamberlaine, who m. Rev. William Murphy, of Wilmington, Del.

HARRIET REBECCA CHAMBERLAINE, dau. of Samuel and Henrietta Maria Hollyday Chamberlaine, m. Levin Gale, of Cecil, and had child., viz., Henrietta Maria,—Samuel Chamberlaine (who m. Mrs. Jenkins, *née* Morton, and had child., viz., Morton,—George,—Littleton,—Henry, and Bessie Gale), and Levin Gale, who m. Sally Dorsey, and had child., viz., Levin,—Warren,—Dorsey,—Samuel Chamberlaine,—Charles, —Harriet Rebecca, and William Collins Gale.

HON. JAMES HOLLYDAY (b. 1st Nov. 1758, d. 8th of Jan'y 1807), of Readbourne, Queen Anne's, son of Henry and Anna Maria Robins Hollyday, was Associate Judge of the Circuit composed of Cecil, Kent, Queen Anne's and Talbot counties, and a member of the Convention of Maryland which ratified the Constitution of the United States in 1788, m. Susanna Tilghman, dau. of Judge James and Susanna Steuart Tilghman, and had child., viz., James,—Anna Maria Chew,—Henry,—George Steuart,—Frisby,—William, and Richard Tilghman Hollyday.

ANNA MARIA CHEW HOLLYDAY, dau. of Jas. and Susanna Tilghman Hollyday, m. Arthur Tilghman Jones, of Swann Point, Kent, the only son of Richard Ireland Jones, and had child., viz., Arthur Tilghman,—Ann Eloise,—Maria Susanna, —Richard,—William, and Alfred Jones.

HENRY HOLLYDAY (b. 15th of Jan. 1798, d. in 1865), of Readbourne, son of James and Susanna Tilghman Hollyday,

m. 18th April 1826, Anna Maria Hollyday, dau. of Henry and Ann Carmichael Hollyday, and had nine child. His 2nd wife (m. 1st June 1858) was Margaretta Goldsborough, dau. of Col. Nicholas Goldsborough and Elizabeth Tench Tilghman, dau. of Col. Tench Tilghman.

GEORGE STEUART HOLLYDAY, son of James and Susanna Steuart Hollyday, was twice a member of the Maryland Legislature, a member of the Constitutional Convention of 1864, and for years the Chief Judge of the Orphans' Court of Kent. He was an intelligent and enthusiastic agriculturist, and organized and was the President of the Agricultural Club of Kent. He was a gentleman of the olden school, polite, well-bred, and hospitable. He m. Caroline M. Carvill, of Kent, and had child., viz., George S., *d.*,—John C., d.,—Caroline M. (who m. Dr. C. C. Harper, of Queen Anne's),—John W.,—Anna M., d., and George T. Hollyday.

GEORGE T. HOLLYDAY, son of George Steuart and Caroline M. Carvill Hollyday, m. 29th Jan'y 1867, Alexina B. Chamberlain, dau. of Alexander B. Chamberlain, of Baltimore, and had child., viz., Caroline R.,—Alice C., d.,—Luella C.,—George T., and John S. Hollyday.

WILLIAM HOLLYDAY (b. 19th of May 1804), of Washington County, son of James and Susanna Tilghman Hollyday, m. 31st Aug. 1830, his cousin, Ann Cheston Tilghman, dau. of Frisby and Anna Maria Ringgold Tilghman, and had child., viz., James Frisby, who d. 1st of June 1849, and Nancy Ringgold Hollyday, who d. 16th of Dec. 1849. She d. 21st of Jan'y 1834, and he m. again 12th Sept. 1837, Louisa Lamar Tilghman, the half sister of his 1st wife, dau. of Frisby and Louisa Lamar Tilghman, and had child., viz., William Henry, a gallant soldier of the Second Maryland Infantry, C. S. A., who was slain in battle, 3d of June 1864, at Cold Harbor,—Mary Tilghman (who m. James Steuart, and had a son William Hollyday Steuart),—Lamar,—Louisa Lamar, b. 28th of Dec. 1843, d. 1st of March 1855,—George Tilghman,—Floyd Sprigg,—Alfred,—Tilghman, d. 20th March 1876 in the 24th year of his age,—Margaret, b. 16th Jan'y 1855, d. 27th of Dec. 1871,—Susan Davis (who m. 27th Jan'y 1876 Walter Sharp), and Henrietta Frisby Hollyday, d. William Hollyday d. 16th of July 1868, and was buried at Greenmount Cemetery.

LAMAR HOLLYDAY, son of William and Louisa Lamar Tilghman Hollyday, m. 23d April 1868, J. Georgie Thelin, and had child., viz., Louisa,—Eloise, and Margaret Hollyday.

Richard Tilghman Hollyday, son of James and Susanna Tilghman Hollyday, m. Susan Ragan, and had child., viz., Elizabeth, — Henry, — Amelia,— Susan,— Geiger, and Anna Maria Hollyday.

Henry Hollyday (b. 11th Sept. 1771, d. 20th March 1850), of Ratcliffe, Talbot, son of Henry and Anna Maria Robins Hollyday, m. 11th Oct. 1798, Ann Carmichael, who was b. 30th June 1776, d. 24th Feb'y 1761, the dau. of Richard Bennet Carmichael, of Bennet's Choice, and had child., viz., Anna Maria, b. 22d March 1800, d. 8th of Jan'y 1804,—Catharine Ann,—Henry James, b. 8th April 1804, d. 4th Aug. 1820,—Anna Maria, b. 9th Oct. 1805, d. 5th March 1815,—Sarah Elizabeth, b. 21st June 1809, d. 21st March 1849,— Richard Carmichael, — Henrietta Maria, — Thomas Robins,—Elizabeth Margaret,—William Murray, and Rebecca Harriet Hollyday.

Hon. Richard Carmichael Hollyday, of Ratcliffe, Talbot, son of Henry and Ann Carmichael Hollyday, m. 24th Nov. 1858, Marietta F. Powell, of Middleburg, Loudon Co., Va., and had child., viz., Richard C.,—Ann Holmes, b. Jan'y 1861, died Sept. 1864, and Marietta Powell Hollyday. He has been the able and efficient Secretary of the State of Maryland during the administrations of Governors Philip Francis Thomas, Oden Bowie, William Pinckney Whyte, James Black Groome, and John Lee Carroll.

William Murray Hollyday, son of Henry and Ann Carmichael Hollyday, m. in Jan'y 1852, R. Louisa Powell, sister of his brother Richard's wife, and has child., viz., Nannie,—Rosalie,—Powell,—Virginia,—Thomas, and Carmichael Hollyday.

Elizabeth Margarett Hollyday, dau. of Henry and Ann Carmichael Hollyday, m. 20th of Aug. 1835, Hon. Richard Bennet Carmichael, b. 25th of Dec. 1807, the son of William Carmichael and his wife Sarah Downs, of Queen Anne's. William Carmichael d. in 1853, and was b. 27th of Jan'y 1775, the son of Richard Bennett and Katharine Murray Carmichael, before mentioned. They had child., viz., Richard Bennet,—William,—Nancy Murray,—Elizabeth Hollyday,— Sarah Katharine, b. July 1849, d. Aug. 1850,—Sarah Downs,— Katharine Virginia, and Fannie Carmichael.

Margaret Robins (b. 20th of April 1734), dau. of George and Henrietta Maria Tilghman Robins, m. William Hayward, of Bailey's Neck, and had child., viz., George (who m. Margaret Smyth, dau. of Thos. Smith, merchant of Chestertown), and Thomas Hayward.

THOMAS HAYWARD, son of William and Margaret Robins Hayward, m. Mary Smyth, a sister of his brother's wife, and had child., viz., William,—Thomas,—Margaret,—Mary Ann, —Elizabeth and Sarah. He m. 2ndly Mary Bond, who d. *sine prole.*

SUSANNA ROBINS (b. 10th June 1738, d. 1815), dau. of George and Henrietta Maria Tilghman Robins, m. Col. Thomas Chamberlaine, and had one son, Thomas, who d. young. She m. a 2nd time, Col. Robert Lloyd Nicols, and had child., viz., Lloyd (who m. Susanna Gulley),—Susanna,—Henrietta Maria, and Eliza Nicols.

SUSANNA NICOLS, dau. of Col. Robert Lloyd and Susanna Robins Chamberlaine Nicols, m. Hon. Bond Martin, of Cambridge, Chief Judge of the Fourth Judicial District of Md., and had child., viz., Bond,—Robert Nicols,—Henrietta Martin, —Susanna, and Martin. He fell in a duel, fought near Baltimore, with Mr. Carr, of Virginia. His son, Hon. Robert Nicols Martin, was Chief Justice of the Western Circuit of Maryland.

SEC. 98, E. ANNA MARIA TILGHMAN (b. 15th Nov. 1709, d. 30th Aug. 1763), dau. of Richard, 2d of the Hermitage, and Anna Maria Lloyd Tilghman, m. twice, 1st William Hemsley, and had child., viz., Philemon,—William, and Anna Maria Hemsley; 2ndly, Col. Robert Lloyd, and had child., viz., Richard,—Deborah (who m. Peregrine Tilghman),—and Anna Maria Lloyd, who m. William Tilghman.

WILLIAM HEMSLEY, son of William and Anna Maria Tilghman Hemsley, m. 3 times. His 1st wife was Henrietta Maria Earle, dau. of James and Mary Tilghman Earle, and had child., viz., William (who m. Maria Lloyd, dau. of Maj. James Lloyd),—Mary and Charlotte Hemsley. His 2nd wife was Sarah Williamson, of Kent, and had child., viz., Philemon, —Thomas,—Alexander,—James Tilghman,—Sarah,—Henrietta Maria (who m. Thomas Chamberlaine Earle,) and Ann Hemsley. His 3rd wife was Anna Maria Tilghman (dau. of his uncle, James Tilghman), who left one dau., Anna Maria Hemsley, who d. at an advanced age, *sine prole.*

MARY HEMSLEY, dau. of William and Henrietta Maria Earle Hemsley, m. Joseph Forman, and had child., viz., William,—Ezekiel,—Harriet Maria, and Augustine Forman.

PHILEMON HEMSLEY, son of William and his 2nd wife, Sarah Williamson Hemsley, m. Elizabeth Lloyd, twin sister of his half brother William Hemsley's wife, and had child., viz., William,—Maria Lloyd, and Philemon Hemsley. By his 2nd wife, Ann Hemsley, he had child., viz., Martha,—Richard, and Philemon Hemsley.

THOMAS HEMSLEY, son of William and his 2nd wife, Sarah Williamson Hemsley, m. Elizabeth Tilghman, dau. of James Tilghman, of Talbot, and had child., viz., William,—Tilghman,—Thomas, and Elizabeth Hemsley.

ALEXANDER HEMSLEY, son of William and his 2nd wife, Sarah Williamson Hemsley, m. Henrietta Maria Tilghman, dau. of Lloyd Tilghman, and had child, viz., Lloyd Tilghman,—Alexander, and Henrietta Maria Hemsley. His 2nd wife was Elizabeth West, of Phila., and had child., viz., Francis West, and Alexander Hemsley.

SARAH HEMSLEY, dau. of William and his 2nd wife, Sarah Williamson Hemsley, m. Doctor John Irvine Troup, of Darley, and had child., viz., Henry,—Henrietta Maria,—Margaret, and Elizabeth Troup.

ANN HEMSLEY, dau. of William and his 2nd wife, Sarah Williamson Hemsley, m. Gen. Thomas Emory of Poplar Grove, Queen Anne's, and had child., viz., Thomas A.,—William H.,—Robert,—John,—Albert,—Frederick,—Blanchard,—Sarah,—Ann,—Henrietta Earle, and Augusta Forman Emory.

SEC. 98, F. WILLIAM TILGHMAN (b. 22nd Sept. 1711, d. in 1782), of Groces, Talbot, son of the 2nd Richard of the Hermitage and Anna Maria Lloyd Tilghman, m. Margaret Lloyd (dau. of James Lloyd and Ann Grundy; James was the 3rd son of Philemon Lloyd of Wye House, Talbot), was at one time Deputy Commissary of Queen Anne's, and had child, viz., Robert Lloyd,—Richard,—James,—Anna Maria,—Margaret (who m. Richard, son of Hon. Mathew Tilghman),—Henrietta, and Mary Tilghman, who m. Edward Roberts, of Talbot.

RICHARD TILGHMAN, son of William and Margaret Lloyd Tilghman, m. Mary Gibson, of Talbot, and had child., viz., William Gibson and John Lloyd Tilghman.

WILLIAM GIBSON TILGHMAN, of Groces, son of Richard and Mary Gibson Tilghman, m. Ann (or Araminta?) Polk, of New Castle County, Delaware, and had child., viz., Charles Henry,—Richard Lloyd,—George Logan,—Mary,—Margaret,—Elizabeth (who m. 1848, Charles Gilmore, of Balto.),—Anna Maria,—Louisa, and Catharine Tilghman, who m. Dr. Charles Lowndes, son of Commodore Lowndes, of Talbot.

ANNA MARIA TILGHMAN, dau. of William Gibson and Ann Polk Tilghman, m. in 1839, Col. Kennedy R. Owen, and had child., viz., Agnes Owen, who m. Richard Cooke, son of Henry Cooke Tilghman,—William Tilghman Owen, who m. Mary T. Buchanan, dau. of Admiral Buchanan,—Kennedy R. Owen, who m. Miss Hilliard, of Baltimore, and Margaret Owen, who m. Owen Norris.

RICHARD LLOYD TILGHMAN, son of William Gibson and Ann Polk Tilghman, was an officer of the United States army, resigned in 1861 and d. in 1867. He resided at Groces, m. Agnes M. Owen, and had child., viz., Charles H.,—Richard Lloyd, who d. when 12 or 13 years of age, in 1863,—Mary,—Sally,—Agnes,—Anna,—Henrietta and Lina Tilghman.

JOHN LLOYD TILGHMAN, son of Richard and Mary Gibson Tilghman, m. Maria Gibson, of Annapolis, lived at Bennett's Point, Queen Anne's, and had child., viz., John Lloyd,—William,—Horatio,—Samuel Ogle, and Mary Tilghman.

SAMUEL OGLE TILGHMAN, son of John Lloyd and Maria Gibson Tilghman, m. Mary Fairbairn, and had a son, Samuel Ogle Tilghman and several daus., one of whom, Anna Maria, m. Richard E. Davidson.

ANNA MARIA TILGHMAN, dau. of William and Margaret Lloyd Tilghman, of Groces, Talbot, m. Charles Goldsborough, of Dorchester, and had two sons, viz., Charles, b. 15th July 1765,—and William Tilghman Goldsborough, b. in Dec. 1766, and d. in 1787, *sine prole.* (See GOLDSBOROUGH.)

SEC. 98, G. COL. EDWARD TILGHMAN, of Wye (b. 3d July 1713, d. 9th of Oct. 1785), son of the 2nd Richard of the Hermitage and Anna Maria Lloyd Tilghman, lived at Wye, Queen Anne's, was a member of the Stamp Act Congress of 1765, and one of the committee which drew up the remonstrance to Parliament. The members of that Congress from Maryland were Col. Edward Tilghman, William Murdock and Thomas Ringgold, and were governed by instructions drawn up by a committee appointed by the General Assembly of Maryland, consisting of James Hollyday, Thomas Johnson, Edmund Key, John Goldsborough, John Hammond, Daniel Wolstenholme and John Hanson. He m. Ann Turbutt, dau. of Maj. William Turbutt, and had one dau. Anna Maria, who m. Bennett Chew, and had a son Edward Chew, who d. *sine prole.* His 2nd wife was Elizabeth Chew, of Dover, Delaware, and had child., viz., Richard, —Edward, b. 11th Dec. 1750,—Benjamin,—Elizabeth, and Anna Maria Tilghman. His 3rd wife was Julianna Carroll,

m. in May 1759, and had child., viz., Matthew,—Benjamin, b. Dec. 1764,—Mary (who m, Richard, son of Matthew and Anna Lloyd Tilghman), and Susanna Tilghman, who m. Richard Ireland Jones, an Englishman, who lived near Chestertown, and had a son Arthur Tilghman Jones, who m. Anna Maria Chew Hollyday.

EDWARD TILGHMAN (b. 11th Dec. 1750, d. 1st Nov. 1815), son of Edward and Elizabeth Chew Tilghman, m. Elizabeth Chew, dau. of Benjamin Chew, of Phila. He received his legal education in the Middle Temple, and was an eminent lawyer, resided in Phila., and had child., viz., Edward, b. 27th Feb'y 1779,—Benjamin, b. 6th of Jan'y 1785,—Elizabeth (who m. William Cooke), and Mary Tilghman, who m. William Rawle, of Phila., and had child., viz., William Brooke and Elizabeth Rawle.

EDWARD TILGHMAN (b. 27th Feb'y 1779), of Phila., son of the 2nd Edward and Elizabeth Chew Tilghman, m. Rebecca Waln, and had child., viz., Edward,—Rebecca,—Elizabeth,—Ann, and Jane Tilghman.

BENJAMIN TILGHMAN (b. 6th Jan'y 1785), attorney-at-law, Phila., son of the 2nd Edward and Elizabeth Chew Tilghman, m. Anna Maria McMurtree, and had child., viz., Edward,—William M., who m. C. Ingersoll,—Benjamin,—Richard,—Maria,—Elizabeth, and Ann Tilghman.

ELIZABETH TILGHMAN, dau. of the 1st Edward Tilghman, of Wye, and his 2nd wife, Elizabeth Chew Tilghman, m. Richard, son of Richard and Susanna Frisby Tilghman, and left one son, Richard, the 5th and last Richard Tilghman of the Hermitage.

ANNA MARIA TILGHMAN, dau. of Edward Tilghman, of Wye, and his 2nd wife, Elizabeth Chew, m. Charles Goldsborough, of Talbot. Her 2nd husband was the Rt. Rev. Bishop Smith, of Charleston, South Carolina, and had two sons, viz., Robert and William Smith, who m. sisters of the name of Pringle, of South Carolina, and had child.

MATTHEW TILGHMAN, son of Edward Tilghman, of Wye, and his 3rd wife, Julianna Carroll, m. about 1788, Sarah Smyth, dau. of Thomas Smyth, of Chestertown, and had child., viz., Edward,—Henry (who m. Martha Hall, dau. of Dr. Benjamin Hall), and Sarah Tilghman, who m. Francis Hall, of Queen Anne's.

EDWARD TILGHMAN, son of Matthew and Sarah Smyth Tilghman, m. Anna Maria Tilghman, of the White House, dau. of William Tilghman, the 4th son of the 3rd Richard of the Hermitage, and had one dau., Eleanor Sarah Tilghman, who m. Matthew Tilghman Goldsborough, of Talbot, the grandson of Col. Tench Tilghman.

SEC. 98, H. JAMES TILGHMAN (b. 6th Dec. 1716, d. 24th of Aug. 1793), son of Richard, 2nd of the Hermitage, and Anna Maria Lloyd, removed to Phila., was attorney to the Lord Proprietor, a member of Penn's Council, and Secretary of the Proprietary Land Office of Pennsylvania. He m. Anna Francis, dau. of Tench Francis, of Fausley, Talbot. He was a lawyer of high standing. After his m. he resided for a time at Fausley, then in Phila., and subsequently in Chestertown, where he d. He had child., viz., Tench, b. 25th Dec. 1744,—Richard, b. 17th Dec. 1746, d. 24th Nov. 1796,—James, b. 1st Jan'y 1748,—William, b. 12th Aug. 1756,—Philemon, b. 29th of Nov. 1760,—Thomas Ringgold, b. 17th of Aug. 1765, d. 29th of Dec. 1789.—Anna Maria,—Elizabeth,—Mary, and Henrietta Maria.

COL. TENCH TILGHMAN (b. 25th Dec. 1744, d. 18th April 1786), son of James and Ann Francis Tilghman, differing in political sentiments from most of the prominent members of his family, was a member of the Flying Camp, of 1776, afterwards Aid de Camp to Gen. Washington and was honored with his esteem, confidence and friendship. He was a brave and efficient officer, and as a reward for his gallantry was selected to bear to Congress the tidings of the surrender of Cornwallis. On the 29th Oct. 1781, Congress gave to his brilliant services a vote of thanks, and presented to him a horse properly caparisoned and an elegant sword. He m. Anna Maria, dau. of his uncle, Matthew Tilghman, youngest son of the 2nd Richard Tilghman of the Hermitage, and had child., viz., Ann Margaretta Tilghman, who m. Tench Tilghman, of Hope, and Elizabeth Tench Tilghman, who m. 25th April 1801, Col. Nicholas Goldsborough (see GOLDSBOROUGH).

RICHARD TILGHMAN (b. 17th Dec. 1746, d. 24th Nov. 1796), son of James and Anna Francis Tilghman, was educated in England, returned home and studied law under Danl. Dulany. At the solicitation of his relative, Sir Philip Francis, the reputed author of the Letters of Junius, he went to Bengal, India, via England. In respect of his political sentiments and proclivities he was permitted to depart, in June 1776, in company with Gov. Robert Eden, in the British sloop-of-war Fowey, Captain Montague. He d. on his 2nd voyage from India.

James Tilghman (b. 2d Jan'y 1748, d. 24th Nov. 1796), son of James and Anna Francis Tilghman, m. Elizabeth Buely, and had child., viz., James, b. 1st of May 1792, d. 22d March 1824,—Elizabeth,—Maria,—Anna Maria, and Margaret Tilghman, who m. Henry Goldsborough (see Goldsborough).

Elizabeth Tilghman, dau. of James and Elizabeth Buely Tilghman, m. Thomas Hemsley, son of William Hemsley, of Clover Fields, Queen Anne's, and brother of the two Hemsleys, mentioned before, who m. the two Misses Lloyd. She had child., viz., William (who m. Elizabeth Brooke, and afterwards Anne Wright, both of Queen Anne's),—Thomas, and Elizabeth Hemsley.

Anna Maria Tilghman, dau. of James and Elizabeth Buely Tilghman, m. Robert Brown, of Queen Anne's, and had child., viz., James Q.,—Elizabeth (who m. Henry Wilson, of Queen Anne's), and Anna Maria Brown, who m. James Cooke Tilghman.

Hon. William Tilghman (b. 12th of Aug. 1756, d. 30th April 1827), son of James and Anna Francis Tilghman, resided in Phila., was appointed by President John Adams, 3d March 1801, presiding Judge of the Third Circuit, composed of Pennsylvania, New Jersey and Delaware; in 1805 was appointed President of the Courts of the 1st Judicial Circuit of Pennsylvania, and 26th Feb'y 1806 was made Chief Justice of Pennsylvania, and filled that position until his death. He m. Margaret Allen, and had one dau., Elizabeth Tilghman, who m. Benjamin Chew, of Phila., and d. 17th June 1817, leaving a dau. who d. an infant.

Capt. Philemon Tilghman (b. 29th Nov. 1760, d. 11th of Jan'y 1797), son of James and Anna Francis Tilghman, retained his commission in the British Navy during the Revolutionary War. After peace was declared he m. Harriet Milbanke, dau. of Admiral Milbanke of the Royal Navy, returned to America and resided with his father in Chestertown. When his father d. he removed to his estate, Golden Square, in Queen Anne's County, where he d. He had child., viz., Harriet,—Caroline, who d. unm. in 1868,—Charlotte,—Emily, and Richard Tilghman.

Harriet Tilghman, dau. of Capt. Philemon and Harriet Milbanke Tilghman, m. Rev. Richard Cockburn, Prebend of Winchester Cathedral and Vicar of Bosley, Kent, England, and d. in 1856 *sine prole.*

Charlotte Tilghman, dau. of Capt. Philemon and Harriet Milbanke Tilghman, m. Sir Molyneux Hyde Nepean, of Soders, Dorsetshire, England, d. in 1830, and had sixteen child., of whom only two survive, viz., Molyneux, the present Baronet, and Fanny, the widow of Capt. Grove.

Emily Tilghman, dau. of Capt. Philemon and Harriet Milbanke Tilghman, m. Jeremiah Hoffman, of Baltimore, and had two child., viz., William Hoffman, who d. in infancy, and Harriet Emily Hoffman, who m. Henry Weld, of Archer's Lodge, England, now of Alleghany Co., Md. Mrs. Emily Tilghman Hoffman d. in 1818.

Richard Tilghman, son of Capt. Philemon Tilghman and Harriet Milbanke, m. in India, Augusta, dau. of Lord Elphinstone, and had five child, viz., Caroline,—Emily,—Harriet,—William Huskisson, and Richard Tilghman, who d. in 1865, *sine prole.*

William Huskisson Tilghman, son of Richard Tilghman and Augusta Elphinstone, took the name of and inherited the estate of his God-father, Mr. Huskisson (the eminent English Statesman, who m. Emily, youngest dau. of Admiral Milbanke), and d. in 1863 *sine prole.*

Sec. 98, I. Hon. Matthew Tilghman (b. 17th Feb'y 1718, d. 4th May 1790), the youngest son of the 2nd Richard Tilghman, of the Hermitage, and Anna Maria Lloyd Tilghman, m. Anna Lloyd, sister of Margaret Lloyd, wife of his brother, William Tilghman, and dau. of James Lloyd and Ann Grundy, and had child., viz., Matthew Ward,—Richard, b. 28th Jan'y 1746,—Lloyd,—Margaret, who m. Charles Carroll, barrister (see Carroll), and Anna Maria Tilghman, who was b. 17th July 1755, m. Col. Tench Tilghman, and d. 13th Jan'y 1843.

Hon. Matthew Tilghman was adopted by his cousin, Matthew Tilghman Ward, and inherited from him the large landed estate, Bayside, in Talbot County, Md. He entered public life at the early age of twenty-three years, and had charge of a troop of horse, which was organized for the protection of the exposed settlements from the incursions of the Indians who lingered upon the Eastern Shore of Md. In 1741 he was appointed by the Governor of the Province, Samuel Ogle, one of the Worshipful Commissioners and Justices of the Peace of Talbot County, Md., a position highly honorable and of great responsibility in those days. In 1751 he was sent as a Delegate to the General Assembly of Maryland, and continued to represent his native county until the overthrow of the Proprietary Government, and was Speaker of the Lower House of the Assemblies in 1773–74 and '75. When the circular letter of the General Court of Massachusetts was brought before the Legislature, for consideration, he was appointed one of the committee to draft a petition to the King remonstrating against the obnoxious taxes imposed upon imported articles. The committee was appointed 8th June 1768, and consisted of William Murdock, of Prince George's, Thomas Johnson, of Anne Arundel, Thomas Ringgold, of Kent, James Hollyday, of Queen Anne's, Matthew Tilghman, of Talbot, and Thomas Jennings, of Frederick.

He was chosen, with Edward Lloyd, Nicholas Thomas and Robert Goldsborough to represent Talbot County in the Convention which assembled at Annapolis, 22d June 1774, and upon its organization was elected its President. This Convention appointed Matthew Tilghman, Thomas Johnson, Robert Goldsborough, William Paca and Samuel Chase, Esqs., delegates to the Continental Congress which assembled in Philadelphia the Sept. following.

At the Provincial Meeting of Deputies held at Annapolis, 21st Nov. 1774, he was Chairman. The proceedings of Congress were read and unanimously approved.

At a meeting of the Deputies of the several counties of the Province of Maryland, at Annapolis, 8th Dec. 1774, Matthew Tilghman, Thomas Johnson, John Hall, Samuel Chase, Charles Carroll, of Carrollton, William Paca, and Charles Carroll, barrister, were appointed the Committee of Correspondence for the Province of Maryland. It was also

Resolved unanimously, That the honorable Matthew Tilghman, and Thomas Johnson, Robert Goldsborough, William Paca, Samuel Chase, John Hall, and Thomas Stone, Esquires, be delegates to represent the Province in the next Continental Congress.

At the meeting of the Deputies, at Annapolis, 24th April 1775, Hon. Matthew Tilghman was the Chairman, and the above-named delegates to Congress were formally and solemnly instructed to join with the delegates of the other Colonies and Provinces and concur with them in such measures as shall be thought necessary for the defence and protection thereof, and most conducive to the public welfare. The Maryland delegation obeyed with cheerful alacrity these instructions, and one of them, Thomas Johnson, on the 15th of June 1775, moved the appointment of George Washington as Commander-in-Chief of the American Army.

At the meeting of delegates of the counties of the Province of Maryland, at Annapolis, 26th of July 1775, Matthew Tilghman was chosen Chairman. A Council of Safety for the Province was organized, and Matthew Tilghman and Thomas Johnson were made members of it also. Again, Matthew Tilghman, Thomas Johnson, Robert Goldsborough, William Paca, Samuel Chase, Thomas Stone and John Hall were appointed Deputies to the Continental Congress.

At the Convention of Delegates, chosen by the several counties of the Province of Maryland, which met at Annapolis, Thursday, 7th Dec. 1775, he was unanimously chosen President.

Tuesday, 21st May 1776, Hon. Matthew Tilghman, Thomas Johnson, Robert Alexander, Samuel Chase, Robert Goldsborough, William Paca, Thomas Stone and John Rogers were elected to represent Maryland in that Congress which passed and issued to the world the Declaration of Independence. Permission to vote for such a Declaration was granted to the delegates, by a unanimous resolution, Friday, 28th June 1776.

Thursday, the 4th of July 1776, Hon. Matthew Tilghman, Thomas Johnson, William Paca, Samuel Chase, Thomas Stone, Charles Carroll, of Carrollton, and Robert Alexander were elected by ballot Deputies to represent Maryland in the Continental Congress. At this time, also, Matthew Tilghman was President of the Maryland Convention.

On this same day, 4th July 1776, in the city of Philadelphia, was adopted, by the Continental Congress, the *Declaration of Independence;* which was afterwards signed, on the part of Maryland, by Samuel Chase, William Paca, Thomas Stone, and Charles Carroll, of Carrollton.

Why are not the names of Matthew Tilghman and Thomas Johnson affixed to the Declaration? We have seen that they were members of the Congress which passed and which signed it. We know that Matthew Tilghman was detained at Annapolis by the duties incumbent upon him as President of the Convention. His eminent abilities made his presence necessary to the State of Maryland. Thomas Johnson was required at home by the extreme illness of a member of his family (see JOHNSON). Matthew Tilghman and Thomas Johnson were the two foremost men, at this time, in Maryland; they, more than any others, formed and moulded public opinion, guided the energies, and directed the actions of the people of Maryland. They were wise and practical workers, and although they did not write their names upon the conspicuous and aspiring shaft of the monument of our liberties, their marks are inwrought and indelibly imprinted upon the solid, imperishable, and more enduring foundations.

Hon. Matthew Tilghman was unanimously elected President of the Constitutional Convention which assembled in Annapolis, 14th Aug. 1776, and was also by it chosen by ballot Chairman of the Committee to prepare a Declaration and charter of rights and a form of Government for this State. He continued in public life until the advances of age compelled him, in 1783, to resign his seat in the Senate of Maryland, after having devoted more than forty years to the public service of his native State.

Speaking of the eventful period of the Revolution, the Historian, McMahon, observes that Matthew Tilghman "seems to have been the *patriarch* of the colony."

RICHARD TILGHMAN (b. 28th Jan'y 1746, d. 28th May 1805), son of Hon. Matthew and Anna Lloyd Tilghman, m. Margaret, the 2nd dau. of his uncle, William Tilghman, of Groces, Talbot, and had child., viz., Matthew, b. 20th Sept. 1777,—Anna Maria (who m. Judge Nicholas Brice, see BRICE), and Mary Elizabeth Tilghman, who m. George Hoffman, of Balto. His 2nd wife was Mary, the eldest dau. of Edward Tilghman (of Wye) and Julianna Carroll, and had child., viz., Julianna (who m. John Paca, son of William Paca, who signed the Declaration of Independence),—Harriet, who m. Henry Brice, of Baltimore,—Mary, who m. John Tilghman, and Mary Tilghman, who m. Charles C. Tilghman.

MATTHEW TILGHMAN (b. 20th Sept. 1777, d. 21st Oct. 1828), son of Richard and Margaret Tilghman, m. twice. His 1st wife was Elenor Rosier, of Prince George's. His 2nd wife was Harriet Hynson, dau. of Richard and Araminta Hynson (see HYNSON), and had child., viz., Richard Lloyd, who was lost at sea in the United States sloop-of-war Hornet, which foundered off Tampico, 12th Sept. 1829,—James Bowers, b. 27th Jan'y 1816,—William Matthew, b. 12th July 1820,—Tench, b. 30th Dec. 1824, d. in California, Aug. 1870,—Henrietta Louisa,—Anna Maria (who was the 1st wife of Dr. Benjamin F. Houston),—Harriet Eliza (who m. William Brice Tilghman), and Catharine Araminta Eloise Tilghman.

JAMES BOWERS TILGHMAN, son of Matthew and Harriet Hynson Tilghman, m. 1st of July 1841, Virginia Wills, of Richmond, Va., and had child., viz., James Bowers,—William Bowers,—Charles Carroll, and Robert Lee Tilghman. They reside near Weldon, North Carolina.

WILLIAM MATTHEW TILGHMAN, son of Matthew and Harriet Hynson Tilghman, emigrated West, and m. in 1846, Miss Sheppard, of Keokuk, Iowa, and had child., viz., Richard Lloyd, — Tench Sheppard, — William Matthew, and John Tilghman.

HENRIETTA LOUISA TILGHMAN, dau. of Matthew and Harriet Hynson Tilghman, m. 2nd of Nov. 1835, William Bowers Everett, son of Joseph, the son of Hales Everett. He d. 29th April 1841. She d. 10th April 1870, in the 58th year of her age, and left two child., viz., William B., and Henrietta Maria Lloyd Everett.

REV. WILLIAM B. EVERETT, M. D., son of William Bowers and Henrietta Louisa Tilghman Everett, m. Jan'y 19, 1865, Ellen S. Whilten, dau. of Edward and Mary Ellen Whilten, of Va., and had child., viz., Mary Ellen,—Henrietta Louisa,—William Bowers,—Lellie,—Lelia Creme, and Lloyd Tilghman Everett.

CATHARINE ARAMINTA ELOISE TILGHMAN, dau. of Matthew and Harriet Hynson Tilghman, m. 10th June 1850, James Lambert Davis, and had child., viz., Harriet Althea,—Anna Catharine,—James Tilghman,—Mary Virginia,—Henrietta Louisa, and David Padget Davis.

HARRIET ALTHEA DAVIS, dau. of James Lambert and Catharine Araminta Eloise Tilghman Davis, m. 10th of June 1875, William Emory Perkins, son of Benjamin Bond and Margaret H. Emory Perkins.

LLOYD TILGHMAN, son of Hon. Matthew and Anna Lloyd Tilghman, m. Henrietta Maria Tilghman, dau. of James and Anna Francis Tilghman, and had child., viz., Anne (who m. John Tilghman),— Henrietta Maria,— Mary,— Matthew,— James,—Elizabeth, and Lloyd Tilghman.

HENRIETTA MARIA TILGHMAN, dau. of Lloyd and Henrietta Maria Tilghman, m. Alexander Hemsley, and had child., viz., Henrietta Maria, who m. Dr. Frisby Tilghman, son of Col. Frisby Tilghman,—Lloyd, and Alexander Hemsley.

JAMES TILGHMAN, son of Lloyd and Henrietta Maria Tilghman, m. Ann C. Shoemaker, of Phila., and had child., viz., Lloyd,—Caroline,—Henrietta Maria, and Ann (or Nina) Tilghman, who m. Mr. Montgomery, of Phila.

MAJ. GEN. LLOYD TILGHMAN (b. 30th Jan'y 1816, d. in battle 16th May 1863), son of James and Ann C. Shoemaker Tilghman, was a graduate of West Point (of 1836), and after several years' services resigned his commission, but rëentered the United States Army during the Mexican war, and served with distinction. At the close of the war he again resigned. Subsequently he entered the Army of the Confederate States, was captured at Fort Henry, in Tennessee, and confined as prisoner of war in Fort Warren; was exchanged, then promoted to a Major General, and slain in battle at Vicksburgh, Miss.,—a cannon ball passing through his body, the 16th of May 1863. He m., in 1842, Augusta Boyd, of Maine, and had child., viz., Lloyd, killed by a kick from his horse while in the Confederate Army,—Frederick Boyd,—Southgate,—Siddell,—Charles, and Maria Tilghman; also a dau. who d. in infancy.

CAROLINE TILGHMAN, dau. of James and Ann C. Shoemaker Tilghman, m. Philip W. Lowery, and had child., viz., Robert,—Philip (U. S. N.),—Sophia, and Minnie Lowery.

TILGHMAN ARMS:—Per fesse sable and argent, a lion rampant, regardant, tail forked, countercharged, crowned or.

CREST: A demi-lion sejant sable, crowned or.

MOTTO:—*Spes alit agricolum.*

SEC. 98, J. SUSANNAH STEUART, who m. Judge James Tilghman, was the dau. of Dr. George Steuart, who came to Annapolis, in 1721, from Perthshire, Scotland, and m. Ann Digges, dau. of George Digges, of Warburton, Prince George's County, a descendant of Sir Dudley Digges, who fell, fighting, under the banner of Charles I.

DR. GEORGE STEUART was a graduate of the University of Edinburgh. Gifted with great natural ability and possessed of much and varied learning, he soon rose to distinction and prominence in the Province of Maryland. He was at various times a Judge of the Land Office, of the Court of Admiralty, one of the Council and in the sessions of 1762 and 1763 represented the City of Annapolis in the Legislature, and during the administration of Gov. Horatio Sharpe was Lieut. Col. of the "Horse Militia." Few in this country can claim as ancient, as royal and as authentic a lineage. He was descended from Kennett II.

KENNETT II was crowned King of Scotland in the year 854 A. D., and was succeeded in 855 by his son, CONSTANTINE II; who was succeeded in 892 by his son, DONALD VI; who was succeeded in 946 by his son, MALCOLM I; who was succeeded in 970 by his son, KENNETT III; who was succeeded 1004 by his son, MALCOLM II, who had a dau. Beatrix, who m. Crynan, Ardthane of the Isles, and had a son, DUNCAN, who was murdered by Macbeth, and was succeeded in 1059 by his son, Malcolm III, called Keanmore, who m. Margaret, sister of Edgar Atheling, and had three sons, viz., Edgar,—Alexander and David, and one dau. Matilda, who m. Henry I, of England.

MALCOLM III fell in battle and was succeeded by his son, EDGAR, in Sept. 1097, who d. *sine prole,* and was succeeded 8th Jan'y 1107 by his brother, ALEXANDER I, who, also, dying without child., was succeeded by his brother, 27th April 1124, DAVID I, who is known in history as ST. DAVID.

DAVID I, or ST. DAVID, m. Maud, dau. of Waltheof, Earl of Northumberland, by his wife, Judith, niece of William the Conqueror, and d. in 1153. His only son, HENRY, Prince of Scotland, m. Lady Adelaide de Warren, sister of the Earl of Warren and Surrey, and dying in 1152, before the demise of his father, left three sons, viz., Malcolm,—William, and David.

DAVID, EARL OF HUNTINGDON, son of Henry Prince of Scotland, m. Maud, dau. of Hugh, Earl of Chester, and had four sons and four daus., viz., Henry,—David,—Robert,—John,—Margaret,—Isabel,—Maud, and Ada.

ISABEL, dau. of David, Earl of Huntingdon, m. Robert Bruce, Lord of Annandale, and had a son Robert Bruce, who claimed, unsuccessfully, the throne of Scotland.

ROBERT BRUCE, Lord of Annandale, son of Robert Bruce and Isabel, the grand-dau. of David I, m. Isabel de Clare, and d. 1295, leaving a son Robert Bruce, who was afterwards Earl of Carrick.

ROBERT BRUCE, Earl of Carrick, m. Margaret, Countess of Carrick, d. 1303, and had 5 sons and 7 daus., the eldest of whom was Robert Bruce, the BRUCE OF BANNOCKBURN.

ROBERT BRUCE, eldest son of Robert Bruce and Margaret, Countess of Carrick, ascended the throne of Scotland Palm Sunday, 27th March 1306, and bore the title of ROBERT I. He m. Isabel, dau. of Donald, Earl of Marr, and had a dau. Margery Bruce.

MARGERY BRUCE, dau. of Robert I, m. 1315 Walter, the High Steward of Scotland. He was b. 1293, and was a man of influence and military prowess. It was he who brought decisive aid to Robert I, and, with Sir James Douglas, held command of the Third Division of the army, 24th June 1314, at the battle of Bannockburn. Shortly afterwards he was selected to receive, on the border, the Queen, with the Princess Margery and other illustrious prisoners, just released from captivity, in England. When King ROBERT I went to Ireland he appointed Walter, the High Steward, and Sir James Douglas, Governors of Scotland, and, in 1318, when Berwick was captured, it was entrusted to his keeping. In the following year he defended it with signal gallantry against Edward II. In 1320 he was one of the patriots who signed the famous letter to the Pope. In 1322 he surprised, at Byeland Abbey, in Yorkshire, the King of England, who escaped with the utmost difficulty to York. The High Steward d. 9th of April 1326, in the 33rd year of his age. He was married twice. His first wife was Alice, dau. of Sir John Erskine, and had a dau. Jean, who m. Hugh, Earl of Ross. His second wife, the Princess Margery, d. in 1317 and left one son, Robert Stewart, afterwards King ROBERT II.

ROBERT STEWART, the 9th Hereditary Lord High Steward of Scotland, only child of Walter and the Princess Margery, b. 2d March 1316, had command of the Second Division of the Scottish Army, at Halledour Hill, and was one of the few who escaped the carnage of that disastrous day. His gallant efforts in the cause of his uncle, David II, in whose absence he acted as Regent of the Kingdom, were as successful as they were disinterested, and resulted in his soverign's deliverance from captivity. At length that monarch dying, *sine prole*, he ascended the throne of his grandfather, the 22d of March 1371, and is known in history as Robert II.

ROBERT II m. Elizabeth, dau. of Sir Adam Muir, of Rowallam, and had four sons, viz., John, Earl of Carrick,—Walter, Earl of Fife,—Robert, Duke of Albany, and Sir Alexander Stewart, of Badenach.

ROBERT STEWART, Duke of Albany, the third son of Robert II, the celebrated Governor of Scotland, b. about the year 1339, m. Margaret, Countess of Menteth, and had seven child., the eldest of whom, Murdoch, being the one through whom the Stewart line was transmitted.

MURDOCH STEWART, the 2nd Duke of Albany, son of Robert and Margaret, m. Isabel, the eldest dau. and heir of Duncan, Earl of Lennox, and had sons, viz., Robert Walter,—Alexander, and James Stewart, who was called the Gross on account of his gigantic stature. He was arrested and executed, with his sons Walter and Alexander, in the year 1425. His son James, the Gross, hearing of his father's arrest, came down from the Highlands with a competent force, burnt the town of Dumbarton, and killed Sir John Stewart, Governor of the Castle, with many others. For which he was obliged to fly to Ireland, where he died previous to the year 1451, leaving a son, James Stewart, called James Beg, because he was not as big as his father, perhaps small in stature, who m. Annabel

Buchanan, and had two child., viz., William, and Janet Stewart, who inherited the Lands of Lettir, and m. William Stirling.

William Stewart, son of James (Beg) and Annabel Buchanan Stewart, inherited Baldorran, and m. Marion Campbell, and had three child., viz., Walter,—John, and Andrew Stewart.

Walter Stewart, eldest son of William and Marion Campbell Stewart, m. Eupham Reddoch, dau. of James Reddoch, Burgess of Stirling, Comptroller of Scotland and Laird of Cultibragan, and had three sons, viz., William,—John, and James Stewart. Walter Stewart having by a grant dated the 14th of Sept. 1500, received a charter of the lands of Duchlash from King James IV, sold in 1504 the estate of Baldorran to William Livingston.

James Stewart, only surviving son of William and Eupham Reddoch Stewart, inherited the estate and lands of Duchlash, and m. Miss Stewart, dau. of Patrick Stewart, in Glenbucky, and had five child., viz., William Stewart, who d. *sine prole*,—Alexander Stewart (who purchased Ardvorlich, m. Margaret Drummond, and had four child., viz., James,—William,—Duncan, and Isabel, who m. John Stewart),—John Stewart, whose son Alexander purchased Annat,—James Stewart, who m. Katharine Murray, and Patrick Stewart.

Alexander Stewart, son of John, the 3rd son of James Stewart, of Duchlash, purchased the estate Annat from James Muschet, of Burnbank, in the year 1621. He m. Miss Mac Nab, dau. of Aucbarn, and had child., viz., John,—Walter,—Andrew,—James, and Archibald.

John Stewart, of Annat, son of Alexander and ——— Mac Nab Stewart, was twice m. His 1st wife was Janet Graham, dau. of Gespard Graham, of Gartur, and had child., viz., Alexander Stewart, his heir, and Duncan Stewart, who purchased Ballachallam, and had a son George Stewart, who m. Mary Hume (or Home), dau. of Harry Hume (or Home), of Argaty, Perth, Scotland, and had two sons, viz., David Stewart, of Ballachallam, and Dr. George Stewart, of Annapolis, Maryland.

Note.—The aforegoing *Lineage* is carefully extracted and drawn out from a small quarto volume of 214 pages, which is esteemed in Scotland of the highest authority. It commences with Kennett II and traces, with minute fidelity, his descendants down to and including Dr. George Stewart, and speaks of him as a Surgeon residing in the Province of Maryland. The title of this work (a copy of which is in possession of Gen. George Hume Steuart) is as follows: "A Short Historical and Genealogical Account of the Royal Family of Scotland from K. Kennett 2nd, who conquered the Picts. And of the Surname of Stewart, From the first founder of that name, Containing A Short Account of the Lives of the Kings of Scotland from that Period; and the Origin and Descent of all the Families of the name of Stewart that are now extant, and the most considerable of those that are extinct. To which is prefixed—A Genealogical and Chronological Tree of the Royal Family, and the Name of Stewart, By Duncan Stewart, M. A. *Ne quid falsi dicere audeat, ne quid veri non audeat.* Edinburgh. Printed by W. Sands, A. Brymer, A. Murray, and J. Cochran. Sold by A. Brymer and the other Booksellers in Edingburgh, and by A. Stalker and J. Barry in Glasgow. 1739." This book was the source from which Sir Walter Scott drew his accurate genealogical lore.

It will be observed that Dr. George Stewart changed the spelling of his name; in which change all his descendants have acquiesced. Many others of the family did the same, in compliment, as is supposed, to the unfortunate Queen Mary, who, while living at the Court of France, substituted the letter *u* for *w* in her surname.

SEC. 98, K. DR. GEORGE STEUART, son of George Stewart and Mary Hume, dau. of Harry Hume, of Argatty, m. Ann Digges, a descendant of Sir Dudley Digges, and had child., viz., George Hume, b. in 1747, d. in Scotland in 1800,—Susanna, b. in 1749, d. 24th Oct. 1774 (who m. Judge James Tilghman, see TILGHMAN),—Charles, b. in 1750, d. in 1802,—David, b. in 1751, d. in 1814,—William, b. in 1754, d. 1838,—James, b. in 1755, d. 1845,—Ann, b. in 1757, d. in 1767,—Mary, b. in 1759, d. in 1776, and Jean Steuart, b. in 1761 and d. in 1778. Dr. Steuart purchased the estate of Dodon, which still remains in the family, from Nicholas Carroll in 1725.

GEORGE HUME STEUART, eldest son of Dr. George and Ann Digges Steuart, was taken by his father to Scotland in 1758, to be educated. When he arrived at manhood, with the consent of his father, who had a life estate therein, he took possession of the estate of Argaty, also Ballachallam and Annat, and assumed the surname of Hume. He m. twice. His 1st wife was a niece of Lord Rolls. She was a great heiress and owned the famous battle-field of Bannockburn, with coal and iron mines of great value. She d., and, four years after her decease, he m. Sophia Monroe, and had a dau., Sophia Hume.

SOPHIA HUME, dau. of George Hume (formerly Steuart) and Sophia Monroe Hume, m. Capt. Binning, of the British army (Indian Service), and had child., viz., George Hume Binning, and Alexander Monroe Binning. George Hume Binning changed his name, by virtue of Act of Parliament, to George Binning Hume or Home, and upon him was settled Argaty. Alexander Monroe Binning changed his name to Alexander Binning Monroe, m. and his eldest son, David Monroe, was a Fellow of Oxford.

CHARLES STEUART, son of Dr. George Steuart and Ann Digges, m. Elizabeth Calvert, dau. of Benedict Calvert, son of Lord Frederick Calvert, and had child., viz., George,—Benedict,—Charles, and Edward Steuart.

CHARLES STEUART, son of Charles Steuart and Elizabeth Calvert, m. Ann Biscoe, and had child., viz., Dr. William Frederick,—George Biscoe, and Charles Calvert Steuart.

DR. WILLIAM FREDERICK STEUART, son of Charles Steuart and Ann Biscoe, m. 27th Feb'y 1840, Ann Hall, dau. of Henry Hall and Mary Stevenson, and had child., viz., Capt. Harry Augustus, C. S. A., d. 1861, aged 20 years,—Charles,—William Frederick (who m. Louisa Du Bignon),—Anne,—Louis Edward,—a 2nd Charles,—Richard Estep (who m. Isabel Murphy, and had child., viz., Roy Campbell and Harry Steuart),—Mary Stevenson (who m. Sept. 1874, William Henry Purcell, of Dublin, Ireland, and had a dau. Anne Purcell), — Eleanor, — George Biscoe, and Cœcillius Calvert Steuart.

GEORGE BISCOE STEUART, son of Charles Steuart and Ann Biscoe, m. Louisa Darnall, and had child., viz., Rose,—Louisa,—George,—Henry Darnall,—Estep Hall, and Virginia Steuart.

CHARLES CALVERT STEUART, son of Charles Steuart and and Ann Biscoe, m. 1st Elizabeth Frances Steele, dau. of Henry Maynadier Steele and Maria Lloyd (see p. 37), and had a dau., Alice Key Steuart. He m. 2ndly April 1853, Hannah Margaret Maynadier Murray, and had child., viz., Helen Steuart, and Sarah Murray Steuart.

MRS. HANNAH MARGARET MAYNADIER MURRAY STEUART is descended from John Murray, Marquis of Tullibardine, who was attainted and fled to Barbadoes in 1716. His son, Dr. William Murray, b. 15th July 1708, settled in Chestertown and m., 22d Jan'y 1740, Ann Smith, of Chestertown, who was b. 7th Dec. 1720, d. 18th Aug. 1807. Dr. William Murray d. 13th April 1769, and had child., viz., James, b.

2d Jan'y 1741, d. 1st Dec. 1819,—Elizabeth, b. 7th Oct. 1743 (who m. John Thompson, of Chestertown, and d. March 1840), —Ann, b. 5th Sept. 1745, d. 1808,—Sarah, b. 12th Nov. 1747 (who m. John Thomas, and d. 1824),—Katharine, b. 27th Feb'y 1749 (who m. Richard Carmichael, and d. 1785),—Dr. William, b. 12th July 1752 and d. 25th Sept. 1842,—Commodore Alexander, b. 12th July 1754, d. Oct. 1821, and Mary Murray, b. 7th Jan'y 1757, d. 23d May 1760.

DR. JAMES MURRAY, of Annapolis, son of William Murray and Ann Smith, m. Sarah Maynadier, and had child., viz., Daniel,—James,—Sally Scott (who m. Gov. Edward Lloyd, see LLOYD),—Anne (who m. Gen. John Mason, of Va.), and Sarah Catharine Murray, who m. the celebrated Richard Rush, of Philadelphia.

DANIEL MURRAY, of Elkridge, son of Dr. James Murray and Sarah Maynadier, m. Mary Dorsey, and had child., viz., Dr. James Murray, of West River,—Sally Scott (who m. Dr. James Cheston),—Mary (who m. Dr. Worthington),—Col. Edward, U. S. A., C. S. A., d. 1872,—Capt. Francis Key, d., —Dr. Robert, U. S. A.,—Anne Maria,—Caroline (who m. Mr. McMurtree),—Harriet (who m. Mr. Talbot),—Priscilla (who m. John Bohlen), and Henry Maynadier Murray.

JAMES MURRAY, son of Dr. James Murray and Sarah Maynadier, m. Charlotte Ratcliffe, and had child., viz., Keturah,—Charlotte Rider,—Sarah Henry Maynadier (who m. Mr. Howison, d.),—Henry M.,—Hannah Margaret Maynadier (who m., April 1853, Charles Calvert Steuart), and James D. Murray, Pay Director U. S. N.

CHARLOTTE RIDER MURRAY, dau. of James Murray and Charlotte Ratcliffe, m., April 1837, Dr. Charles Hutchins Steele, and had child., viz., Charlotte Ratcliffe (who m., 21st Oct. 1856, James Cheston, Jr., and had child., viz., James,—Ratcliffe,—Charlotte Ratcliffe,—Mary Steele,—Margaret Cary Cheston),—Charles H., d. in C. S. A., 1864,—Mary N., d.,—Nevett, and Dr. John Murray Steele, U. S. N.

JAMES D. MURRAY, U. S. N., son of James and Charlotte Ratcliffe, m. 1st Catharine Spencer, and had a dau., Eva Murray. He m. 2ndly Elizabeth Murray Spencer, and had child., viz., James Daniel,—Catharine Spencer,—Charlotte Ratcliffe, and William Spencer Murray.

ANNA MARIA MURRAY, dau. of Dr. James Murray and Sarah Maynadier, m. Genl. John Mason, of Analostan Island, son of Col. George Mason, of Gunston Hall, Virginia, and had child., viz., John,—James M.,—Maria,—Virginia (who

m. George Mason),—Catharine,—Eilbeck (who m. Virginia Magee),—Murray,—Maynadier,—Anna M., and Barlow Mason, A. D. C. to Genl. Joseph E. Johnston, C. S. A., at the Battle of Manassas, who was severely wounded and d. at Warrenton, unm.

COL. GEORGE MASON was the Solon and Cato of Virginia. "The Bill of Rights and the Constitution of Virginia are lasting monuments to his memory." In the former he uttered those memorable words which will never be forgotten in America: "that no man or set of men is entitled to exclusive " or separate emoluments, or privileges from the community, " but in consideration of public services; which not being " descendible, neither ought the offices of magistrate, legisla- " tor, or judge to be hereditary."

JOHN MASON, son of Genl. John Mason and Anna Maria Murray, was private secretary to Mr. Poinsett, U. S. Minister to Mexico, m. Catharine Macomb, dau. of Genl. Alexander Macomb, U. S. A., and had child., viz., John (who m. in N. York),—Eilbeck,—Macomb,—Alexander,—Anna,—Poinsett,—Daniel M., and George Mason.

HON. JAMES M. MASON, son of Genl. John Mason and Anna Maria Murray (for many years a distinguished member of the U. S. Senate, afterwards the accredited Minister Plenipotentiary of the Confederate States, with Mr. Slidell, to Great Britain) m. Eliza Chew, dau. of Benjamin Chew, of Phila., and had child., viz, Anna (who m. John Ambler),—Benjamin,—Catharine (who m. John B. Dorsey),—George (who m. in Texas),—Virginia,—Ida,—James M. (who m. Miss Hill) and John Mason.

MARIA MASON, dau. of Genl. John Mason and Anna Maria Murray, m. Samuel Cooper, Adjutant General U. S. A. (afterwards Adjutant General C. S. A.), and had child., viz., Maria (who m. Lieut. Frank Wheaton, U. S. A.),—Virginia (who m. Nicholas Dawson) and Samuel Cooper.

CATHARINE MASON, dau. of Genl. John Mason and Anna Maria Murray, m. Cecilius C. Jamison (Cashier, and afterwards for many years President of the Bank of Baltimore), and had child., viz., John Mason and Eliza Mason Jamison.

LIEUT. MURRAY MASON, U. S. N., Capt. C. S. N., son of Genl. John Mason and Anna Maria Murray, m. Clara Forsyth (dau. of Hon. John Forsyth, Secretary of State from 27th June 1834 to 5th March 1841), and had child., viz., Fannie Forsyth,—Clara (who m. John Maguire),—Virginia (who m.

A. Peter Bower), and Anna M. Mason, who m. Capt. Samuel Davis, C. S. A.

MAYNADIER MASON, son of Genl. John Mason and Anna Maria Murray, m. Virginia French, and had child., viz., Maynadier,— Murray,— John,— Charles,— Robert (who m. Miss Cooke),—Mariamne (who m. Dr. Emmlin Marsteller), and W. Virginius Mason (who m. Eva Marsteller). He m. 2ndly, Mary Fitzhugh, and had a son, James M. Mason.

ANNA M. MASON, dau. of Gen. John Mason and Anna Maria Murray, m. Lieut. Smith Lee, U. S. N., afterwards Captain in the Confederate service (a brother of Gen. Robert E. Lee, C. S. A.), and had child., viz., Gen. Fitzhugh Lee, C. S. A. (who m. Ellen Fowle),—Smith Lee,—John Lee (who m. Nora Bankhead),—Henry Lee (who m. Sallie Johnston),—Daniel Murray Lee (who m. Nannie Ficklin), and Robert Lee.

DR. WILLIAM MURRAY, son of William Murray and Ann Smith, m. Harriet Hesselius, and had child., viz., Mary Ann Caroline,—William Henry (who m. Isabella Maria Sterling, and had child., who are now living, Sterling and Alexander Murray),—and Alexander John Murray, who m. twice: 1st, Miss Addison, and had a dau., Elizabeth, and 2ndly Mary Clapham, of Baltimore, dau. of Jonas Clapham and Catharine Cooke (see COOKE), and had child., viz., Clapham Murray,—William H. Murray, b. 30th April 1839, at West River, was killed at Gettysburg, 3rd July 1863, while commanding Company A of the 2nd Maryland Infantry, C. S. A.,—Mary Ann Caroline Murray, and Alexander Murray.

DR. JAMES STEUART, son of Dr. George and Ann Digges Steuart, was taken by his father to Scotland, at the early age of 8 years, and did not return until he had completed his professional education at Edinburgh. He practiced his profession for several years in Annapolis, with success and reputation, residing in the house in which he was born, the celebrated mansion which was built by his father in 1750, widely known in after years as "Mrs. Green's Boarding House," until it was removed to give place for the present Executive Mansion. He removed to Baltimore in 1794, and immediately enjoyed the fruit of his deserved reputation, a lucrative practice. In 1805 he retired from practice and devoted himself to the cultivation and improvement of his estate, Sparrow's Point, a part of which is now known as Holly Grove; where he passed much of his life, preferring the quiet of nature to the gay and bustling scenes of a city. He m. in 1787, Rebecca Sprigg, who was b. at Strawberry Hill, Anne Arundel Co., the dau. of

Richard Sprigg, of Cedar Park, West River, Md., and his wife, Margaret Caile, and had child., viz., George Hume, b. in 1790, d. 1867,—Margaret, b. 1795, d. 1832,—Sophia, b. 1796,—Richard Sprigg, b. 1797,—James, b. 1798, d. 1804,—Henry, b. 1799, d. 1804,—Henrietta, b. 1801, and Elizabeth Steuart, b. in 1802.

RICHARD SPRIGG, of Cedar Park, m. in 1765, Margaret Caile, dau. of John Caile an Englishman, and his wife, Rebecca Ennalls, and had child., viz., Sophia, b. 1766, d. 1812,—Rebecca, b. 1767, who m. 1787, Dr. James Steuart, and d. in 1806,—Elizabeth, b. 1770, who m. 1795, Hugh Thompson, and d. 1813,—Henrietta, b. 1775, d. 1791, and Margaret Sprigg, b. 1790, and d. 1864.

SOPHIA SPRIGG, dau. of Richard and Margaret Caile Sprigg, m. 1785, Col. John Francis Mercer, of the Revolutionary Army. At the time of his marriage he was a member of Congress, from his native State, Virginia, and resided on his estate, "Marlboro," on the Potomac. There his children were born. His wife inherited Cedar Park about the year 1799, and he removed to Maryland. He was an intimate and trusted friend of Thomas Jefferson, and warmly espousing the political doctrines of that great Statesman; and possessing rare eloquence, he, in a short time attained eminence, popularity and influence in Maryland, and was elected Governor of the State in 1801. He d. in 1821, in Philadelphia, and had child., viz., John,—a son who d. in 1810, at sea, 19 years of age,—and Margaret Mercer, a lady of unusual culture and refinement, who was widely known as the "Hannah More of America."

COL. JOHN MERCER, son of Gov. John Francis and Sophia Sprigg Mercer, m. Mary Swann, of Alexandria, Va., and had ten child., viz., John Francis, who d. aged 19 years,—Dr. Thomas S. Mercer, who m. Violetta Carroll, and had 2 sons,—Richard S. Mercer, who m. E. Cox, and had 6 child.,—Monroe Mercer, who m. Ella Hopkins, and had 3 sons,—William, who m. Mary Chapman, and had several child.,—George Douglas Mercer,—Wilson C. Mercer,—Jane Bird Mercer, who m. Peter McCall, of Phila., and had 4 child.,—Sophy Mercer, who m. ——— Strong, of La., and Mary Mercer, who m. Dr. Arthur Brogden.

GENERAL GEORGE HUME STEUART, son of Dr. James and Rebecca Sprigg Steuart, b. in Annapolis 1st Nov. 1790, accompanied his father to Baltimore in 1794, was educated at Princeton College, read Law in the office of Gen. W. H. Winder, and practiced in the Courts of Baltimore and Annapolis during the greater portion of his life. He was twice elected to the Legislature of Maryland. When only 22 years of age he raised a company and marched it, as part of Col. Sterrett's 5th Regiment, to the field of the battle of Bladensburg, and while gallantly resisting the advance of the enemy at North Point was wounded in the leg by a musket ball. He afterwards rose to the rank of Major General of the Volunteer Forces of the State of Maryland. In 1850–51 he visited Europe, and was treated with distinguished consideration by the highest nobility of England.

When the late war broke out he went South, and remained there during the whole struggle; and, too aged to serve, spent most of his time with the army and was present in many battles. At the conclusion of the war he went to Europe to reside, but returned in 1867, and died the same year at the residence of his son, Gen. George H. Steuart. He m. Ann Jane Edmondson (eldest dau. of Thomas Edmondson, who came from the North of England, and was a successful merchant in Baltimore), and had child., viz., George Hume,—Isaac Edmondson,—William James, who d. from wounds received in the battle of the Wilderness, 1864, while serving with gallantry in the Confederate Army,—Thomas Edmondson d. 1865,--James Henry,--Charles David,--Mary Elizabeth d. 1861,—Ann Rebecca, d. 1865,—Margaret Sophia, d. 1860, and Henrietta Elizabeth Steuart, d. 1867.

Gen. George Hume Steuart, son of Gen. George Hume and Ann Jane Edmondson Steuart, entered the Military Academy at West Point in 1844, was graduated in 1848, and was for many years engaged in active and arduous service on the Indian frontier, in Texas, Kansas and Nebraska. He was a Lieutenant in the 2d Regiment of Dragoons U. S. A., and subsequently a Captain in the 1st Regiment of Cavalry, U. S. A., and served with credit until, at the breaking out of the late Civil War, he resigned his commission, and, like many other sons of Maryland, went South, and was commissioned a Captain in the Confederate Army. In June 1861 the First Maryland Confederate Regiment was organized, at Harper's Ferry, with the following officers, viz., Col., Arnold Elzey,—Lieut. Col., George Hume Steuart,—Maj., Bradley T. Johnson, and acting Adjt., Frank X. Ward. He commanded the Regiment on the 21st July 1861 at the first battle of Manassas, holding the right of the line and greatly distinguished himself. His zeal, ability and courage were recognized, and in the Spring of 1862 he was commissioned a Brigadier General and assigned to the command of a Brigade in the immortal Corps of Stonewall Jackson, and participated actively all through in the brilliant campaigns of the Valley of Virginia, and was conspicuous in the battles at Winchester and Cross Keys. In the latter battle he was severely wounded. After his recovery he was assigned to the command of the Maryland Line, at Winchester, and was the commandant of the post; after which he was placed in command of a Brigade in the Division of Gen. Edward Johnson and led his men, with great gallantry, in the battles of the 2nd Winchester, Gettysburgh, Mine Run, Spottsylvania and the Wilderness. His last military service was performed in command of a Brigade in Picket's Division, and was surrendered at Appomattox, April 1865.

Genl. George Hume Steuart m. 14th Jan'y 1858, Maria Kinzie (dau. of Col. Robert A. Kinzie, U. S. A., a son of John Kinzie, famous as one of the first settlers of Chicago), and had two child., viz., Maria Hunter, and Ann Mary Steuart.

MRS. MARIA KINZIE STEUART was the dau. of Col. Robert A. Kinzie, U. S. A., and his wife, Miss Whistler, a dau. of Genl. William Whistler, U. S. A. Col. Robert A. Kinzie was a son of John Kinzie, who was the owner of the site, the first permanent settler and the founder of the City of Chicago.

MARGARET STEUART, dau. of Dr. James and Rebecca Sprigg Steuart, m. John H. B. Latrobe, a distinguished lawyer of Baltimore, and had a son, Henry B. Latrobe. Mr. Latrobe, m. a 2nd time and had several child. One of his sons, Genl. Ferdinand C. Latrobe is the present (1876) worthy Mayor of the City of Baltimore. JOHN H. B. LATROBE and SAMUEL M. SHOEMAKER were the United States Centennial Commissioners for Maryland.

SOPHIA STEUART, dau. of Dr. James and Rebecca Sprigg Steuart, m. John C. Delprat, a Hollander, and had child., viz., Paul,—Fanny,—Henrietta, who m. her cousin, Steuart Thorndike, son of Augustus and Henrietta Steuart Thorndike, of Boston,— Margaret, who m. Robert Remsen,— Charles,— Richard, and James Steuart Delprat, who m. Miss Morris, of New York.

DR. RICHARD SPRIGG STEUART, son of Dr. James and Rebecca Sprigg Steuart, was b. 1st Nov. 1797, in the City of Baltimore, and educated at St. Mary's College. At the age of 17 years he was present at the battle of North Point, engaged in escorting supplies to his father and elder brother (Genl. George H. Steuart), while they were in the heat of action with the enemy. In 1816 he commenced the study of Law in the office of Genl. Winder, where he continued until the year 1818, when, without the knowledge of his father, he began the study of Medicine with Dr. William Donaldson, and was graduated in the University of Maryland (School of Medicine) in March 1822. With Dr. Donaldson he subsequently entered into partnership and finally, when the health of his beloved preceptor, partner and friend failed, succeeded to his entire practice, and rose to the head of his profession in Baltimore. In 1838 he inherited a large landed estate and many slaves, and retired to the repose of plantation life to recuperate his health, which had become impaired. In 1849, with restored health, he returned to the practice of his profession. He again retired to the country in 1854, and remained there until 1862, with the exception of one or two Winters spent in the city. After the death of Dr. Fonerden, Medical Superintendent Resident of the Maryland Hospital for the Insane, he assumed the position to which he had been, originally, elected in 1828, as Medical Superintendent of the Hospital and President of the Board, and removed to the residence attached to the institution.

The necessity for larger and better accommodations for the Insane than the old Hospital, on Broadway, afforded, at length became so apparent that the Legislature, in 1852, was induced, after great effort, to take the initiative, and it appropriated five thousand dollars for the purchase of a site and created a Commission to build a new Hospital. The Commission, when organized, consisted of Dr. Richard Sprigg Steuart,—Gen. Benjamin C. Howard,—Col. Alexander B. Hanson,—Cahil Humphries, and Dr. Washington Duvall. A beautiful site, Spring Grove, was immediately selected, containing about 136 acres, and costing $14,500.00.

Dr. Steuart by his own exertions among his friends, by volunteer contributions, raised the sum of twelve thousand five hundred dollars and presented it to the State to pay for the site and to begin the work of construction. To his efforts is mainly due the erection of the present magnificent Hospital, which was twenty years in building, at a cost of $850,000.00. It will accommodate three hundred patients, and is equal to the best Institutions of the kind in this country.

For twenty-six years Dr. Steuart served the Hospital without salary or compensation of any kind, and frequently, out of his own, then slender, means advanced the money which fed and supported the inmates, from day to day, and gave his individual obligations to defray the expense of necessary improvements, amounting to thousands of dollars, trusting solely to the liberality of the State for repayment. He m. 27th Jan'y 1824, Maria Louisa, eldest dau. of the Chevalier De Bernabeu, Consul General of Spain, at Philadelphia, and had child., viz., Mary,—Elizabeth,—James A.,—Louisa,—Emily, —Isabella,—John B.,—William Donaldson, and Richard Sprigg Steuart. He d. in the City of Baltimore 13th July 1876, and was buried in the family cemetery at Dodon, Anne Arundel County.

DR. JAMES A. STEUART, the present (1876) Health Commissioner of the City of Baltimore, son of Dr. Richard Sprigg and Maria Louisa Bernabeu Steuart, m. 25th of Feb'y 1851, Sarah Elizabeth Baxter, dau. of Arthur and Emily Mahool Baxter, and had child., viz., Louisa,—Emily,—Arthur,—Richard, d., and James Steuart. Emily Mahool Baxter was b. 23rd Aug. 1808, the dau. of Capt. Thomas Mahool and Elizabeth Burnside, who was the dau. of James Burnside, who came to America in 1795. His elder brother, —— Burnside, had previously m. and settled in one of the Western States. Arthur Baxter's father was engaged in one of the rebellions in Ireland and fled to this country for safety. After the birth of her son, Arthur Baxter, his wife followed him to America. She was formerly a Miss Nelson, from near Belfast, Ireland. His family was of consanguinity with the Rev. Richard Baxter, the author of "Baxter's Call," which is read and deeply prized by the devout wherever our noble language is read.

JOHN B. STEUART, son of Dr. Richard Sprigg and Maria Louisa Bernabeu Steuart, m. Mrs. Georgianna Gist Steuart, the widow of his d. brother Richard Steuart, and had child., viz., Sprigg, and Margaret Steuart.

WILLIAM DONALDSON STEUART, son of Dr. Richard Sprigg and Maria Louisa Bernabeu Steuart, m. in 1859, Matilda Montell, dau. of Francis Montell, and had child., viz., Mary,—Frank,—Zaidee,—Annie,—William,—Louisa,—Fanny and Archibald Steuart.

HENRIETTA STEUART, dau. of Dr. James and Rebecca Sprigg Steuart, m. Augustus Thorndike, of Boston, and had child., viz., Steuart, who m. his cousin, Henrietta Delprat, dau. of John H. and Sophia Steuart Delprat, of Boston,—Rebecca, who m. Lt. Marin, U. S. N.,—Charles, who m. Mary Edgar, and Augusta Thorndike.

ELIZABETH STEUART, dau. of Dr. James and Rebecca Sprigg Steuart, m. George H. Calvert, son of George Calvert, of River's Dale, near Bladensburg, Md.

SEC. 98, L. CHARLES GOLDSBOROUGH, of Horn's Point, Dorchester Co., who m. Anna Maria Tilghman, dau. of William and Margaret Lloyd Tilghman, of Groces, was descended from Nicholas Goldsborough.

NICHOLAS GOLDSBOROUGH, the Progenitor of the Goldsborough Family of Maryland, was b. 1640–1641, at Malcolm Regis, near Weymouth, in the County of Dorset, England, and m. 1659, Margaret Howes, the only dau. of Abraham Howes, son of William Howes, of Newbury, in the County of Berks, England. He had three child., viz., Robert Goldsborough, b. Advent Sunday 1660, at Blandford, Dorset County, England, and d. Christmas Day 1746,—Nicholas Goldsborough, who d. 1705, and Judith Goldsborough. The first-named Nicholas Goldsborough left England in 1669 and went to Barbadoes, thence to New England, and finally, early in 1670, settled on Kent Island, where he d., and was buried on the plantation of Tobias Wells. His wife survived him, and m. 1672, George Robins, of Talbot County, and had a son, Thomas Robins, who m. twice. He married first, 3d Feb'y 1696, Susannah Vaughan, and had a son, George Robins. His 2d wife was Elizabeth Standley, and had child., viz., Thomas, b. 11th Oct. 1705,—William and John, twins, b. 22d Dec. 1709,—Elizabeth,—Lambert and Standley Robins, who m. 6th Jan'y 1742, Sarah Goldsborough. Thomas Robins d. 29th Dec. 1721.

ROBERT GOLDSBOROUGH, of Ashby, Talbot County, Md., son of Nicholas and Margaret Howes Goldsborough, came to Maryland in 1678, and m. 2d Sept. 1697, Elizabeth Greenbury, dau. of Col. Nicholas Greenbury and Ann, his wife, of Greenbury's Point, near Annapolis. She was b. 23d Sept. 1678, in Anne Arundel Co., d. 2d March 1719, and had child., viz., Ann, b. 13th July 1698, d. 24th Feb'y 1708, —Elizabeth, b. 13th Feb'y 1700, d. 17th Jan'y 1708,—Mary, b. 14th Dec. 1702, d. 15th Jan'y 1742,—Robert, b. 17th Feb'y 1704, d. 30th April 1777,—Nicholas, twin brother of Robert, b. 17th Feb'y 1704, d. 14th Nov. 1757,—Charles, b. 26th June 1707, d. 4th July 1767,—William, b. 6th July 1709, d. in Sept. 1760,—John, b. 12th Oct. 1711, d. 18th Jan'y 1778,—Greenbury, b. 16th Nov. 1713, d. 2d Feb'y 1716,—Howes, b. 14th Nov. 1715, d. 30th March 1746,—a 2nd Greenbury, b. 15th Nov. 1717, d. 20th Nov. 1717, and a 3rd Greenbury Goldsborough, b. 19th Nov. 1718, who d. three hours after birth.

SEC. 98, M. MARY GOLDSBOROUGH, dau. of Robert and Elizabeth Greenbury Goldsborough, m. ——— Mooney, and had child., viz., Mary,—Elizabeth, and Ann Kesiah Mooney.

MARY MOONEY, dau. of Mary Goldsborough Mooney, m. 16th June 1751, Thomas Sherwood, and had a son, Maj. Hugh Sherwood, who m. 10th Dec. 1795, Elizabeth Tilghman, dau. of Richard Tilghman.

ANN KESIAH MOONEY, dau. of Mary Goldsborough Mooney, m. 8th Dec. 1763, Daniel Feddeman, and had child., viz., Mary, b. 29th June 1766,—Anne, b. 19th April 1768, and Daniel Feddeman, b. 9th Jan'y 1770, d. 25th Feb'y 1832.

DANIEL FEDDEMAN, son of Daniel and Ann Kesiah Mooney Feddeman, m. 16th March 1794, Rebecca Sherwood Wrightson, who d. 15th Oct. 1842, and had child., viz., Mary Mooney, b. 3d Feb'y 1795,—Ann Kesiah, b. 13th Feb'y 1797, —Richard, b. 8th May 1800,—Elizabeth, b. 8th Jan'y 1805,—Mary, b. 8th May 1807,—Jane Maynadier, b. 27th May 1809, —Emma, b. 18th Dec. 1811,—Philemon Henry, b. 3d Aug. 1814,—Daniel Maynadier, b. 24th Jan'y 1817, who m. 27th April 1865, Alice Colbert, and Dorothy Feddeman, b. 4th Feb'y 1819.

ANN KESIAH FEDDEMAN, dau. of Daniel and Rebecca Sherwood Wrightson Feddeman, m. 25th Nov. 1813, Philemon Williamson Hemsley, and had child., viz., Philemon Feddeman, b. 8th Sept. 1814, d. young,—Martha Ann, b. 23d Dec. 1815, who m. Alexander Mackey,—Philemon Feddeman, b. 1st Oct. 1817, who m. Mary Hambleton, and Richard Feddeman Hemsley, b. 19th July 1819, d. 17th April 1854.

PHILEMON (PHILIP) HENRY FEDDEMAN, son of Daniel and Rebecca Wrightson Feddeman, m. 25th Nov. 1840, Anna Matilda Groome, dau. of Samuel and Deborah Morris Groome, and had one son, Morris Groome Feddeman. Samuel Groome was the son of Charles and Sarah Kennard Groome. Charles Groome, the Register of Chester Parish, Kent Co., Md., was the son of Samuel and Margaret Groome. The last named Samuel Groome was a Church Warder in St. Paul's Parish, Kent Co., Md., in the year 1726.

SEC. 98, N. ROBERT GOLDSBOROUGH, son of Robert and Elizabeth Greenbury Goldsborough, m. twice. He m. 5th Nov. 1739, Sarah Nicols, dau. of Rev. Henry Nicols, Rector of St. Michael's Parish, Talbot Co., and had one son, Robert Goldsborough, b. 8th Nov. 1740, d. 1798,—Mrs. Sarah Nicols Goldsborough d. Saturday, 15th Nov. 1740. He m. again 8th July 1742, Mrs. Mary Ann Turbutt Robins, widow of John

Robins, attorney-at-law, who d. in 1739, and the dau. of Foster and Bridget Turbutt. She d. 29th Aug. 1794.

Robert Goldsborough and his 2nd wife had child., viz., Elizabeth, b. 29th April 1745, d. 29th April 1748,—Howes, b. 4th Sept. 1747, d. 30th Jan'y 1797,—William, b. 17th March 1750, d. 23d Jan'y 1801, and Mary Ann Turbutt Goldsborough, b. 21st Oct. 1752, d. unm. 18th April 1811.

ROBERT GOLDSBOROUGH, of Myrtle Grove, son of Robert and his 1st wife, m. 22d Sept. 1768, Mary Emerson Trippe, youngest dau. of Henry Trippe, of Dorchester Co., and had child., viz., Robert, b. 21st March 1771, d. 1st April following,—Robert Henry, b. 9th Feb'y 1774, d. 18th Sept. 1777,—Elizabeth, b. 30th July 1776, d. 14th Aug. 1798, and a 2nd Robert Henry Goldsborough, b. 4th Jan'y 1779, d. 5th Oct. 1836.

ELIZABETH GOLDSBOROUGH, dau. of Robert and Mary Emerson Trippe Goldsborough, m. 22d Sept. 1793, Governor Charles Goldsborough, and had child., viz., Elizabeth Greenbury and Anna Maria Goldsborough.

HON. ROBERT HENRY GOLDSBOROUGH, son of Robert and Mary Emerson Trippe Goldsborough, United States Senator from 21st May 1813 to 21st Dec. 1819, m. 16th Jan'y 1800, Henrietta Maria Nicols, dau. of Col. Robert Lloyd Nicols and his wife, Susannah Robins Chamberlaine Nicols, and had child., viz., Robert William, b. 18th Oct. 1800,—William, b. 20th April 1802,—Charles Henry, b. 12th April 1804,—Susan Elizabeth, b. 4th Jan'y 1806, who m. Mr. Coolidge, of Boston, and d. 14th Jan'y 1838,—Mary Caroline, b. 11th Nov. 1808,—Henrietta Maria, b. 31st Jan'y 1811,—John McDowell, b. 4th Oct. 1813,—Mary McDowell,—Eliza, b. 19th Sept. 1815, and George Robins Goldsborough, b. 11th April 1821.

Col. Robert Lloyd Nicols was the son of Jeremiah Nicols and Deborah Lloyd. Deborah Lloyd was the dau. of James Lloyd and Ann Grundy (see LLOYD). Susannah Robins Chamberlaine, when she m. in Aug. 1775, Col. Robert Lloyd Nicols, was the widow of Thomas Chamberlaine. She was the dau. of George Robins and Henrietta Maria Tilghman, who m. 22d April 1721. Henrietta Maria Tilghman was the dau. of Richard and Anna Maria Lloyd Tilghman of the Hermitage (see TILGHMAN).

HOWES GOLDSBOROUGH, son of Robert and his 2nd wife, Mary Ann Turbutt Robins Goldsborough, m. 16th Nov. 1773, Rebecca Goldsborough, dau. of Robert and Sarah Yerbury

Goldsborough, and had child., viz., Sarah, b. 5th Oct. 1774,—Robert, b. 6th March 1776, d. 5th Dec. 1777,—Mary Ann, b. 23d Feb'y 1778,—Charles, b. 4th June 1779, d. 13th Aug. 1824,—Robert Yerbury, b. 24th Jan'y 1782,—Henry Turbutt, b. 11th Dec. 1783, d. 2d Feb'y 1785,—William Henry, b. 6th May 1785, d. 14th Aug. 1842,—Ann, b. 11th May 1787, who m. 30th May 1810, Charles Louis Pascault, of Baltimore, and d. 24th Dec. 1855,—Howes, b. 11th March 1789, who m. Maria Ward,—Rebecca, b. 25th Nov. 1790, d. Sept. 1792,—Elizabeth, b. 8th Feb'y 1791, d. 19th Feb'y 1791, and Henry Goldsborough, b. 16th Feb'y 1792, d. 1832.

SARAH GOLDSBOROUGH, dau. of Howes and Rebecca Goldsborough, m. 25th March 1802, Dr. Samuel Y. Keene, and had child., viz., John Henry, and Mary Ann Keene, who m. —— Hollingsworth.

MARY ANN GOLDSBOROUGH, dau. of Howes and Rebecca Goldsborough, m. 4th March 1804, Dr. Tristram Thomas, of Easton, Md., and had child., viz., Juliana, b. 20th Dec. 1804, and Robert T. Goldsborough Thomas, who m. in March 1831, Mary Isabella Willson, dau. of James and Mary Jacob Willson.

CHARLES GOLDSBOROUGH, son of Howes and Rebecca Goldsborough, m. 2nd Nov. 1802, Sarah Keene, b. 16th Dec. 1789, d. 26th Nov. 1819, the dau. of Vachel Keene, who was a brother of the Rev. Samuel Keene, of Talbot, and had child., viz., Howes,—Eleanor,—Charles, b. 1st June 1807,—Samuel, and Sarah Goldsborough.

HENRY GOLDSBOROUGH, son of Howes and Rebecca Goldsborough, m. 4 times, viz., 1st, 24th April 1817, Eliza Ann Thomas, of Queen Anne's, who d. 24th Aug. 1817,—2dly, Susannah Shippley, and had 2 sons and a dau.,—3rdly, 18th May 1823, Anne Keene, who d. 9th June 1824,—and 4thly, 15th Nov. 1825, Margaret Tilghman, dau. of James Tilghman, son of James Tilghman, of Phila. Mrs. Margaret Tilghman Goldsborough survived her husband, m. 22d June 1817, John Goldsborough, son of John and Caroline Goldsborough, of Four Square.

SEC. 98, O. NICHOLAS GOLDSBOROUGH, son of Robert and Elizabeth Greenbury Goldsborough, and twin brother of Robert, m. 7th April 1746, Mrs. Jane Banning, widow of James Banning, and d. 14th Nov. 1756. Having no child. of his own, he adopted those of his wife, and in his Will, dated 20th Oct. 1756, left to them his property. The names of his adopted children were Jeremiah,—Henry, and Anthony Banning.

SEC. 98, P. CHARLES GOLDSBOROUGH, son of Robert and Elizabeth Greenbury Goldsborough, m. twice. He m. 18th July 1730, Elizabeth Ennalls, sister of Col. Joseph Ennalls, and had two child., viz., Elizabeth Greenbury, b. 4th July 1731, who m. William Ennalls, son of the said Col. Joseph Ennalls,—and Robert Goldsborough, b. 3rd Dec. 1733, d. 20th Dec. 1788. He married again 2nd Aug. 1739, Elizabeth Dickinson, a half-sister of John Dickinson, of Phila., and had one son, Charles Goldsborough, b. 2nd April 1740.

HON. ROBERT GOLDSBOROUGH, barrister, son of Charles and Elizabeth Ennalls Goldsborough, was a very distinguished gentleman. He was appointed a delegate to the Continental Congress by the several Conventions of Maryland, which were held in Annapolis, 22d of June 1774, 8th Dec. 1774, 7th Dec. 1775, and 8th of May 1776. He was a member of the "Council of Safety," and also of the Convention of the Province of Maryland, held at Annapolis, 14th Aug. 1776, to form a Constitution for the STATE OF MARYLAND. He m. in England, 27th March 1755, Sarah Yerbury, dau. of Richard Yerbury, of Bassing-Hall Street, London, who d. 20th Dec. 1788, in Cambridge, and had child., viz., Charles, b. 19th Dec. 1755, d. 29th Dec. 1758,—Rebecca, b. 4th July 1757, d. 26th June 1802 (who m. 16th Nov. 1773, Howes Goldsborough),—Sarah, b. 11th Oct. 1758, who m. Henry Ennalls, of Dorchester Co., and d. 21st April 1821, *sine prole*,—Elizabeth, b. 3d June 1760, and d. 6th Nov. 1827,—Charles, b. 21st Nov. 1761, d. June 1801,—William, b. 5th Aug. 1762, d. 22d May 1826,—John, b. 19th Dec. 1763, d. 10th May 1767, —Robert, b. 1766, and drowned in 1791,—Richard, b. 13th Aug. 1768,—Rachel, b. 10th Dec. 1769, who m. Horatio Ridout, of Anne Arundel Co., and left a son, John Ridout,—John, b. 28th Oct. 1772, d. Oct. 1788, and Howes Goldsborough, b. 18th Feb'y 1775, who m. Mary Rodgers.

ELIZABETH GOLDSBOROUGH, dau. of Hon. Robert and Sarah Yerbury Goldsborough, m. Dr. James Sykes, of Delaware, and had child., viz., James, b. in 1794,—William, b. 1798,—Alfred, b. 1801, and Anna Matilda Sykes, b. 1805, d. 1812.

CHARLES GOLDSBOROUGH, of Horn's Point, son of Hon. Robert and Sarah Yerbury Goldsborough, m. thrice. His 1st wife was Williamina Smith, dau. of Dr. William Smith, of Phila., and had child., viz., Robert, b. 1785, d. 1817,—William, b. 1787, d. 1812, and Sarah Yerbury Goldsborough, b. 1789, who m. Gov. Charles Goldsborough. His 2nd wife was Elizabeth Greenbury Goldsborough, dau. of John and Caroline Goldsborough, who d. 7th April 1797. His 3rd wife was Mrs. Anna McKeel Stevens, and had a son, Charles Goldsborough, of Lewistown, Delaware. She survived him, and m. Dr. Alward White, of Cambridge, Md., and had child., viz., John and Dr. Alward McKeel White.

REV. WILLIAM SMITH, D. D., was the last Principal of the celebrated Free School at Chestertown. He was afterwards the first Principal of Washington College, near Chestertown, and subsequently Provost of the University of Pennsylvania.

Washington College, the corner-stone of which was laid 15th of May 1783, had the honor, during the administration of Dr. Smith, of conferring the degree of L.L. D. upon George Washington, who, it is recorded, upon one of his visits to Chestertown, "by invitation, took the chair and presided at a meeting of the Visitors and Governors of the College."

ROBERT GOLDSBOROUGH, son of Charles and Williamina Smith Goldsborough, m. Mary Nixon, of Dover, Delaware. She survived him and m. Gardiner Bailey, of Cambridge.

WILLIAM GOLDSBOROUGH, son of Hon. Robert and Sarah Yerbury Goldsborough, m. 8th Nov. 1792, Sarah Worthington, dau. of Nicholas Worthington, of Anne Arundel, and in 1795 removed to Frederick Co. and purchased an estate called "Richfield." Several years before his death he resided in Frederick City, and d. 26th May 1826, in the 63rd year of his age. He had child., viz., William, b. 1793, d. 1813,—Nicholas Worthington, b. 1795,—Dr. Edward Yerbury, b. 5th Dec. 1797, d. 14th Nov. 1850,—Dr. Charles Henry, b. 14th Feb'y 1800, d. 17th Aug. 1862,—Dr. Leander W., b. 21st May 1804, and Catharine Goldsborough, b. 25th of March 1807, who m. 15th Nov. 1827, Thomas Duckett, of Prince George's, and had child., viz., Richard, and Allen Bowie Duckett.

DR. EDWARD YERBURY GOLDSBOROUGH, son of William and Sarah Worthington Goldsborough, m. 21st Nov. 1826, Margaret Schley, dau. of John and Mary Schley, and had child., viz., Mary Catharine, — William, b. 29th Nov. 1830, d. 14th May 1853,—Eliza Margaret, b. 25th Feb'y 1833, d. 25th Aug. 1834, — John, — Edward, b. 28th Feb'y 1833, d. 18th March 1839,—Edward Yerbury,—Robert Henry, and a 2nd Eliza Margaret Goldsborough, b. 10th April 1845, d. 15th Aug. 1845. Mrs. Margaret Schley Goldsborough d. 28th Dec. 1876, in the 73rd year of her age.

DR. JOHN GOLDSBOROUGH, son of Dr. Edward Yerbury and Margaret Schley Goldsborough, m. 8th Dec. 1863, Julianna Strider, and had child., viz., John Schley and Edward Yerbury, *twins*, and Julianna Goldsborough.

EDWARD YERBURY GOLDSBOROUGH, U. S. Marshal (1876) in Baltimore, son of Dr. Edward Yerbury and Margaret Schley Goldsborough, m. 10th June 1874, Amy Ralston Auld (a grand-niece of Hon. Salmon P. Chase, late U. S. Chief Justice), dau. of Robert and Jane Chase Auld, of Ohio.

DR. CHARLES HENRY GOLDSBOROUGH, son of William and Sarah Worthington Goldsborough, m. 24th of Nov. 1836, Amelia Poe, and had child., viz., Catharine Duckett, who m. 27th Dec. 1866, Professor Alfred M. Mayer, the distinguished Chemist, and d. 2nd May 1868, — Charles Worthington, — Sarah Worthington, b. 6th April 1846, d. 10th Dec. 1868,— Josephine (who m. 17th Jan'y 1871, Lewis Trail, and d. 17th Nov. 1871), and Amelia Goldsborough.

DR. CHARLES WORTHINGTON GOLDSBOROUGH, son of Dr. Charles Henry and Amelia Poe Goldsborough, m. 9th Nov. 1866, Henrietta Bedinger Lee, dau. of Edmond J. Lee, of Va., and had child., viz., Charles, — Edmond Lee, — Catharine Duckett,—Edward Gray, and Neilson Poe Goldsborough.

DR. LEANDER W. GOLDSBOROUGH, son of William and Sarah Worthington Goldsborough, m. 1830, Sarah Duncan, and had child., viz., Maj. William (C. S. A.),—Dr. Charles,—Leander, —Lewis,—Eugene, and Alice Goldsborough.

CATHARINE GOLDSBOROUGH, dau. of William and Sarah Worthington Goldsborough, m. 15th Nov. 1827, Thomas Duckett, of Prince George's Co., Md., and had child., viz., Sarah, — Richard, who m. ——— ———, and Allen Bowie Duckett.

DR. RICHARD GOLDSBOROUGH, son of Hon. Robert and Sarah Yerbury Goldsborough, m. Achsah Worthington, and had child., viz., Catharine, b. in 1794 (who m. James B. Patterson, and afterwards Sykes R. Robinson, of Winchester, Va.), —Richard Yerbury, b. 1796,—Robert, b. 1797, d. 1809,— Sarah, b. 1799, who m. Ephraim Gaither, of Montgomery Co., —Nicholas, b. 1800, who m. Jane Edelin,—Brice John, b. 1803 (who m. Leah Goldsborough, dau. of James Goldsborough, and had 2 sons, Richard and Worthington),—Elizabeth, b. 1805,— Charles and William, *twins*, b. 1808, and Matilda Goldsborough.

CHARLES GOLDSBOROUGH, of Horn's Point, son of Charles and his 2nd wife, Elizabeth Dickinson Goldsborough, m. Anna Maria Tilghman, dau. of William and Margaret Lloyd Tilghman, of Groces, and had child., viz., Charles b. 15th

July 1765, and William Tilghman Goldsborough, b. Dec. 1766, d. 1787, *sine prole.*

HON. CHARLES GOLDSBOROUGH (b. 15th July 1765, d. 13th Dec. 1834), of Hunting Creek, son of Charles and Anna Maria Tilghman Goldsborough, was Governor of Maryland in 1818, m. twice. He m. first, 22d of Sept. 1793, Elizabeth Goldsborough, dau. of Judge Robert Goldsborough, of Myrtle Grove, Talbot County, Md., and had child., viz., Elizabeth Greenbury, b. 20th Aug. 1794, and Anna Maria Sarah Goldsborough, b. 15th Nov. 1796 (who m. 10th Jan'y 1814, William Henry Fitzhugh, of Va). He m. a 2nd time, 22d of May 1804, Sarah Yerbury Goldsborough, dau. of Charles Goldsborough, of Horn's Point, the eldest son of Charles Goldsborough, of Cambridge.

Gov. Charles Goldsborough and his 2nd wife, Sarah Yerbury Goldsborough, had child., viz., Charles Yerbury, b. Feb'y 1805, d. in 1807,—John McDowell, b. 22d Aug. 1806, d. 24th Aug. 1807,—William Tilghman, b. 5th of March 1808, d. 23d of Jan'y 1876,—George Washington, b. 20th Jan'y 1810, d. 27th Sept. 1812,—Charles McDowell, b. 27th Oct. 1811, d. 24th May 1815,—Williamina Elizabeth Cadwalader, b. 30th of March 1813, d. 9th of Feb'y 1865,—Robert Henry, b. 31st Dec. 1814, d. 9th Sept. 1819,—Mary Tilghman,—William Henry Fitzhugh, b. 15th of Aug. 1818, d. 9th of Oct. 1819,—Caroline,—Robert Fitzhugh, b. 28th of Aug. 1822, d. 20th Sept. 1824,—Sarah Yerbury, b. 31st Aug. 1824, d. 26th July 1825,—Richard Tilghman,—Henrietta Maria, b. 29th of Aug. 1828, d., and Charles Fitzhugh Goldsborough.

ELIZABETH GREENBURY GOLDSBOROUGH, dau. of Gov'r. Charles and his 1st wife, m. 30th of Oct. 1828, Hon. John Leeds Kerr, of Easton, Md. She d. in Baltimore in 1870, at the advanced age of 80 years. He d. in Feb'y 1844. They had child., viz., Elizabeth Goldsborough,—Charles Goldsborough, and Edward Leeds Kerr.

HON. CHARLES GOLDSBOROUGH KERR, of Baltimore, son of Hon. John Leeds and Elizabeth Greenbury Goldsborough Kerr, with whom the writer was a fellow student at Dane Hall, University of Cambridge, Massachusetts, in 1853, m. 25th of April 1867, Ella Johnson, dau. of Hon. Reverdy Johnson, the eminent lawyer and distinguished Statesman and Diplomatist, and had child., viz., Mary Bowie Kerr,—Ella Johnson Kerr, and Charles Goldsborough Kerr.

HON. REVERDY JOHNSON, of Baltimore, b. at Annapolis 21st of May 1796, was the son of Chancellor John Johnson.

His first public position was Deputy of the Attorney General in Prince George's Co., Md. In Nov. 1817, he removed to Baltimore. In 1821 he was elected to the Senate of Maryland, and, serving with distinction and ability, was reëlected. In 1845 he was sent to the United States Senate, but resigned in 1849 to accept the position of Attorney General, tendered him by President Taylor. In the Winter of 1860–61 he was a member of the Peace Convention. In 1861 he again was in the State Senate, from Baltimore County; and in the Winter of 1862–63 was elected a second time to the Senate of the United States. In 1868 he was appointed Minister to the Court of St. James, and was so warmly received and entertained by the English people of all ranks and conditions that Lord Clarendon, writing to a friend in America, said that "Mr. Johnson was the only Diplomatic Representative that had ever brought out the true friendly feeling of the British people for those of the United States."

Hon. Reverdy Johnson died suddenly, 10th of Feb'y 1876, from the effects of an accidental fall, received while walking, in the dusk of evening, in the grounds of the Executive Mansion at Annapolis.

The sad event was communicated to the Legislature of Maryland, then in session, by the Governor, with the following special message:

STATE OF MARYLAND, EXECUTIVE DEPARTMENT,
ANNAPOLIS, MD., Feb'y 11.

Gentlemen of the Senate and House of Delegates:

The melancholy duty devolves on me of informing you, by an official communication, of the death of the Hon. Reverdy Johnson. This sad event occurred last evening at the Executive Mansion from an unaccountable and unwitnessed accident. The distinguished abilities of Mr. Johnson as a jurist and statesman have long made him the pride of his native State. And on this most sad occasion the General Assembly of Maryland may deem it proper to pay to his memory that tribute of respect to which his faithful services to his State and his country so justly entitle him.

JOHN LEE CARROLL.

Hon. John Leeds Kerr, father of Hon. Charles Goldsborough Kerr, was the son of David Kerr, who came from Scotland, while yet a young man, and settled first in Falmouth,

Va., on the Rappahannock River. From thence he came to Maryland and m. in Annapolis, Mrs. Hammond, who soon d., leaving no child. He subsequently settled in Talbot County, Md., and m. Rachel Leeds Bozman, a sister of John Leeds Bozman, the Historian of Maryland, and had several child., one of whom was the Hon. John Leeds Kerr. David Kerr held many prominent positions and was a member of the Maryland Legislature in 1793.

HON. JOHN LEEDS KERR represented his county in the House of Delegates and Senate of Maryland, was three times in the House of Representatives, and a member of the United States Senate from the 5th of Jan'y 1841, to the 4th of March 1843. His 1st wife (8th April 1801) was Sarah Hollyday Chamberlaine, dau. of Samuel and Henrietta Maria Hollyday Chamberlaine, of Talbot, and had child., John Bozman,—Rev. Samuel C.,—David,—Sophia, who m. Mr. Leigh,—Henrietta Maria, who m. General Tench Tilghman, and Rachel Ann Kerr, who m. William H. Done. His 2nd wife was Elizabeth Greenbury Goldsborough.

HON. WILLIAM TILGHMAN GOLDSBOROUGH (b. 5th March 1808, d. 23rd Jan'y 1876), of Horn's Point, Dorchester Co., son of Gov. Charles and Sarah Yerbury Goldsborough, m. 26th of Oct. 1837, Mary Ellen Lloyd, dau. of Col. Edward Lloyd, of Wye House, Talbot, and Sarah Scott Murray Lloyd, and had child., viz., Charles,—William Tilghman,—Edward Lloyd, b. 15th Dec. 1843, d. 29th March 1861,—Ellen Lloyd,—Fitzhugh,—Nannie Lloyd,—Sally Murray, b. 27th Jan'y 1855, d. 6th Dec. 1856,—Richard Tilghman,—Alice Lloyd, and Mary Lee Goldsborough.

HON. WILLIAM TILGHMAN GOLDSBOROUGH, d. at his late residence, No. 130 Cathedral street, Baltimore, Sunday, 23d Jan'y 1876, and was buried (11 o'clock, 26th of Jan'y 1876) in Greenmount Cemetery.

He was physically a splendid specimen of a man, 6 feet 4 inches in height, and in other respects a superb type of the gentry of the Eastern Shore of Maryland of the olden time. He early distinguished himself in the Senate of Maryland. In 1847 he was the candidate of the Whig party for Governor, but was defeated, by a small majority, by Hon. Philip Francis Thomas. In 1850 he was again elected to the State Senate. In 1860–61 he was a member of the Peace Convention which met in Washington. In 1867 he represented his county in the Constitutional Convention of Maryland. As a Director of the Chesapeake and Ohio Canal Co. he was identified with the great public works of the State.

CHARLES GOLDSBOROUGH, son of Hon. William Tilghman and Mary Ellen Lloyd Goldsborough, m. 7th of Nov. 1865, Mary C. Galt, of Va., and had child., viz., Mary C.,—Ellen Lloyd,—Charles,—William Fitzhugh, and Robert Galt Goldsborough.

WILLIAMINA ELIZABETH CADWALADER GOLDSBOROUGH, dau. of Gov. Charles and Sarah Yerbury Goldsborough, m. June 1837, William Laird, and had child., viz., Winder, b. in Oct. 1838, who d. a soldier in the Confederate Army,—William Henry, who m. Miss Packard,—Martha, who m. Washington Elwell Goldsborough, and Philip Laird.

MARY TILGHMAN GOLDSBOROUGH, dau. of Gov. Charles and Sarah Yerbury Goldsborough, m. William Goldsborough, of Myrtle Grove, and had child., viz., Susan,—Robert,—William,—Charles, and Mary Goldsborough.

CAROLINE GOLDSBOROUGH, dau. of Gov. Charles and Sarah Yerbury Goldsborough, m. Philip Pendleton Dandridge, of Virginia, and had child., viz., Mary Lee,—Nannie,—Lilly,—Philip,—Charles,—William, and Caroline Dandridge.

HENRIETTA MARIA GOLDSBOROUGH, dau. of Gov. Charles and Sarah Yerbury Goldsborough, m. Daniel Henry, of Dorchester County.

RICHARD TILGHMAN GOLDSBOROUGH, son of Gov. Charles and Sarah Yerbury Goldsborough, m. Mary Henry, sister of Daniel Henry.

CHARLES FITZHUGH GOLDSBOROUGH, son of Gov. Charles and Sarah Yerbury Goldsborough, m. Charlotte Henry, sister of Daniel Henry, and had child., viz., Charlotte,—Charles,—Daniel, and Sterling Goldsborough.

SEC. 98, Q. WILLIAM GOLDSBOROUGH, son of Robert and Elizabeth Greenbury Goldsborough, m. 1734, Elizabeth Robins, dau. of Thomas Robins, who d. 29th Dec. 1721, the son of George Robins, who d. 12th May 1677.

[The last named George Robins came to America and settled in Talbot Co., Md., in 1670, upon a tract of one thousand acres of land originally patented to Job Nutt, called "Job's Content," adjacent to Capt. Miles Cook's patent for "Cook's Hope." This homestead was subsequently called "Peach-Blossom," because of the number of peach and other trees planted there by George Robins, son of Thomas, who being sent to England, for commercial training, formed a life-long friendship with Peter Collison, then, world-renowned as a naturalist and botanist. Many fruits and flowers were here first introduced into America, having been sent by Collison, who procured them from Persia and the East. The peach tree was cultivated in Kent County, Md., as early as 1650 —see page 20.]

William and Elizabeth Robins Goldsborough had child., viz., Greenbury,—Henrietta Maria,—William, and Elizabeth Goldsborough, b. 28th July 1743. William Goldsborough m. again 2nd Sept. 1747, Mrs. Henrietta Maria Tilghman Robins, widow of George Robins, who d. 6th Dec. 1742. She was b. 18th Aug. 1707, the dau. of Richard Tilghman, 2d of the Hermitage, d. 7th Nov. 1771,—William Goldsborough, d. 1760.

SEC. 98, R. JOHN GOLDSBOROUGH, of Four Square, Talbot, son of Robert and Elizabeth Greenbury Goldsborough, m. 31st Oct. 1733, Ann Turbutt, b. 29th April 1715, dau. of Foster Turbutt and Bridget, his wife. Foster Turbutt, for many years Clerk of Talbot Co., b. 13th Nov. 1679, was the son of Michael Turbutt and Sarah, his wife. Michael Turbutt was one of the Justices of Talbot in 1688, and d. in 1696. Foster Turbutt d. 21st Feb'y 1720. Bridget Turbutt d. 18th Oct. 1719.

John and Ann Turbutt Goldsborough had child., viz., Elizabeth, b. 22d Jan'y 1735,—Robert, b. 7th Feb'y 1736, d. 2d Jan'y 1770,—John, b. 26th March 1740, d. 18th Nov. 1803,—Greenbury, b. 22d April 1742, d. 19th Feb'y 1829,—Charles, b. 16th June 1744, m. Ann Tilghman, dau. of Edward Tilghman, and was accidentally killed by a gun in 1774,—Anne, b. 2d Jan'y 1751, m. Vincent Loockerman, of Dover, Delaware, and d. 15th May 1781, leaving a dau., Susan Hall Loockerman, who m. Mr. Stoops,—Henrietta Maria, b. 6th Dec. 1752,—Mary, b. 19th Oct. 1755, d. 20th March 1796, and Capt. William Goldsborough, of the Revolutionary Army, who was b. 2d June 1759, and d. 22d Dec. 1794, *sine prole.* Mrs. Ann Turbutt Goldsborough d. 11th Nov. 1766, aged 51 years.

John Goldsborough m. 2ndly Mrs. Mary Skinner Loockerman, widow of John, son of Jacob Loockerman, who d. in 1732, and had 2 child., viz., Anna, who m. Arthur Emory, of Queen Anne's Co., and left a dau., Mary Emory, who m. Perry Wilmer,—and Robert Goldsborough.

ELIZABETH GOLDSBOROUGH, dau. of John and Ann Turbutt Goldsborough, m. 3 times. Her 1st husband was John Campbell, and had child., viz., Ann, d. young, and Margaret Campbell. Her 2nd husband was Benton Staunton, of Caroline Co. Her 3rd husband was Richard Kennard, who d. 1796. She d. 20th March 1796.

MARGARET CAMPBELL, dau. of John and Elizabeth Goldsborough Campbell, m. Hon. John Henry, Governor of Maryland in 1797, and d. 1789, leaving two sons, John Campbell Henry, who m. Miss Steele,—and Francis Jenkins Henry.

JOHN GOLDSBOROUGH, of Four Square, son of John and Ann Turbutt Goldsborough, m. 26th Oct. 1762, Caroline Goldsborough, dau. of Howes and Rosannah Piper Goldsborough, and had child., viz., John, b. 2d May 1767, d. 12th Aug. 1840,—Howes, b. 20th Nov. 1771, d. 20th Oct. 1804,—Robert, b. 5th April 1775, who m. Sarah Potter, of Phila., and d. 16th April 1811,—Elizabeth Greenbury, b. 5th April 1775, who m. Charles, son of Hon. Robert and Sarah Yerbury Goldsborough, and d. 7th April 1797,—Charles Washington, b. 18th April 1777, d. 14th Dec. 1843,—Horatio, b. 26th Dec. 1778, d. 16th Dec. 1812, and Matthew and Samuel Goldsborough, *twins*, b. 1st June 1784, d. in infancy. John Goldsborough was Deputy Commissary of Dorchester County under the Provincial Government, and after the Revolution, was for many years Register of Wills.

JOHN GOLDSBOROUGH, son of John and Caroline Goldsborough, of Four Square, m. 24th Jan'y 1797, Anna Maria Chamberlaine, and had child., viz., John, b. 1797,—Henrietta Maria, b. 16th Oct. 1798, d. 13th Oct. 1799,—John Chamberlaine, b. 22nd Sept. 1800,—a 2nd Henrietta Maria, b. 2nd Nov. 1805, d. 17th Aug. 1826,—Samuel Chamberlaine, b. 1807, d. 27th Sept. 1828,—Elizabeth Greenbury, b. 1st Jan'y 1803, d. 1st Dec. 1860,—Robert Lloyd, b. 26th Aug. 1810,—James Kemp, b. 14th Feb'y 1813, drowned in Treadavon Creek, and buried 21st April 1864,—Marion Caroline, b. 31st Jan'y 1815, and Henry Hollyday Goldsborough, b. 22d June 1817. He m. 2ndly, 28th Nov. 1837, Mrs. Margaret Goldsborough, the widow and 4th wife of Henry, son of Howes and Rebecca Goldsborough.

Samuel Chamberlaine, who m. 15th Jan'y 1772, Henrietta Maria Hollyday, the father of Anna Maria Chamberlaine, above mentioned, was b. 23d Aug. 1742, the son of Samuel Chamberlaine, of Plain Dealing, Talbot Co., who was b. 17th May 1697, settled at Oxford, Talbot, 1714, and was the son of Thomas Chamberlaine, b. 1658, and his 1st wife, Ann Penketh, who had five child., viz., Thomas,—John,—Samuel,—Mary, and Esther Chamberlaine.

Samuel Chamberlaine, of Plain Dealing, m. twice. His first wife, Mary Ungle, dau. of Robert Ungle, who d. *sine prole*, and he m. 22d Jan'y 1729, Henrietta Maria Lloyd, dau. of Col. James Lloyd and Ann Grundy, dau. of Robert Grundy. He d. 30th April 1773, and his wife d. 29th March 1748. They had child., viz., Thomas Chamberlaine, b. 25th May 1731, who m. 1st Oct. 1761, Susannah Robins, dau. of George Robins and Henrietta Maria Tilghman,—James Lloyd Chamberlaine, b. 11th Oct. 1732, who m. 16th April 1757, Henrietta Maria Robins, a sister of his brother Thomas' wife,—Ann Chamberlaine, b. 23d Oct. 1734, who m. Richard Tilghman Earle, of Queen Anne's,—Henrietta Maria Chamberlaine, b. 21st March 1736, d. 17th May 1737,—a 2nd Henrietta Maria, b. 28th Oct. 1739, who m. 21st May 1760, William Nicols,—Samuel Chamberlaine, b. 23d Aug. 1742, and Robert Lloyd Chamberlaine, b. 14th Sept. 1745, d. 27th July 1756.

Samuel Chamberlaine, son of Samuel and Henrietta Maria Lloyd Chamberlaine, m. 15th Jan'y 1772, Henrietta Maria Hollyday, dau. of Henry and Anna Maria Robins Hollyday; and had child., viz., Anna Maria, who m. 24th Jan'y 1797, John Goldsborough, of Easton,—Lloyd,—May, —Sarah Hollyday, who m. Hon. John Leeds Kerr, on the 8th April 1801,—Harriet Rebecca, who m. Hon. Levin Gale, of Cecil Co.,—Samuel,—James Lloyd, of "Bondfield," who m. Anna Maria Hammond, dau. of Nicholas Hammond, a distinguished lawyer of Talbot Co., and his wife, Rebecca Hollyday, dau. of Henry and Anna Maria Robins Hollyday, and Henry Chamberlaine, of "Richmond Hill," who m. Henrietta Gale, dau. of Hon. George Gale, who was a member of the 1st Congress held under the Constitution of the United States. Mr. Henry Chamberlaine, a truly Christian gentleman, departed this life, on the 30th Dec. 30th 1863, while on a visit to his nephew, James Lloyd Chamberlaine, of Island Creek Neck, in Talbot, respected and lamented by all who knew him.

John Chamberlaine Goldsborough, son of John and Anna Maria Chamberlaine Goldsborough, m. 3d April 1827, Eliza Bishop Emory, dau. of Charles and Francis Bishop Emory. Francis Bishop Emory was the dau. of William Bishop, of Greenbury's Point Farm, near Annapolis. They had child., viz., John,—Charles Emory,—Henrietta Maria, b. 7th March 1833, d. 11th April 1847,—Henry Chamberlaine,

—Samuel Chamberlaine, b. 15th June 1839, d. 2d July 1844, and Francis Emory Goldsborough, b. 5th July 1843.

ROBERT LLOYD GOLDSBOROUGH, son of John and Anna Maria Chamberlaine Goldsborough, m. Oct. 1836, Fanny Miller, dau. of Alexander Miller, of Phila., and had child., viz., Alexander Miller,—John,—Alfred,—William Miller, and Henry Chamberlaine Goldsborough.

MARION CAROLINE GOLDSBOROUGH, dau. of John and Anna Maria Chamberlaine Goldsborough, m. 6th June 1837, Dr. Alward McKeel White (son of Alward White and Mrs. Anna McKeel Goldsborough White, who was the widow and 3rd wife of Charles Goldsborough, of Horn's Point, whose maiden name was Anna McKeel, and whose 1st husband was John Stevens, and was the 2nd wife of Dr. Alward McKeel White; his 1st wife was ——— Warfield, dau. of Rev. Mr. Lot Warfield, of Easton), and had child., viz., Anna Maria, b. 31st March 1838, d. 29th Sept. 1839,—Henrietta Maria, who m. Henry Chamberlaine,—Sally,—John Goldsborough, —Alward,—Anna Maria,—Fanny, and Charles White.

HON. HENRY HOLLYDAY GOLDSBOROUGH, son of John and Anna Maria Chamberlaine Goldsborough, has been a prominent politician. In 1841 and 1845 he was the defeated Whig candidate for the Legislature. In 1852 he was defeated as one of the Electoral Ticket for Scott and Graham. In 1855 he was the Democratic candidate for Commissioner of Public Works, and was defeated. In 1856 he was elected one of the Democratic Electors for Buchanan and Breckenridge. In 1857 he was elected, by the Democrats, to the House of Delegates of Md., and, in 1859, by the same party, to the Senate of Md., and in 1861 was made President of that honorable body. In 1862 he was Commandant of the Military Post near Easton, Md., with the rank of Brigadier General, and had command of the militia of the Eastern Shore of Md., called into the service of the United States. In 1863 he was Comptroller of the Treasury of Md. In 1864 he was President of the Convention which formed a Constitution for the State, and was elected Elector at Large for Lincoln and Johnson; and, in the same year, was made Judge (*vice* Judge Carmichael, forcibly and brutally removed by the military), of the 11th Judicial Circuit, composed of the Counties of Talbot and Caroline, and served three years. In 1867 he was the defeated candidate, of the Union Party, for Attorney General; and, in 1868, was a defeated Elector for Grant and Colfax. In 1874 he was appointed U. S. Appraiser of

Merchandise, at and for the Port of Baltimore, which position he now (1876) holds.

He m. 25th Jan'y 1853, Anna Maria Kennard, dau. of Samuel Thomas and Elizabeth Thomas Kennard (Elizabeth Thomas Kennard was the dau. of William Dawson Thomas), and had child., viz., Henry Hollyday, b. 8th Nov. 1853, d. 20th July 1854,—Samuel Kennard, b. 31st Oct. 1855, d. 30th July 1856,—Louis Piper,—Anna Maria,—Elizabeth Kennard,—Mary Hammond,—Charles Carroll, and John Whittingham Goldsborough, b. 15th July 1868, d. 31st July 1868. His 1st wife d. 31st July 1868, and he m. a 2nd time, 1st June 1871, Kate Haly Caldwell, of Lynn, Massachusetts, dau. of Daniel and Mary Lord Caldwell, (Mary Lord Caldwell was the dau. of Capt. John Lord and his wife, Lucy Perkins, of Ipswich, Mass.), and had child., viz., Kate,—Henry Caldwell, b. 3d Aug. 1873, d. 30th Aug. 1874, and Anita Goldsborough.

Howes Goldsborough, son of John and Caroline Goldsborough, m. Mary McCallmont, of New Castle, Delaware, who was b. 1774, and d. 14th March 1821, and had child., viz., Francis McCallmont, d.,—Robert, d.,—Ann Caroline (who m. May 1823, Dr. Nicholas Hammond, son of Nicholas and Rebecca Hammond, d. leaving child., viz., Nicholas,—Charles,—James, and Mary G. Hammond), and Charles Howes Goldsborough.

Charles Washington Goldsborough, son of John and Caroline Goldsborough, m. 28th Aug. 1802, Catharine Roberts, of Phila., and had child., viz., Caroline, b. 9th Jan'y 1804,—Louis Malesherbes, b. 18th Feb'y 1805,—Charles Henry, b. 22d Dec. 1806,—John Roberts, b. 2d July 1809, who m. Mary Pennington, of Phila., and Hugh Allen Goldsborough, b. 17th Aug. 1813, who m. Mrs. Ellen K. Leslie.

Caroline Goldsborough, dau. of Charles Washington and Catharine Roberts Goldsborough, m. 6th Oct. 1825, John Lane Gardner, U. S. A., and had child., viz., Elizabeth Greenbury,—Caroline Goldsborough,—Catharine Francis,—and Henry W. Gardner.

Admiral Malesherbes Goldsborough, U. S. N., son of Charles Washington and Catharine Roberts Goldsborough, m. 1st Nov. 1831, Elizabeth G. Wirt, dau. of Hon. William and Elizabeth Wirt, and had child., viz., William Wirt,—Louis Malesherbes, and Elizabeth Wirt Goldsborough.

Henrietta Maria Goldsborough, dau. of John and Ann Turbutt Goldsborough, m. Philip Francis, son of Tench Francis (Clerk of Talbot County from 1726 to 1734) and

Elizabeth Turbutt, and had child., viz., John Francis, who was lost at sea, and Maria Francis.

Foster Turbutt and, Bridget, his wife had child., viz , Mary, b. 15th Jan'y 1703,—Sarah, b. 2nd Dec. 1706, who m. 25th Jan'y, Nicholas Goldsborough, — Elizabeth, b. 17th March 1708, who m. 29th Dec. 1724, Tench Francis,—Mary Anne, b. 13th July 1711, who m. 9th Feb'y 1730, John Robins, and afterwards Robert Goldsborough,—Mary Turbutt, b. 9th Sept. 1713, who m. Edward Tilghman,—Ann, b. 29th April 1715, who m. 31st Oct. 1733, John Goldsborough,—Rachel Turbutt, b. 26th Sept. 1718, who m. 8th May 1735, Thomas Bullen.

MARIA FRANCIS, dau. of Philip and Henrietta Maria Goldsborough Francis, m. in 1809, Dr. Tristram Thomas, and had child., viz., Philip Francis, b. 24th Sept. 1810,—Charles, b. 30th Nov. 1812,—Henrietta Maria, b. 8th July 1815,—Ellen Francis, b. 25th May 1817,—Mary Moore, and Ann Thomas.

HON. PHILIP FRANCIS THOMAS, son of Dr. Tristram and Maria Francis Thomas, succeeded Hon. Thomas G. Pratt as Governor of Maryland in 1847, and was Secretary of the Treasury in the Administration of President Buchanan.

MARY GOLDSBOROUGH, dau. of John and Ann Turbutt Goldsborough, m. Jan'y 1775, Benedict Brice, son of John and Sarah Frisby Brice, and had a dau. Sarah Goldsborough Brice, b. 10th Aug. 1776, who m. Andrew Price. Benedict Brice d. 1786, and she m. Dr. James Cooke, d. 20th March 1796, leaving two child., viz., Susan Loockerman Cooke, b. 28th Dec. 1790, and Mary Elizabeth Cooke, b. 1st March 1793. Dr. James Cooke d. 1794.

SUSAN LOOCKERMAN COOKE, dau. of Dr. James and Mary Goldsborough Brice Cooke, m. Greenbury Turbutt, and had child., viz., James Edward,--Anna Maria, and Samuel Turbutt.

MARY ELIZABETH COOKE, dau. of Dr. James and Mary Goldsborough Brice Cooke, m. Jan'y 1828, Jeremiah Mullikin, and had a son, Arthur Cooke Mullikin.

DR. ROBERT GOLDSBOROUGH, of Centreville, Queen Anne's Co., Md., son of John and Mary Skinner Loockerman Goldsborough, m. Mrs. Henrietta Nicholson Bracco, widow of Dr. John Bracco, dau. of Joseph and Mary Nicholson, of Kent, and left one son, Robert Goldsborough.

ROBERT GOLDSBOROUGH, son of Dr. Robert and Henrietta Nicholson Bracco Goldsborough, m. Eleanora Dall Lux, dau. of Darby and Mary Lux, and had child., viz., Robert,—John, —Joseph Nicholson,—Henrietta, who m. Philemon B. Hopper,—Ellen Ridgely,—Edward Ridgely,—Mary Nicholson,—

Jacob Loockerman,—William Lux,—Thomas Henry,—Mary Rebecca,—Anna Maria, and Francis Spencer Goldsborough.

SEC. 98, S. HOWES GOLDSBOROUGH, son of Robert and Elizabeth Greenbury Goldsborough, m. Rosannah Piper, dau. of a Protestant Episcopal clergyman, the Rev. Michael Piper and Rosannah B. Piper, and had a dau., Caroline Goldsborough, who m. 26th Oct. 1762, her cousin, John Goldsborough, son of John and Ann Turbutt Goldsborough, and d. 10th March 1816. Howes Goldsborough d. 30th March 1746. His widow, Rosannah Piper Goldsborough, m. in 1747, James Auld. In 1765 they removed to Halifax, in Halifax Co., North Carolina. They had child., viz., James Auld, b. 14th Oct. 1747, d. 30th June 1751,—Anne Auld, b. 26th Dec. 1749, d. unm. 1st March 1822,—John Auld, b. 30th May 1752 (who m. 17th Aug. 1775, Elizabeth Scurlock, d. 28th Dec. 1796, and had eight child., viz., 1st Elizabeth, b. 29th May 1776, 2d James Sherwood, b. 15th Jan'y 1778, d. in Alabama in 1827, 3d Henry W., b. in 1781, 4th Elizabeth, b. 1st March 1783, m. James Graves, and d. in 1803, 5th Sarah, b. in 1785, d. in 1788, 6th Charles, b. 13th Dec. 1787, d. 30th Jan'y 1797, 7th Alexander, b. 16th Sept. 1789, d. 1822, and 8th Sarah Scurlock, b. 25th Dec. 1792, m. May 1811, Dr. James Bogle),—Rosannah Auld, b. 2d Dec. 1754 (who m. 31st July 1776, an Englishman, Henry William Harrington, of South Carolina, d. 13th Oct. 1828, and had nine child., viz., 1st Rosannah, b. 2d Feb'y 1778, m. 21st Jan'y 1800, Robert Troy, and d. 30th March 1838, 2d Henrietta, b. 29th Oct. 1779, d. 16th Sept. 1780, 3d Henry W., b. 14th March 1782, d. 23d March 1792, 4th James Auld, b. 11th Aug. 1785, m. 28th Dec. 1808, Eleanor Willson, dau. of John Willson, she d. 12th Sept. 1843, he d. 21st March 1834, 5th Henrietta, b. 24th Jan'y 1788, d. 2d Oct. 1791, 6th Michael, b. 5th Dec. 1790, d. 43th Jan'y 1794, 7th Henry Williams, b. 5th July 1793, 8th Harriett, b. 22d Nov. 1795, m. 15th Feb'y 1815, Beld William String, killed in a duel 27th May 1815, and 9th Caroline Harrington, b. 8th Nov. 1798, m. 2nd Dec. 1821, Otho Chambers, and d. 10th April 1829),—Michael Auld, b. 3d March 1757, d. 18th Sept. 1788 (who m. Sidney Fields, and left a son, John Fields Auld, who m. Mary Jackson, and had child., viz., Rosamond, Elizabeth, Michael, James, Susan, and Sidney Auld),—Mary Auld, b. 14th Oct. 1761, d. 25th Oct. 1837 (who m. twice, 1st 22d May 1794, Hartwell Ayer, and had two child., viz., Michael, b. in 1795, d. 1796, and Henry William Ayer, b. 6th May 1797, d. 4th Aug. 1839,

2ndly James Blakeney),—Elizabeth Auld, b. 11th Nov. 1764, d. 30th Dec. 1847, and James Auld, b. in North Carolina, 30th Nov. 1766, and d. 21st Jan'y 1770. All the child. of James and Rosannah Piper Goldsborough Auld except the last were born in Dorchester County.

Sec. 98, T. Nicholas Goldsborough, son of Nicholas and Margaret Howes Goldsborough, was Deputy Sheriff of Talbot County, 1689, under Samuel Withers, and was a Justice of the County Court for several years prior to his death in 1705. His 1st wife, Ann Goldsborough, left three child., viz., Nicholas, b. 1687, d. Sept. 1766,—Rachel, who m. 30th March 1712, Samuel Turbutt,—and Robert Goldsborough. His 2nd wife, Elizabeth, in her will dated 6th Dec. 1708, mentions *her* two daus., Mary and Elizabeth, who appear to have been the child. of a former husband.

Nicholas Goldsborough, son of Nicholas and Ann Goldsborough, m. 25th Jan'y 1721, Mrs. Sarah Jolly Turbutt, widow of Samuel Turbutt and dau. of Peter Jolly, and had child., viz., Ann, b. 8th Feb. 1722, who m. Edward Oldham, son of John Oldham, who was the grandfather of the late Gen. Daniel Martin and the late Edward Martin,—Sarah, b. 26th Dec. 1724, m. 6th Jan'y 1742, Standley Robins, who d. 1749, leaving a son, Standley Robins, who m. Mary Greene,—Nicholas, b. 3rd July 1726,—Thomas, b. 24th Feb'y 1728, d. March 1793,—Racbel,—Robert,—Foster,—Elizabeth,—Bridget,—and Mary Goldsborough, b. 1st May 1741, d. 11th Oct. 1812.

Nicholas Goldsborough, son of Nicholas and Sarah Jolly Turbutt Goldsborough, m. Mary Thomas (dau. of William Thomas and Elizabeth Allen, who were m. 11th May 1732), d. 31st May 1777, and had child, viz., Nicholas, b. 25th Feb'y 1759, who m. in 1787, Sarah Harrison, and d. 6th May 1788, leaving a son, Col. Nicholas Goldsborough, of Otwell, b. 30th June 1787, m. 25th April 1801, Elizabeth Tench Tilghman, dau. of Col. Tench Tilghman,—James,—Elizabeth, who m. Thomas Coward,—Mary, who d. unm. 1821,—and Anna Goldsborough, who m. 25th Feb'y 1765, and became the 2nd wife of John Singleton, whose 1st wife was Bridget Goldsborough. John Singleton d. 15th March 1819.

Col. Nicholas Goldsborough, of Otwell, Talbot, son of Nicholas and Mary Thomas Goldsborough, m. 25th April 1801, Elizabeth Tench Tilghman, dau. of Col. Tench Tilghman (see Tilghman), and had child., viz., Matthew Tilghman (who m. Eleanor Sarah Tilghman, dau. of Edward and Anna Maria Tilghman),—James Nicholas,—Tench,—Richard Henry,—

Ann Margaretta (who m. Henry Hollyday),—Anna Maria,—Sally,—Clara (who m. Dr. John Charles Earle), and Mary Goldsborough.

JAMES GOLDSBOROUGH, son of Nicholas and Mary Thomas Goldsborough, lived at a place called "Boston," in Talbot. His 1st wife was Miss Elbert. He m. 2ndly, 20th June 1789, Ann Martin, dau. of Thomas and Mary Ennalls Martin, and had child., viz., Mary, b. 27th June 1790, d. 3rd Sept. 1828,—Jane, b. 1st Aug. 1799, who m. Nicholas Thomas, and d. in May 1856,—Ann, b. 17th Feb'y 1804, d. 15th May 1856,—Leah, b. 26th June 1806, who m. Brice John Goldsborough,—Martin, b. 20th Jan'y 1808, who m. Ann Hayward, of Cambridge, Md.,—Elizabeth, b. 5th June 1812, who m. Wm. F. Rudestein,—and Tench Goldsborough. His 3rd wife was Margaret Patterson, and d. 1st March 1827.

THOMAS GOLDSBOROUGH, son of Nicholas and Sarah Jolly Turbutt Goldsborough, m. Catharine Fauntleroy, of Va., a niece of Genl. George Washington, and had child., viz., Thomas, who m. 2d Oct. 1801, Maria Thomas, dau. of Hon. James Thomas, of Annapolis,—Sarah Fauntleroy, who m. 1808, Dr. John Barnett,—Griffin Goldsborough, and Catharine Goldsborough, who m. 3d June 1798, Dr. Nathaniel Potter, of Baltimore. Thomas Goldsborough d. March 1793.

RACHEL GOLDSBOROUGH, dau. of Nicholas and Sarah Jolly Turbutt Goldsborough, m. 4th May 1768, the Rev. John Barclay, Rector of Saint Peter's Church, Talbot, who d. 13th Sept. 1772, the son of David and Christiana Barclay, of Kingcaird County, Scotland, and had a dau., Sarah Barclay, b. 1st Aug. 1771, who m. 23d Oct. 1788, Joseph Haskins, for many years Cashier of the Branch Bank, of the Farmers' Bank of Maryland, at Easton, Md., and had child., viz., Barclay Haskins, who m. in 1842, Elizabeth Robins Hayward, and 2ndly, Mary Trippe, dau. of Richard Trippe, of Baylies Neck,—and Anna Haskins, who m. John Bowie, and had child., viz., Joseph Haskins Bowie,—Louisa Emily Bowie, who m. Charles P. Craig,—Isabella Dallas Bowie, and Josephine Haskins Bowie, who m. in 1854, Thomas Smyth Hayward (she was his 2d wife), and had child., viz., Henrietta Maria Robins,—Elizabeth Haskins,—William,—Thomas Smyth, and Dallas Bowie Hayward.

Thomas Smyth Hayward was the son of Thomas Hayward, who was b. 8th Oct. 1771, and m. 12th May 1795, Mary Smyth, of Kent, d. July 1838, the son of William Hayward, of Locust Grove, in Baylies Neck, Talbot, who m. 29th Nov.

1760, Margaret Robins, dau. of George and Henrietta Maria Tilghman Robins. Joseph Haskins was the son of Capt. William Haskins and Sarah, dau. of Rev. Thomas and Elizabeth Airey.

FOSTER GOLDSBOROUGH, son of Nicholas and Sarah Jolly Turbutt Goldsborough, m. Rachel Bruff, of Caroline Co., and had a son, Foster Goldsborough, who m. Miss Potter, a sister of Col. William Potter, and had two child., viz., Thomas and Sophia Goldsborough.

BRIDGET GOLDSBOROUGH, dau. of Nicholas and Sarah Jolly Goldsborough, m. 14th Feb'y 1774 (and was the 1st wife of) John Singleton, who was b. 28th Dec. 1750, at Whitehaven, England.

SEC. 98, U. TENCH FRANCIS, the father of Anna Francis Tilghman, wife of James Tilghman, received a learned and legal education in England, and came to America about the year ——, and settled in Kent. After his marriage he removed to Phila. In 1744 he was appointed Attorney General and held that position till 1752. He was Recorder of the City of Philadelphia from 1750 to 1754. He was descended from

PHILIP FRANCIS, who was Mayor of Plymouth 1644, whose son, the Very Rev. John Francis, D. D., was Dean of Leighlin and sat in the Convention at Dublin in 1704. His son,

The Very REV. JOHN FRANCIS, Dean of Lismore in 1722, and Rector of St. Mary's Church, Dublin, m. Miss Tench, and had child., viz., Tench Francis,—Richard Francis, an eminent lawyer, author of "Maxims in Equity," and Rev. Philip Francis, D. D., whose son was the celebrated SIR PHILIP FRANCIS, K. G. C. B., the reputed author of *Junius*, b. at Dublin in 1740.

TENCH FRANCIS, eldest son of the Very Rev. John Francis and Miss Tench, while acting as the Attorney for Lord Baltimore in Kent, m. 29th Dec. 1724, Elizabeth Turbutt, b. 17th March 1708, dau. of Foster and Bridget Turbutt, and had child., viz., John b. 1726,—Anna, b. 1727, who m. James Tilghman (see TILGHMAN),—Mary, b. 1729,—Tench, b. 1730, d. 1800,—Elizabeth, b. 1733, d. 1800,—Margaret, b. 1735, d. 1794, who m. Chief Justice Edward Shippen, (see SHIPPEN),—Rachael, b. 1737, who m. 1st John Retfe, 2d Matthew Pearce,—Turbutt, b. 1740, d. 1797, and Philip Francis, b. 1748, who m. Henrietta Maria Goldsborough, dau. of John and Ann Turbutt Goldsborough. (See GOLDSBOROUGH.)

MARY FRANCIS, dau. of Tench Francis and Elizabeth Turbutt, m. William Coxe, of New Jersey, and had child., viz., Tench, who m. Miss McCall,—John, a Judge of the District Court,—William,—Daniel, who m. Margaret Burd, dau. of Maj. Edward Burd and Elizabeth Shippen,—Sarah, who m. Andrew Allen, and Rebecca Coxe, who m. Dr. William McIlvaine.

TENCH FRANCIS, son of Tench Francis and Elizabeth Turbutt, m. 1762, Anne, eldest dau. of Charles and Anne Willing, and had child., viz., John, b. 1763, who m. Abby, dau. of Hon. John Brown, and was the father of Gov. John Brown Francis, U. S. Senator from Rhode Island,—Thomas Willing, b. 1767 (who m. Dorothy, dau. of Hon. Thomas Willing, and had child., viz., Elizabeth, who m. Hon. John Brown Francis, and Anne Francis, who m. Hon. James A. Bayard, U. S. Senator from Delaware),—Sophia, who m. George Harrison, and d. 1851,—Charles, b. 1771, d. 1845 *sine prole*, and Elizabeth Powell Francis, b. 1777 (who m. 1806, Joshua Fisher, and had a son, J. Francis Fisher, who m. Elizabeth, dau. of Hon. Henry Middleton, Governor of South Carolina.

ELIZABETH FRANCIS, dau. of Tench Francis and Elizabeth Turbutt, m. John Lawrence, and had one dau., Elizabeth Lawrence, who m. James Allen, son of Chief Justice Allen, and had child., viz., James, — Anne Penn, who m. James Greenleaf,—Margaret, who m. Chief Justice Tilghman, and Mary Allen, who m. Harry Walter Livingstone, of Livingstone's Manor, New York.

COL. TURBUTT FRANCIS, son of Tench Francis and Elizabeth Turbutt, was an officer in the British Continental Army, m. Rebecca, the only dau. of Samuel Mifflin, and had child., viz., Tench, — Samuel, who took the name of his grandfather Mifflin, and m. Elizabeth Davis, and Rebecca Francis, who m. Matthias Harrison, and had a dau. Rebecca, who m. James McMurtree.

1675–'76.

SEC. 99. At a Court holden for ye County of Kent, January ye 25th 1675.

Present—Mr. Joseph Wickes, Mr. Henry Hosier,
Mr. James Ringold, Mr. Tobias Coes,
Mr. John Hynson, Comrs.

It is ordered by this Court yt Thomas Warren, Junior; Christopher Andrews, Henry Carter and Thomas Brite be summoned to ye next Court to take ye oath of Constables. Afterwards, Christopher Andrews was sworn Constable for Chester hundred; Thomas Warren, Jun., for Langsord's Bay; Henry Carter, for ye Upper hundred for Kent; and Thomas Brite for ye Lower hundred for Kent.

SEC. 100. At a Court holden for ye County of Kent, March ye 25th, 1676, and adjourned untill ye 20th April 1676.

Present—Mr. Joseph Wickes, Mr. Henry Hosier,
Mr. James Ringold, Mr. William Lawrence,
Mr. John Hinson, Commissioners,

Mr. Joseph Wickes brought a woman servant to Court yt came in without Indentures, named Christian Gordan who doth declare in open Court yt she is nineteen years old. This Court doth order yt ye sd servant doe serve according to Act of Assembly wch. is six years from her first Arrivall.

SEC. 101. At a Court holden for ye County of Kent, June ye 27th 1676,

Present—Mr. Joseph Wickes, Mr. Nathaniell Evatts,
Mr. John Hinson, Mr. Samuell Tovy,
Mr. Thomas Hosier, Mr. Cornelius Comegys,
Mr. William Lawrence, Mr. Desboro Bennett,
Commissioners.

Whereas Patrick Gordon hath made it appeare to ye Court yt there is due unto him out of ye estate of Edward Joanes the sum of Eighty pounds of Tob., this Court doth order yt present payment be made out of ye Estate by ye Administrator, els execution.

Gave Patrick Gordon a copy o this Order ye 27th of Sept. 1677.

SEC. 102. At a Court holden for ye County of Kent, August ye 22d, 1676.

Whereas Mr. Joseph Wickes one of ye Commissioners of ye Court hath complained to ye Court against John Bowles for divers slanderous words yt said Bowles hath spoken agst ye sd Mr. Wickes. Whereas it is ordered by ye Court yt ye Sheriff of ye County doe take John Bowles into his custody himself untill he finds sufficient security, such as ye Court shall approve for his good behaviour for a twelvemonth and yt sd Bowles appeare at Every Court, or in default of his good behaviour to forfeit twenty pounds sterling to ye Lord Proprietor.

Thomas Warren, Jun., became bound, for John Bowles, in Tenn pounds sterling unto ye Lord Proprietor.

SEC. 103. The following extracts are taken from Liber J, Court Proceedings from 3rd of January 1676 *o. s.* to 29th of June 1698:

At a Court holden for ye County of Kent, the 6th of April 1676—

Present—Mr. Joseph Wickes, Mr. John Hinson,
Mr. James Ringgold, Mr. Nath. Ewett,
Mr. Henry Hosier, Mr. Cornelius Comegys,
Commissioners.

Ordered that ye present Clarke (Benjamin Randall) do make a list of all the Records and papers received from Charles Banckes, Late Clarke.

1677.

SEC. 104. At a Court holden for ye County of Kent ye 30th day of October 1677.

Present—Col. Henry Coursey, Esq., Mr. John Hinson,
Mr. Joseph Wickes, Mr. Samuel Tovey,
Mr. James Ringgold, Mr. Nathl. Evetts,
Commissioners.

This Day being appoynted for Laying of ye County Levy and is as followeth: Publick Levy for 298 persons at 136 per poll.

Robert Smith was admitted to be an Attorney in this Court.

1678.

SEC. 105. At a Court held for Kent County ye 2d day of April 1678.

John Errickson is admitted to be an Attorney in this Court, he was sworn accordingly.

There were 313 Taxable persons in the County this year: the County Levy was 201 lbs. of Tobacco per poll.

SEC. 106. The Court Proceedings from the year 1678 to 1685 appear to be lost; but in Liber B, For Transcribing Old Records, Fols. 33 and 34, the following is recorded:

Kent, July ye 13th 1680.

May it please your Lordship,

We the Justices of this County Court having had the perusall of a Letter from your Lordship directed to Maj. James Ringgold dated the sixth Day of Aprill 1680 wherein your

Lordship hath signified that the Court house and prison of this County ought to be Conveyed to your Lordship for the use and benefitt of this County. In Compliance of which, we do humbly present unto your Lordship the Copy of the Conveyance drawn by the Expertest Councill we Could procure, which if your Lordship shall think it not sufficient Conveyance We humbly desire your Lordship would be pleased to order one of your Clerks to send up one which your Lordship shall approve of, which shall be willingly and Readily signed and performed by

Your Lordship's most humble servants

Henry Hosier	James Ringgold
Nathl. Evetts	Saml. Tovy
Conl. Comegys	Wm. Lawrence.

Vera Copia.—Elias King, Clerk.

SEC. 107.—

A PROCLAMATION

For His Majesties Province of Maryland.

Whereas it hath pleased Almighty God to call to his mercy ye late Sovereign Lord King Charles ye second of most blessed memory, by whose Demise ye Imperiall Crownes of England, Scotland, France & Ireland, as also the supreme Dominion & Sovereigne Right of ye Province of Maryland & all other his late Majesties territories & Dominions in America are soly & Rightfully Come to yt High and Mighty Prince James Duke of York & Albany, his Majesties only Brother and heir;

We Doe therefore with ye * * * Officers and Inhabitants of ye Province aforesaid Doe now hereby with our Full Voyce and Consent of ye tongues & hearts Publish and Proclaime; That ye High & Mighty Prince James ye second is now by ye Death of ye Late Soveraign of happy memory become our only Lawful, Lineall & Rightfull Liege Lord, James the second by ye Grace of God King of England, Scotland, France & Ireland, Defender of ye Faith, supreme Lord of ye Province of Maryland, and all other his Late Majesties Territories & Dominions in America &c.

To whom we Doe acknowledge all faith and Constant obedience with all hearty and humble obedience and affections beseaching God by whom Kings Reigne to bless ye Royal King James ye second with Long and happy yeares to Reigne, &c.

God save King James ye Second!

Henry Darnall
Wm. Digges.

The above written is a true Copy of ye Printed Proclamation sent from England for proclaiming of his Majestic King James ye second in ye Province in testimony whereof is affixed ye great seale of This sd Province this Day of June Annoq Dom 1685.

To ye Sheriff of Kent County—These

Recorded
Elias King,
Clk. Com. Kent.

SEC. 108—

October ye 28th 1685.

At a special Court called this day, by virtue of a writt to the Sheriff appointing a day for Electing two Delegates for the said County for the Assembly to be convened the last Tuesday in March next. Present—

Col. Henry Coursey, Mr. William Frisby,
Mr. John Hinson, Mr. Charles Tilden.

Ordered yt ye first Tuesday in November is appointed for electing the sd Delegates or Burgesses for the sd County and ordered yt the Sheriff make known the same in the sd County.

Elias King, Clk.

Att a Court called and held for the electing Delegates for the sd county this third Day of November 1685 & likewise for Laying the County Levy

By virtue of a New Commission directed to Capt. Wm. Lawrence & others to be Commissioners and Justices of the Peace for the sd County of Kent,—Capt. Wm. Lawrence, Mr. John Hynson and Mr. Charles Tilden took the Oath of Commissioners and Justices of the Peace, and were duly sworne at the house of Mr. Allen Smyth in Kent Island the fourth of this November, and this day (November ye 10th 1685) were sworne on the sd Commission Mr. Cornelius Comegys, Mr. Hans Hanson and Mr. Daniel Norist.

Mr. Philip Conner being called to take the oath refused it.

By a just and free Election of the Freemen of the sd County, Mr. Henry Hosier and Mr. Michael Miller were chosen Burgesses for this said County of Kent.

The Court adjourned untill to-morrow morning for Laying the County Levy.

Judges present—

Mr. John Hinson, Mr. Hans Hanson,
Mr. Charles Tilden, Mr. Daniel Norist.

On Folio 39 is the following memorandum :

James Frisby son of William and Mary Frisby, born at Sassafras river in Cecil county on Thursday near nine of the clock at night, September ye third 1685. Baptized by Mr. John Tillingston at the house lately belonging unto Mr. Simon Carpenter ye 18th of April 1686.

Col. Henry Coursey & Mr. Henry Coursey Godfathers and Mrs. Elizabeth Coursey Godmother.

SEC. 108, A. CHARLES TILDEN, or more properly CHARLES TYLDEN, was the second son of MARMADUKE TYLDEN, who was seated at Great Oak Manor, in Kent County, Md., in or about the year 1658. Marmaduke Tylden was first cousin of Sir Richard Tylden, of Milsted, who d. in 1659, and a grandson of Sir William Tylden, of Great Tyldens, in the Parish of Marden, Kent County, England.

The following *lineage* is prepared from papers of the late Sir John Cotgreave, Knight, &c., copies of which were certified by his widow, Lady Harriet Cotgreave,—from the pedigrees of the Cotgreaves, Gamul and Cowper de Elton, and from memoirs collected with much care by Richard Tylden, Esq., of Milsted, and continued by his son, Sir John M. Tylden, who says:

"In relation to the Tildens of Great Oak Manor, County "Kent, Maryland, and the founder of that branch of the "Tilden family, I have, after mature investigation and due "reflection, arrived at the conclusion that the head of that "branch of the family was at one period principal proprietor "of the large estate, Great Tyldens, near Marden, South "Kent, England, as the large means which he possessed and "the portion he transferred to America (these matters are set "forth in the records, both in the counties of Kent, England, "and Kent in Maryland) justify me in arriving at this con-"clusion. * * * * * The principal of the American "branch appears to have been a cousin of Sir Richard Tylden, "of Milsted, who d. in 1659, and is buried in Milsted church. "* * * It appears to have been the custom of the Tyldens, "who are descended from Nathaniel Tylden (who left Kent, "England, in 1628, as shown by the records in Tenterden, "Kent, and settled at Scituate, near Cape Cod, Massachusetts), "to write their name TILDEN. This is supposed to be owing "to the mutations of the English language, about the time of "the first planting of the colonies. The elder branch in Eng-"land have never indulged in that practice, not seeing any "advantage, but rather many objections."

Sir Bernard Burke, in his *Landed Gentry*, says:

"The family of Tyldens, one of great antiquity, has been seated in Kent for several centuries. Of the three distinct branches into which it separated, the eldest branch became possessed of Milsted in that county; the second removed into Sussex, and one of its members, emigrating, founded the numerous Tildens of America, while the youngest branch settled at Ifield. The family anciently possessed lands in the parishes of Brenchly, Otterden, Kinnington and Tilmanstone, and as far back as the reign of Edward III, we find William Tylden paying aid for the lands in Kent, when the Black Prince was knighted."

Definition of the arms of the Tylden family, of Great Tyldens, Milsted, and Great Oak Manor, Maryland:

ARMS.—Azure, a saltier ermine, between four pheons, or.

CREST.—A battle-axe, erect, entwined with a snake, proper.

MOTTO.—Truth and Liberty.

SIR WILLIAM TYLDEN, of Great Tyldens, the grandfather of Marmaduke Tylden, of Great Oak Manor, Kent County, Maryland, was descended from Sir RICHARD TYLDEN, who was living in the reign of Henry II, and Richard I. He was seneschal to Hugh de Lacy, Constable of Chester, during the reign of Henry II, and afterwards accompanied Cœur de Lion to the Holy Land, and fought under him at ye battle of Ascalon against the Sultan Saladin, Anno 1190.

SIR RICHARD TYLDEN de Sittenbourne, in Kent and Congleton in Cheshire, m. Gertrude, dau. of Sir William Vernon, Lord de Frodsham in Cheshire.

SIR HENRY TYLDEN, son of the above, m. Phillipa, dau. of Sir Richard Boteler de Warrington, Lancaster.

SIR WILLIAM TYLDEN, son of Sir Henry, was living temp. Edward III, and fought in ye van of ye English armye, commanded by ye Lord Audley under ye Black Prince, at ye battle of Poictiers, Anno 1356." He m. Constance, dau. of Rudulphus Gamul, Lord de Mollington, Cheshire.

SIR WILLIAM TYLDEN, son of Sir William, m. Angharad, dau. of Sir Matthew Ellis, de Overleigh, near Chester, England.

SIR THOMAS TYLDEN, son of the above, m. Alice, dau. of Robert del Holme, Lord of Tranmore, Cheshire.

SIR JOHN TYLDEN, son of Sir Thomas, m. Isabel, dau. of Sir Roger Cotgreave, Lord de Hargrave, of Tarrin and Tuttenhall, Cheshire.

SIR WILLIAM TYLDEN, son of the above, m. Elizabeth, dau. of James Yonge, *gentleman*, of Tunstal, County Kent. He was of Great Tyldens, in the parish of Marden. He sold a portion of Great Tyldens in the reign of Henry VI and bought Chatts Place, which continued in the family until the Revolution. He removed to Worms hill, in the early part of the reign of Queen Elizabeth, d. 23d June 1613, and is buried in the back chancel of the church. He was the ancestor of the Tyldens, of Milsted and of Great Oak Manor, Kent Co., Md.

This part of the Tylden pedigree was obtained from the "Papers of the late Sir John Cotgreave, Knight, &c., in which are found Pedigrees of the Cotgreaves, Gamul and Cowper de Elton; compiled by William Camden in 1591, and drawn out by Randal Holme in 1670. The armorial bearings are curious, and show that Sir Richard Tylden's ancestors had intermarried with the family of Fitzhugh, Baron Lord Malpas, and nephew to Hugh Lupers, first Norman Earl of Chester, temp. William the Conqueror; also with the family of Crews of Montel, now Mould, chez Flint." The remainder of the pedigree is compiled chiefly from Burke's *Landed Gentry*, and papers in the possession of the family, now living in England.

Sir Richard Tylden, son of Sir William Tylden and his wife Elizabeth Tonge, purchased 16th Sept. 9th Charles I, from Edward Chute, Esq., of Bethersden, the manor and advowson of Milsted, Kent Co., England, and m. Elizabeth, dau. of John Toke, Esq., of Godington, of consanguinity to Archbishop Chichele, the founder of All Souls' College. He d. in 1659, leaving a son, William Tylden.

William Tylden, Esq., of Milsted, son of Sir Richard and his wife, Elizabeth Toke, m. Hannah, dau. of Sir Thomas Manby, of Lincolnshire, and d. in 1703, leaving an only son, Richard Tylden.

Richard Tylden, Esq., of Milsted, son of William and Hannah Manby Tylden, m. in 1710, Elizabeth, dau. of Thomas Osborne, Esq., of Place House, Kent Co., England, and coheir to her brother. She d. in 1766, aged 79. He d. in 1763, and had child., viz., Richard Osborne, his heir,—Hannah, who m. Edward Belcher, Esq., of Ulcomb, and had two child., viz., Mary, who m. in April 1748, Rev. Thomas Bland, A. M., Vicar of Sittenbourne, and Phillipa Tylden.

The Rev. Richard Osborne Tylden, of Milsted, and Rector thereof, son of Richard and Elizabeth Osborne Tylden, m. in Oct. 1754, Deborah, dau. and heiress of Daniel May, Esq., d. in 1766, aged 44 years, leaving his widow, who afterwards m. Rev. Edward Smith, Rector of Milsted, and had

Tylden.

child., viz., Richard, his heir,—Osborne,—Richard,—Cooke, —Manby Mary, and Elizabeth Tylden.

ELIZABETH TYLDEN, youngest dau. of the Rev. Richard Osborne and Deborah May Tylden, m. twice. Her 1st husband was Vallyer Baker, Esq., of Sittingbourne, and had a son, Vallyer Baker. Her 2nd husband was John Withers, Esq., of London.

REV. RICHARD COOKE TYLDEN, Rector of Milsted and Frinsted, 3rd son of the Rev. Richard Osborne and Deborah May Tylden, assumed the surname and arms of Pattenson, in compliance with the testamentary injunction of William Pattenson, of Ibornden, Biddenden.

OSBORNE TYLDEN, of Torry Hill, Milsted, 2nd son of the Rev. Richard Osborne and Deborah May Tylden, m. Anne Withers, of London, and d. in 1827, leaving child., viz., Osborne, who d. unm.,—Charles, Lieut. R. M., d.,—John, Lieut. Gen. and Col. R. A., who d. in 1866, leaving child., viz., Henry, Lieut. R. N.,—Mary (Madame Maillie),—Eliza, —Emily, who m. 1840, Lieut. Col. Pattenson, of Ibornden,— Isabella, who m. Capt. Luke Alen, son of the late Col. Alen, C. B., of St. Wolstans, representative of Archbishop Alen, and Imogene Tylden, who m. Capt. Lempriere, R. A.

RICHARD TYLDEN, ESQ., of Milsted Manor House, eldest son and heir of the Rev. Richard Osborne and Deborah May Tylden, was m. twice. His 1st wife was Catharine Rolphe, of Ashford, and had one son, Richard Osborne Tylden. His 2nd wife was Jane, dau. of the Rev. Samuel Auchmuty, at one time Rector of Trinity, New York, U. S., a sister of Lieut. Gen. Sir Samuel Auchmuty, G. C. B., and had child., viz., Sir John Maxwell,—Gen. William Burton, and Mary Isabella Tylden, who m. Rev. Ralph Price, Rector of Lyminge, Kent, England. Richard Tylden, Esq., d. 2d Feb'y 1832.

REV. RICHARD OSBORNE TYLDEN, son of Richard and his 1st wife, Mary Rolphe Tylden, was for the period of fifty-three years Vicar of Chilham with Moldash, Kent, England. He m. twice. His 1st wife was Francis, 2nd dau. of William Fairman. She d. in 1849, and had two daus., who survived, viz., Frances Jane Kemp, who m. in 1857, John Blyth, Esq., and Annabella Tylden. He m. a 2nd time, in May 1851, Harriet Lenora Frances, dau. of James Stanley Ireland, Esq., and had child., viz., Richard, b. May 1858, and Catharine Matilda Tylden. Rev. Richard Osborne Tylden d. in March 1862.

Sir John Maxwell Tylden, Knt., of Milsted, J. P. and D. L., son of Richard and Jane Auchmuty Tylden, b. Sept. 25th 1787, m. twice. His 1st wife, m. in 1829, was Elizabeth, only dau. of the Rev. Henry Lomax Walsh, LL. D., of Grimblesthorpe, Lincolnshire, England, who d. in 1839, leaving a dau., Jane Elizabeth Tylden, who m. in 1860, Charles Wright, Esq., who took the surname of Tylden before Wright. She d. in 1860. His 2nd wife was Charlotte, dau. of Sir Robert Lynge, Bart.

He served twenty years in the British Army with distinction, and was formerly Lieut. Col. in command of the Fifty-Second Regiment of the Line (of Corunna celebrity), and received the Order of Knighthood in 1812, at an installation of the Knights of the Bath. Sir John Maxwell Tylden d. May 18th 1866.

Genl. William Burton Tylden, son of Richard and Jane Auchmuty Tylden, late Brigadier General in the British Army, and Col. R. E., was twice m. He m. 1st, Aug. 20th 1817, Lucilina, eldest dau. of William Baldwin, Esq., of Steed Hill, Kent Co., England, and had two sons, viz., William, now of Milsted, and Richard Tylden, Col. R. E., C. B., and A. D. C. to the Queen, who died on his passage home, after the Crimean war, from wounds received in the trenches before Sebastopol. He m. a 2nd time in 1851, Mary, widow of Capt. J. H. Baldwin, dau. of the late Rev. George Dinely Goodeve.

Gen. William Burton Tylden was mortally wounded at the battle of Alma, and d. the day after, Sept. 21st 1854, and his widow, now Lady Mary Tylden, was raised to the same rank as if her husband had survived to be made a Knight Commander of the Bath.

Rev. William Tylden, of the Milsted Manor House, Sittingbourne, Kent County, England, Vicar of Stanford, near Hythe, was b. July 3d 1818, m. Nov. 30th 1852, Eleanor Coates, 2nd dau. of Rev. James W. Ballamy, Vicar of Sallindge, and had child., viz., Richard, b. in 1853,—William, b. in 1854, and Harry John Tylden, b. in 1856.

☞ Gov. Samuel J. Tilden, of New York (descended from Nathaniel Tilden, mentioned on page 302), was the candidate of the Democratic Party for the Presidency of the United States in Nov. 1876. The following congratulatory address was issued 13th Dec. 1876 :

" WASHINGTON, Dec. 13.

" The following congratulatory address was issued to-day:

" *Rooms of the National Democratic Committee, Washington,*
" *Dec.* 13*th*, 1876—*To the People of the United States:*

" The National Democratic Committee announce as the " result of the Presidential election held on the 7th of " November, the election of Samuel J. Tilden, of New York, " as President, and Thomas A. Hendricks, of Indiana, as Vice " President of the United States. We congratulate you on this " victory for reform. It now only remains for the two Houses " of Congress, in the performance of their duty, on the second " Wednesday in February next, to give effect to the will of the " people thus expressed in the constitutional mode by a " majority of the electoral votes, and confirmed by a majority " of all the States, as well as by an overwhelming majority of " all the people of the United States. By order of the Exec- " utive Committee.

" ABRAM S. HEWITT, Chairman.

" FREDERICK O. PRINCE, Secretary."

SEC. 108, B. MARMADUKE TYLDEN, of Great Oak Manor, d. Sept. 1671, and left three sons, viz., Marmaduke,—Charles, and John Tilden.

MARMADUKE TILDEN, son of Marmaduke Tylden, was a very large land owner in Kent, perhaps the largest. He owned at one time, in the year 1709, thirty-one thousand and three hundred and fifty acres. He m. Rebecca Wilmer, dau. of Lambert and Ann Wilmer, and d. 20th June 1726, and had child., viz., Marmaduke,—Jane,—Mary (who m. Thomas Ringgold),—Wealthy Ann,—Charles and Martha Tilden.

MARMADUKE TILDEN, son of Marmaduke and Rebecca Wilmer Tilden, d. in 1768. In his will, dated 29th Oct. 1767, he mentions his wife, Sarah Tilden, and his child., viz., Marmaduke,—Charles,—Mary Ann,—Tabitha,—Martha, and Mary Tilden, who m. Edward Worrell. Mrs. Sarah Tilden d. in 1774.

MARMADUKE TILDEN, eldest son of Marmaduke and Sarah Tilden, d. in 1816, and had child., viz., Marmaduke and Mary F. Tilden, who m. George D. S. Handy, and d. March 1851, leaving child., viz., Esther Ann,—Susan L., and Marmaduke P. Handy.

MARMADUKE TILDEN, son of Marmaduke Tilden, m. Sarah Bowers. He d. before his father, and left child., viz., Thomas

Bowers, and Anna Maria Tilden, who m. Joseph W. Brice, and d. 6th July 1846.

CAPT. THOMAS BOWERS TILDEN, son of Marmaduke and Sarah Bowers Tilden, m. 8th Dec. 1852, Catharine R. Wing, who was b. 26th Sept. 1828, and d. 20th Feb'y 1863. He d. 23d of Oct. 1875, *sine prole.*

SEC. 108, C. WEALTHY ANN TILDEN, dau. of Marmaduke and Rebecca Wilmer Tilden, m. 19th Oct. 1710, Thomas Hynson (see HYNSON) and had child., viz., Margarett, b. 13th Jan'y 1712,—Charles, b. 14th Jan'y 1713,—Martha Waltham, and Mary Hynson, who m. ——— Jones, and had a son, Thomas Jones.

CHARLES HYNSON, son of Thomas and Wealthy Ann Tilden Hynson, m. 30th of Nov. 1739, Phoebe Carvill, and d. in 1782, and had child., viz., Charles, b. 9th Oct. 1741,—Charles Carvill, b. 11th Dec. 1743,—Mary, b. 21st of May 1746,—Phoebe, b. 3d Dec. 1747,—Richard, b. 3d Feb'y 1749, and John Carvill Hynson.

MARY HYNSON, dau. of Charles and Phoebe Carvill Hynson, m. Hans Hanson (son of Hans Hanson, son of Judge Frederick Hanson and Mary Lowder, see HANSON) and d. 1st Feb'y 1774. Hans Hanson d. in 1777. They left two child., viz., Martha and William Hanson.

MARTHA HANSON, dau. of Hans and Mary Hynson Hanson, m. Dr. William Ringgold, son of Major William Ringgold, of Eastern Neck, who was b. 23rd Feb'y 1723, the son of Thomas Ringgold, who was b. 9th Aug. 1693, d. 27th Aug. 1728, the son of Thomas Ringgold, the son of Maj. James Ringgold, of Huntingfield, who was the son of Thomas Ringgold, one of the Justices for Kent County as early as "ye 12th Jan'y 1651." (See RINGGOLD.)

Dr. William and Martha Hanson Ringgold had child., viz., William, b. 1794,—Peregrine, b. 1796,—Harriet Rebecca, b. 1798,—James Alexander, b. 1800,—Frederick Gustavus, b. 1801, and Mary Hanson Ringgold, b. 10th of Sept. 1803.

MARY HANSON RINGGOLD, dau. of Dr. William Ringgold and Martha Hanson, m. 9th Oct. 1821, Hon. James Hodges, of Liberty Hall, Kent, who was descended from William Hodges (a member of the English Church, of Kentish parentage) who came to Maryland, from Virginia, about 1665, and settled near Gray's Inn (anciently known as Gravesend) in

Kent, on a tract of land "near Huntingfield and lying along the road that was called Yarmouth Race Ground."

HODGES ARMS.

ARMS: Or, three crescents sable, on a canton of the second, a ducal crown of the first.

CREST: Out of a ducal coronet or an heraldic antelope's head argent, horned and tufted gold.

MOTTO: DANT LUCEM CRESCENTIBUS ORTI.

SEC. 108, D. WILLIAM HODGES d. May 1697. In his Will, dated 15th Feb'y 1696–7, he mentions his 3 sons, viz., Robert Hodges,—William Hodges (who m. 23rd Dec. 1736, Frances Bradshaw, and had child., viz., William b. 23rd Dec. 1739,—Robert, b. 16th Jan'y 1741, who m. Sarah Ayres,—Sarah, b. 7th May 1758,—Frances Rebecca, d. 1767, and Hannah Hodges, who m. Mr. Winters) and d. 1777, more than 90 years of age,—and John Hodges, who m. ye 10th May 1699, Mary Newes, and had a son, John Hodges baptized, at St. Paul's, Kent, 24th Feb'y 1703.

ROBERT HODGES, of Liberty Hall, eldest son of William Hodges, had child., viz., William,—Martha, b. 15th Jan'y 1715,—Robert, b. 27th Aug. 1718,—Priscilla, b. 9th Sept. 1720,—Stephen, b. 28th Feb'y 1722,—Samuel, b. 25th Dec. 1724,—Rebecca, b. 24th Nov. 1727,—Sarah, b. 4th Aug. 1728,—John, b. 1730, and James Hodges, b. 22nd Feb'y 1732, the natal day of George Washington. Robert Hodges d. 1735. In his Will, dated 20th Nov. 1734, he mentions his "loving wife, Tamer Hodges" and surviving child., viz, William,—Robert,—John and James Hodges.

CAPT. JAMES HODGES, of the Revolution, son of Robert and Tamer Hodges, of Liberty Hall, m. Sarah Granger, and had child., viz., James, b. 6th Jan'y 1759,—John, b. 21st June 1761,—Martha, b. 30th Jan'y 1764 (who m. 13th Oct. 1785, William Gale),—Richard, b. 23d June 1766,—Robert, b. 23rd March 1769,—Stephen, b. 2nd Feb'y 1773,—Ann, b. 23rd June 1775 (who m. Thomas Gale), and William Hodges, b. 3rd July 1778. Capt. James Hodges d. Jan'y 1816, and was buried in the family burial-ground, at Liberty Hall. A portrait of him is in the possession of his great grandson, James James.

JAMES HODGES, of Liberty Hall, son of Capt. James Hodges and Sarah Granger, m. Mary Claypoole, and d. 1815, leaving a son, James Hodges.

MARY CLAYPOOLE HODGES was descended from James Claypoole, a notable personage at the time of the founding of Philadelphia in 1683, and the author of several books and pamphlets, published during the early period of that city, now in the Friend's Library, on Arch street. James Claypoole was "an admired friend of William Penn, the Quaker," long before his emigration to America. He was the son of Adam Claypoole, Esq., who was seated at the Manor of Norborough, Northampton County, England, in 1610 and also owned Waldram Parks and Gray's Inn, estates in the same County, and was an uncle of Lord John Claypoole, who m. Elizabeth, the favorite dau. of Oliver Cromwell. The abovenamed Adam Claypoole m. Dorothy, dau. of Robert Wingfield and Elizabeth Cecil, sister of William Cecil, Lord Burleigh, and Prime Minister of England in the reign of Queen Elizabeth.

HON. JAMES HODGES, of Liberty Hall, son of James and Mary Claypoole Hodges, m. 9th Oct. 1821, Mary Hanson Ringgold, dau. of Dr. William and Martha Hanson Ringgold, and d. 14th Feb'y 1832. He was a member of the Legislature of Maryland in the sessions of 1823 and 1824, and left child., viz., James, b. 11th Aug. 1822,—William Ringgold, b. 27th July 1824,—Mary, b. 19th July 1826,—Frances Harriet, b. 18th Sept. 1828, and Robert Hodges, b. 14th Feb'y 1831.

FRANCES HARRIET HODGES, youngest dau. of Hon. James and Mary Hanson Ringgold Hodges, m. 1st July 1852, William Ringgold Constable (see CONSTABLE), and had child., viz., Harrie Clarence,—William Stevenson,—Charles Hodges,—Mary Rebecca,—Roberta Hodges, and Martha Hanson Constable.

MARY HODGES, eldest dau. of Hon. James and Mary Hanson Ringgold Hodges, m. 7th June 1853, Alfred Henry Fisher, son of Dr. Jacob and Mary Ann Ringgold Fisher (see FISHER), and d. 9th July 1854, leaving an only dau., Mary Hodges Fisher.

WILLIAM RINGGOLD HODGES, son of Hon. James and Mary Hanson Ringgold Hodges m. 19th April 1860, Matilda Phillips, dau. of S. H. Phillips, and had child., viz., Cora Ringgold,—William Hanson, and Robert Beverly Hodges.

JAMES HODGES, eldest son of Hon. James and Mary Hanson Ringgold Hodges, m. 30th Nov. 1847, Josephine A. Bash, dau. of Henry M. Bash, and had child., viz., Mary Ella,—Ida Virginia,—Lillie Hanson, and William Ringgold Hodges.

Claypoole.

Granted to JAMES CLAYPOOLE of Waldram-Parks, Northamptonshire, England, by ROBERT COOKE, Clarencieux King-of-arms, June 17, 1588

MARY ELLA HODGES, dau. of James and Josephine Augusta Bash Hodges, m. 16th of April 1874, George A. Kirby, of Baltimore, Md., son of William and Ann Sewell Kirby, and had child., viz., Bessie Sewell, and Mary Hanson Kirby.

The ancestors of the parents of George A. Kirby settled at an early period in Maryland, on the banks of the Severn. The family still possesses the original homestead.

IDA VIRGINIA HODGES, dau. of James and Josephine Augusta Bash Hodges, m. 12th of January 1875, Dr. St. George W. Teackle, of Baltimore, son of St. George W. Teackle and Catharine Hays, and has a son, St. George Williamson Teackle.

SEC. 108, E. DR. ST. GEORGE W. TEACKLE is descended from the Rev. Thomas Teackle, a clergyman of the Church of England, who was b. 1624, in Gloucestershire, England, whose father was slain in battle, fighting under the banner of Charles I. Being persecuted by the Cromwellites, he came to America in 1656, and settled at Craddock, an estate in Accomac County, Virginia, where he performed the functions of his sacred calling until the 26th of Jan'y 1695, the day of his death.

REV. THOMAS TEACKLE, of Craddock, m. Margaret Nelson, dau. of Robert Nelson, merchant of London, and had nine child., only three of whom left descendants, viz., John,—Elizabeth, and Catharine Teackle.

JOHN TEACKLE, of Craddock, son of Rev. Thomas and Margaret Nelson Teackle, b. 2d Sept. 1693, m. 2d Nov. 1710, Susanna Upshur, dau. of Arthur and Sarah Upshur, and d. 3d Dec. 1721, at York Town, Va., and left five sons and one dau. viz., Thomas, b. 11th Nov. 1711, d. 20th July 1769,—John, b. 5th Aug. 1713, d. 3d May 1760 *sine prole*,—Caleb, b. 13th Dec. 1714, d. Nov. 1739, on the Island of St. Croix, *sine prole*,—Levin, b. 12th March 1718, d. 28th Sept. 1794,—Upshur, b. 26th Feb'y 1719, who m. Mrs. Margaret Scarborough, and d. in Sept. 1774, and Margaret Teackle, b. 14th March 1720, who m. Col. Edward Robins, and d. 8th Oct. 1794.

THOMAS TEACKLE, of Craddock, eldest son of John and Susanna Upshur Teackle, m. Elizabeth Custis, and had three sons and six daus., viz., Thomas,—Caleb, who m. Elizabeth Harmanson,—Severn, who m. Lucretia Edmondson, of Talbot,—Elizabeth, who m. Isaac Smith, of Northampton Co., Va.,—Margaret, who m. George Hack,—Sarah, who m. Bowdoin Kendall,—Ann, who m. Hillery Stringer, and Susanna

Teackle, who m. Daniel Gore, of Accomac Co., Va. Thomas Teackle d. at his seat, Craddock, 20th July 1769.

THOMAS TEACKLE, of Craddock, eldest son of Thomas and Elizabeth Custis Teackle, m. Elizabeth Upshur, and d. 15th April 1784, leaving child., viz., Sarah, b. 14th Aug. 1759, who m. Dr. John Boisnard,—John, b. 12th Jan'y 1762,—Thomas, b. 30th Oct. 1763, who m. Catharine Stockley,—Susannah, b. 18th March 1766, who m. Col. John Robins,—Catharine, b. 17th Aug. 1768, who m. Charles Smith,—George, b. 30th April 1770, who m. Francis Bowdoin, dau. of John Bowdoin, of Northampton Co., Va.,—Margaret, b. 28th Feb'y 1771, who m. Thomas Savage, and d. Sept. 1846,—Elizabeth, b. 17th March 1776, and Leah Teackle, b. 4th Aug. 1780, d. in Feb'y 1851. Mrs. Elizabeth Upshur Teackle d. 14th Jan'y 1782.

JOHN TEACKLE, of Craddock, eldest son of Thomas and Elizabeth Upshur Teackle, m. 18th Dec. 1783, Ann Upshur, dau. of Thomas Upshur, d. 18th Feb'y 1811, and had child., viz., Elizabeth, b. 26th Sept. 1784, who m. Harrison Ball, of Richmond Co., Va., and d. 6th April 1806,—Thomas Upshur, b. 1786, d. 3d Aug. 1787,—Ann Stockley, b. 17th March 1788, who m. Isaac Smith, and d. 11th Dec. 1862,—Mary Upshur, b. 29th April 1790, who m. John Pender, of Baltimore, and d. Aug. 1846,—Lavinia Upshur, b. 11th Oct. 1792, who m. Capt. William Graham, of Baltimore, and d. 25th March 1853,—Sarah Upshur, b. 7th May 1795, who m. William G. Lawson, of Baltimore,—a 2d Thomas Upshur, b. 2d Nov. 1797, who sold Craddock, m. Emma Wilson, dau. of Thomas Wilson, of Baltimore,—Susannah Brown Upshur, b. 26th April 1800, who m. Francis Hopkinson Smith,—Dr. John Upshur, b. 15th Oct. 1803, d. 1st June 1851, and St. George Williamson Teackle, b. 26th Jan'y 1806, and d. 26th March 1874.

ST. GEORGE WILLIAMSON TEACKLE, son of John and Ann Upshur Teackle, m. 27th Oct. 1836, Catharine Hays, and had child., viz., Ann Upshur Teackle, — John Teackle, — Ellen Teackle, and Dr. St. George W. Teackle. Ellen Teackle m. 17th Dec. 1868, William Cadwalader Schley, Attorney-at-law, Baltimore, son of William Schley and Ann Cadwalader Ringgold (see RINGGOLD), and a descendant on his mother's side of Thomas Ringgold and Rebecca Wilmer. Dr. St. George W. Teackle m. 12th Jan'y 1875, Ida V. Hodges, dau. of James Hodges, a descendant of the same Thomas Ringgold and Rebecca Wilmer. (See RINGGOLD and HODGES.)

DOCTOR ST. GEORGE W. TEACKLE is at present (1876) the Visiting Physician at Bayview Asylum, near Baltimore, and attending Physician to the Baltimore General Dispensary. In 1870 and 1872, he was the House Surgeon of the Charity Hospital, Blackwell's Island, N. Y., and Resident Surgeon of the Work-House on Blackwell's Island. During the same period he was Visiting Physician to the New York City Penitentiary, and Resident Physician of the New York Alms-House.

SEC. 108, F. CHARLES TILDEN (the 2nd son of the first named Marmaduke Tilden), was one of the Judges of Kent County Court, 28th Oct. 1685, on the 24th day of January 1693, was elected one of the first vestry of St. Paul's Parish, and was also, in 1693, High Sheriff of Kent. He left two child., viz., a son, John Tilden, and a dau., Ann, who m. Mr. Wilson.

JOHN TILDEN, son of Charles Tilden, m. 27th July 1722, Catharine Blay, dau. of Col. William Blay and his wife Isabella Pearce, and had child., viz., Charles, b. 11th May 1723,—John,—Catharine, who m. Gustavus Hanson, son of Judge Frederick Hanson and Mary Lowder (see HANSON), Mary, b. 10th March 1728, and William Blay Tilden.

COL. WILLIAM BLAY, of Blay's Range, the only son of Col. Edward and Ann Blay, was for many years a vestryman of Shrewsbury Parish, and represented Kent in the Legislature of Maryland in the sessions of 1714 and 1715. He m. Isabella Pearce, dau. of Judge William and Isabella Pearce, and had child., viz., Rachel, b. 24th Oct. 1703,—Catharine, who m. John Tilden,—Edward, b. 31st Jan'y 1707,—Isabella, and William Blay, b. 22d Oct. 1714.

COL. EDWARD BLAY was a distinguished and zealous member of the Episcopal Church, and a vestryman of Shrewsbury Parish. In 1709–10 he gave to that Parish two acres of land, the ground upon which the church edifice stands. In after years his great-grandson, Dr. William Blay Tilden, gave more land and increased the church yard to its present ample dimensions. Col. Edward Blay was a delegate from Cecil in the Legislature of Maryland in the sessions of 1706 and 1707, and represented Kent in the Legislature in 1713. His wife, Madame Ann Blay, was buried at Shrewsbury 27th Aug. 1712.

ISABELLA BLAY, youngest dau. of Col. William and Isabella Pearce Blay, m. Richard Wethered, son of Samuel and Dolly Lewin Wethered (see WETHERED).

RACHEL BLAY, dau. of Col. William and Isabella Pearce Blay, m. John Brown, Collector of the Pocomoke District, and had one son, Peregrine Brown. Her 2nd husband was Edward Scott. Her 3rd husband was Mr. Paca.

PEREGRINE BROWN, son of John and Rachel Blay Brown, m. Miss Baker, and had child., viz., Peregrine, and Sophia C. Brown, b. 11th Aug. 1752, who m. 1st Mr. Massy, and 2ndly Cornelius Comegys, and left a dau., Anna Maria Comegys, b. 27th March 1783.

ANNA MARIA COMEGYS, dau. of Cornelius and Sophia C. Brown Comegys, m. 3d April 1804, Dr. Edward Scott, and had 13 child. Mrs. Anna Maria Comegys Scott d. 27th Jan'y 1857, leaving ten child., seven of whom are now (Feb'y 1876) living, the most of whom are in the Western States. Cornelius J. Scott remains in Kent, at Galena. He m. 10th Dec. 1857, Mary E. Kennard, dau. of Samuel E. Kennard, and has three child., a son, Edward A. Scott, and two daus.

SEC. 108, G. DR. WILLIAM BLAY TILDEN, son of John and Catharine Blay Tilden, m. Sarah ——— ——— and had child., viz., William Blay, b. 20th Feb'y 1764,—John, b. 24th of Dec. 1765,—Katherine, b. 26th Oct. 1767, who m. Mr. Hynson,—Charles, b. 31st Aug. 1769,—Edward Blay, and Mary Tilden. Dr. William Blay Tilden d. 22d Feb'y 1800.

DR. WILLIAM BLAY TILDEN, son of Dr. William Blay Tilden and Sarah Tilden, m. Mary Buchanan, dau. of Robert Buchanan, and had child., viz., Louisa, who m. George, son of Edward Ringgold, and afterwards Dr. Peregrine Wroth, and d. *sine prole*,—Isabella,—William Blay, and Charles Tilden.

ROBERT BUCHANAN was a Delegate from Kent County in the Maryland Legislature in the sessions of 1765, 1766 and 1767, and was a member of the Convention of the Province of Maryland which assembled at Annapolis, Tuesday, 21st June 1776.

DR. CHARLES TILDEN, son of Dr. William Blay and Sarah Tilden, m. Anna Maria Buchanan, dau. of the above-mentioned Robert Buchanan, and had child., viz., Catharine (who m. 27th Jan'y 1829, William Henry Page Worrell, see WORRELL), —Harriet Buchanan,—William,—Robert,—Anna Maria, and Mary Elizabeth Tilden.

ANNA MARIA TILDEN, dau. of Dr. Charles and Anna Maria Buchanan Tilden, m. 17th Oct. 1843, and was the 2nd wife of George Bergen Westcott, and had one son, Charles Tylden Westcott.

CHARLES TYLDEN WESTCOTT, son of George Bergen Westcott and Anna Maria Tilden, m. 17th Sept. 1873, Mary S.

Guion, dau. of Dr. John A. and Susan S. Roberts Guion, of New Berne, North Carolina, and had a son, Tylden Westcott.

MARY ELIZABETH TILDEN, dau. of Dr. Charles and Anna Maria Buchanan Tilden, m 25th Nov. 1845, Nicholas Godfrey Westcott, and had child., viz., Harriet Tilden,—Samuel Buck,—Charlotte,—George Bergen,—William Henry,—Mary Louisa, and Alice Westcott.

HARRIET TILDEN WESTCOTT, dau. of Nicholas Godfrey Westcott and Mary Elizabeth Tilden, m. 20th Oct. 1875, the Reverend Stephen C. Roberts, the much beloved Rector of Chester Parish, Kent. He was from North Carolina and a brother of Mrs. Susan S. Roberts Guion, mentioned above.

SEC. 108, G. MARY TILDEN, dau. of Dr. William Blay and Sarah Tilden, m. twice. Her 1st husband was Mr. Hurtt. Her 2d husband was John Ireland, and had child., viz., Tilden,—Charles Tilden,—Catherine Tilden,—Mary, and Alethea Ireland.

JOHN IRELAND was the son of Joseph Ireland, who was b. 17th June 1727, near Halifax, Yorkshire, England, and was m. by the Rev. Mr. Sterling, 10th July 1761, to Alethea Comegys, dau. of William and Ann Cosden Comegys (see COMEGYS), and had child., viz., William, b. 28th June 1762,—Joseph, b. 8th March 1765,—John, b. 9th March 1767,—Jesse Comegys, and Alphonso Cosden Ireland.

CATHERINE TILDEN IRELAND, dau. of John and Mary Tilden Ireland, b. 23d Nov. 1804, m. 27th Nov. 1821, Daniel Jones, and d. 26th of Sept. 1858. Daniel Jones was b. 10th Oct. 1796, d. 23d April 1865. They had ten child., two of whom d. in infancy, viz., William Ireland, and William Blay Tilden Jones, d. 11th June 1851, in the 11th year of his age. The following survive, viz., Mary Elizabeth,—Jacob Alfred,—Sarah Catherine,—John Wesley,—George Washington,—Anna Alethea,—Jane Louisa, and Daniel Jones.

DANIEL JONES was the son of Jacob Jones, Jr. and Elizabeth Gale. Jacob Jones, Jr. was High Sheriff of Kent in 1783, and was the son of Capt. Jacob and Elizabeth Jones.

ELIZABETH GALE was descended from George Gale, who was b. in 1670, in Kent Co., England, and came to Maryland in 1690, d. in Aug. 1712, leaving 3 sons, viz., Levin Gale, whose dau., Leah, m. Mr. Wilson (descendants of whom now reside in Washington, D. C.),—George Gale, and John Gale, who came to Kent in 1718, and left a son, John Gale, whose 2nd wife was a dau. of John Rasin, and left two child., viz., a dau. and Rasin Gale. Col. George Gale, of Still Pond, Kent, is now, 1876, the oldest living representative of the emigrant.

RASIN GALE, son of John Gale, m. in 1756, Martha Moore, and had child., viz., William Gale (who m. 13th Oct. 1785, Martha Hodges, dau. of Capt. James Hodges and Sarah Granger),—Elizabeth Gale (who m. Jacob Jones, Jr.),—George Gale,—John Gale,—Rasin Gale,—Rachel Gale,—Mary Gale (who m. Mr. Cann),—Asenath Gale (who m. Mr. Newell), and Thomas Gale, who m. Ann Hodges, a sister of the above-named Martha Hodges.

MARY ELIZABETH JONES, dau. of Daniel and Catherine Tilden Ireland Jones, m. 18th Oct. 1849, George Washington Mears, and had child., viz., Lelia Anna Catherine,—Mary Elizabeth,—George Washington, d. 31st July 1856,—Sarah Blay Tylden,—Edward Clarence, d. 23d July 1860,—Daniel Henry, and Edward Blay Tylden Mears. George Washington Mears was born 30th Nov. 1827, the son of Henry Haller Mears and Ann Barbard Birkenbine, b. 13th Oct. 1800, m. 22d Sept. 1824. Henry Haller Mears, b. 31st July 1797, d. 10th Dec. 1870, was the son of William Mears and Elizabeth Haller, b. 24th March 1761, m. in April 1786, d. 1849. William Mears, b. 9th March 1761, d. 11th June 1825, was the son of John Mears and Susanna Townsend, b. 14th Dec. 1737, m. in Phila. 1760, d. 1817. John Mears, b. 4th June 1738, d. 1819, was the son of William Mears and Elizabeth Gilbert, b. 19th Dec. 1715, d. 14th Sept. 1796. William Mears, b. 1710, m. about 1735, at Everton, England, came to America with Gen. Oglethorpe's expedition, and was lost at sea in 1738.

JACOB ALFRED JONES, son of Daniel and Catherine Tilden Ireland Jones, m. 30th Dec. 1856, Martha A. Price, dau. of Perry and Elizabeth Price, and had child., viz., William Alfred, d. 12th June 1866,—Hyland Tylden,—Lizzie Howard, d. 11th Nov. 1867,—Daniel Bazard, and Howard Price Jones, who d. 23d Sept. 1874.

SARAH CATHERINE JONES, dau. of Daniel and Catherine Tilden Ireland Jones, m. 7th Oct. 1852, Thomas Marshall, son of James and Mary R. Marshall, and had child., viz., Catherine Tylden, d. 1st July 1854,—Mary Tylden,—Sallie Virginia,—Anna Lelia,—Carrie Louisa,—Ida Kate, d. 1st Aug. 1865,—Charles Tylden,—George Washington, and Clarence Linnard Marshall.

JOHN WESLEY JONES, son of Daniel and Catherine Tilden Ireland Jones, m. 22d Oct. 1867, Mary Billmeyer Murphey, dau. of John A. and Mary Murphey, and had child., viz., Helen Blay,—Florence Tylden, and Charles Tylden Jones. He received, in 1862, the appointment of Secretary to the President of the Philadelphia and Reading Railroad Company, a confidential position of responsibility. Afterwards, he successively filled the positions of General Freight Clerk,—Auditor,—Secretary,—Secretary and Comptroller,—and, in May 1873, was elected First Vice President of the Company, the position which he now (1876) ably fills.

George Washington Jones, son of Daniel and Catherine Tilden Ireland Jones, m. 15th Dec. 1863, Anna Amelia Howard, dau. of Joseph and Susannah K. Howard, and had child., viz., Daniel Howard, d. 20th July 1865,—Mary Catherine,—Susanna Wesley,—George Washington, d. 12th Sept. 1872,—Anna Elizabeth, d. 22d. Nov. 1874, and Ida Josephine Jones.

Anna Alethea Jones, dau. of Daniel and Catherine Tilden Ireland Jones, m. 11th April 1865, Rev. William Henry Hopkins, son of William Henry and Mary J. Hopkins, and had child., viz., William Glenmore,—Nettie Lee,—Harry Tylden,—John Edward, d., and Howard Blay Hopkins, d.

Jane Louisa Jones, dau. of Daniel and Catherine Tilden Ireland Jones, m. 11th May 1869, Henry Churchill Cutler, son of Lemuel and Elizabeth Cutler, and had a son, Henry Churchill Cutler, d.

Daniel Jones, son of Daniel and Catherine Tilden Ireland Jones, m. 22nd Oct. 1873, Hannah Elizabeth Rush, dau. of Stephen P. and Elizabeth Ketcham Rush, and had one child, William Rush Jones.

Charles Nehemiah Tilden (a descendant of John Tilden, son of the first named Marmaduke Tylden) and his wife, Sarah Jane Tilden, had child., viz., Charles Nehemiah,—Elizabeth,—William P.,—Josephine,—Sarah Jane,—Mary,—Thomas Ware, and Edwin Marmaduke Tilden.

Edwin Marmaduke Tilden, son of Charles Nehemiah and Sarah Jane Tilden, m. 31st Jan'y 1854, Williamina Tatem, and had a son, William Tatem Tilden.

Williamina Tatem was the dau. of William Alexander and Martha Washington Tabélé, who were m. 19th May 1824. William Alexander Tatem was the son of Samuel Tatem and Mary Alexander, who were m. 1799. Samuel Tatem was the son of William Tatem and Susan Ashbrook.

Sec. 108, H. Richard Wethered, who m. Isabella Blay, was descended from James Wethered, Esq., who left a son, John Wethered, and two other child.

JOHN WETHERED, son of John, had 3 child., viz., James,—Agnes, who m. Sawnder Avery in 1542, and Sisley Wethered, who m. in 1545, George Evely.

JAMES WETHERED, son of John, m. Alice ———, and had child., viz., Margaret, b. 1539,—Tone, b. 1541,—Edmund, b. 1542,—Tone, b. 1545, d. 1557, and Francis Wethered, b. 1547.

FRANCIS WETHERED, son of James and Alice Wethered, m. 1571, Agnes ———, was a member of Parliament in 1619, and left a son, Francis Wethered.

FRANCIS WETHERED, son of Francis and Agnes Wethered, m. Margaret Bargclaw, d. 1667, leaving two child., viz., Elizabeth Wethered, b. 1600, who m. Henry Guy Tring, and had a dau., Elizabeth Tring (who m. Sir Anderson de Pendecy, Knight of the Golden Spurs, and a son, Henry Tring), and Thomas Wethered, b. 1606, d. 1671. Henry Guy Tring was Groom of the Bed Chamber, Clerk of the Treasury, and a member of Parliament.

THOMAS WETHERED, son of Francis and Margaret Bargclaw Wethered, m. in 1626, Elizabeth ———, and had child., viz., Francis and Samuel Wethered.

COL. SAMUEL WETHERED, R. A., son of Thomas and Elizabeth Wethered, left three sons, viz., Thomas, who sold the family estate to Lord Tankerville, and d. in Italy,—William and Samuel Wethered, Esqs.

SAMUEL WETHERED, ESQ., of London, son of Col. Samuel Wethered, m. Dolly Lewin, and d. 1719, leaving child., viz., Samuel,—Lewin, Governor of Cape Coast Castle, Africa,—George,—Richard,—Henry, lost at sea,—Sarah, and Mary Wethered. All these child., excepting Lewin and George Wethered, came to America with their mother in 1720.

SAMUEL WETHERED, son of Samuel and Dolly Lewin Wethered, returned to England, and m. Miss Thornton, and had child., viz., Col. William,—Col. Samuel, R. A.,—John,—Thomas,—Sarah, who m. Mr. Law, Commissary R. A., at Fort Cumberland,—Catharine, who m. Capt. Dixon, R. A.,—and Polly Wethered, who m. Sir Arthur Loftus, R. A.

COL. WILLIAM WETHERED, R. A., son of Samuel Wethered, was present at Braddock's defeat, m. Miss Cochrane, and had child., viz., Samuel and William Wethered, R. N., lost at sea in H. B. M. Rockingham,—Thomas Wethered, Commissary General, R. A. (who m. Miss Kirwin, and had two child., viz., Thomas, Surgeon, R. A., and Henrietta, who m. Dr. Bernard Duffy, and had a dau., Arabella Duffy),—Molly Wethered, and Dolly Wethered, who m. Capt. Quintin, R. A.

RICHARD WETHERED, son of Samuel and Dolly Lewin Wethered, m. Isabella Blay, dau. of Col. William and Isabella Pearce Blay, of Blay's Range, Kent, and had child., viz., William (who m. Miss Hurt, removed to Virginia, and had a son, Peregrine, who m. Miss Turpin, and had a son, Turpin Wethered),—John,—Samuel, and a 2nd John Wethered.

JOHN WETHERED, son of Richard and Isabella Blay Wethered, m. Mary Sykes, dau. of Judge J. Sykes, of Delaware, and had child., viz., Peregrine, who d. 1857,—Samuel,—Lewin,—Mary,—Sarah Isabella,—Ann Catharine,—Catharine Matilda,—Harriet C., and Caroline Wethered.

PEREGRINE WETHERED, son of John and Mary Sykes Wethered, m. Hannah Medford, and had child., viz., John Lathem and Mary Elizabeth Wethered.

JOHN LATHEM WETHERED, son of Peregrine and Hannah Medford Wethered, m. 16th Jan'y 1862, Charlotte Spencer, dau. of George and Margaretta Ringgold Spencer (see SPENCER), and had child., viz., Margaretta Spencer,—Mary Elizabeth, and John Lathem Wethered.

MARY ELIZABETH WETHERED, dau. of Peregrine and Hannah Medford Wethered, m. William Janvier, who d. 26th April 1876, and had child., viz., William,—John Wethered, and Mary C. Janvier.

SAMUEL WETHERED, son of John and Mary Sykes Wethered, m. Eliza Yeates, dau. of Col. Yeates, of Kent, and had child., viz., John D.,—George H., who m. Ann Irwin,—Matilda,—Lewina,—Elizabeth,—Sally, and Samuel Wethered, who m. Elizabeth Evans, and had child., viz., George,—Mary,—Eliza, and Hugh Wethered.

LEWIN WETHERED, son of John and Mary Sykes Wethered, m. Elizabeth Ellicott, dau. of Elias Ellicott, and had child., viz., Peregrine Wethered,— Charles C. Wethered, who m. Elizabeth Bathurst, and had a son, Charles, b. 1837, d. 1840, —Hon. John Wethered, who m. Mary Thomas, dau. of Philip E. Thomas, the first President of the Baltimore and Ohio Railroad Company in 1827,—Samuel Wethered,—Mary Lewin Wethered (who m. Wm. G. Thomas, and had child., viz., Philip Thomas, who m. Susette Marigny, and had two child., viz., Susette and Philip,—Ann Thomas, who m. William Bell, and had 3 child., viz., Mary Lewin, Rebecca and Ann Bell, —Lewin W. Thomas,—Mary Lewin Thomas,—Evan Thomas, Elizabeth Thomas,—Harriet Thomas and Wethered Thomas), —Ann Wethered (who m. Henry Carvill, and had child., viz., Mary and John Carvill),— Lewin Wethered,— Elizabeth

Wethered (who m. Hon. D. N. Barringer, Minister Plenipotentiary and Envoy Extraordinary in 1850 to Spain, and had child., viz., Lewin, Elizabeth, Paul, Moreau and Samuel Barringer),—and James S. Wethered, who m. Mary Woodworth, and had child., viz., Lewina,—Carrie,—Molly, and Woodworth Wethered.

PEREGRINE WETHERED, son of Lewin and Elizabeth Ellicott Wethered, m. Louisa Maria Wickes, dau. of Lambert and Alethea Ireland Wickes, and had child., viz., Lewin and Ann Elizabeth Wethered, who m. W. N. E. Wickes. (See WICKES.)

ANN CATHARINE WETHERED, dau. of John and Mary Sykes Wethered, m. Robert C. Ludlow, U. S. N., and had child., viz., Bainbridge Ludlow, U. S. N.,—Augustus Ludlow, who m. A. Crook, and had child., viz., Mary C., Sally, Charlotte, Kate and Rose,—Mary Ludlow, who m. James Carroll (see CARROLL), and Catharine Ludlow.

CATHARINE MATILDA WETHERED, dau. of John and Mary Sykes Wethered, m. George Jaffrey, and had two child., viz., Matilda, d. 1850, and Mary Jaffrey, who m. Capt. H. Field, U. S. A.

HARRIET C. WETHERED, dau. of John and Mary Sykes Wethered, m. Admiral William B. Shubrick, U. S. N., and had two child., viz., Mary Shubrick, who m. Dr. George Clymer, Surgeon, U. S. N., and had a dau., Mary W. B. Shubrick Clymer, and Harriet Shubrick, d. 1830.

POLLY LEWIN, who m. Samuel Wethered, was descended from John Lewin, Esq., whose son, John, m. Miss Plomer, dau. of an Alderman of London, and had 4 child., viz., Elizabeth,—Mary,—John, and Thomas Lewin.

JOHN LEWIN, b. 1538, m. Sybil Allen, dau. of Sir William Allen, Knt., of London, who had a son, William, who had a son, Samuel Lewin, Esq., of London, whose son, Sir William Lewin, Knt., b. in 1664, Sheriff of London in 1713, m. Lady Susanna Champion, d. 1737, and had child., viz., Polly Lewin, who m. Samuel Wethered,—Richard Lewin, Esq., Sheriff of Kent in 1726,—Sarah Lewin, who m. Lord Colchester, and Catharine Lewin, who m. Sergeant Maynard, M. P.

The above (SEC. 108, H.) is taken, excepting a few particulars, from a lithographed chart, in the possession of Hon. John Wethered and other members of the family, entitled "Genealogy of the Wethered Family, Ashline Hall, Hertfordshire and Buckinghamshire, Great Berkhamsted, England."

SEC. 109. At a Court holden for the County of Kent at the Towne of New Yarmouth, the 22d day of June, By his Lordships Commissioners 1686;

Present—CAPT. WM. LAWRENCE

MR. JOHN HINSON	MR. ISAAC WINCHESTER
MR. WM. FRISBY	MR. CORN. COMEGYS
MR. CHARLES TILDEN	MR. HANS HANSON
MR. CHRISTE GOODHAND	MR. DANIEL NORIST.

Mr. Michael Turbutt produced a Commission appointing him Clerk of the County. Mr. Phillip Everett was Foreman of the Grand Jury at this Court. Mr. Edward Sweatman was the High Sheriff of Kent this year.

At the September Term the Court established and ordered the following to be published.

The Rates or Prices of Liquors Sett by this Court for the Ordinary.

	Lbs. Tobacco.
Brandy per gall	100
Rum per gall	080
Brandy Burnt per gall	100
Cider per gall	020
Quince drink & Perry per gall	025
Sherry Wines per gall	120
Port, a Port Wine per gall	060
Claret & white Wine per gall	060
Canary per Gall	150
A Bowl of Punch with one quart of Rum and Ingredients	040
Ditto Brandy	060
Madeira Wines per gall	076
Molasses beer per gall	012
Mault Beer—strong—per gall,	020

This Court Orders the Clarke to draw out and put up A Copy of the above Rates of Liquors in the Court house.

Tho. Joce, Clk.

There were 401 taxable persons in Kent in the year 1686.

Among the appropriations this year were the following interesting particulars:

To Valentine Southern for Expenses on the TOWNE ON KENT ISLAND, 400 lbs. of Tobacco.

To Mr. Anthony Workman for Expenses on the Towne on Kent Island, 380 lbs. Tob.

To Wm. Elliott for Laboring 6 days on the Towne on said Island, at 10—60 lbs. Tobacco.

SEC. 110. At a Court holden for Kent County the 22d day of March in the Twelfth year of the Dominion of the Rt. Honble Charles Lord Baron of Baltimore. Annoq Domi. 1686-7.

The Court Orders and appoints Constables for the year ensuing:

Thomas Seward, Constable for Eastern Neck. Benjamin Ricaud, Constable for Swan Creek. James Wattson, Henry Hosier, William Bateman, Constables for Langford's Bay. Richard Jones, Constable, Upper Hundred, Kent Island. Edward Jones ordered to remain until sufficient cause to the Court, showed to the contrary as aforesaid.

This Court orders that Mr. Wm. Harris who is bound for England, to buy and bring for the County of Kent the weights and scales according to Law for each Towne in said County and the costs and charge shall be allowed him in said County Levy.

1688.

At a Court holden for Kent County ye 25th day of Sept., Anno 1688. Mr. Charles Bass was Clerk.

1693

SEC. 111. Att their Majesties Court holden for Kent County the 28th day of November in ye fifth year of their Majesties Reigne 1693.

Present—CAPT. HANS HANSON MR. EDW. SWEATMAN
MR. DAN. NORRIS MR. JOHN COPEDGE,
Justices.

Mr. Charles Tilden sworne Sheriff. Mr. Charles Hynson, Clarke. Mr. Elias King sworne one of ye Justices of the Peace.

December ye 4th being ye Day appointed for Laying the County Levy, Mr. Hans Hanson, Mr. Daniel Norris, Mr. Elias King appearing, for want of another Justice adjourned to ye house of Mr. Edward Sweatman on ye 6th of this instant.

At a Court holden for Kent County for Laying ye Levy at ye house of Mr. Edward Sweatman ye sixth day of December in ye 5th year of their Majesties Reign Anno 1693.

Ordered by ye Court that ye 19th of this instant, December, be ye Day appointed for electing ye Vestrymen at ye Towne of New Yarmouth.

There were 476 Taxables in the County this year.

SEC. 112. At a Court holden by their Majesties Justices for Kent County at the Town of New Yarmouth, for Laying out ye Upper part of this County into parishes, this 19th day of December, in ye 5th year of their Majesties (William and Mary), Annoq Dom. 1693.

The Justices, with the advice of ye most principal freeholders present doe lay out ye upper part of this County for one District or Parish by ye name of St. Peters (now St. Paul's), to begin at ye Lower end of Eastern Neck, bounded by Chester River and ye Bay, so far as ye plantation that formerly did belong to Plarness and from thence by ye Division Line between Kent and Cecil county.

Entered pr. Charles Bass, Clk.

Their Majesties Justices do appoint ye 24th day of January for electing Vestrymen at the Town of New Yarmouth.

At their Majesties Court holden for Kent County ye 23d day of January in ye 5th year of their Majesties Reign Annoq. Dom. 1693.

Upon motion of Thomas Ringold to this Court it is ye opinion of this Court that a servant Judged at eighteen years should serve seven years.

The Court adjourns till to-morrow nine o'clock.

January ye 24th the Court is again sat.

Present—CAPT. HANS HANSON
MR. ELIAS KING MR. DANIEL NORRIS,
Justices.

These Justices for want of ye Justices from Kent Island and ye Sub Sheriff to Return his Writs from thence, doe order the Sheriff to keep all writts and processes in his custody till ye next Court.

The Court adjourns till ye fourth Tuesday in March.

SEC. 113. January ye 24th 1693–4 Being the day appointed, according to a former order of Justices of this County for the Electing and Chusing of Vestrymen for St. Peter's Parish, on which day at a meeting of ye most principal Freeholders and Justices, as aforesaid, at ye house of Mr. Thomas Joyce at ye

Towne of New Yarmouth, doth by a Free Election elect 6 Vestrymen, viz:

MR. THOMAS SMITH	MR. CHAS. TILDEN
MR. WM. FRISBY	MR. MICH. MILLER
MR. HANS HANSON	MR. SIMON WILMER.

On this day the Justices determined not to transact any business on the fourth Thursday in March next, but to adjourne the Court, then, until further notice. This was owing to a "distemper" which was raging and rendered the inhabitants incapable of attending.

1694.

SEC. 114. Att their Majesties Court holden for Kent County the 17th day of April in the sixth yeare of their Majesties Reign Annoq. Dom. 1694.

The Grand Jury called and sworne.

ABRAHAM SOUTHERN, Foreman,

ROBERT DEAVENISH	WM. OSBOURN
BENJAMIN RICAUD	ROBT BLUNT
JOSEPH SUDLER	JNO CHASE
EDW ROGERS	BENJ. BLACKLEACH
ROBERT PEARL	GRIFFITH JONES
WALTER BARLEY	RICHARD LOWDER

JOHN IVIOT.

Coroners called, both appear. Constables called: Isaack Bowles, Constable of Chester upper hundred, cont. Britton Queeny of Chester lower hundred, cont. Thomas Stevens appointed Constable of Langfords Bay hundred, sworne in open Court. Wm. Wright, Constable of Swan Creek hundred, cont. Joseph Wickes appointed Constable of Eastern Neck hundred. Edward Rawlins, Constable of ye Lower hundred of Kent Island. Anth. Workman, Constable of ye upper hundred, cont.

SEC. 115. Att their Majesties Court holden for Kent County, the 26th day of June in the sixth year of their Majesties Reigne Anno. 1694.

Present—CAPT. HANS HANSON,

MR. DANLL NORRIS	MR. ED. SWEATMAN
MR. ELIAS KING	MR. JOHN COPEDGE

Justices.

To the Worshipfull ye Justices of Kent County:

The Humble petition of John Hynson, Executor, Executor of Major Wickes late of Kent County, deceased:

Humbly sheweth, that on ye Island of Kent in ye jurisdiction of this Court, Major Wickes died possessed of a Certaine Tract of land commonly called and known by ye name of Love Point, upon which tract of land, by ye inhabitants of ye said Island there have and dayley are diveres incursions and trespasses, upon ye same caused by means of a Road that is made, and leads to ye point, not being to any other plantation nor to any publique Landing, nor to any publique advantage, but wholly to ye damage of your petitioner and them to whom ye heritage may descend, being within the inclosures of your petitioner & them concerned:

Prays order of this Court that ye long continued injuryes may cease and that there may noe Road be within the inclosures any more for ye persons, above, allowed, &c.

On the 27th of November 1694 Mr. Simon Wilmer took the Oath of Allegiance and abhorrency and qualified as Clerk of the County in the place of Charles Hynson.

Sec. 115, A. Simon Wilmer and Rebecca Wilmer, his wife, were the progenitors of the Wilmer Family of Kent. Simon Wilmer was a very prominent man in Old Kent. On the 24th of Jan'y 1693, he was elected one of the 1st Vestry of St. Paul's Parish, and represented Kent in 1698, in the Legislature of Maryland. He had child., viz., Simon Wilmer,—Lambert Wilmer,—Rebecca Wilmer, who m. Thomas Ringgold (see Ringgold), and Frances Wilmer, who m. Samuel Wickes (see Wickes).

Lambert Wilmer, son of Simon and Rebecca Wilmer, was a Vestryman of Shewsbury Parish, 10th April 1721, d. 1732, leaving his wife, Ann Wilmer, and had child., viz., Rebecca Wilmer, b. 4th March 1703, who m. Marmaduke Tilden (see Tilden),—Ann Wilmer, b. 23d Sept. 1705,—Mary Wilmer, b. 22d Oct. 1708,—Frances Wilmer, b. 24th March 1710,—Simon Wilmer, b. 12th April 1713,—Martha Wilmer, b. 24th Oct. 1715, and Lambert Wilmer.

Simon Wilmer, son of Lambert and Ann Wilmer, had child., viz., Edward Price Wilmer, b. 23d Sept. 1737,—Mary Wilmer, b. 17th Feb'y 1738, who m. William Geddes,—Simon Wilmer, b. 23d Aug. 1743,—John Lambert Wilmer, b. 8th June 1747,—James Jones Wilmer, b. 15th Jan'y 1749, and Ann Wilmer, b. 18th Jan'y 1755. His wife's name was Mary Wilmer.

EDWARD PRICE WILMER, son of Simon and Mary Wilmer, had child., viz., Simon, b. 8th Aug. 1766,—Lambert Wilmer, b. 8th Aug., 1768, and Edward Price Wilmer. His wife's name was Mary Wilmer.

EDWARD PRICE WILMER, son of Edward Price and Mary Wilmer, m. Rachel Wilson, dau. of George and Susan Holliday Wilson, and had child., viz., Henrietta,—Susan Elizabeth,—William Carmichael, and Edwin Wilmer.

HENRIETTA WILMER, dau. of Edward Price and Rachel Wilson Wilmer, m. Rev. Pennell Coombe and had child., viz., Cora Eugenia (who m. Rev. Thomas Poulson), Pennell Thomas, and Henrietta Wilmer Coombe.

SUSAN ELIZABETH WILMER, dau. of Edward Price and Rachel Wilson Wilmer, m. Lambson Farrow, and had child., viz., Charles Alfred and Laura Jane Farrow, who m. John Megredy McLenahan.

EDWIN WILMER, son of Edwin Price and Rachel Wilson Wilmer, m. Hannah Elizabeth Megredy, and had child., viz., Mary Rachel,—Emma Wilson,—Emma Rasin,—Laura Freeman,—Edwin Megredy,—Ellen Moor Reynolds, and Florence Zeilin Wilmer.

SIMON WILMER, son of Simon and Rebecca Wilmer, d. 1737, and left child., viz., William Wilmer,—Lambert Wilmer,—Dorcas Wilmer,—Margaret Wilmer,—Simon Wilmer,—a dau. who m. James Moore, and had a son, James Moore,—and Mary Wilmer, who m. Mr. Clay, and after his death m. 30th Oct. 1746, Rev. George William Forester, Rector of Shrewsbury Parish, and had child., viz., George William Forester, b. 22nd March 1748 (who m. 29th Aug. 1779, Temperance Redgrave, and had a dau., Mary Wilmer Forester, b. at 8 P. M. 8th June 1780),—Catharine Margaretta Forester, b. 17th Jan'y 1753, and Francis Dorcas Forester, b. 10th March 1755.

WILLIAM WILMER, son of the above-named Simon Wilmer, m. Rosa Blackiston, and had child., viz., Lambert,—William,—Mary, who m. Maj. William Ringgold, of Eastern Neck (see RINGGOLD),—Margaret, who m. James Frisby,—Frances, who m. Richard Miller,—and Martha Wilmer, who m. Mr. Bond.

BLACKISTON WILMER (son of William Wilmer and Rosa Blackiston) and Sarah Williamson, were m. 19th Feb'y 1778, and had child., viz., Elizabeth Wilmer, b. 4th Feb'y 1779 (who m. 7th Nov. 1805, Robert Tate, and had a dau. Sarah Maria, b. 5th Sept. 1806, who m. J. Frisby Gordon),—Maria

Wilmer, b. 22d Dec. 1780,—Sarah R. Wilmer, b. 14th Jan'y 1783,—Harriet Wilmer, b. 20th March 1785,—John Williamson Wilmer, b. 17th Dec. 1787, and William Blackiston Wilmer, b. 27th April 1791, d. 30th Jan'y 1853.

JOHN WILLIAMSON was b. 21st Feb'y 1717, m. 3d May 1738, Elizabeth Holt, who was b. 4th Sept. 1719. He d. 27th Oct. 1765. She d. 13th April 1786. They had child., viz., Maria Williamson. b. 9th Sept. 1739, d. 29th Sept. 1739,—Elizabeth Williamson, b. 22d March 1740-1, d. 29th Feb'y 1741-2,—John Holt Williamson, b. 26th Nov. 1742, d. 26th Feb'y 1742-3,—Ann Williamson, b. 25th Aug. 1744, d. 5th Sept. 1744,—Sarah Williamson, b. 26th May 1747, who m. 19th Feb'y 1778, Blackiston Wilmer, and d. 14th June 1827, and Mary Williamson, b. 19th June 1750.

JOHN WILLIAMSON WILMER, son of Blackiston Wilmer and Sarah Williamson, b. 17th Oct. 1787, m. 22nd Aug. 1809, Elizabeth Gittings Croxall, who was b. 9th March 1789, the dau. of Thomas and Eleanor Croxall. He d. 15th Dec. 1861. She d. 10th Feb'y 1845. They had child., viz., James Gittings Wilmer, b. 11th June 1810,—Ellen Wilmer, b. 5th Sept. 1811, d. 10th May 1870,—Elizabeth Williamson Wilmer, who m. 1st Aug. 1839 George R. Vickers (see VICKERS),—Sarah Jane Wilmer, b. 8th July 1815,—a 2nd Sarah Jane Wilmer, b. 13th Feb'y 1817, d. 31st Jan'y 1853,—Williamson Wilmer, b. 10th Sept. 1818,—a 2nd Williamson Wilmer, b. 8th Dec. 1819,—Harriet Wilmer, who m. 3d Oct. 1865, John S. Constable,—Rebecca Ann Wilmer, b. 10th Jan'y 1823, d. 27th Aug. 1849,—John Charles Wilmer, b. 3d Nov. 1825,—Edward Palmer Wilmer, b. 2d May 1827, d. 19th Aug. 1836,—Charles Wilmer, and William John Wilmer, who m. 29th Nov. 1855, Sarah Jane Gaskings, dau. of Samuel Gaskins, of Baltimore, and has a son, Samuel Gaskins Wilmer.

CHARLES WILMER, son of John Williamson Wilmer and Elizabeth Gittings Croxall, m. 31st Oct. 1860, Harriet M. Rogers, dau. of Lloyd N. Rogers, of Druid Hill, Baltimore County. She d. 16th April 1862 *sine prole*, and he m. 10th Nov. 1864, Mary A. Whittingham, dau. of Rt. Rev. William Rollinson Whittingham, Bishop of Maryland, and Hannah Harrison, of Orange, Essex County, New Jersey, and had child., viz., Phoebe Harrison Wilmer,—William Rollinson Whittingham Wilmer,—Elizabeth Croxall Wilmer,—Charles Wilmer, b. 19th Jan'y 1770, d., and Mary Condit Wilmer.

WILLIAM BLACKISTON WILMER, son of Blackiston and Sarah Williamson Wilmer, m. 16th April 1816, Mary Ann

Taylor, who was b. 22d Feb'y 1798, the only child of Philip Taylor and Annie James, and had child., viz., Sallie Anne Wilmer, who m. 23d Dec. 1847, George D. S. Handy,—William Blackiston, James Taylor Wilmer,—John Williamson Wilmer,—Mary Elizabeth Wilmer, who m. 18th Nov. 1869, Luther Handy, — Ellen Olivia, and Richard Cox Wilmer.

WILLIAM B. WILMER, son of William Blackiston and Mary Ann Taylor Wilmer, m. 11th Oct. 1852, Mary A. Brooks, and had child., viz., Alice Medford,—Mary Brooks,—Philip George,—William Thomas,—Helena Taylor,—John Handy, and William Blackiston William.

JOHN WILLIAMSON WILMER, son of William Blackiston Wilmer and Mary Ann Taylor, m. in Dec. 1859, Sallie Nicholson, of Queen Anne's, and had child., viz., Josephine,—Mary Taylor, Mary Anne Taylor, and Sallie Wilmer.

LAMBERT WILMER, son of Simon, and grandson of Simon and Rebecca Wilmer, m. Ann Elizabeth ———, d. in 1755, and had child., viz., Rebecca, and Simon Wilmer, b. 30th Aug. 1749, who d. 19th Oct. 1798, at the "White House Farm," near Chestertown, and was there buried.

SIMON WILMER, of the "White House Farm," son of Lambert and Ann Elizabeth Wilmer, m. 17th of May 1772, Ann Ringgold (dau. of James and Mary Ringgold), who was b. 17th Feb'y 1746, and had child., viz., Ann Eliza Wilmer, b. 29th Jan'y 1773, d. 13th March 1798 (who m. Mr. Miller, of Kent, and had a dau., Martha Rebecca),—Lambert Wilmer, b. 21st March 1774, d. in April 1775,—James Wilmer, b. Aug. 1775, d. 10th April 1831, in Phila., buried in Christ Church Cemetery,—Lambert Wilmer, b. March 1778, d. Sept. 1786,—Simon, b. 25th Dec. 1779,—William Henry Wilmer, b. 29th Oct. 1782, who m. Harriet Ringgold, d. 25th July, 1827, at Williamsburg, Va.,—John Ringgold Wilmer, b. 9th March 1784, m. Ann E. Eccleston, d. 22nd June 1823, buried at "White House Farm,—Peregrine Wilmer, b. Aug. 1786, and d. Sept. 1786,—and Mary Wilmer, b. 1788. Mrs. Ann Ringgold Wilmer d. 3rd April 1789, and was buried at the "White House Farm." Simon Wilmer m. again, Mary Dunn, and had child., viz., Peregrine, b. 19th June, 1791, d. 4th Feb'y 1836,—Sarah, b. in 1792, d. 25th Aug. 1824, at Alexandria, Va.,—Lemuel, b. 1st Jan'y 1795, d. 10th March 1869, and Anne Eliza Wilmer. Mrs. Mary Dunn Wilmer d. 29th March 1831, at Alexandria, Va.

SARAH WILMER, dau. of Simon Wilmer and his 2nd wife, Mary Dunn, m. Isaac Cannell, and had child., viz., Mary Susannah d., and Wilmer Cannell, who m. Sally Skipwith (sister of Helen Skipwith, wife of Bishop Joseph Pere Bell Wilmer, of Louisiana), and d. in 1873, leaving child., viz., Skipwith, who m. Miss Miller, of Phila.,—Wilmer,—Sally,—Virginia (who m. Mr. Wheeler, of Phila.),—Mary (who m. Howard Peterson, of Phila., and has one child),—Annie and Gertrude Cannell.

REVEREND LEMUEL WILMER, son of Simon Wilmer and his 2nd wife, Mary Dunn, was the Rector of Port Tobacco Parish, Charles County. "He had been in active charge of this parish nearly forty-seven (47) years, having entered upon its duties on the 1st of July 1822. He faithfully and laboriously cultivated this vineyard with almost the same burning zeal and energy in his last years that shone so brightly in his early ministry. Of his zeal and efficiency, the best evidence is found in the flourishing condition of the parish under his pastoral charge. He was enabled to meet almost without failure his weekly appointments every Sunday in two churches, at the distance of ten miles apart. And yet he was spared to a good old age, and in his seventy-fifth year he honorably and nobly fell with his harness on. To his persevering zeal and pious liberality St. Paul's Chapel, a beautiful temple, will be an enduring monument. The very day on which he was seized with his last sickness, he read the service and preached twice, administered the Holy Communion, and rode twenty miles." He was b. at the "White House Farm" in Kent County, 1st Jan'y 1795, and d. 10th March 1869. He m. Jane Henrietta Frisby, of Kent, who was b. 15th Jan'y 1795, and d. in Charles County, 23d Sept. 1865, and had child., viz., Lemuel Wilmer,—John Frisby Wilmer.—Henrietta Williamson Wilmer,—Ann Elizabeth Wilmer, who were b. in Kent, and the following child. b. in Charles, viz., Pere Wilmer,—William R. Wilmer, a 2nd Lemuel Wilmer,—Rebecca Frisby Wilmer, and Mary Jane Wilmer.

PERE WILMER, son of Rev. Lemuel Wilmer and Jane Henrietta Frisby, m. twice. His 1st wife was Susan Roberts, of Charles County, and had child., viz., Lemuel Allison Wilmer, Attorney, Baltimore, — Pere Wilmer, of Charles County, and Joseph Ringgold Wilmer, U. S. N. His 2nd wife was Alice Lilly, of Baltimore, and had child., viz., Ruth and Edith Wilmer.

DR. WILLIAM R. WILMER, son of Rev. Lemuel Wilmer and Jane Henrietta Frisby, m. Elizabeth M. Day, of Bridgeport, Conn., and had one son, Guy Wilmer.

LEMUEL WILMER, son of Rev. Lemuel Wilmer and Jane Henrietta Frisby, m. 10th July 1861, Henrietta M. Brawner, dau. of Henry Middleton Brawner and Catharine Robertson (see ROBERTSON), and had child., viz., Jane,—Catharine,—William Ringgold,—Henrietta Maria, and Lemuel Wilmer.

JAMES WILMER, son of Simon Wilmer and his 1st wife Ann Ringgold, m. 15th Sept. 1797, Ann Emerson, of Easton (dau. of Thomas Emerson, of England), and had child., viz., Elizabeth (who m. 20th May 1823, Lynford Lardner, who d. in 1834, leaving one son, John Lardner),—Nancy,—Margaret,—Robert, who m. Miss Heath, of Phila.,—James, who d. 1840,—John Ringgold,—Mary Louisa, who m. William Lippincott, of Phila., and Ellen Wilmer.

NANCY WILMER, dau. of James and Ann Emerson Wilmer, m. Samuel Rush, son of Dr. Benjamin Rush of Phila., and had child., viz., William Rush and Julia Rush, who m. Alexander Biddle, of Phila., and had child., viz., Alexander William,—Henry,—Julia Rush,—Wilmer,—Lewis,—Marriamne, and Lynford Biddle.

MARGARET WILMER, dau. of James and Ann Emerson Wilmer, m. Admiral James Lardner, U. S. N., and d. in 1845, leaving two child., viz., Lynford Lardner (who m. Ella Sweetser, of Boston, and had a dau. Margaret), and Margaret Lardner, who m. Edward Reakirt, of Phila. ADMIRAL JAMES LARDNER survived his wife, Margaret Wilmer Lardner, and m. in 1851, her sister, Ellen Wilmer, and had child., viz., Ringgold Wilmer Lardner and James Lardner.

JOHN RINGGOLD WILMER, son of James and Ann Emerson Wilmer, m. Miss Teissiere, of Phila., who d. 1852 *sine prole*. His 2nd wife, m. 1855, was Nathalie Chazournes, and had child., viz., Marie Louisa,—James,—John Ringgold,—Charles B., and Marie Eliza Nathalie Wilmer.

REVEREND SIMON WILMER, son of Simon and Ann Ringgold, m. Rebecca Frisby, and had child., viz., John Ringgold Wilmer,—Joseph Pere Bell Wilmer,—Mary Ann Wilmer, and William L. Wilmer. His 2nd wife was Mrs. Eleanor Tubman, and had child., viz., Mary Rebecca Frisby Wilmer, and Elizabeth Wilmer.

RT. REV. JOSEPH PERE BELL WILMER, son of Rev. Simon Wilmer and his 1st wife, Rebecca Frisby, was consecrated in Christ Church, New Orleans, Wednesday, 7th Nov. 1866,

Bishop of Louisiana, being the 80th in the succession of American Bishops, of the Protestant Episcopal Church. He m. Helen Skipwith, of Mechlenburg County, Va., and had child., viz., Skipwith,—Rebecca,—Joseph,—Helen Skipwith,—William Nivison, and John Ravenscroft Wilmer. Helen Skipwith was the dau. of Hon. Humberston Skipwith and Sarah Nivison. Hon. Humberston Skipwith was the 2nd son of Sir Peyton and Lady Jean Skipwith.

SKIPWITH WILMER, son of Rt. Rev. Joseph Pere Bell Wilmer and Helen Skipwith, m. 15th June 1871, Delia Jarvis Tudor, dau. of Frederick and Euphemia Tudor, of Boston, and had child., viz., Euphemia Fenno, b. 28th April 1872, d. 5th May 1873,—Joseph Pere Bell, d. 2nd June 1874, and Helen Skipwith Wilmer.

JOHN RINGGOLD Wilmer, son of Rev. Simon Wilmer and his 1st wife, Rebecca Frisby, m. Lydia Longstreth, and had child., viz., William Craig and John R. Wilmer.

MARY REBECCA WILMER, dau. of Rev. Simon Wilmer and his 2nd wife. Eleanor Tubman, m. Dr. James Burd Peale, of Holmesburg, Phila., son of Rubens Peale and Eliza Patterson, of Germantown, Pa., and had child., viz., Eleanor Wilmer Peale,—Caroline Elise Peale, and Elizabeth Burd Peale. (See PEALE.)

REV. WILLIAM HENRY WILMER, D. D., son of Simon and Ann Ringgold Wilmer, was President of the "General Convention of the Bishops, the Clergy and the Laity of the Protestant Episcopal Church in the United States," President of William and Mary College, and also a Professor in the Virginia Theological Seminary. He m. three times. His 1st wife was Harriet Ringgold, dau. of James Ringgold. His 2d wife was Miss Cox, and had child., viz., William Wilmer d.,—the Right Reverend Richard Hooker Wilmer, D. D., who was consecrated Bishop of Alabama, 6th of March 1862,—Rev. George Wilmer, D. D.,—Jane Eliza Wilmer, who m. Rev. Samuel Buel, D. D., Professor in the General Theological Seminary, New York,—Marion Wilmer, who m. Rev. R. Templeton Brown, and Maria Wilmer. His 3d wife was Anne Fitzhugh, and had several child., of whom, only one is living, Elizabeth Wilmer. He d. 25th July 1827.

SEC. 115, B. DR. JAMES BURD PEALE, who m. Mary Rebecca Frisby Wilmer, was descended from the world-renowned artist, Charles Willson Peale, and William Shippen.

WILLIAM SHIPPEN, of Yorkshire, England, had child., viz., a dau., who m. Mr. Leybourne, of Yorkshire,—Rev. William

Shippen, Rector of St. Mary's Church, Stockport, and Edward Shippen, who was b. in 1639, and emigrated to America.

EDWARD SHIPPEN and his 1st wife, Elizabeth Lybrand, of Boston, had child., viz., Frances, b. at Boston, 2d Feb'y 1672, d. 9th April 1673,—Edward, b., same place, 2nd Oct. 1674, d. 2d Nov. 1674,—William, b, same place, 4th Oct. 1675, d. 1676,—Eliza, b. Aug. 1676, d. young,—Edward, b., at Boston, 10th Dec. 1677, d., at Philadelphia, 26th Dec. 1712 (who m. Anna Francina Vanderleyden, and had a dau., Margaret, who m. John Jekyl, Collector of the port of Boston, and had child., viz., Francis Jekyl, who m. William Hicks, and Margaret, who m. Mr. Chalmers),—Joseph, b., at Boston, 28th Feb'y 1678-9,—Mary, b. 6th May 1681, d. 1688, and Anne Shippen, b., at Boston, 17th June 1684, who m. 10th July 1706, Thomas Story, and d. *sine prole.*

JOSEPH SHIPPEN, son of Edward Shippen and Elizabeth Lybrand, m., in Boston, 28th July 1702, Abigail Grosse, dau. of Thomas and Elizabeth Grosse. She d. 28th June 1716, at Phila. They had child., viz., Edward, b., in Boston, 9th July 1703,—Elizabeth, b., in Phila., 17th April 1765, d. 8th June 1714,—Joseph, b., in Phila., 28th Nov. 1706, m. Mary Kearney, and d. in June 1793,—William, b. 31st Aug. 1708, d. 29th Dec. 1710,—Anne, b. 5th Aug. 1710, m. 21st Jan'y 1731, Charles Willing, who was b. 18th May 1710, at Bristol, England, and d., in Phila., 30th Nov. 1754, where she also d. 23d June 1790,—William, b. 1st Oct. 1712, and Elizabeth Shippen, b. 28th Sept. 1714, d. 3d Dec. 1714.

EDWARD SHIPPEN, eldest son of Joseph Shippen and Abigail Grosse, m. at Philadelphia, 20th Sept. 1726, Sarah Plumley, dau. of Charles and Rose Plumley, who was b. in Philadelphia, 8th Nov. 1706, d. 28th April 1735. They had child., viz., Elizabeth, b. 17th Aug. 1726, d. 29th Aug. 1726,—Joseph and William, *twins*, b. and d. Sept. 1727,—Edward, b. 16th Feb'y 1728-9, Chief Justice of Pennsylvania (who m. Margaret Francis, dau. of Tench Francis and Elizabeth Turbutt, and had 9 child., viz., Elizabeth (who m. Maj. Edward Burd, son of Col. James Burd and Sarah Shippen, and had child., viz., Edward Stephen Burd, who m. Miss Sims, Margaret Burd, who m. D. W. Coxe, and Sarah Burd),—Sarah (who m. Thomas Lea, and had child., viz., Robert Lea, Margaret Lea, who m. Dominick Lynch, Jane Lea, who m. Julius Izard Pringle, of S. C., Dominick Lea, who m. Antonio Aquimba, Margaret Shippen Lea, who m. Stewart C. Maitland, and George Harrison Lea),—Edward (who m. Elizabeth Footman, and had child., viz., Edward, Margaret, Elizabeth, Richard, Mary and Fanny Shippen),—Mary (who m. Dr. William McIlvaine, and had child., viz., William, Edward Bloomfield, Maria, and Margaret McIlvaine),—James,—Margaret (who m. 8th April 1779, Genl. Benedict Arnold, and left many descendants, now living in England),—Sarah, b. 22d Feb'y 1730,—Joseph, b. 30th Oct. 1732, and Rose Shippen, b. 10th Sept. 1734, d. young.

SARAH SHIPPEN, dau. of Edward Shippen and Sarah Plumley, m. Col. James Burd, the 3rd son of Edward Burd, of Ormiston, near Edingburgh, Scotland, and his wife, Jane Halliburton, a dau. of the Lord Provost of Edingburgh. Col. Burd and his wife d. at his estate of Tinian, near Harrisburg. He was elected 18th Sept. 1773, Colonel of a Regiment in the Revolutionary Army. They had child., viz., Sarah Burd, who m. Judge Jasper Yeates,—Edward Burd (who m. his cousin, Elizabeth Shippen, dau. of Chief Justice Edward Shippen and Margaret Francis),—Jane Burd, who m. GEORGE PATTERSON,—Margaret Burd, who m. Jacob Hubley,—James Burd, who m. Elizabeth Baker, and Joseph Burd, who m. 1st Kitty Cochrane, 2dly Harriet Bailey.

SEC. 115, C. ELIZA PATTERSON, dau. of George Patterson and Jane Burd, m. Rubens Peale, son of Charles Willson Peale and Rachel Brewer, and had child., viz., Charles Willson,—George Patterson,—William,—Mary,—James Burd, and Edward Burd Peale, who m. 9th Nov. 1859, Louisa Harriet Hubley, dau. of Hon. Francis Hubley, and had child., viz., Anna Frances and Rubens Peale.

DR. JAMES BURD PEALE, son of Rubens Peale and Eliza Patterson, m. Mary C. M. Burney, and had two child., viz., Mary Burd and Jane Peale. He m. a 2nd time Mary Rebecca Frisby Wilmer, dau. of Rev. Simon Wilmer and Eleanor Tubman, and had child., viz., Eleanor Wilmer,—Caroline,—Elise, and Elizabeth Burd Peale.

RUBENS PEALE, the father of Dr. James Burd Peale, was descended from the Rev. Charles Peale, Rector of Edith Weston, County of Rutland, England, heir-in-tail to the manor of Wootten, Oxfordshire, the estate of Charles Willson, Doctor of Physic, who d. in Stamford, Lincolnshire, in March 1724. The Rev. Charles Peale left a son, Charles Peale, who came to this country, and a dau., Margaret Jane Peale.

CHARLES PEALE settled in Kent and was for many years a teacher in the celebrated Free School at Chestertown. He was an accomplished scholar and a polished gentleman. In the absence of the clergyman of the parish he occasionally officiated at divine service. He d. in 1750, leaving a widow and five child., viz., Charles Willson Peale,—Margaret Jane Peale, who m. Col. Nathaniel Ramsay, of the British Army, —St. George Peale, who was distinguished as the head of the Land Office,—Elizabeth Digby Peale, who m. Capt. Polk, and James Peale, the celebrated painter of miniatures and still life.

CHARLES WILLSON PEALE was b. in Chestertown 16th April 1741, and at an early age went to Annapolis and engaged in the saddler, coach, clock, watch making, and silversmith business. While on a visit to Norfolk he saw some pictures, painted by a Mr. Frazier, which were so far below his idea of art, which had been formed by the contemplation of a portrait of Lord Baltimore, at Annapolis, that he was inspired with a hope of excelling, and, at once, determined to be an artist.

Upon his return with the materials to be found in a coach factory of that day, he painted a landscape and portrait of himself, holding a palette and brushes in his hand, with a clock in the back-ground. He afterwards visited England and received instruction from Mr. West and Mr. Flaxman. In 1776 he settled in Phila. as an artist, but soon became deeply interested and actively engaged in the patriotic movements of the people. He raised a company of volunteers, was elected Captain, and served in the battles of Trenton and Germantown.

In 1786 the idea of forming a Museum of Natural History was suggested to his mind by some bones of the Mammoth, which were brought to him to make drawings from. In 1810 he succeeded in establishing an Academy of the Fine Arts. He m. 3 times. His 1st wife was Rachel Brewer. He d. in 1827, and left child., viz., Raphael,—Angelica Kaufman,— Rembrandt,—Rubens,—Sophonisba,—Carriera,—Linaeus,— Franklin,—Sybilla,—Meriam,—Elizabeth, and Titian Peale.

RUBENS PEALE, son of Charles Willson Peale and Rachel Brewer, m. Eliza Patterson, and had child. before-mentioned.

SEC. 115, D. GEORGE R. VICKERS, who m. Elizabeth Williamson Wilmer, was descended from George Vickers, who m. Rebecca, dau. of David Phipery, emigrated from England to Mass., and d. about 1679, leaving sons, viz., George,—Isaac, and Jonathan Vickers.

GEORGE VICKERS, son of George Vickers and Rebecca Phipery, m. Lucy ———, and had child., viz., Silvanus, b. 13th June 1683,—Hannah, b. 9th Sept. 1685,—George, b. 14th Aug. 1688,—Elizabeth, b. 1693,—Lucy, b. 20th Oct.

1695, d. 2d Aug. 1698,—Israel, b. 30th Nov. 1698, d. 28th Jan'y 1699, and a 2nd Israel, b. 17th Dec. 1699.

GEORGE VICKERS, son of George and Lucy Vickers, m. 10th Dec. 1710, Elizabeth Binney, and had child., viz., Mercy, b. 14th Sept. 1711, and George Vickers, b. 12th Nov. 1713.

GEORGE VICKERS, son of George Vickers and Elizabeth Binney, m. 1730, Lydia Tower, removed to the Eastern Shore of Maryland, and had child., viz., Jesse Vickers, b. 16th Oct. 1737 (who m. Jennie Clothier, and had child., viz., Benjamin, Celia, Milly, and Sarah),—Abner Vickers, b. 6th Nov. 1740, who had child., viz., Asa and Rosa,—Benjamin Vickers, b. 26th Jan'y 1742,—William Vickers, b. 8th Jan'y 1746,—George Vickers, b. 6th Nov. 1747,—Lydia Vickers, b. 30th May 1749 (who m. Jacob Shaffer, and had child., viz., Barbara and Elizabeth Shaffer), and James Vickers, b. 22nd July 1752, m. Avis Rollison, and had child., viz., Ella, and Elizabeth Vickers, who m. John Atkisson. Lydia Tower was b. 1st May 1713, the dau. of Hezekiah Tower and Elizabeth, dau. of Mathew Whiton. Hezekiah Tower was the son of Ibrook Tower and Margaret, dau. of John Hardin. Ibrook Tower was the son of John Tower, who m. 13th Feb'y 1639, Margaret Ibrook, and John Tower was the son of Robert Tower and Dorothy Dawson, who were m. 1607, in Norfolk Co., England.

BENJAMIN VICKERS, son of George Vickers and Lydia Tower, m. Rachel Roberts, and had child., viz., David, b. 16th Oct. 1765,—Ann, b. 16th Sept. 1767, who m. Samuel Beck, and d. 1839,—Elizabeth, b. 20th Dec. 1771, d. 12th Jan'y 1832,—Captain Joel, b. 14th Aug. 1774, d. 2nd Dec. 1860,—Samuel, b. 6th Sept. 1776, d. 31st Aug. 1802,—Benjamin, b. 28th Oct. 1778, d. an infant,—William, b. 18th Feb'y 1783, d. 23rd Feb'y 1865, *sine prole*,—Sophia, b. 16th Jan'y 1786, d. an infant,—John R. Vickers, b. 18th Dec. 1787, lost at sea, 1811, and Mary Vickers, b. 16th Jan'y 1781, who m. William Voss, and had child., viz., Elizabeth Rachel,—Hester Ann (who m. Rev. George Barton, and d. 1840, leaving a son, George I. Barton),—Mary Jane (who m. James W. Phillips, and d. 21st May 1852, leaving child., viz., Wealthy Anne, d., Hester Ann, Geraldine, Mary Jane, and John W. Phillips, d.), Sophia V. Voss, who d. unm. 10th Sept. 1832.

CAPT. JOEL VICKERS, son of Benjamin Vickers and Rachel Roberts, m. Ada Beck, of Kent, removed to Baltimore, and had child., viz., Geraldine Vickers, d.,—Celena Vickers, who m. Charles Jessup,—George R. Vickers (who m. 1st Aug.

1839, Elizabeth Williamson Wilmer, dau. of John W. Wilmer, of Baltimore, d. 1875, and had child., viz., Joel, Ada, George, Samuel Roberts, and William H. Collins Vickers),—Benjamin Albert Vickers (who m. Mary I., dau. of Francis Foreman, and had child., viz., Benjamin Albert, Annie, Robert J. Walker, Geraldine Sarah, Mary, Frances, and Charles Jessup Vickers), and a 2nd Geraldine Vickers.

WILLIAM VICKERS, son of George and Lydia Tower Vickers, m. Margaret Bordley, and had child., viz., Capt. James, b. 22d Feb'y 1776,—Mary, who m. Richard Ayres, and had a dau., Elizabeth Ayres, and Jesse Vickers, who m. Mary Redgrave, and left a son, Jesse Vickers.

CAPT. JAMES VICKERS, son of William Vickers and Margaret Bordley, participated in the battle of Caulks' Field, and was one of the gallant few who remained all night upon the ground to succor the wounded. He m. Ann Davis, of Queen Anne's, who d. 1827. He d. Oct. 1818. They had sons, viz., William, d. an infant, and Gen. George Vickers, b. 19th Nov. 1801.

GENERAL GEORGE VICKERS, of Chestertown, son of Capt. James Vickers and Ann Davis, was admitted to the bar of Kent in 1832, in 1836 was one of twenty-one Whig members of the Senatorial College, and subsequently declined the appointment of Judge tendered by Governors Bradford and Hicks. In 1864 he was a Presidential Elector. In 1865 he was elected a member of the Senate of Maryland. In 1868 he was elected a Senator of the United States, voted for the acquittal of President Johnson, and filed a written statement of the reasons for his vote. In 1861 he was appointed by Gov. Hicks, Maj. General of the Maryland Militia. He m. 5th Jan'y 1826, Mary, dau. of James Mansfield, of Chestertown, and had eleven child., viz., George Jefferson Vickers, b. 30th Nov. 1826, d. 28th April 1864,—James Mansfield Vickers,—William Albert Vickers, b. 28th July 1831, d. 17th Oct. 1832,—a 2nd William Albert Vickers, b. 29th April 1834, (who m. Mary Emma Boon, dau. of James Boon, and d. 30th April 1874, leaving child., viz., George Smith, Percy Bates, and James Boon Vickers),—Benjamin Clothier Vickers, b. 29th April 1836 (who entered the Regiment of General (Bishop) Polk, C. S. A., was mortally wounded at Shiloh, and d. at Memphis in June 1862),—Annette Tower Vickers, b. 17th May 1839, d. 30th Sept. 1842,—Harrison Wilson Vickers, b. 28th Jan'y 1841, d. 11th Oct. 1842,—a second Annette Tower Vickers (who m. John Henry White, and had child., viz., George Vickers, John Cleveland, and Mary Clara White), —a 2nd Harrison Wilson Vickers (the present, 1876, State's Attorney for Kent, who m. Jennie Yates Barber Shemwell, of St. Mary's Co., and has child., viz., Mary Barber and Jennie Vickers),—Polly Vickers, b. 12th June 1848, d. 12th Sept. 1848, and Mary Clara Vickers, who m. 24th Aug. 1871, Jefferson Rives, of Washington, D. C. He was b. 4th Feb'y 1847, and d. 20th Dec. 1874, *sine prole.*

George Vickers, son of George and Lydia Tower Vickers, m. Margaret Price, of Cecil, and had child., viz., George, d. unm.,—Abraham, d. unm.,—Sarah (who m. Thomas Bishop, and had child., viz., Thomas V. and Charles Bishop),—Margaret (who m. John Hurtt, of Kent, and left a dau., Margaret Hurtt),—Rebecca, d. unm.,—Thomas (who m. Maria Edes, and left child., viz., John R., Margaret, Mary Frances, Annie, and Thomas),—Samuel (who m. 1st Miss Hardcastle, of Caroline, had a son, Rev. John Thomas Vickers, and 2ndly Miss Roberts, of Queen Anne's),—Martha (who m. Darius Dunn), and Elizabeth Vickers, who m. twice, 1st Jeremiah Glenn and 2ndly Christopher Goodhand.

Sec. 116. At their Majesties Court holden for Kent County, the twenty-eighth day of August, in the sixth year of their Majesties Reign, Anno 1694,

Present—Capt. Hans Hanson Mr. Edward Sweatman
Mr. Elias King, Mr. John Copidge.

This Court doth confirme the meeting of the three Justices, the 15th of this instant, having then appointed the twenty-ninth of this instant to be the day for the Electing and Choosing of four Deputys or Delegates for this County.

By Virtue of a Writt, directed to the Sheriff of this County for the Electing and chusing of four Deputys or Delegates for this County, the said Writt being Read in Order, for the Election:

The Freemen of this County doth Elect,
Mr. William Frisby, Mr. John Hynson,
Mr. Hans Hanson, Mr. Tho. Smith,
to serve as Burgesses for this County.

When the Court met, on the 22d day of January 1694–95, it was found that, "by reason of the hard and Frosty weather," the inhabitants of Kent Island could not possibly come over to the Court, and the writs and processes could not be returned from thence. The Court adjourned without transacting any business.

SEC. 117. At a session of the Court 28th Nov. 1694, The following Order was passed:

By reason of a great and dangerous mortalitie in the neighboring Province of Pennsilvania, it is by this Court ordered that no person inhabiting in the Countie doe entertaine any stranger, travelling from any part out of this Province. And that no person inhabiting in this Countie may Travel into any part of Pennsilvania or the Territories thereunto belonging untill January Court next upon pain and penaltie of being proceeded against according to Law in that case made and provided, and all Constables are hereby required to give notice to the inhabitants of their respective hundred.

There were 458 Taxables in the County this year.

1695.

SEC. 118. At a Court held for Kent County ye 27th day of August in this 7th year of their Majesties reigne Annoq. Dom. 1695.

Present—LIEUT. COLL. HANS HANSON,
MAJ. THOMAS SMITH, CAPT. EDWARD SWEATMAN,
CAPT. JOHN COPEDGE, CAPT. THOMAS RINGGOLD,
Justices.

Saml. Glenn prefers a petition to this Court, viz:

That your petitioner being intermarried with the youngest daughter of John Wodge of this County, deceased, and there being due to your Petitioner out of ye Estate of Philip Davis late of this County, deceased: two Cowes and Calves, Now for it, that Edward Walvin having married the Executrix of Philip Davis and having ye said Cattle in his possession and denying the delivery of the same to your Petitioner, and Considering that all the other daughters of the said Wodge after their several marriages having had their respective parts except your Petitioner; humbly supplicates to grant your Petitioner an order for the said Two Cowes and Calves as aforesaid, and he shall ever pray as in duty bound.

his
SAMUEL x GLENN.
mark

And the said Glenn having produced to the Court a Certificate of Marriage Betwixt him and Eliz. Wodge, bearing date the first day of January Anno Dom. 1694 and attested under the Seale of the County of Kent, one of the Counties annexed to the Province of Pennsilvania and signed by William

Rodeny, Clk of the said County, the 22d day of August, Anno Dom. 1695, which is approved by this Court.

This Court have ordered that Samuel Glenn have Two Cowes and Calves out of the Estate of Philip Davis, late of this county, deceased, now in possession of Edward Walvin, who married with the relict of the said Philip Davis.

SIMON WILMER, Clk.

There were 467 Taxable persons in the County this year.

1696.

At a Court held for Kent County the 25th day of June in ye Eighth year of the Reign of William the 3d, Annoq. Dom. 1696, at ye house of Mr. Daniel Norris.

Mr. William Hemsley produced a Commission from the Attorney General to be Clerk of Indictments and he was sworn according to Law.

There were 515 taxable persons in Kent county in the year 1696.

At the following January Term of the Court Mr. Michael Earle and Mr. Richard Marklin petitioned the Court to be permitted to practice as Attorneys in this Court, which was allowed.

Capt. Edward Sweatman was High Sheriff of Kent county this year.

1697.

SEC. 119. At a Court held for Kent County ye 22d day of June in the ninth yeare of the Reigne of William the Third Annoq. Dom. 1697,

Ordered, by this Court that the Writts be returned by the Sheriff to the Clerk by eight of the clock on the morning of each respective Court-day, and that the Clerk be then ready to produce them, and that upon default of either the sd Sheriff or Clerk, offending against the said Order be fined the sum of one thousand pounds of tobacco to be disposed of as the Justices of this Court shall see fit.

SEC. 120. To the Worshipfull his Majesties Justices of the Peace for Kent County, the humble Petition of William Brewer humbly showeth:

That whereas your Petitioner came into the Country as a Servant sould to Major Joseph Wickes and served him in his life time three years and since his Death he hath served Coll. St. Ledger Codd four years, the just time adjudged for him to serve: May it please your Worships, your Petitioner came into the Country on the 20th day of April 1690.

Therefore your humble Petitioner humbly prays your Worships to take the case of your sd Petitioner into your serious and mature consideration, whose property is to doe justice, &c.

The Court having considered the above Petition and it appearing to them that the said Wm. Brewer has served his full and due time.

It is therefore considered by this Court that William Brewer do recover, from Coll. St. Ledger Codd, Corn and Clothes according to the Custome and usage of this Province in such cases.

Sec. 121. At a Court held for Kent County the 24th day of August in the ninth yeare of the Reigne of King William the Third, Annoq. Dom. 1697.

Capt. Edward Sweatman produceth to this Court a new Commission for the Justices of Court, which is by this Court ordered to be read and is accordingly performed and hereunder Recorded:

William the Third, by the Grace of God, of England, Scotland, France and Ireland, King, Defender of the Faith &c.

To Mr. William Frisby, Mr. John Hinson, Mr. Hans Hanson, Mr. Thos. Smyth, Mr. James Smith, Mr. John Whittington, Mr. Charles Hynson, Mr. Thomas Ringgold, Mr. Philip Hopkins, of Kent County, Gent.:

Know ye for the great trust and confidence We have in your Fidelitie, circumspection, prudence and Wisdom, have constituted, ordained and appointed and by these presents Doe constitute Ordaine and appoint you the said William Frisby, John Hynson, Hans Hanson, Thomas Smyth, James Smith, Charles Hynson, Thomas Ringgold and Philip Hopkins, Commissioners, joyntly and severally to keepe the Peace in Kent County and to keep and cause to be kept all Lawes and orders for the conservation of the peace and for the quiet rule and Government of the people, in all and every Articles of the same and so Chastize and punish all persons offending against the forme of any of the Lawes and Orders of this our Province, or any of them in Kent County aforesaid, according to the Lawes and Orders, shall be fit to be done.

Wee have also constituted and appointed you and every four or more of you of which you the said William Frisby, John Hynson, Hans Hanson and Thomas Smyth or one of you are allways to be one of the Commissioners to Enquire of the

Oaths of good and Lawfull men of your County, aforesaid, of all manner of Felonies, Witchcrafts, Inchantments, Soceries, Magick art, Trespasses, Forestallings, Ingrossings, and Extortions whatsoever, and of all and singular other misdeeds and offences, whatsoever, of which Justices of the Peace, in England, may or ought Lawfully to Enquire, by whomsoever or wheresoever done or perpetrated, or which hereafter shall be done or perpetrated in the county aforesaid, against the Lawes and Orders of this Province, *Provided* you proceed not in any of the cases aforesaid to the life or Members, But that in every such case you send the Prisoners with their Indictments and the whole matter depending before you to the next Provincial Court to be holden for this our Province, whensoever and wheresoever to be holden, there to be Tryed. And further Wee doe hereby Authorize and Impower you to issue out Writts, Process, and Attachments, and to hold Plea of Oyer and Terminor, in all actions, real, personal and mixt, and after Judgment, Execution to award in all causes civil, according to the Lawes, orders and reasonable customes made and provided in this our Province of Maryland except in matters relating to Titles of Land. In which cause civil soe to be Tryed, Excepting as before Excepted, Wee do constitute and appoint You the several and respective persons aforesaid to be Judges as aforesaid: And therefore Wee doe Commend You, that you diligently Intend the keeping of the Lawes and Orders of all and singular other the premises, and at certain dayes appointed, according to Act of Assembly, in such case made and provided, and at such place as You or any Four or more of you as aforesaid, shall in that behalfe appoint, you make Inquiry upon the premises and perform and fulfill the same in forme aforesaid, doing therein what to Justice appertaineth according to the Lawes, Orders and reasonable Customes of this our Province, and therefore Wee Command the Sheriff of our County by virtue of these presents, that at the place and on the dayes, aforesaid, that you or any such four or more of you as aforesaid, shall make knowne to him that he give his attendance on you, and, if need require, he cause to come before you, or any such four or more of you, such and so many good and Lawfull men of your County by whom the truth of the premises may the better be knowne and inquired. And chiefly you shall cause to be brought before you on the days and at the place aforesaid the writts, proofs, process, and Indictments to your Court and Jurisdiction belonging, that the same may be Inspected and by due Course determined.

Witness our Trusty and Well beloved Francis Nicholson, Esq. our Capt. General and Governor in Chief in and over our Province and Territory of Maryland this sixteenth day of June in the ninth year of our Reigne, Annoq. Dom. 1697.

(Seal) FR. NICHOLSON.

William the Third, by the grace of God of England, Scotland, France and Ireland, King Defender of the Faith, to Mr. John Hynson, and Mr. Hans Hanson and Thomas Smyth of Kent County, Gent. *Greeting:* Wee doe authorise you the said Hans Hanson and Thomas Smyth or either of you to Administer the Oathes appointed by Act of Parliament, instead of the Oathes of Allegiance and Supremacy, as alsoe the Oath of Justice to the said John Hinson, And you the said John Hynson having taken the said Oathes are to administer the same unto the said Hans Hanson and Thomas Smyth and the rest of the Justices and Commissioners of the said County, respectively as they are nominated in the within written Commission. And that you and every of you doe severally subscribe the test, and for soe Doeing this shall be your sufficient Authority hereof, fail not and when you have soe done you are to Certifie the same under your hands and seals, unto to us in our High Court of Chancery, with all convenient speed.

Witness our Trusty and well beloved Francis Nicholson Esq. Capt. General and Governor in Chief in and over our Province and Territory of Maryland this sixteenth day of June in the ninth yeare of our Reigne, Annoq. Dom 1697.

(Seal) FR. NICHOLSON.

The above Commission and Dedimus Potestatem being distinctly read Lieutenant Coll. Hans Hanson administered the Oathes appointed by Act of Parliament instead of the Oathes of Allegiance and abhorrency, as alsoe the Oath of Justice unto Coll. John Hynson who likewise administered the said Oathes to the rest of the Justices, as they are nominated in the above Cond. all but Capt. James Smith who came not then to Court.

Capt. Edward Sweatman read several orders of Council and Acts of Assembly.

SEC. 122. The County Levy was laid, the 8th of Nov. 1697, upon the basis of 538 Taxable persons.

Immediately after it is recorded the following:

William the Third, by the Grace of God, King of England, Scotland, France and Ireland, Defender of the Faith, &c.

To the Sheriff of Kent County, Greeting;

Whereas at a Court held, at the house of Isaac Caulk, the 8th of November, Anno Dom. 1697, by our Justices of our County of Kent, for assessing the sd County Levy or Tax, and that it doth appear that the late Tax or charge amounts to the sum of Twenty Four Thousand seven hundred forty and eight pounds of tobacco and alsoe that there is assessed upon every taxable person the sum of forty pounds of tobacco per poll, by virtue of an Act of Assembly made at the Port of Annapolis the tenth day of July Anno Dom. 1696 (chap. xviii) Entitled an Act for the Service of Almighty God and Establishment of the Protestant Religion, both which sums amounts to the sum of Forty Six Thousand two hundred sixty and eight pounds of tobacco at Eighty and six pounds of tobacco per poll, there being returned five hundred ninety and eight Taxables for our said County of Kent. Wee Command you therefore that of every taxable person within the same that you Levy by way of Execution on their persons or Estates the sd sum of Eighty six pounds of Tobacco per poll and that first of the said sumes being 24748 lbs. of tobacco you make punctual and speedy payment thereof to the persons above named according to the several proportions to them allotted as abovesaid and the other sume being 21520 lbs. of tobacco, You pay according as in the said Act is expressed; hereof fail not at your peril, and for so doing this shall be your Warrant.

1698.

Sec. 123. At a Court held for Kent County the 28th day of June in the 10th year of the Reigne of William the Third, &c. Annoq. Dom. 1698.

At the meeting of this Court, the proceedings of which are the last recorded in Liber I nothing was done, worthy of mention, excepting the following order:

"Whereas Sydwick Whittworth, Griffith Jones, William Pickett, and Nicholas Cloude, being by this Court admitted to Practice as Attorneys, but not giving such attendance as is, from such persons, required, this Court hath thought fitt to suspend, and discharge them, therefrom."

Simon Wilmer, Clk.

Sec. 123, A. Col. Edward Wilkins (see p. 20), the celebrated peach-grower of Kent, now the U. S. Collector of the Port of Baltimore, m. twice. His 1st wife, m. 29th Feb'y

1838, was Deborah Jones, and had child., viz., Juliana (who m. Capt. Robert S. Emory, and had child., viz., Edward Wilkins,—Maria Ella,—Julia,—Isabelle, and Robert Juliene Emory),—Mifflin (who m. Mary Anna Merritt, and had child., viz., Susan Carter, Fanny Louise and Jenny),—and Maria Wilkins, who m. James Russell, and had child., viz., James,—Olive and Maria Russell. He m. 2ndly, 28th March 1848, Frances Olivia Merritt and had child., viz., Samuel Merritt, —Fanny Louise (who m. Edward B. Jones),—Ben Nowland Starck, and Franck Wilkins.

CAPT. ROBERT S. EMORY was the first one, in Maryland, to engage extensively in the culture of the pear, and has now (1876) 15,000 trees in his beautiful orchards.

ST. PAUL'S PARISH.

SEC. 124.—The following are extracts from the "Church Record of St. Paul's Parish, from 30th Jan'y 1693 to 11th April 1726":

Pursuant to an Act of Assembly (1692, Chap. II.), entitled *An Act for the Service of Almighty* GOD, *and the Establishment of the Protestant Religion in this Province*, wherein it is ordered that its counties within the province of Maryland shall be divided into parishes, and likewise, by the same law, it is ordered that the justices of the county, with the freeholders, shall chose six vestrymen of each respective parish, which accordingly was done and performed the twenty-fourth day of January, Annoque Domini, 1693.

Whose names are hereunder inserted, viz.:

Jan'y 30, 1693. { MR. THOS. SMITH, MR. CHAS. TILDEN,
MR. WM. FRISBY, MR. MICHAEL MILLER,
MR. HANS HANSON, MR. SIMON WILMER.

By a meeting of the vestry at the house of Mr. Thos. Joce, for the Parish of St. Paul's, on the north side of Chester river, agreed about the dimensions of a church to be built upon part of a tract of land belonging to Mr. Michael Miller, which is called the main branch of Broadnox Creek, viz.: Fifty feet long, &c., wherein Mr. Norris was desired to consider of and present the charges to the vestry, the fifteenth day of February next.

FEBRUARY THE 15TH, 1693.

At a meeting of the vestry, MR. MICHAEL MILLER and MR. WM. FRISBY, being chosen principals, MR. HANS HANSON, MR. CHARLES TILDEN, MR. THOS. SMITH, and MR. SIMON WILMER, at the House of Mr. Thos. Joce, aforesaid, Mr. Norris did then and there deliver an account of the charge, which was by the vestry considered to be too great for the parish, therefore, the said vestry only agreed with Mr. Norris for the making of one hundred and thirty thousand bricks, fifteen hundred tile of ten inches square and two inches thick, for which they are to give him thirty thousand ———

Therefore, it is ordered by the vestry that Mr. Charles Tilden, Sheriff, pay to Mr. Daniel Norris what tobacco he shall have occasion for, according to the assessment of forty pounds tobacco per poll, for this present year, and likewise ordered that Mr. Simon Wilmer take an obligation from the said Norris to perform his work.

1694.

9th b. 7th. MR. LAWRENCE VANDERBUSH having offered himself to officiate as Minister, was accepted at a salary of 800 lbs. of tobacco per annum. Mr. John Leigh was appointed clerk of the Vestry.

1695.

15th April. At a meeting of the Vestry at the house of Thos. Joce, at New Yarmouth. The Vestry "agreed with " Mr. Daniel Norris to build a Church according to the fol- " lowing dimensions, viz., forty foot long, and twenty and " four foot wide, and ten foot chancel, to be paved with tile, " and a six foot Isle, the length of chancel to be paved with " tile, and from the door to the Isle six foot. In considera- " tion of twenty-one thousand pounds of tobacco."

8th August. Philip Hopkins qualified as Church Warden.

7th Jan'y *o. s.* Philip Hopkins and Thos. Ringgold were elected Church Wardens.

18th Feb'y *o. s.* The Vestry chose Matt. Tilghman Ward to be Clerk, and agreed to give him 1,200 lbs. of tob. for the ensuing year.

1696.

7th Feb'y. At a meeting of the Vestry,

Present—MR. WM. FRISBY, MR. THOS. SMYTH,
MR. MICHAEL MILLER, MR. CHAS. TILDEN,
COL. HANS HANSON, MR. SIMON WILMER.

"Whereas the Church was built upon a parcel of land belonging to Michl. Miller, being part of a Tract of land called Arcadia, lying at the head of Broadnox Creek, bounding on the South with a parcel of land called the Fork, formerly laid out for Henry Hawkins, and on the North with a parcel of land formerly laid out for Jas. Ringgold, and on the West with John Ward's land, the Vestry have agreed with the said Mr. Mich'l. Miller to give him two thousand pounds of Tobacco for the aforsd land, and the said Mich'l. Miller doth oblige himself to make over the said land at March Court next."

"The Vestry have appointed Mr. Simon Wilmer to represent to Robert Norris what there is to be done to the Church, viz., to pail in a Church Yard, one hundred foot square, and to new cover the said Church. The chancel to be railed in, and to build a pulpit and reading pew."

William Bateman and Morgan Jones were elected Church Wardens.

1697.

At a meeting of the Vestry, at the Church of St. Paul's, on the north-side Chester River, July 2d, 1697.

Present—Mr. Michl Miller, Mr. Chas. Tilden,
Col. Hans Hanson, Mr. Simon Wilmer,
Maj. Thos. Smith.

"This day came Mr. Stephen Bordley, who produced an order from his Excellency the Governor to the Vestry, viz.,

"Gent. The bearer hereof is the Reverend Stephen Bordley, " who is sent by Right Honble and Right Rev'd Father " in God, Henry Lord Bishop of London, in order to officiate " as a Clergyman of the Church of England in this his " Magesties Province of Maryland. I do therefore, in his " Majesty's Name, appoint the same Mr. Stephen Bordley to " Officiate as a Clergyman of the Church of England in the " Parish of St. Paul's in Kent County.

"Given under my hand and Seal at the Port of Annapolis " this 23d Day of June, in the 9th Year of the Reign of our " Sovereign Lord William the third, by the Grace of God, of " England, Scotland, France and Ireland King, defender of " the Faith, &c., Anno Domini 1697.

" Fr. Nicholson. *****
Seal
*****

" To the Vestrymen of St. Paul's Parish, in Kent County—
" These."

18th Nov. Col. John Hynson was chosen a Vestryman. 27th Jan'y, "Agreed with Robert Norris to build thirteen pews in the Church, and a gallery at the West end." Charles Hynson and Elias King were chosen Church Wardens. Capt. Edward Sweatman was High Sheriff.

1698.

5th Dec. At a meeting of the Vestry at the Court House, ordered, "That Robert Mehrson, John Wade, Robert Devonish, Benjamin Ricaud, William Smith, & Robert Dunn have notice to meet the Vestry at the Parish Church, 12th day of December next, to the levying of a parish tax, if necessity requires, according as the law directs."

24th Jan'y. William Smith and Robert Devonish were chosen Church Wardens. William Pearce was High Sheriff of Cecil County at this time.

1699.

April ye 9th. "Maj. Thomas Smyth doth present the Parish of St. Paul's, on the North side Chester River, as a gift, one Callice of Silver and one Plate of Silver."

Oct. ye 1st. William Glanville qualified as Church Warden, *vice* Robert Devonish, d.

Oct. ye 23d. Mr. William Harris and Mr. Charles Hynson were appointed Vestrymen.

Nov. 11th. KENT COUNTY: "We the undersigned sworn " by Elias King Sheriff of Kent County to value two acres " of land, adjacent to the Parish Church of St. Paul's, on the " North side Chester River, We do value the said two acres of " land at five hundred pounds of tobacco: Witness our " hands this Eleventh Day of November Anno Domini 1699."

WM. SMITH,	RICE JONES,
GEO. SMITH,	JNO. BLACKISTON,
JAMES WATSON,	BENJ. RICAUD,
THOMAS HIX,	THOMAS RICAUD,
DAVID DAVIS,	RICHARD MASON,
SAMUEL THOMAS,	JOHN HODGES.

Elias King was Sheriff of Kent, and John Carvill of Cecil County. George Smith was chosen Church Warden, and William Glanvill continued.

1700.

20th April. "This Vestry hath empowered Col. Hans Hanson to agree with workmen to lay the Church with tile and to finish Robert Norris' work." George Worsley was sworn clerk. 14th Sept. "Ordered that Maj. Thomas Smyth draw a note on Mr. William Harris, payable to John Salter for glazing the church windows."

1701.

25th June. Ordered, "that a note be set up at the Church door concerning the payment of Tobacco for seats in the pews." 5th July. Ordered, "that the clerk go to Edward Plesto and dispute him concerning underpinning the Church with stone," "that Mr. Harris doth speak to Robert White for to look after and to clean the Church,"—that "each Vestryman and Church Warden doth collect a contribution of the Inhabitants of the Parish towards the repairing and beautifying the Church." 17th Jan'y. Samuel Thomas and Michael Miller were chosen Church Wardens.

1702.

6th April. "This Vestry hath this day agreed with Mr. Alexander Greaves to take down the Brick work belonging to the Church, to the foundation and to build it up with stone." 1st Sept. Mr. Elias King was elected Vestryman. 2nd Feb'y. "This day was presented a petition to this Vestry from the Gentlemen of the Parish of Shrewsbury, in Cecil County, Requesting Mr. Stephen Bordley to preach there every third Sunday." 2nd March. "This Vestry hath empowered Lieu. Col. Thos. Smyth to agree with William Mackey to pale in the Church Yard,"—"that Mr. Elias King do provide Linnen for the Communion: one table cloth and two napkins,"—"that the Clk write a note to Col. Hynson to request him to order his Joyner to make a Communion Table, four foot square, with a drawer underneath to put the Church Books in, & to make it of black walnut."

1703.

5th April. Capt. Thomas Ringgold and Mr. Robt. Dunn were elected Vestrymen, and Wm. Worrell and Saml. Tovey Church Wardens. Three of them "took the Oath of Allegiance & Abhorrency and qualified the same day." Saml. Tovey qualified, 11th April. 1st June. "Eliner Smyth, the wife of Thos. Smyth, this Day was pleased to present the Church with a Pulpit Cloth and a Cushion."

Mr. Giles Bond is requested to provide a chest to put the Pulpit Cloth, Cushion & Church Books in, and Col. Hans Hanson is impowered to agree with Jacob Young to alter the

Pulpit Door and Stair-case, Rails & fit it for to hang the Pulpit Cloth. Mr. John Hawkins was High Sheriff.

1704.

18th April. Mr. John Wills and Mr. Wm. Glanvill were elected Vestrymen in the Room of Col. Hans Hanson, d., and Capt. Thomas Ringgold. Edward Skidmore and Edward Rogers where chosen Church Wardens.

1705.

15th April. Thomas Covington and John Fanning were chosen Church Wardens. "Ordered that it be moved to the Justices, of the Court in Kent County, for the Assessment of a Parish Tax, Pursuant to Act of Assembly for Repairing the Church, in that part of the Parish, lying in Kent County, five Pounds tobacco pr. Poll, According to the List of Number of Taxables. Ordered, that it be moved to the Justices of Cecil County Court, for the Assessment of a Parish Tax, Pursuant to an Act of Assembly for Repairing the Church, in that Part, of the Parish of St. Paul's on the north side of Chester River, that lyeth in Cecil County; seven Pounds Tob. pr. Poll, according to the List & Number of Taxables, it being Omitted for three years."

1706.

9th Jan'y. This day it was moved to the Vestry by Mr. Stephen Bordley to continue preaching, the first Sabbath in the month, at Sassafras Church.

1707.

14th April. Mr. Wm. Harris, Col. Nathl. Hynson, and Mr. Wm. Potts were elected Vestrymen, and Abraham Ambrose and John Hurt were chosen Church Wardens.

4th Aug. *Ordered*, that the Clk. write to the Commissary for a copy of the Will of Wm. Pearle. 27th Nov. 1707. At a meeting of the Vestry at the Town & Port of Chester, *Ordered*, "that Charles Ringgold be paid Two Thousand Pounds Tobacco for what Timber was cut off his Land & Used Building the Church and five Hundred Pounds Tobacco for two Acres of Land that the Church is Built on, by Order of a Jury."

1708.

6th April. Mr. Chas. Hynson, Mr. Thos. Covington, and Mr. William Ringgold were elected Vestrymen, and Samuel Thomas chosen Church Warden.

1709.

26th April. Maj. Thos. Ringgold, Capt. Jas. Harris, and Capt. Edward Scott were elected Vestrymen, and Messrs. George Smyth and Michael Miller chosen Church Wardens.

1710.

10th April. Col. Thos. Smith and Mr. Wm. Scott were elected Vestrymen, and Messrs. Michl Miller and Wm. Crow chosen Church Wardens. 19th July 1710. "*Ordered*, that the Clk set up a Note at East Mill to give Notice that the Plantation which belongs to the Minister is to be Lett. *Ordered*, that the Clk search the Record for the Lines of the Land which William Pearle left to the Poor of this Parish, lying in Langford's Bay called Spensex!"

1711.

2d April. Mr. Wm. Frisby and Maj. Wm. Harris were elected Vestrymen, and Messrs. Jas. Smith and Jno. Blackiston chosen Church Wardens—10th May Rev. Alexander Williamson presented his credentials and was received as the Minister of St. Paul's, *vice* Rev. Stephen Bordley, d.

27th Aug. At a meeting of the Vestry—Present:

Rev. Alexander Williamson	Mr. Wm. Scott
Capt. Edward Scott	Mr. Wm. Harris
Capt. Jas. Harris	Mr. Wm. Frisby

"This Vestry doth agree with Mr. James Harris, as Under-
" taker to Build a Church for the use of the Parish of St.
" Paul's in Kent County, According to the Dimensions follow-
" ing, vizt. 40 feet long in the Clear & 20 feet Wide in the
" Clear, to be 16 feet from the Ground, 5 Windows, 2 Doors
" & Cases, the Brick Wall to be 2½ Bricks thick to the Water
" Table, & 2 Bricks thick from thence Upward, a Circle to be
" at the East End for the Communion: The Windows &
" Doors & Cornish & other Work to be all Proportionable &
" suitable to such a Building & in Consideration this Vestry
" will agree to pay Mr. Jas. Harris Seventy Thousand pds of
" Tob."

18th March. "This Vestry hath rented the Plantation which was Wm. Pearle's, lying in Langford's Bay, called Spensex unto Capt. Edwd Scott for seven Years, commencing from this Day, & the sd. Capt. Scott to pay to the Vestry Three Hundred pounds of Tob. pr. annum." Capt. Jas. Harris was Sheriff.

1712.

21st April. Capt. St. Ledger Codd & Mr. Wm. Ringgold were elected Vestrymen, and Messrs. Edward Worrell & Jacob Glenn chosen Church Wardens—9th Sept. "This day Mr. Alex. Williamson procures an Order, from the President & Council, for the whole Year's Revenue in the year 1711, vizt.,

"By the honble President & Council, August 19th, 1712, " upon the Petition of Mr. Alexander Williamson, rector of " St. Paul's Parish, in Kent County, Praying the Direction " of this Board, that the Vestry of his Parish, and Sheriff of " the said County Pay unto him the 40 lbs. Tob., per poll " arising in that Parish in the year 1711; Ordered that the sd " Vestry & Sheriff Pay unto the sd Williamson the whole 40 " lbs. Tob. per Poll, arising that year, saving so much as will " be sufficient to satisfy the Reader, if any employed, accord- " ing to the Term he officiated."

1713.

6th April Col. Nath. Hynson & Mr. Michael Miller were elected Vestrymen, and Messrs. Edward Skidmore and Wm. Bateman were elected Church Wardens. 2nd Feb'y. This Day Capt. James Harris having complied with his obligation to the Vestry about Building the Church, hath made his Delivery of the sd Church to this Vestry,

" *Ordered*, that Notice be given at Church, the next Sab- " bath Day, & Notes set up at the Mills, for those Inhabitants " of this Parish that are Desirous to have seats in Pews, to " meet the Vestry at the said Parish Church the 20th day of " this month and to give in their names, it being the day " appointed to consult concerning the erection of pews."

20th February. " *Ordered*, by the Vestry, that every Per- " son that hath taken a pew this day shall be obliged to pitch " upon a family that hath subscribed towards Building the " Church, between this & Easter Monday, to be partners in the " same Pew; Otherwise the Vestry will take care to place " them their places, so that every one that hath subscribed " will have seats therein."

1714.

29th March. *Ordered*, that the price of each pew in the New Church be one thousand pounds of tobacco. Capt. Wm. Pott and Mr. Robert Dunn were elected Vestrymen, and Messrs. Thos. Hynson & Michael Hacket, chosen Church Wardens.

1715.

18th April. Messrs. Edward Scott and Jas. Harris were elected Vestrymen, and Messrs. Marmaduke Tilden and Thos. Ringgold chosen Church Wardens.

"*Ordered*, that Wm. Deane hath leave to pull down the old church & to have the Nails for his Pains."

1716.

2d April. Messrs. Saml. Tovey and Saml. Thomas were elected Vestrymen, and Messrs. Abram. Ambrose & Hans Hanson Church Wardens. 14th Oct. 1716 Capt. Jas. Harris and Mr. Jas. Smith were elected Vestrymen. 27th Feb'y 1716 Messrs. Arthur Miller and Edward Worrell were elected Vestrymen.

1717.

22d April. Messrs. Thomas Ringgold, Arthur Miller and Thomas Piner were elected Vestrymen, and James Murphy and Matthew Piner chosen Church Wardens.

1718.

14th April. Mr. Marmaduke Tilden was elected Vestryman and Messrs. Josias Sannum and Wm. Crow chosen Church Wardens.

1719.

30th March. Messrs. Robert Dunn and Chas. Ringgold were elected Vestrymen and Messrs. Frederick Hanson and John Evans Church Wardens.

1720.

18th April. Messrs. William Ringgold & Wm. Crow were elected Vestrymen, and John Brown and Daniel Ferrell Church Wardens.

At this period the pew-holders were as follows, viz., Pew, No. 1, Alexander Williamson and Nathl. Hynson; No. 2, Thomas Smyth; No. 3, John Marsh and Solomon Wright; No. 4, James Smyth and Thomas Brown; No. 5, James Harris; No. 6, Edward Scott; No. 7, William Pott and Richard Simmons; No. 8, John Moll and William Bateman; No. 9, Samuel Thomas, Edward Davis and John Evans; No. 10, Simon Wilmer, Thomas Piner; No. 11, John Fulston, Richard Fulston, William Jones, John Williams; No. 12, William Worrell, Saml. Tovey; No. 13, Rebecca Wilmer, Thomas Ringgold, Charles Hynson; No. 14, William Frisby, James

Frisby; No. 15, William Glanville, William Pope; No. 16, Frances Crawford, Ann Frisby; No. 17, Oliver Higgenbotham, John Green, John Rolph; No. 18, Marmaduke Tilden, Thomas Hynson; No. 19, Arthur Miller, Edward Worrell; No. 20, John Moore, John Fanning; No. 21, St. Ledger Codd, Hans Hanson; No. 22, Daniel Duffy, John Hynson; No. 23, James Murphey, Jacob Glenn; No. 24, Michael Hacket, Philip Davis; No. 25, Ebenezer Blackiston, John Blackiston; No. 26, John Rogers, John Tilden; No. 27, Michael Miller, Samuel Berry; No. 28, Robert Dunn, Wm. Dunn; No. 29, John Taylor, William Simcock; No. 30, William Ringgold, Charles Ringgold; No. 31, Edward Rogers, Jr., Samuel Wickes; No. 32, George Hanson, Frederick Hanson; No. 33, For the Minister, Thos. Bordley, Stephen Bordley; No. 34, Richard Phillingan, Saml. Gooden, Edward Jarvis.

In 1721 Gideon Pearce was Sheriff of Kent.

1722.

26th March. Messrs. Simon Wilmer and Thos. Hynson were elected Vestrymen, and Messrs. Michl. Hacket and Jno. Derrick Church Wardens.

1723.

15th April. Messrs. Jas. Smith and Thos. Ringgold were elected Vestrymen, and Messrs. Thos. Joce and Arthur Foreman Church Wardens.

1724.

6th April. Col. Edward Scott and Mr. Simon Wilmer were elected Vestrymen, and Messrs. Daniel Ferrill and Vincent Hatchison Church Wardens.

1725.

29th March. Messrs. Jas. Harris and Edward Worrell were elected Vestrymen, and Messrs. Robert Dunn and Chas. Smith, Church Wardens.

At a meeting of the Vestry of St. Paul's Parish, in Kent County, at the Church, the 23rd Feb'y 1725.

Mr. Alexander Williamson	Mr. Edward Worrell
Mr. James Smith	Mr. Simon Wilmer

This day the afsd Vestry ordereth that four of the Principal Vestrymen go to view the Library.

Four of the Principal Vestry of St. Paul's Parish, according to Act of Assembly, viz., Mr. Thos. Ringgold, Mr. James

Smith, Mr. Simon Wilmer and Mr. Edward Worrell, went to view the Library of this Parish, March the seventh 1725, in the presence of Thomas Bordley and William Everett.

1726.

11th April. Messrs. Jas. Smith and Joseph Young were elected Vestrymen, and Messrs. Elias Ringgold and Samuel Groome, Church Wardens.

SAML. ANDREWS Clk.

I, Charles G. Ricaud, Register of St. Paul's Parish of Kent Co., Md., do hereby certify that I have examined the aforegoing extracts, made by Col. George A. Hanson, from the Records of said Parish and find them to contain a true History of St. Paul's Parish.

CHAS. G. RICAUD, *Register,*
St. Paul's Parish, Kent Co., Md.

SHREWSBURY PARISH.

SEC. 125.—The oldest extant Record of this Parish commences on "ye 8th day of November 1701 at ye Church of Shrewsbury." There was a meeting of the Vestry in April 1702, but the record of its minutes are mutilated, as also to a more or less extent are the proceedings until the 3d of Aug. 1714.

1703, 4th April. Col. Edward Blay, Philip Hopkins, Wm. Husband and Abraham Redgrave were present.

1704. Col. William Pearce, Col. Edward Blay, Philip Hopkins, Wm. Comegys, Saml. Wallis and James Wilson were Vestrymen, and, 6th March, agreed to pay Josias Sutton 1800 lbs. Tob., "to weather-board the old part of ye aforsd Church all round with good feather edge plank and to make a new door and new shutters for the windows and find hinges for them." In 1705 John Hynson was Sheriff. In 1706, 3d Sept., Col. Edward Blay, Philip Hopkins, James Wilson, Humphrey Tillton, Philip Burgan, George Browning were Vestrymen; Ed. Holdman, Church Warden, and Abraham Redgrave, Clerk. The Vestry ordered that 4000 lbs. Tob. be paid to Rev. Stephen Bordley for "his last year's attendance." In 1707, William Comegys and Thomas Christian were sworn of the Vestry. 7th Sept. 1708, Mr. Abraham Redgrave being inducted reader was allowed "the moiety of ye forty per poll raised in sd. Parish, for his attendance as Reader the ensuing year."

"May ye 20th 1709,

"Gentlemen, upon the Vacancy of your Parish, I Request
" you to admitt of the Reverend Mr. Sewell to officiate till
" such time as you shall be otherwise provided by ye Right
" Honorable & Reverend Father in GOD, Henry, Lord Bishop
" of London, and to allow him a handsome Compensation,
" which I shall take as a favor, to your Friend to serve ye.

"JO: SEYMORE

" To the Vestry of Shrewsbury Parish, In Kent County."

28th May 1709. The above letter was read and "received ye consent of the vestry of North Sassafras Parish." In 1709-10 COL. EDWARD BLAY presented to the Parish two acres of land. (Upon which the present Church now stands.) In 1710, William Comegys, Philip Hopkins, James Hudson, Col. William Blay, George Browning were Vestrymen, and Luther Middleton Church Warden. 2d May 1710 Abraham Redgrave was inducted Reader of the Parish.

1711, 2d April. John Wilson and Henry Knock were elected Vestrymen ; Thomas Medford and James Wait were chosen Church Wardens.

1712, 21st April. Col. Edward Blay, Samuel Wallis were elected Vestrymen ; George Browning and James Campbell chosen Church Wardens.

1712, 15th Dec. The Vestry agreed to give Rev. James Crawford 20,000 lbs. Tob. yearly, "during ye sd. Crawford's continuing amongst us."

1713, 5th May. Vestry met. Present, Rev. Jas. Crawford, Rich. Campbell, Henry Knock, John Wilson, Saml. Wallis, James Wilson and Lambert Wilmer, Vestrymen, and Jon. Ridson and Wm. Milborn, Church Wardens.

Luther Burgan was elected Sexton, and for "Keeping clean of ye Church and Yard, for ye full space of one full year and to garnish ye Church at ye three Great Festivals, that is to say Christmas, Easter and Whitsuntide, for which ye vestry is to pay him ye said Luther Burgan Three hundred pounds of Tobacco."

1713, 4th Aug. It is recorded: "The fifth day of July, last, came James Campbell to ye Communion table and asked pardon of Col. Blay and Mr. William Comegys for Calling them murderers of ye parish; at ye same place the aforesaid Campbell did condescend to pay what Charge should Increw upon the Writ that was served upon him for ye above fault."

1713, 25th Sept. The Rev. James Williamson was inducted Rector of the Parish.

1714, 29th March. Gideon Pearce and William Boyer were elected Vestrymen, and Thomas Medford and John Dining chosen Church Wardens.

1715, 18th April. John Hall and Col. William Blay were elected Vestrymen, and Edward Holdman and Richard Skegs chosen Church Wardens.

1715, 3d May. The following letter to William Frisby, Sheriff, is recorded:

"Sir, Know by this time we Greatly admire that you take " no Care at all to pay our Minister his tobacco: it is a very " great Wrong and Injustice Done him to detain his tobacco " in good times and to pay him in bad: this is insufferable " and unaccountable; we will not see him so served, let him " have his tobacco without fail. Take these things to your " Consideration, and we desire for your own good and Credit " to Comply with him as soon as possible. Pray do not give " us opportunity of taking other measures with you. If you " do not regard what we have said, in making him speedy " payment, as ye Law directs, you may expect to be put to " Greater trouble by ye Vestry of Shrewsbury Parish."

"*Signed per order* Abrah. Redgrave Clk."

1716, 2d April. Henry Lowe and William Comegys were elected Vestrymen, and Thomas Heborn and Nicholas Riley chosen Church Wardens.

1717, 22d April. Capt. Daniel Pearce and Thomas Heborn were elected Vestrymen, and John Jones and John Cole chosen Church Wardens.

1718, 14th April. Samuel Wallis and Edward Holdman were elected Vestrymen, and William Debrewster and Matthias Day chosen Church Wardens.

1719, 30th March. John Hall and John Wilson were elected Vestrymen, and Thomas Chandler and John Clark chosen Church Wardens.

1720, 18th April. Henry Lowe and John Dining were elected Vestrymen, and George Reed and John Brooks chosen Church Wardens.

1721, 10th April. Lambert Wilmer and John Brooks were elected Vestrymen, and Roger Hailes and Roger Hicks chosen Church Wardens.

1721, 4th Oct. John Johnson was elected Vestryman, *vice* Henry Lowe, d. "Then was ordered yt Roger Hailes should give Madame Lowe notice to come and take ye pew down, she has built in ye Church, without consent of ye Vestry and Church Wardens; otherwise she may expect to have it pulled down by order of the Vestry of said Parish: it being an agreviance to the parishioners."

1721, Oct. 10th. "A letter appearing from Madame Lowe, relating to the Pew, fixed in the Church, on which the Vestry debating, Mr. James Williamson, ye Minister, rather than the Vestry should be offended, does oblige himself and his friend to contribute the sum of twenty-five pounds sterling towards the building of a New Church, and thereto he has put his hand."

(Signed) JAMES WILLIAMSON

"And that for ye above consideration the Vestry and Church Wardens do order and direct the said Pew, built by Madame Lowe stand as it now is."

"Then was ordered by ye Vestry yt the lock that is on ye pew door yt was formerly called Col. Blay's pew shall be and remain on as it now is."

"Further appointed also by ye Vestry and Church Wardens of ye Parish yt ye Parishioners should appear at ye Church, on Thursday, being ye 26th day of this instant, to see what contributions they will give towards ye building of a NEW CHURCH, and ye Reverend James Williamson has promised to preach a sermon, on ye same day, answerable."

The letter of Reverend Mr. Willkinson sent to ye Reverend Mr. James Williamson, bearing date ye 26th of September 1721, was ordered to be recorded, which is as followeth:

"DEAR BR. I desire your Company at ye Consecration of Wye Church on St. Luke's Day of ye next Month, and intend to have a visitation the day following at ye same place, and expect one of your Church Wardens there. Be pleased to bring your Gown with you and lodge at my house ye night before."

"I have a Complaint preferred agst you by a very Great "man, the matter of it is (if I have not forgotten) that you "frequently employ your Clark to read ye prayers of ye "Church, and to babtize ye children privately; If I had "really believed ye report, I should have sent you word of "it before now. But, however, that you may not be mistaken "in your friends, and take them to be such, who are really

" otherwise, I guess ye SHE LOWE to be your accuser. Col. " Ward sent me word of it. Pray acquit yourself of this " Imputation, and me also, for I, openly, vindicated you from " ye aspersion. I am your humble servant."

"CHRIS. WILLKINSON."

The Vestry and Church Warden's Letter, in answer to Reverend Mr. Christopher Willkinson is as followeth:

"REVEREND SIR, The Reverend Mr. James Williamson, " of our Parish, was pleased to communicate to us, the Vestry " and Church Wardens of Shrewsbury Parish, ye contents of " your letter, which we declare and proved to be altogether " false, unjust and lying assertions; & that to our Knowledge, " he was never guilty of these Crimes laid to his charge, We " are, May it please your Reverence your must humble " servants"

CAPT. DANIEL PEARCE — MR. LAMBERT WILMER
MR. SAMUEL WALLIS — MR. JOHN BROOKS
MR. JOHN HALL — MR. JOHN JOHNSON

ROGER HICKS and ROGER HAILES Church Wardens.

The Reverend Mr. Christopher Willkinson
Commissary of ye Eastern Shore of Maryland.
Signed per order ABRAH. REDGRAVE Clk.

1722, March ye 26th. Roger Hicks and William Milborn were elected Vestrymen, and Philip Brooks and William Smothers chosen Church Wardens.

1722, Sept. ye 15th. Then was ordered that Gideon Pearce (High Sheriff) should pay unto William Thornton thirty shillings and 250 lbs. Tob. for carrying &c. to his Excellency ye Governor, at Annapolis, the following letter:

" May it please your Excellency:"

"The Vestry of Shrewsbury, in Kent County, having " received an Information yt a certain Mr. Thos. Thomson, a " Minister, at present of Dorset County, has made application " to your Excellency to be inducted in this Parish, it created a " great uneasiness in ye inhabitants of ye Parish, in generall, " and which has given your Excellency trouble; of this, " desiring, on ye behalf of themselves & ye rest of ye parish- " ioners, that your Excellency would as well have a tender " regard to them of the laity as of ye promotion of some of the

" clergy, whose business, of Late, has been, more to gape after
" ye fleece than any Great Desire of Directing their flocks—
" some of which I beg leave to acquaint your Excellency, that,
" there have been too late an Instance of such unchristian
" practices.—The Character of Mr. Thomson (if ye Report
" given of him be true) is soe bad yt he is rediculous even
" under the Denomination of a Layman, but far worse of a
" Clergyman, whose actions are Publick marks for ye enemies
" of ye Church to point at, and it is on presumption yt your
" Excellency might be unacquainted with the Gentleman's
" Credit that they give the trouble of this Relation.

"The bad life & Corrupt principles of their last minister
" they presume has been more than a little injurious to Religion
" in General & especially to their parish; ye whole of ye par-
" ishioners not Careing to come to Divine Service during his
" Stay amongst them, and some others wholly leaving ye
" Church & now constantly attend ye Quaker Meetings, &
" sometimes giving their reasons for soe doing & say there can
" be little Religion in a man who preaches against a sin on ye
" Sunday which he so often practices the rest of the Week.

"Your Excellency may perceive, by this, how unhappy
" they have been by loosing some of ye members of ye Church
" for want of a good Minister, & may probably lose more, if
" not prevented by your Excellency's favour, to recommend
" such a one, to reside among them, as a minister, whose life
" & actions may keep up ye Character of a good Christian &
" Clergyman, & may tend to ye support of the true Protestant
" Church & ye Glory of GOD,—otherwise they beg your
" Excellency to wait for awhile that they may apply themselves
" to some friends in England to recommend such a person, to
" your Excellency, for an Induction, as may Endeavour the
" Service of GOD, the propogation of RELIGION, & the unity
" and welfare of his flock.

"This which I am ordered to lay before your Excellency
" for your concurrence & that they are with all due obedience.
"Your Excellency's most humble servants"

Signed per order ABRAH. REDGRAVE.

$172\frac{2}{3}$, 19th Feb'y. The Vestry order 2000 lbs. Tob. to be paid to Rev. Mr. Robert Walker for preaching three or four Sundays.

1723, April ye 15th. Lambert Wilmer and John Hall were elected Vestrymen, and Daniel Perkins and Peter Massy Church Wardens.

1723, Sept. ye 3rd. Rev. Mr. Richard Sewell was inducted Rector of the Parish.

1724, April ye 6th. Thomas Hepbourn, John Wilson and Daniel Perkins were elected Vestrymen, and Jarvis Spencer and Christopher Hall, Church Wardens.

1725, March ye 29th. Christopher Hall and John Dunnington were elected Vestrymen, and Joseph Hall and George Wilson, Church Wardens.

1726, March ye 3rd. John Tilden and George Wilson were elected Vestrymen and John Rogers and Mathias Howard, Church Wardens. Thomas Medford was elected Vestryman.

1727, April ye 3rd. Jarvis Spencer and Mathias Howard were elected Vertrymen and William Woodland and Sutton Burgan, Church Wardens.

1728, April 21st. Sutton Burgan and William Woodland were elected Vestrymen, and Lambert Wilmer and John Hall, Church Wardens. William Thornton was sworn Clerk to the Vestry.

1729, April ye 7th. John Hall and Henry Evens were elected Vestrymen, and Christopher Hall and Griffeth Jones, Church Wardens.

1730, March ye 30th. James Stavely and Saml. Norris were elected Vestrymen. The Record of proceedings of the Vestry from 1730 to 1745 appears to be lost.

1745, Aug. 6th. Rev. Mr. George William Forester was the Rector. Griffith Jones, Christopher Bellikin, John Gleaves and Christopher Hall were elected Vestrymen, and George Medford and Nicholas Massy, Church Wardens, and Obadiah Fisher, Clerk.

1746, March 31st. Fardiando Hull and George Medford were elected Vestrymen, and Thomas Chandler and John Donaldson chosen Church Wardens.

1747, April 20th. Nicholas Massy and Saml. Mansfield were elected Vestrymen and Wm. Comegys Jr., and George Wilson, Church Wardens.

1748, April 11th. Lambert Wilmer and John Donaldson were elected Vestrymen, and Peter Massy and Lambert Davis Church Wardens.

1749, March 27th. Philip Hudson and John Hicks were elected Vestrymen, and William Smith and Dorobable French, Church Wardens.

1750, April 16th. William Comegys and Peter Massy were elected Vestrymen, and Frederick Hanson and Richard Boyer, Church Wardens.

1751, April 8th. John Wallis and Hugh Wallis were elected Vestrymen, and Ebenezer Reyner and William Stoops, Church Wardens. 4th June, Richard Wilson qualified as Vestryman, *vice* Philip Hudson.

1752, March 30th. William Woodland and Thomas Perkins were elected Vestrymen, and Jonathan Turner and John Browning, Church Wardens.

1753, March 23d. Nicholas Smith and Cornelius Comegys were elected Vestrymen, and Philip Brooks and William Symonds, Church Wardens.

1754, April 15th. William Comegys Jr. and Thos. Chandler were elected Vestrymen, and John Crew and Jesse Cosden, Church Wardens.

1755, March 31st. Alexand Baird and John Angier were elected Vestrymen, and Thomas Sewell and John Clayton, Church Wardens.

1755, June 3d. The Vestry agreed there should be a subscription bond to build the addition to the Church.

1756, March 19th. William Haley and Ebenezer Reyner were elected Vestrymen, and James Pearce and William Kenton, Church Wardens.

1757, April 11th. Augustine Boyer, Jr. and Andrew Hynson were elected Vestrymen, and Samuel Davis and Isaac Freeman, Church Wardens.

1758, March 7th. Samuel Davis and Joseph Rasin were elected Vestrymen, and Robert Hatchison and Benjamin Hazel, Church Wardens.

1759, April 16th. Robert Hatchison and Jonathan Turner were elected Vestrymen, and Jos. Briscoe and Richard Riley, Church Wardens.

1759, Aug. 7th. William Haley was elected Clerk, *vice* Ebenezer Reyner, *resigned.*

1760, Oct. ye 7th. Isaac Freeman & Daniel Massy were elected Vestrymen, and Joseph Briscoe and Richard Riley, Church Wardens.

1761, March 23d. Henry Clark and John Comegys were elected Vestrymen, and Christopher Hall and John Stavely, Church Wardens.

1762, April 12th. Joseph Briscoe and John Eccleston were elected Vestrymen, and Joseph Redgrave and Rasin Gale, Church Wardens.

1763, April 4th. Joseph Redgrave and William Comegys were elected Vestrymen, and Bartus Piner and Nicholas Riley, Church Wardens.

1764, April 23d. Isaac Spencer, Rasin Gale and Christopher Hall were elected Vestrymen, and Joseph Reyner and Michael Jobson, Church Wardens.

1765, April 5th. Henry Trulock and Holeman Johnson were elected Vestrymen, and Thomas Boyer and Hezekiah Cooper, Church Wardens.

1766. William Weathered, William Keating, James Pearce and Ebenezer Reyner were elected Vestrymen, and Bartus Comegys and Jas. Stavely, Church Wardens.

1767, April 20th. Saml. Davis and Wm. Weithered were elected Vestrymen, and Thos. Boyer, Jr. and Wm. Merritt, Church Wardens.

1768, April 4th. Wm. Woodland and Isaac Freeman were elected Vestrymen, and George Medford and Benjamin Riley, Church Wardens.

1769, March 27th. William Blay Tilden and John Comegys were elected Vestrymen, and Joseph Stavely and John Wilson, Church Wardens.

1770, April 16th. Samuel Thompson, Jas. Stavely, Jas. Hynson were elected Vestrymen, and Wm. Ford and Ebenezer Massy, Church Wardens. Ebenezer Reyner was elected and qualified as Clerk of the Vestry, *vice* Wm. Haley.

1771, April 1st. Wm. Merritt and Ebenezer Massy were elected Vestrymen, and Wm. Briscoe and Jos. Massy, Church Wardens.

1772, April 20th. Wm. Briscoe and Jos. Massy were elected Vestrymen, and John Wilmer and Joseph Ireland, Church Wardens.

1773, April 12th. Benj. Riley and John Wilson were elected Vestrymen, and Jesse Cosden and Jos. Massy, son of Daniel, Church Wardens.

1774, April 4th. Jos. Stavely and George Medford were elected Vestrymen, and Elijah Massy and Acquila Page, Church Wardens.

1774, Nov. 12th. Reverend George William Forester d. this day.

1775, Feb'y 7th. Rev. Mr. John Montgomery was inducted Rector of the Parish.

1775, April 17th. Peter Massy and Jesse Cosden were elected Vestrymen, and Oliver Smith and George Wilson, Church Wardens.

1775, Oct. 3d. George Maffit qualified as Vestryman, *vice* Joseph Massy, d.

1776, Jan'y 2d. The Vestry agreed to employ Messrs. Jas.

Hollyday and Joseph Earle to defend the Glebe Land of the Parish.

1776, April 8th. James Pearce and George Wilson were elected Vestrymen, and John Hurt and Archable Wright, Church Wardens.

1777, Jan'y 21st. Isaac Spencer was elected Vestryman, *vice* Peter Massy, d.

1777, March 31st. Wm. Wethered and John Hurt were elected Vestrymen, and Bartus Piner and Thos. Boyer, Jr., Church Wardens.

1778, April 20th. Bartus Piner, Isaac Freeman and Samuel Davis were elected Vestrymen, and Thomas Pearce and William Blay Tilden, Church Wardens.

1779, April 5th. Wm. Blay Tilden was elected Vestryman, and Wm. Keating and Jas. Hynson, son of Thomas, Church Wardens.

" *To the Vestrymen and Church Wardens of the Parish of* " *Shrewsbury, Gentlemen:*

" I find myself, by my present low and enfeebled situation, " incapable of performing my duty as Minister of the Parish " of Shrewsbury, and beg leave to resign the care of the said " parish into the hands of some worthier successor. Should it " please GOD shortly to bestow me to health, I am willing, with " your consent, to contribute my services until the obligations " I am under shall call upon me to attend elsewhere. I hope, " Gentlemen, my present sickness will be a sufficient apology " for my non-attendance this day.

" I am, Gentlemen, Your very humble servant,

" Oct. 4th, 1779. THOS. HOPKINSON."

The Answer.

" The Vestry of Shrewsbury Parish, Kent County, has " desired me to inform you that they received yours wherein " you informed them that your state of Health will not Per- " mit you to Discharge your Duty as Minister of this Parish, " and Begg leave to Resign. They also desire me to inform " you that they accept your Resignation and hope you will be " Better Provided for elsewhere. They shall endeavor to " provide themselves, and shall not want any More of your " Services till some things layd to your Charge are cleared up.

"*By order of the Vestry,*

" Oct. 4th, 1779. EBEN. REYNER, *Reg.*"

SEC. 126. DR. PEREGRINE WROTH has permitted me to illustrate these pages with the following "Memoirs of Physicions of Kent County" which were written in 1852, but have never been published. In the manuscript preface, Dr. Wroth says: "The following brief Memoirs were prepared at the suggestion and at the request of George C. M. Roberts, M. D. and D. D., Professor of Obstetrics in the Washington Medical College of Baltimore. He contemplated a Work on the Members of the Medical and Chirurgical Faculty of Maryland."

SEC. 127. "DR. JAMES M. ANDERSON. In the period embraced by these Memoirs, the first among the Members of the Medical and Chirurgical Faculty of Kent County, is the venerable name of Dr. James M. Anderson. He was a son of Dr. James Anderson, who was born in Scotland and emigrated, thence, to Chestertown, but at what time is not remembered. He lived in and probably built the house still standing in the upper part of Cannon Street, in Chestertown, where his son, the subject of this memoir—his grandson Dr. James M. Anderson, Jr., and his great-grandson Dr. Alexander M. Anderson were born, lived and practiced Medicine. I have heard my preceptor, Dr. Browne, say that he remembered the Emigrant well, and he was considered eminent in his day. When his son, the subject of this memoir, grew up to manhood he was sent to Edinburgh,—the most celebrated Medical School in the world,—under those great men, Drs. Cullen and Monro—the former Professor of the Practice of Medicine, the latter Professor of Anatomy. How long he remained in Edinburgh, and how many courses of Lectures he attended is not known. He returned to Chestertown without a regular Diploma, but armed with an ample and very flattering Certificate, signed by the Faculty of the University.

"The theatre of his professional life was Chestertown and the surrounding country, including part of Queen Anne's County, on the opposite side of Chester river. His residence was in the Town for many years, until his son grew up and married, when he removed to his farm, distant about three miles, where, with a short interval of return, after the death of his son's wife, he remained until the close of his life in 1820, in the 70th year of his age, having practiced Medicine nearly half a century.

"In his long professional life he achieved, and most justly, a reputation, at home and abroad, which few, before or since, have enjoyed, and an extent of practice limited only by his ability to attend to it. Though much his Junior, I remember to have attended with him in some cases. In a clear and satisfactory way it was his custom, in Consultation with his brethren, to discuss the cases brought under his attention, their sources, morbid condition, and treatment, and I do not hesitate to say that it was more profitable to the young practitioners to listen to him on such occasions than to study the most elaborate treatise on the same subject by the best author. His language was clear and chaste, learned and eminently fitted to instruct. In one feature of his character he excelled all whom I have known. His piety was deep and sincere, and his whole walk, social, professional and religious, was such as attracted the attention and commanded the admiration of all. In all bad cases it was his custom to kneel by the bed of his patient in earnest prayer to God for help, and for the recovery and spiritual welfare of the sick, and of the family to which he belonged.

"Towards the end of his life he was so feeble that when he arrived at the house of the sick he was frequently obliged to lie down before he could prescribe. He refused no call while he was able to get into his sulky, a kind of single carriage then altogether used by physicians. When at last he was unable to rise from his bed, he sent for his son, Dr. James M. Anderson, Jr., Dr. Browne and myself. We all promptly obeyed the call, and, when assembled in his chamber, he addressed us, if my memory be correct after a lapse of 40 years, in the following words. In fact, he said much more, but these words are distinctly remembered:

"'I have sent for you, Gentlemen, believing it to be my 'duty to use the means placed in our hands for my recovery, 'if it be the Lord's Will. I promise to obey your orders and 'take everything you may prescribe. But I know that all 'your skill and all your efforts will be in vain, and I am sat- 'isfied that it should be so. I am willing and ready to die 'when it may please the Lord to call me.'

"It was a sad but beautiful sight to look upon that calm and venerable face,—his hoary locks falling over his breast and shoulders,—his dark eye beaming with intelligence and love. He had 'finished his course'—he had 'kept the faith,' and was calmly and submissively waiting for his crown. We all had known him long. We admired him for his learning and eminent talents, but we loved him for the kindness and tenderness of his heart.

"During his last illness an affecting incident occurred. Two ladies, Mrs. Alphonsa Blake and her sister-in-law, Miss

Jane Blake, who had often felt the benefit of his skill—and the kindness of his attentions, in his character as a Christian, went to see him, and though Roman Catholics, such was their confidence in his piety, that they kneeled by his bed-side and asked his blessing. The good old man stretched out his arms, laid his hands on their heads and earnestly prayed that the blessing of God would rest upon them.

"From early youth Dr. Anderson had united himself with the Methodists, then in their infancy in Kent County, and for many years was the acknowledged head of that religious society in Chestertown.

"His dress was a gray cloth coat, long-waisted, single or shad-breasted, standing collar, long skirts, reaching from below the knee, with ample pockets. He wore olive coloured velvet breeches, very loose, buckled at the knee with silver buckles,—gray woolen stockings, home knit, long vamped short quartered shoes with large silver buckles, a low-crowned broad brimmed beaver hat, and around his neck a white lawn stock (neck-cloth) plaited in many folds and fastened behind his neck with a silver buckle. In winter, when going out he wore red-topped boots.

"Dr. Anderson was rather below the middle stature, slender, and with a limping gait; having had several bones broken by falls from his sulky. His whole appearance, though dignified was unique, forming a *tout ensemble,* which, once seen, was not soon forgotten. With a dignity never laid aside, for it was natural, he combined a child-like simplicity of character which secured to him a degree of respect, reverence and love which very few ever reach.

"I enjoyed the privilege of an intimate acquaintance with this venerable patriarch, and shall ever remember with grateful pride that though young, comparatively unknown, he took some notice of me."

Sec. 128. "Dr. James M. Anderson, Jr., son of Dr. James M. Anderson, was educated at Washington College, Chestertown, and received a classical and liberal training. He was of the medium size, well proportioned, of comely and graceful person, lordly in his carriage and general deportment, exceedingly careful and particular in his dress, which always consisted of the most costly materials, fashionably cut, while on his high intellectual forehead was written in legible characters: '*Odi profanum vulgus et arceo!*'

"With those whom he considered his equals, socially, he was affable and friendly—to all he showed himself to be a well-bred gentleman.

"Dr. Anderson pursued the study of Medicine under the immediate tuition of Dr. Rush, Professor of the Practice of Medicine in the University of Pennsylvania. He commenced the practice of his profession in connexion with his father, in Chestertown, and was considered, and justly, as a young man of fine promise. While still young he married, and his father, finding that from his advancing years and infirmities he needed repose, retired to his farm in the neighborhood of Chestertown. His son succeeded to all his father's business. His practice was select and profitable. The Doctor was a great reader, and though he spent much time with the lighter literature of the day, he kept himself well posted in the progress of his profession by means of the Medical Quarterly Journals. All his life he enjoyed the reputation of a good Physician, and always held a respectable rank among his professional brethren. In his genial moods his conversation was seasoned with wit and humor; and, having at command an inexhaustible fund of anecdotes, was the life of every social circle into which he might be thrown. He was quick at repartee, and enjoyed the society of kindred spirits so keenly that I have seen him almost fall from his chair in convulsions of laughter. He was, consequently, very popular as a social companion, and was greatly admired by his patients as second to none in judgment. Dr. Anderson died 31st May 1830, in the 55th year of his age, very suddenly, as was supposed of disease of the heart, after returning one evening to his house from visiting some patients. The previous existence of the disease had not, as far as I know, been suspected. After he got home he complained of feeling badly, and laid down on his bed. Soon afterwards, his wife being with him, he felt his wrist, and, finding that his pulse had ceased to beat, he remarked that he was gone—and died."

SEC. 128, A. DR. JAMES MOAT ANDERSON, JR. was m. twice. His 1st wife, m. 16th Feb'y 1796, was Elizabeth Bedingfield Hands, dau. of Thomas B. and Mary Hands, and had child., viz., Anna Maria, b. 29th Nov. 1797, d. 14th Oct. 1800,—James M., b. 16th Jan'y 1799, d. 9th Oct. 1800,—Thomas Bedingfield Hands, b. 8th Oct. 1800, d. 14th Sept. 1803,—a 2nd James M., b. 5th July 1803, d. 5th May 1805. Mrs. Elizabeth Bedingfield Hands Anderson d. 26th Feb'y 1804. His 2d wife, m. 13th Nov. 1806, was Elizabeth Smith, and had child., viz., Mary, b. 25th July 1807, d. 27th Aug. 1807,—William Smith, b. 4th Oct. 1808, d. 30th Aug. 1809,—John Brown Hackett, b. 5th Dec. 1809, d. 6th Sept. 1863,—

Francis, b. 18th Sept. 1811,—Elizabeth, b. 22d July 1813, d. 27th Sept. 1815,—a 3rd James Moat, b. 2d Sept. 1814, d. 20th Sept. 1815,—Alexander Moat, b. 25th Sept. 1816, d. 7th Sept. 1859,—Ann Margaret, b. 27th Dec. 1818,—Edward, b. 14th June 1822, and Caroline Elizabeth Anderson, b. 11th Dec. 1824, d. 26th Oct. 1828. Mrs. Elizabeth Smith Anderson d. 25th Dec. 1853.

Dr. Alexander Moat Anderson, son of Dr. James M. and Elizabeth Smith Anderson m. 28th Dec. 1852, Susan R. Frisby, dau. of James Frisby and Rebecca Stoops, a descendant of Col. Hans Hanson, and had child., viz., Alexander Moat, b. 30th March 1856, d. 25th Nov. 1856, and James Frisby Anderson, b. 25th Sept. 1857.

Ann Margaret Anderson, dau. of Dr. James M. and Elizabeth Smith Anderson, m. 25th April 1843, John Rodgers Gray, and had child., viz., Helen,—James M.,—Andrew,—Alexander,—John A.,—Rebecca F.,—Fannie,—Elizabeth Frisby, and John Hampden Gray.

Andrew Gray, son of John Rodgers and Ann Margaret Gray, m. 26th Nov. 1872, Sophie Pinckney, dau. of Hon. Frederick Pinckney (a distinguished member of the Bar of Baltimore), and had child., viz., Isabel and Ethel Gray, *twins*, and Bertha Gray.

John Brown Hackett Anderson, son of Dr. James M. and Elizabeth Smith Anderson, m. 10th Aug. 1835, Elizabeth Frisby, sister of Susan R. Frisby. She d. March 1862, and had child., viz., William Frisby,—Mary E.,—Emma Caroline,—James Moat, and John Stoops Anderson.

William Frisby Anderson, son of John B. H. Anderson and Elizabeth Frisby, m. 19th April 1865, Victoria Louise Starlings, and had child., viz., Anna Virginia,—Elizabeth Frisby,—Georgia Louise, and Herbert Willson Anderson.

Mary Elizabeth Anderson, dau. of John B. H. Anderson and Elizabeth Frisby, m. 22d Dec. 1863, James Bateman Hopkins, and had child., viz., John Anderson, b. 18th April 1865, d. 1st Nov. 1865,—Alice Gertrude,—Mary Anderson,—Daniel,—James Bateman,—Maggie, b. 12th Sept. 1872, d. 3d Nov. 1873,—Alexander, b. 12th Aug. 1874, d., and Edward Hopkins.

Emma Caroline Anderson, dau. of John B. H. Anderson and Elizabeth Frisby, m. Dec. 1865, Charles E. Tolson, and had child., viz., John Stoops, d.,—Elizabeth Frisby,—Charles Eareckson, and Percy Tolson.

SEC. 129. "DR. EDWARD WORRELL, the younger of two sons of Mr. William Worrell, of Fairy Meadow, near Chestertown, received a classical education at the old Free School, as it was called,—a large brick building on the hill, above the Spring, still known as the Free School Spring, on the road from Chestertown to Washington College, which was built since. A Free School only in name (though such it might have been originally before my time), all paid for their tuition. It was then the best Seminary of learning in the County, and was under the care of teachers eminent for their qualifications before Washington College was built, Rev. Dr. Smith and Rev. Mr. Armor.

"Dr. Worrell studied medicine under the care of Dr. Boardley, a respectable physician of that day, in Chestertown; attended lectures in Philadelphia, and commenced the practice of medicine about the year 1784. He had a fine, commanding figure, little, if any, less than six feet in height, somewhat inclined to obesity, but graceful and active in his movements, of a very handsome countenance, courteous and gentlemanly in his bearing, and affable and kind to all. He evidently entertained a high degree of self-respect, and was not disposed to tolerate any exhibition of a want of it in others. He was a great reader, and, though much engaged in a large practice, he found time to keep up with the progress of medical science, to amuse himself with the 'Diversions of Purley' and to maintain an intimate acquaintance with physical science and general literature, ranking with the first literary men of the day.

"Dr. Worrell continued to follow his profession, in Chestertown, with universal satisfaction until 1796, when, by the death of his elder brother, he fell heir to the paternal estate of Fairy Meadow, in the vicinity of Chestertown (where his grandson, Dr. Frederick, now resides). Passionately fond of agriculture, he removed to the country and cultivated his land in connection with his practice, which was extensive, until his premature and lamented death in 1804.

"He was truly an industrious man, out of his bed by the dawn and walking about his farm, planning improvements and attending to their execution, and was far ahead of his neighbors in scientific and practical agriculture. After an early breakfast he was ready to attend to professional calls. He deservedly held a high rank in his professional and social relations, and was considered by all as equal, and by his patients, as superior to the most distinguished of his contemporaries. He was my father's friend and family physician, and it was under his care that I commenced the study of medicine. I continued in his office from July 18th, 1803, to October 18th, 1804, when he died of pneumonia, in the 52nd year of his age, universally lamented.

"Dr. Worrell was the preceptor of Dr. Morgan Browne, of Chestertown; of Dr. Henry Page, of Kent; of Dr. John Groome, then of Kent, afterwards of Elkton, Cecil County. All of whom attained eminence in professional life, which was owing, in part at least, to his strict, frequent and thorough examinations. In all the phases of his character he had few equals—no superiors."

SEC. 130. "DR. MORGAN BROWNE was born in 1769, the eldest son of Mr. Joseph Browne, a respectable farmer and land owner of Kent County. He was liberally educated, partly at the old Free School and partly at Washington College, then just founded. He held a high rank among his classmates for scholarship, and finished his college course without obtaining a diploma—the college, being in its infancy, had not begun to confer its honors. He entered the office of Dr. Worrell, in Chestertown, about the year 1788, and attended lectures in Philadelphia when the distinguished Dr. Kuhn was Professor of the Practice of Medicine.

"During the time he was engaged in study he was frequently called to attend the sick in the absence of his preceptor, and such were his prudence and tact that he won golden opinions, while yet a mere tyro. Towards the close of the course of lectures in February 1791, a general inoculation for small-pox took place in Kent County, and Dr. Worrell, finding it impossible to attend to all who desired inoculation, wrote for his pupil, Browne, to come home and join him in practice. Accordingly, he left before the close of the course of lectures. Though, then, not quite five years old, I well remember the time when Dr. Worrell inoculated my father's family. A few days after he sent Dr. Browne to see whether we had taken the infection. My mother, who was intimate in Dr. Worrell's family, and knew Dr. Browne *as a student*, met him at the door, and said, 'Morgan, what did Dr. Worrell send you here for?' He replied, 'To see if the family had taken the infection, Madam.' 'Well, do you know anything about it?' 'Yes, Madam, I know as much, probably, as Dr. Worrell, for I have been with it in the hospitals, all winter.' 'Well, come in and look at their arms.' This was, perhaps, Dr. Browne's first professional visit, and afterwards he needed no further introduction or commendation. He seemed to have secured the favor of my parents, and during his connection with Dr. Worrell, until 1796, he was received everywhere Dr. Worrell could not attend.

"Dr. Browne having attended not even one full course of lectures, did not obtain a diploma, but was, like many others of that day, styled Doctor by courtesy. Indeed, there was not at that time one M. D. in Kent County. It was not so fashionable as now. It may, however, be said with perfect truth, and the remark has been made by strangers, as well as by the citizens, that Chestertown was peculiarly favored in having physicians of the first rank, as Anderson, Worrell and Browne.

"Young physicians have many difficulties to encounter in their entrance into business. But as Dr. Browne was taken into partnership by his preceptor, which indicated the confidence he reposed in him, he seemed to have no middle state, but sprung at once from youth to maturity. He was a hard student, and having been well educated, had stored his mind with all the riches of the professional lore of that day, as well as the varied wealth of Grecian and Roman literature. Many great works of a prêceding age, works now seldom seen in medical libraries, never read, were laboriously studied by him.

"Dr. Browne was not only popular with his patients, but was highly esteemed by his professional brethren, for the maturity of his judgment. He had a very extensive practice, and his success was equal to, indeed, was the groundwork of his fame.

"He had been in practice from 1791 to 1807, when, after completing my course of study, under his care, after the death of Dr. Worrell, he proposed to me a partnership with him. The offer was, of course, gladly and gratefully accepted. This partnership was terminated by my removal to my farm, about 3 miles from Chestertown, in the year 1813, when an invasion was threatened by the English ships, then lying in the Chesapeake Bay. All persons who had country seats left the town for a time, intending to return when danger was over. I chose, however, to remain in the country, and did so until 1821, when I was driven back to town by the dreadful illness of my family. By that time, Dr. Joseph Browne was in practice with his father.

"About 1841, Dr. Browne had a serious attack of typhoid fever, from which he broke down in physical strength and too evidently marked in his intellectual powers. He soon retired to his farm near St. Paul's Church, where he lingered a year or two and died at the age of 72.

"In person, Dr. Browne was about 5 feet and 8 or 9 inches in height, neat, but not showy in his dress, and in early life was very handsome. In my whole life, now extended to three score and sixteen, I have not known a physician of superior judgment, or more deservedly admired and loved."

SEC. 131. "DR. JACOB FISHER was the third son of the Rev. Mr. Fisher, a Baptist Clergyman, of Sussex County, Delaware. His two elder brothers were named Abraham and Isaac.

"Where he was educated and what was the extent of his learning is not known, but I *do* know that he conversed fluently and correctly and wrote with facility, taste and judgment. While a member of the Kent County Medical Society he presented an essay which would have given a respectable name to a Professor.

"He attended the usual course of lectures in the Medical College of the University of Maryland, in Baltimore, and was graduated with honor as M. D. He also complied with the provisions of the law, in the Act incorporating the Medical and Chirurgical Faculty, and obtained license from the Examiners, thus becoming an L. M.

"Soon after the premature and lamented death of Dr. Henry Page, in 1821, his friends and patients united in an invitation to me to remove from Chestertown and take his place. The invitation was declined, for my friends and patients were unwilling that I should leave them. About this time, 1821 or 1822, Dr. Fisher came from Baltimore, offered himself a candidate for their favor, and was universally accepted.

"For a few years he had an extent of practice too large for any one man, however active and vigorous he might be. The topographical position of the district, consisting of Eastern Neck Island, Pine Neck, Skinner's Neck, Pig Neck, part of Broad Neck, besides a considerable country around St. Paul's Church, the Bayside and Swan Creek, &c., long and narrow slips of land between deep and unfordable creeks, rendered traveling from one to the other tedious and laborious. A competitor, in Dr. William F. Harper, soon appeared, and, settling near St. Paul's, relieved Dr. Fisher of a part of his labors.

"I became acquainted with Dr. Fisher soon after he came to Kent, and found him very clever, well informed in his line of business and conscientiously inclined to keep pace with all the improvements and discoveries in medicine. In my frequent intercourse with him in consultations and otherwise I had good opportunities of becoming satisfied, and so became, that he had a well regulated mind, an amiable disposition, and that he was an example worthy of imitation in his domestic, social and professional relations.

"On the 9th of April 1857, Dr. Fisher suffered an attack of paralysis while in his carriage, on his return from visiting a patient. Though his mind rallied after the first day, and was unaffected by the shock, his physical powers never recovered their tone, and after a long confinement, borne with Christian meekness and cheerfulness, he died 18th of February 1859, in the 64th year of his age. For many years Dr. Fisher had fully sustained the character of a pious and exemplary Christian, and was a prominent member of the Methodist Protestant Church. He was about 5 feet 8 inches high, stout built, and rather inactive in his movements. Of a comely countenance, in which the character he bore for the goodness of his heart, both by nature and grace, was faithfully portrayed, and of a refined and gentlemanly manner. He was a good physician,—and better, a good Christian man.

"The author of this imperfect tribute maintained a most amicable, social and professional intimacy with Dr. Fisher, uninterrupted by a single cloud for six and thirty years, and laments the inadequacy of his power to do justice to his friend.

"P. W."

I. U. PARISH.

SEC. 139. "Be it therefore enacted by the Right Honorable the Lord Proprietary by and with the advice and consent of his Lordships Governor and the Upper and Lower house of Assembly and the authority of the same, That from and after this present Session of Assembly all those parts of St. Pauls Parish and Shrewsbury Parish in Kent County aforesaid that are contained within the bounds hereinafter mentioned and expressed,

"That is to say Beginning in St. Pauls Parish at the mouth of a pond by the Bay-side between Marmaduke Tilden's and William Frisby's (lately John B. Anderson's now Overand's) and running up the pond-side to the head thereof where it intersects the line between said Marmaduke Tilden's and George

Copper's land, thence with that line to the road leading from said Tilden's to Cooter Grffins, thence with that road to intersect the main road leading from the head of Worton Creek by Chestertown and with that main road to a vally in James McClean's plantation leading into the head of the Branch called Fannings Branch thence down that vally and Branch to a small branch issueing out of said Fannings Branch called Bloody-Bridge-Branch thence up said Bloody Bridge Branch to the head thereof and with a straight line to the head of Muddy Creek and down said Creek to Chester River,

"And in Shrewsbury Parish beginning at the mouth of Turners Creek on Sassafras river and running up said Creek to James Louttits Point (now Mrs. Mary Janvier where the Wharf and Granary now stands) and thence with the road leading by John Hawkins into the main County road to Chestertown thence with the said main County road to Thomas Perkins and thence by the Cross roads to Isaac Perkins Mills, and thence by a due south-east line from the said Mills to Chester river shall be taken from St. Pauls Parish and Shrewsbury Parish aforesaid, and created into a new Parish by the name of Chester Parish."

Then follows what appears the first meeting of the Vestry on May 6th, 1766. The following members attended: Aaron Alford, Macall Medford, Joseph Rasin, St. Leger Everett, and Wm. Ringgold, Vestrymen; William Cowarden, Church Warden.

An agreement was made by the above with Charles Tilden, Architect, for the building of a Church 60 feet long and 40 feet wide. The walls to be three bricks from the foundation to the water-table, and two and a half bricks thick from thence to the plate on the sides. The building to have two doors and thirteen arched windows 5½ feet wide and 9 feet high, with double sashes, &c. The articles of agreement contain a minute description of the building and of the materials of which it was to be built, and the whole was to be finished by the 31st day of March, 1768, for which the Vestry agreed to pay to the said Architect, Charles Tilden, the sum of £758 in Spanish milled dollars, estimated at 7 shillings and 6 pence Pennsylvania currency. The articles were signed by the Vestry and the architect.

This building stood precisely on the ground where the present I. U. Church now stands. The long way from east to west, with the main front entrance fronting the south. The Pulpit on the north side fronting the main entrance, with the

Chancel or Communion at the west end. The aisles crossing each other the whole length and width of the building, with 50 large square pews. There was also a door of entrance at the east end, and a stairway immediately inside the door leading to the gallery.

At a meeting of the Vestry, on 10th June, 1766, the following members appeared, viz.:

William Ringgold, Thomas Perkins, St. Leger Everett, and Robert Peacock and William Cowarden, Church Wardens. Charles Tilden agreed to build a brick Vestry-room 18 feet square, and to furnish all the materials for £90 current money. This house stood about 25 or 30 paces from the end of the Church in a north-east direction from the east door.

The Rev. Mathias Harris was the first Rector.

On 21st July, 1769, a special meeting was called at the request of the Rev. Philip Hughes. The following members were present: Richard Frisby, Luke Griffith, Thomas Smith, James Wroth, and Macall Medford. The Rev. Mr. Hughes presented his induction to this Parish to the Vestry, which was read and postponed until the sentiments of a full Vestry could be ascertained.

The next meeting was held July 24th, 1769. Present: Luke Griffith, Robert Buchanan, James Wroth, Macall Medford, and Thos. Smith, Vestrymen; Edward Beck and Thos. Medford, Church Wardens. No decision seems to have been made, but a special meeting was held on the 5th August, when it appears that the Rev. Mathias Harris appeared as Rector and a member of the Vestry. The Vestry ordered the Registrar, Charles Groom, to write to the Rev. Philip Hughes, as follows:

"Dear Sir: I am directed by the Vestry to acquaint you that they have ordered me to Register your Induction whenever you please to produce it, and have given orders for your admission into the Church any time when you will attend. And the Vestry would be glad if you will preach at the Church to-morrow Aug. 5th 1769.

"CHARLES GROOM."

Agreeably to the order of the last Vestry the Rev. Philip Hughes has produced his induction, and it was entered on the Book of Records, as follows:

"Maryland St. FREDERICK, absolute Lord and Proprietary of the Province of Maryland, and Avalon Lord Baron of Baltimore &c. to Rev. Philip Hughes sendeth Greeting:

"We do hereby constitute and appoint you, said Philip Hughes, to be Rector of the Church of Chester Parish, in Kent County, to have hold and enjoy the said Church together with all the rights, profits and advantages whatsoever appertaining to a Minister of said Parish and do hereby require the Church Wardens, Vestrymen and other the Parishioners to receive, acknowledge and assist you the said Philip Hughes in all matters relating to the discharge of your functions.

"Witness our well beloved Robert Eden Esquire Governor and Commander in Chief in and over the said Province this 15th day of July in the 19th year of our dominion Anno Domini 1769.

"Signed by order U. SCOTT, Clk. Con."

"I hereby certify that the Rev. Philip Hughes qualified as Rector of Chester Parish by taking the several oaths directed by the Act of Assembly and subscribing the test this 7th day of August 1769 before

"THOMAS SMITH."

The Freeholders of the Parish met this day, April 20th, 1772, at the Parish Church, and elected Thomas Wilkins and Simon Worrell Vestrymen in the room of Thomas Smith and Macall Medford, late Vestrymen, now left out, and Edward Beck and Josias Ringgold, Church Wardens, in the room and place of John Anger and Rasin Gale, late Church Wardens, now left out.

A meeting of the Vestry is recorded held Nov. 10th, 1772, when were present Rev. Philip Hughes, D. D., St. Leger Everett, Wm. Cowerden, John Duyer, Thos. Wilkins, and Joseph Rasin, Vestrymen; and Edward Beck, Church Warden.

This appears to be the last meeting at which the Rev. Philip Hughes, D. D., presided as Rector on March 14th, 1773. At a meeting of the Vestry the Rev. Mathias Harris presented his induction to this Parish. It was ordered to be read and entered on the Parish Register.

The name of Rev. John Patterson is recorded as present, in 1773, 1774, and again 1775.

On page 29, Old Register, is recorded that the Rev. Samuel Keene agrees to officiate in the Parish Church, I. U., every third Sunday, and at the Chapel in Chestertown every third Sunday. Joseph Couden agrees to act as Lay Reader on the other three Sundays in said Churches. Nothing is said of the residence of Mr. Keene, but there is a condition that he should remove his family to Kent County. The date of this agreement is Nov. 8th, 1779.

The war of the Revolution going on at this time, there appears to have been very irregular services, nearly all the Episcopal clergy being of English birth, and sympathising with the mother country, were obliged to leave their churches, and this so continued in a greater or less degree for many years. The Methodists about this period took their rise and were nearly the only preachers in Kent County. This state of affairs continued for some time after the consecration of Dr. White, who was the first Bishop in America of any denomination. At the time of rëestablishing of the Episcopal Church, 1787, the Church in this county was well-nigh extinct. And the writer of this can remember, from 1816 to 1825, when a room of 10 feet square would, perhaps, hold every Episcopalian in Kent County. Yet there were spasmodic efforts to keep the Church alive. We find at a Vestry meeting, June 4th, 1781, John Sturgges agrees to act as Clerk in the church and chapel, to keep the church clean and ring the bell (perhaps the same old bell that now summons the people to worship at the old church in Chestertown) at a salary of 60 bushels of wheat. The Vestry at this time were Dr. John Scott, Dr. Thos. Vandyke, John Bolton, John Kennard, St. Leger Everett; Church Warden, Marmaduke Medford; and Charles Groome, Register.

At a special Vestry meeting held December, 1789, an invitation was sent to *Baltimore town*, to the Rev. John Roberson, to come over and officiate for one month on trial.

At a subsequent meeting, 1st Feb. 1790, when Jeremiah Nicols, St. Leger Everett, John Kennard and Doctor Edward Worrell, Vestrymen, were present, it was resolved to employ Rev. Mr. Roberson for six months, and if at the expiration of that time Mr. Roberson should incline to continue for the year, the Vestry would assign to him the whole of the subscription.

August 22d, 1790. A certificate is given by the Vestry, Church Warden, and Register to Samuel Keene, Jun., recommending him to the Standing Committee of the Diocese for Priest's orders.

October 14th, 1790. Vestrymen present, Dr. Jno. Scott, Dr. Edward Worrell, Hales Everett, St. Leger Everett, and John Kennard. Ordered and agreed by the Vestry to employ the Rev. Samuel Armor to officiate in this Parish for one year, to commence from the 31st of this instant, Oct., and that the said Samuel Armor shall officiate every other Sunday at I. U. and chapel in Chestertown, or oftener, if convenient for said clergymen to do so. Samuel Armor was Register at this time. There is no more entry in the old book until 4th April, 1796. Samuel Chew was elected Lay Delegate to a Convention to be held in Easton that year. The Vestry adjourned to meet in Chestertown; John Gale, Reg.

May 4th, 1796. Vestry present: St. Leger Everett, John Chew, John Wethered, Benjamin Chambers, James Corse; Wardens, John Hyland and Joseph Everett.

Rev. Archibald Walker was called on to know upon what terms he would agree to officiate. Mr. Walker said for £150 if the Vestry would insure the payment; they declined. The Vestry and Church Wardens living in Chestertown, viz.: John Wethered, John Chew, John Hyland, Benj. Chambers and Dr. Edward Worrell, do agree to pay the Rev. A. Walker at the rate of £100 for officiating in the chapel in Chestertown every Sunday for one year. John Gale was Register.

April 10th, 1798. Thomas Worrell, John Scott were elected in the room of John Chew and John Hyland put out, and in place of St. Leger Everett, deceased. Thomas Wilkins was elected Church Warden; James Wroth, Register. At an adjourned meeting held July 14th, 1800, the following contract was made with Rev. George Dashields, viz.: to obtain such subscription for him as we can, and to use legal measures to collect the same; also to allow said Dashields to preach at St. Paul's at such times as a Joint Committee of both Parishes may agree upon.

From the last mentioned date, the new names that appear on the Register as Vestrymen until 1811 are, Wm. Smith, Isaac Connell, Jun., Simon Wilmer, Samuel Ringgold, Wm. Graves, Wm. Barroll, Unit Anger, Thos. B. Hands, Richard Barroll, James Scott, Gen. Philip Reed, Dr. Benson, B. Blake, Stephen Crane, Wm. Skirvin, James Bowers, Wm. H. Wilmer, Isaac Spencer, Joseph Wicks, John Carvill.

From 1800 to 1811, the following Clergymen are mentioned as having officiated or as having been called to officiate at I. U. and the chapel at Chestertown. Rev. Mr. Ball, Rev. Mr. Davis, Rev. Simon Wilmer, Rev. John Kewley. The induction of Mr. Kewley was performed at the chapel in Chestertown, and it was ordered that the keys of I. U. Church be brought to the chapel on that occasion. Rev. William H. Wilmer was the last Rector of Chester Parish that held regular service at I. U. The building becoming so dilapidated, the house was abandoned. The writer of this remembers the old church from 1816 to 1834, with its roof fallen in, doors off the hinges, and a shelter for the sheep and other animals in hot or bad weather. The pews and walls were during that period in good condition. In that condition it was sold to Mr. Benjamin Howard, who hauled the bricks away, and built a dwelling in 1835, on his farm near Turner's Creek, now belonging to Mrs. Hamman, his daughter. She is the widow of the late Dr. Hamman. So ends this brief history of old I. U.

The new church, now standing on the precise spot from which the old church was taken, was built and completed between the years 1856 and 1859. Rev. Mr. Stokes, Rector, of Chestertown, had frequent services during the warm weather under the shade at old I. U., and mainly through his influence the people got in the notion to rebuild a church. Those that mostly interested themselves were Dr. Wm. M. Gemmill, Dr. Thos. G. Wroth, Anthony Bell, Nathaniel T. Hynson, Wm. F. Baker, Edward T. Wroth, Dr. Thos. C. Wroth, Isaac Perkins, John P. Davidson, &c. Mr. Stokes held regular services there as long as he remained in Chestertown every Sunday P. M. When he left, the gentleman above-named called Rev. Ambrose Clark and petitioned the Convention to set them off as a separate Parish, to be called I. U. This was done, and on the 11th day of May, 1863, they were fully organized with the above-named gentlemen as its first Vestry; Wm. R. Davidson, Register.

The bounds of I. U. Parish are as follows: Beginning at the mouth of a pond by the Bay-side in the farm of John B. H. Anderson, that is to say, at a point where the boundary line of Chester and St. Paul's Parish, begins and running by and with said line to a point where it intersects the 3rd and 4th Election Districts of Kent County, in the main road leading from Worton's Creek to Chestertown, near the residence of J. C. Parsons, and thence by a due east line until it intersects the boundary line of Shrewsbury Parish, thence by and with said line to its beginning, at the mouth of Turner's Creek on Sassafras River.

The Rev. Mr. Perryman, of Shrewsbury Parish was the next Minister at I. U., holding service in the P. M. of each Sabbath. The church at I. U. was consecrated by the Rt. Rev. Bishop Whittingham, about 1860, and called Christ Church of I. U. Parish. I forgot to mention in its place the entire territory of I. U. Parish was taken from Chester Parish.

Next to Mr. Perryman was Rev. Dr. Charles Goodrich, of Shrewsbury Parish; after him Rev. Mr. Jaycock; then the

Rev. Mr. Goodwin, of Chestertown; then the Rev. Mr. Perryman, of St. Paul's Parish; then the Rev. Mr. Hendly, of said Parish; and lastly, Rev. Sewell S. Hepbron, of St. Paul's, since July 1874 until now.

The last named personage was recommended by the Vestry of I. U. as a suitable person for the Ministry in 1866.

The Rev. Perregrine Wroth and Rev. Edward Wroth, now in Virginia, are both offshoots of I. U. Parish.

SEWELL HEPBRON, Reg. I. U. Parish.

Dec. 31st, 1875.

SEC. 140—

A LIST OF MEMBERS OF THE LEGISLATURE OF MARYLAND, WHOSE NAMES OR FAMILIES HAVE BEEN MENTIONED:

CECIL COUNTY.

Abraham Weld—1674.
Henry Ward—1674.
St. Ledger Codd—1694, 1702.
John Thompson—1694.
Casper Augustine Herman—1694.
William Pearce—1694, 1706, 1707.
Col. Hans Hanson—1699, see Kent County.
Edward Blay—1706, 1707, see Kent County.
Thomas Frisby—1706.
Matthias Vanderleyden—1709, 1713, 1715, 1716.
John Ward—1715, 1716.
Ephram Augustine Herman—1715, 1716, 1728, 1731.
James Frisby—1715, 1716, 1719.
Peregrine Frisby—1713.
Stephen Knight—1728, 1731.
Benjamin Pearce—1740, 1745, 1746, 1754.
Michael Earle—1757, 1765.
Henry Ward—1757.

DORCHESTER COUNTY.

Richard Preston—1669.
Daniel Clark—1671, 1674.
Henry Trippe—1671, 1674.
William Ford—1671, 1674.
John Potterd—1694.
Henry Hooper—1694.
Thomas Ennalls—1694.
Henry Ennalls—1712, 1713.
William Ennalls—1728, 1731.
Bartholomew Ennalls—1745.
Thomas Robins—1750.
Charles Goldsborough—1752, 1763.
Robert Goldsborough 3rd—1765, 1766.

KENT COUNTY.

Christopher Thomas—1638.
Nicholas Browne—1638.
Joseph Wickes—1659.
Thomas Hynson—1659.
Henry Morgan—1659.
John Russell—1659.
Thomas Haywell—1661.
William Leeds—1661.
Capt. Robert Vaughan—1649, 1661.
Richard Blunt—1661, 1666, 1669.
Nicholas Picard—1666.
Robert Dunn—1669.
Arthur Wright—1671, 1674.
William Bishop—1671, 1674.
William Frisby—1694, 1695, 1696, 1697, 1706, 1707.
Col. Hans Hanson—1694, 1695, 1696, 1697, see Cecil County.
John Hynson—1694, 1695, 1696, 1697.
Thomas Smith—1694, 1695, 1696, 1697.
Simon Wilmer—1698.
Elias King—1706.
James Wells—1706, 1707.
Daniel Pearce—1709, 1711, 1712, 1713.
Edward Scott—1711, 1712, 1713, 1714, 1716.
Capt. St. Ledger Codd—1712, 1713, 1714, 1715, 1716, 1719, 1720.
Col. Edward Blay—1713, see Cecil County.
William Blay—1714, 1715.
Nathaniel Hynson—1716, 1719, 1720, 1721.
James Smith—1719, 1720, 1721, 1728.
Lambert Wilmer—1719, 1720, 1721.
Capt. James Harris—1715, 1716, 1728, 1734.
Samuel Wallis—1722.
Robert Dunn—1722.
Philip Kennard—1722, 1728, 1734.
William Blackiston—1722.
George Wilson—1728, 1731, 1732, 1734, 1735, 1736, 1740, 1745, 1746, 1747.
Ebenezer Blackiston—1728, 1732, 1733.
Matthew Howard—1732, 1733.
Christopher Hall—1732, 1733, 1734, 1735, 1736.
William Harris—1739, 1740.
Charles Hynson—1739, 1740.
John Gresham—1745, 1746, 1747.
Richard Gresham—1745, 1746, 1747, 1753, 1754, 1768.
Matthias Harris—1745, 1746, 1747.
Nicholas Smith—1750.
Richard Lloyd—1750, 1762, 1765, 1766.
Simon Wilmer—1750.
Alexander Williamson—1752, 1753, 1754, 1757, 1758.
William Hynson—1757, 1758, 1762, 1763.
William Rasin—1757.
Thomas Ringgold—1762, 1763, 1765, 1766, 1768.
Robert Buchanan—1765, 1766, 1768.
Stephen Boardley—1768.

QUEEN ANNE'S COUNTY.

Philemon Hemsley — 1709, 1711.
John Salter—1709, 1711.
John Whittington — 1709, 1711.
Solomon Wright--1709, 1711.
Solomon Clayton--1715, 1732.
James Earle—1719, 1721.
William Hemsley — 1721, 1729, 1731, 1732, 1734, 1735, 1736.
William Turbutt--1721, 1729, 1731.
Edward Wright—1732.
William Tilghman — 1734, 1735, 1736, 1737, 1738.
Grundy Pemberton — 1737, 1738.
Capt. William Hopper—1746, 1747, 1748.
Col. Edward Tilghman--1746, 1747, 1749, 1757, 1758, 1762, 1765, 1766, 1768.
Thomas Hammond — 1746, 1747, 1848.
James Hollyday—1752, 1753, 1765, 1766, 1768.
Robert Lloyd—1757, 1758, 1762, 1763, 1765.
Thomas Knight—1762.

SOMERSET COUNTY.

William Stevens—1669.
Paul Marsh—1671, 1674.
Roger Woolford—1671, 1674.
Robert Woolford—1674.
John Bozman—1694.
Matthew Scarborough—1694.
Thomas Dixon—1694.
John Waters—1706.
Joseph Grey—1706.
John Jones—1706.
Major George Gale—1709.
Levin Gale—1728, 1734.
William Hayward—1768.

TALBOT COUNTY.

Lt. Col. Richard Woolman—1661, 1669, 1671, 1674.
William Coursey—1666.
William Hamilton—1666.
William Hambleton — 1669, 1671, 1674.
Daniel Clark—1669.
Philemon Lloyd—1671, 1674,
Joseph Weeks—1669, 1671, 1674.
Henry Coursey—1694.
Robert Smith—1694.
Thomas Smithson — 1694, 1706.
Richard Tilghman — 1698, 1699, 1701, 1702.
Foster Turbutt—1715, 1716.
Thomas Emerson—1717.
James Hollyday—1728, 1729, 1731.
George Robins—1728, 1729, 1731.
James Chamberlaine—1728.
Samuel Chamberlaine—1731.
Nicholas Goldsborough — 1732, 1734, 1735, 1745, 1747, 1748, 1749, 1750.
Tench Francis—1734.
Edward Lloyd—1739.
Robert Lloyd — 1740, 1745, 1746, 1748, 1749, 1750.
William Thomas--1745, 1746.

Philemon Lloyd—1701, 1702.
Robert Goldsborough—1706, 1707.
Thomas Robins—1709, 1712, 1713, 1714, 1715, 1716, 1717.
Robert Ungle—1712, 1713, 1715, 1716.
Matthew Tilghman Ward—1712, 1713, 1714, 1715, 1716.
James Lloyd —1712, 1713, 1714, 1717, 1719, 1720, 1722.
John Goldsborough — 1745, 1749, 1750, 1752, 1753, 1754, 1755, 1762, 1765, 1766.
Charles Goldsborough—1749.
Matthew Tilghman — 1751, 1752, 1753, 1754, 1758, 1768.
James Tilghman—1762.
Henry Hollyday—1765.

WORCESTER COUNTY.

Thomas Robins—1748.

ANNAPOLIS.

Dr. Charles Carroll—1738.
Dr. George Steuart — 1762, 1763.

CHARLES COUNTY.

Samuel Hanson—1716, 1728.
Robert Hanson—1719, 1720, 1728, 1732, 1734, 1739, 1740.
Alexander Contee—1724.
John Hanson, Jr—1757, 1758, 1765.
John Contee — 1735, 1737, 1738.
Richard Harrison—1742.

SEC. 141. ADDITIONS and CORRECTIONS. On page 2, line 12th, read submit instead of *snubmit,*—on page 20, Sec. 8, A, read Col. Edward Wilkins, instead of *Wilkens,*—on page 124, line 22nd, read John B. Morris, instead of *Norris,*—on page 128, line 4th, read Adolphe de Contee, intead of *Comtee,*—Mrs. Mary L. Barraud, mentioned on page 168, d. 24th Dec. 1876, in the 80th year of her age,—Mrs. Anna W. Comegys, mentioned on page 225, d. 19th Dec. 1876, in the 76th year of her age,—on page 244, line 16th, read Jonas Clapham, instead of *James,*—on same page, line 36th, read Richard Lowndes Ogle, instead of *Cooke,*—on page 251, line 1st, read Thomas Smyth, instead of *Smith,*—on page 266, read Argaty, instead of *Argatty,*—on page 273, read John H. Delprat, instead of *John C. Delprat,*—on page 353, line 15th, read Richard Phillingham, instead of *Phillingan,*—on same page, read John Denick, instead of *Derrick,* and on page 375, read Charles Groome, instead of *Groom.*

THE END.

INDEX.

Names marked (*) with an asterisk are of persons from whom information was obtained.

N.

www.ingramcontent.com/pod-product-compliance
Lightning Source LLC
Chambersburg PA
CBHW072041020426
42334CB00017B/1351

* 9 7 8 0 8 0 6 3 4 6 3 2 8 *